AQA GCSE MATHS

FOUNDATION

TEACHER COMPANION

OXFORD
UNIVERSITY PRESS

OXFORD
UNIVERSITY PRESS

Great Clarendon Street, Oxford, OX2 6DP, United Kingdom

Oxford University Press is a department of the University of Oxford.
It furthers the University's objective of excellence in research, scholarship,
and education by publishing worldwide. Oxford is a registered trade mark of
Oxford University Press in the UK and in certain other countries.

First published in 2015

British Library Cataloguing in Publication Data
Data available

978-0-19-835171-9

10 9 8 7 6 5 4 3 2

Paper used in the production of this book is a natural, recyclable product made
from wood grown in sustainable forests. The manufacturing process conforms to
the environmental regulations of the country of origin.

Printed in Great Britain by Ashford Colour Press Ltd, Gosport

Contents

13 Factors, powers and roots

14 Graphs 1

15 Working in 3D

16 Handling data 2

17 Calculations 2

18 Graphs 2

19 Pythagoras and trigonometry

20 The probability of combined events

21 Sequences

22 Units and proportionality

About this book

This Teacher Companion is part of the *AQA GCSE Maths* series which has been specifically written for the new GCSE Mathematics (8300) specification from AQA. The Companion accompanies the Foundation GCSE student book in the same series, and is designed to help you to plan and deliver lessons, and to support your Foundation tier students' learning in conjunction with this book.

The author team brings a wealth of classroom experience to the Teacher Companion meaning that you can plan and deliver lessons with confidence.

The structure of the Companion closely follows that of the student book for coherence and ease of navigation.

In this Companion you will find:

- Clear **learning outcomes** taken from the specification, so you can be confident of full coverage when planning each topic
- **Links to *MyMaths*,** as well as **assessment and InvisiPen video resources** on the associated online Kerboodle product, to give fully blended support
- Suggested **starters, teaching notes and plenaries** to help you deliver your lessons effectively
- **Exercise commentaries**, with a handy narrative identifying misconceptions and guidance hints for the questions, so you can intervene before your students get stuck
- **Simplification and extension** guidance for each lesson, so you can support the full range of abilities in your Foundation classes
- Summarised key outcomes with a **Quick Check** feature, so you can assess your students' mastery of the topic
- Summarised **misconceptions and challenges** for each topic, with suggested strategies for intervention, for ensuring your students overcome any obstacles to learning
- **Worked solutions and mark schemes** for assessment and revision exercises, to help you and your students gain familiarity with the new requirements and grading, and work towards the best possible grade

Finally, you can download a version of this book in Word format, so you can customise the material to suit your own departmental and individual needs. To download this file, you will simply need to go to the series page, where the file is available: www.oxfordsecondary.co.uk/AQAGCSEMaths

Look for the link to the file, then use this password: AGMFTCoxford!

Calculations 1

Learning outcomes

N1 Order positive and negative integers, decimals and [fractions]; use the symbols =, ≠, <, >, ≤, ≥.

N2 Apply the four operations, including formal written methods, to integers, decimals – all both positive and negative; understand and use place value (e.g. when working with very large or very small numbers, and when calculating with decimals).

N3 Use conventional notation for priority of operations, including brackets, powers, roots [and reciprocals].

N5 Apply systematic listing strategies.

N15 Round numbers and measures to an appropriate degree of accuracy (e.g. to a specified number of decimal places or significant figures)

Prior knowledge

Check-in skill

- Understand place value.
- Use mental methods to add, subtract, multiply, divide.
- Order positive and negative numbers.

Online resources

MyMaths 1001, 1004, 1005, 1007, 1020,1028, 1068, 1069, 1072, 1103, 1167, 1392, 1393, 1916, 1917

InvisiPen videos

Skills: 01Sa – q Applications: 01Aa – f

Kerboodle assessment

Online Skills Test 1 Chapter Test 1

Development and links

Negative numbers have a wide application in the sciences and finance. Apart from the obvious uses in recording temperatures, they have applications in electronics when working with voltages and in accounting and bookkeeping to record debits or credits. The accounting phrase 'in the red' originates from the standard practice of writing negative values or debits in red ink.

Chapter investigation

Students will be familiar with decimal or denary numbers, base 10, and the algorithms for comparing, rounding and carrying out arithmetic operations on them. Looking at binary numbers, base 2, allows a fresh approach to a potentially stale topic and an opportunity to see why the various algorithms work.

Start by explaining how binary numbers work and how to convert between binary and decimal numbers: focus on the significance of a digits place value [**1.1**].

$1011_2 = 1 \times 2^3 + 0 \times 2^2 + 1 \times 2^1 + 1 \times 2^0 = 8 + 2 + 1 = 11_{10}$

Ask students for suggestions on how to go from decimal to binary notation. Finding the largest power of two less than or equal to the number is one approach as is repeated division by 2

$37_{10} = 32_{10} + 5_{10} = 100000_2 + 4_{10} + 1 = 100000_2 + 100_2 + 1 = 100101_2$

$37 \div 2 = 18$ r **1**; $18 \div 2 = 9$ r **0**; $9 \div 2 = 4$ r **1**; $4 \div 2 = 2$ r **0**; $2 \div 2 = $ **1** r **0** $\Rightarrow 37_{10} = 100101_2$

Consolidate understanding of place value by looking at comparing numbers. This can be extended to decimals and negative numbers.

Rounding of decimals is based on looking at the 'next digit': 0, 1, 2, 3, 4 ⇒ 'round down', 5, 6, 7, 8, 9 ⇒ 'round up' [**1.2**]. The same idea applies to binary: 0 ⇒ 'round down', 1 ⇒ 'round up'.

Addition and subtraction [**1.3**] use the same algorithm for binary and decimal numbers: here the focus should be on carry and borrow digits and what they actually mean.

For multiplication and division [**1.4**] students may be surprised at how easy it is in binary.

Binary numbers were first formalized by Gottfried Leibnitz in 1693 but they have a long pre-history. However it was not until modern electronic computers arrived with on (1) and off (0) switches that binary arithmetic took off.

1.1 Place value

Objectives

① **N1** Order positive and negative integers and decimals

② **N1** Use the symbols =, ≠, <, >, ≤, ≥

Useful resources

Place value table, number line, mini whiteboards, number fans

Starter – Skills

Show numbers 3567, 735.6, –53.76, 603 570, 37065, 5.637 and –7605.3

Ask students to say each number in words.

Challenge students to find the number you are thinking of from clues given. For example, I am the largest number; I am the only number with ten thousands; I am the only number with zero tens; etc.

Emphasise that all the numbers contain the same digits and discuss what changes the size of the number. Establish that the place value of each digit determines its size.

Teaching notes – Skills

① Emphasise that on a number line:

- Positive numbers are to the right of zero
- **Negative numbers** are to the left of zero

Discuss temperature as an example of where negative numbers appear in the real world.

Reinforce that on a thermometer:

- Positive numbers are above zero
- Negative numbers are below zero

Discuss how to order the numbers 105, 7, 16, 123.

Establish that you compare the number of hundreds, then tens, and then units.

Ask students for some decimal numbers with different numbers of decimal places. Discuss how each number can be written in a place value table, and focus on the value of each digit in turn.

Ensure that students understand that the 1 in 0.31 is a different magnitude to the 1 in 0.13.

Emphasise the importance of being systematic when ordering decimals: first non-zero digit, then the second, etc.

② Look at the difference between the pairs of **symbols**, = and ≠, < and >, and ≤ and < (or ≥ and >).

Students may first need to practise inserting the **inequality sign** between simple pairs of numbers. They could remember that the larger end of the inequality sign is beside the larger number if they struggle to distinguish < from >; and that the ≤ and ≥ signs include a partial 'equals' sign.

Plenary – Skills

In pairs or small groups, ask students to write statements about what is the same and what is different about several numbers; for example,

5.6, –5.6, 5.06 and 5.60.

Exercise commentary – Skills

A common misconception with place value is believing that the length of a number determines its size regardless of the position of the decimal point. Recognising that any number has a decimal point is an important concept, whether you can see the point or not.

Questions 1 and **2** Encourage students to check spelling, and to remember to consider the place value of any zero digits.

Questions 3 and **4** A number line could help here. Students may benefit from saying each number aloud to give context to the digits and place value.

Question 5 Students may want to call 9.50 'nine point fifty'. Is this correct?

Question 6 Students need to be clear about the meaning of each inequality sign. Students may benefit from writing 'less than' or 'greater than' in addition to the symbols as this will make it clear whether an incorrect answer is due to an ordering error or a misuse of the symbol. Students should take extra care with the negative numbers in parts **g** to **j**.

Question 7 Students may revert back to 'adding or removing a zero'. This can be addressed by formalising their work with digits in place value columns and showing the shift. Students may confuse which direction the digits move in and will benefit from an example to refer to.

Question 8 A number line will help.

Question 9 Students should again consider each pair on a number line.

Simplification – Skills

Allow students to gain confidence with examples using positive numbers only, to begin with, rather than negative; and with integers rather than decimals. Give students sets of numbers with the same number of digits to order. This enables them to concentrate on the place values.

Extension – Skills

Students work in pairs with an example of an incorrect list in ascending order, to spot the error and decide why that mistake was made. Then they write an incorrect list and ask their partner to explain the mistake. Repeat this task with a list in descending order.

Recap – Applications

1 Order the numbers from largest to smallest.

3.6005 0.3602 3.59 3.601 0.3659 3.6

(3.601 3.6005 3.6 3.59 0.3659 0.3602)

2 Place < or > between each pair of numbers.

a 24 42 (<) **b** 16 1.6 (>)

c −3 5 (<) **d** 6 −7 (>)

3 Place = or ≠ between each pair of numbers.

a 705 seven hundred and fifty (≠)

b −2 + 7 8 − 3 (=)

4 a 5.3 × 1000 (5300)

b 100 × 0.32 (32)

c 10 × 0.075 (0.75)

d 1 ÷ 100 (0.01)

e 0.667 ÷ 10 (0.0667)

f 0.0032 ÷ 10 000 (0.000 000 32)

Plenary – Applications

Show minimum and maximum temperatures of different world cities.

City	Minimum temperature	Maximum temperature
London	−6 °C	32 °C
New York	−10 °C	35 °C
Paris	−4 °C	38 °C

Ask students questions based upon minimum and maximum temperatures. Which city has the lowest/highest temperature?

Discuss the decimal system and link to other words that use the ‘dec’ prefix: decathlon, decade, etc.

Exercise commentary – Applications

Question 1 Students can ignore the other digits in the bill and just consider the difference between 6.2 and 2.6.

Question 2 There may be some language issues here, and encourage students to extract the relevant information. Students will need to know the conversion between mm and cm. A sketch will help in part **c**.

Question 3 Remind students that the fastest time is the smallest number. In part **c**, students may add 0.03 instead of subtracting.

Question 4 In part **a**, ask students to use a mental method to add the scores together. Extent to questions such as 5 + 70 + 200 + 1100 + 4100 + 11 000 where each place value of the answer can be found in turn.

Question 5 Extend this by posing a similar example where the rule is multiply by ten, add ten.

Question 6 In part **c**, ask students how they can calculate the increase without working out the price of the shares before and after the price change.

Simplification – Applications

The world of sport provides many applications of ordering numbers. Race times such as 10.2 sec, 9.9 sec, make an easy introduction to this topic. Ask students to distinguish between using times in ascending order to place the runners in a race, and distances in descending order to place competitors in, for example, a long jump.

Extension – Applications

Encourage students to investigate other number systems such as binary or hexadecimal. Ask them: what would each place value component represent, and how would you order numbers written in these systems?

1.2 Rounding

Objectives

① **N1** Round to a specified number of decimal places or significant figures

Useful resources

Place value table, number line, mini whiteboards, number fans

Starter – Skills

Distribute number fans and ask students to use these to answer the following questions.

Ask for a variety of numbers to be given to: the nearest 10; nearest whole number; nearest 100, and so on.

Also, ask for a number which to the nearest 10 is ..., and so on, exploring the range of answers offered and the range possible.

Teaching notes – Skills

② Ask students to think how they would **round** 4369 to the nearest 10, 100 and 1000; ask them what rounding strategies they would use.

Highlight that a ten has one zero as the last digit, a hundred has two zeros as the last digits, and so on.

Demonstrate the process:

- Consider which two tens, hundreds or thousands the number lies between.
- Use the *next* place value digit (the **decider digit**) to decide whether to round up or down.
- If that digit is *below* 5, then round down.
- If that digit is 5 (*halfway*) *or above*, then round up.

Demonstrate notation: $364 \approx 400$ (to the nearest 100).

Progress to consider rounding a **decimal** number to the nearest whole number (**integer**).

Discuss how to round to 1 **decimal place**. Emphasise that the hundredths digit is the decider.

Extend to 2 dp and 3 dp.

Discuss **significant figures**, and ask students to name the first, second, third … significant digit of a variety of integers and decimal numbers. Include numbers less than 1.

Show how you can use significant figures to estimate the answer to decimal calculations.

Discuss when you might use rounding and highlight these uses:

- To estimate a calculation – link to mental starter.
- When the exact size of a number is unknown – refer to the populations of cities.
- When an approximate answer is good enough.

Plenary – Skills

Repeat the starter activity, but include sf, dp and max/min values for any given number, exploring as before the reasoning behind the answers offered.

Exercise commentary – Skills

In all questions they should be encouraged to consider a number's position on a number line. Some students may look at the wrong digit to help them decide whether to round up or down, for example rounding 7.3 to 8 because $7 > 5$. Similarly they may 'forget' which degree they are rounding to. Encouraging them to first consider the two *tens* or *hundreds* or *thousands* the number is between before rounding up or down can help fix the degree. Supportive questioning can be used – which two thousands is this between?

Question 4 Check that students return to the original number before rounding a second time, for example part **a**: $3472 = 3000$ to nearest $1000 \neq (3500$ to nearest $100)$ to nearest $1000 = 4000$.

Question 5 In parts **j**–**l**, check that students understand how to 'cascade' the effect of rounding up a 9.

Questions 6 and **7** Decimal numbers can confuse students. Recall that most of the digits are irrelevant – they need only be interested in the decider digit.

Question 8 Remind students to add place-holder zeros to preserve the size of the number.

Question 11 Students could also use these values to round to 1, 2 and 3 dp.

Question 12 Remind students to read each part carefully as they may confuse dp and sf.

Simplification – Skills

Students may benefit from access to empty place value columns to reinforce the value of the digits in each number. By placing each number to be rounded in its place value columns, students will be able to focus on the digit to be rounded up or down and the decider digit.

Extension – Skills

Students could be given further examples where approximating is used to estimate the answers to calculations. These could be considerably harder, or much longer, strings of numbers.

Recap – Applications

1 Round 245.367 to 2 dp. (245.37)

2 Round these numbers to each accuracy.

a 32	nearest 10	(30)
b 56	nearest 100	(100)
c 4320	nearest 1000	(4000)
d 8	nearest 10	(10)
e 4.4	nearest 10	(0)
f 8	nearest 100	(0)
g 4.8	nearest whole number	(5)
h 0.48	nearest whole number	(0)

3 Round the numbers to

i 1 dp **ii** 2 dp **iii** 1 sf **iv** 3 sf

a 26.573	(26.6, 26.57, 30, 26.6)
b 0.3264	(0.3, 0.33, 0.3, 0.326)
c 10 000.719	(10000.7, 10000.72, 10000, 10000)
d 0.07175	(0.1, 0.07, 0.07, 0.0718)

Plenary – Applications

Show students an imaginary headline: '60 000 attend Arctic Monkeys concert'.

Discuss a likely degree of accuracy for this figure and minimum and maximum attendance if the figure has been rounded to the nearest 1000.

Exercise commentary – Applications

Question 2 Discuss the largest degree of accuracy that the numbers could be rounded to while still being able to order the numbers in both questions.

Question 3 Recap that finding 10% is the same as dividing by 10.

Question 4 Ask students to choose their own numbers and pose questions such as: I have two numbers that are the same when rounded to 2 dp, but different when rounded to 3 sf. Find my numbers.

Question 5 Discuss the advantages and disadvantages of rounding to higher degrees of accuracy. Students should round the final answer, not the length and width of the room – refer students to the first example.

Question 6 Make sure students can use the square root and cube functions on their calculator.

Question 7 Extend the question by posing: would you pay more or less tax if you found the total and then rounded down to the nearest pound?

Simplification – Applications

Students should concentrate on consolidating their ability to round simple numbers to a given degree of accuracy. They should leave 'tricky' roundings until they are secure with the basic principles.

Extension – Applications

Provide students with a list of 'complicated' calculations and a jumbled set of accurate answers and challenge them to match question and answer without resorting to doing the detailed calculation.

1.3 Adding and subtracting

Objectives

① **N2** Apply addition and subtraction, including formal written methods, to integers, decimals – both positive and negative

② **N2** Understand and use place value when calculating with decimals

Useful resources

Number line, place value table, digit cards, mini whiteboards

Starter – Skills

Give out nine cards to each pair of students: four should contain digits, four should be subtraction signs and one should be an addition sign. Challenge the students to make number sentences resulting in the largest and smallest possible numbers.

Allow five minutes for this and then discuss the results and the effects of putting signs together.

Challenge students to find a result nearest to zero.

Teaching notes – Skills

① Write the **addition** 37 + 28 on the board and ask students to work out the answer using a **mental method**. Use a number line to illustrate the start number and possible strategies. Ask students for suggestions. For example:

- Method 1: Start at 37, partition 28 into 10, 10 and 8 and take each smaller jump separately.
- Method 2: Start at 37, jump 30 and compensate for the extra 2 units by subtracting 2 at the end.
- Method 3: Partition both numbers into place value components and deal with tens and units separately.

Repeat with a **subtraction** calculation and illustrate as above for different methods. Discuss whether the compensation method is appropriate and how you would use it; emphasise that it is most useful when a number is close to a multiple of 10 or 100.

Discuss how to use a written method for the **addition** 287 + 344, and then the **subtraction** 3518 – 765. Encourage students to approximate the answers by rounding. Highlight the importance of: writing the number you are taking away from at the top, in subtraction; lining up the digits according to place value; working from right to left; **carrying over** tens into the next column in addition; and **borrowing** a ten from the next column when a subtraction is not possible.

Use a number line and show adding and subtracting positive numbers, before working with **negative numbers**. Highlight the start number as *position* on the number line, and operation as *direction*.

Progress to calculations including negatives. For example, –4 + 7 and 6 – –4. Ask students to demonstrate the calculation, reinforcing start number and direction of jump.

② Discuss whether the **decimal** calculation 2.4 + 5 + 1.68 = 251.72 is correct. Discuss how to estimate an answer and how to calculate an accurate answer. Use a number line to demonstrate, starting at 2.4 and partitioning 1.68 into its **place value** components and taking each jump separately: 2.4 + 5 + 1 + 0.6 + 0.08

Also demonstrate using the column addition method, highlighting the key points as for non-decimal calculations above.

Explain how 'filling in the blanks' can help the calculation, for example 2.4 = 2.40 and 5 = 5.00

Discuss a subtraction calculation in the same way, for example: 23.5 – 8.6

Plenary – Skills

Ask each student to write advice for themselves about tackling addition and subtraction problems using mental and written methods without a calculator. Share and discuss their thoughts. Save a record of students' advice for display.

Exercise commentary – Skills

Encourage students to use the strategy they feel most confident with. Support students who are unsure about any method, using prompts and suggestions to tease out the common sense aspects of the method.

Question 2 Students will need the usual reminder that subtracting (a minus number) is the same as adding. Beware of the phrase 'minus a minus is a plus' as this causes confusion (as it is applied differently with multiplication/division), often leading to –3 – 4 = +7

Questions 3 and **4** Students could work in pairs and discuss the best strategy for each calculation. Compensation can be confusing to some students. For example, in the calculation 257 + 98 they may perform 257 + 100 and then add another 2. Encourage them to refer to the original question (and relating to money can help – 'I've added £100 instead of £98, so I need to take back £2'). Using jotted number lines will also help remind students of the steps they have taken. In parts **o** to **r**, several values are involved in each calculation and students may prefer written methods. However, students must read questions carefully as occasionally addition and subtraction are combined. Here they should be encouraged to calculate each part separately.

Questions 5 to **8** The remaining questions extend to calculations where students will need to carry and borrow. In particular, students have difficulty with subtractions and will typically reverse the digits so no borrowing is necessary; instead of 5 – 8, they will calculate 8 – 5. Students must be reminded that you cannot change the order of a subtraction: 2 – 1 is not the same as 1 – 2. (Link to negative numbers.) Encourage students to write each calculation in large writing, leaving sufficient space between the digits to enable them to record any borrowing clearly. Throughout the exercise encourage students to approximate an answer first to highlight any mistakes.

Question 9 Ask students to carry out the subtraction using their method and then compare with the question. Ask students to explain why carrying from the top line is equivalent to adding to the second line.

Simplification – Skills

Students should consolidate their skills with one- and two-digit numbers rather than larger numbers; with positive numbers rather than negative numbers; with integers rather than decimals; or with decimals to one dp rather than more decimal places.

Extension – Skills

Students could work out the answers to harder and/or mixed addition and subtraction calculations, such as those involving some or all of these: negative numbers, decimals, longer strings of four or five numbers to calculate with.

Recap – Applications

1 **a** 27 – 14 (13) **b** 325 + 419 (744)
c 4006 – 2327 (1679)

2 **a** 17 + –2 (15) **b** –7 + 14 (7)
c 11 + –19 (–8) **d** –7 + –4 (–11)
e –3 – –1 (–2) **f** –5 – –11 (6)

3 **a** 72.4 + 121.64 (194.04)
b 8.6 – 7.75 (0.85)
c –13.7 + 18.61 (4.91)
d –23.6 + –17.4 (–41)

Plenary – Applications

Challenge students to write a number sentence which has an answer of –1.5

The sentence must include at least three numbers and three symbols (+ and/or –). Swap the sentences around for other students to check.

Exercise commentary – Applications

Question 1 Ask students to suggest different strategies for adding list of number using mental methods and jottings. Such as grouping together number pairs that add up to multiples of ten.

Question 2 Remind students to include carry digits on the calculations and work from right to left. Students may struggle to fill in the tens column in part **a**, ask students to think about how they end up with a '2' in the hundreds column in the answer.

Question 3 Students can create their own number pyramids and challenge a partner.

Question 4 Prompt students to work out the cost of the books first. A mother may buy more than one copy of each book.

Question 5 Explore different strategies for accurately calculating multiple additions.

Question 6 Extend by posing question such as: How many points does Edward need to be top of the league? How many points would Asha need to beat Callum in the league?

Question 7 This can be time-consuming. It is a suitable question for working in pairs. The most able could extend the task further by inventing similar problems.

Question 8 Students should attempt to add the four weights in a single calculation, prompt students to add extra zeros to keep their columns aligned correctly.

Simplification – Applications

Students should work on problem-solving examples with fewer stages and smaller, positive and/or simple decimal numbers only; with the emphasis on ensuring correct application of the methods learned.

Extension – Applications

Students could work on problem-solving examples with a negative decimal answer or with multiple stages. Or they could complete further word problems.

1.4 Multiplying and dividing

Objectives

① **N2** Apply multiplication and division, including formal written methods, to integers and decimals – both positive and negative

② **N2** Understand and use place value and relationships between operations when calculating

③ **N3** Use conventional notation for priority of operations, including brackets and powers

Useful resources

Number line, place value table, multiplication squares, mini whiteboards, blank grid templates

Starter – Skills

Write up the statement: 'Multiplying a value by something makes the value larger.'

Ask students to discuss in pairs and decide on the truth or otherwise of this statement, with reasons. Share some of the results and reasons.

Follow this with the statement: 'Multiplying by 0.1 is the same as dividing by 10'.

Teaching notes – Skills

① Discuss different **mental methods** for tackling both **multiplication** and **division**.

- **Factors**: $7 \times 16 = 7 \times 8 \times 2$, $48 \div 16 = 48 \div 2 \div 8$
- **Compensation**: $17 \times 9 = 17 \times 10 - 17$
- **Partitioning**: $256 \times 3 = (200 + 50 + 6) \times 3$ or $134 \div 2 = (100 + 30 + 4) \div 2$

Discuss which method would be best for 21×9, 23×6, 23×7, $342 \div 3$, $138 \div 6$ and $756 \div 7$

Demonstrate **standard written methods** of **multiplication** and **division** and emphasise the importance of **estimating** each calculation first.

Use examples to illustrate how to multiply and divide with **negative numbers**. Generalise rules for:

- positive by negative/negative by positive (−)
- positive by positive/negative by negative (+)

② Ask students to think how they could **simplify a calculation** such as 1.8×0.25 (no calculators).

Encourage and praise recognition of 0.25 as $\frac{1}{4}$ or the equivalence of 0.9×0.5, $1.8 \div 4$, etc.

Give further calculations for similar thinking and sharing of strategies.

③ Challenge students to make 46 and 34 using all three numbers 12, 11 and 2 and any operation.

$(12 + 11) \times 2 = 46$ and $12 + 11 \times 2 = 34$

Highlight that you use the same digits and operations. Remind students of the use of brackets to determine which operation is done first.

Highlight **BIDMAS** as a tool for recalling the **order of operations**. Write the calculation $3 + 4^2 \times 5$ and discuss how to evaluate it. Encourage students to work through the order systematically: Are there any brackets? Are there any powers? etc.

Plenary – Skills

Ask students to write advice for themselves on tackling multiplication and division problems effectively and efficiently without a calculator. These might cover anything they have found challenging in relation to mental or written methods, or calculations involving negative numbers and/or decimals. Share and discuss some of these points.

Exercise commentary – Skills

Questions 1 to **3** Students may feel that the direction signs get in the way when multiplying and dividing. Explore what happens in a few examples, then ask students find their own way of doing these accurately and more quickly. This is likely to result in students formulating their own 'rules', which are likely to have more relevance for a student than any given in a book.

Question 4 Misconceptions often surround the expectations of what constitutes a mental method or a written method. Mental strategies can involve jottings, and encourage this if it helps students. Similarly, jottings can adequately support written methods. These points need to be made clear to help students' progress.

Question 5 Students could use a formal method for each part or a written version of their answer to check. For example it is equally appropriate to do 17×19 as long multiplication or as $(17 \times 20) - 17$. The important aspect here is that students feel confident and are competent with a written approach of their own choice.

Questions 6 to **10** Encourage estimation to check the answer is reasonable. Sometimes pattern-spotting is useful. $200 \div 50 = 4$, $200 \div 5 = 40$ so $200 \div 0.4$ must be 400

Questions 11 to **14** Misconceptions and errors will occur where calculations have no brackets, as students will read and calculate in a linear manner. Encourage looking at the whole statement first before calculating.

Question 15 The questions are a good test of calculator work. Students who get the answer wrong using a calculator must estimate the answer to spot any errors and may need more practice!

Simplification – Skills

Students should focus on calculations involving one- and two-digit numbers rather than larger, positive rather than negative, integers or one-place decimals rather than more complex decimals.

Extension – Skills

Students could research alternative calculation methods such as those used by the Egyptians or the 'Russian method'. Puzzles such as 'four fours' could also be given to students who are confident in their application of the order of operations.

Recap – Applications

1 **a** $7 - 6$ (−42)

b -7×-6 (42)

c $36 \div -9$ (−4)

d $-36 \div -9$ (4)

2 Use a written method to calculate

a 51.6×3.82 (197.112)

b 42.5×31.6 (1343)

c $126.84 \div 2.8$ (45.3)

d $44.631 \div 0.57$ (78.3)

3 $26 \times 91 = 2366$ Write down the values of

a 2.6×9.1 (23.66)

b 2600×910 (2 366 000)

c $23.66 \div 2.6$ (9.1)

d $0.2366 \div 0.91$ (0.26)

4 Using BIDMAS, work out the values of:

a $3 + 4 \times 5$ (23)

b $7(13 - 4 \div 2)$ (77)

c $4^3 - (3^2 + 2^2)$ (51)

d $4^3 - (3 \times 2)^2$ (28)

e $7 + (15 - (2 + 9))$ (11)

f $\dfrac{6^2}{3^2 - 5}$ (9)

g $144 \div (6^2 \times (4^2 \div 2^3))$ (2)

Plenary – Applications

Show a calculation with its answer, for example:

$4.2 \times 17 = 71.4$

Ask students in pairs or groups to list three to five equivalent calculations and three to five calculations that follow from this statement. For example:

- Equivalent: $42 \times 1.7 = 71.4$ or $71.4 \div 17 = 42$
- Follow on: $42 \times 17 = 714$ or $2.1 \times 17 = 35.7$

Select some to display to the whole group, asking students to explain the equivalence. Encourage using related-fact strategies such as doubling, halving and links to powers of 10, connections with 10 and 5, etc.

Exercise commentary – Applications

Questions 1 and **2** Fairly simple problems involving multiplication. Language and culture may be an issue in question **1** – substitute forwards count as forwards.

Question 3 This question refers to units of area. Some students will struggle with part **c**, which requires a 'common sense' response: students should note that it is cheaper to buy 5 bags than 4.

Question 4 There is a lot of information given in this problem. Students will need to realise that there are two types of pack.

Question 5 This question also gives a lot of information, and involves area in square feet. Students will need to assume that the room is rectangular, and use the formula for area of a rectangle. Encourage use of scaling (in this case × 3.5). Part **c** involves percentage increase.

Question 6 Missing digits in standard methods of multiplication and division – these are more challenging than the addition and subtraction problems encountered in an earlier exercise, but can be done by careful deduction (and maybe a little trial and error!)

Question 7 This involves conversion between metric and imperial units of capacity. There may be some language issues, so ensure all students understand the question.

Simplification – Applications

Students should be given further examples to consolidate multiplication and division techniques, and practise them on problems that are no more than two-stage, and involve smaller and simpler numbers.

Extension – Applications

Students could work on more complex and multi-stage problems requiring the correct application of BIDMAS. They could also be challenged to invent (complicated) problems that yield a particular given answer.

1 Calculations 1

Key outcomes	Quick check
N1 Order positive and negative integers and decimals; use the symbols =, ≠, <, >, ≤, ≥.	**1** Put each list of numbers in order, starting with the smallest. **a** 3.5 3.497 3.54 3.07 3.47 (3.07, 3.47, 3.497, 3.5, 3.54) **b** – 10 8 0 –3 –21 (–21, –10, –3, 0, 8) **2** Write > or < between each pair of numbers. **a** 730 795 (730 < 795) **b** 8.3 8.1 (8.3 > 8.1) **c** 4.03 4.51 (4.03 < 4.51) **d** 0.652 0.67 (0.652 < 0.67)
N2 Apply the four operations, including formal written methods, to both positive and negative integers and decimals; understand and use place value (e.g. when working with very large or very small numbers, and when calculating with decimals).	**3** Calculate using mental or written methods. **a** 924 + 312 (1236) **b** 12.8 + 62. (74.8) **c** 2.58 + 13.3 (15.88) **d** 1205 – 720 (485) **e** 834.5 – 38.9 (795.6) **f** 27.64 – 3.9 (23.74) **4** Calculate. **a** –8 + –1 (–9) **b** –3 – –5 (2) **c** –4 × +7 (–28) **d** –8 × –7 (56) **e** –39 ÷ +3 (–13) **f** –48 ÷ –12 (4) **5** Calculate using mental methods. **a** 30 × 15 (450) **b** 24 × 7 (168) **c** 400 ÷ 8 (50) **d** 540 ÷ 90 (6) **6** Calculate using written methods. **a** 89 × 63 (5607) **b** 9.5 × 14.9 (141.55) **c** 182 ÷ 7 (26) **d** 322 ÷ 1.4 (230) **7** Work out the value of **a** 9.48 × 100 (948) **b** 0.67 × 1000 (670) **c** 870 ÷ 100 (8.7) **d** 80.1 ÷ 1000 (0.0801)
N3 Use conventional notation for priority of operations, including brackets, powers	**8** Evaluate these without using a calculator. **a** 35 – 16 ÷ 8 (33) **b** 3 × (7 + 3) (30) **c** 3 × 42 (126) **d** $19 + \sqrt{100}$ (29)
N15 Round numbers and measures to an appropriate degree of accuracy (e.g. to a specified number of decimal places or significant figures).	**9** Round **a** 905 to the nearest 10 (910) **b** 68.7 to the nearest whole number (69) **c** 3.427 to 1 dp (3.4) **d** 0.587 to 2 dp (0.59) **e** 803 to 1 sf (800) **f** 9354 to 2 sf (9400) **g** 0.79 to 1 sf (0.8) **h** 0.0805 to 2 sf (0.081)

Misconceptions and challenges	Solutions
Students often struggle with ordering negative decimals. For example, they will think that –2 < –2.5.	Show the number line as a reflection around 0. This will help students to see that –2 is greater than –2.5.
Many students are reluctant to apply BIDMAS, as they are used to calculating from left to right. They may try to reorder an expression, with all the divisions to the left and the subtractions last of all.	Work in reverse: start with something simple, 4 + 4, and build up its complexity, 4 + 4 = (16 – 12) + 4 = (4 × 4 – 12) + 8 ÷ 2... Once students grasp BIDMAS they will have a more thorough understanding of algebraic expressions.
Students will often interpret '=' as a request for an answer as a result of seeing calculations like '21 + 35 = ?' in their formative years.	Encourage students to see the equals sign as a 'balance point', meaning 'is the same as'. Students will have difficulty with even simple equations and recording multi-step workings until they understand this distinction.

Misconceptions and challenges	Solutions
Students may not have secure recall of times-tables and often view times tables work as patronising or embarrassing.	Repeatedly use the same multiplication fact, for example 7 × 8, in a series of lessons, or the 6 times table in a whole series of problems about area of shapes. This will improve students' fluency and increase their willingness to tackle problems that are more complex.

Review question commentary

Do not use calculators in this exercise except for question **15**.

Question 1 (1.1) – A possible misconception is to simply add zeros on the end of the number when multiplying by powers of 10. Encourage students to think about place value.

Question 2 (1.1) – Remind students not to write an unnecessary zero at the end in part **b**.

Question 3 (1.1) – Remind students that the open side of the inequality sign indicates the larger number.

Question 4 (1.1) – Remind students to line up the numbers with the decimal point in part **b**.

Questions 5 and **6 (1.2)** – Remind students to check that their answers are sensible approximations.

Question 7 (1.3) – Encourage students to think about their starting number and then work out which the direction to move on the number line.

Questions 8 and **9 (1.3)** – Parts **a** and **b** could be done mentally but for **c** and **d** students should use column methods, making sure to line up the digits and decimal point.

Question 10 (1.4) – Make links between multiplying and dividing negative numbers.

Ask students to rewrite parts **a** and **b** as division facts and parts **c** and **d** as multiplication facts.

Question 11 (1.4) – Remind students of the different mental methods for multiplying and dividing: halving and doubling, repeated doubling and using related calculations.

Questions 12 and **13 (1.4)** – Students should use formal written methods and show their working. Students might find it easier to take out decimal points in **13** and put them back in at the end.

Questions 14 and **15 (1.4)** – Both question rely on the use of 'BIDMAS', **15** tests the appropriate use of a calculator.

Review answers

1 **a** 6 700 **b** 85.2 **c** 240 **d** 5

2 **a** 45 **b** 6.21 **c** 0.079 **d** 0.006

3 **a** 905 < 961 **b** 14.7 < 14.9
c 0.7 > 0.09 **d** 0.214 < 0.22

4 **a** 53 099, 53 909, 503 099, 503 909 530 909
b 4.09, 4.289, 4.29, 4.3, 4.32
c –14, –8, –4, 0, 9

5 **a** 850 **b** 25 **c** 0.8 **d** 62.94

6 **a** 400 **b** 5 100 **c** 45.7 **d** 0.08
e 0.090 **f** 1

7 **a** –1 **b** –5 **c** 6 **d** 2
e 0 **f** –3

8 **a** 1 358 **b** 38.4 **c** 914.07 **d** 7.401

9 **a** 513 **b** 268 **c** 219.2 **d** 3.67

10 **a** –21 **b** 32 **c** –5 **d** 13

11 **a** 240 **b** 400 **c** 40 **d** 8

12 **a** 2 961 **b** 14 976 **c** 28 **d** 26

13 **a** 17.92 **b** 11.637 **c** 2.45 **d** 5.65

14 **a** 33 **b** 17 **c** 55 **d** 45
e 18 **f** 14

15 **a** 36 **b** 2

Assessment 1

Question 1 – 6 marks

a $-33 < 8$ [M1]

$-33, 8, 19, 44, 303, 576$

Lose 1 mark for each error. [A2]

b $-576 < -19$ [M1]

$-576, -19, 8, 33, 44, 303$

Lose 1 mark for each error. [A2]

Question 2 – 4 marks

$42 \div 100 = 0.42$	$0.3 \times 10 = 3$
$4236 \div 1000 = 4.236$	$516 \div 10 = 51.6$
$42 \times 100 = 4200$	$216 \times 1000 = 216\,000$

[M1, A2]

The numbers are ordered correctly. [F1]

Question 3 – 6 marks

a

2	−4	2
−2	**−2**	
−4		

[B3]

b

−9	**−16**	2
−25	−14	
−39		

[B3]

Question 4 – 6 marks

a 24 [B1]

b [B5]

7	**12**	**5**
6	8	10
11	**4**	**9**

Question 5 – 2 marks

a No, 271.75 cm < 271.775 cm

Must see a reason. [B1]

b No, 233.345 cm > 233.3415 cm

Must see a reason. [B1]

Question 6 – 5 marks

a Yes [B1]

[36 = 40 (1 sf) and 44 = 40 (1 sf)]

b 36 + 1 = 37 = 40 (1 sf)

44 + 1 = 45 = 50 (1 sf) [M1]

No [A1]

c 36 + 9 = 45 = 50 (1 sf) but 44 = 40 (1 sf)

44 + 9 = 53 = 50 (1 sf) but 52 = 50 (1 sf) [M1]

Dave is 45, Jane is 53. [A1]

Question 7 – 8 marks

a Abena 13 000 (2 sf) [B1]

Edward 8100 (2 sf) [B1]

b Abena $3.142 \times 13\,000 = 40\,846$ km

Edward $3.142 \times 8100 = 25\,450$ km [M1]

$40\,864 - 25\,450$ [M1]

$= 15\,414$ km [A1]

OR

$3.142 \times (13\,000 - 8100)$ [M1]

$= 3.142 \times 4900$ [M1]

$= 15395.8$ [A1]

c Abena 10 000 (1 sf)

Edward 10 000 (1 sf) [M1]

Difference = 0 [M1]

Estimate would be inaccurate. [A1]

Question 8 – 4 marks

a C [$27.65 \neq 27.6$] [B1]

b B [$33.18 \neq 33.12$] [B1]

c B [$4.6 \neq 4.575$] [B1]

d A [$11.11 \neq 11.1$] [B1]

Question 9 – 10 marks

A (20.16, 29.6) [B1]

B (6.8, 17.71) [B1]

C (29.6, 9.76) [B1]

D (17.71, 12.2) [B1]

E (46.27, 5.4) [B1]

F (9.76, 46.27) [B1]

G (12.2, 20.16) [B1]

H (5.4, 6.8) [B1]

Any cycle of A, C, F, E, H, B, D, G

Lose 1 mark for each error. [F2]

Question 10 – 3 marks

Distance = 850×2.5 [M1]

$85 \times 25 = 2\,125$ m [M1, A1]

Accept any valid written multiplication method.

Question 11 – 4 marks

a $113 - 0.5 = 112.5$

$112.5 \div 4.5 = 25$ sweets [M1, A1]

b $135\,400 \div 5.4 = 25\,074.07...$ [M1]

$= 25\,000$ (nearest 1000) [A1]

Question 12 – 2 marks

a $(3 + 4) \times 5 + 2 = 37$ [B1]

b $60 \div (5 + 7) + 5 = 10$ [B1]

Expressions

Learning outcomes

A1 Use and interpret algebraic notation, including:
- ab in place of $a \times b$
- $3y$ in place of $y + y + y$ and $3 \times y$
- a^2 in place of $a \times a$, a^3 in place of $a \times a \times a$, a^2b in place of $a \times a \times b$
- a/b in place of $a \div b$
- coefficients written as fractions rather than as decimals
- brackets.

A2 Substitute numerical values into formulae and expressions.

A3 Understand and use the concepts and vocabulary of expressions, equations, formulae terms, and factors.

A4 Simplify and manipulate algebraic expressions (including those involving surds) by:
- collecting like terms
- multiplying a single term over a bracket
- taking out common factors
- simplifying expressions involving sums, products and powers, including the laws of indices.

Prior knowledge

Check-in skill

- Understand index notation.
- Understand word problems.
- Apply the four operations to positive and negative integers.
- Find common factors.

Online resources

MyMaths 1033, 1155, 1158, 1178, 1179, 1186, 1187, 1247

InvisiPen videos
Skills: 02Sa – f Applications: 02Aa – f

Kerboodle assessment
Online Skills Test 2 Chapter Test 2

Development and links

Scientists and engineers write expressions to model phenomena in the real world. Numbers are represented by symbols and then can be manipulated using a series of strict algebraic rules. This links with ideas used in computer programming. A computer game programmer represents a character in a game as a string of symbols. He then uses a series of commands to tell the computer what to do with the string of symbols to manipulate the character around the screen.

Chapter investigation

This is a classic type of puzzle so students may have encountered something similar before but it is worth pursuing. Allow students to investigate and realise that they always obtain 2 (even if they use negative numbers, decimals or fractions). Explain that 'algebra' provides a language for generalising and understanding why the puzzle works for *any* number. Formulating the puzzle will require knowledge of algebraic notation and language, the order of precedence of operations and the use of brackets [**2.1, 2.4**]. It may help to think of dividing by two as multiplying by a half. The interpretation of the algebra should be reinforced by substituting numbers for the unknown and evaluating. As students become confident, challenge them to create their own puzzles *and* explanations.

Pose a second type of puzzle: think of a number; double it; take away 10; add three times the original number; divide the answer by 5; add 2; what do you get? (The original number). Use this as an introduction to simplifying expressions and collecting like terms [**2.2**] and develop the idea to the case of several variables.

Pose a third type of puzzle: think of a number; triple it; square your answer; divide your answer by 9; divide your answer by the original number; what do you get? (The original number). Use this as an introduction to basic index notation and rules of indices [**2.3**]. Rather than develop convoluted problems it will be easier to treat indices as a 'digression' and investigate their properties in their own right.

2.1 Terms and expressions

Objectives

① **A2** Substitute numerical values into formulae and expressions

②**A3** Understand and use the concepts and vocabulary of expressions, equations and formulae

Useful resources

Dice

Starter – Skills

Write on the board $d + 3$ Roll a dice to generate the number for d. Students must evaluate the expression taking d to be this number. The student who correctly evaluates the expression gets to roll the dice. Repeat with different expressions: $d - 1$, $d + 3$, extending to multiplications: $2d$, $3d$ and combinations: $2d + 1$, and so on.

Teaching notes – Skills

Ask students what they understand by the term 'substitution'. Refer to a football match where one player replaces another.

Refer to the mental starter. Explain that students were substituting a value for the symbol d to evaluate the expression. Discuss how to evaluate expressions with two variables, such as $x + y$ where $x = 8$ and $y = 7$. Demonstrate working out and replacing the variables with the values before evaluating the expression. Extend to consider $y - 2x$ and recall order of operations. Ensure students understand multiplication must be done before addition and subtraction.

Plenary – Skills

Draw an equilateral triangle on the board with equal side notation and one dimension labelled x. Invite students to consider the expression for the perimeter of the rectangle. Highlight multiplication as repeated addition and emphasise the idea of collecting like terms to simplify. Ask students to suggest different values for x and work out the perimeter.

Exercise commentary – Skills

Question 1 In this question students have to match a description of an expression with the actual expression. In this question only one operation is used. Pupils may need to be told that n stands for the unknown number and that $\frac{n}{2}$ means $n \div 2$.

Questions 2, 3 and **4** In these questions students need to demonstrate that they can correctly write expressions given in words using algebra, in each case only one operation has been used. Working through the first example given on page 26 before asking students to attempt these questions may be advisable. Some students may give the answer to question **4 f** as $\frac{3}{4}x$ and others may give it as $\frac{3x}{4}$ discuss how both answers are acceptable and mean the same thing.

Question 5 This question is a progression of the first question and involves students matching expressions involving two operations. Students may need to be reminded that if you wish to add or subtract before multiplying then brackets need to be used and also the convention of placing the number that needs to be multiplied on the left of the brackets.

Question 6 A variety of common misconceptions are raised here – ensure students are clear that $7a$ means $7 \times a$ and that x^2 means $x \times x$.

Questions 7 and **8** These questions involve simple substitutions of just one variable. Ensure students realise that the use of a fraction line is another way of writing a division. Encourage students to show evidence of working out too. The second example given on page 26 may aid with these questions.

Question 9 This question uses substitution of one more than one variable. Negative numbers need to be substituted and some answers are negative – students should not be put off by this. Ensure they are clear about the rules of multiplying and dividing negative numbers and that xy means $x \times y$. Any students that are finding this topic difficult could look at the final example on page 26.

Question 10 Here students need to substitute numbers into expressions that involve the need to square. Often students think that when you square a negative number the answer is also negative, explain why this is not the case.

Question 11 Emphasise that in the expression $2x^2$, x^2 has to be calculated before multiplying by 2, whereas when you have $(2x)^2$ you would need to multiply by 2 before squaring. It would be worth reminding pupils of the order of operations and linking this topic to that

Question 12 This would make a suitable question to cover as a whole class. Discuss what the perimeter of any shape is and demonstrate by drawing a rectangle and labelling the sides a and b that the formula for the perimeter given can be derived.

Simplification – Skills

Students can practise substituting values into expressions which involve only one letter and a sequence of plus and minus terms.

Extension – Skills

Challenge students to come up with their own expressions (as easy or difficult as they like) and substitute a range of numbers into them. These numbers could be as easy or difficult as *you* like.

Recap – Applications

1 a Are the following statements true or false?

i $3a = 3 \times a$ (T) ii $a + a = a^2$ (F)

iii $5a = a + 5$ (F) iv $3 - a = -3a$ (F)

v If $c = 3$, then $7c = 21$ (T)

vi If $s = 5$, then $s^3 = 35$ (F)

b b is squared and then multiplied by 5.

Which of the following shows correct result?

i $10b$ ii $2b^5$ iii $b^2 + 5$ iv $5b^2$ (iv)

c Write algebraic expressions for the following:

i 3 added to x and the result multiplied by 7 ($7(x + 3)$)

ii 5 multiplied by y and added to z multiplied by 12 ($5y + 12z$)

2 If $d = 4$; $e = -2$, $f = 0$ and $g = 5$, find the values of

a $5e$ (-10) b g^3 (125)

c de (-8) d $defg$ (0)

e e^2 (4) f $2d + 4e - 5f - 6g$ (-30)

g d^2e (-32) h $f \div g$ (0)

i $d^2e^3 \div g^2$ (-5.12) j $\frac{d}{e} + \frac{g}{d}$ (-0.75)

3 a A square has side length m.

Write expressions for the area and perimeter. ($A = m^2, P = 4m$)

b A rectangle has sides of lengths m and n. Write expressions for its area and perimeter. ($A = mn, P = 2(m + n)$)

c An isosceles triangle has two sides of length $4x - 3y$ and a third side of length $2x + 4y$. Write an expression for its perimeter. ($P = 10x - 2y$)

d An isosceles triangle has two sides of length $3p - 4q$. The perimeter is $5p - 7q$, find the length of the third side. ($-p + q$)

Plenary

A real-life application of substituting values into an expression is the conversion of Celsius to Fahrenheit temperatures. Give students the approximate formula: $F = 2C + 30$.

Invite students to mentally calculate Fahrenheit temperatures for various Celsius temperatures.

Exercise commentary

Question 1 This question involves matching equivalent expressions. As well as linking an expression given in symbols to words it may also be worth reminding students of the link between multiplication and addition, ie $n + n + n = 3n$.

Question 2 This involves substituting a number into a given expression in order to compare the cost of two possible options. Emphasise that students must show all stages of their working out.

Question 3 Here students need to demonstrate that they fully understand the effect each term in the expression has. In part **a,** encourage students to find the cost of 1, 2 and 3 days. What do they notice? In part **c**, trial and error may be the most accessible method.

Question 4 A fun task that involves discovering a coded word. Students could be challenged to create their own versions of this activity.

Question 5 A question that involves forming an expression based on given information. Ask students to find an expression for the number of DVDs Lisa has first.

Question 6 Students should be reminded to read this question carefully, easy to mix up 'times' and 'more'. They may be confused by the wording of the questions and be looking to find a number answer, stress that an expression is needed for the number of texts Kris sends.

Question 7 This question is a similar style to that of the second example given on page 28. Students should be encouraged to 'test' their expression as shown in the example.

Question 8 This is similar to the previous question but for parts **c** and **d** there are 3 variables involved. Once again, promote the benefit of testing the expression found.

Question 9 Here a common misconception is explored. This would make a good class discussion, why do we square before multiplying? It is worth emphasising this concept as it is often answered incorrectly yet is encountered frequently.

Question 10 Tell students to translate what each person is saying into symbols as shown in the final example on page 28. In order to know whether Cerys is correct or not encourage the substitution of the 1st equation into the 2nd equation. Students could be challenged to pose problems of a similar style for each other.

Simplification

Students will benefit from access to a number line (–20 to 20) and should be encouraged to consider starting number and direction in any addition and subtraction calculations.

Extension

Ask students to find other conversions, such as stones to kilograms, and substitute values.

2.2 Simplifying expressions

Objectives

① **A4** Simplify and manipulate algebraic expressions by collecting like terms

Useful resources

Mini whiteboards

Starter – Skills

Here are six statements about repeated addition and subtraction.

Invite students to decide which are true and which are false.

1. $5 + 5 + 5 + 5 + 5 + 5 = 6 \times 5$ (T)
2. $3 + 3 + 3 - 3 + 3 + 3 - 3 + 3 = 4 \times 3$ (T)
3. $7 + 7 + 7 - 7 + 7 - 7 = 0$ (F)
4. $4 - 4 + 4 + 4 - 4 + 4 = 6 \times 4$ (F)
5. $8 + 8 + 9 - 8 - 9 + 8 + 9 = 2 \times 8 + 9$ (T)
6. $11 + 12 - 11 + 11 + 12 + 12 = 11 + 3 \times 12$ (T)

Ask students to make up a seventh statement, which may be true or false, using three different numbers and addition/subtraction signs. Pick some of these to be shared with the class.

Link this to algebraic *expressions* made up from several *terms*.

Teaching notes – Skills

Draw a square on the board. Ask students how long each side is. Say that it is unknown and remind students a letter can be used to represent such an unknown. Emphasise that the same letter can be used on each side because the lengths are equal. Ask students to write an expression for the perimeter on mini whiteboards.

Emphasise $t + t + t + t$ is 4 lots of t and can be written simpler as $4 \times t$. Recall algebraic convention of 'hidden' multiplication and link to $4t$.

Discuss the total perimeter of two identical squares.

Highlight 4 lots of t and 4 lots of t makes 8 lots of t.

Formalise: 'like' terms have been collected together to *simplify* the expression.

Discuss how to simplify $4p + 8p - 3p$, ensuring students note the subtraction.

Discuss the meaning of 5^2. Ensure students understand that powers are used when a number multiplies by itself. Highlight the power as the number of times it multiplies by itself. Link to algebra $b^2 = b \times b$ and emphasise the powers notation makes the expression simpler.

Plenary – Skills

Draw a rectangle on the board with height labelled x and length labelled $x + 5$.

Invite students to consider the expression for the perimeter of the rectangle.

Highlight you can only collect like terms; numbers with numbers, and xs with xs.

Exercise commentary – Skills

Question 1 Students may need to be reminded that d on its own represents $1d$, in parts **g** and **h** you may need to reinforce the point that only like terms can be simplified, that x and 2 are not like terms.

Question 2 This question covers a key point, that $k + k = 2k$ whilst $k \times k = k^2$.

Question 3 Here students need to collect like terms where towards the end of the question more than one type of term is given. Demonstrate how this can be achieved by first circling like terms in the same colour ensuring you include the sign before the term.

Question 4 As an extension to this question you could ask students to find two expressions that simplify to given $4a + 7b$.

Question 5 Emphasise that only like terms can be simplified.

Question 6 Further practise at collecting like terms where more than one type of term is given. You could demonstrate how to rearrange the expression so that like terms are together before simplifying.

Question 7 This question is similar to question **6** but this time some of the terms are negative. Stress that the sign before belongs to the term in front of it.

Question 8 As an extension you could ask students to simplify an expression such as $4ab + 3bc - 2ba - bc$.

Question 9 Another misconception is investigated in this question. You could as students to find the term that to itself and the itself again to make $6a$.

Questions 10 and **11** It may be worthwhile reinforcing the fact that $x^2y + y^2x$ cannot be simplified as the terms in the expression are not like terms.

Question 12 This would be a good question to answer collectively as a class. One student could pose a possible answer and the others could decide if this would be a correct possibility or not.

Question 13 Remind students that when you add fractions with the same denominator to just add the numerator, and that if the denominators are different you will first need to find equivalent fractions that have the same denominator.

Question 14 Discuss as a whole how an expression such as $5 + 6x \times 3$ can be simplified and suggest that they look through the final example on page 30 before attempting this question.

Question 15 Explain that the $\sqrt{2}$ means the square root of 2 but that if should be treated in the same way as a variable such as x or y, just like x and y, $\sqrt{2}$ and $\sqrt{3}$ are not counted as like terms.

Question 16 Ensure students simplify all of the terms in the numerator and all of the terms in the denominator first before attempting to simplify further. Demonstrate how 24 in the numerator will simplify with 6 in the denominator at this stage.

Simplification – Skills

Students should be given further examples where terms in only one letter are added. Only then should subtracting terms be introduced.

Extension – Skills

Student could be given further examples which involve expressions of the form *ab* or which involve squared terms.

Recap – Applications

1 Which of the following are like terms and which are unlike terms?

Simplify the expressions which have like terms.

a $4a + 6a$ $(10a)$	**b** $5a + 7b$
c $14ab + 62ab$ $(76ab)$	**d** $24ab + 26ba$ $(50ab)$
e $a^5 + 5a$	**f** $5pq + -3qp$ $(2pq)$
g $7p^3 + 5p^3$ $(12p^3)$	**h** $8c^2 + 9c^3$
i $4t^4 + -4t^4$ (0)	**j** $4gh + 3g$

2 Simplify these expressions:

a $3d + 4e - 5e + 9d$ $(12d - e)$

b $24fg - 13gf + 5fg - 12gf$ $(4fg)$

c $4p^2 + 9q^2 - 5p^2$ $(9q^2 - p^2)$

d $2a - 6b + 7a - 9$ $(9a - 6b - 9)$

e $3w^3 + 9w^3 - 12$ $(12w^3 - 12)$

f $c \times v \div b$ $\left(\frac{cv}{b}\right)$

g $15 \div 3e$ $\left(\frac{5}{e}\right)$

Plenary – Applications

Write $6x + 8y$ in a bubble on the board. Invite students to give expressions that would simplify to this: $4x + 2x + 3y + 5y$. Encourage students to extend to subtractions: $4x - 2x + 10y + 4x - 2y$. Develop to include alternative unknowns: $4x - 2x + 10y + 4x - 2y + 8d - 8d$.

Exercise commentary – Applications

Question 1 In this question expressions have to be formed to represent given information. A reminder that $1x$ need simply be written as x may be beneficial here.

Question 2 Here students need to match up equivalent expressions. In each box one expression will not match up with the others. It will be worth emphasising that the sign before the term belongs to the term in front of it and that the order of the terms does not matter, $7x + 2y$ is the same as $2y + 7x$

Question 3 This question reinforces the message that only 'like' terms can be simplified, $3m$ and 5 are not 'like terms'.

Question 4 Encourage students to write down possibilities, isolate 'like terms' and simplify. In part **b** do not mistakenly treat the cards as if they are written within brackets.

Question 5 A quick recap on how to find the perimeter and area of a rectangle may be needed here. Emphasise that although $4p \times 8$ can be simplified $4p + 8$ cannot. In order to answer part **b** it may be helpful to demonstrate to students that once you have found the length and width of a rectangle you can double this to get the perimeter. Fortunately the answer is the most obvious solution. Part **c** would be suitable questions to discuss as a whole class. As an extension question you could ask more able students to find as many different perimeters as possible for the rectangles in this question.

Question 6 Students should recognise that the area of the shape will be found by finding the area of the smaller rectangle and subtracting this from the area of the larger one. They may benefit from looking through the second example as the method is similar though the second stage in the question will be to subtract.

Question 7 Students may initially struggle with part **a** and may need to be prompted to name the type of triangle and what this means for the side lengths. Parts **b** and **c** provide good opportunity for discussion work and students could be asked to explain and justify their reasoning.

Simplification – Applications

Students should concentrate on examples which are just addition in the first instance. If subtraction is introduced, ensure that the final coefficients of the variables are positive numbers.

Extension – Applications

Students could be asked to create their own sets of equivalent expressions and challenge a partner to identify which go together, or they could challenge a partner to create an expression which is equivalent to one they make up.

Indices

Objectives

ⒹA4 Simplifying expressions involving sums, products and powers, including the laws of indices.

Useful resources

Mini whiteboards

Starter – Skills

Ask students to write any two terms which will multiply to give $12x^3$ on whiteboards. Select some students to add their versions to a group display.

After taking a few suggestions, ask the students to think of more unusual possibilities. Now add these to the display.

Give the students a different expression: $18a^2b$. Ask them to write on whiteboards, in a given time limit, as many different pairs of terms as they can which will produce this result in a given time limit. Ask students to compare their versions with a neighbour.

Teaching notes – Skills

Explain that you add indices when multiplying powers of the same number.

This can be written algebraically as $x^a \times x^b = x^{a+b}$.

The letters emphasise that x can be any number but must be the same number in both terms.

How can you simplify $6^5 \div 6^2$? With $6^5 \div 6^2$ you are cancelling out 2 of the 6's. So it leaves only 6^3. It is worth showing the cancelling on the board.

Test understanding using $7^6 \div 7^4 = 7^2$.

Again it is worth showing the cancelling on the board.

What shortcut rule could you use?

Dividing means *subtract* the indices.

This can be written algebraically as $x^a \div x^b = x^{a-b}$.

Discuss the power 0.

Using the subtraction rule $4^3 \div 4^3 = 4^{3-3} = 4^0$.

But any number divided by itself gives the answer 1, so $4^0 = 1$. More generally $x^0 = 1$

Discuss the power 1. $x^1 = x$ for all x.

Ask for volunteers to demonstrate this.

Plenary – Skills

Discuss answers to questions that involve both multiplication and division, with a mixture of base numbers. Make sure students are clear that they can only apply the index laws to powers of the same base.

Exercise commentary – Skills

Question 1 Students may need to be prompted to give their answers using index notation and may benefit from being given a few examples on this topic before embarking on this question.

Question 2 Ensure students realise that in this question they have to find the actual value of these expressions, you may need to remind students that when you cube a number it will remain negative and how to multiply fractions together.

Question 3 You could introduce this question by addressing a common misconception, Sally thinks that $4^3 \times 4^2 = 4^6$, do you agree? Show students that $4^3 \times 4^2 = 4 \times 4 \times 4 \times 4 \times 4 = 4^5$ so that they can fully understand what is happening here. The first part of the first example also demonstrates this.

Question 4 These questions could be introduced in a similar way to question **3**, 'Jo thinks that $5^{12} \div 5^3 = 5^4$. Do you agree? Explain and justify your answer.' The second part of the first example shows how this index law is derived. You could also show that part **a** could alternatively be written as $\frac{5^6}{5^3}$.

Question 7 This question addresses a very common misconception and provides students with an opportunity to demonstrate that they are clear how to apply the first index law covered.

Question 9 Students may initially not spot what is wrong with Tracey's attempt as the indices have been added. It may be helpful to write both terms out in the long unsimplified form in order to spot the error.

Question 10 For the final part students may incorrectly give $12st^7$ as the answer. This provides an opportunity for whole class discussion, ' who can justify why this is not the case?' (These powers do not have the same bases).

Question 11 It may be beneficial to set out this question as a division written using a fraction sign and each term given in its unsimplified version. This should make it clear to students that although the powers are subtracted the coefficients of each term are divided.

Question 12 Promote the approach of dealing with the whole numbers first and then with the powers, encourage students to double check their answers.

Questions 13 and **14** Students should set out their working in a similar style to that shown in part **e** in the second example on page 34, e.g. Expand $(3a^4)^2$, $3^2 = 9$, $(a^4)^2 = a^8$, $(3a^4)^2 = 9a^8$.

Questions 15 and **16** A quick recap on the rules of adding, subtracting and multiplying negative numbers may be needed prior to this question.

Questions 17 and **18** Ensure students show every stage of their working out so that mistakes can be minimised. In the final part of the final question you may need to remind students that to simplify the numerator first before attempting to divide by the denominator.

Simplification – Skills

Encourage students to write divisions out in fraction form to help them see the cancelling more clearly.

Extension – Skills

Ask students to use the index laws to work out the answer to $3^2 \div 3^3$. Ask them to interpret the meaning of the negative power and investigate other examples of this type.

Recap – Applications

1 Write these expressions using index notation.

a $s \times s \times s \times s$ (s^4) **b** $4 \times n \times n$ ($4n^2$)

c $5 \times u \times 5 \times u \times u$ ($25u^3$)

2 Simplify **a** $a^3 \times a^2$ (a^5)

b $b^4 \div b^2$ (b^2) **c** $(c^2)^5$ (c^{10})

d $(d^3)^{-5}$ (d^{15}) **e** $3e^4 \times 5e^2$ ($15e^6$)

f $\dfrac{f^2 \times f^8}{f^3}$ (f^7) **g** $\dfrac{4h^5 \times 3h^4}{6h^2}$ ($2h^7$)

3 Fill in the gaps (?) in the following statements:

a $5b \times ? = 15b^4$ ($3b^3$)

b $35pq \div ? = 5q$ ($7p$)

c $4a + ? - 3b - ? = 7a + 2b$ ($3a, -5b$)

d $3mn \times ? = -18m^3n^5$ ($-6m^2n^4$)

e $5f^3 \times ? = 35f^7$ ($7f^4$)

Plenary – Applications

What is the value of x in each equation?

$$x^{\frac{1}{2}} = 1, x^3 = 1, x^{-2} = 1$$

(x always equals 1)

What does this mean about 1 to any power? (Answer is always 1)

Summarise all three rules

Exercise commentary – Applications

Question 1 If students pick a card with an unsimplified expression they will find it will simplify to give an expression found on a different card.

Question 2 Students may need to start by considering how they find the volume of a cube where each side is say '5'. Remind them to apply the same method in this situation, some students may use $2xy^2 \times 2xy^2 \times 2xy^2$ whilst others may use $(2xy^2)^3$. A good opportunity to demonstrate and discuss why these are equivalent.

Question 3 Ask pupils to describe in words how they would find the area of shape. Encourage all stages of working out to be shown. Suggest students who are finding this question difficult look carefully through the first part of the first example on page 36. Ensure they realise that the final stage involves adding (part **a**) and subtracting (part **b**) but that this can only be done as the bases are the same prior to this.

Questions 4 and **5** Remind students to apply one index law at a time. Some students may find question **5** challenging, remind students to simplify the terms inside the brackets first and to treat numbers and letters separately.

Questions 6 and **7** These are problem solving style questions that may be easier to visualise by first drawing a diagram. In question **7** students will need to consider how they find the area of a square and then how they would do the reverse, find the side lengths when they know the area. It will be helpful to separate each part and ask 'what multiplies by itself to make 16?' 'what multiplies by itself to make a^2?' etc... Some will recognise that they are finding the square root here.

Question 8 Cards have to be rearranged to make statements correct. Part **b** may on first glance seem tricky but then students should realise that one side of the equation will need to be $4x^3y^3$ and will then need to consider how the coefficient '4' can be formed.

Question 9 Encourage students to write out the formula for the area of a triangle before substituting in the side lengths given. They should do each part of the calculation step by step.

Question 10 This question demonstrates to students that sometimes the expression will simplify to give a negative power.

Question 11 In this question tell students to apply what they have learnt so far about index laws. Part **h** is particularly challenging and would make a suitable extension question for more able students or may be best tackled as a whole class, show students that $4^6 \times 4^1 = 4^7$ and that $2x = 6$ leaving $x = 3$.

Question 12 Remind students to apply the final law covered and multiply the powers together.

Question 13 Tell students to apply the laws one at a time and show all stages of their working out.

Simplification – Applications

Ensure students have sufficient practice at combining indices when there are only two terms. Further examples may be required to ensure a full understanding.

Extension – Applications

Ask students to complete examples which include addition and subtraction. Are there equivalent rules for combining powers when two terms are added or subtracted? (No)

2.4 Expanding and factorising 1

Objectives

① **A4** Simplify and manipulate algebraic expressions by collecting like terms, multiplying a single term over a bracket and taking out common factors

Useful resources

Mini whiteboards

Starter – Skills

Say to the students that you are going to make them all think of the number 3.

They should use mini whiteboards and start with any number they wish; now add 2; now multiply by 5; subtract 4; add the first number thought of; halve this result; now take away 3 lots of the first number.

Check with all the students that 'it worked'. Ask them to discuss with a neighbour why it worked.

Go through the instructions briefly again, recording each stage simply on the board. Share some of the students' explanations. Encourage those who have not done so to allocate a symbol for the variable, and record the expressions.

Teaching notes – Skills

Using the activity in the mental starter, check the result of writing the expression for the stage 'multiply by 5'. Share with the whole group that it may be recorded as $5(x + 2)$ or $5x + 10$.

Remind the students of grid multiplication, and draw up the corresponding grid.

$\times$	$x + 2$
5	$5x + 10$

Formalise how to multiply a single term over a bracket.

Progress to factorising, and describe the process as being the inverse of expansion. Illustrate with the expression $24t + 36$, and ask students to suggest equivalent expressions involving brackets.

Emphasise that the number outside the bracket is a common factor of each term.

Plenary – Skills

Display this multiplication grid to the entire group.

$\times$	?
?	$16n + 24$

Ask each student to suggest possible products to produce this result. Share some of the findings. There are three possible answer groups. Repeat for another expression.

Exercise commentary – Skills

Question 1 Using arrows as shown in the introductory section is a good way to ensure you remember to multiply by both terms. You may like to show any students that find this method difficult to employ the grid method.

Question 2 This question highlights a common error and this is just to multiply the term on the outside by the first term on the inside of the brackets. Ask students to state what the answer should be.

Questions 3 and **4** Emphasise that the sign before a term belongs to the term in front of it and remind students of the rules involving multiplying negative numbers

Questions 5 and **6** Recap that $y \times y = y^2$. Question **6** reminds students to multiply the term on the outside by all the terms on the inside.

Question 7 It will be worth emphasising that $x \times x^2 = x \times x \times x = x^3$ and it would be advisable to go through the final part of this question as a whole class, students may be unsure how to treat the fraction.

Question 8 A common oversight when expanding and simplifying these types of expressions is to forget to allow for the negative sign given. Place emphasis on the fact that the sign before a term belongs to the term in front of it.

Question 9 The HCF could be a number, a letter or even both – it may be worth discussing the final part of this question to highlight the latter.

Question 10 Tell students that integers are whole numbers. Ensure they realise that they can check their answer by expanding the brackets.

Question 12 Discuss why an answer such as $2(3w + 27)$ would not be correct for the final part.

Question 13 Emphasise that an expression cannot be factorised if it does not contain any common factors.

Questions 14, 15 and **16** Encourage students to think about the numbers first and then the letters. Stress the importance of expanding the brackets to double check the final answer.

Question 17 This question could be answered by expanding brackets or factorising and therefore provides an effective illustration of the fact that factorising is the reverse process of expanding brackets.

Simplification – Skills

Ask students to work through several numerical examples of the form, $5 \times 13 = 65$ and $5 \times (10 + 3) = 5 \times 10 + 5 \times 3 = 50 + 15 = 65$, before agreeing on what is the correct procedure for expanding a single bracket.

Extension – Skills

Give students more questions which require simplification after the expansion, for example where like terms need collecting, squared terms may appear and multiple brackets may be involved.

Recap – Applications

1 a Does $4(g-3) = 4g-3$? (No)

b Does $4(g-3) = 4g+12$? (No)

2 Expand

a $5(r+9)$ $(5r+45)$

b $6(s-2)$ $(6s-12)$

c $-7(f+3)$ $(-7f-21)$

d $-2(2s-1)$ $(-4s+2)$

e $6(3p-5d)$ $(18p-30d)$

f $-3(4z-3y)$ $(-12z+9y)$

g $12c(4c+5d)$ $(48c^2+60cd)$

h $-15e(-4f+3e^2)$ $(60ef-45e^3)$

i $12(3v-4w)-9(7v-5w)$ $(-27v-3w)$

3 Completely factorise these statements.

a $15p+25q-35r$ $(5(3p+5q-7r))$

b a^2+3a $(a(a+3))$

c $14v^3w^2+35vw^3$ $(7vw^2(2v^2+5w))$

d $16d^3e-8de^2$ $(8de(2d^2-e))$

e $6z+8zw-z^3$ $(z(6+8w-z^2))$

Plenary – Applications

On the board, present this incorrect algebra:

$$\begin{aligned} 3(4x+8)+4(2x-3) &= 12x+24+8x-12 \\ &= 20x-12 \\ &= 2(10x-6) \end{aligned}$$

Ask students to work in pairs and identify the errors in the reasoning. Share and discuss the students' comments.

Exercise commentary – Applications

Question 1 Suggest students abbreviate Lucy, Mary and Nat to 'L', 'M' and 'N'. They will probably understand that the expression that represents the amount that Nat picks will be $n+5$ multiplied by 3 but may need some prompting to understand that brackets will need to be used here.

Question 2 This question may initially seem confusing to students as there is a lot of information to read but soon they should realise that they will only need to read one sentence at a time in order to form the required expression for the age of each person. Some may give the age of Jake's grandmother as $2(4n-2)$ whereas others may expand the brackets to give $8n-4$, this may provide a useful discussion point and an opportunity to discuss the fact that these are equivalent. In part **b** students will need to expand brackets taking care with negative signs and then simplify like terms.

Question 3 Students may spot that both Kate's attempt at factorising and Bryn's attempt expand to give the original expression. This provides a chance to emphasise the fact that when you factorise you should find the HCF (Highest Common Factor).

Question 4 Students should compare the x terms and then the constant terms, they should also be reminded to check their final answers by expanding.

Question 5 This question provides an opportunity to recap on the difference between an expression and an equation and also that when you rearrange equations you should perform the same operation to both sides of the equation.

Question 6 This question makes a suitable one for whole class discussion. In part **a** 'what process would lead us to a solution?' In part **b** 'how can we ensure that we get a number other than 1 on the outside of the brackets?'

Question 7 Here students should be prompted to simplify their expression before factorising.

Question 8 It is easy for students to make mistakes and the importance of showing every stage of their working out should be stressed.

Question 9 Remind students to factorise the given expression to find possible solutions.

Questions 10 and **11** Pose the same sort of question but where the volume is a whole number. 'How would you then find possible side lengths?' They should realise that they can be found by finding factors that multiply together to make the required volume. Hopefully this will then enable them to access this question with the awareness that they will need to factorise the given expression. Allow students to use a calculator for the final part of the last question. They should soon realise that if y is outside of this range that an impossible volume results (i.e. one equal to 0 or a negative value), discuss the reason the value of x has no impact.

Question 12 Students may need to be given the formula for the area of the trapezium here. It will be much easier for them to expand their brackets if they have simplified as much as possible prior to this.

Simplification – Applications

Initially students should practise taking out numerical factors only to ensure that they understand the principle of finding the highest common factor (HCF). Avoid common factors with both letters *and* numbers until they fully understand the factorisation process.

Extension – Applications

Students could be given examples which involve more than one letter per term and where the common factor is more complicated. An example of this could be $4abc+6ab$

2 Expressions

Key outcomes	Quick check
A1 Use and interpret algebraic notation, including: - ab in place of $a \times b$ -$3y$ in place of $y + y + y$ and $3 \times y$ - a^2 in place of $a \times a$ - a^3 in place of $a \times a \times a$ - a^2b in place of $a \times a \times b$ - brackets	**1** Write each of these expressions in the simplest way possible **a** $c \times d$ (cd) **b** $f + f + f + f + f$ $(5f)$ **c** $e \times e$ (e^2) **d** $5x \times 9y$ $(45xy)$ **2** Simplify the following expressions by collecting like term **a** $9s + 8s$ $(17s)$ **b** $3m + 2n + m + 5n$ $(4m + 7n)$ **c** $8p - 5p - 4q - q$ $(3p - 5q)$ **d** $5y^2 + 3y^2 + 3y + 4y$ $(8y^2 + 7y)$
A2 Substitute numerical values into formulae and expressions, including scientific formulae.	**3** Substitute $r = 2$ to find the value of these expressions **a** $8r$ (16) **b** $r + 14$ (16) **c** $5r - 30$ (–20) **d** r^3 (8) **4** Use the formula $V = a + 2b$ to calculate V when **a** $a = 3$ and $b = 7$ (17) **b** $a = 8$ and $b = -2$ (4)
A3 Understand and use the concepts and vocabulary of expressions, equations, formulae, terms, factors.	**5** $5x + 4 = 9$ $D = ST$ $8x + 11$ Give an example of each of these from the cloud above **a** expression $(8x + 11)$ **b** equation $(5x + 4 = 9)$ **c** formula $(D = ST)$
A4 simplify and manipulate algebraic expressions (including those involving surds) by: - collecting like terms - multiplying a single term over a bracket - taking out common factors - simplifying expressions involving sums, products and powers, including the laws of indices.	**6** Expand the brackets in these expressions **a** $5(w - 4)$ $(5w - 20)$ **b** $9(2u + 3v)$ $(18u + 27v)$ **c** $-6(4d - 6)$ $(-24d + 36)$ **d** $2r(r + 1)$ $(2r^2 + 2r)$ **7** Factorise these expressions **a** $16 + 24a$ $(8(2 + 3a))$ **b** $22b - 11$ $(11(2b - 1))$ **c** $12x^2 + 6x$ $(6x(2x + 1))$ **d** $5cd - 15c$ $(5c(d - 3))$ **8** Simplify these expressions involving indices **a** $a^3 \times a^6$ (a^9) **b** $f^5 \div f^2$ (f^3) **c** $(c^5)^4$ (c^{20}) **d** $u^{-9} \times u^4$ (u^{-13}) **e** $8v^4 \times 2v$ $(16v^5)$ **f** $\frac{16w^5}{4w^2}$ $(4w^3)$

Misconceptions and challenges	Solutions
Students easily grasp that $2a$ means $a + a$ or 'two 'a's', and $7t$ means 'seven 't's', but lose confidence if pushed too quickly with more complex expressions.	Use visual problems to build confidence. For example, use squares or other regular shapes with side length x, and get students to write algebraic expressions for their perimeters ($x + x + x + x$, or $4x$). Then move on to irregular shapes.
Students do not have a secure understanding of adding and subtracting directed numbers. This causes them to make technical mistakes and appear to have misunderstood the algebraic content, when in fact their arithmetic is at fault.	Encourage a mental image of a number line for adding and subtracting negative numbers, and link this explicitly to simplifying algebraic expressions. To help students draw a number line with intervals marked with algebraic units ($-5a, -4a, -3a, ..., 0, a, 2a, ...$).
Students lose confidence once there is a range of terms and they then miss negative coefficients. For example, $2x + 5$ or $2a + 5b + 3s - 2b$	Ask the students to write each term on a card, including the operation (+ or –) and then physically re-arrange the cards so that they can be simplified more easily. Pay particular attention to 'invisible' operations like the hidden '+' on the first term of $2a + 5b + 3s - 2b$

Misconceptions and challenges	Solutions
Students confuse $2a$ and a^2.	Give students frequent practice with square numbers, including images of why they are square. Use starters and plenaries to compare $p^2 = 9$ and $2p = 9$, and then link this to simplifying expressions.
$3(2x - 5)$ is given incorrectly as $6x - 5$ or $2x - 15$	Look at a numerical example to help explain why we multiply all the terms in the bracket. For example, $3(4 + 5) = 12 + 15$.
Students do not understand that a subtraction is equivalent to adding a negative.	Pose problems such as: 'What is $-3 - 4$? What is $-3 - -4$?'. Stretch their understanding further by looking at '$-3 - - - -4$', then apply similar reasoning to algebraic expressions.
Students often make mistakes by trying to combine different powers. For example, $3p + 6p^2 = 9p^2$	Use numerical substitutions to 'prove' that such simplifications are not accurate.
Students struggle to see the common factors where they have a coefficient and an algebraic element. For example, for $2x^2 + 8x$ they give the common factor as only x or 2.	Give students a number of strategies. Some will respond well to thinking of this as an informal checklist ('numbers...letters'). Some will rewrite the expression without powers ('$2x^2 + 8x$' as '$2xx + 8x$').Some will link this with their method for finding HCF. Have the students explain their method to their peers.

Review question commentary

Question 2 (2.1) – Make links between writing a numerical expression and writing an algebraic expression

Question 3 (2.1) – Make sure that students understand what each expression means, in particular $5t$ means $5 \times t$.

Question 4 (2.1) – In part **c** students should first square -4 (gives 16 not -16) then multiply by 2. Incorrect order of operations could give ± 64.

Question 5 (2.1) – Make sure that students don't forget negative signs when working out these expressions, especially in part **c**.

Question 6 (2.1) – Students may have a limited understanding of the words equation, formula and expression. Extend them by asking them to write further examples of their own.

Question 7 (2.1) – Make sure that students include negative and positive signs in their list of terms.

Question 8 (2.2) – Discuss reasons for not generally using multiplication signs in algebra.

Question 9 (2.2) – Ensure students pay attention to the sign immediately preceding each term by drawing coloured circles around like terms. In part **d** emphasize that x^2 terms and x terms are not alike and can't be simplified together.

Question 10 (2.3) – In **f** students should write $3v$ not $3v^1$.

Question 11 (2.4) – Students should take care with negative signs, particularly in part **c**. A common error is to neglect to multiply the second term in the bracket.

Question 12 (2.4) – The expressions should be fully factorised as students are told to find the highest common factor. Partial factorisations include: **b** $2(4 - 2c)$, **c** $3(x^2 + 6x)$, **d** $4(ab - 3b)$. Check that students understand that letters can be a common factor.

Review answers

1 a $13y$ **b** $7xy$ **c** $3x$ **d** y^3
e $\frac{1}{2}x$ **f** $5xy$

2 a £1.35 **b** $15y$

3 a 35 **b** 15 **c** -4 **d** 49

4 a -28 **b** -12 **c** 32 **d** 18
e 1 **f** 34

5 a 6 **b** -4 **c** -2 **d** 2
e -2 **f** 6

6 a $3x - 2 = 7$ **b** $S = \frac{D}{T}$ **c** $5x - y$

7 a $+5f, +6g, -2h$ **b** $+5p, -6q, +q^2$

8 a $5ab$ **b** $4c$ **c** d^3 **d** $10fg$
e $8e - 15$ **f** $a^3 + a^2 + 3$

9 a $2r$ **b** $5a + 6b$ **c** $5d - 7e$ **d** $3x^2 + x$

10 a c^6 **b** d^5 **c** r^{12} **d** t^6
e $6u^8$ **f** $3v$

11 a $2a + 2$ **b** $32b - 16c$ **c** $-15d + 20$ **d** $h^2 + 2h$

12 a $7(2b + 1)$ **b** $4(2 - c)$ **c** $3x(x + 2)$ **d** $4b(a - 3)$

Assessment 2

Question 1 – 2 marks

They are both right. [B1]

$c + c + c + c$ means 'add c to itself four times' which is the same as $4c$. [B1]

Question 2 – 5 marks

a $V - 4$ years old [B1]

b $\frac{1}{2}V$ or $\frac{V}{2}$ years old [B1]

c $\frac{1}{2}V + 5$ years old [B1]

d $V + \frac{1}{2}V$ [M1]

$= \frac{3}{2}V$ years old. [A1]

Question 3 – 5 marks

a The DVD costs £8. [B1]

b The Blu-ray is £7 more expensive than the DVD. [B1]

c The book is half the cost of the DVD. [B1]

d The DVD and the Blu-ray together cost £23. [B1]

e The total cost of all three items is £27. [B1]

Accept equivalent statements.

Question 4 – 4marks

a $l + l + w + w$ OR $2l + 2w$ [B1]

b $l + 5 + l + 5 + w - 5 + w - 5$

OR $2(l + 5) + 2(w - 5)$ [B1]

c $2(l + 5) + 2(w - 5) = 2l + 10 + 2w - 10$

$= 2l + 2w$ [M1]

They have the same perimeter. [A1]

Question 5 – 8 marks

a $A = \pi \times 5 \times 10 = 50\pi$ [M1]

$= 157\ \text{cm}^2$ [A1]

b $45 = \pi \times r \times 4$ [M1]

$r = 45 \div 4\pi$ [M1]

$= 3.58$ m. [A1]

c $126.4 = \pi \times 12.3 \times l$ [M1]

$l = 126.4 \div 12.3\pi$ [M1]

$= 3.27$ in [A1]

Question 6 – 1 mark

Fiona

$9x - 4x + 2 = (9 - 4)x + 2 = 5x + 2$

$9x$ and $4x$ are like terms and 2 is not. [B1]

Question 7 – 11 marks

a $C = 62S + 93L$ [B2]

b $C = 4 \times 62 + 2 \times 93$ [M1]

$= 248 + 186 = 434$p [A1]

c $C = 5 \times 62 + 3 \times 93$ [M1]

$= 310 + 279 = 589$p

Julie's post costs £5.89 [A1]

d $C = 26 \times 62 + 5 \times 93 = 1612 + 465$ [M1]

$= 2077$p or £20.77 [A1]

e The two items are large letter size. [B1]

$C = 3 \times 62 + 4 \times 93$ [M1]

$= 186 + 372 = 558$p or £5.58 [F1]

Question 8 – 3 marks

$A = \dfrac{(2z^2 + 3z^2) \times 4z}{2}$ [M1]

$= (2z^2 + 3z^2) \times 2z$

$= 5z^2 \times 2z$ [M1]

$= 10z^3$ [A1]

Question 9 – 8 marks

a $\text{SA} = y^2 + y^2 + 20 \times y + 20 \times y + 20 \times y + 20 \times y$

$= 2y^2 + 4 \times 20y$ [M3]

$= 2y^2 + 80y$ [A1]

b $\text{V} = y \times y \times 20 = 20y^2$ [M1]

$20y^2 = 200$ [M1]

$y^2 = 10$ [M1]

$y = \sqrt{10}$ or 3.162...

No, he is incorrect. [A1]

Question 10 – 9 marks

a Brothers' age $= 2W - 5$ [B1]

Total ages $= 2(2W - 5) + W$ [M1]

$= 5W - 10$ [A1]

$= 5(W - 2)$ [F1]

b Dad's age $= 4W + 3$ [B1]

Mum age $= 4W + 3 - 2$ [B1]

$= 4W + 1$ [B1]

Parents' ages $= 4W + 3 + 4W + 1$ [M1]

$= 8W + 4$

$= 4(2W + 1)$ [F1]

Question 11 – 6 marks

$(10 - w) + (3w - 5) = w$ [M1]

$2w + 5 = w$ [M1]

$w + 5 = 0$ [M1]

$w = -5$ [A1]

w cannot be negative as it is a length. [B1]

Greta's diagram cannot be correct. [B1]

Question 12 – 5 marks

Area of base $= 2p \times 5p$ [M1]

$= 10p^2$ [A1]

Total area $= 10p^2 + 2 \times 2p(3p + 2) + 2 \times 5p(p - 3)$ [M1]

$= 10p^2 + 12p^2 + 8p + 10p^2 - 30p$ [M1]

$= 32p^2 - 22p$

OR $= 2p(16p - 11)$ [F1]

Question 13 – 8 marks

a $\text{DC} = a + 4 + 9$

$= a + 13$ [M1]

No [A1]

b $P = a + (a + 13) + a + (a + 13)$

$= 2a + 2(a + 13)$ [M1]

$= 2a + 2a + 26$ [A1]

$= 2(2a + 13)$ [F1]

c Area rectangle = width × length [M1]

Area of AEFD $= a \times (a + 4) = a(a + 4)$ [A1]

Area of EBCF $= 9 \times a = 9a$ [A1]

Angles and polygons

Learning outcomes

G1 Use conventional terms and notations: points, lines, [vertices, edges, planes,] parallel lines, perpendicular lines, right angles, use the standard conventions for labelling and referring to the sides and angles of triangles; draw diagrams from written description.

G3 Apply the properties of angles at a point, angles at a point on a straight line, vertically opposite angles; understand and use alternate and corresponding angles on parallel lines; derive and use the sum of angles in a triangle (e.g. to deduce and use the angle sum in any polygon, and to derive properties of regular polygons)

G4 Derive and apply the properties and definitions of: special types of quadrilaterals, including square, rectangle, parallelogram, trapezium, kite and rhombus; and triangles and other plane figures using appropriate language

G5 Use the basic congruence criteria for triangles (SSS, SAS, ASA, RHS).

G6 Apply angle facts, triangle congruence, similarity and properties of quadrilaterals to conjecture and derive results about angles and sides, [including Pythagoras' Theorem] and the fact that the base angles of an isosceles triangle are equal, and use known results to obtain simple proofs.

G11 Solve geometrical problems on coordinate axes.

G15 Use of bearings.

G19 Apply the concepts of congruence and similarity, including the relationships between lengths, in similar figures.

Prior knowledge

Check-in skill

- Measure a line segment in mm and cm.
- Estimate the size of an angle.
- Recognise right angles, angles at a point and angles on a line.

Online resources

MyMaths 1082, 1086, 1100, 1102, 1109, 1119, 1130, 1320, 1141, 1148

InvisiPen videos
Skills: 03Sa – j Applications: 03Aa – h

Kerboodle assessment
Online Skills Test 3 Chapter Test 3

Development and links

The angle properties of 2D shapes have applications in art and are important in construction and all forms of technological design. Many structures including bridges and roof trusses employ triangles in their construction to give them strength.

Bearings are used universally for air and sea navigation where the locus of all the points at a certain distance from an object or on a particular bearing from an object is called a line of position. A navigator measures the bearing or distance of visible objects using a compass or rangefinder. She draws the lines of position on the map or chart and finds her current position as the point at which the lines cross.

Chapter investigation

The students will need square dotty paper and you may need to clarify that they are only using a 3 × 3 square.

Allow students to compile lists of quadrilaterals. As a class, compile a list of the shapes and agree how to classify them based on their properties: lengths of sides, parallel sides, sizes of angles [**3.2**].

Focus attention on a parallelogram and ask students, what can you say about the various angles? Use this question to expand on the properties of the angles associated with parallel lines together with angles at a point, on a line and at an intersection [**3.1**].

An associated development is the use of angles to specify directions using bearings [**3.1**].

Return to the original problem and ask if the position or size of the shape matters. Use this as an introduction to congruent and similar shapes [**3.3**]. For example, there are nine possible 1 × 1 squares which are congruent to one another, four possible 2 × 2 squares which are congruent to one another and one possible 3 × 3 square. The 1 × 1, 2 × 2 and 3 × 3 squares are all similar to one another. Establish criteria for similarity and congruence: focus on component triangles as the simplest case and as a way to 'derive' properties of special quadrilaterals.

Ask, what is the sum of the interior and exterior angles in each quadrilateral? (360° and 360°). How does this change for triangles or other polygons? [**3.4**]

3.1 Angles and lines

Objectives

① **G1** Use conventional terms and notations: points, lines, parallel lines, perpendicular lines, right angles

② **G3** Apply the properties of angles at a point, angles at a point on a straight line

③ **G3** Use bearings

Useful resources

IWB images to support visualisations (Power Point or a Dynamic Geometry package), OHT/whiteboard file of a (local) map, 360° protractors, mini whiteboards, display of directional modelling using a geometry package or LOGO, trundle wheel, some directional compasses

Starter – Skills

Ask students to listen carefully and create a mind picture from the instructions you will read to them. To help with 'seeing', students may prefer to close their eyes, or look down. Give instructions for a visualisation which begins with a pair of parallel lines, then includes a transverse line, which can lie over the parallel lines. To help students who struggle with imaging from words, repeat while modelling with appropriate images. Question students about their images of intersections, angles, names of angle pairs, which are equal, and so on.

Teaching notes – Skills

Show a map of the local area. Mark two points of interest with a cross. Discuss how to direct someone from point A to point B using only angle of turn and distance to move. Establish that you need to know in which direction the person is facing and will be turning before considering the angle and direction to turn. Emphasise that the person will be facing North and will turn clockwise.

Repeat with other points of interest.

Emphasise that students have been using bearings; an angle measured from North. Highlight that bearings and distances are used to describe an exact journey when there are no other reference points, and are often used at sea. Highlight that bearings:

- are measured from North
- are measured clockwise
- have three digits.

Ask students to sketch on whiteboards some examples of bearings: the bearing of B from A is 090, 330, 175. What is the bearing of A from B?

Discuss use of the 360° protractor. Highlight:

- the central target of the protractor sits on the starting point ('from A to B' means start at A).
- North/0° and 360° point directly upward – encourage students to draw the North line first.
- the protractor is read in a clockwise direction.

Plenary – Skills

Refer to the map of the local area. Ask students to provide bearings from one place of interest to another. Invite them to demonstrate use of the protractor. Encourage students to calculate direct distances using the scale of the map.

Exercise commentary – Skills

Weaker students sometimes do not realise that lower-case letters represent unknown angles in diagrams, so this may need to be made clear.

Students do rely on the visual messages of drawings, and will tend to estimate angles visually rather than calculate them, so this may also need to be addressed.

Students should appreciate that the reason is as important as the correct numerical value. The reason should be given in words rather than as a calculation; for example, 'angles on a straight line'. Students often find angle values confidently, but avoid giving reasons, often because they are not sure how to write such reasons down. Providing model reasons will help, together with emphasis on marking which relies on reasoning.

Questions 1 and **2** Refer to the first worked example. In Question **1d**, remind students of the right angle symbol.

Question 3 There are many ways of finding these angles. They can be found in alphabetical order but they do not have to be.

Question 4 Refer to the second worked example. Ask students to look for the F and Z shapes.

Questions 6 to **8** Ask students to look for the F and Z shapes.

Question 8 Students may be tempted to use parallel line facts for the lines which are not parallel. It is a good question to work through as a whole class after students have attempted it.

Simplification – Skills

Students could be placed in supporting pairs to ensure correct use of protractors and accurate drawing. Students may also be given further diagrams to measure bearings on rather than moving on to draw bearings.

Extension – Skills

Students could be invited to create a 'treasure map' and mark certain features on it. They could then instruct a partner where the treasure is buried using information given as bearings.

Recap – Applications

1 Which angles are

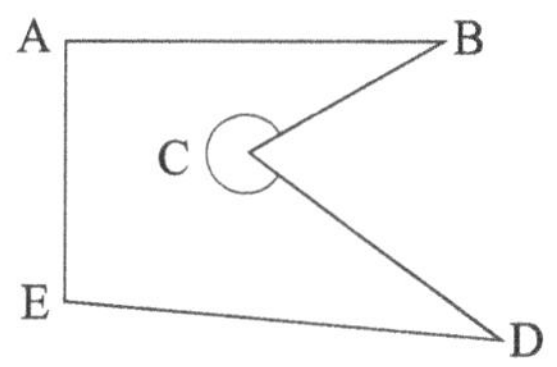

a obtuse	(E)	**b** right-angled	(A)
c reflex	(C)	**d** acute?	(B and D)

Plenary – Applications

Pick a student. Give him/her instructions to visit other students and/or places in the room. The other students interpret the moves by estimating/counting into bearing instructions for recording (say on IWB). The instructions can also be modelled at the same time using geometry or other software. Repeat the activity. Ask as many students as possible to respond with details or ask questions.

Exercise commentary – Applications

Emphasise that a sketch is not an accurate diagram, but neither should it be slapdash. It should give a good representation of the situation and it is often added to as the problem unfolds.

Students who find such exercises difficult can be helped by emphasising the notation in diagrams. Encouraging students to look carefully at diagrams, twist and turn them if necessary, and write directly onto the diagrams as well, will help to develop confidence.

Setting out the reasons for any conclusions is an opportunity to demonstrate reasoning skills.

Question 1 Students will find a sketch easier to draw on square grid paper. In part **b**, emphasise that all bearings are made clockwise. Students will find bearings above 180° easier to find with a 360° protractor.

Question 2 Students use their sketch from Question **1a**. Ask then how many degrees there are in half a right angle.

Question 3 Ask what fraction of the clock face lies in the sector between two adjacent digits. Have students find this angle. Their work can then be based on their answer.

Question 4 Ask students if something is missing from the diagram. Ask them how they would find the angle between Kate and Neil.

Question 5 Students need a good knowledge of angles on parallel lines and angles at a point. After help with part **a**, students will be better prepared for the much harder part **b**.

Questions 6 to **8** Refer to the second worked example on page 50. These questions deal with finding 'back bearings'. Questions **7** and **8** need students to draw good diagrams.

Question 9 Students need a good diagram to find their answers. It is not an easy question and a whole-class discussion would be useful.

Question 10 This question builds on Questions **5** to **9**. Students need to use the angle skills of the previous section, especially those for parallel lines, full turns and straight lines.

Question 11 Knowing that the sum of the angles of a triangle is 180° is needed in the following section on triangles. To illustrate this question, students could draw, cut out and reposition a dissected triangle as shown, but they need to know that this dissection merely illustrates the fact; it does not prove it

Simplification – Applications

Students should practise measuring bearings carefully. Provide pre-drawn diagrams for questions if necessary.

Extension – Applications

Challenge students to draw a scale map of various key locations around their school using the idea of bearings. A trundle wheel will be a useful tool to help measure the distances.

3.2 Triangles and quadrilaterals

Objectives

① **G3** Derive and use the sum of angles in a triangle

② **G4** Derive and apply the properties and definitions of special types of quadrilaterals

③ **G6** Apply angle facts to conjecture and derive results about angles

Useful resources

Coordinate grid, squared paper

Starter – Skills

Challenge students to guess each of the shapes you are describing:

- I have three sides. Two of my sides are equal, two of my angles are equal, and I have one line of symmetry. (isosceles triangle)
- I have four sides, four right angles. I do not have four equal sides. (rectangle)
- I have four sides, no right angles. Only two of my sides are parallel. (trapezium)
- I have four sides, two pairs of equal sides, two pairs of equal angles and two pairs of parallel sides. (parallelogram)

Invite students to the board to sketch each shape and mark equal sides and angles. Remind them of notation for parallel sides and equal sides.

Teaching notes – Skills

Define a quadrilateral as a shape with four sides and four angles.

Link quad to four and highlight other words that use this prefix: quad-bike, quadruped and quadruplet.

Invite students to give the names and spelling of other quadrilaterals they know and discuss angle, side and symmetry properties of each.

Ensure students recall that parallel lines are the same distance apart (equidistant) and will never meet.

Discuss properties of diagonals of a rhombus and a kite. Ensure students recall that perpendicular lines intersect at right angles and a line that bisects an angle cuts it exactly in half.

Plenary – Skills

Discuss the sum of the angles in a square.

Repeat for a rectangle.

Demonstrate how a quadrilateral can be split into two triangles and encourage students to consider what this indicates.

Elicit from students' responses that the sum of angles in any quadrilateral must be 360° since any quadrilateral is made from two triangles.

Exercise commentary – Skills

The diagrams are not drawn to scale, so answers must be calculated, not measured. Some questions have more than one method for finding the answers.

A decision could be made to find the answers by mental/written methods or using a calculator.

Question 1 Ask students for their reason for saying 'yes' or 'no'.

Questions 2 and **3** Refer to the bullet points at the top of page 52.

Question 4 Students will need at least two of the angles facts from page 52.

Questions 5 and **6** Refer to the facts on the previous page. In Question **5**, weaker students will find question **5**, part **b** more difficult than part **a**.

Question 7 Students can be shown two methods one uses a triangle and a quadrilateral, the other uses two (overlapping) triangles.

Question 8 Students may offer the line symmetry of a kite as their explanation. A formal proof results from the base angles of the isosceles triangles. Discuss the difference been an explanation and a proof.

Simplification – Skills

Students may need further practice at applying the simple rule of angles in a quadrilateral. Avoid questions where equations need to be formed until the students have understood the basics.

Extension – Skills

Students could be given further examples that require a combination of the angle facts and properties of triangles and quadrilaterals.

Recap – Applications

1 Look at these statements about triangles and quadrilaterals. Write down if each statement is true or false. If the statement is false explain why.

a A triangle can have two right angles.

b A triangle can have one right angle, one acute angle and one obtuse angle.

c A quadrilateral can have four right angles

d A quadrilateral can only have one pair of parallel sides

e A quadrilateral can have two pairs of parallel sides and four equal sides

Answer

a False. Two right angles make 180° which would make the third angle 0°

b False. The total would be more than 180°

c True

d False. A trapezium has only one pair but parallelograms, squares and rhombi have two pairs

e True (rhombus, square)

2 Find the values of the angles a to g.

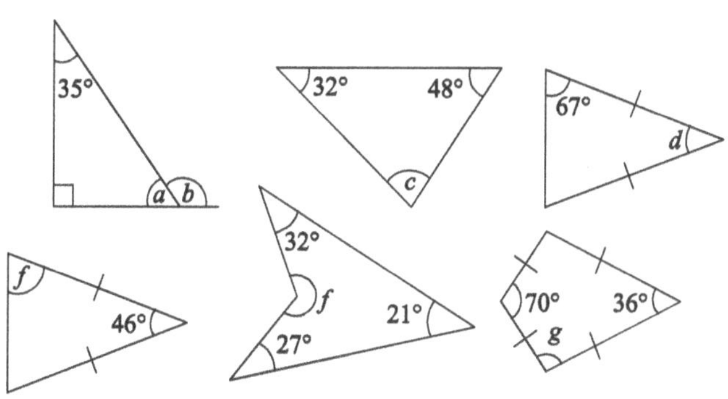

($a = 55°$; $b = 125°$; $c = 100°$; $d = 46°$; $e = 67°$; $f = 280°$; $g = 127°$)

Plenary – Applications

Extend a geometrical problem on coordinate axes where different combinations of angle facts can be used. Encourage students to work through the problem, explaining their reasoning throughout. Invite students with different methods to the board to show calculations and in each case discuss the clarity of workings, stressing the importance of clear working.

Exercise commentary – Applications

As before, the diagrams are not drawn to scale, so answers must be calculated, not measured.

Encourage students to consider what they see in the diagram and decide which angle facts they might need to use before starting the problem. Demonstrate that they can 'hide' part of the picture allowing them to focus on one part at a time. Working in pairs may be beneficial at this stage, but students must be encouraged to explain their reasoning both verbally and in their written work.

Students need square grid paper for questions **6** and **8**.

Question 1 Students should draw a sketch for each part and put the given information on it. Refer students to page 52 for some of the basic facts.

Question 2 This question is suitable for paired work. Students need several cut-out squares and equilateral triangles (with all sides equal). They experiment and then draw their solutions (which all comprise two squares and three triangles).

Question 3 requires all the angle facts learned so far in 31 and 3.2 (pages 50 and 52). Make a list of the facts for the students.

Questions 7 and **8** Students could draw their shapes on square grid paper rather than plain paper.

Question 9 A common error will be to take AB and DC as parallel. A strategy could be discussed as a whole class.

Simplification – Applications

Remind students of strategies to help with calculations, using the column method/number line jottings to add and subtract.

Extension – Applications

Students could draw triangles and quadrilaterals of certain types on a coordinate grid. They could identify the coordinates of the vertices which correspond to each one.

3.3 Congruence and similarity

Objectives

① **G5** Use the basic congruence criteria for triangles

② **G6** Apply angle facts, triangle congruence, similarity and properties of quadrilaterals to conjure and derive results about angles and sides

③ **G6** Apply the concepts of congruence and similarity, including the relationships between lengths

Useful resources

Set of large triangles cut from card (three congruent right-angled triangles, one enlargement and one non-congruent/non-similar right-angled triangle). diagram showing two congruent shapes and two similar shapes, copies of shapes for matching

Starter – Skills

Display two similar triangles, sides marked a, b, c and p, q, r. Explain that the triangles are similar; one is an enlargement of the other. Record that these triangles are in the ratio 1: 3. Students respond to questions using whiteboards: 'What is the scale factor of a to p? p to a?' 'If b is 5 cm long, what is the length of q?' 'If angle ... is... what size is this angle?' and so on. Now change the ratio to 2 : 3 and repeat the questioning.

Teaching notes – Skills

On the board, draw different-sized circles and one oval. Discuss which is the odd one out.

Remind students of the keyword *similar* and define as exactly the same shape, but different in size.

Pin up or stick the triangle shapes on the board. Discuss which two shapes are the odd ones out.

Introduce students to the keyword *congruent* and define it as exactly the same shape AND size. Congruent shapes are identical. Emphasise that congruent shapes may be in a different orientation, and briefly recap the types of transformations that students know. Illustrate these by reflecting, rotating and translating the congruent triangle shapes on the board. Say that there are particular conditions that relate to triangles.

Discuss the four conditions in turn, using the standard acronyms (SSS, SAS, ASA and RHS). Encourage students to realise that in each case they are given three pieces of information relating to angles and lengths.

Plenary – Skills

Give students a visual image of two congruent shapes and two similar shapes. Ask them to suggest two things that are the same about congruent and similar shapes, and two things that are different.

Allow thinking time before the recording and then ask students to compare responses. Select some of the comments for sharing with the whole group.

Finish with clear definitions of both congruent and similar. Link to the transformations. Ask students which transformation will produce similar shapes.

Exercise commentary – Skills

The main difficulty students have with the definition of congruency is that of confusion with similarity. It is important to talk about *both* the words together, so that the similarities and differences are explicit. Emphasise that congruent shapes will fit exactly on each other (as they have the same shape and size) and that shapes are similar if one is an enlargement of the other (as they have the same shape but different sizes). Card cut into congruent and similar triangles can be used to ask questions of the whole class before they attempt the exercise.

Question 1 A tracing of shapes A and B could test whether the other shapes have identical angles or not.

Question 2 Sometimes students should look at which pairs of angles and sides are opposite each other (parts **a**, **c**, **d**) and sometimes what order the angles and sides are (part **b**). Refer to the first worked example on page 56.

Question 4 The reasons should include the scale factors.

Question 5 Refer to the second worked example on page 56.

Question 6 With a scale factor of $24/8 = 3$, a common error will be to think that CE is $3 \times 5 = 15$ cm. A cut-out triangle of ABC can show that it has to flip over to fit the angles of triangle CDE. Colour equal angles in different colours to make the same point. These considerations also apply to question **7**.

Simplification – Skills

Students could be given copies of shapes on card and asked to match them physically.

Extension – Skills

Challenge students to complete examples where the two triangles are 'nested'.

Recap – Applications

1 For each pair of triangles, decide if they are congruent. Explain your answer.

a

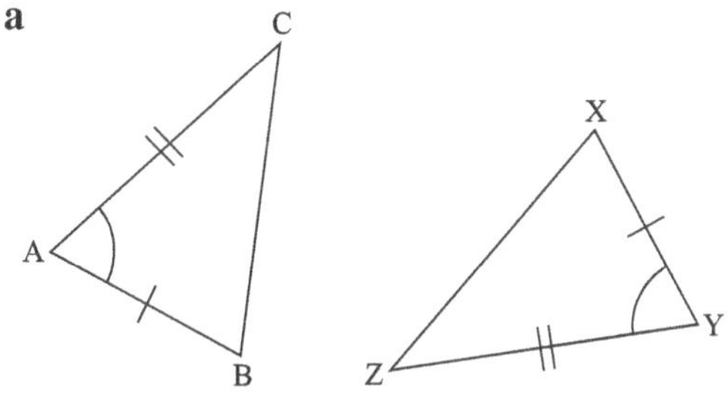

(Yes ASA)

b

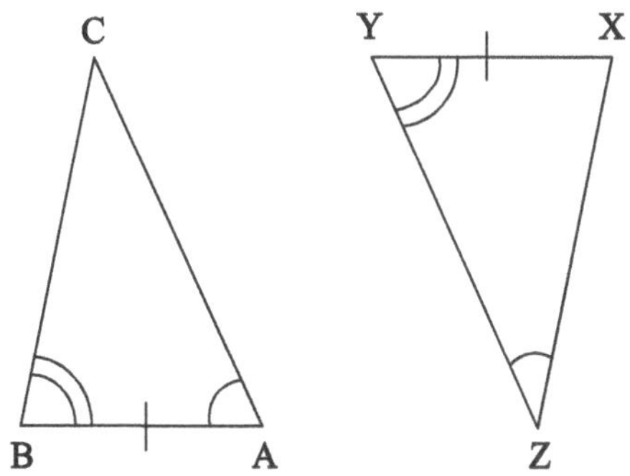

(No, angles not corresponding)

2

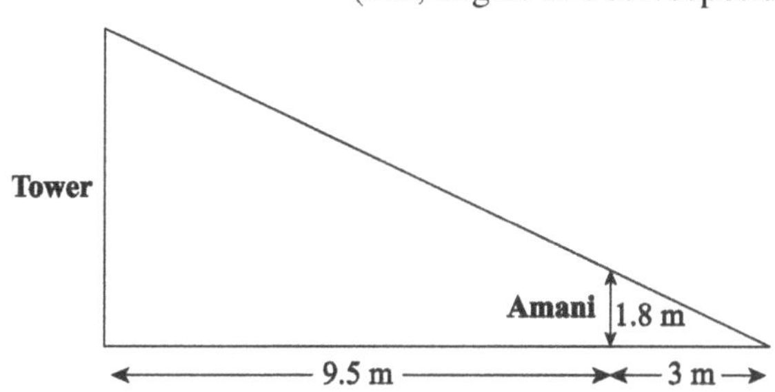

Amani, who is 1.8 m tall, is standing 9.5 m from the base of a tower. The Sun over the tower gives Amani a shadow 3 m long.

Work out the height of the tower. (7.5 m)

Plenary – Applications

Can congruent triangles be used to tessellate? Divide the class into seven groupings. Assign one type to each group: equilateral, obtuse-angled isosceles, right-angled isosceles, acute-angled isosceles, obtuse-angled scalene, right-angled scalene, acute-angled scalene. Conclude that all triangles tessellate.

Exercise commentary – Applications

Questions 1 and **2** The use of the words 'enlargement' (as in the first example on page 58) when the image is larger than the object and 'reduction' when it is smaller will help students – especially when linked with scale factors greater than 1 and less than 1. Question **2** particularly needs careful explanation.

Questions 4 and **5** The word 'proof' is not used in this exercise, but these two questions are essentially proofs. Remind students that that they must give a chain of reasoning in which each statement is derived from previous statements or facts known to be true. Also emphasise that they should start from the definitions of the shapes that are given in 3.2 on page 52 (and not assume any other facts until they are proven).

Question 7 provides two possible methods. The first and very laborious method is to find the linear scale factor for each pair of sizes. For example, for the mini and small sizes, the width scale factor (30/24=1.25) differs from the height scale factor (40/30=1.33...), so they are not similar. But there are 10 possible pairs of sizes and much work to find the scale factors. The second method works with the ratio of width to height for each shape. Only five ratios have to be calculated. This question could be explored as a whole class.

Question 9 Students could colour the three matching pairs of sides in different colours before using the scale factor.

Question 10 This could be whole-class exploration. Take A3 to A6 sheets and have students measure and compare their dimensions. Find the dimensions of A1 and A2 and confirm the pattern discovered for A3 to A6.

Simplification – Applications

Students should be encouraged to write down all of the facts that they know, in terms of what angles and sides are equal in the diagrams, before trying to match this information with the conditions. Working in supported pairs will also help.

Extension – Applications

Students could discuss the conditions required to demonstrate the congruence of three-dimensional solid shapes such as spheres, pyramids and prisms.

3.4 Angles in polygons

Objectives

① **G3** Derive and use the sum of angles in a triangle (e.g. to deduce and use the angle sum in any polygon, and to derive properties of regular polygons)

Useful resources

MOW written on paper, mirrors, board compasses and protractor, squared and isometric paper

Starter – Skills

Write the words MUM, DID, HAH and HIDE on the board and discuss what they have in common – lines of reflection symmetry. Challenge students to give other words with lines of reflection symmetry.

Display the word MOW and discuss whether it has symmetry. Invite students to suggest what *type* of symmetry it has. Rotate the word to show its rotational symmetry.

Teaching notes – Skills

Highlight that a triangle is so called because it has three angles. Link to triathlon and triplets. Emphasise that quad, as in quadrilateral, means four and link to quadruplets and quad-bike.

Discuss other polygons, linking where possible with similarly prefixed words: Pentagon: pentathlon; Heptagon: heptathlon; Octagon: octopus.

Highlight that all these shapes are polygons and emphasise that poly means many and so polygons are many-sided shapes.

Emphasise that an equilateral triangle and a square are examples of regular polygons and ask students to define ‘regular’. Establish that a regular polygon has equal sides and equal angles.

Demonstrate how a hexagon is formed from six congruent isosceles triangles meeting at a central point. Discuss the sum of the angles at the central point. Highlight it must be 360° since it is a full turn. Discuss the value of each individual angle and establish: $360° \div 6 = 60°$.

Use board compasses and a board protractor to demonstrate accurate construction of a hexagon. Challenge students to find the missing angles of each triangle, and how to calculate the interior and exterior angles of the hexagon.

Repeat with construction of an octagon. Highlight, in this case, the angles of each triangle are not equal (the hexagon is a special example).

Plenary – Skills

Draw up a simple table and invite students to consider the angle sum of other polygons given the number of triangles each can be divided into.

Shape	No. of sides/ angles	No. of triangles	Sum of interior angles
triangle	3	1	180°
quadrilateral	4	2	360°
pentagon	5	3	540°
hexagon	6	4	720°

Encourage students to predict the number of triangles a decagon can be divided into and the sum of the angles in a decagon.

Exercise commentary – Skills

In each question, the first step is to note whether the question is about regular polygons or polygons which are not regular.

Question 1 Refer to the first worked example on page 60.

Question 3 The second worked example on page 60 gives two methods for completing this table.

Questions 4 and **5** Ask students to be wary and watch for the word *regular*. These two questions are **not** about regular polygons. Questions **6** to **10** are all about **regular** polygons.

Questions 6 and **7** Refer to the second worked example on page 60 for these two methods.

Question 8 Refer to the second worked example on page 60.

Question 9 This method of finding an internal angle of a regular polygon can be compared with that using the formula $(n - 2) \times 180°$ and with that using exterior angles, both found on page 60 and in question **6**. Students now have three methods of finding the internal angle of a regular polygon.

It could be useful for students to see all three methods written out next to each other and then, as a whole class, to show their working for each method on their mini whiteboards for (say) a regular decagon.

Simplification – Skills

Students may find a glossary of the names (and angle rules) for the polygons useful.

Extension – Skills

Students could be asked to generate a formula connecting the number of sides with the interior angle sum and write it down.

Sum of the interior angles of an n-sided polygon is $(n - 2) \times 180°$ or $2n - 4$ right angles.

Recap – Applications

1 a What is the sum of the exterior angles in any polygon? (360°)

b What is the name given to a regular

i triangle (equilateral)

ii quadrilateral? (square)

c What size is the exterior angle of a regular pentagon? (72°)

d What size is the interior angle of a regular nonagon? (140°)

e What is the interior angle of a regular polygon containing 100 sides? (176.4°)

2 a A quadrilateral has angles of 133°, 44° and 127°. What size is the other angle? (56°)

b A decagon has 6 angles each of 142°. The other 4 angles are equal. What size are they? (147°)

c A pentagon has 3 angles of 75° each. The remaining angles are $w + 60$ and $w - 55$. What is the value of w? (155°)

Plenary – Applications

Show an isosceles trapezium. Challenge students to add an identical trapezium in such a way that the resulting shape has 2 lines of symmetry:

For example: 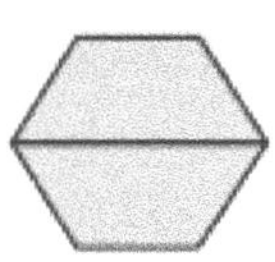

Challenge students to add three more identical trapeziums in such a way that the resulting shape has no lines of symmetry/one line of symmetry, for example:

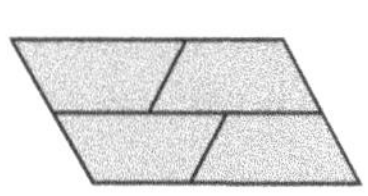

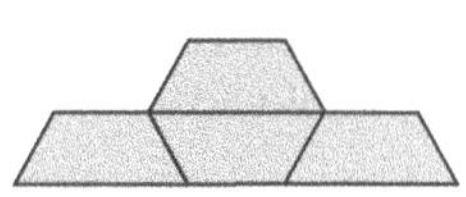

Exercise commentary – Applications

Questions 1 to **3** Refer students to the first worked example on page 62.

Question 4 Refer to the second worked example, part **a** on page 62.

Question 5 is suitable for paired work with cut-out shapes. Refer students to the table in question **4**.

Questions 6 to **8** Students can copy the diagrams and, as a start, enter interior angles from the table in question **4**.

Question 9 is based on angles meeting at a point and adding to make a full turn of 360°.

Question 10 Explain where the 'inside and outside polygons' are to be found in the diagram. This question is easier with prepared cut-out pieces than by drawing.

Simplification – Applications

Some students find it hard to visualise symmetry in shapes. Encourage them to consider the lines of symmetry of shapes like rectangles, squares and regular pentagons to give them a reference to work from. Access to mirrors to enable students to use trial and error will be beneficial.

Extension – Applications

Students could be invited to draw their own shapes, on squared or isometric paper, that conform to certain symmetry rules. Encourage them to be creative in their designs, adding colour if appropriate while maintaining the symmetry. These designs can make excellent display pieces.

3 Angles and polygons

Key outcomes	Quick check
G1 Use conventional terms and notations: points, lines, vertices, edges, planes, parallel lines, perpendicular lines, right angles, polygons, regular polygons and polygons with reflection and/or rotation symmetries; use the standard conventions for labelling and referring to the sides and angles of triangles; draw diagrams from written description.	**1** Calculate the size of angles a, b, c, d, and e. 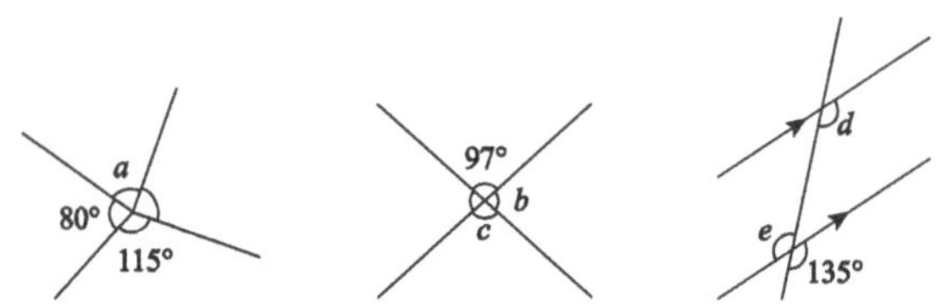 ($a = 75°$, $b = 97°$, $c = 83°$, $d = 135°$, $e = 135°$) **2** Calculate the size of angle BAC (30°) 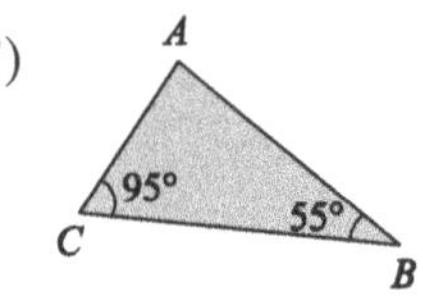 **3** What do the interior angles of a hexagon add up to? Show how you worked it out. (720°) **4** The bearing of A from B is 065°. What is the bearing of B from A? (245°)
G3 Apply the properties of angles at a point, angles at a point on a straight line, vertically opposite angles; understand and use alternate and corresponding angles on parallel lines; derive and use the sum of angles in a triangle (e.g. to deduce and use the angle sum in any polygon, and to derive properties of regular polygons)	
G15 Use bearings.	
G4 Derive and apply the properties and definitions of: special types of quadrilaterals, including square, rectangle, parallelogram, trapezium, kite and rhombus; and triangles and other plane figures using appropriate language.	**5** Which quadrilateral is described below? Draw each shape, use correct notation for parallel and equal sides. **a** Four equal sides, two pairs of parallel sides and two pairs of equal angles. (rhombus) **b** Two pairs of equal and parallel sides and four equal angles. (rectangle) **6** Calculate the size of angles a and b in the parallelogram. ($a = 135°$, $b = 45°$) 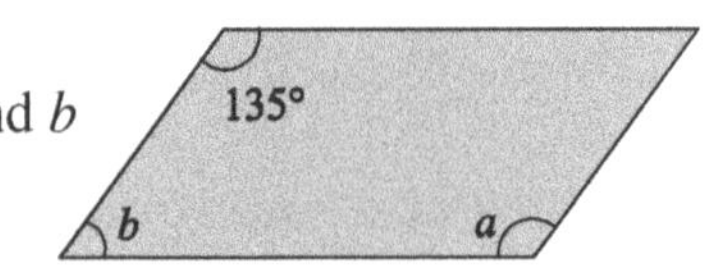
G5 Use the basic congruence criteria for triangles (SSS, SAS, ASA, RHS).	**7** Are these two triangles congruent? Give a reason for your answer. 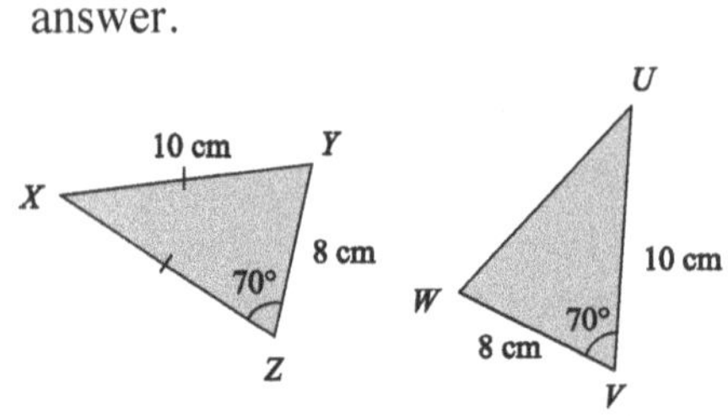 (Yes – $\angle XYZ = 70°$ as triangle XYZ is isosceles so $\angle XYZ = \angle UVW$, also $XY = UV$ and $YZ = VW$ so the triangles are congruent with SAS defined.)
G6 Apply angle facts, triangle congruence, similarity and properties of quadrilaterals to conjecture and derive results about angles and sides, and the fact that the base angles of an isosceles triangle are equal, and use known results to obtain simple proofs.	
G19 Apply the concepts of congruence and similarity, including the relationships between lengths.	**10** These rectangles are similar, what is the length of EH? 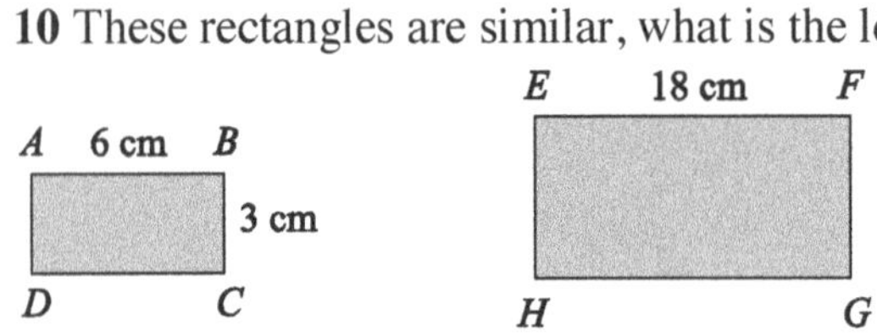 ($EH = 9$ cm)

Misconceptions and challenges	Solutions
Students know the angle facts but do not know how to apply them to a question.	Give students opportunities to discuss their reasons for how they found the value of the missing angle.
Students don't know when to measure and when to calculate an angle and don't understand the significance of 'Not drawn to scale'.	Frequently use 'badly drawn diagrams' in examples or draw two diagrams and have ask students which of two diagrams has been drawn to scale.
Students show 'working' rather than 'reasons'.	Give students a fact, and then a range of options for the reason why it is true. Ask them to identify which are mathematical reasons (use of specific terminology such as 'corresponding angles'), and which are workings ('Because when I worked it out it had the answer 135').
Students confuse the terms congruent and similar.	Quick starters are an ideal time to reinforce these terms and ideas. Show an image of a pair of shapes for a period of only one or two seconds before asking students to decide if they are similar or congruent.
Students struggle to recall key facts about polygons.	Give students regular opportunities to solve problems using kites, trapezia, and parallelograms in context. Use the diagram of a shape as a context for other areas of mathematics. For example, find the missing angles in a parallelogram with angles labelled in multiples of x.
When finding a missing angle students may jump to conclusions, or guess at an answer, using false visual clues, rather than taking the logical steps required.	Build students' stamina by classifying missing angles problems as one-step, two-step, three-step etc. Challenge them to invent their own 4 or 5-step problems that include a variety of different angle facts.

Review question commentary

Make students aware that in general diagrams are not 'drawn to scale'.

Question 1 (3.1) – In part **b**, students need to know that the box indicates a right angle.

Question 2 (3.1) – Encourage students to give clear, mathematically correct reasons for their answers.

Question 3 (3.2) – Make sure that students understand why the angle is called 'angle *ABC*' and not 'angle *B*'.

Question 4 (3.2) – Check that students know that this triangle is isosceles.

Question 5 (3.2) – Encourage students to label the vertices.

Question 6 (3.2) – Students must use knowledge of the angle properties of a rhombus to first give size of angle **a**. Make a link here to angles in parallel lines.

Question 7 (3.2) – Part **a** could also describe a rhombus, rectangle or square. Challenge students to give additional descriptions that would apply to these quadrilaterals but not a parallelogram.

Question 8 (3.2) – If students are stuck remind them of the different types of triangles and ask them how they would check each of their properties.

Question 9 (3.3) – You could use peer assessment to review the clarity of their explanations.

Question 10 (3.3) – Remind students that similar shapes are enlargements of each other and ask them to identify the scale factor (2).

Question 11 (3.4) – Remind students that a pentagon can be split by two diagonals into 3 triangles, each with an angle sum of 180°.

Review answers

1 **a** = 70° (ASL) **b** = 120° (AP)
c = 65° (VO) **d** = 115° (ASL)

2 **a** = 55° (CA) **b** = 100° (AA)

3 35°

4 *DF*

5 2 × 180° = 360°

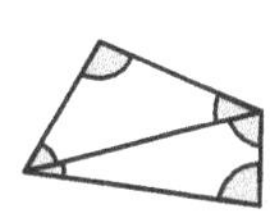

6 **a** = 50° **b** = 130°

7 **a** Parallelogram **b** Trapezium **c** Kite

8 Isosceles.

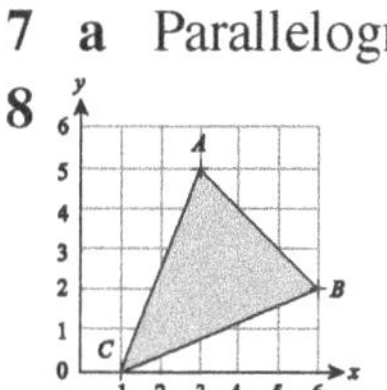

9 Yes, $\angle ZXY = \angle WUV$, $XY = UV$,
$\angle XYZ = \angle UVW$ (ASA)

10 10 cm

11 540°

65 marks

Assessment 3

Question 1 – 5 marks

a $\frac{8}{12}$ [M1]

$=\frac{2}{3}$ [A1]

b $\frac{9}{12}$ [M1]

$=\frac{3}{4}$ [A1]

c 3 [B1]

Question 2 – 3 marks

a $\frac{5}{12}\times 360° = 150°$ [B1]

b $\frac{2.5}{12}\times 360°$ [M1]

$= 75°$ [A1]

Question 3 – 2 marks

130° – 70° [M1]

= 60° clockwise [A1]

Question 4 – 5 marks

a 75° + 55° = 130° [A1]

b 180°+ 75° [M1]

= 255° [A1]

c 360° – 105° – 40°

OR 180° + (75° – 40°) [M1]

= 215° [A1]

Question 5 – 1 mark

Rafa was south of Sunita.

OR

Rafa was facing Sunita. [B1]

Question 6 – 2 marks

64° + 59° + 56° = 179° ≠ 180°. [M1]

No [A1]

Question 7 – 12 marks

a a = 180° – 90° – 56° = 34°

Angle sum of a triangle = 180°. [M1]

Incorrect [A1]

b b = 180° – 34° – 71° = 75°

Angle sum of a triangle = 180°. [M1]

Correct [A1]

c c = 180° – 67° – 67° = 46°

Isosceles triangles have two equal angles and angle sum of a triangle = 180°. [M1]

Correct [A1]

d d = [180° – 32°] ÷ 2 = 74°

Isosceles triangles have two equal angles and angle sum of a triangle = 180°. [M1]

Incorrect [A1]

e e = 121°

Vertically opposite angles are equal. [M1]

Correct. [A1]

f = 180°– 121° = 59°

Angles on a straight line add up to 180°. [M1]

Incorrect [A1]

Question 8 – 8 marks

a Two obtuse angles add to more than180° which is the sum of the three angles in a triangle. [M1]

False [A1]

b Students' drawing of an obtuse-angled triangle. [M1]

True [A1]

c Right angle + obtuse angle + acute angle

> 90° + 90° + 0° > 180° [M1]

False [A1]

d Students' drawing of a right-angled triangle. [M1]

True [A1]

Question 9 – 2 marks

$\hat{X}$ = 48° [=180° – 65° – 67°] [B1]

$\hat{Y}$ = 65°, $\hat{Z}$ = 67° [B1]

Question 10 – 2 marks

Using similar triangles

Height = 10 × 1.5 [M1]

= 15 m [A1]

Question 11 – 12 marks

a Sum of interior angles of a pentagon

= (5 – 2) × 180° [M1]

= 540° [A1]

Remaining angles total

= 540°– 125°– 155°– 74° [M1]

= 186° [A1]

Angles = 186° ÷ 2 = 93° [A1]

b Sum of interior angles of an octagon

= (8 – 2) × 180° [M1]

=1080° [A1]

Sum of three angles = 1080° – 5 × 114° [M1]

= 510° [A1]

Angle = 510° ÷ 3 = 170° [A1]

c Sum of interior angles of a hexagon

= (6 – 2) × 180° = 720° [B1]

Remaining angles total

= 720° – 3 × 137° = 309° [B1]

= $w + w + 120 + w - 30$

= $3w + 90 = 309$ [M1]

$3w$ = 309°– 90° = 219°

w = 219 ÷ 3 = 73° [A1]

d Exterior angle = 360° ÷ 60 = 6° [M1]

Interior angle = 180°– 6° = 174° [A1]

Question 12 – 11 marks

a UV $\nparallel$ WY and VW $\nparallel$ UY [M1]

No [A1]

b i 360° ÷ 6 [M1]

= 60° [A1]

ii 180° – 60° [M1]

= 120° [A1]

c $\measuredangle$VWX =$\measuredangle$WXY = 120°. [B1]

Δ VWX is isosceles

$\measuredangle$VXW = (180°– 120°) ÷ 2 = 30° [M1]

$\measuredangle$VXY = 120°– 30° [M1]

= 90° [A1]

d No, equilateral triangle. [B1]

Handling data 1

Learning outcomes

S1 Infer properties of populations or distributions from a sample, whilst knowing the limitations of sampling.

S2 Interpret and tables, charts and diagrams, including frequency tables, bar charts, pie charts and pictograms for categorical data, vertical line charts for ungrouped discrete numerical data, and know their appropriate use.

S4 Interpret, analyse and compare the distributions of data sets from univariate empirical distributions through:
- appropriate graphical representation involving discrete, [continuous and grouped] data;
- appropriate measures of central tendency (median, mean, mode [and modal class]) and spread (range, including consideration of outliers).

S5 Apply statistics to describe a population.

Prior knowledge

Check-in skill

- Order positive numbers.
- Add, subtract and divide.
- Calculate the value of an angle at a point.

Online resources

MyMaths 1192, 1193, 1202, 1205, 1206, 1207, 1214, 1215, 1254

InvisiPen videos

Skills: 04Sa – n Applications: 04Aa – e

Kerboodle assessment

Online Skills Test 4 Chapter Test 4

Development and links

Techniques for graphical presentation are used throughout the sciences, social sciences, finance, etc. Most companies produce an annual report containing statistical diagrams, the media reports the results of polls and surveys, and scientists, health professionals, chemists and pharmaceutical researchers report their findings in diagrammatical form. The ability to draw and interpret statistical charts is vital for students to use statistics for their own reports, to draw inferences or to persuade others of a need for action or change.

Chapter investigation

The question is likely to illicit some quick responses, such as, 'fourteen and a half'. Press students on how they can be certain/how they can check the claim. Guide students towards collecting actual data.

In the first instance suggest using a tally chart/frequency table, split into years and months [**4.1**]. As a refinement consider a two-way table based on age and gender. Check understanding of the tables using questions on their interpretation and also by looking at 'data' for other classes.

As a second step look at getting a 'feel' for the data using various graphical representations: pictograms, bar charts and dual bar charts [**4.2**]. Move on to showing the data in a pie chart [**4.3**]. Here it may help to group the data into, for example, quarter years in order to reduce the number of categories. Since the numbers in the class are likely to be awkward (not nice factors of 360°) have available fake data with which to illustrate the calculations. Take time to discuss what the various graphs show and what they do not.

As a third step look at calculating averages mode, median and mean (and range) for the class data [**4.4**]. Look at how the averages compare to one another and the expectations from looking at the various graphs. Are the averages sensitive to 'outliers' or 'coincidences'?

Students should be encouraged to pose their own questions and collect their own data to investigate.

4.1 Organising data

Objectives

① **S2** Interpret and construct tables and diagrams

Useful resources

Mini whiteboards

Starter – Skills

Record the hair colours of students in a simple frequency table. Ask questions based on the data and discuss the most common hair colour. Repeat this for eye colour. Discuss what proportion of the class have brown eyes. Link this to fractions. Recall the link between '1 out of 4' and $\frac{1}{4}$ Repeat for blue eyes and green eyes.

What is the most common combination of hair and eye colour? Ask students whether they have the necessary data to answer this question accurately from their tables. Discuss how you could collect and record data for this

Teaching notes – Skills

② Refer to the starter. Highlight the simple **frequency tables** used to record each characteristic. Recall how two types of information about the same population can be combined in a **two-way table**. Draw this table for students to copy and complete:

	Blue eyes	Brown eyes	Green eyes
Black hair			
Brown hair			
Blond hair			
Red hair			

Refer back to the original question and ask students which is the most common combination. Ask other questions based on the combined data and demonstrate finding the appropriate cell. Discuss how many students with blue/brown/green eyes there are in total. Emphasise that it is often useful to extend the table to include **totals**.

Recall how to record data in a **tally chart**. Highlight it as an example of a data collection sheet. Remind students about grouping the tallies into 5s and discuss tactics of organising data into a tally chart:

- crossing off each value once it has been recorded
- checking that the total frequency equals the total number of raw values.

Plenary – Skills

Show an incomplete two-way table and ask students to complete, justifying their answers:

	Girls	Boys	Total
Meat-eater	7		15
Vegetarian			
Total	20		34

Exercise commentary – Skills

Question 1 Remember that, in order to produce a frequency chart, the student should be encouraged to go through the data once only. For example, rather than going through the data looking for all of the 0s, then again looking for all of the 1s, etc., it is good practice to tally 1, 0, 2, 0, 1..., then get the totals - it's faster and more accurate.

Questions 2 and **3** are similar questions to question **1**, but get the student to do progressively more of the work. Once the totals have been obtained, the grand total should be found and then, as a minimum check, see that it corresponds to the total number of observations. Remember that, for the purposes of the exam, the data collection sheet refers to the table without any observations recorded.

These are ideas that have been introduced earlier but now in the context of presentation of data. In all of this work it should be emphasised that raw data is generally unmanageable and, without being re-presented in tables and charts, difficult to interpret.

Question 4 Remember, in producing tally charts, go through the data only once, tallying each item in order.

Question 6 Ensure that the student understands the table as it's given first – for example, that there are 31 adults in cinema 1, ... then encourage the habit that, as soon as a bivariate (or two-way) table is given, the marginal totals and the grand total should be calculated and recorded. Then check that the students understand what information the marginal totals give; for example, that there are a total of 78 adults in the two cinemas. Finally, use all the checks available – for example, that the sum of the horizontal marginals is the same as the sum of the vertical marginals, which equals the grand total.

Simplification – Skills

Students should work with small, simple data sets that are straightforward to sort and interpret.

Extension – Skills

Students could complete other unfinished two-way tables similar to the one given in the plenary.

Recap – Applications

1 Jasmine surveys the colours on different national flags and rearranges the data into a frequency table.

Colour	Black	Blue	Green	Red	White	Yellow
Frequency	3	11	8	10	14	4

Which is the

a most **b** least common colour?

(**a** White **b** Black)

2 A survey into mobile phone ownership of 100 primary school students, secondary school students and adults was taken. There were 45 secondary students; 38 *i*-phones. Of the primary school students, 5 had *i*-phones and 7 Samsung phones. Of the adults, 10 had Nokia phones and 20 Samsung phones. 10 of the secondary school students had Nokia phones.

a Draw a two-way table to illustrate this data.

b How many Nokia phones were there altogether?

c How many adults were there in the sample?

d How many secondary students had *i*-phones?

(Answer

a

PHONE	Primary	Secondary	Adults	Total
i	5	28	5	38
Nokia	8	10	10	28
Samsung	7	7	20	34
Total	20	45	35	100

b 28 **d** 35 **e** 28)

Plenary – Applications

Present this hypothesis: 'Most goals are scored in the last 10 minutes of a match.' Ask students to consider what information would need to be collected to test this and how they would collect it. Brainstorm what type of data collection sheet could be used. Invite students to demonstrate their suggestions. Ask other students to comment.

Exercise commentary – Applications

Before attempting questions **1** and **2**, it may be useful to discuss question **6** in **4.1S**.

Question 3 Tests the students' understanding of this theory by requiring them to construct a two-way table from a frequency distribution and some descriptions. It may be necessary to give them a hint: 'this is a one-way table but in a section on two-way tables. What do you think you should do?'

Question 4 A precursor to calculating the mean from a frequency distribution. As such, it is well worth spending time discussing the detail of this question – 'there are 6 students who own 2 DVDs each. How many DVDs altogether is that?', etc. First, though, make sure that they don't think that the total number of DVDs is $0 + 1 + \ldots + 5$, or similar errors.

Question 5 Can act as a precursor to the later material on experimental probabilities. It is clearly solved by calculating proportions and it may be useful at this point to introduce the idea that proportions can be used to estimate probabilities. Keep the examples simple though. For example, 14 heads in 20 throws of a coin. Do you think that the coin is fair?

Question 6 Maybe use this question to prepare students to do some project work involving simple data collection and analysis.

Simplification – Applications

Use an example to check students understand that the rows and columns of a two-way table must add up. Give them questions with just one or two missing entries. Students may also need some smaller frequency tables. Use a total frequency of 10 or 20 to simplify the arithmetic.

Extension – Applications

Students could be asked to collect their own data in the form of a two-way table and pose questions.

4.2 Representing data 1

Objectives

① **S2** Interpret and construct charts and diagrams, including pictograms and bar charts

Useful resources

Mini whiteboards, pictogram, bar chart

Starter – Skills

Show students this pictogram with no title or key.

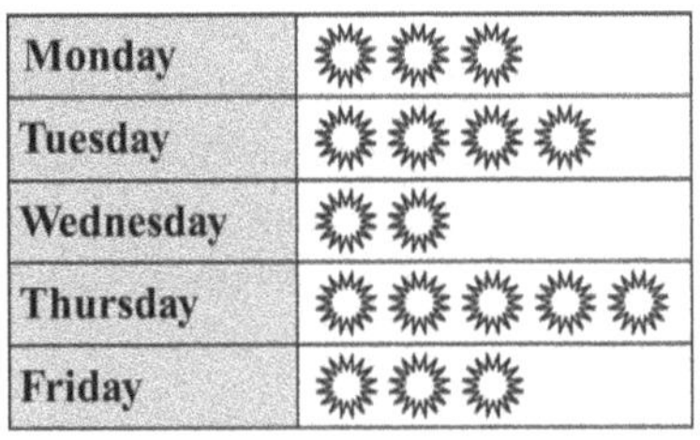

Discuss what the pictogram might show and highlight that with no title it is meaningless. Write a title: 'The number of hours of sunshine during a week'. Discuss what the pictogram now shows. Highlight that whilst you can compare categories, with no key the details of the data are unknown. Decide on a reasonable key, and write this on.

Teaching notes – Skills

② Discuss how a picture can give a lot of information immediately and that charts, tables and graphs can represent different kinds of data visually.

Refer to the starter and highlight that a **pictogram** uses pictures to represent numbers.

Look at the first example in the student book. Explain that in the key one car **symbol** represents four units. Two identical cars are drawn for eight units. One and a half cars show six units. Discuss how to show other units and the difficulty of interpreting a pictogram which contains portions of the chosen symbol. Using identical symbols enables us to compare different categories at a glance.

Discuss what other visual methods can be used to display data clearly. Look at the **bar chart** example from the student book. Highlight that, instead of pictures, it uses bars to show the size of each category. Show how the bars can be **vertical or horizontal** but must be the same width. Discuss the **scale** in the example; when the values are large it is not sensible to show each unit. Highlight that a bar chart gives a clear general picture of how each category compares with the rest, as well as a way of reading exact values from the chart. Discuss how many people responded for each pet. Encourage students to share their reasoning. Now consider how many were asked in total. Ask: What frequencies would you expect if you asked twice as many people? Discuss how you could change the vertical axis scale to be more appropriate for larger numbers. Finally, discuss the **modal category** and recall that the modal category is the one with the highest frequency. Ensure that students differentiate between the categories themselves and the *frequency* of the modal category.

Show that a **bar-line chart** is a variation on a bar chart, and that **dual bar charts** can show two sets of data on the same diagram for easier comparison.

Plenary – Skills

Show a bar chart without title or axes labelled. Ask students to suggest what it might show. Encourage them to consider the general trend of the chart, to count the number of bars, and so on. Elicit one or more plausible scenarios for the data.

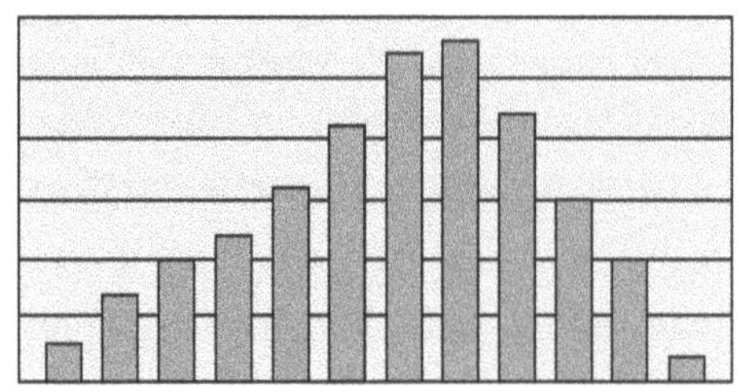

Agree and add a title, such as 'Average monthly temperature in the UK'. Agree and add axis and scale labels, such as : x-axis 'Months' and 'J, F, M, A …'; y-axis '°C' and '0, 5, 15 …'. Ask students to read off monthly temperatures from the graph.

Exercise commentary – Skills

Questions 1 to **3** These diagrams are useful because the theory is so accessible but it may be worth discussing their limitations and students should be able to come up with these in a discussion. Most of the limitations will probably be related to accuracy and time needed to produce them. For example, with 1 car representing 1000 cars produced by a factory, how do you represent 1050 cars? Also, it takes a while to draw 10 cars.

Questions 4 to **6** It may be worth starting a discussion about the similarities between pictograms and bar charts. In question **3** of this exercise, the total length of the diagram representing the Spanish teachers is longer than that for the Russian teachers because there are more Spanish teachers. Bar charts build on this idea because the length of the line in a bar chart is proportional to the frequency it represents.

Question 7 Investigatory task, perhaps involving some online research, the students could be asked to learn the meanings of the median and range (if they don't know or can't recall already) and then find their values for this data.

Simplification – Skills

Students could be given copies of pictograms and bar charts and simply required to complete them.

Extension – Skills

Students could complete their own comparative bar charts and start to make descriptive comparisons.

Recap – Applications

1 The distance, to the nearest mile, that patients had to travel to visit a hospital clinic was recorded. Draw a bar chart of this data.

Distance	0 - 2	3 - 4	5 - 6	7 - 8	9 - 10
Patient numbers	16	15	11	9	6

2 The number of DVDs sold in a shop over a week is shown. Draw a pictogram to illustrate this data. Include a suitable key.

Day	Mon	Tue	Wed	Thurs	Fri	Sat	Sun
DVDs	29	34	30	25	29	36	17

Plenary – Applications

Show this comparative, dual bar chart:

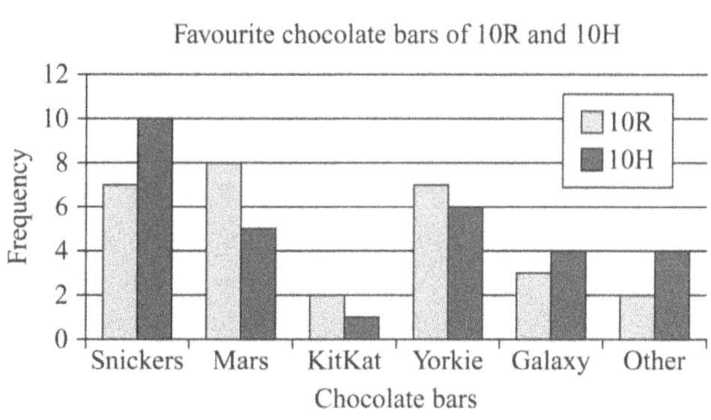

Highlight that this chart allows *comparison* of two sets of data. Invite students to make descriptive sentences comparing the two data sets.

Exercise commentary – Applications

Question 2 Could be done in three stages: a discussion about how the population changes for village **a**, then the same for **b**, then how the difference between the populations changes. With questions like this, encourage the students to study the diagram first without much consideration of the questions being asked – only move on to the questions when they feel that they fully understand the diagram.

Question 3 Before doing this question it may be worth considering questions **4** and **5** in exercise **4.3S** where we compared pictograms with bar charts.

Question 4 Unlike the previous questions, this one is about dividing a total number of items into exhaustive and mutually-exclusive categories. As such, a pie chart is also suitable here. This idea could be introduced here, preparing the students for the material in the next section.

Question 5 A good question for discussion and one which will probably lead to the conclusion that, in general, bar charts are more useful than pictograms.

Simplification – Applications

Students could be given a writing frame for their responses or work in groups for support.

Extension – Applications

Students could be given a comparative bar chart or a composite bar chart, and asked to describe the significant features.

Representing data 2

Objectives

① **S2** Interpret and construct charts and diagrams, including pie charts

Useful resources

Mini whiteboards, calculators, clock face for starter activity, protractors, pre-drawn circles

Starter – Skills

Show a clock face. Ensure students understand a full turn is 360°. Show a hand pointing to 12 and discuss where it will be after various turns: 90° clockwise, 270° clockwise. Repeat with different start numbers and different turns in both directions.

Teaching notes – Skills

② Recall that a **pie chart** shows information as different-sized parts of a circle. It is a clear visual picture, and especially good for showing the **proportion** of each category of the whole. Look at the first example in the student book. Discuss which fruit is the most popular. Elicit that the angle of the sector represents the size of the category. Use the clock face from the starter to show how the angle point is the centre of the circle. Encourage students to make statements about the information. Discuss how many people were asked in total. Highlight that a pie chart does not give this information directly, but it allows comparison of proportions.

Discuss and model how to construct a pie chart:

- Divide the full circle (360°) by the total number of respondents to find out the angle representing one respondent
- Multiply the angle for one person by the number of people in each category
- Construct a start line from the centre of the circle
- Use a protractor to measure the first angle
- Place the protractor on the new line to measure the second angle, and so on.

Look at the student book example about vehicles. Highlight that the full circle represents 60 vehicles. Encourage students to calculate the number of vehicles in the Lorries and Vans categories by considering each as a quarter of the whole and linking this to the starter. Discuss the **modal type** of vehicle. Recall that it is represented by the largest sector of the circle. Discuss how to calculate the exact value of each remaining category, by reversing the earlier steps:

- Divide the 360° by the total number of vehicles to find out the angle representing one vehicle
- Divide the angle for each category by the number of degrees for each vehicle.

Plenary – Skills

Present this data and ask students how they would represent it on a pie chart.

Colour of car	Blue	Red	Silver	Black
Frequency	12	6	8	4

Ask them to think in pairs about how to work out the angles, how to draw it, a suitable title and how to show a key before drawing the pie chart.

Exercise commentary – Skills

Drawing good diagrams is not a skill which comes naturally to many students. It may well be worth spending half a lesson on using a pair of compasses before starting this exercise and then using the exercise to develop further these skills.

Questions 1 and **2** Students could attempt question **2** first as it talks the students through the construction of the pie chart. As in all of these problems, once the student has identified the total number of items being represented and found the angle corresponding to one item, the rest of the problem is generally fairly straightforward.

Question 3 The first question to ask for a pie chart to be drawn from data given in a table and one which provides an opportunity to teach the student how to extend the table by adding a column headed 'angle'. This tabular presentation, as well as increasing clarity, enables the student to find easily the total number of days (if it wasn't given at the beginning of the question) and to check that the total of the angles is 360°.

Question 4 Ask your students whether it's necessary to do part **a** since the times are given in the chart. The answer is yes because there might be time unaccounted for which has to be included in the calculation.

Questions 5 and **6** two similar questions, both essentially changing angles into numbers. Question **5** gives a gentle introduction to the idea since the angles are either 90° or 180°. Once the general principle is understood, the students should find question **6** more manageable.

Question 7 The same idea as in the previous questions. At this point, as the student is becoming more familiar with the principles, it may be worth emphasising again that pie charts primarily deal with proportions but these can be turned into numbers of items if the total number is known.

Simplification – Skills

Students could be given the required angles for all questions so that they can practise drawing the pie chart correctly. Pre-drawn circles would also help. Students could use calculators to help them focus on the pie charts.

Extension – Skills

Students could be given data that is not easily divisible into 360 and asked to consider the implications of rounding the angles. They could then proceed to draw a pie chart from the data.

Recap – Applications

The number of viewers watching a film at each of the 5 screens at a cinema complex is shown in the pie chart.

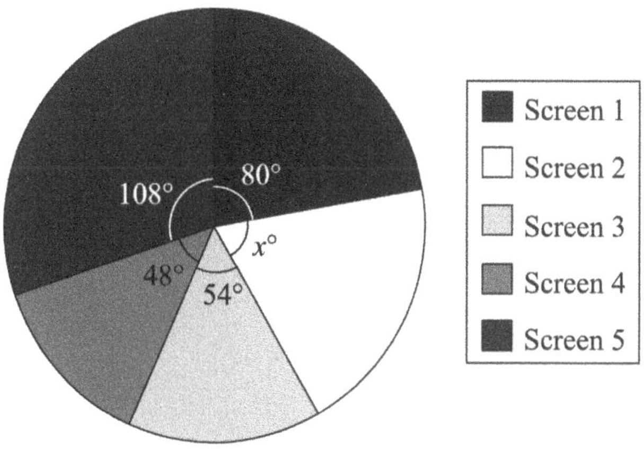

a Work out the value of x. (70)

b There were a total of 540 viewers in the cinema at the time. How many were watching the film at each screen? (Screen 1: 120; Screen 2: 105; Screen 3: 81; Screen 4: 72; Screen 5: 162.)

Plenary – Applications

Show students a pie chart with no title or key. Ask students what it might show, and highlight how little it means with no labelling. Elicit possible scenarios for the data, then give it a title: 'Votes for the major UK parties in 2005'. Write up the three main party names and 'Other'. Discuss which party is likely to be which on the pie chart (Labour won the election) and label accordingly. Extend this to a comparative application of pie charts by displaying a similarly unlabelled pie chart of the 2010 election. Discuss and elicit what this might show (the Conservatives were the largest single party), and label accordingly.

Exercise commentary – Applications

Question 1 Gest the students' understanding of proportion in general as well as in relation to pie charts. Perhaps use the unitary method – with the unit being 1000 tourists – to find the angle corresponding to 225000 tourists. The remaining angle can be found by subtraction.

Questions 2 and **3** These questions look similar but are in fact rather different. The type of data in question **2** is appropriate for a pie chart in that there is a clearly defined total number of items, the drinks sold, which are divided into a set of different categories. The problem is that there are too many categories. In question **3** the total number of marks obtained doesn't have the same significance – why would anyone want to add up all of the marks of five students then calculate the proportions of that quantity obtained by each? A subtle point which may be worth making to a few students.

Question 4 Probably the best question to illustrate the idea that pie charts deal with proportions not totals. It may be a good time to introduce the idea that totals can be dealt with in comparative pie charts by letting area be proportional to total.

Question 5 A good question because, at some point in the near future, students will have to make of choice of statistical diagrams in project work. Emphasise to students that, while more than one type of diagram may be possible in a particular context, some may be better than others and the decision on which to use partly depends upon what is being illustrated.

Simplification – Applications

Students should work with data that is easily divided into 360. They should work out the angles and check the total is 360 before drawing their charts.

Extension – Applications

Give students further examples where the steps are not clearly scaffolded or the total frequencies are larger and more difficult to deal with mentally.

Averages and spread 1

Objectives

① **S4** Interpret, analyse and compare the distributions of data sets

② **S4** Interpret the range

③ **S5** Apply statistics to describe a population

Useful resources

Mini whiteboards, calculators

Starter – Skills

Write a data set of colours of cars: blue, red, yellow, blue, black, blue, red, yellow, grey, black.

Ask 'What is the average car colour?' Establish that the only possible answer for this data is the mode.

Write a data set of the number of siblings of seven students: 1, 2, 1, 3, 4, 2 and 7. Ask 'What is the average number of siblings' Explore the different averages and elicit the mode, median and mean averages for this data set and how to find them.

Teaching notes – Skills

① Refer to the starter and recap the three types of average: **mean**, **median** and **mode**. Ensure that students recall how to find each one. Emphasise that an average is a single value that in some way **represents** a whole data set and that the mean and median can only be used with numerical data – data that can be added, subtracted and ordered.

Refer to the frequency table in one of the student book examples and discuss how to find the **mode** (or **modal value**). Highlight that this is clear to see from the table: it is the value with the highest **frequency**. Ensure students recognise that the modal value is not the **frequency** itself (this indicates how many times the value appears).

Use the set 3, 1, 2, 6, 7 to illustrate that there are data sets with no mode, and the set 6, 2, 3, 3, 6 to illustrate that there can be more than one mode.

Discuss what students recall about the **mean** and remind students that it is normally called the 'average'. Highlight that the total is *shared equally* – as if it has been levelled. Ensure students understand that to find the mean, first add the values and then divide this total by the number of values.

Discuss how to find the **median**, making sure students understand that the median is the *middle* value. Highlight the need to **order the data** from smallest to largest *before* finding the middle value. Give a more complete definition, that the median is the middle value once the values have been ordered.

Demonstrate crossing off one value from each side of an ordered list until the middle value is left. Recap that in the case of an even number of items in the data set the median is the midpoint of the two middle values. Recall that to calculate the midpoint, add the numbers and divide by 2.

② Refer to one of the data sets in the student book and recall how to find the **range** of data. Discuss real-life applications of the word. Emphasise that range is a measure of spread, telling you how much difference there is between the highest and lowest values. Formalise that the range is *one* value:

range = highest value – lowest value.

③ Joe and Kane went fishing and each caught ten fish. The lengths of their fish, in cm, were:

Joe	3	5	7	8	8	9	9	10	12	17
Kane	6	6	7	7	8	10	1	11	12	14

Discuss how to compare their catches by finding the means, medians and ranges.

Kane's averages are slightly higher than Joe's. His smaller range shows his fish have a more consistent length. Discuss examples where consistency might be more important than a high average.

Plenary – Skills

Challenge students to think of (different) data sets of six values with, for example:

- a median of 4
- a mean, median and mode of 5
- a mode of 3 and a range of 11.

Discuss strategies. Elicit deductions about each set.

Exercise commentary – Skills

Questions 1 to **3** A set of three questions which can be used in two different ways. In order to develop skills in calculating these quantities, they could be set one after the other; that is, do all of the mean questions, then all of the median questions, then the mode and range questions. This is quite old fashioned but has lots to recommend it. The danger here is that, if that's all that is done, once they start question **2** they forget the theory for question **1**, etc. So, once the techniques have been established, the students could be asked to do a mixed set of questions, say **1b**, **3d**, **2bii**, **3e**,... This will fix in the students' heads the different measures and how to calculate each.

Question 4 Consolidates ideas relating to the interpretation of frequency distributions and the different measures of location and spread.

Question 5 Provides a good opportunity to relate data to a real-life situation. Ask the students to imagine that these 25 students are typical of all of the students in the school. Are we impressed by the attendance patterns demonstrated within this school? Perhaps complete a similar table for the students within the class and compare

Question 7 For the brightest students, this could be an excellent introduction to coding, a technique which was very important in the days before calculators and computers and is still important for theoretical reasons, for example, in normalizing variables. For these students, in part **c**, don't stop at the range; calculate the other measures and investigate how this coding could be useful.

Simplification – Skills

Allow students to use a calculator to check their mean calculations. For the median, mode and range they could be given pre-ordered data.

Extension – Skills

Students could work out the mean, median, mode and range of grouped data by extending the table rather than writing the data values in a list.

Recap – Applications

Work out the mean, median and mode of this frequency distribution of sales of ladies' dress sizes.

Dress size	8	10	12	14	16	18
Frequency	5	11	15	16	11	2

(Mode = 14; Median = 12; Mean = 766 ÷ 60 = 12.8 (3sf))

Plenary – Applications

Ask students to work in small groups. Ask how they would select, say, athletes or players for a sports event. Provide them with sample data including different patterns of spread (for example, on running times, goal averages etc). Given such statistics for each individual's performance, ask students how they could use the data to make the best selections. Prompt students to think about useful methods of analysing the data, including the different averages and measures of spread. Allow thinking time. Share final responses and the reasoning behind them.

Exercise commentary – Applications

Questions 1 and **2** These 'compare sets of data' questions demonstrate that statistical concepts are not an end in themselves but intended to inform us about practical matters. In question **1**, the student has to recognise that it is the spread of the data which is important. In question **2** it is 'typical values' that have to be considered. This question could usefully start a discussion along the lines, 'is it sensible to calculate all three measures of location and if not, which one is most useful here?'

Questions 3 and **4** Focus first on the meaning of the relevant measure; in this case, range for question **3** and range, median and mode for question **4**.

Question 5 A question well worth spending some time on as it involves several important techniques. First, discourage students from solving the problem by writing all of the values out; rather, work from the frequency distribution. Then, to find the mean, get them to add an extra row for mark × frequency. For the median, this might be the right time to emphasise that, since they can't get the middle value by 'counting in from the outsides', they should use the $\left(\frac{n+1}{2}\right)$th value.

To convince them that this works, note that the middle value of 3 numbers is not the 1½th value but the 2nd.

Question 7 Emphasise that totals as well as means can be found from frequency diagrams and that totals can be found from means; in other words, using standard formulae in a slightly unusual way.

Question 8 The comments for question **7** also apply to this question which is a good introduction to the concept of weighted mean.

Simplification – Applications

Students could be given values for the mean, median, mode and range for two data sets and asked to compare them, rather than having to calculate them first. Ensure that students write their answers in full sentences with reasoning.

Extension – Applications

Challenge students to create a set of five numbers with a specific mean, median, mode and range of their choice. Students can then swap questions and work out each others set of numbers. Negative numbers are allowed!

4 Handling data 1

<table>
<tr><th>Key outcomes</th><th>Quick check</th></tr>
<tr><td>S1 Infer properties of populations or distributions from a sample, whilst knowing the limitations of sampling.</td><td>
1 A sample is taken of people visiting a shop one day. This is done by surveying all the people that leave between 11 and 11:15 am. The number of items bought by each is recorded.
5, 11, 28, 4, 13, 35, 17, 13, 4, 2, 11
a Use this sample to estimate the mean number of items bought per person that day. (143 ÷ 11 = 13)
b What are the possible issues with estimating the mean in this way? (sample too small, could be biased)
</td></tr>
<tr><td>S2 Interpret and construct tables, charts and diagrams, including frequency tables, bar charts, pie charts and pictograms for categorical data and know their appropriate use.</td><td rowspan="3">
2 The age (in years) of a number of hamsters is given, record this information in a frequency table.
1, 5, 2, 3, 1, 2, 2, 3, 4, 3, 2, 2, 2, 4, 1, 1
<table><tr><th>Age</th><th>Frequency</th></tr><tr><td>1</td><td>4</td></tr><tr><td>2</td><td>5</td></tr><tr><td>3</td><td>3</td></tr><tr><td>4</td><td>2</td></tr><tr><td>5</td><td>1</td></tr></table>
3 The number of students in a class in a particular school is recorded.
30, 25, 29, 12, 19, 31, 17, 32, 29, 30, 23, 33, 29, 14, 28, 31, 26, 28, 25, 30, 27
Work out the
a highest number (33) **b** range (21)
c mode (29) **d** median. (28)
In a different school, the median number of students in a class is 25 and the range is 24.
e Compare the class sizes in the two schools.
(2nd school has lower median (average) class size but a slightly greater range (spread) of class sizes)
4 For this set of numbers work out the 1, 5, 4, 5, 3, 7, 9, 5, 0, 2
a mean (4.1) **b** median (4.5)
c mode (5) **d** range. (9)
5 Draw a bar chart to represent the data in question **1**.
(bar chart for data in question **1**, include labels, equally spaced scale and gaps between bars)
6 The pie chart shows the favourite vegetable of 200 people. How many people prefer
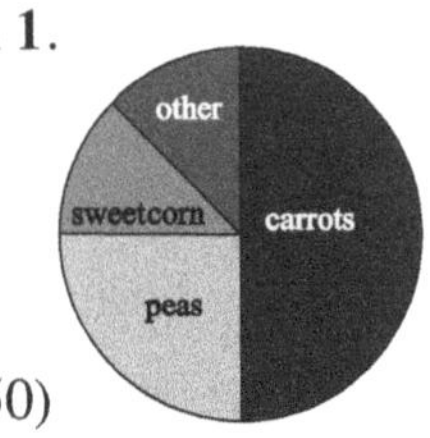

a carrots (200) **b** sweetcorn? (50)
</td></tr>
<tr><td>S4 Interpret, analyse and compare the distributions of data sets from univariate empirical distributions through:
- appropriate graphical representation involving discrete data;
- appropriate measures of central tendency (median, mean, mode and modal class) and spread (range, including consideration of outliers).</td></tr>
<tr><td>5 Apply statistics to describe a population.</td></tr>
</table>

Misconceptions and challenges	Solutions
Students make mistakes during the tallying process or misuse tally marks.	Encourage students to list systematically to improve accuracy.
Students do not remember the difference between mean, mode and median because all three words begin with the same letter.	Have students develop a 'memory trick' specific to themselves or the class, to help them remember. There are various songs that students can learn, or, better still, compose themselves.
Students are unable to extract data from tables, graphs or everyday sources and then use it to draw simple inferences.	Build understanding by comparing two contrasting data-sources, and look at their similarities and differences before making inferences.

Misconceptions and challenges	Solutions
Students often leave uneven gaps between bars, use unequal bar widths when drawing bar charts and are careless when labelling the scales on the axes.	Students have used bar charts since KS1, and may see them as pictures rather than mathematical diagrams. Look specifically at the accuracies of scales, and of the bars.
Students remember the algorithm for finding the mean but have great difficulty in reversing it to find the overall sum.	Use other mathematical topics as a context. For example, when learning about negative numbers, challenge students to find a set of numbers with a mode of –5 and a mean of –3.5.
Students find it difficult to choose which graphs to use because they do not understand that different graphs highlight different properties of the data.	From one set of data draw (or attempt to draw) a range of charts: bar, pie, line graph, and then discuss which are relevant to the data and the problem given, and why.
Students can extract data from graphs accurately, but have difficulty in creating, or judging the veracity of, statements based upon data or graphs.	Students at this level will benefit from plenty of past-paper practice where they are required to extract data from tables, graphs or from everyday sources and use it to draw and support inferences.

Review question commentary

Students will need rulers, protractors and pencils.

Question 1 (**4.1**) – Remind students to use a tally chart before creating their frequency table.

Question 2 (**4.1**) – If students are stuck have them work out the total of each of the rows and columns and label each answer.

Question 3 (**4.2**) – Get students to split each football in quarters and label how much each is worth.

Question 4 (**4.2**) – Peer assessment could be used to check charts have titles, labels and correct (equally spaced) scales

Question 5 (**4.3**) – Encourage students to use fractions $\frac{1}{2}$, $\frac{1}{4}$ and $\frac{1}{8}$ in this question rather than measuring each angle.

Question 6 (**4.3**) – It may help students to first put the information in a table and calculate the angles. Sectors in the pie chart need to be labelled or a key provided.

Question 7 (**4.4**) – The total for the mean is 72. For the median students may forget to write in order and get an incorrect answer of 6 (average of 9 and 3).

Question 8 (**4.4**) – Discuss how bias could occur in this sample, e.g. several people could arrive together and be similar ages, time of day could affect the age of people visiting, e.g. during school time children less likely to be visiting.

Question 9 (**4.4**) – Remind students that they need to put the numbers in order to find the median. This will also help them to find the mode and range.

Review answers

1

Number	Frequency
1	2
2	4
3	8
4	5

2 **a** 30 **b** 13 **c** 2 **d** 27

3 **a i** 16 **ii** 9

b i $2\frac{1}{2}$ footballs **ii** $3\frac{3}{4}$ footballs

4

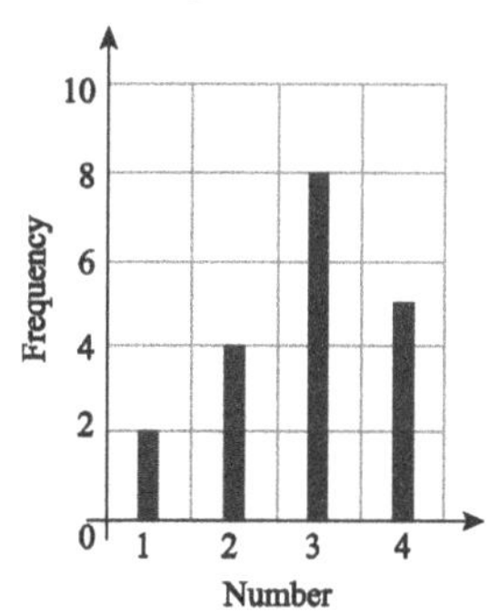

5 **a** 40 **b** 10

6 Snack 36°, Magazine 108°, Savings 216°.

7 **a** 6 **b** 6.5 **c** 7 **d** 6

8 **a** 44 **b** Sample is biased and too small

9 **a** 35 **b** 34 **c** 11 **d** 12

e The 2nd zoo has a higher median number of birds per aviary and its range is smaller.

Assessment 4

Question 1 – 6 marks

a

Milk	Frequency
0	6
1	14
2	13
3	7
4	7
5	2
6	1

Table with correct categories 0 6 [M1]
Correct frequencies; lose 1 mark for each error. [A2]

b y-axis labelled 'Frequency', x-axis labelled 'Pints of milk' [B1]
Correctly drawn bars: 0 (6), 1 (14), 2 (13), 3 (7), 4 (7), 5 (4), 6(2) [B1]
Gaps between bars. [B1]

Question 2 – 4 marks

a 35 [15 + 20] [B1]
b 16 [B1]
c 3 [3 – 0] [B1]
d Information may be accessed in multiple ways. [B1]

Question 3 – 4 marks

	Glasses	No glasses
Left-handed	1	4
Right-handed	14	16

Correctly labelled table [M1]
Correct frequencies; lose 1 mark for each error. [A3]

Question 4 – 13 marks

a **i** $1030 \div 10$ [M1]
$= 103$ miles [A1]
ii $(90 + 109) \div 10$ [M1]
$= 99.5$ miles [A1]
iii 88 miles [B1]

b You do not know how many journeys are made in one day. [M1]
Therefore you cannot tell. [A1]

c $163 - 56$ [M1]
$= 107$ miles [A1]

d The mean increases.
The total has increased not the number of journeys. [B1]
The median increases
98 replaces 90 as one of the two middle numbers. [B1]
There is no mode.
Each number occurs only once. [B1]
The range is unchanged.
The highest and lowest numbers are unaffected. [B1]
Must see reasons given for each answer.

Question 5 – 15 marks

a

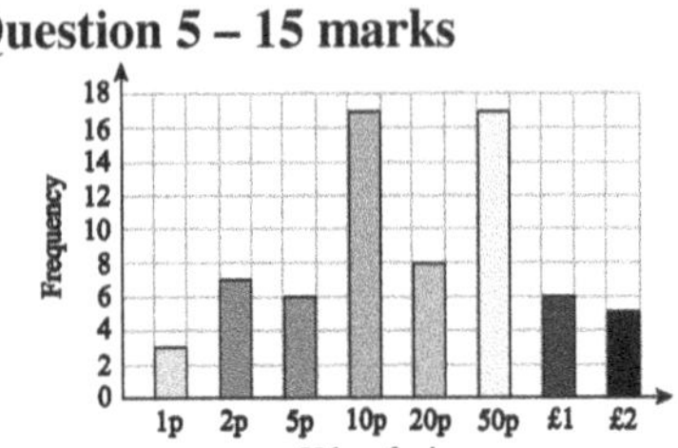

Lose 1 mark for each incorrectly drawn bar. [B2]

b

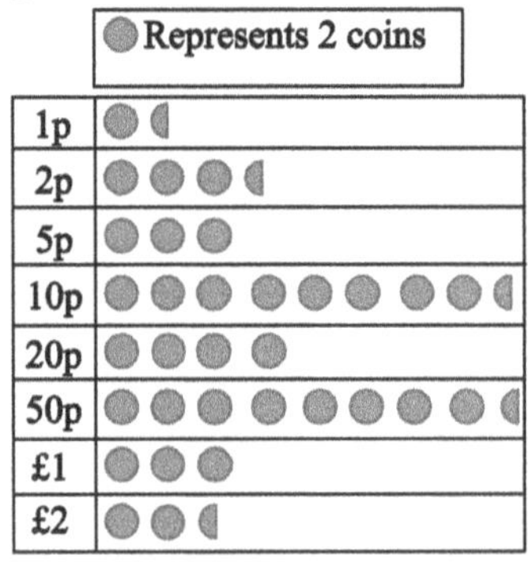

Pictogram with correct categories [M1]
Must include a key [M1]
Correct frequencies; lose 1 mark for each error [A2]

c 10p and 50p [B1]

d Median coin = (Number of coins + 1) ÷ 2 [M1]
Median coin = (69 + 1) ÷ 2 = 35th coin [A1]
$3 + 7 + 6 + 17 = 33 < 35$, $33 + 8 = 41 > 35$
20p [A1]

e Value of coins
$= 1 \times 3 + 2 \times 7 + 5 \times 6 + 10 \times 17 + 20 \times 8 + 50 \times 17 + 100 \times 6 + 200 \times 5$ [M1]
$= 2827$ [A1]
Number of coins
$= 3 + 7 + 6 + 17 + 8 + 17 + 6 + 5$ [M1]
$= 69$ [A1]
$= 2827 \div 69$
$= 40.971\ldots = 41$p [A1]

Question 6 – 5 marks

Sector angles: frequency × (360° ÷ total frequency)
= frequency × 4.5° [M1]
Child 27°, First 63°, Business 76.5°, Standard 81°, Senior 112.5° [A2]
Accurate drawing (±1°) [B1]
Correctly labelled [B1]

Question 7 – 8 marks

a Walk [B1]
b Car [B1]
c $\frac{90°}{360°}$ [M1]
$= 25\%$ [A1]
d Sector 45° [B1]
$\frac{45°}{360°} \times 1200$ [M1]
$= 150$ people [A1]
e None [B1]

Question 8 – 10 marks

a $5 + 2 + 0 + 1 + 1$ [M1]
$= 9$ [A1]
b 2 [B1]
c $5 + 2 + 1 + 0 + 0$ [M1]
$= 8$ [A1]
d Zero [B1]
e Number of pets
$= 10 \times 0 + 9 \times 1 + 8 \times 2 + 2 \times 3 + 0 \times 4 + 1 \times 5$ [M1]
$= 36$ [A1]
Number of families
$= 10 + 9 + 8 + 2 + 0 + 1 = 30$ [A1]
$36 \div 28 = 1.2$ [A1]

Fractions, decimals and percentages

Learning outcomes

A1 Use and interpret algebraic notation, including:
- coefficients written as fractions rather than as decimals.

N1 Order positive [and negative integers,] decimals and fractions; use the symbols =, ≠, <, >, ≤, ≥.

N2 Apply the four operations +, −, ×, ÷, including formal written methods, to [integers, decimals and] simple fractions (proper and improper), and mixed numbers.

N3 Recognise and use relationships between operations, including inverse operations (e.g. cancellation to simplify calculations and expressions); and reciprocals.

N10 Work interchangeably with terminating decimals and their corresponding fractions (such as 3.5 and 7/2 or 0.375 or 3/8).

N12 Interpret fractions and percentages as operators.

R3 Express one quantity as a fraction of another, where the fraction is less than 1 [or greater than 1].

R9 Define percentage as 'number of parts per hundred'; interpret percentages 100%.

Prior knowledge

Check-in skill

- Multiply and divide by 10.
- Round numbers to 2 decimal places.
- Order decimal numbers.

Online resources

MyMaths 1015, 1016, 1017, 1018, 1019, 1029, 1030, 1031, 1040, 1042, 1046, 1047, 1075

InvisiPen videos

Skills: 05Sa – h Applications: 05Aa – e

Kerboodle assessment

Online Skills Test 5 Chapter Test 5

Development and links

Fractions and percentages are widely encountered when working with measure. They are used in pie charts to describe the results of statistical enquiries, in recipes, on food packaging to describe the nutritional value of the contents, to compare measurements and concentrations of liquids and to determine taxes. In everyday life, percentage change is used to calculate interest due on bank and building society accounts, to calculate VAT and to calculate price increases and reductions.

Chapter investigation

Invite students to investigate the challenge for smallish numbers of divisions before drawing out a number of issues. Do the sections have to be the same size? (Yes) Is the answer unique? (No. Quarters can be created with 3 horizontal, or vertical lines, or 2 perpendicular lines through the rectangle's centre.) Use the second question to discuss how you decide if two fractions are equal. For equal denominators simply compare the numerators – this easily extends to ordering fractions [**5.1**]. For unequal denominators an understanding of equivalent fractions is required: this translates to grouping or subdividing existing unit-fraction sections. Extend the discussion to cover improper (top-heavy) fractions and mixed numbers. Converting to equivalent decimals can be done using equivalent fractions with denominators of tenths, hundredths, etc. This works well for denominators of the form $2^n \times 5^m$. Show that this can also be done by arithmetic division which allows all denominators to be treated.

Introduce percentages, and their notation, as fractions with denominator 100 [**5.2, 5.4**]
Viewed as repeated addition calculating a fraction of an integer has a simple interpretation using shaded shapes with an equivalent arithmetic procedure [**5.2**]. An understanding of arithmetic with fractions can be achieved using equivalent fractions and shaded shapes and this 'concrete' approach should be encouraged [**5.3**].It is straightforward for addition and subtraction. Multiplication of $\frac{a}{b}$ by $\frac{c}{d}$ can be explained as follows. Think of $\frac{a}{b}$ as a rectangle with b equal parts a of which are shaded. You want to divide each of the $\frac{1}{b}$ divisions into d parts, from each of which you want c parts. That is you want $a \times c$ parts out of $b \times d$.
Division can be introduced as what you have to do to undo a multiplication, $1 = \frac{a}{b} \div \frac{a}{b} = \frac{a}{b} \times \frac{b}{a}$, or using equivalent fractions with the same denominator, $\frac{a}{b} \div \frac{c}{d} = \frac{ad}{bd} \div \frac{bc}{bd} = \frac{ad}{bc}$.

5.1 Decimals and fractions

Objectives

① **(Pre-GCSE)** Identify, name and write equivalent fractions of a given fraction, represented visually

② **(Pre-GCSE)** Recognise mixed numbers and improper fractions and convert from one form to the other

③ **N10** Work interchangeably with terminating decimals and their corresponding fractions

④ **N1** Order positive decimals and fractions and use the symbols $=, \neq, <, >$

Useful resources

Number line, place value table, magnetic fractions (parts of circle, etc.), mini whiteboards, calculators

Starter – Skills

Ask students various questions based around the fraction $\frac{1}{2}$: What's half of 44, 200, 32, 460, ...?

Repeat with the fraction $\frac{1}{4}$ and various numbers.

Teaching notes – Skills

① Revise the terms **numerator** and **denominator**.

Discuss different **representations of fractions**, highlighting the number shaded/indicated as a fraction of the whole and the number of equal parts in total. Highlight the need to divide a shape into equal parts first. Build confidence in writing one amount as a fraction of the whole using groups within the class. For example, what fraction of students have brown hair? Link the phrase 'out of' to fractions: '19 *out of* 30 students are girls'= $\frac{19}{30}$.

Ask students to write these fractions in their simplest form: $\frac{5}{10}, \frac{2}{20}, \frac{3}{15}, \frac{10}{1000}, \frac{4}{16}$ $\left(\frac{1}{2}, \frac{1}{10}, \frac{1}{5}, \frac{1}{100}, \frac{1}{4}\right)$

Compare answers and discuss strategies for **simplifying fractions**. Elicit that you need to find **common factors** (ideally finding the HCF to begin with) and **cancel** (divide top and bottom by the common factor). When no further cancelling is possible, a fraction is in its **simplest form**.

② Ask students to convert **improper fractions to mixed numbers**: $\frac{4}{3}, \frac{6}{5}, \frac{7}{5}, \frac{8}{4}$. Encourage them to explain their reasoning: for example, there are three thirds in a whole so four thirds is one whole and one third. Highlight that mixed numbers are considered the simplest form of improper fractions.

③ Discuss strategies for converting mixed numbers to improper fractions.

Draw a line from 0 to 1 divided into 10 equal intervals. Ask students to label any interval marker with a decimal or fraction. Link to previous work on fractions (each interval as $\frac{1}{10}$) and to the first decimal place value column (tenths). Divide one interval into 10 and ask students to count up, say, 0.31, 0.32, 0.33... Discuss how to convert **decimals to fractions**, referring back to place value columns and their use as denominator. To convert **fractions to decimals**, emphasise fractions as a division and demonstrate (using a calculator if needed) dividing numerator by denominator.

④ Review students' knowledge of equivalent fractions. Use this to order a collection of fractions. Emphasise the need for a *common denominator*.

Write statements such as $\frac{1}{3} < \frac{5}{12}$ and discuss whether this is true or false. Include an example of the use of the symbol $\neq$. E.g. $\frac{5}{6} \neq \frac{3}{8}$

Plenary – Skills

Give groups of students a set of five different digits. Ask them to make as many different fractions as they can with the digits, using each one as numerator and/or denominator (e.g. using 1 and 2: $\frac{1}{1}, \frac{1}{2}, \frac{2}{1}, \frac{2}{2}$). Then ask students to group their list of fractions by similarity in any ways they can. Use target vocabulary to discuss the groups of fractions.

Exercise commentary – Skills

Students need to be able to visualise fractions, and previous classroom experiences should be revisited. While students usually have few problems in simplifying equivalent fractions, using them to compare sizes, or for addition and subtraction, does not come readily. Ordering fractions close to each other is a challenge. Be aware of the student who sees $\frac{4}{5}$ and $\frac{6}{7}$ as the same because there is only 1 between numerator and denominator, or they might argue only 1 away from a whole, rather than $\frac{1}{5}$ away and $\frac{1}{7}$ away.

Question 1 Some students will see the numerator as shaded whilst the denominator represents the number unshaded, for example $\frac{2}{3}$ instead of $\frac{2}{5}$. This is discussed throughout the lesson but also ensure there is a visual example for students to refer back to.

Question 2 Students must find a fraction on a line. Encourage them to consider how many parts their line must be divided into, and 'walk' the number of parts required from zero. J is in between two marks on the scale in **c**; invite students to think how many parts the line is divided into if you include halfway points.

Question 4 Encourage students to consider the HCF of the two numbers.

Question 7 This links to proportional reasoning; it may be helpful for students to imagine scaling up or down.

Question 8 Students should be encouraged to draw a place value table, and then rewrite as a fraction with denominator a power of 10.

Question 9 Students should not use a calculator. Where the fraction does not immediately offer equivalence with denominator 10 or 100 (for example, $\frac{2}{8}$), encourage students to first simplify the fraction.

Question 12 Encourage weaker students to 'fill the gaps' so they are comparing decimal numbers with the same number of digits, for example 2.2 as 2.20.

Simplification – Skills

Give students further examples of fractions given as diagrams before moving on to the word problems. Students should also practise simplifying (and un-simplifying) proper fractions before moving on to improper fractions; and simple fraction–decimal conversions with one or two place decimals.

Extension – Skills

Students could be given further examples of fraction–decimal conversion that require division (and possibly rounding).

Recap – Applications

1 a Write each fraction in its simplest form:

i $\frac{6}{24}$ **ii** $\frac{72}{108}$ **iii** $\frac{17}{72}$

(**i** $\frac{1}{4}$ **ii** $\frac{2}{3}$ **iii** $\frac{17}{72}$)

b Convert each fraction into an improper fraction:

i $4\frac{7}{11}$ **ii** $15\frac{5}{12}$ **iii** $24\frac{2}{7}$

(**i** $\frac{51}{11}$ **ii** $\frac{185}{12}$ **iii** $\frac{170}{7}$)

c Convert each fraction into a mixed number:

i $\frac{19}{4}$ **ii** $\frac{55}{12}$ **iii** $\frac{113}{15}$

(**i** $4\frac{3}{4}$ **ii** $4\frac{7}{12}$ **iii** $7\frac{8}{15}$)

2 Write these lists of numbers in ascending order:

a $\frac{5}{9}$ 0.5 $\frac{27}{50}$ 0.53 $\frac{14}{25}$

(0.5 0.53 $\frac{27}{50}$ $\frac{5}{9}$ $\frac{14}{25}$)

b $\frac{85}{42}$ 2.125 $\frac{53}{25}$ 2.25 $2\frac{3}{10}$

($\frac{85}{42}$ $\frac{53}{25}$ 2.125 2.25 $2\frac{3}{10}$)

Plenary – Applications

Refer to $\frac{12}{24}$ as equivalent to $\frac{1}{2}$. Find the equivalent fractions (with denominator 24) to $\frac{1}{4}$ and $\frac{2}{3}$.

Exercise commentary – Applications

Question 2 Refer students to the first example.

Question 3 Makes links between fractions and probability.

Question 4 Students could try to explain what mistake Eric has made and why he is incorrect.

Question 5 Refer students to the second example. Student could approach the problem mentally by considering whether each shape is less than, equal to, or less than half shaded.

Question 6 Students could make the cards and then do the task. The important thing is to ensure that they convert to the same type of quantity – easier to compare decimals in this case. Encourage simplification of fractions, particularly 20/32 which should not need a calculator to evaluate as a decimal.

Questions 7 and **8** Students may convert to decimals or convert the fractions into fractions with a common denominator and then compare.

Question 9 Extend the question by asking students what would happen if the CDs represented one-third of the collection.

Question 10 This task involves algebra, which some Foundation students will find challenging. You may need to recap collecting like terms – students should be encouraged to do this with the expressions on the left.

Simplification – Applications

Use examples with easy numbers so that each fraction can be simplified.

Extension – Applications

Students could work on multi-stage problems or those involving fractions with larger numbers and/or needing extensive cancelling.

Fractions and percentages

Objectives

① **N12** Interpret fractions and percentages as operators

② **R9** Define percentage as 'number of parts per hundred' and interpret percentages as a fraction

Useful resources

Number line, place value table, magnetic fractions (parts of circle, fraction walls), multiplication squares, mini whiteboards, calculators

Starter – Skills

Fraction and percentage bingo.

Ask students to each fill in a 3 × 3 grid with numbers chosen from the range 1–20. Ask simple fraction and percentage questions; e.g. $\frac{1}{2}$ of 32, 25% of 40. Students cross off answers in their grid. The first to complete a row in any direction wins.

Teaching notes – Skills

① What do we mean by $\frac{3}{5}$ of £50? (Divide 50 into five equal parts and take three of the parts.)

What do we mean by 70% of 10 cm? (Divide 10 into ten equal parts and take seven of the parts.)

Refer to the bingo starter. Discuss how to find **fractions of amounts**. Start with $\frac{1}{2}$ and $\frac{1}{4}$ of an amount and extend to $\frac{1}{3}$ and $\frac{1}{8}$. Encourage students to generalise using algebra (to find $\frac{1}{n}$, divide by n).

Discuss how to find $\frac{2}{3}$ of 36. Encourage students to say the calculation aloud, reinforcing the denominator as the *size* of the parts, and the numerator as the *number* of parts. Emphasise that $\frac{2}{3}$ means 2 lots of $\frac{1}{3}$, so divide by 3 to find $\frac{1}{3}$, then multiply by 2 to find $\frac{2}{3}$. Generalise: divide by the denominator then multiply by the numerator.

Discuss what 'of' means when finding a fraction of something. Use a simple integer example; say, '3 lots *of* 4' to link to multiplication. Ensure students understand that $\frac{2}{3}$ of $36 \equiv \frac{2}{3} \times 36$

② Discuss how to find **percentages of amounts**. Highlight key points:

- 50% is the same as $\frac{1}{2}$, so you divide by 2
- 25% is equivalent to $\frac{1}{4}$ so divide by 4 (or half of 50%, so halve the 50% value)
- 10% is the same as $\frac{1}{10}$, so you divide by 10
- 5% is half of 10%, so you halve the 10% value
- 1% is the same as $\frac{1}{100}$, so you divide by 100

Discuss how to extend calculating 10% of a number to calculating 20%, 2.5% and then 15%.

Discuss why 1% is an important value to find. Highlight that any number is a multiple of 1%, so this value can be multiplied up as necessary.

Plenary – Skills

Demonstrate how one calculation can be considered in many different ways:

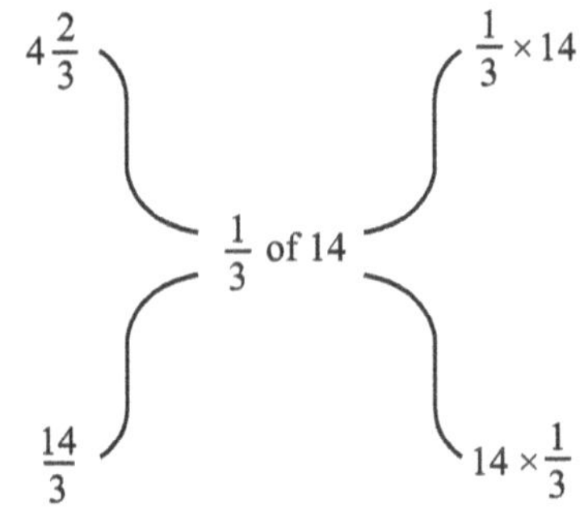

Ask students to suggest additional legs, involving percentages. Then ask students to complete similar diagrams in pairs or groups.

Exercise commentary – Skills

Question 1 Suggest to students that 'of' usually means multiply.

Questions 2 and **3** The example on page 100 shows a good way to set out workings, particularly for the non-unitary fractions in question **3**.

Question 4 Students might need the hint that 1/10 = 10%

Question 5 These should all be possible to work out mentally, and will reinforce strategies for the main percentages: 1, 5, 10, 20, 25, 50.

Question 6 Parts **d** and **h** work out as mixed numbers. Encourage students to give the correct units in all these questions.

Question 7 Students may wish to use a calculator here – check they're using it properly.

Question 8 These develop the strategies from questions **5** and **6**. Encourage students to think confidently and creatively about how they can work out a particular percentage. If they can do 1%, then why not 2%? If they know 10%, 5% and 2%, how can they work out 13%?

Question 10 Ask students to come up with rules for finding 1%, 5%, 25% and so on.

Simplification – Skills

Students should focus on unitary fractions that divide simply into the amount; finding simple percentages before moving on to complicated ones. A multiplication square might help.

Extension – Skills

Students could be asked to solve problems which involve finding percentages of quantities where the percentage is greater than 100.

Recap – Applications

1 Use a mental method to find:

a $\frac{3}{4}$ of 12 **b** $\frac{5}{6}$ of 54

c $\frac{3}{8}$ of 28 (**a** 9 **b** 45 **c** 10.5)

2 Giving answers, where appropriate, to 3sf, Calculate:
a 24% of 56 km **b** 65% of 3 l 100 ml
(**a** 13.44 km **b** 2 l 15 ml)

3 0.435 of a Pizza is the base; 35% is Cheese and $\frac{1}{8}$ is Pepperoni. What Percentage of the Pizza contains the rest of the ingredients? (9%)

Plenary – Applications

Discuss fractional and percentage increases.

- The value of a house increases by $\frac{1}{5}$ of its original selling price in 2 years. It originally cost £200 000. How much is it worth after 2 years?
- A jumper originally costing £18 is reduced by 10%. What is its sale price?

Ensure students understand they must first calculate the fractional/percentage increase/decrease before adjusting the original quantity by this amount.

Highlight increase as addition, decrease as subtraction.

Exercise commentary – Applications

Question 2 Remind students that you find 20% by dividing by 10, then multiplying by 2 (not dividing by 20!).

Question 3 This might involve a bit of trial-and-error at the start, but should quickly fall into place.

Questions 4 and **5** Refer students to the second example. These questions could be extended by including examples that contain fractions and percentages.

Question 6 Students may find the increase and then add it to $47 800, whereas students who are more confident with percentage increases may recall that you can use a single calculation to find the new salary.

Question 7 Prompt students to find the total amount of saturated fat in one bar, and then think of four squares as one-eighth of the bar.

Question 9 Students could discuss how they arrived at their answer. Did they find the fraction represented by the ‘others’ and then work out the angle, or did they work out the angles for each sector and subtract from 360°?

Question 10 Discuss as a class. Ask students how the problem would change if Farmer Macdonald had died leaving 35 horses. The neighbour wold end up with two horses!

Simplification – Applications

Students should work with simple percentages securing mental and written methods before attempting more complicated examples.

Extension – Applications

Students could be given multi-stage problems to solve. They could also investigate reverse fractional or percentage change when given the final amount and asked to find the original when told what fraction/ percentage it has been increased by.

Calculations with fractions

Objectives

① **N2** Apply the four operations to simple fractions (proper and improper), and mixed numbers

Useful resources

OHT/whiteboard file of shapes for starter activity, mini whiteboards, calculators

Starter – Skills

Show students five fraction diagrams and ask them to identify the odd one out, justifying their answer:

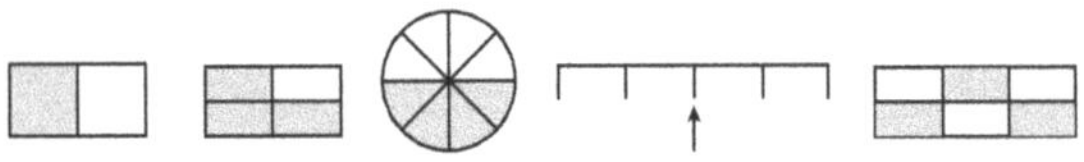

Highlight that all the fractions but one are equivalent to a half: $\frac{1}{2}=\frac{2}{4}=\frac{4}{8}=\frac{3}{6}$

Give each group of students a unitary or other simple fraction to find as many equivalent fractions as they can. Discuss strategies for generating them.

Teaching notes – Skills

① Highlight the importance, when **adding** and **subtracting** fractions, of being confident with using equivalent fractions and finding the **lowest common denominator** (LCM). Ask students to find the LCM of two or three numbers. Emphasise finding the *lowest* common multiple to keep the numbers as simple as possible. Show students two **additions** and discuss which is correct:

$\frac{1}{8}+\frac{2}{8}=\frac{3}{16}$ or $\frac{1}{8}+\frac{2}{8}=\frac{3}{8}$

Highlight that when the denominator is the same, you just add the numerators together.

Display the calculation: $\frac{2}{3}+\frac{3}{5}=\frac{5}{8}$

Ask students to decide whether the statement is true or false. Explore the responses and draw out that, just by estimating or using common sense, it *can't* be right. Use visual models to illustrate that the result must be more than 1. Ask students what would be the right answer, and why? Model the use of equivalent fractions as a strategy.

Change the operation in the original statement to **subtraction**. Explore how to use the same strategy.

Recall the link between 'of' and **multiplication**. Ask students how else this question could be written: 'What is half of two and a half?' Collect responses and prompt further versions; for example, to include $2\frac{1}{2}\times\frac{1}{2}$, $\frac{1}{2}\times2\frac{1}{2}$, $2\frac{1}{2}\div2$, $\frac{1}{2}\times\frac{5}{2}$. Draw out the equivalence of, for example, $\times\ \frac{1}{2}$ and $\div\ 2$. Also explore related-fact strategies for additional versions: so $\frac{1}{2}\times2\frac{1}{2}\equiv1\times1\frac{1}{4}$

Use examples such as $\frac{1}{2}\times\frac{1}{4}$ to revise the method of multiplying numerators and denominators together.

Do a similar initial activity for **division**, asking students how else this question could be written: 'How many halves in 10 and a half?' Then ask students to work out the answers to similar questions (with unitary fractions only) and to look for relationships between the question (particularly the denominator) and the answer. Draw out the equivalence of, for example, $\div\ \frac{1}{2}$ and $\times\ 2$, which might lead on to a discussion of how to invert the divisor as a strategy.

Plenary – Skills

Explain that the ancient Egyptians used only unit fractions, such as $\frac{1}{2}$, $\frac{1}{4}$, $\frac{1}{5}$, $\frac{1}{10}$ ... If they wanted any other fraction, they added different unit fractions together. But they always used as few unit fractions as possible in the sum. So, for example, for $\frac{3}{4}$ they wrote $\frac{1}{2}+\frac{1}{4}$, not $\frac{1}{4}+\frac{1}{4}+\frac{1}{4}$. How could they write, for example, $\frac{7}{10}$? $\frac{5}{6}$? ($\frac{1}{2}+\frac{1}{5}$, $\frac{1}{2}+\frac{1}{3}$, ...)

Exercise commentary – Skills

Make sure students set their work out clearly, even if they still have misgivings with fraction calculations. It will help you (and them) to identify where they are getting stuck.

Question 1 Focuses on recapping equivalent fractions. Encourage students to identify the LCM of the denominators.

Questions 3 and **4** Some students can quickly learn routines for converting between mixed numbers and improper fractions, but need reminding. One way to check whether they've got it right is to try to convert it back – do they end up with what they started with?

Question 5 To help avoid students getting bogged down with all the converting, they could try to solve these just by drawing number lines.

Question 6 Each of these will need both fractions converting to an equivalent fraction. All answers are proper fractions. Students should not use a calculator.

Questions 7 to **9** Focus on multiplying and dividing with fractions. Students should appreciate that dividing by ½ is the same as doubling.

Question 10 Parts **e** and **f** may cause problems for students who deal with the whole parts and fractions separately.

Question 12 Students may cancel first and then multiply or leave cancelling until the end. Discuss which way is better.

Question 14 Encourage students to simplify before multiplying.

Simplification – Skills

Students may benefit from a multiplication square to identify common factors. They should concentrate on the idea of equivalent fractions before working on comparing fractions and simple additions.

Extension – Skills

Students could try addition and subtraction calculations that involve three or more fractions, provided that any common denominator is reasonably easy to spot/not too large. They could also try fraction multiplications or divisions where one (or both) of the fractions is top-heavy.

Recap – Applications

1 a Rewrite as improper fractions:

i $5\frac{3}{4}$ **ii** $12\frac{2}{5}$

iii $8\frac{5}{8}$ (**i** $\frac{23}{4}$ **ii** $\frac{62}{5}$ **iii** $\frac{69}{8}$)

b Rewrite as mixed numbers:

i $\frac{63}{5}$ **ii** $\frac{81}{6}$ **iii** $\frac{93}{11}$ (**i** $12\frac{3}{5}$ **ii** $13\frac{3}{6}$ **iii** $8\frac{5}{11}$)

2 Calculate these additions and subtractions:

a $2\frac{1}{16}+4\frac{1}{2}$ **b** $2\frac{1}{3}-1\frac{1}{8}$ (**a** $6\frac{9}{16}$ **b** $1\frac{5}{24}$)

3 Calculate these multiplications and divisions:

a $\frac{3}{10}\times\frac{2}{5}$ **b** $2\frac{1}{3}\div 1\frac{1}{4}$ (**a** $\frac{3}{25}$ **b** $\frac{28}{15}$)

Plenary – Applications

Write these figures on the board:

$\frac{2}{3}, \frac{1}{4}, \frac{2}{5}, \frac{1}{2}, 1\frac{3}{5}, \frac{4}{5}, \frac{3}{4}, \frac{3}{8}$

£382.50, £45, £75, £187.50, £50, £200

Explain that the fractions are to be calculated as fractions of £225. Ask students, in groups, to calculate these amounts and then put the whole list in ascending order.

(45, 50, $\frac{1}{4}\times 225 = 56.25$, 75, $\frac{3}{8}\times 225 = 84.38$,

$\frac{2}{5}\times 225 = 90$, $\frac{1}{2}\times 225 = 122.50$, $\frac{2}{3}\times 225 = 150$,

$\frac{3}{4}\times 225 = 168.75$, $\frac{4}{5}\times 225 = 180$, 187.50, 200,

$1\frac{3}{5}\times 225 = 360$, 382.50)

Exercise commentary – Applications

These questions will really test students' ability to work with fractions, drawing together all the skills they have learned and applying them to real-life problems.

Question 1 Students may prefer to add the number and fraction parts separately. This approach may be more straightforward for students who are prone to making errors when multiplying larger numbers.

Question 2 Students could use a 3 by 4 grid to explain why the answer is incorrect.

Question 3 Remind students to round their final answer down to the nearest whole number. Ask students to write a corresponding question where you would round the final answer up (for example, how many smaller paint pots would you need to buy to fill the larger container).

Question 4 Some students may prefer to calculate the number of hours that she is paid for ($11\frac{7}{8}$) and then multiply by £15 per hour. Ask students to justify why this method is the same as multiplying $9\frac{1}{2}$ by the weekend rate of £18.75/hour.

Question 5 Ensure that students simplify their answers fully.

Question 6 Students may need to reminded of the meaning of the word reciprocal.

Question 7 Students may try to subtract the fractions to find the shaded region. The task could be extended by asking students to explain why the answer is equivalent to the sum of the fractions – 1.

Question 8 Challenge students to create their own puzzles.

Question 9 Extend the question by asking students what would happen to the height of the pule if you kept adding sheets of paper that are half as thick as the previous sheet. Would the pile ever be exactly one inch tall?

Simplification – Applications

Give students plenty of practice at adding and subtracting simple fractions using a common denominator. Avoid mixed numbers at this stage. Students should also work on simple multiplication and division examples. Encourage them to show their working very clearly at all times.

Extension – Applications

Ask students how they might approach a problem where there are three fractions multiplied together. (Left to right) What if there was a combination of multiplying and dividing in longer strings? (Left to right) What about if addition and subtraction were included as well? (BIDMAS.)

Fractions, decimals and percentages

Objectives

① **N10** Work interchangeably with decimals and their corresponding fractions

② **N1** Order positive decimals and fractions and use the symbols =, ≠, <, >

③ **R9** Interpret percentages as a fraction or a decimal and compare two quantities using percentages (or decimals)

Useful resources

Number line, FDP value cards, 10 × 10 grid, mini whiteboards

Starter – Skills

Draw a line 0–1 with ten equal intervals. Label $\frac{1}{2}$ and ask students to offer equivalent fractions, decimals or percentages. Point at the first interval and ask students to offer its label. Encourage all decimal, percentage and fractional values. Repeat with all other tenth values and ask students to offer any additional values they know; e.g. $\frac{1}{4}$, $\frac{3}{4}$.

Teaching notes – Skills

① Refer again to the number line. Highlight that fractions, percentages and decimals are different ways of writing the same thing. Write the headings percentage, decimal and fraction as vertices of a triangle and write up methods between the headings on the board, using arrows to demonstrate the direction. Elicit these **conversions**:

- **percentage to decimal**: divide by 100
- **decimal to percentage**: multiply by 100
- **percentage to fraction**: write with denominator 100 and then cancel
- **fraction to percentage**: write as an equivalent fraction with denominator 100
- **fraction to decimal**: divide the numerator by the denominator.
- **decimal to fraction**: use place value to write as a fraction with the appropriate denominator.

Highlight:

- 'per cent' as meaning 'out of 100'
- the movement of digits two places when multiplying (left) or dividing (right) by 100
- the need to simplify the basic fraction (e.g. $\frac{60}{100}$) by cancelling common factors from numerator and denominator
- the simplest form of a fraction: when no further cancelling is possible.

② Discuss how to **order a set of numbers**. Demonstrate converting each number to its equivalent decimal. Ensure that students are confident converting between fractions, decimals and percentages before attempting to order them.

③ Introduce the use of percentages for making a comparison. Use this example: A survey of the students at two schools gave these results.

School A: 500 students of whom 45 had been to the cinema last week

School B: 650 students of whom 52 had been to the cinema last week

Work out percentages. School A had 9% who went to the cinema and school B had 8%.

Plenary – Skills

Distribute sets of FDP value cards, one per pair, for students to place in order, or on a number line. Discuss the results by asking for the largest to be raised, then the smallest. Ask students to look at the three values: $\frac{7}{20}$, 0.34, 38%. Explore how these were placed, and why.

Exercise commentary – Skills

Support students as they practice the conversion processes set out on page 108. Encourage clear layout of workings.

Students could design their own mini-poster by way of an aide-memoire to show how to convert between the three forms.

Question 2 In part **d**, beware students confusing 3% and 30%, or even 0.03%.

Question 3 Reinforce place value (3 decimal places means denominator 1000), also reducing to simplest form.

Question 4 Students could use a calculator for parts **c** to **f**. Encourage conversion to denominator 100 in part **b**.

Question 6 Students can leave their answer as a mixed number, so only need focus on the decimal part.

Question 7 the challenge here is to not use a calculator. Students could use division, but it will probably be better to convert to an equivalent fraction, which may take more than one step (e.g. where the denominator is 75).

Questions 8 to **13** These give more challenging practice in converting between the three forms. You may need to remind students about rounding numbers.

Questions 14 and **15** Refer students to the third example. Ensure that students read the question carefully to make sure that they are ordering from lowest to highest or highest to lowest.

Question 16 Students should use long or short division, and should quickly find that they are doing the same calculation, or sequence of calculations (ensure they don't spend hours on this!). Encourage correct use of recurring notation.

Simplification – Skills

Students should concentrate on examples where the percentage is in tens or fives and where the denominator of the fraction divides into 10 or 100 exactly. They should initially avoid questions involving ordering, then concentrate on comparing two numbers only. These can be a mix of fractions, decimals and percentages but should be easy to convert and clearly different.
A 10 × 10 grid might be helpful for conversions involving percentages.

Extension – Skills

Students could be given further examples where the denominator of the fraction does not divide into 10 or 100 exactly, and other fractions; e.g. eighths. Students could be asked to convert from fractions to decimals using a long division method through adding zeros after the decimal point. Or they could be given longer strings of numbers to order that require a more difficult-to-find common denominator. Discourage the use of calculators.

Recap – Applications

1 Write the following list in ascending order.

$\frac{3}{4}$ 70.01% 0.73 $\frac{18}{25}$ 69.9% $\frac{29}{40}$

(69.9% 70.01% $\frac{18}{25}$ $\frac{29}{40}$ 0.73 $\frac{3}{4}$)

Plenary – Applications

Discuss where students have experience of percentages: exam marks, sales etc. Use the scenario of exam marks to highlight the importance of using percentages to compare different quantities. Emphasise that percentages are easy to compare because they are all out of 100.

Discuss which is the best exam mark:

History	$\frac{17}{20}$	French	$\frac{22}{25}$
Maths	92%	English	$\frac{42}{50}$

Exercise commentary – Applications

Question 1 Ask students: if the manager's claim was true, what is the maximum number of customers who waited for more than 5 minutes?

Question 2 Students must convert all numbers to the same form before comparison. Discuss which is easiest: fractions, decimals or percentages?

Questions 4 to **7** Ask students to explain their reasoning and highlight that there are often many different ways to solve a problem solving question.

Question 8 Ask students to create their own versions of this question and challenge a partner.

Simplification – Applications

Practise one-step problems such as:

1 The total mark in a science test is 60. The pass mark is 42. What percentage is this?

2 A rug is priced at £85. In the sale, the price is reduced by 20%. How much is the reduction? Or, moving to two-step problems, what is the sale price?

Keep the numbers simple. Concentrate on methods.

Where appropriate, encourage swapping between % and fraction, e.g. 20% $=\frac{1}{5}$.

Extension – Applications

Students could be introduced to the concept of two successive percentage changes, for example:

In 2010 the population of a village was 1200 people. By 2012 the population had increased by 15%. This increased again by 15% over the next two years. Jess is working out the population in 2014 and says that she can do this by finding 30% of 1200 and adding it on. Explain why Jess is wrong and work out the correct answer. (1587)

5 Fractions, decimals and percentages

<table>
<tr><th>Key outcomes</th><th>Quick check</th></tr>
<tr><td>N1 Order positive fractions; use the symbols =, ≠, <, >, ≤, ≥.</td><td>1 For each pair of fractions, write < or > between them.
a $\frac{2}{9}\square\frac{1}{7}$ $\left(\frac{2}{9}>\frac{1}{7}\right)$ b $\frac{8}{5}\square\frac{21}{11}$ $\left(\frac{8}{5}<\frac{21}{11}\right)$</td></tr>
<tr><td>N2 Apply the four operations +, −, ×, ÷, including formal written methods, to simple fractions (proper and improper), and mixed numbers.</td><td>2 Calculate and simplify your answers where possible.
a $\frac{3}{7}\times\frac{1}{9}$ $\left(\frac{1}{21}\right)$ b $7\times\frac{3}{8}$ $\left(\frac{21}{8}\text{ or }2\frac{5}{8}\right)$
c $\frac{5}{16}+\frac{2}{16}$ $\left(\frac{7}{16}\right)$ d $\frac{11}{12}-\frac{3}{4}$ $\left(\frac{1}{6}\right)$
e $\frac{1}{6}+\frac{4}{5}$ $\left(\frac{29}{30}\right)$ f $2\frac{1}{3}-\frac{2}{7}$ $\left(\frac{43}{21}\text{ or }2\frac{1}{21}\right)$</td></tr>
<tr><td>N10 Work interchangeably with terminating decimals and their corresponding fractions (such as 3.5 and 7/2 or 0.375 or 3/8).</td><td>3 Write these decimals as fractions in their simplest form.
a 0.9 $\left(\frac{9}{10}\right)$ b 0.75 $\left(\frac{3}{4}\right)$ c 0.46 $\left(\frac{23}{50}\right)$
4 Convert these fractions to decimals.
a $\frac{1}{4}$ (0.25) b $\frac{7}{100}$ (0.07) c $\frac{19}{20}$ (0.95)</td></tr>
<tr><td>N12 Interpret fractions and percentages as operators.</td><td>5 Calculate the following fractions of amounts.
a $\frac{1}{6}$ of 18 (3) b $\frac{4}{9}$ of 27 (12) c $1\frac{1}{4}$ of 80 (100)
6 Calculate the following percentages of amounts
a 50% of 18 (9) b 30% of 110 (33)
c 35% of 200 (70) d 150% of 60 (90)
7 Convert these mixed numbers to improper fractions and vice versa.
a $2\frac{3}{9}$ $\left(\frac{11}{4}\right)$ b $1\frac{4}{5}$ $\left(\frac{9}{5}\right)$ c $\frac{7}{6}$ $\left(1\frac{1}{6}\right)$ d $\frac{31}{8}$ $\left(3\frac{7}{8}\right)$</td></tr>
<tr><td>R9 Define percentage as 'number of parts per hundred'; interpret percentages as a fraction or a decimal.</td><td>8 Copy and complete the table. Simplify fractions fully.<table><tr><th>Fraction</th><th>Decimal</th><th>Percentage</th></tr><tr><td>$\frac{4}{5}$</td><td>(0.8)</td><td>(80%)</td></tr><tr><td>$\left(\frac{17}{20}\right)$</td><td>0.85</td><td>(85%)</td></tr><tr><td>$\left(\frac{1}{25}\right)$</td><td>(0.04)</td><td>3%</td></tr><tr><td>$\left(\frac{957}{1000}\right)$</td><td>0.957</td><td>(95.7%)</td></tr></table></td></tr>
</table>

Misconceptions and challenges	Solutions
Students do not understand the link between division and fractions.	Look at the symbol for division and show how the dots above and below the line in the middle of '÷' represent the general idea of a fraction with a numerator and a denominator.
Students think of fractions as part of a whole but not as numbers in their own right.	Make the link between fractions of amounts (shaded parts of a diagram) and fractions on a number line. Have students count in fractions, or set homework on the $\frac{1}{6}$ times-table.
Students are confused, when converting fractions and decimals, by the fact that different numbers of decimal places are required.	Develop a method of showing that 0.5 is the same as 0.50, and 0.500, … Encourage students to compare decimals by finding the 'ghost zeros'.

Misconceptions and challenges	Solutions
Students become confused when converting between mixed numbers and improper fractions, about what represents the denominator, and about why the two fractions are equivalent.	Use symbolic representations of mixed numbers alongside algorithms for converting between mixed numbers and improper fractions. For example, have students draw out $\frac{13}{6}$ as $\frac{6}{6}+\frac{6}{6}+\frac{1}{6}$ using diagrams of 2×3 arrays.
When ordering fractions students sometimes think that a larger denominator means the fraction is larger.	Compare $\frac{1}{2}$ with $\frac{1}{10000000}$. Also consider examples of non-unit fractions, for example, which is larger $\frac{3}{1000}$ or $\frac{3}{4}$?
When finding fractions of an amount, some students can only find halves, quarters, etc. by repeated division by 2. This leaves them unprepared to find fractions such as thirds.	The concept of a 'half' can come to dominate a students' early understanding of fractions, and have implications later on. Challenge this misconception directly, and also have students list cases where halving repeatedly is useful: $\frac{1}{8}$, $\frac{1}{16}$, …
Students are unsure of how to add and subtract fractions because the methods appear different when the denominators are the same or different.	A sound understanding of equivalent fractions is vital for this. Use visual diagrams to aid conceptual understanding. Students need to see that $\frac{2}{5}+\frac{3}{7}$ requires the use of equivalent fractions.
When multiplying and dividing fractions, students misapply what they have learnt for adding and subtracting fractions.	Students will have been using language like 'two-thirds of…' since KS2. Encourage students to see how 'of' links with multiplication: e.g. $\frac{2}{3}\times 12$ is the same as '$\frac{2}{3}$ of 12'.

Review question commentary

Students should not use a calculator.

Questions 1 and **2 (5.1)** – Diagrams will help students to understand how to do these.

Question 3 (5.1) – Encourage students to write as decimal fractions first then simplify fully.

Question 4 (5.1) – In part **d** one possible method is to convert to a decimal fraction first.

Question 5 (5.1) – Students need to find equivalent fractions with common denominators.

Question 6 (5.2) – Reinforce to students that they need to divide by the denominator and multiply by the numerator. In part **c**, they could find $\frac{1}{3}$ of 6 and add this on, or they could convert the mixed number to an improper fraction.

Question 7 (5.2) – No calculators to be used here, can discuss their differing methods for each one.

Question 8 (5.3) – Part **b, e** and **f** can also be written as $3\frac{1}{5}$, $1\frac{1}{24}$ and $\frac{23}{20}$. Discuss how the LCM of the two denominators gives the new denominator in **d**, **e** and **f**.

Question 9 (5.3) – Encourage students to cancel before multiplying.

Question 10 (5.3) – Students often forget to 'flip' the second fraction and cancel too early.

Question 11 (5.4) – You can write $\frac{6}{5}$ as $1\frac{1}{5}$.

Review answers

1 **a** $\frac{7}{5}$ **b** $\frac{25}{7}$

2 **a** $2\frac{1}{4}$ **b** $1\frac{5}{6}$

3 **a** $\frac{3}{10}$ **b** $\frac{1}{4}$ **c** $\frac{22}{25}$ **d** $\frac{1}{20}$

4 **a** 0.5 **b** 0.7 **c** 0.02 **d** 0.625

5 **a** $\frac{2}{7}$ **b** $\frac{8}{3}$

6 **a** 9 **b** 12 **c** 8 **d** 36

7 **a** 16 **b** 48 **c** 12 **d** 99

8 **a** $\frac{7}{11}$ **b** $\frac{7}{10}$ **c** $\frac{25}{24}$ **d** $1\frac{3}{20}$
e $2\frac{11}{12}$ **f** $4\frac{1}{2}$

9 **a** $\frac{5}{2}=2\frac{1}{2}$ **b** $\frac{2}{35}$ **c** $\frac{3}{10}$ **d** $\frac{25}{18}=1\frac{7}{18}$

10 **a** $\frac{4}{50}=\frac{2}{25}$ **b** $\frac{2}{3}$ **c** 20 **d** $\frac{14}{5}=2\frac{4}{5}$
e $\frac{5}{4}=1\frac{1}{4}$ **f** $\frac{49}{4}=12\frac{1}{4}$

11 $\frac{3}{5}$, *0.6*, *60%*; $\frac{1}{100}$, 0.01, *1%*; $\frac{13}{20}$, *0.65*, 65%; $\frac{6}{5}$, 1.2, *120%*

85 marks

Assessment 5

Question 1 – 4 marks

0, $b=\frac{1}{6}$, $a=\frac{2}{5}$, 0.5, $d=\frac{2}{3}$, $c=\frac{8}{10}$, 1

Lose 1 mark for each error [B4]

Question 2 – 4 marks

a $\frac{4}{5}=\frac{12}{15}$ or $\frac{2}{3}=\frac{10}{15}$ [M1]
No [A1]

b A fraction = numerator ÷ denominator
and any number goes into itself exactly once. [B1]
Yes. [B1]

Question 3 – 4 marks

a $\frac{1}{4}$ [B1]

b Ben has treated the 6s as factors.
Only factors can be cancelled,
16 is not 1 × 6 and 64 is not 4 × 6. [B2]

c Student examples, for example, $\frac{15}{65}=\frac{3}{13}\neq\frac{1}{6}$ [B1]

Question 4 – 6 marks

a 5 580, 558.0, 55.80, 5.580, 0.5580, 0.055 80 [B1]
No [B1]

b **i** Yes [B1]
ii No, 9.55 [B1]
iii No, 2.205 [B1]
iv No, 6.995 [B1]

Question 5 – 5 marks

a 40% [B1]

b 15% [B1]

c $\frac{45}{100}=\frac{9}{20}$ [B1]

d 45% > 40%, apples and > 15%, pears [M1]
Bananas [A1]

Question 6 – 2 marks

The first pair (one quarter off) [B1]
One quarter off = 25% discount > 20% discount [B1]

Question 7 – 13 marks

a 0.3 × 400 [M1]
= £120 [A1]

b 0.7 × 54 [M1]
= £37.80 [A1]

c 0.3 × 90 + 0.05 × 90 or equivalent [M1]
= £31.50 [A1]

d 0.2 × 65 + 0.02 × 65 or equivalent [M2]
= £14.30 [A1]

e 0.36 × 1 = £0.36 [B1]

f 0.4 × 800 + 0.07 × 800 + 0.005 × 800
or equivalent [M2]
= £380 [A1]

Question 8 – 2 marks

1.2 × 50 [M1]
= 60 [A1]

Question 9 – 6 marks

a Redyonder [20% of 20 = 4] [B1]

b Air [20% of 25 = 5] [B1]

c 20% of (25 + 20) = 9 [M1]
Chat-Chat [3 + 6 = 9] [A1]

d 8 is 32% of 25 but 40% of 20. [M1]
Branson was wrong. [A1]

Question 10 – 4 marks

a $\frac{4}{11}\times100=36.4\%$ (3 sf) [M1, A1]

b $\frac{35}{250}\times100=14\%$ [M1, A1]

Question 11 – 4 marks

a 1 – 0.25 – 0.28 – 0.35= 0.12 [M1, A1]

b Fourth [B1]

c Third [B1]

Question 12 – 3 marks

$3\frac{3}{4}\times\frac{2}{5}=\frac{15}{4}\times\frac{2}{5}=\frac{3}{2}\times\frac{1}{1}$ [M2]

$1\frac{1}{2}$ hectares [A1]

Question 13 – 4 marks

$\frac{5}{9}+\frac{7}{20}=\frac{100+63}{180}$ [M1]

$=\frac{160}{180}$ [A1]

$=\left(1-\frac{163}{180}\right)\times90=\frac{17}{180}\times90$ OR $90-\frac{163}{180}\times90$ [M1]

= 8.5 yards [A1]

Question 14 – 5 marks

a 540× 0.27= 145.8 m^2. [M1, A1]

b 540 – 145.8 = 394.2 m^2 [M1]
0.36 × 394.2 [M1]
= 141.912 = 142 m^2 (3 sf) [F1]

Question 15 – 2 marks

$\frac{8}{11}\times\frac{3}{4}\times\frac{5}{9}=\frac{10}{33}$ [M1, A1]

Question 16 – 4 marks

Small area = 12.5 × 7.5 = 93.75 cm^2
Large area = 15 × 10 = 150 cm^2 [M1, A1]
$\frac{150}{93.75}$ × 100 – 100 = 60% [M1]
They are correct. [F1]

Question 17 – 8 marks

a $\frac{1}{3}=1\div3=0.3333...=0.\dot{3}$ [M1, A1]

b $\frac{5}{9}=5\div9=0.5555...=0.\dot{5}$ [M1, A1]

c $\frac{6}{7}=6\div7=0.8571428571...=0.\dot{8}5714\dot{2}$ [M1, A1]

d $\frac{7}{11}=7\div11=0.6363...=0.\dot{6}\dot{3}$ [M1, A1]

Question 18 – 5 marks

Convert to a common format [M1]

$\frac{3}{8}$ = 0.325 33.3% = 0.333 $33\frac{1}{3}\%$ = 0.333...

0.334 0.34 $\frac{5}{14}$ = 0.35714..... [A2]

$\frac{3}{8}$ 33.3% $33\frac{1}{3}\%$ 0.334 0.34 $\frac{5}{14}$ [A2]

Lose 1 mark for each error.

Formulae and functions

Learning outcomes

A2 Substitute numerical values into formulae and expressions, including scientific formulae.

A3 Understand and use the concepts and vocabulary of expressions, equations, formulae, inequalities, terms, factors and identities.

A4 Simplify and manipulate algebraic expressions [(including those involving surds)] by:
- collecting like terms
- expanding products of two binomials
- factorising quadratic expressions of the form $x^2 + bx + c$, including the difference of two squares.

A5 Understand and use standard mathematical formulae; rearrange formulae to change the subject.

A6 Know the difference between an equation and an identity; argue mathematically to show algebraic expressions are equivalent, and use algebra to support and construct arguments.

A7 Where appropriate, interpret simple expressions as functions with inputs and outputs.

Prior knowledge

Check-in skill

- Use BIDMAS in multi-stage calculations.
- Multiply a single term over a bracket.
- Take out common factors in an expression.

Online resources

MyMaths 1150, 1151, 1155, 1157, 1158, 1159, 1167, 1171, 1186, 1187, 1247

InvisiPen videos

Skills: 06Sa – m Applications: 06Aa – d

Kerboodle assessment

Online Skills Test 6 Chapter Test 6

Development and links

Formulae are widely used in science, mathematics and engineering. They are used in daily life to calculate the cost of tickets, mobile phone charges, gas and electricity bills and when working with computer-based spreadsheets. Real-life graphs can be used to identify trends in data and to predict future behaviour. Distance–time graphs have wide applications in mechanics and are used in motors ports to analyse the performance of the driver and the car from data collected during a lap. Another form of a distance–time graph is a tachograph which records the speed of a lorry or coach during a journey and is used to calculate the driver's speed, distance travelled and hours worked.

Chapter investigation

Students should enjoy trying to spot magic squares and will be solving lots of intuitive mathematical equations along the way.

You might need to give the students some partially completed magic squares to get them going.

	9	2
8		

6		
	5	
8		

They should spot that the number 5 appears in the middle and that the different magic squares are essentially rotations and reflections of the one given.

They could investigate a 4 × 4 magic square and see if they could identify the magic number (34).

Requiring the diagonals to sum to the same number as the rows and columns forces the central square to be one third of the 'sum number'. If the sum number is $3s$ and two other numbers, X and Y, are given then there is a unique completion of the grid.

For example ($X + Y < 3s$ for positive entries)

X	$4s - 2X - Y$	$X + Y - s$
Y	s	$2s - Y$
$3s - X - Y$	$2X + Y - 2s$	$2s - X$

For the numbers 1 to 9, the sum number is $(1 + 2 + \ldots + 9)/3 = 15$ so $s = 5$. Substituting values for X and Y allows various magic squares to be created [**6.1**]. Given a value for a square, the formulae can be rearranged to give X and or Y [**6.2**]. Testing the general grid works is essentially verifying identities, such as, $X + (4s - 2X - Y) + (X + Y - s) \equiv 4s$ [**6.3**].

Since X and Y can be any expressions it is possible to explore substituting into and rearranging more complex formulae together with checking more involved identities.

Rather tenuously the 3 × 3 grid can also be used to organise multiplying out double brackets and in the reverse process of factorising quadratics [**6.4**].

Substituting into formulae

Objectives

① A2 Substitute numerical values into formulae and expressions, including scientific formulae

② A5 Understand and use standard mathematical formulae; rearrange formulae to change the subject

Useful resources

Mini whiteboard

Starter – Skills

Write on the board $2d + 5$. Roll a dice to generate the number for d. Students must evaluate the expression choosing d to be this number. The first student who correctly evaluates the expression gets to roll the dice. Change the expression to include divisions (noting algebraic notation) and subtractions.

Ensure students recall the order of operations (multiplication before addition).

Teaching notes – Skills

Refer to the starter and ensure students understand algebraic conventions: the hidden times sign in multiplication; use of the divisor line to represent division.
Draw several rectangles on the board with dimensions 8 cm × 6 cm, 8 × 3, 7 × 10, etc.
Encourage students to recall the formula.

Area = length × width

Highlight the fact that students have been substituting different values for length and width to evaluate the area. Link to the starter activity.

Formalise length and width as variables (values that vary) and highlight the fact that area depends on these values. Demonstrate how to use letters to represent length and width, and simplify using a 'hidden' times sign.

Plenary – Skills

Draw a rectangle with dimensions labelled 'length' and 'width'. Discuss how to calculate the perimeter. Collect all suggestions:

Perimeter = length + width + length + width

Perimeter = 2(length + width)

$P = 2(l + w)$

Discuss use of brackets and ensure students recall these are evaluated first.

Invite students to calculate the perimeter given various dimensions.

Exercise commentary – Skills

Questions 1 and **2** Simple substitution involving just one variable. Make sure students are clear that the variable has to be replaced with the value given.

Question 3 This question challenges a common misconception. You may wish to discuss why Ian is incorrect as a whole class. Make sure students are clear that $5w$ means $5 \times w$.

Question 4 This question should be fairly easy for students to access as long as they are clear that $5p$ means $5 \times p$, the final part of the first example covers this concept. You may wish to remind students of the rules of multiplying by negative numbers.

Question 5 It is important that the students are clear that a fraction line is another way of setting out a division. Ask 'is the answer to part **f** 2 or 0.5?'

Question 6 The same value of a is substituted into a number of different formulae, now involving more than one operation. Emphasise the importance of showing the method. Students may need to be reminded to apply the principles of BIDMAS, particularly in part **e**.

Question 7 Here one formula is given but different values of a and b need to substituted each time. You may wish to go through a few examples using a similar style of question, stress the importance of being careful when substituting negative numbers.

Question 8 Remind students that at means$a \times t$. In parts **c**, **d** and **e** a variable that is not the subject of the formula needs to be calculated. It is probably easier if students substitute in the values that they know first rather than rearrange the formula. You may wish to demonstrate how to do this.

Question 9 A recap on how to find fractions of amounts may be needed here. As an extension to this question students could convert a few other temperatures given in degrees Celsius into Fahrenheit, they could even draw a conversion graph. This will be much easier if the temperatures chosen to convert are multiples of 5.

Question 10 In this question students need to derive a formula to represent the relationship. Discuss how in part **f** brackets will be needed as you need to add 7 first before multiplying by 3.

Question 11 Encourage students to read the written information given in the question and ask them to state in words how the circumference is calculated. Then ask them to replace the words with the symbols given, remind them that in algebra we don't write the multiplication sign. As an extension you could ask students if they can rearrange the formula so that the subject is the diameter, they can then test their formula using the values given and found in part **b**.

Question 12 You will need to allow students the use of a calculator for this extension question and you may need to show students how to use the π button. Discuss the order of operations that will need to be applied here.

Question 13 This would be an appropriate question to cover as a whole class. You could ask if anyone can explain why the formula given in part **b** is correct. For part **c** discuss what the total of a and b need to be.

Simplification – Skills

Students should concentrate on one-operation formulae and substitutions should be integer values only.

Extension – Skills

Students could be introduced to formulae which contain squared terms such as that for the area of a square.

Recap – Applications

1 Write down the formula for each of these statements.

- **a** A is equal to 9 less than T
- **b** B is equal to twice U
- **c** C is equal to half of V
- **d** D is equal to W cubed
- **e** E is equal to 5 times X minus 13
- **f** F is equal to 2 times Y multiplied by 3
- **g** G is equal to $3Z$ minus 2, all multiplied by -5

(**a** $T-9$ **b** $2U$ **c** $\frac{V}{2}$ **d** W^3

e $5X-13$ **f** $6Y$ **g** $-5(3Z-2)$)

2 Dougal is making porridge for breakfast.

He uses the formula '**100 g porridge needs 33 g oats and 67 ml milk**'.

Write a formula connecting P, the mass of porridge made, O, the mass of oats and M, the mass of milk. ($P = 33O + 67M$)

Plenary – Applications

Give students a formula for cooking chicken (or another dish if vegetarian):

cooking time = 40 min per kilogram
+ extra 20 min

Discuss cooking times for a 3 kg, 5 kg and 2.5 kg chicken. Challenge students to calculate at what time a 3 kg chicken should be put in the oven for eating at 2.30 pm.

Exercise commentary – Applications

Question 1 In this question students need to show that they can substitute values into a formula used in real life. Allow them to use calculators and make sure they are familiar with where the π button is. Discuss the order that the operations need to be calculated, in particular that you would need to square before multiplying by the other terms. Ensure students set out all stages of their working out in the same way that is shown in the first example on page 118.

Question 2 Here five different formulae are given both in words and in symbols. Ask students to first decide which of the five formulae they need to use, write down the correct formula using symbols and then substitute in the given information. Allow them to use calculators to find the answers. Looking through the final example on page 118 may assist any students that are finding this question difficult. In part **e** they will need to take care to ensure that they put the negative value for v in brackets before squaring. You may wish to cover the final part as a class, discussing which variables are equivalent in this context and why this is the case.

Question 3 You may like to go through the first part of this question with the whole group. You could help them to derive the formula by considering simple concepts – what units do we normally use when measuring speed? What would the speed be if a car travels 80 miles in 2 hours? How have you worked out this answer? Hopefully students will be able to spot that they have divided the distance by the time to get the speed and hence be able to derive the formula. Students should be asked to attempt this question without a calculator but remind them to take care with units.

Question 4 Ensure students spot that Current uses the symbol I and Charge has the symbol Q. In part **d** encourage students to substitute in the information that they have been given in the question, they should then be able to work out I without the need to rearrange the formula. In the final part students will need to take the given formula for Energy and then substitute in the formula for Voltage.

Question 5 This question addresses a number of misconceptions and common errors – not substituting in correct values, not applying BIDMAS and multiplying by 0 incorrectly. As an extension students could be given different values for u, t and a and asked to find s.

Question 6 You may need to show students how to use the power button on their calculators. Emphasise the correct order of operations. There are a lot of opportunities for students to make errors with the compound interest formula – ensure they realise that they need to divide before adding within the brackets and that they apply the power before multiplying by A.

Simplification – Applications

Students should concentrate on one-step examples and small number substitutions. Students might find it helpful to work in pairs.

Extension – Applications

Students could be given further examples involving two (or even three) steps and asked to substitute various numbers into these formulae.

6.2 Using standard formulae

Objectives

① A2 Substitute numerical values into formulae and expressions, including scientific formulae

② A5 Understand and use standard mathematical formulae; rearrange formulae to change the subject

③ A7 Where appropriate, interpret simple expressions as functions with inputs and output

Useful resources

Mini whiteboards, blank function machine

Starter – Skills

Draw a function machine on the board, say + 7. Give students various input values, they must provide the output values. Repeat with a different machine, say × 3, and different input values.

Teaching notes – Skills

Explain that a function takes a starting number and changes it into another number.

in → × 7 → out

This simply multiplies the input by 7. how do we find the input if the output is 28?

(Divide by 7 to get 4.) So to reverse the machine, we use the inverse operation.

Take a simple equation, say $y = 3x + 4$, and ask students, on whiteboards, to give the two operations that this involves in order.

Check and record responses as a function machine

input (x) → × 3 → + 4 → output (y)

Demonstrate reversing this process, stage by stage, resulting in $x = (y - 4) \div 3$. Ask students to check that it is a true reversal by asking them what y is if x is 4, then using this value of y to find x.

Ask students to give the reverse operation, on whiteboards, of multiply by 5, divide by 2, add 8, square, multiply by –3, etc. Discuss the 'rearranging' of the equation with the students.

Now show a typical question that states 'rearrange', for example '$v = u + at$, rearrange to make t the subject'. Discuss that this means $t = \ldots$ hence the need to focus on what is happening to t.

Ask students to try this on whiteboards, and invite one or two to write this as a function machine on the large board. Prompt through to the conclusion of the question:

$$t = \frac{v-u}{a}$$

Plenary – Skills

Take the formula

$$C = \frac{5(F-32)}{9}$$

and say that it is the formula to change temperature from Fahrenheit to Celsius. Ask students to record each step of the transformation on whiteboards, and transfer each step to a function machine. Finally, ask the students to write a formula for changing Celsius to Fahrenheit. Share responses and discuss.

Exercise commentary – Skills

Question 1 This question should be easy to answer as long as students are clear that the 'inverse of addition is subtraction' and that the 'inverse of multiplying is dividing' (and vice-versa in each case).

Questions 2 and **3** Emphasise the fact that a and then x need to become the subject of the formula. Tell students that they need to work out which operation is currently being applied to a or x and then apply the inverse of this to both sides so that a or x becomes the subject.

Question 4 Remind students to deal with the operations in reverse order.

Question 5 Here the formulae that need to be rearranged involve more than one operation. Students often find it difficult to know which operation to 'deal with' first when rearranging. Encourage them to say in words what is happening to the letter that needs to be made the subject – in question **5a** p is being multiplied by 2 and then 5 is being added. Tell them to apply the inverse operations in the reverse order – subtract 5 (from A) and then divide by 2. They could organise their method in the same way as shown in the second example on page 120. Alternatively they could represent what is happening as a function machine, create the inverse machine and then convert their answer into algebra.

Question 6 The same principles and methods apply here but students may be put off by the fact that some squared terms have been introduced. They may incorrectly and unnecessarily try and 'undo' the squaring by 'square rooting' both sides. As an extension activity or as part of a whole class discussion you could challenge students to create a question to be rearranged that would involve square rooting.

Question 7 It would be worthwhile covering one of these questions or an example of a similar style with the whole group. Demonstrate how creating a function machine and then the corresponding inverse machine partially rearranges the formula in this case.

Question 8 This question addresses a common error which is to not take into account the negative sign before the term that needs to be made the subject of the formula.

Question 9 Encourage students to make the first step in rearranging to be to 'add x' to both sides.

Question 10 Students may need to be prompted to first make D the subject. Discuss as a whole class what S, D and T stand for and link this to using a formula triangle as a tool for rearranging this type of formula.

Question 11 In each case encourage students to first make the numerator of the fraction the subject. What do they notice each time when they get the final answer?
Question 12 Encourage students to use SAMDIB (reverse order of BIDMAS) when rearranging this formula, they will need to subtract 3 from both sides first, then multiply both sides by y (using brackets on the left hand side) and finally divide both sides by $A - 3$.
Question 13 In this question students become familiar with the concept that the inverse of squaring is square rooting (and vice versa). Remind them to think carefully about the order of operations when rearranging particularly in the latter parts of this question.
Questions *14 and **15** In these questions more complex formulae that involve more variables and operations are given to be rearranged. Question **14** needs to be factorised in order to make x the subject. Both questions are probably best demonstrated as a whole class or given to the more able as extension questions.

Simplification – Skills

Students should practise further examples using simple arithmetic skills to finding outputs before being introduced to the idea of 'inverse'.

Extension – Skills

Challenge students to rearrange harder formulae that involve squares or square roots. An example could be making x the subject in $y = 3x^2 - 2$.

Recap – Applications

1 Write down the inverse operation for each of these operations.

a $+5$	(-5)	**b** -7	$(+7)$
c $\div 9$	$(\times 9)$	**d** $\times 2$	$(\div 2)$
e $\times -3$	$(\div -3)$	**f** $+\frac{1}{4}$	$(-\frac{1}{4})$
g $-\frac{2}{3}$	$(+\frac{2}{3})$	**h** $\div\frac{1}{3}$	$(\times\frac{1}{3})$

2 Make x the subject of the formulae.

a $y = x + 3$	$(x = 3 - y)$
b $y = x \div 5$	$(x = 5y)$
c $y = 7x + 6$	$(x = \frac{y-6}{7})$
d $y = 8 - 9x$	$(x = \frac{8-y}{9})$

Plenary – Applications

Read the following. Challenge students to write an equation and solve it.

I have a number, I add 3 and then I multiplyit by 2. The answer is 16.

Recall use of brackets to determine order of operations in an equation.

Invite students to solve similar equations:

$3(x + 4) = 27$

Exercise commentary – Applications

Question 1 Ensure students recognise that in order to answer this question the formulae will need to be rearranged so that u is the subject, they may benefit from looking through the second part of the first example on page 122 to get a reminder of the process needed to do this. You may wish to allow students to use a calculator for this question or alternatively you could discuss the fact that dividing by 0.1 is equivalent to multiplying by 10.
Question 2 Tell students to apply the same operation to both sides when rearranging. You may need to hint that ***f** needs factorising as part of the process.
Question 3 Students should recognise that their part **a** answer will help with part **b**.
Question 4 Remind students to treat ax as one term and to not try and separate these two variables.
Questions 5 and **6** These questions are comparable to the second example given on page 122, it would be worthwhile looking thought this example as a whole group so that students are clear about the process before attempting these questions. Ensure students spot that πneeds to be subject of the formula in question **6**.
Question 7 Discuss that in order to make b the subject you will first need to subtract a^2 from both sides and then square root both sides. Ensure students are aware that $\sqrt{c^2 - a^2}$ does not equal $c - a$.
Question 8 This could be tackled well in a whole class discussion. Emphasise that the first stage in rearranging – either expanding the brackets or dividing by a – are both correct options.
Question 9 Students may need guidance on how to input formulae into a spreadsheet.

Simplification – Applications

Students may need further practice at using one-step inverse function machines before moving on to the two-step variety.

Extension – Applications

Students could make up their own two-stage 'think of a number' problems and challenge a partner.

6.3 Equations, identities and functions

Objectives

① A3 Understand and use the concepts and vocabulary of expressions, equations, formulae, identities, inequalities, terms and factors

② A6 Know the difference between an equation and an identity; argue mathematically to show algebraic expressions are equivalent, and use algebra to support and construct arguments

Useful resources

Mini whiteboards

Starter – Skills

Ask students to work in pairs in order to sort these expressions into three categories: formula, equation and expression. $2x + 5$ $V = IR$ $v = u + at$ $2w - 1 = 3w + 4$ $3x + 1 = 7$ $ab + cd$

Select pairs of students to share results. Discuss the groupings and the reasons for any decisions. Display the three keywords and ask student pairs to describe each. Add their descriptions to the display.

Teaching notes – Skills

Can you solve $4x + 2 = 2(2x + 1)$?

What values work for x? (All values.)

Why is this? (Because the two sides are identical.)

This is called an identity and you use three lines ≡ so you write $4x + 2 \equiv 2(2x + 1)$

Give an example of a more complex identity, such as

$$5(2x + 3) + 4(2x - 1) \equiv 18x + 11$$

Draw out that you need to expand and simplify to show that the two sides are identical.

Can you solve $A = \pi r^2$? (No, because you need a value for radius 'r' to find the area 'A' of the circle.)

This is not an equation where you can find an answer; it is a formula that calculates a variable when you know the value of the other variables in the formula.

Can you solve $2x + 1 = 5$? (Yes, $x = 2$)

This is an equation, because it can be solved for a particular value of x.

So you can have identities, formulae and equations.

Plenary – Skills

Write an equation on the board: $3x + 7 = 25$ and ask the students to say whether it is an equation or an identity. Select students to give an explanation of their choice and the difference between the two words. Refer back to statements made earlier in the lesson. Equations are only true for particular values of x; ask the students to find the value of x which makes this equation true.

Exercise commentary – Skills

Questions 1 and **2** It is essential that students are clear about how to identify inequalities, equations, formulae and identities. It would be worth spending a bit of time going through the introductory section and first example on page 124. These would be suitable questions to go through as a whole class – getting students to justify their answers.

Questions 3 and **4** Students need to know that the same rules for simplifying algebraic expressions also apply to identities. Remind them to use the 'identically equal to' sign in each case. There are lots of possibilities for the final part on question **4**, you could discuss whether answers provided are acceptable or not with the group, asking students to justify why in each case.

Question 5 Recap on how to expand brackets. Demonstrate that in order to state whether these are true or not they will need to show that the number on the outside of the brackets is being multiplied by both of the terms on the inside, students should do this in the same way as shown in the first part of the final example on page 124.

Question 6 A brief reminder on how to factorise may be necessary. Show students how to prove the factorisation, for part **a**, $5a + 10 \equiv 5 \times a + 5 \times 2 \equiv 5(a + 2)$. An explanation concerning the difference of two squares may be necessary for students who attempt the final part of this question.

Questions 7 and **8** Students will need to show every stage of their working though they may find it quicker to use arrows when expanding the brackets. They will need to make sure that they only simplify 'like terms' and that they pay attention to negative terms.

Question 9 Further practice on classifying expressions given as equations, identities and formulae. Emphasise that a formula involves several variables and an identity is true for all possible values of the unknown letter(s).

Question 10 Students could find other formulae in common use that can be written in more than one way, for example, the formula for the perimeter of a square or the area of a triangle.

Simplification – Skills

Students may be confused by the distinctions between formula and equation, and between equation and identity. Give plenty of simple examples to ensure they understand the concepts.

Extension – Skills

Challenge students to come up with their own identities (as easy or difficult as they like) and substitute a range of numbers into them to show they are identities.

Recap – Applications

1 Decide if each of these statements is an equation, a formula or an identity.

- **a** $C = 2\pi r$ (Formula)
- **b** $c \times c \times c = c^3$ (Identity)
- **c** $3(x - 4) = 3x - 12$ (Identity)
- **d** $x^2 - 3x - 7 = 0$ (Equation)
- **e** $5(q + 3) = 7$ (Equation)
- **f** $6x^2 + 4x = 2x(3x + 2)$ (Identity)
- **g** $4x + 1 = 7$ (Equation)
- **h** $A = 4\pi r^2$ (Formula)

2 Complete these identities:

- **a** $8u - 10u - 7u \equiv \boxed{?}$ ($\boxed{?} = -9u$)
- **b** $6v^2 + 9v^2 \equiv \boxed{?}$ ($\boxed{?} = 15v^2$)
- **c** $3x - 7y + 4x \equiv \boxed{?}$ ($\boxed{?} = 7(x - y)$)
- **d** $5a - 17b - 3a + 14b \equiv \boxed{?}$ ($\boxed{?} = 2a - 3b$)
- **e** $4(x - 1) \equiv \boxed{?}$ ($\boxed{?} = 4x - 4$)
- **f** $3a^3 + 6 \equiv \boxed{?}$ ($\boxed{?} = 3(a^3 + 2)$)
- **g** $7bc + 21c \equiv \boxed{?}$ ($\boxed{?} = 7c(b + 3)$)
- **h** $g^2 + 6g \equiv \boxed{?}\ (g + 6)$ ($\boxed{?} = g$)
- **i** $c^2 - 9 \equiv (c + \boxed{?})(c - \boxed{?})$ ($\boxed{?} = 3$)

3 Are these identities true or false?

Give reasons for any you think are false.

- **a** $5(b - 15) \equiv 5b - 75$ (True)
- **b** $6(c + 1) \equiv 6c + 1$ (False)
- **c** $d(5 - d^2) \equiv 5d - d^2$ (False)
- **d** $3y(y + 3) \equiv 3y^2 + 3y$ (False)
- **e** $x(x - 4) \equiv x^2 - 4x$ (True)

Plenary – Applications

Ask students to work in pairs to discuss the statement '$x = 4$ is the same as $4 = x$'.

Share some of the comments before replacing this statement with '$x > 4$ is the same as $4 > x$' Ask pairs to discuss this statement before exploring the reasoning here. How would this statement need to be changed to be correct?

Exercise commentary – Applications

Questions 1 and **2** As a whole class ask students to describe in words how they would find the area of the shapes made from the rectangles shown. Some students will describe finding the area of each individual small rectangle and then adding the answers, others may opt for finding the area of the big rectangle. Apply these methods with the side lengths given and then it should be easier for students to see how the identical expressions are formed. Ensure students are clear that an identity applies to all values of the unknown whereas an equation just applies to some values.

Question 3 This first part of this question addresses a common misconception that $(2a)^2 = 2a^2$. Hopefully students will be able to see that $(2a)^2 = 2a \times 2a = 4a^2$.

Questions 4 and **5** Hopefully most students will recognise that they have to expand bracket and factorise to find the missing values. Insist that final answers are checked by expanding the brackets. The second example on page 126 demonstrates effectively the thinking process students will need to apply when solving this type of problem.

Question 6 Ask students to read once more the definitions of these terms, they are given at the top of page 126. In situations which are sometimes true or never true ask students to explain their reasoning. This question would work well as a whole class discussion.

Question *7 Invite students to suggest different ways the shapes could be split into rectangles. Demonstrate how you would then find the area of each part and then add (or subtract if such approach is taken) to get the total area. These different methods will result in the same area and hence an identity can be formed. In each case what is the minimum value that the area could be? Considering this question should enable students to write an identity too. For part **i** students should be able to see that they cannot work out the values of x. However they do know some limits on the value of x and can use these to create an inequality.

Simplification – Applications

Students may need more practice with using two rectangles to form an identity. Keep the numbers small, so that multiplication problems do not confuse the basic idea of the large rectangle being equal to the sum of the two smaller ones. This should help students to answer these types of questions. Vary the letters used but avoid complications. Use questions to check on understanding of the key words and as an opportunity for discussion.

Extension – Applications

Challenge students to produce identities from expressions, including x^3 and possibly higher powers. They can then ask another student to check their identities by substituting two different numbers into them to show they are true identities (or not). Some students will know that the easiest number to substitute is 1 but they may find that substituting 1 gives a false validity which is disproved by using any other number. This makes a good discussion point, leading to the realisation that $1^n \equiv 1$ for any value of n, but 2^n will take different values.

Expanding and factorising 2

Objectives

① A4 Simplify and manipulate algebraic expressions by expanding products of two or more binomials and factorising quadratic expressions of the form $x^2 + bx + c$

Useful resources

Mini whiteboards, display of a multiplication grid

Starter – Skills

Ask students to evaluate 3×10^2 (300)

Remind students of the rules of BIDMAS if necessary, which is indices/powers before multiplication.

The algebraic expression $3x^2 - 8x - 35$ can also be written as $(3x + 7)(x - 5)$. The two expressions give the same numerical answer for all values of x.

Split the class in half and ask each half to evaluate one of the expressions with $x = 7$. As soon as a student has the result they should raise their hand. Why is the second calculation easier and quicker? (56; The brackets mean fewer and easier calculations.)

Teaching notes – Skills

There are different methods for multiplying two brackets together, for example the FOIL method and using a multiplication grid. There are several others which students may have encountered before. It may be helpful to discuss each method for the same example and then discuss the advantages and disadvantages of each method.

Use a method of choice to expand and simplify

$$(3x - 1)(2x + 4) = 6x^2 + 12x - 2x - 4$$
$$= 6x^2 + 10x - 4$$

Emphasise the different phrases which can be used to describe the process, for example 'expand', 'multiply out', 'remove the brackets'.

Show different quadratic expressions and ask what they all have in common.

$$2x^2 + 3x, \quad 4x^2 + 4x - 1, \quad x^2 + 12, \quad -7x^2$$

They all have an x^2 term as the highest power of x; they are all quadratics.

Demonstrate how some quadratics can be factorised (put back into brackets).

Look at $(x + 1)(x + 7) = x^2 + x + 7x + 7 = x^2 + 8x + 7$

Where did the x^2 come from?

(The $x \times x$ at the beginning of each bracket.)

Where did the 7 come from?

(The 1×7 at the ends of the brackets.)

Where did the $8x$ come from?

(The $1x$ and $7x$ made from multiplying out the brackets.)

Show students how examples of the form $(x^2 - a^2)$ can be factorised (the 'difference of two squares').

Plenary – Skills

A quadratic like $x^2 + 6x + 8$ factorises into two brackets $(x + 2)(x + 4)$.

What might a cubic like $x^3 + 4x^2 + 5x + 2$ factorise into? (Three brackets)

Expand $(x + 1)(x + 1)(x + 2)$ and see if this is the factorised form of the cubic expression.

$$(x^2 + 2x + 1)(x + 2) = x^3 + 2x^2 + 2x^2 + 4x + x + 2$$
$$= x^3 + 4x^2 + 5x + 2 \text{ (it works!)}$$

Exercise commentary – Skills

Questions 1 and **2** Spend some time ensuring students are confident applying the FOIL method as shown at the top of page 128. An alternative method would be to use a grid – the same type as some use for multiplication. Discuss why $x^2 + 18$ is not the correct answer to **2** part **a**.

Question 3 This question emphasises the importance of remembering to multiply all the terms by each other and not accidently adding.

Questions 4 and **5** Practice at expanding double brackets where one of the terms is negative. Recap on the rules of multiplying with negative numbers

Questions 6 and **7** This time double brackets need to be expanded involving two negative terms are found. Remind students that when you multiply two negative numbers together the result is a positive number

Question 8 It would be very easy to give the incorrect answer of $x^2 + 9$ to the first part of this question, ask students to explain why this is not correct.

Questions 9 and **10** Emphasise that the expressions need to be factorised completely. Why would the answer $2(6x^2 + 3x)$ only be a partially factorised expression for the final part of question **10**?

Questions 11 and **12** You may wish to introduce this topic by asking students to expand and simplify some simple expressions given as double brackets and comment on what they notice, e.g. $(x + 1)(x + 1)$, $(x + 1)(x + 2)$, $(x + 2)(x + 2)$, etc.

Hopefully they will then discover for themselves that you can multiply the numbers to get the constant term and that the coefficient of x is formed when you add the numbers. Promote the strategy of listing factor pairs as shown in the second example on page 128.

Questions 13 to **16** Further practise on factorising quadratics. In each case at least one term is negative. Some students may find that using a 'grid approach' as shown in the examples makes these questions easier.

Question 17 Students may initially not know how to factorise these types of expressions. You could lead them towards the correct solution by asking them to expand $(x + 1)(x - 1)$, $(x + 2)(x - 2)$, etc. Hopefully they will see for themselves that the x termscancel out and so discover the difference of two squares.

Question 18 In this question students need to expand expressions where the coefficient of x is greater than 1. Emphasise the importance of multiplying the numbers first and then dealing with the letters, being careful with negative terms and showing all stages of your working.

Simplification – Skills

Ensure students are happy with simple expansions before moving on any further. More examples may be needed and students may need to be guided through the process more slowly. A writing frame may help where they only have to fill in the various numbers and letters as they go through the examples.

Extension – Skills

Ask students to think about factorising more complicated quadratics where the coefficient of the x^2 term is not 1. Can they spot a method 'by eye'?

Recap – Applications

1 Expand and simplify:

a $v(v + 5)$ **b** $(v + 3)(v + 9)$

c $(v - 15)(v + 2)$ **d** $(v + 4)^2$

e $(v - 5)^2$ **f** $(3v + 4)(5v + 9)$

(**a** $v^2 + 5v$ **b** $v^2 + 12v + 27$

c $v^2 - 13v - 30$ **d** $v^2 + 8v + 16$

e $v^2 - 10v + 25$ **f** $15v^2 + 47v + 36$)

2 Factorise.

a $3w^2 - 15$ **b** $5w^2 + 20w$

c $w^2 - 5w + 6$ **d** $w^2 - 3w - 54$

e $16w^2 - 25$ **f** $w^2 - x^2$

(**a** $3(w^2 - 5)$ **b** $5w(w + 4)$

c $(w - 2)(w - 3)$ **d** $(w - 9)(w + 6)$

e $(4w + 5)(4w - 5)$ **f** $(w + x)(w - x)$)

Plenary – Applications

Factorise these. $3x^2 + 2x$ (one bracket: $x(3x + 2)$)
$x^2 - 1$ (two brackets: $(x - 1)(x + 1)$)
How do you know when to use one or two brackets? Look for a common factor in every term. If you can see it, remove it, then put a bracket after. If you cannot see a common factor, use two brackets.

Now try this: $ax + bx + ay + by$

(No common factor for all terms, but with expressions with four terms you can look to see whether there is a common factor for each pair of terms. $x(a + b) + y(a + b) = (a + b)(x + y)$)

Try factorising $xy + xp - ky - kp = (x - k)(y + p)$

Exercise commentary – Applications

Questions 1 and **2** Here students should recognise that $(x + 3)(x + 4)$ means $(x + 3) \times (x + 4)$ and realise that this can be represented as an area problem. They will need to show that if they find the area of each coloured section in the shape independently and then add the areas together this will simplify to give the second expression given within each question.

Question 3 The example on page 130 shows how this question relates to the difference of two squares.

Question 4 It may be worthwhile completing part **a** as a class to ensure that everyone has the correct expansion. Make sure students can identify which number is equivalent to a and b in the second part of this question.

Question 5 This question addresses a common misconception – incorrectly multiplying to get the coefficient of x and adding to get the constant term.

Question 6 Students will need to think carefully about how the coefficient of x is formed and how the constant term is formed and use this to find the missing terms in the brackets. They should then expand the brackets to find the missing term in the expanded expression.

Question 7 This question involves a combination of expanding brackets, rearranging the equation and then factorising to get the required expression given.

Question 8 It may be helpful to cover this question as a whole group or at least start the question by drawing a diagram to represent the information given. You could discuss why adding 1 to one of the current side lengths and then multiplying would be an incorrect approach that gives $(x + 3)(x + 4)$.

Question 9 The second part of this question makes a suitable question for class discussion. Invite students to suggest possible combinations that would multiply together to make $4x^2 - 4x$. Why would '4' not be a suitable number to place in the brick and immediately below and to the right of the top brick? Model how to check answers by expanding brackets.

Question *10 Demonstrate how to factorise the numerator (or denominator in part **d**) and then cancel out common factors to simplify the fraction given.

Simplification – Applications

Students will need plenty of practice at factorising quadratic expressions.

Extension – Applications

Students could be challenged to complete further examples where expansion and simplification is needed to arrive at a quadratic expression, which can then be factorised.

6 Formulae and functions

Key outcomes		Quick check
A2	Substitute numerical values into formulae and expressions, including scientific formulae.	**1** Substitute $x = -3$, $y = 2$ into these expressions. **a** $8x$ (–24) **b** xy (–6) **c** $3x^2$ (27) **d** $7x - 4y$ (–29) **2** The formula $F = ma$ gives the relationship between Force (F), mass (m) and acceleration (a). Calculate **a** the force when $m = 25$ kg and $a = 2$ m/s^{-2} (50N) **b** the force when $m = 6$ kg and $a = 0.3$ m/s^{-2}. (1.8N)
A3	Understand and use the concepts and vocabulary of expressions, equations, formulae, terms, and identities.	**3** $y = 2x - 2$ $2x - 3 = 7$ $V = IR$ $7y + 2b + 2b \equiv 3b$ Give an example of **a** an expression ($7y + 2$) **b** an equation ($2x - 3 = 7$) **c** a formula ($V = IR$) **d** an identity ($b + 2b \equiv 3b$) **e** a function. ($y = 2x - 2$)
A4	Simplify and manipulate algebraic expressions by: - collecting like terms - expanding products of two binomials - factorising quadratic expressions of the form $x^2 + bx + c$, including the difference of two squares.	**4** Expand the brackets and simplify. **a** $(y + 8)(y + 4)$ $(y^2 + 12y + 32)$ **b** $(y - 3)(y - 1)$ $(y^2 - 4y + 3)$ **c** $(y + 9)(y - 2)$ $(y^2 + 7y - 18)$ **d** $(5y + 2)(y - 4)$ $(5y^2 - 18y - 8)$ **5** Factorise these quadratic expressions. **a** $4x^2 - 2x$ $2x(2x - 1)$ **b** $x^2 + 9x + 8$ $(x + 8)(x + 1)$ **c** $x^2 + 13x$ $x(x + 13)$ **d** $x^2 + 6x - 7$ $(x + 7)(x - 1)$ **e** $x^2 - 49$ $(x + 7)(x - 7)$ **f** $x^2 - x - 12$ $(x - 4)(x + 3)$
A5	Understand and use standard mathematical formulae; rearrange formulae to change the subject.	**6** Rearrange each formula to make X the subject. **a** $X - 7 = Y$ $(X = Y + 7)$ **b** $3X = z$ $(X = \frac{z}{3})$ **c** $4X + 9 = w$ $(X = \frac{w - 9}{4})$ **d** $\frac{X - t}{3} = V$ $(X = 3V + t)$
A6	Know the difference between an equation and an identity; argue mathematically to show algebraic expressions are equivalent, and use algebra to support and construct arguments.	**7** Show that this identity is true. $3x(x + 2) - 2(3x + 1) \equiv 3x^2 - 2$ $(3x(x + 2) - 2(3x + 1) = 3x^2 + 6x - 6x - 2 = 3x^2 - 2)$
A7	Where appropriate, interpret simple expressions as functions with inputs and outputs.	**8** Write each of these expressions as function machines. **a** $x - 3$ (–3) **b** $7x$ (×7) **c** $\frac{x}{5}$ (÷5) **d** $2x + 3$ (×2, +3)

Misconceptions and challenges	Solutions
Students do not understand '=' in terms of balance and have great difficulty rearranging formulae and demonstrating equivalence of algebraic expressions.	Use scales or a seesaw as visual images to support understanding. Beware! It requires a conceptual leap to imagine adding or subtracting a weight of –5 kg.
When re-arranging formulae, students do not notice if they make a mistake such as cancelling $-5x$ with $-5x$ rather than $5x$.	Teach students how to rearrange using cancelling rather than moving expressions from one side of an equation to the other, as this will help them understand the process more.

Misconceptions and challenges	Solutions
Common errors occur when factorising quadratic expressions such as $x^2 + 7x + 6$ where the factors include 1.	Make 1 the first factor to check for (it is also the easiest to remember).
Students lose track of negative coefficients. For example, giving $(x - 4)(x - 5)$ as $x^2 - 9x - 20$.	Students need a checklist when tackling algebraic problems. They should check every time whether there are any negatives, and deal with them appropriately.
Constructing proofs using algebra will require an understanding of what algebraic expressions represent, not merely how to manipulate them.	Use familiar mathematical contexts, such as odd and even numbers, to introduce how algebra expresses generality. Introduce expressions such as $2n$, and $2m + 1$ to represent odd and even numbers and use them in various conjectures.
Students make errors if the algebraic element appears in the 'second position' of brackets. For example, $(4 - x)(x - 5)$.	Introduce this positioning early on alongside expressions where the algebraic terms appear first in the brackets. They are both equally valid.

Review question commentary

Question 1 (6.1) – Students could discuss what the units of the answer would be (g/cm^3).

Question 2 (6.1) – Discuss where formula could have come from (area of a triangle).

Question 3 (6.1) – Students need to use inverse operations for part **b.**

Question 4 (6.2) – Use function machines to help weaker students understand these questions by considering inverse operations.

Question 5 (6.3) – Challenge students by asking them to write further examples.

Question 6 (6.3) – Encourage students to lay out their argument clearly and then peer assess their answers. Discuss how the identity sign indicates that the statement is true for all values of x.

Question 7 (6.4) – Make students aware that whatever method they use they will always get 4 terms and then need to simplify the resulting expression. Students may make errors with negative signs so it is worth revising this.

Question 8 (6.4) – Students should find the HCF of the terms and factorise using a single set of brackets.

Question 9 (6.4) – Many mistakes are possible here. For example, adding the constants in the brackets to give the constant term in expression. In parts **c** and **d** students may get the signs the wrong way round. Encourage students to expand the brackets to check their answers.

Question 10 (6.4) – Students need to spot these are the differences of two squares.

Review answers

1 **a** 3 g/cm^3 **b** 12.5 g/cm^3

2 **a** 16 **b** 22.5

3 **a i** $2x$ **ii** $x - y$ **b** £15

4 **a** $A = b - 3$ **b** $A = \dfrac{d}{2}$

c $A = \dfrac{F + c}{5}$ **d** $A = 2J - h$

e $A = \sqrt{L + 2K}$ **f** $A = \dfrac{2}{b}$

5 **a** $2y + 3 = 7$ **b** $3b \times 4b \equiv 12b^2$

c $4z + 2$ **d** $F = ma$

e $y = 3x + 4$

6 $2(3x + 1) - 4 = 6x + 2 - 4 = 6x - 2$ as required.

7 **a** $x^2 + 8x + 15$ **b** $x^2 - 8x + 12$

c $x^2 - 3x - 28$ **d** $6x^2 + 13x - 5$

8 **a** $x(x + 5)$ **b** $3x(4x - 1)$

9 **a** $(x + 4)(x + 1)$ **b** $(x - 6)(x - 1)$

c $(x - 4)(x + 2)$ **d** $(x + 5)(x - 2)$

10 **a** $(x + 6)(x - 6)$ **b** $(2x + 5)(2x - 5)$

Assessment 6

Question 1 – 4 marks

a $m = t \div 5$ OR $t = 5m$ [B1]
b **i** 3 miles [$15 \div 5$] [B1]
ii 0.5 miles [$2.5 \div 5$] [B1]
iii 12.5 s [2.5×5] [B1]

Question 2 – 9 marks

a $J = 0.45R + 0.55S$ [B1]
b 4×0.45 [M1]
$= 1.8$ kg [A1]
c 6×0.55 [M1]
$= 3.3$ kg [A1]
d Raspberries: 9×0.45 Sugar: 9×0.55 [M1]
$= 4.05$ kg $= 4.95$ kg [A1]
e $2.25 \div 0.45$ [M1]
$= 5$ kg [A1]

Question 3 – 9 marks

a **i** $15 - 0.75 \times 2$ [M1]
$= 13.5$ hours OR 13 hr 30 min [A1]
ii $15 - 0.75 \times 10$
$= 7.5$ hours OR 7 hr 30 min [B1]
b **i** $6 = 15 - 0.75a$ [M1]
$a = (15 - 6) \div 0.75$ [M1]
$= 12$ years [A1]
ii $a = (15 - 9) \div 0.75$
$= 8$ years [B1]
c $15 - 0.75 \times 18 = 1$ hr 30 min [M1]
No, this is too little sleep. [A1]

Question 4 – 3 marks

a **i** Yes [$7^2 = 49$] [B1]
ii No [B1]
± 11 [B1]

Question 5 – 11 marks

a **i** No – Must see a valid reason. [B1]
$p^2 - 11p + 28$ [B1]
ii No – Must see a valid reason. [B1]
$(v^2 + 2v - 63) + (25v^2 - 40v + 16)$ [B3]
$26v^2 - 38v - 47$ [B1]
b **i** Yes Must see workings [B1]
$z \times z + 4 \times z + 9 \times z + 4 \times 9$ [B1]
ii No – Must see a valid reason [B1]
$v^2 - 100 = (v + 10)(v - 10)$
OR $(v - 10)^2 = v^2 - 20v + 100$ [B1]

Question 6 – 2 marks

a $W = 7D$ [B1]
b $C = 50 + 250D$ [B1]

Question 7 – 15 marks

a **i** $P = 15m$ [B1]
ii $P = 12m$ [B1]
iii $P = 14n$ [B1]
b **i** 13:15 ⇒ peak time [B1]
3 min 20 sec → 4 min [B1]
$P = 15 \times 4 + 14 \times 8$ [M1]
$= 60 + 112$
$= £1.72$ [A1]
ii 08:01 ⇒ off-peak, 09:01 ⇒ peak [B1]
6 min 10 sec → 7 min
14 min 1 sec → 15 min [B1]
$P = 15 \times 15 + 12 \times 7 + 14 \times 17$ [M1]
$= 225 + 84 + 238$ [A1]
$= 547$p OR £5.47 [A1]
c 2 min 43 sec → 3 min 7 min 17 sec → 8 min
23 min 42 sec → 24 min 4 min 55 sec → 5 min [B1]
$P = 12 \times 3 + 12 \times 8 + 12 \times 24 + 12 \times 5 + 14 \times 25$
$= 12 \times 40 + 14 \times 25$ [M1]
$= 480 + 350$
$= 830$p OR £8.30 [A1]

Question 8 – 10 marks

Must see a reason or counter example.

a False $5 \times 4 = 20$ [B1]
b False 5 has two factors, 1 and 5 [B1]
c True Let the two numbers be $2x$ and $2y$
$2x + 2y = 2(x + y)$ so the sum is even. [B2]
d False $0^2 = 0$ [B1]
e False $2 \times 7 = 14$ [B1]
f True Let the numbers be $2x$, $2x + 2$ and $2x + 4$.
$2x + 2x + 2 + 2x + 4 = 6x + 6 = 6(x + 1)$,
is divisible by 6. [B2]
g True $p^2 (p > 1)$ has 3 factors, 1, p and p^2 [B2]
($1 = 1^2$ is not prime.)

Question 9 – 4 marks

a $y = 4x + 1$ [B2]
b $y = x \div 3 - 2$ [B2]

Question 10 – 8 marks

a $S = 100^2 \div 170$ [M1]
$= 58.8$ m (1 dp) [A1]
b $S_1 = 70^2 \div 170$ $S_2 = 52^2 \div 170$ [M1]
$= 28.8235\ldots$ $= 15.9058\ldots$ [A1]
$S_{min} = S_1 + S_2$ [M1]
$= 44.7$ m (3 sf) [A1]
c $v = \sqrt{170S}$ [B1]
$= \sqrt{170 \times 60}$
$= 101$ km/h (3 sf) [F1]

Working in 2D

Learning outcomes

A5 Understand and use standard mathematical formulae; rearrange formulae to change the subject.

G1 Draw diagrams from written description.

G7 Identify, describe and construct congruent and similar shapes, including on coordinate axes, by considering rotation, reflection, translation and enlargement (including fractional scale factors).

G14 Use standard units of measure and related concepts (length, area, [volume/capacity, mass, time, money, etc.)].

G15 Measure line segments and angles in geometric figures, including interpreting maps and scale drawings and use of bearings.

G16 Know and apply formulae to calculate: area of triangles, parallelograms, trapezia.

G24 Describe translations as 2D vectors.

R2 Use [scale factors,] scale diagrams and maps.

Prior knowledge

Check-in skill

- Multiply fractions and mixed numbers.
- Add decimals.
- Measure a line segment in mm and cm.

Online resources

MyMaths 1086, 1099, 1103, 1108, 1113, 1115, 1117, 1125, 1127, 1128, 1129, 1146

InvisiPen videos

Skills: 07Sa – m Applications: 07Aa – e

Kerboodle assessment

Online Skills Test 7 Chapter Test 7

Development and links

Transformations have many applications in real life. Graphic designers use transformations to create patterns, sushi bars use conveyors to translate dishes in front of customers and web designers use enlargements to transform images. Observation wheels such as the London Eye rotate around a central axis but the individual capsules rotate in the opposite direction around their own axes of rotation. As a result, the people inside the capsules remain upright.

Chapter investigation

Explain that you wish to create a giant Koch snowflake in the school's gym/playground/playing field/... and that you wish to plan it using a scale drawing [**7.1**]. Use an accurately drawn diagram as a basis for calculating real-life lengths of sides and distances between various points. Suggest using bearings as a way to give instructions on which directions to travel. This can be done as a practical activity using chalk and taut string to draw lines.

Suggest that you now want to paint the snowflake and therefore need to know its area. Taking a hexagram as a starting shape it is possible to join points to create rectangles, parallelograms, trapezia and various triangles. Establish formulae for the areas of these basic shapes [**7.2**] and calculate the area of the hexagram as a composite shape; there are many different decompositions, allowing all formulae to be applied. This approach naturally lends itself to motivating several of the formula using dissections and rearrangements to make simpler *base* shapes such as a rectangle.

At each stage the snowflake has many symmetries so that it can be created by transforming one small 'edge' triangle [**7.3**]. Investigate how to do this by defining and apply rotations, reflections and translations. It is also possible to spot similar triangles that are enlargements of one another: discuss how enlargements are defined and applied.

As well as looking at single transformations students should be encouraged to look at combinations of transformations [**7.4**].

7.1 Measuring lengths and angles

Objectives

① G14 Use standard units of measure and related concepts

② G15 Measure line segments and angles in geometric figures, including interpreting maps and scale drawings and use of bearings

Useful resources

Clock-face, protractors, board protractor

Starter – Skills

Show students various angles using the clock-face (at this stage with horizontal or vertical base lines of angles). Discuss what type of angle: right angle, acute, obtuse and reflex angles. After deciding what type of angle it is, challenge students to give estimations of each angle. Encourage students to think about what half a right angle would be. Is this angle more than or less than 45°?

Use a board protractor to demonstrate how to measure angles accurately.

Teaching notes – Skills

Ask students to look at their rulers and discuss how many millimetres in a centimetre.

Ask students to use their rulers to construct a line of 28 mm. Invite students to check one another's work. Repeat for 5.4 cm. Ensure students line up the zero mark of their ruler with the start of their line. Discuss whether the mm or cm scale of the ruler must be used to measure a line of 28 mm.

Sketch an acute angle on the board. Use the board protractor to highlight the two scales on a protractor. Measure the angle and discuss how to decide whether the angle is, say, 30° or 150°. Highlight that deciding what type of angle it is and a quick estimation can help with this decision.

Using a board protractor, highlighting:

- The central cross of the protractor should be exactly on the point of the angle.
- The base line of the protractor must line up with the angle base line.
- The angle should be measured from zero.

Sketch an angle in two different positions, one with a horizontal base (0°) line, another with the base line facing 'north'. Which angle is easier to measure?

Plenary – Skills

Sketch a reflex angle on the board and label it (inaccurately) 230°. Invite a student to use the board protractor to measure the obtuse angle and then discuss whether the reflex angle measurement can be correct and why. Highlight that angles around a point (making a full turn) must add up to 360°, if not, then one measurement must be incorrect. Discuss how to use the obtuse angle to calculate the reflex angle.

Exercise commentary – Skills

Each student will need tracing paper, ruler, protractor and a short piece of thin string or cotton.

Questions 1 and **2** Students could measure the lengths in cm or mm or both. If a 360° protractor is available discuss how to measure reflex angles using both a 360° and a 180° protractor.

Question 3 Students may not notice the change of units for real distances.

Question 5 Students must trace the maps and draw north lines and other directions on the tracing paper. Ask them what 1mm represents if 1 cm ≡ 50 km. Tracing the maps on squared or lined paper may help students orientate their north lines accurately.
When using a semi-circular protractor for bearings, students should orientate the protractor with the 0° line pointing due north. Some students get into difficulties when they line up the 90° line with due north. For bearings greater than 180°, the protractor is positioned to the left of the north line.

Question 6 Students will need a short piece of thin string for this question.

Question 7 Students will find drawing the scale diagram easier on squared paper. Some students may require help to convert the decimal lengths.

Simplification – Skills

Measuring from the 1 cm mark is a common mistake. Practise this during the lesson. Students may have difficulty using a protractor and may need help lining up the target point and the base line. Students often use the wrong scale when measuring. Using a table to write down the type of angle and an estimate will help them to check their answer.

Extension – Skills

Students could investigate alternative measures of angle. Some protractors and calculators have scales in grads (400 in a full turn) while radian measure is related to the circle (2π radians in a full turn).

Recap – Applications

1 Make an accurate drawing of these lines and angles.

a

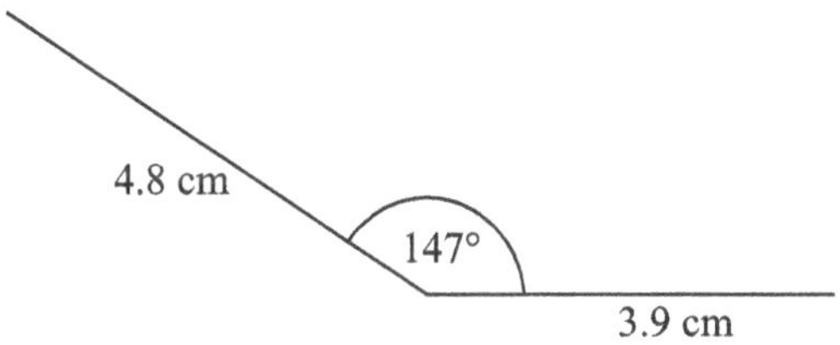

b

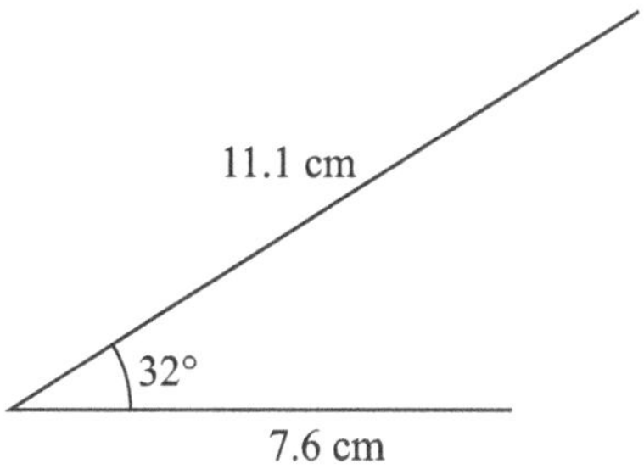

c

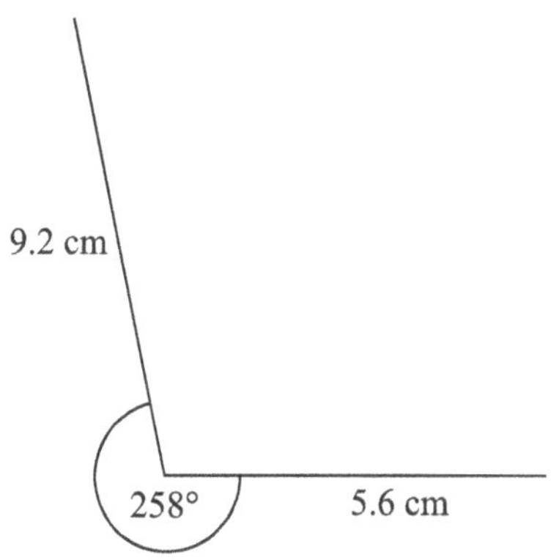

2 Three cities, A, B, and C are the vertices of the triangle shown.

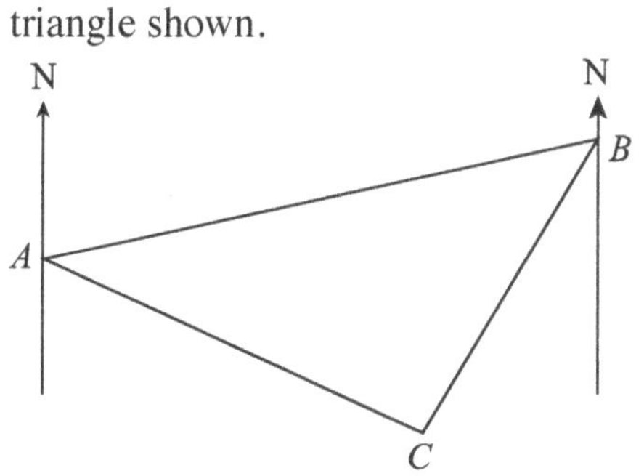

The bearing of B from A is 055°.

The bearing of C from A is 140°.

The bearing of C from B is 205°.

Work out and write down the bearings of:

a B from C **b** A from C **c** A from B

(**a** 025° **b** 320° **c** 235°)

Plenary – Applications

Sketch an obtuse-angled triangle. Label the shorter sides 3.2 cm and 4.7 cm. Discuss which of these are possible lengths of the third side: 8.4 cm, 2.8 cm, 6.5 cm. This leads to the concept of 'Is my answer reasonable' which gives a check on the accuracy of the drawing.

Exercise commentary – Applications

Each student will need tracing paper, ruler, protractor and a short piece of thin string or cotton. When drawing plans to scale, students will find it easier to use squared paper rather than plain paper. Circular, rather than semi-circular, protractors would simplify the measurement of bearings above 180°.

Emphasise that the words 'the bearing of A from B' emphasise that the student is at B and looking away from B towards A, so that centre of the protractor is placed on B when measuring the bearing.

Question 1 A whole-class discussion on how to start drawing the scale diagram will avoid the later frustration if the diagram were to drop off the edge of the paper! Have students sketch the journey from A to B to give the overall shape of the scale diagram. The sketch will help students to decide on the scale to use and also where to locate the starting point of the journey on the paper.

Question 2 Two north lines are needed, one at Mevagissey and the other at the chapel (+) on Rame Head. Encourage students to draw these north lines before they measure the bearings.

Question 3 This question is best explored through an initial whole-class discussion. One method would be to choose a scale, draw the bedroom on square grid paper, cut out smaller rectangles for the furniture to the same scale and then re-arrange them. There may be more than one realistic answer.

Question 5 Students could use a ruler to get a first approximation for each day's journey and then use cotton or thin string to refine the distance.

Simplification – Applications

Sketch an obtuse-angled triangle. Label the shorter sides 3.2 cm and 4.7 cm. Discuss which of these are possible lengths of the third side: 8.4 cm, 2.8 cm, 6.5 cm. This leads to the concept of 'Is my answer reasonable' which gives a check on the accuracy of the drawing.

Extension – Applications

Set up a three-leg journey, such as: $A \rightarrow B$ is 5 km on 282°, $B \rightarrow C$ is 4 km on 196°, $C \rightarrow D$ is 2.5 km on 115°. Ask students to find the distance and bearing of A from D. (Answer approx. 5.3 km on 043°) Students could then work in pairs, setting similar problems for each other.

7.2 Area of a 2D shape

Objectives

①G16 Know and apply formulae to calculate: area of triangles, parallelograms, trapezia

Useful resources

Mini whiteboards, OHT or whiteboard file of area of a triangle, parallelogram and trapezium, scissors

Starter – Skills

Using mini whiteboards ask students to sketch a standard parallelogram. Now sketch a different one. Now sketch a more unusual one. Ask students to show their examples, and look at each others'. Draw attention to any features, and correct any errors, emphasising the basic parallelogram properties.

Repeat the activity requesting standard, different and unusual trapeziums.

Teaching notes – Skills

Draw a 4×6 right-angled triangle on the board. Discuss how to calculate its area. Highlight that the squares can be counted, matching fractions of squares to create wholes. Then demonstrate the rectangle that can be drawn to enclose the triangle and make sure all understand that the triangle has half the area of the rectangle.

Derive the formula and emphasise that the height is perpendicular to the base.

Ask students, in pairs, to explore different ways in which they might calculate the area of a parallelogram. Remind them that 'cutting' a shape into others may help. Take feedback from the students' work, ensuring that at least three different ways are shared and establish the same result. Check/prompt students to use correct area units.

Enquire what would be the 'easiest' or quickest way to find the area. Arrive at the formula.

After some consolidation work, perhaps matching different parallelograms to different areas, a similar activity can help to establish the area of a trapezium. Display the formulae for the area of a trapezium and parallelogram. Use an example of a composite shape to discuss splitting a shape into smaller shapes to find the area.

Plenary – Skills

Challenge students to list all the right-angled triangles with an area of 24 cm^2.

Discuss strategies: trial and error or considering rectangles with an area of 48 cm^2 and looking for factor pairs of 48.

Exercise commentary – Skills

Question 1 This question gives students only the measurements they need to answer the question.

Question 2 This question gives students some unnecessary bits of information to test their understanding of the area formulae. Remind students that the perpendicular height (not the slant height) is used to find area. Some students may benefit from further examples to show why this is the case.

Question 3 Some students will have difficulty with some of the computation involving fractions. They could look at the examples on page 100 to help and estimate the answer to each area to check that their answers are reasonable.

Question 4 For this question students either need to rearrange the area formulae or work backwards to find the required dimensions. The second example on page 144 gives an example of this for a triangle.

Questions 5 Part **a** of the first worked example on page 144 will give students a good idea of how to lay out their working for this type of question.

Question 6 This questions is similar to question **4** as it requires rearrangement of formulae.

Question *7 Part **b** of the first worked example on page 144 will give students a good idea of how to lay out their working for this type of question. Note the mixture of units in both shapes. As a first step, students must decide which unit to use.

Simplification – Skills

Students should continue routine practice on simple shapes before moving on to composite shapes.

Extension – Skills

Students could be provided with examples where the parallelograms and trapeziums are not in a standard orientation. This will encourage them to visualise the various lengths clearly before applying the formulae.

Recap – Applications

1 Find the areas of these shapes.

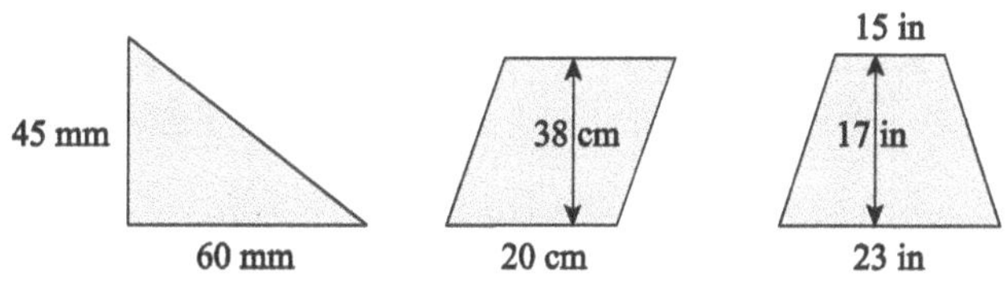

(1350 mm^2; 760 cm^2; 323 in^2)

Plenary – Applications

Take a composite shape and ask students to find three different ways of calculating its area.

Stress that the answer is not what is required, just the ways of working it out. When gathering feedback from the class, include a method that involves subtraction as well as one(s) that involve addition.

Exercise commentary – Applications

Question 1 In part **a**, emphasise that a clear and methodical lay-out of workings including an explanation is necessary for a complete answer. Part **b** requires a whole-class discussion. Accept answers which ask about the accuracy of the measurements, 'are they to the nearest whole metre?', and whether the land is likely to have perfectly straight edges. Students may forget to answer the question posed in part **a**.

Question 2 For these composite shapes, refer to the first field in the worked example on page 146.

Question 3 The purple area can be dissected in several different ways. Students could compare answers from different methods.

Question 4 This question provides a useful test of students' ability to plot coordinates. Different methods to solve this question include splitting the arrow into a rectangle and three triangles and using a variety of triangles, rectangles, parallelograms and trapezia. Challenge more able students to try a subtraction method.

Question *5 This question involves a mixture of units. Students may decide that working in centimetres is easiest. Sketching the diagram and adding measurements to complete the perimeter will help. As in question **1a** students should lay out their workings methodically and explain their reasoning where necessary.

Question *6 This question assumes that the map runs to the edge of the paper and that there is no empty border. Amy's words need careful reading and a sketch of the map will help students to 'see' the method of subtracting the area of two rectangles.

Simplification – Applications

Students could be given further examples where they need to apply the standard formulae rather than expecting them to work backwards.

Extension – Applications

Pose questions involving composite shapes or shapes with holes cut out of them.

7.3 Transformations 1

Objectives

① G7 Identify, describe and construct congruent and similar shapes, including on coordinate axes, by considering rotation, reflection, translation and enlargement

Useful resources

Mini whiteboards, OHT/whiteboard slide of coordinate grid (all four quadrants), tracing paper, squared paper, set of congruent shapes on coordinate grid

Starter – Skills

Display a coordinate grid showing all four quadrants. Place a circle, representing a robot, at any point, say (1, 3). Ask students to give the robot position after various 'moves': 2 up/2 right/1 down, extending to two-step instructions.

Place two circles at a start position and end position. Ask students to describe the move as simply as possible (for example, as a combination of only two moves).

Repeat using different start and end coordinates.

Teaching notes – Skills

Display a coordinate grid (four quadrants). Join points (0, 4), (2, 3) and (3, 0). Discuss reflection of the shape in the y-axis. Remind students to take each point separately and ensure equidistance from the mirror line. Repeat for reflection in the x-axis.

Draw this flag, and its reflection about a horizontal line through the centre. Discuss whether this has been rotated.

Highlight that whilst the pole of the flag could be seen to be rotated through 180°, the flag itself has not; instead it is a reflection.

Draw a right-angled triangle on the board. Model it rotating clockwise 90° about one of its vertices.

Repeat with different centres of rotation. Emphasise that for any rotation you need: a centre of rotation; a direction; an angle.

Introduce *translation* as a sliding movement. This moves a shape, by sliding right/left, up/down, without changing its size, shape or which way round it is drawn.

Introduce students to translation vector notation. Moving a shape by vector $\binom{4}{2}$ means moving the original shape 4 units right and 2 units up. Vector $\binom{-1}{-5}$ means 1 left and 5 down. The first number (top) is always right/left, the second (bottom) is always up/down.

Plenary – Skills

Challenge students to give translations to move the blocks of picture 1, to create the 'fish' in picture 2:

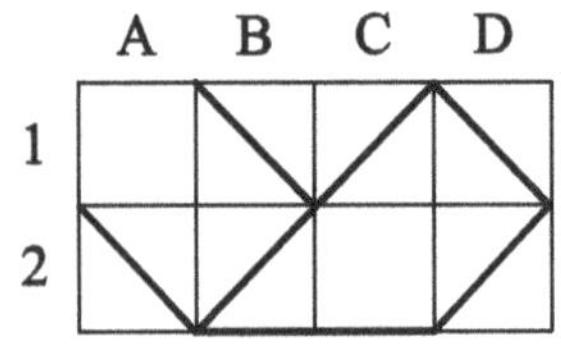

Picture 1

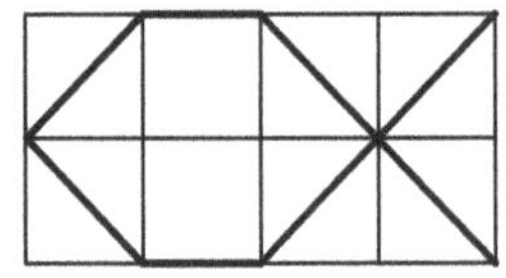
Picture 2

Exercise commentary – Skills

Squared paper is required for this exercise. Students will need tracing paper for rotations and they can also use it to check reflections and translations.

Questions 1 and **2** Remind students that they can use tracing paper to help with their reflections and rotations.

Question 3 Remind students of the signs in a vector, the top number moves parallel to the x-axis (right +, left –) and the bottom number moves parallel to the y-axis (up +, down –). Students should translate each vertex on the object in turn to create the image.

Question 4 Students should first draw the 'rays' out from the centre. They then count along the grid (or measure with a ruler) to move each vertex of the object by multiplying the distance from the centre by the scale factor. A common error is to move the vertex by counting (or measuring) from the object rather than from the centre of the enlargement.

Questions 5 and **6** Draw students' attention to the fact that a rotation needs three items of data to define it completely, an angle, a direction and a centre of rotation. Ask what a reflection needs to define it completely, refer to question **5**.

Question 7 Students should translate each vertex on the object in turn to create the image. Some students confuse the words *translation* and *transformation*. It might help them to think that, as a *translation* from French to English moves a word from one language to another, so a translation moves a shape (without rotation or reflection) from one place to another.

Question 8 In part **b**, students should first draw the 'rays' out from the centre (see the dotted lines on the diagram on page 148). They then count along the grid (or measure with a ruler) to move each vertex of the object by multiplying the distance from the centre by the scale factor. A common error is to move the vertex by counting (or measuring) from the object rather than from the centre of the enlargement.

Question *9 Use a large scale on both axes. A sharp pencil will also help! In part **c**, use tracing paper to join a vertex (say, A) to the centre (0, 1) and watch this line as it rotates.

Question 10 Refer students to the points and lines listed as invariant on page 148. Students should then be able to work backwards to find the transformation. Some students may benefit from drawing a grid and a shape, marking the point that is invariant and then checking different transformations.

Simplification – Skills

Students could be given pre-drawn shapes on fixed axes in order to emphasise that the important part of this topic is the transformation, not the drawing of graphs/coordinates.

Extension – Skills

Students could be invited to draw their own shapes on a coordinate grid and to challenge a partner to draw the image when reflected in a given mirror line, or to rotate the shape about a given point.

Recap – Applications

1 Copy each shape and draw its reflection in the mirror line given.

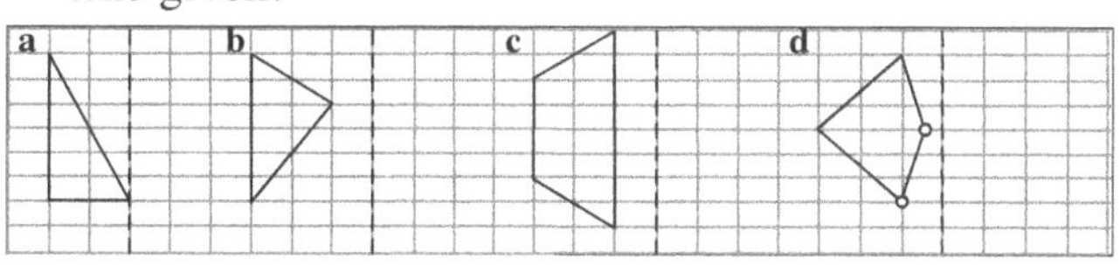

2 Copy this diagram and draw the shape that has been rotated

i 90° clockwise about point O

ii 90° anticlockwise about point O

iii 180° about point O

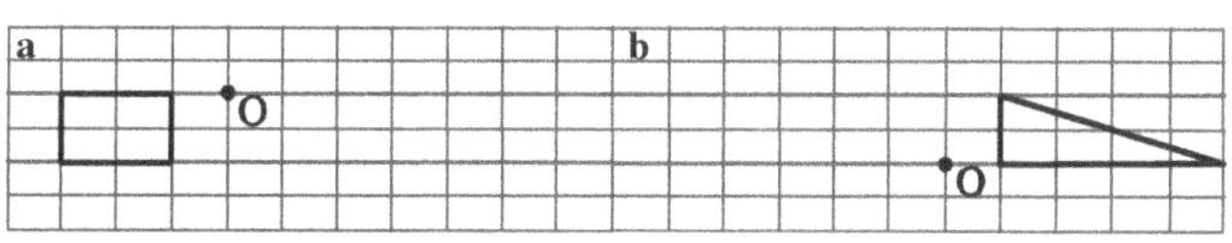

3 a Copy this diagram.

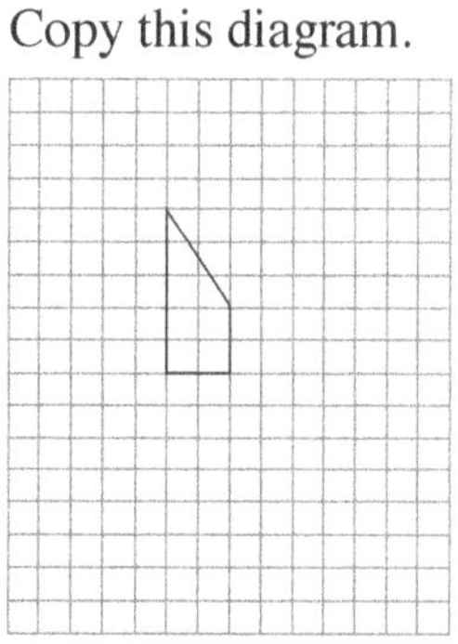

Draw this shape with the following translations:

a 4 to the right and 2 upwards

b 7 to the left and 6 downwards

c 4 to the right and –3 upwards

d –5 to the right and –4 upwards

e $\begin{pmatrix} 5 \\ -4 \end{pmatrix}$

Plenary – Applications

Display a set of congruent shapes and ask students to consider how, say, shape A could be transformed to shape E. The responses should be written on mini whiteboards, allowing for the selection of some for discussion. Repeat for other pairs.

Try to involve all three of the transformations in this activity.

Exercise commentary – Applications

Squared paper and tracing paper will be needed throughout the exercise.

Questions 1 and **2** These questions cover three of the transformations, reflection, rotation and translation. Remind students that 'describing' a transformation is more than just naming it – the properties of the transformation must also be given.

Question 3 Copies of this diagram would be useful for students, as they will need to draw on it. Remind students that they can use tracing paper. The recap box on page 150 lists the points and lines that are invariant.

Question 4 Students who cannot visualise the answer to part **a** will need to draw a diagram for part **b**. Some students may be able to use the description of what has happened to the coordinates to deduce that this is an enlargement scale factor 3 centre (0, 0).

Question 5 This question asks students todraw this transformation in order to describe it because it is an enlargement with a centre that is not (0, 0).

Question 6 For part **b**, ask students to think initially of the hour hand during one hour.

Question *7 Tracing paper will help students to see that the coordinates of the centre of rotation are not integer values.

Question *8 Students should be able to use tracing paper to experiment with finding centres of rotation and mirror lines for these transformations. As an extension they could try and find two transformations that combine to produce the image *B*, for example, two reflections.

Question 9 Students need to consider a few points, find their images and compare the coordinates of object and image points.

Simplification – Applications

Encourage students to label corresponding corners of shapes in order to enable them to identify and describe the transformation correctly.

Extension – Applications

Students could be asked to write down the reverse translation that maps the image to the original. Can they identify the (simple) pattern?

Transformations 2

Objectives

① G7 Identify, describe and construct congruent and similar shapes, including on coordinate axes, by considering rotation, reflection, translation and enlargement

Useful resources

OHT/whiteboard file of recipe in starter activity, squared paper, blown up copies of the diagrams from the exercise, display showing two similar kites

Starter – Skills

Show a recipe for Spaghetti Bolognese for 4 people:

600 g	spaghetti
500 g	lean mince
2	onions
2 tins	tomatoes
3 cloves	garlic
4	carrots
12	mushrooms

Discuss how much of each ingredient would be required for 8 people, 12 people, 40 people.

Teaching notes – Skills

Refer to the starter. Highlight that to enlarge the recipe for more people, every ingredient had to be increased proportionally.

Display a 4 × 2 rectangle. Discuss how to enlarge the 4 × 2 rectangle to one with a base of 12. Discuss the multiplier of the length and introduce the keyword *scale factor*. Enlarge the rectangle.

Next to this enlargement draw a 6 × 12 rectangle and discuss whether it is similar. Highlight that changing the orientation of the image does not alter its similarity.

Draw an isosceles triangle (base 2 cm). Discuss how to enlarge it to a triangle with a 6 cm base. Establish that the scale factor is 3 and encourage students to explain how this could be calculated:

$$2 \times ? = 6 \quad \text{so} \quad ? = 6 \div 2 = 3$$

Highlight that:

- angles stay the same
- lengths increase in proportion.

What would enlarging with a factor of $\frac{1}{2}$ do?

(Halves all dimensions.) Note that this is still called enlargement, not reduction!

Demonstrate enlargement from different centres of enlargement. Emphasise the importance of counting from the centre of enlargement to points on the object and image to describe or construct an enlargement.

Plenary – Skills

Display a diagram showing two similar kites, saying clearly that these are similar shapes, therefore one is an enlargement of the other.

Ask students to look carefully at the diagram and to record two things that are the *same* in both kites. After giving thinking time, discuss the results.

Now ask students to record two things that are *different* in both kites. Follow up this discussion with questions about some of the lengths and the scale factor.

Exercise commentary – Skills

This exercise practises the many different ways that two successive transformations can be equivalent to one single transformation. Diagrams can become complicated and are easier to draw and interpret if they are not too small. Squared paper and tracing paper are needed throughout.

Question 1 Refer students to parts **a** and **b** of the worked example on page 152. Students need to draw ‘rays’ out from the centre of enlargement to the object and beyond.

Questions 2 and **3** Students could use tracing paper to help them with the rotations and reflections in these two questions.

Question 4 This question is very similar to the worked example on page 152 as it involves an enlargement with scale factor $\frac{1}{2}$ and a translation. In both questions, students then need to find the transformation that maps the final image back to the original object.

Questions 5 to **7** Students should draw large diagrams and take care to label the corners of the object and images correctly. They may notice that part **e** of question ***7** is the inverse of part **d**.

Simplification – Skills

Students may benefit from copies of the diagrams that are blown up to make the measurements of side lengths and angles easier.

Extension – Skills

Students could be given examples where the object and image of an enlargement is given and asked to find the centre of enlargement by drawing rays.

Recap – Applications

1 Mark a square grid with values of x and y from -6 to 6. On it draw a triangle with vertices (1, 1), (1, 3) and (2, 1)

On your grid, draw the enlargement of the given triangle with scale factor 3 from the origin.

(Triangle with vertices (3, 3), (3, 9) and (6, 3))

Plenary – Applications

Show a pair of shapes, one an enlargement of the other. Ask pairs of students to discuss and decide where the centre of enlargement is, and the scale factor involved. Select a pair to demonstrate their findings.

Repeat with other shape pairs, and also a shape and a centre of enlargement with the image to be produced.

Exercise commentary – Applications

Squared paper and tracing paper will be needed throughout this exercise.

Questions 1 to **5** When students are describing a transformation, they should refer to the recap box on page 154 to help them identify the transformation and what information is needed to describe it.

Question 1 A worded description such as 'move one square left, one square down' is not sufficient for the translation, it must be expressed as a vector.

Question 2 There are many different angles and directions that could have caused the pattern, 45° clockwise is the most obvious. Challenge students to find all the possible rotations.

Questions 3 and **4** A whole-class discussion could discuss the general results of these two questions. Two reflections in parallel mirrors produces a translation by twice the distance between the mirror lines and two reflections in perpendicular mirrors produces a 180° rotation about the point of intersection. Students should notice that reversing the order of the transformations reverses the direction of the combined transformation. As an extension students could investigate what happens if the two mirrors are at an angle, for example, 45°. The result is a rotation about the point of intersection of the mirror lines through twice the angle between the mirror lines.

Question 5 This question has an infinite number of valid answers. Students could be challenged to find more than one solution.

Question 6 Students should take an appropriate shape of their choosing to perform the transformations, a square is not suitable as it is regular and so difficult to see which vertex on the object has mapped onto which vertex on the image.

Question 7 Students need to decide which is the initial object shape and which is the final image shape. There are several possible valid answers.

Questions *8 and **9** These questions could be discussed as a whole class. Note that, in question **9** part **b**, the object is subject to *three* enlargements in succession.

Question 10: Students need access to a range of wallpaper, fabric, tile patterns and kaleidoscopes for this investigation. When designing their own patterns, a variety of different grids on lined and dotty paper is essential for them to use. The results of students working in pairs could be shared by the whole class. If students work with reflections, ask them what happens when an object shape crosses a mirror line. If students work with rotations or enlargements, ask them what happens when the centre is inside the object shape or on its perimeter.

Simplification – Applications

Students could be given prepared diagrams to avoid any problems of incorrect copying. They may need guidance for the first few examples on enlargement; ensure they are drawing the rays correctly.

Students should be encouraged to count squares on the sides of the shapes to work out the scale factor.

Extension – Applications

Ask students to discuss where you might use fractional scale factors in the real world. Ask them to give specific examples.

7 Working in 2D

Key outcomes	Quick check
G1 Use the standard conventions for labelling and referring to the sides and angles of triangles; draw diagrams from written description. G7 Identify, describe and construct congruent and similar shapes, including on coordinate axes, by considering rotation, reflection, translation and enlargement (including fractional scale factors). G11 Solve geometrical problems on coordinate axes. G24 Describe translations as 2D vectors.	**1** Copy the diagram. **a** Reflect triangle A in the y-axis and label the image B. **b** Rotate triangle B 180° clockwise about (0, 0) and label the image C. **c** Describe the single transformation that maps A to C. **d** Translate C by the vector $\begin{pmatrix}-5\\2\end{pmatrix}$ and label the image D. 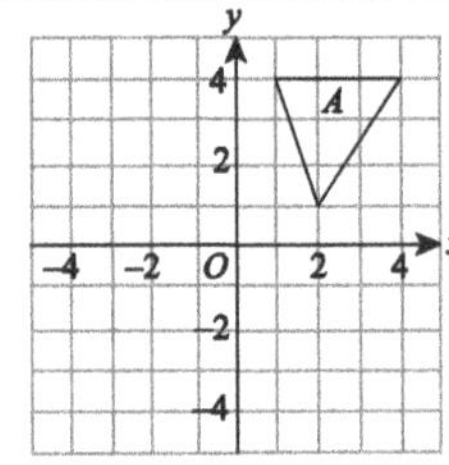 **2 a** Enlarge A by scale factor 0.5 from centre of enlargement (0, 0) and label the image B. **b** Describe the transformation that maps B back onto A. 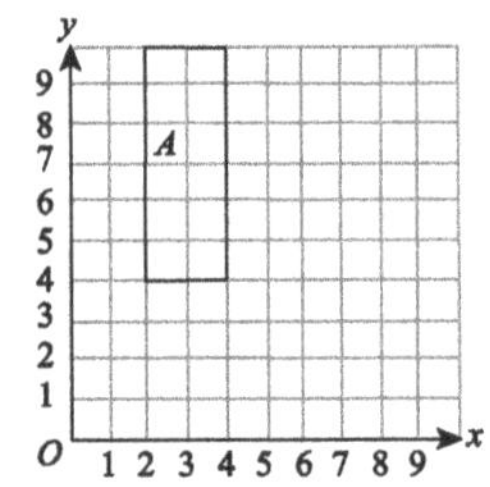 Solution 1 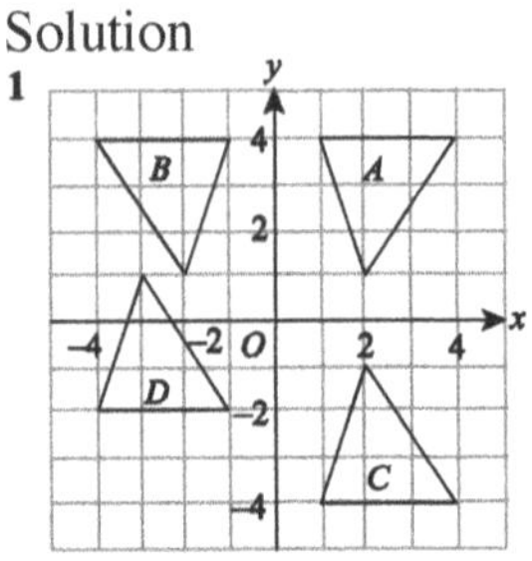 2 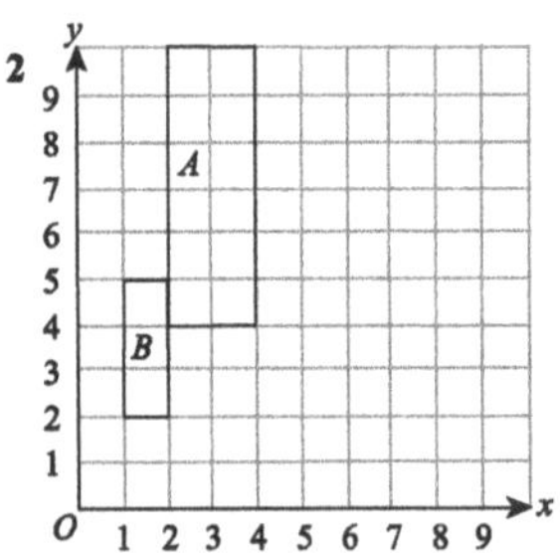 **c** Reflection in x-axis. **b** Enlargement scale factor 2, centre of enlargement (0, 0).
R2 Use scale diagrams and maps. G15 Measure line segments and angles in geometric figures, including interpreting maps and scale drawings and use of bearings.	**3** The diagram below is drawn to scale where 1 cm = 3 km. **a** What is the bearing of B from A? **b** What is the bearing of A from B? **c** What is the length of AB in real life? (055°, 235°,13.5 km) 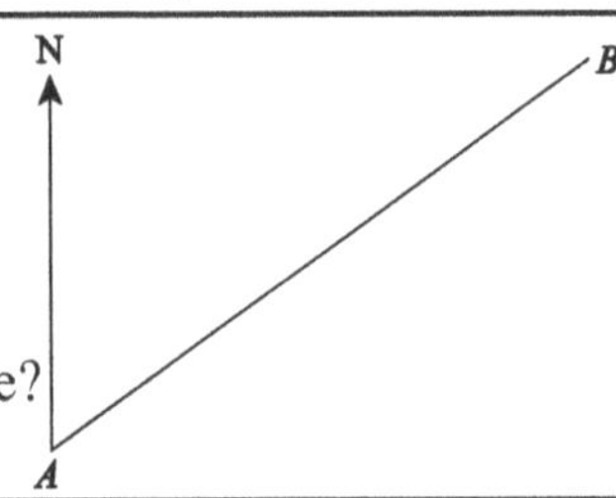
A5 Understand and use standard mathematical formulae. G14 Use standard units of measure and related concepts (length, area). G16 Know and apply formulae to calculate: area of triangles, parallelograms, trapezia.	**4** Work out the area of these shapes. 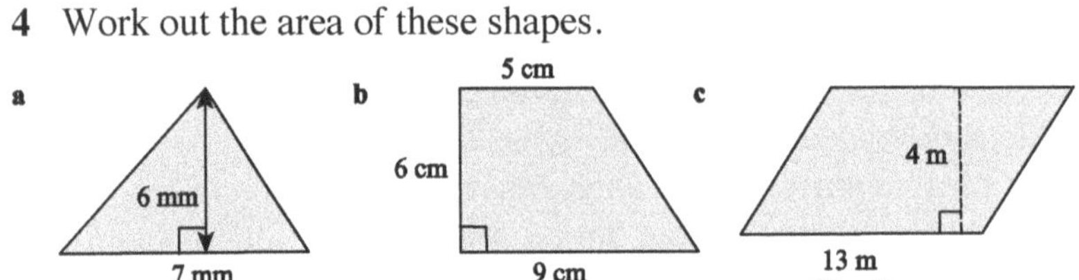 (21 mm²) (42 cm²) (52 m²)

Misconceptions and challenges	Solutions
Students find it difficult to remember and apply the formulae for area of 2D shapes and get them mixed up.	Use images and animations to demonstrate why the formulae work. Set regular homework to learn one or two formulae and give students a small test at the end of each week.
Students expect to be able to use a formula to solve a problem in one go. This causes problems when they are calculating the area of composite shapes.	Begin with simple composite shapes and build up to more complex, composite shapes. This will help students to understand that composite shapes maintain the combined areas of the smaller shapes but not their perimeters.

Misconceptions and challenges	Solutions
When measuring angles, students are not sure whether to use the inner or the outer scale of a protractor.	Ask students to decide whether the angle is acute, obtuse or reflex. This will help them to select which side of the protractor to use.
Students think that angle measurement is a measure of size rather than of rotation.	When demonstrating how to measure angles, model how to find the centre of rotation and follow the sweep of rotation round.
Students do not recognise trapezia if the parallel sides are not horizontal.	Regularly use shapes in unfamiliar rotations. Set students the challenge of sketching a trapezium that is different from the rest of the class.
Students assume the centre of enlargement or rotation is always at the origin.	Begin with other centres, and then look at the specific case of enlargement from the origin.
Students assume that enlargement is always from smaller to larger, and so find fractional scale factors difficult.	Use this as an opportunity to develop students' understanding of proportionality, and apply the skills of multiplying by fractions in context.
Vector notation can seem arbitrary and confusing to students, as it is so similar to coordinate notation.	Give students frequent practise of using vectors including a combination of fractional and negative translations. Look at the effect of doubling the x-translator or halving the y-translator.

Review question commentary

Students will require a pencil, ruler and possibly tracing paper for this exercise.

Questions 1 and **2** (**7.1**) – Make sure students state the units of their answer. Allow ±2° and ±2 mm, bearing must have 3 digits.

Question 3 (**7.2**) – Students must remember to state the units of their answers. Part **b** may catch some out, emphasise that the dimensions multiplied must always be perpendicular.

Questions 4 and **5** (**7.3**) – Tracing paper can be used if necessary. For the descriptions ensure all relevant information is given.

Question 6 (**7.4**) – Students need to appreciate that an enlargement can make a shape smaller.

Review answers

1 **a** 55° **b** 5.1 cm

2 Check $AC = 5.7$ cm, $\angle BAC = 73°$, $\angle BCA = 42°$.

3 **a** 28 m^2 **b** 6 cm^2 **c** 20 mm^2

d 25 cm^2 **e** 55 m^2

4 **a, b**

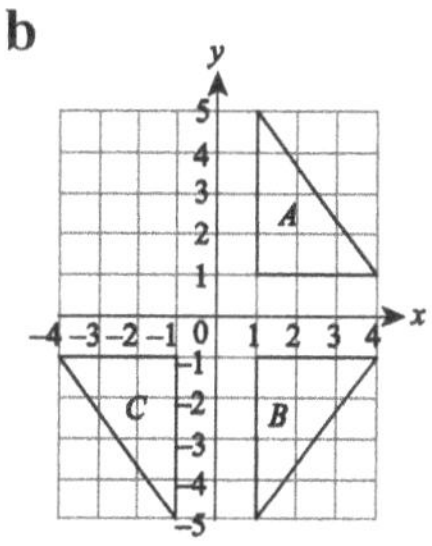

c Reflection in the y-axis

5 **a**

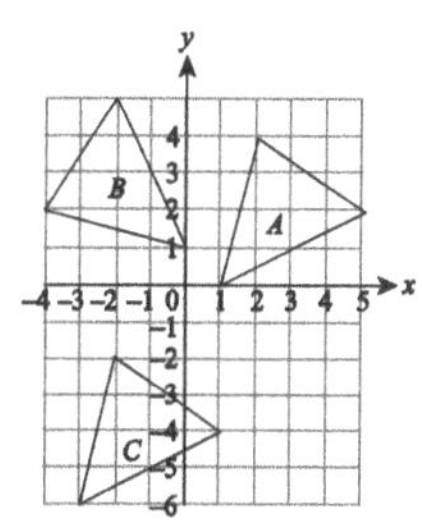

b Rotation 90° clockwise about (0, 0).

6 **a**

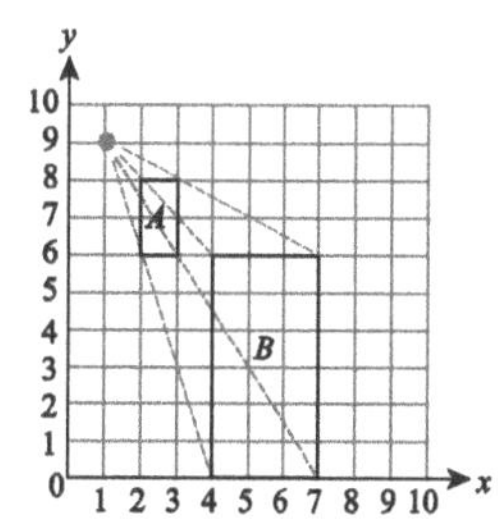

b Enlargement, scale factor $\frac{1}{3}$, centre of enlargement (1, 9).

Assessment 7

Question 1 – 2 marks

a Karl [B1]
b Neither. Multiply by 1 000 000. [B1]

Question 2 – 8 marks

a Check student's drawing.
BC, AD and DC correct to within ±3 mm [B1]
∡ADC and ∡BCD correct to within ±3° [B1]
b **i** 6.5 cm ± 2 mm [B1]
ii 60° ± 3° [B1]
iii 135° ± 3° [B1]
c Kite [B1]
d Correct drawing [B1]
Rectangle [B1]

Question 3 – 11 marks

Each answer must be accompanied by a reason.

a Yes, it's between 90° and 180°. [B1]
b No, it's a right angle. [B1]
c Yes, it's less than 90°. [B1]
d Yes, it's greater than 180°. [B1]
e Yes, it's between 90° and 180°. [B1]
f No, it's less than 90° so acute. [B1]
g No, it's a right angle. [B1]
h No, it's less than 90° so acute. [B1]
i Yes, it's between 90° and 180°. [B1]
j No, it's less than 90° so acute. [B1]
k No, it's greater than 180° so reflex. [B1]

Question 4 – 9 marks

a 180° + 15° [M1]
= 195° [A1]
b 65° + 45° [M1]
= 110° [A1]
c 015° [Alternate angles] [B1]
d 180 + (65 + 45) [M1]
= 290° [A1]
e 180 + 65° [M1]
= 245° [A1]

Question 5 – 18 marks

a Area = 2 × 3.5 [M1]
= 7 cm^2
Yes [A1]
b Area = $\frac{1}{2}$ × 3.5 × 1.5 [M1]
= 2.625 cm^2
No [A1]
[2.1 = $\frac{1}{2}$ × 3.5 × 1.2]
c Area = 19.6 × 15 [M1]
= 294 cm^2
Yes [A1]
d Area = $\frac{1}{2}$ × (7.8 + 5.4) × 3.2 [M1]
= 21.12 cm^2 [A1]
No [A1]
[42.24 = (7.8 + 5.4) × 3.2]
e Area = $\pi \times 7.6^2$ [M1]
= π × 7.6 × 7.6 = 181.5 cm^2 [A1]
Yes [A1]
f Area = $\frac{1}{2}$ × 3.2 × 2.9 [M1]
= 4.64 cm^2
No [A1]
[6.09 = $\frac{1}{2}$ × 4.2 × 2.9
g No, 22 cm [B1]
h No, 22 cm [B1]
i No, 12 cm [B1]
j No, 20 cm [B1]

Question 6 – 8 marks

a 49 [7 × 7] [B1]
b No, plus a valid reason. [M1]
2 or 3 is not a factor of 7
OR $2^2 = 4$ or $3^2 = 9$ is not a factor of 49 [A2]
c No, plus a valid reason. [M1]
Each 7 m side must include two 2 × 2 slabs and one 3 × 3 slab.There are only three ways of arranging slabs around the edges, all of which include gaps or overlap. [M1]

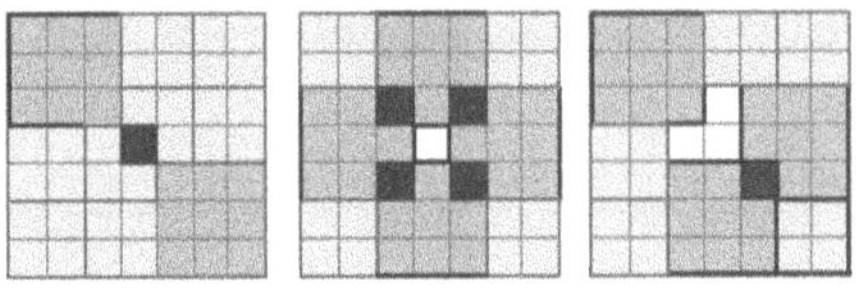

[A2]

Question 7 – 9 marks

a	4	[B1]	**b**	1	[B1]
c	7	[B1]	**d**	6	[B1]
e	5	[B1]	**f**	3	[B1]
g	2	[B1]	**h**	10	[B1]
i	8	[B1]			

Question 8 – 9 marks

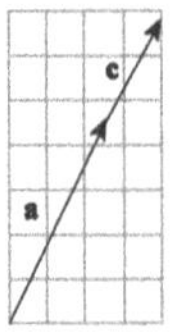

a One mark each component. [B2]
c One mark each component. [B2]
OR
The reflection of this in a vertical line

b $\begin{pmatrix}\pm25\\45\end{pmatrix}$ [B1] **d** $\begin{pmatrix}\pm15\\20\end{pmatrix}$ [B1]

e $\begin{pmatrix}\pm40\\65\end{pmatrix}$ [B2]

f $\begin{pmatrix}\pm25\\45\end{pmatrix}+\begin{pmatrix}\pm15\\20\end{pmatrix}=\begin{pmatrix}\pm40\\65\end{pmatrix}$ [F1]

Question 9 – 11 marks

a Rotation [B1]
180° [B1]
About the point (0, 0) [B1]

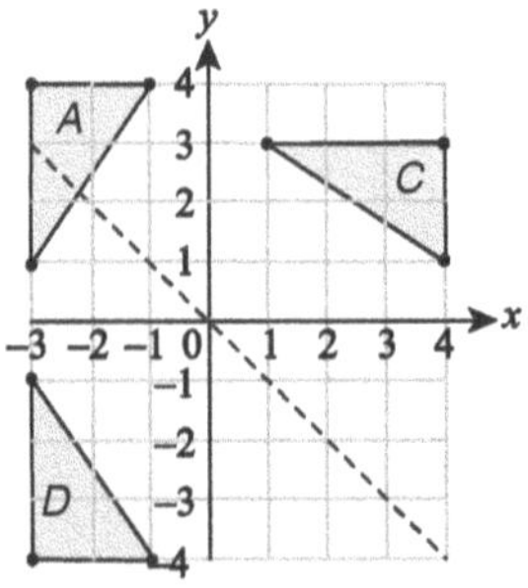

b Correct angle and direction [B1]
Correct orientation [B1]
Correct position [B1]
c Correct orientation [B1]
Correct position [B2]
d Reflection [B1]
in the *x*-axis [B1]

Probability

Learning outcomes

P1 Record, describe and analyse the frequency of outcomes of probability experiments using tables.

P2 Apply ideas of randomness, fairness and equally likely events to calculate expected outcomes of multiple future experiments.

P3 Relate relative expected frequencies to theoretical probability, using appropriate language and the 0 - 1 probability scale.

P4 Apply the property that the probabilities of an exhaustive set of outcomes sum to one; apply the property that the probabilities of an exhaustive set of mutually exclusive events sum to one.

P5 Understand that empirical unbiased samples tend towards theoretical probability distributions, with increasing sample size.

Prior knowledge

Check-in skill

- Cancel fractions to their simplest form.
- Order decimal numbers.
- Add and subtract fractions and decimals.

Online resources

MyMaths 1209, 1210, 1211, 1262, 1263, 1264

InvisiPen videos

Skills: 08Sa – f   Applications: 08Aa – e

Kerboodle assessment

Online Skills Test 8   Chapter Test 8

Development and links

Probability has applications wherever it is necessary to predict how likely it is that a random or unpredictable event will happen, for example to produce a weather forecast, to predict the effects of climate change or to predict the chance of winning a prize in any game of chance. It is important in the field of genetics and can be used to explain how genetic features are passed on from one generation to the next.

Probability is important in the workplace as all employers are required by law to carry out risk assessments to minimise the chances of an accident. Companies use probability to make risk/reward assessments for calculating insurance premiums or to determine the likelihood of a product breaking down during a warranty period. Quantum physics is concerned with the behaviour of sub-atomic particles which are so small that the traditional laws of physics do not apply. Their behaviour can only be described in terms of the probability that something will happen.

Chapter investigation

Start by asking students to play the game several times: recording the choices made by the two players in each game. These choices determine who has won. Once data has been collected ask, who is more likely to win? This requires a language of probability to be established and a prescription for calculating probabilities based on relative frequencies [**8.1**]. The relative frequency definition naturally leads to the probability of an impossible event being zero, the probability of a certain event being 1 and the sum of the probabilities of an event happening and not happening being one. The reliability of an event should also be discussed using the idea of pooling results.

Use 'data' from a game played by another player to try to predict how often they would pick the various options in a given number of future games: this leads to expected frequencies [**8.2**].

If the selection of rock, scissors and paper was random – each equally likely – then probabilities could also be calculated theoretically [**8.3**]. The probability of a particular player winning is then $\frac{1}{3}$ which is the same as the probability of a draw. This way of calculating probabilities can be investigated for other chance games such as those using coloured balls taken from a bag, dice or a spinner.

Look at the two ways of calculating probabilities and establish that for mutually exclusive events you simply add the probabilities [**8.4**]. Investigate calculating probabilities for various other chance games.

8.1 Probability experiments

Objectives

① **P1** Record, describe and analyse the frequency of outcomes of probability experiments using tables and frequency trees

Useful resources

Coins, drawing pins (one per pair of students), mini whiteboards

Starter – Skills

A fair dice is rolled 6 times.

Ask students how many:

- sixes
- even numbers
- prime numbers
- square numbers
- they would expect.

Ask 'How would these expected numbers change if the dice was rolled 60 times?'

Teaching notes – Skills

① Ask students what outcomes are possible when tossing two coins. Explore and share possible recording methods to use, and check that students recognise the need to record HT *and* TH. Remind them that it helps to think of two different coins to ensure listing all possibilities. Look at the use of **tables** and **tree diagrams** as recording strategies.

Then ask 'What outcomes are possible when tossing three coins?'. Ask students to work in pairs to discuss and develop their ideas. After thinking and recording time, discuss the recording strategies that students used and demonstrate successful listing and branching techniques to the whole group.

Use the resulting data to work out the probabilities of three heads etc. and explore which recording strategies students find most helpful in identifying all the possible outcomes.

Set up an **experimental probability** task to carry out as a whole group: Estimate the number of times a drawing pin will fall on its head if it is dropped 1500 times. Give each pair of students one drawing pin and ask them to drop the drawing pin 10 times and record the number of times it falls on its head and on its side. Then collect and sum these results from five pairs at a time, recording the total numbers of heads and sides per 50 drops, using a simple table like this:

Number of drops	1st 50	2nd 50	3rd 50
Number of heads			
Number of sides			

Ask students how they could use this data to answer the original question, and whether a better way of recording could be found. Elicit that recording the results cumulatively would be more useful, and model this using a table like this:

TOTAL number of drops	50	100	150
Number of heads			
Number of sides			

Plenary – Skills

Display a table of events with given probabilities. Ask students to write responses to questions such as:

- What is the probability of not getting ... ?
- What is the probability of getting either ... or ... ?
- What is the total probability?

Exercise commentary – Skills

Question 1 This question asks students to use relative frequency to estimate probabilities. This question can be used as a basis for discussion around the meaning of relative frequency as an estimate of theoretical probability.

Question 2 This is a straightforward question on constructing theoretical probabilities, together with practice of converting between fractions, decimals and percentages.

Question 3 This question involves comparing fractions to find which probability is greater. Part **b** does not require conditional probability and has an obvious answer when the question is read carefully.

Question 4 This question leads pupils through a probability experiment from looking at the number of trials in part **a**, finding the relative frequencies in part **b**, calculating the expected frequency in part **c**, and describing how to improve the experiment in part **d**. Encourage students to describe what they are doing in each part using these key words.

Questions 5 and **6** These questions describe two very interesting and similar probability experiments that can be managed in the classroom in a variety of ways. You may consider asking each student to do the experiment once and collect the class's results. The explanation for each part **b** could lead to some interesting discussions about infinite exhaustive events.

Simplification – Skills

Students could be given a prepared tree diagram for questions. Further examples of listing outcomes in this way may be necessary to cement understanding.

Extension – Skills

Students could be asked to complete further examples of three-stage tree diagrams where the probabilities are not equally likely.

Recap – Applications

1 A dice is thrown 200 times and the values shown each time were:

Score	1	2	3	4	5	6
Frequency	34	40	26	32	45	23

Write down the relative frequencies of scoring

a 4 (0.16)

b an even number (0.475)

c a prime number (0.555)

d higher than 3. (0.5)

Plenary – Applications

Draw six equal cards on the board. Ask for a suggestion for a number to write on card A. Repeat for cards B and C. Tell the students a number can be repeated. Gather suggestions to fill all the cards. Ask a question e.g. 'A card is picked at random, what is the probability it is a 5?' The student who answers your question sets the next question. This can be varied as 'What is the probability it is a 5 or a 2?' or an open-ended question, 'The probability is ½, what was the question?'

Exercise commentary – Applications

Question 1 Prepare for this question by considering a fair dice. Ask the students, 'Would you really expect one each of the numbers from 1 – 6 if a fair dice was thrown six times?' If they are not sure, get them to have a go.

Question 2 This question uses the same ideas as question **1** but gives students the opportunity to discuss the idea that the larger the number of trials, the closer the relative frequency is likely to be to the theoretical probability.

Question 3 This question does not rely on the fact that the sum of all possible outcomes must sum to one. Some students may be tempted to calculate the relative frequency of red first – as the relative frequencies do sum to one these students will get the correct answer but not understand the significance of part **a**. These students may benefit from an example where the relative frequencies do not sum to 1. Students could then be asked to draw possible spinners for both questions, the difference being in the second scenario that it would be possible to have a fourth colour on the spinner.

Question 4 This question links theoretical probability with experimental outcomes or experimental probability. You could get the students to look at the frequency distribution and then, in a general class discussion, talk about the characteristics of the dice which produced those results.

Question 5 Another good question for relating theoretical and experimental probability – ideas which are developed in the next section on expected frequency. In this question, focus on the fact that the spinner is fair and discuss the implications of this on the resultant frequency distribution when the spinner is spun a large number of times.

Question *6 An interesting question and one which may result in some fruitful group work. One of the key questions which have to be considered is, 'Can a sample of size 100 be considered large and therefore can we assume relative frequencies and probabilities will be close?' These are difficult ideas to come to grips with and the answer may be that 100 is not large enough to pick up the small effects which may be present here.

Simplification – Applications

Work on experiments with rolling a dice. In pairs, one rolling and one recording, students record on a tally chart their outcomes from 30 rolls. How close are their results to 5, 5, 5, 5, 5, 5? Add together the results from four (or more) pairs of students – are these close to 20, 20, 20, 20, 20, 20? Discuss the evidence that a larger number of experiments gives results closer to the theoretical outcomes.

Extension – Applications

Students could devise, carry out and decide how to record the experimental probabilities for their own experiment.

8.2 Expected outcomes

Objectives

① **P2** Apply ideas of randomness, fairness and equally likely events to calculate expected outcomes of multiple future experiments

Useful resources

(Fair) coins, spinners, dice, results from drawing pin experiment in **8.1**

Starter – Skills

Write these fractional statements on the board and ask students to identify the odd one out.

$\frac{1}{2}$ of 24 $\frac{2}{3}$ of 18 $\frac{1}{5}$ of 60 $\frac{3}{4}$ of 16 $\frac{1}{4}$ of 40

Ensure students understand how to find a fraction of an amount: they should divide by the denominator and then multiply by the numerator.

Teaching notes – Skills

① Discuss what calculation would be used to calculate 3 *lots of* 4 and recall that multiplication is used to calculate 'lots of'. Refer to the starter and highlight that $\frac{1}{4}$ *of* 24 is the same as $\frac{1}{4} \times 24$.

Show students a **fair** coin. Discuss the probability of it landing on tails. Highlight that when tossing a fair coin, heads and tails are **equally likely events**. Discuss how many times you would expect a tail to come up if the coin was tossed 100 times. Ask students to share their reasoning. Elicit that the probability of tails is $\frac{1}{2}$ (or 0.5) and $\frac{1}{2}$ of 100 is 50.

Discuss how many times you would expect a tail to come up if the coin was tossed 500 times, again asking students to share their reasoning. They should arrive at the fact that the probability of tails is $\frac{1}{2}$ (or 0.5) and that $\frac{1}{2}$ of 500 is 250.

Challenge students to generalise the relationship to a formula recalling the link between 'of' and multiplication:

expected frequency = probability × no. of trials

Highlight keywords and phrases: the **expected outcome** (or frequency) is the number of times you expect the outcome to happen; the number of **trials** is the number of times the activity is performed.

Refer to the final example in the student book and illustrate calculation of expected frequency with a non-unitary fraction, recalling the starter again.

Recall the drawing pin experiment carried out in **8.1** and display the cumulative results from the 150 class trials. Ask students how they could use this data to give an **estimated probability** for working out the expected number of heads in 1500 drops. Discuss responses and demonstrate working out the estimated probability as:

number of heads ÷ number of drops,

and the **expected outcome** (or frequency) as:

estimated probability × 1500.

Plenary – Skills

Set this problem for discussion: A set of cards is numbered from 20 to 49 inclusive. A card is picked at random. Ask: What is the probability that it...

is a multiple of 5?

contains the digit 3?

is a prime number? ($\frac{6}{30}$, $\frac{12}{30}$, $\frac{7}{30}$)

Mary says that if you pick a random card 45 times, you will get 18 threes. Is she correct? Explain.

(No. This is the expected frequency. Experimental frequency is unlikely to be the same when the number of experiments is small)

Exercise commentary – Skills

Questions 1 and **3** In these questions, and in subsequent ones, some elementary ideas related to theoretical probability must be considered first. Only then can the formula for expected frequency be used.

Question 2 Here students are predicting frequencies of outcomes based on probability. The relevant formula is given on page 150, expected frequency = number of trials × probability of the event.

Question 4 In this question students first need to spot that if the spinner is spun twelve times you might expect the yellow section to appear 5 times as there are 5 yellow sections.

Questions 5 to **8** Four straightforward questions where the probabilities of the relevant outcomes are given and the students have to simply apply the expected frequency formula.

Questions 9 and **10** It may be worth reminding students that percentages are simply numbers, 30% really is no different from 0.3 or 3/10. Probabilities can therefore be given as percentages, decimals and fractions.

Question 11 This is a tricky question because the students need to recall some number theory about prime numbers, etc.

Simplification – Skills

Students may need further practice at working out the probability of an event happening before moving on to the idea of expected outcomes.

Extension – Skills

Students could be given harder probabilities or numbers of trials to work with. They could consider what you would do if the expected frequency calculation gave a decimal rather than an integer.

Recap – Applications

1 **a** In a school, the probability of passing the cycling proficiency test is 74%.

50 students take the test. How many can be expected to pass? (37)

b A school bus arrives early twice a week (5 days). In a school year of 40 weeks how many times can the bus be expected to arrive early? (80)

c At Gatrow Airport the probability, per minute, of a plane landing between 7am and 9pm is 0.2 and 0.05 outside those times. How many planes are expected to land in any 24 hours? (198)

2 A magician has a pack of cards. The probabilities of drawing each suit are:

Spades	Hearts	Diamonds	Clubs
0.2	0.3	0.4	0.1

20 audience members pick a card at various times.

a How many Hearts are expected to be selected? (6)

b How many times is a card other than Diamonds expected to be selected? (12)

c The same suit is selected 4 times. Which suit is it most likely to be? (Spades)

Plenary – Applications

The angle of the red sector of this spinner is 52°. Asif, Bonny and Cleo each did an experiment to find the probability of the arrow landing in the red sector. Their results are shown.

	Asif	Bonny	Cleo
Red	16	9	29
Not red	84	51	171

Discuss these results: whose results are likely to be closest to the expected outcome? Why? Find the aggregated result and discuss whether this is a fair spinner. Encourage students to explain their decisions mathematically and succinctly.

Exercise commentary – Applications

Question 1 As with other questions, it is necessary to find the relevant probabilities. This question could be used to consolidate earlier ideas of experimental probability.

Question 2 The answer to part **b** of this question doesn't really matter – it is the discussion which it prompts which is important. For example, if the bottom of the box is bigger than the square, some counters will end up outside the square; if the bottom of the box and the square are of the same size, the walls of the box may affect the final position of the counters. In this context, it is the word 'random' which should be focused upon.

Question 5 This question provides an opportunity to introduce, without actually mentioning it by name, the idea of a weighted average. Why, for example, is it not acceptable to conclude that the proportion of fair haired students is 55%?

Question 6 In this question students need to spot that the angle of each shape at the centre determines the size of each section. If students are stuck encourage them to add up Aisha's probabilities to see if they sum to 1.

Question *7 The obvious mistake, and of course the main point of the question, is to assume that because the number of white balls is the same in each case, the number of appearances of white will be about the same. Students should be shown that probabilities, and therefore expected frequencies, depend upon proportions not numbers.

Question *8 A good opportunity to talk about gambling and the concept of a fair game!

Simplification – Applications

Students need to test their understanding of expected outcomes with simple questions, before dealing with sectors or ratios.

Extension – Applications

Students could be asked to sketch their own version of a spinner which would raise money for charity. They must balance a reasonable prospect of winning against the need to make a profit. Ask them to justify their design.

8.3 Theoretical probability

Objectives

① **P3** Relate relative expected frequencies to theoretical probability, using appropriate language and the 0–1 probability scale

② **P5** Understand that unbiased samples tend towards theoretical probability distributions with increasing sample size.

Useful resources

Dice, counters, 'bag of chance', identical bags (1 per group) of c. 20 multilink cubes in 3 or 4 different colours, mini whiteboards

Starter – Skills

Challenge students to give examples of events that are certain, impossible, likely, unlikely and evens (or '50:50'). Draw a 0–1 probability scale and ask students to place events on the scale; for example:

- You will win the lottery this weekend.
- Your teacher will live to be 308.
- You will eat potatoes tonight.

Teaching notes – Skills

① Write a selection of numbers on the board including fractions, decimals, negative numbers and numbers > 1. Ask students which of these can represent probabilities. Discuss answers, refer to the starter and re-emphasise that probability is expressed as a **number between 0 and 1**. Highlight that the larger the number, the more likely the event.

Check students' understanding of the words used in the starter. Ask students to draw and label a **probability scale**, marking on it the words from the starter as well as the numbers 0, $\frac{1}{2}$ and 1. Extend this by getting them to mark on suitable fractions for 'likely' and 'unlikely'. Share and discuss these fractions and the equivalent decimals for all the fractions used, highlighting that probability can equally well be expressed as a decimal. Ask students to draw and label a second 0–1 scale, and mark different dice-rolling outcomes on it, writing short justifications for their answers.

Place 5 counters, 4 red and 1 green, in a 'bag of chance'. Ask 'Do you expect the first counter to be pulled out to be red or green?'. List all the possible outcomes together. Highlight that the probability of the counter being red is 4 out of 5. Write this as a fraction $\left(\frac{4}{5}\right)$. Emphasise that numerator and denominator indicate the number of favourable outcomes and the *total* number of outcomes, respectively. Extend this by adding further counters of different colours to the 'bag of chance'.

② Give an identical bag of, say, 20 multilink cubes in three or four colours to each group of students. Tell students the total number of cubes and the number of colours. The task is to try to work out the number of each colour *without* emptying the bag.

Tell students to guess the numbers of each colour to start, and then carry out 5 trials with replacement, recording the colour each time. Ask for predictions again, and how sure they feel about them compared to their original guesses. Add the results of a further 5 trials to those of the first, and display them on a graph for each colour. Repeat the activity, asking for predictions and how sure students feel about them, until there is a level of sureness being expressed by the students – and indicated in the graph. Translate the results from experimental outcomes to estimated probability and then to work out the number of cubes of each colour. Finally, display the bag contents, and discuss. Elicit that the **greater the number of trials, the more reliable the estimate**.

Plenary – Skills

Place 2 red counters and 4 green into the 'bag of chance'. Offer students different answers for the probability of picking a red one: 2 (there are 2 reds), $\frac{2}{4}$ (2 reds and 4 greens) or $\frac{1}{3}$ (2 reds but 6 counters in total). Discuss which answer is correct and why. Highlight that:

- all probabilities must be between 0 and 1.
- the denominator represents the *total* number of outcomes.
- fractions should be simplified.

Exercise commentary – Skills

Question 1 Students may need reminding what square numbers and factors are.

Question 2 This is an important question because it is crucial to emphasise that the formula for theoretical probability given in this section applies only for equally likely outcomes. This question should be used as a prompt for discussion.

Question 3 This question tests understanding of logical possibilities. It also relies on the fact that the least number of black counters occurs when you have the least number of counters in total in the bag. If the probability of picking a green counter is $\frac{1}{4}$ at the start and then 2 green counters are picked then the least number of counters in the bag is 8.

Question 4 Here, students are using experimental data to calculate relative frequencies. For part **b**, remind students that using all of the available data will produce the best estimate.

Question 5 You could use this question to emphasise the idea that probabilities of 0 and 1 correspond to events which are impossible and certain, respectively. In part **b**, suggest to the students that, because each draw has two possible outcomes, even and odd, they must both have probabilities of $\frac{1}{2}$. If they fail to see the flaw in this argument, refer them to question **2**.

Question 6 This question requires calculating a relative frequency and updating the calculation repeatedly, including more data each time. It is possible to draw a graph of number of trials against relative frequency, and this can help explain the fact that an increase in number of trials will improve our probability estimate.

Question *7 A useful question for discussion, aiming for the conclusion that the best estimates come from using as much data as possible.

Simplification – Skills

Students should concentrate on listing (small) sets of possible outcomes; they may need further practice at this before proceeding to answer the follow-up questions. They could also be given copies of the probability scale in order to ensure focus on the actual questions.

Extension – Skills

Students could be given a 100 number square and asked to work out various probabilities; for example, 'what is the probability of a square number?' They could also be asked to think of a mathematical word and challenge a partner to work out the probabilities of a letter chosen at random being a vowel or a consonant.

Recap – Applications

1 Give a value between 0 and 1 for the probability of each of these events:

   a Selecting a Queen from a pack of cards. $\left(\frac{1}{13}\right)$

   b Selecting a faulty light bulb from a box containing 500 bulbs of which 410 are not faulty. $\left(\frac{9}{50}\right)$

2 Imelda has 25 pairs of shoes; 10 white, 8 blue, 5 red and 2 brown. She selects 2 pairs.
   Work out the probability that

   a they are both white $\left(\frac{10}{25}\times\frac{9}{24}=\frac{3}{20}\right)$

   b neither of them are white $\left(\frac{15}{25}\times\frac{14}{24}=\frac{7}{20}\right)$

   c the first pair is blue and the second brown $\left(\frac{8}{25}\times\frac{2}{24}=\frac{2}{75}\right)$

Explain your answer in each case.

Plenary – Applications

Show a spinner split into 10 equal sections. Invite students to shade the spinner in such a way that:

P(red) = 1 or P(red) = 0 or P(blue) = $\frac{1}{2}$ or P(blue) = $\frac{1}{10}$ or P(red) = $\frac{1}{5}$.

Exercise commentary – Applications

Question 1 This question provides a good opportunity to remind students how two-way table works. It is probably worth teaching students that, almost always in this context, it is helpful to put in the marginal totals and the grand total before even attempting the question.

Question 2 If students say that they can't solve this question, don't give any immediate help but refer them to the first worked example in the skills part of this section.

Question 3 Question **2** of this exercise involved experimental probability. The students should understand that this is a different type of problem – one involving **theoretical** probabilities. Ultimately, this comes down to a simple geometry problem.

Question 4 This question requires students to be able to calculate the area of a quarter circle. As an extension ask students to choose a point at random within the square (itself a good opportunity to discuss the practical problems of choosing points at random) 30 times and use the results to estimate the value of π.

Question 5 A straightforward problem involving equally-likely outcomes. This may be a good time to ask students why the balls should be mixed up well after they are put into one bag and before a ball is chosen. Encourage the students to give probabilities as fractions in their lowest terms.

Question 7 The key to this question is looking at the expected number of sectors for each colour. For both black and red the expected number of sectors is not a whole number, meaning that if the relative frequency is reliable the spinner is biased. Ask students to explain why the question is phrased as 'Explain why the spinner *could* be biased' rather than being definite. Hopefully students will respond that relative frequency is only an estimate of the probabilities and to get a more reliable estimate you need to do more trials.

Simplification – Applications

Students could practise answering more two-way table questions. They could also consider possible bias on a dice, given tables of results from 50 throws.

Extension – Applications

Students could carry out their own experiment with a dice (possibly biased with a bit of blu-tack) and work out the relative frequency of each outcome.

Mutually exclusive events

Objectives

① **P4** Apply the property that the probabilities of an exhaustive set of outcomes sum to 1

② **P4** Apply the property that the probabilities of an exhaustive set of mutually exclusive events sum to 1

Useful resources

'Bag of chance', green and yellow counters, red and blue balls, dice, mini whiteboards

Starter – Skills

Write the number 1 on the board. Spidering off it, write a fraction. Ask students for the fraction you would need to add to get to 1, and write the answer on the opposite 'leg'. Repeat with other fractions. Highlight that, to equal 1, the numerators added together equal the denominator. Once students are confident, extend to one-place decimals.

Teaching notes – Skills

① & ② Show students a 'bag of chance'. Say that there are 5 counters in the bag, some yellow and some green. Tell students that P(yellow) = $\frac{1}{5}$. Challenge them to give P(green) and justify their answer. Highlight that yellow + green = 5, since there are 5 counters in total. If P(yellow) = $\frac{1}{5}$ then there is 1 yellow, so there must be 4 greens. So P(green) = $\frac{4}{5}$. Link to the starter and highlight that $\frac{1}{5}+\frac{4}{5}=1$. Ensure students understand that:

- to add fractions with equal denominators, you just add the numerators.
- when the numerator and denominator are equal, the fraction is equivalent to a whole.

Repeat with 7 counters in the bag. Say P(green) = $\frac{5}{7}$. Challenge students to give P(not green).
Establish that P(not green) = P(yellow). Again, highlight that $\frac{5}{7}+\frac{2}{7}=1$.

Formalise: these are **mutually exclusive events**; that is, they cannot both happen at once.

Emphasise that if you know the probability that an event will occur, you can immediately find the probability that it will *not* occur: the two probabilities should **sum to 1**.

Elicit the simplest and best-known situation involving mutually exclusive events (tossing a fair coin), and challenge students to think of mutually exclusive events when rolling fair dice. Discuss the probability of each event and again highlight that they sum to 1. Extend this to thinking of events in the real world, for example: means of transport to school, weather conditions, hair colour, right-/left-handedness. Discuss different scenarios where these 'events' (in probability terms) may or may not be mutually exclusive, and may or may not cover all possible outcomes (be **exhaustive**).

Return to rolling fair dice. Challenge students to think of sets of two or more events that cover all possible outcomes, but are *not* mutually exclusive, for example: a prime number *vs*. a factor of 6.

Provide practice in calculating 'not' probabilities. Encourage students to focus less on the formal terminology and more on their intuitive understanding of each situation in practical terms.

Plenary – Skills

Write down an event with a given probability. Ask students to write and show the probability of the event *not* happening. Choose a few other events, giving values if necessary. Ask students to say their answers and use the opportunity to strengthen equivalence of fractions, decimals and percentages.

Exercise commentary – Skills

Questions 1 and **2** These questions can cause difficulties for students since they require careful, logical thinking. Get students to imagine the situations described. For example, in question **1** part **a** the student should ask whether it's possible to imagine a girl with red hair and brown eyes. If it is possible, the events are not mutually exclusive.

Question 3 The key to this question is for students to understand that, in this case, 'black' is the same as 'not green'. The A and not-A formula can then be applied.

Question 4 Students should understand that the possible outcomes, green, white or black, are mutually exclusive and exhaustive. Recognising this enables the probability distribution to be drawn. This question requires students to be able to add fractions with different denominators. You may need to consider preliminary work to ensure all students can cope with this.

Question 5 Students need to read the information carefully and make sure they fully understand which cards remain in the pack before answering the questions. The question is then fairly easy, assuming students are comfortable with definitions of multiples and primes.

Question 6 This question require use of the fact that the sum of probabilities of all possible outcomes is 1.

Question 7 This question is not difficult, but requires some knowledge of 2D and 3D shapes, together with careful reading of the relevant criteria.

Question 8 This question is fairly straightforward as soon as students realise that a team other than Olympic, United and City could win the league.

Simplification – Skills

Students should be given further opportunity to practise the basic skills. Avoid too much use of formal language and encourage the students to think about each situation in practical terms.

Extension – Skills

Set this question: In a class the probability of picking a student with green eyes is $\frac{1}{3}$, the probability of picking a boy is $\frac{1}{2}$ and the probability of picking either a girl or a student with green eyes is $\frac{3}{4}$. Are there any girls with green eyes?

Recap – Applications

1 Are these sets of events mutually exclusive?

a Getting a 1 or a 5 in one throw of a dice. (Yes)

b Getting a heads when a coin is tossed and a spade when a pack of cards is cut. (No)

c Getting two tails when two coins are tossed. (No)

Plenary – Applications

Display a situation where A and B are mutually exclusive events, with P(A) and P(B) both given, as well as any other known facts about the situation. Ask students to respond to questions such as: What is the probability of A or B happening? What is the probability of A or B not happening? What is the probability of neither happening?

Exercise commentary – Applications

Question 1 The two-way table should show the difference in each cell. It's worth commenting that the difference is the positive value since no order is suggested.

Questions 2 and **3** The key to these two questions is realising that the probabilities must sum to 1.

Question 4 This question requires use of the fact that the sum of probabilities of all possible outcomes is 1. It is an unusual question that will require careful reading.

Question 5 A good question which gets to the root of mutually exclusive events. If students are finding these ideas difficult, get them to think of the probabilities of obtaining an odd number, an even number and a 4 when a fair dice is thrown.

Questions 6 and **7** Theses two questions could be used for group work or discussion. They should help students to identify and practice the meanings of exhaustive and mutually exclusive. For some students, it may be necessary to introduce the concepts without actually using the words.

Question 8 Negative outcomes are possible in this question. Encourage students to check their work using their two-way table by looking at the patterns which exist in the table – mistakes should be glaringly obvious.

Question 9 This is a good question to reiterate the ideas about probability distributions and probabilities for mutually exclusive events.

Simplification – Applications

Use examples based on 'balls in a bag' to practise finding probabilities of picking any given colour and checking that the probabilities sum to 1. Then reverse the process by giving probabilities to work out how many balls of each colour are in the bag, Start with fractions that have the same denominator.

Extension – Applications

Students could collect some data about the class and use this to make statements about the probability and 'not'-probability of various outcomes.

8 Probability

<table>
<tr><th>Key outcomes</th><th>Quick check</th></tr>
<tr><td>P1 Record describe and analyse the frequency of outcomes of probability experiments using tables.</td><td>1 Kate counts the number of cars of different colours that pass her house one afternoon.
a What is the relative frequency of a white car? ($\frac{9}{30} = \frac{3}{10}$)
b The next day, 75 cars pass her house, how many would you expect to be red? (10)
<table><tr><th>Colour</th><th>Frequency</th></tr><tr><td>Black</td><td>7</td></tr><tr><td>Silver</td><td>4</td></tr><tr><td>White</td><td>9</td></tr><tr><td>Red</td><td>4</td></tr><tr><td>Other</td><td>6</td></tr></table></td></tr>
<tr><td>P2 Apply ideas of randomness, fairness and equally likely events to calculate expected outcomes of multiple future experiments.
P3 Relate relative expected frequencies to theoretical probability, using appropriate language and the 0 - 1 probability scale.
P5 <u>Understand that empirical unbiased samples tend towards theoretical probability distributions, with increasing sample size.</u></td><td>2 A dice is thrown 12 times and the number 6 occurs three times.
a What is the relative frequency of a 6? ($\frac{3}{12} = \frac{1}{4}$)
b What is the theoretical probability of a 6? ($\frac{1}{6}$)
c Is this a fair dice? Give your reason.
(Not enough trials have been done to be able to tell)
3 A bag contains 8 red, 3 blue and 2 orange counters. A counter is selected at random.
What is the probability the counter is
a red $\left(\frac{8}{13}\right)$ b blue or orange $\left(\frac{5}{13}\right)$
c white (0) d not black? (1)</td></tr>
<tr><td>P4 Apply the property that the probabilities of an exhaustive set of mutually exclusive events sum to one.</td><td>4 Lily walks to school 50% of the time and the rest of the time, she either cycles or gets the bus. The probability that she cycles is $\frac{1}{3}$
What is the probability that she gets the bus?
($1 - 50\% - \frac{1}{3} = \frac{1}{6}$)</td></tr>
</table>

Misconceptions and challenges	Solutions
When finding all the possible outcomes of a combination of events, students do not know how to check their work.	Encourage students to write down outcomes carefully using a table or listing systematically.
Students find the 'not rule' difficult to understand and will often add up the probabilities, rather than subtract from 1.	Give students plenty of practice with subtracting decimals and fractions from 1.
Students need to be able to convert accurately between different forms of probability.	Spend time converting between decimals, fractions and percentages.
Students need to know that experimental probabilities are used when an event is biased or in cases where the theoretical outcome is unknown.	Introduce experimental probability where the theoretical probability is unknown. Explain to students that you use relative frequency when the outcomes are not equally likely.
Students have great difficulty in creating, or judging the truth of, statements based upon results or probabilities.	Give students blocks of text that they can use in explanations: 'The expected probability is .... but the relative frequency was...'

Misconceptions and challenges	Solutions
Students misunderstand probabilities as ratios because of everyday language such as 'a 1 in 8 chance'.	Probability calculations should use fractions and decimals but it is worth showing students that the ratio of heads to tails is 1 : 1 and the probability of throwing a head is 0.5 or $\frac{1}{2}$.
Probability often involves dice experiments. This can be difficult for students who want to use decimals as they might mistakenly write $\frac{1}{6}$ as 0.6	Consolidate conversion between decimals and fractions, especially recurring decimals. Give students practice with a calculator and rounding their answer to different levels of accuracy.
Students become confused about when to add and when to multiply when asked to calculate probabilities using tree diagrams.	Discuss with students a way to remember why to multiply along the branches and add vertically.
When students are not confident in adding, multiplying and subtracting fractions, they will have significant difficulties solving probability problems.	Practice the different calculation methods in lessons and set homework on this topic.
Students will be familiar with probability problems involving dice, coins and spinners, but find problems set in unfamiliar contexts difficult.	Be adventurous in your choice of contexts and draw from everyday experiences.
When working out expected outcomes given a theoretical probability, students need to be able to calculate accurately using decimals and large numbers.	Challenge students to come up with the most efficient way of solving a calculation. For example, 0.95×4000 $= 4000 - 0.05 \times 4000$ $= 4000 - \frac{1}{20} \times 4000 = 4000 - 200 = 3800$.

Review question commentary

Ideally, students should give theoretical probabilities as fractions and relative frequencies as decimals.

Question 1 (**8.1**) – The total number of ladybirds sampled is 50.

Question 2 (**8.2**) – Students need to use the fact that the relative frequencies should add up to 1.

Question 3 (**8.3**) – Discuss what is meant by 'unbiased'. What would you expect to happen if the dice was biased?

Question 4 (**8.3**) –The answers to parts **b** and **c** should be given as 0 and 1 respectively, not as fractions (e.g. $\frac{0}{10}, \frac{10}{10}$).

Question 5 (**8.3**) – Discuss what the term 'fair' means in this context. Students should write out all the possible (equally likely) outcomes.

Questions 6 and **7** (**8.3, 8.4**) – Students must use the fact that these events are mutually exclusive and exhaustive and so sum to 1.

Review answers

1 **a** 0.4 **b** 120

2 **a** 0.2 **b** 24

3 **a** 0.1 **b** $\frac{1}{6}$ **c** about $0.16 \approx \frac{1}{6}$

4 **a** $\frac{3}{10}$ **b** 0 **c** 1

5 0.25

6 $\frac{8}{11}$

7 **a** $\frac{2}{7}$ **b** $\frac{4}{7}$

65 marks

Assessment 8

Question 1 – 1 mark
No, this is unlikely but not impossible. [B1]
Must see a reason.

Question 2 – 2 marks
P(H) = 0.5 [B1]
Because each throw is an independent event. [B1]

Question 3 – 2 marks
(14 + 22 + 15) ÷ 100 [M1]
0.51 [A1]

Question 4 – 3 marks
a 200 [1600 ÷ 8] [B1]
b 2 [14 ÷ 8 = 1.75 → 2] [B1]
c 4 [34 ÷ 8 = 4.25 → 4] [B1]

Question 5 – 8 marks
a 2 × 0.2 + (0.14 + 0.26 + 0.22) = 0.4 + 0.62 = 1.02
If x = 0.2 then the total probability = 1.02 > 1 [B1]
$2x + 0.62 = 1$ [M1]
$x = 0.19$ [A1]
b 52 [200 × 0.26] [B1]
c 200 ×(0.19 + 0.26 + 0.19) [M1]
= 128 [A1]
d 200 ×(0.14 + 0.26 + 0.19) [M1]
= 118 [A1]

Question 6 – 5 marks
a Estimate = total number of pea seeds ÷ total number of seeds [M1]
i (5 + 5 + 8 + 3 + 6) ÷ (5 × 30) = 27 ÷ 150
= 0.18 [A1]
ii 51 ÷ (10 × 30) = 51 ÷ 300
= 0.17 [A1]
b The sample with more packets. [M1]
Ben's [A1]

Question 7 – 3 marks
a 4 ÷ 20 = 0.2 or $\frac{1}{5}$ [B1]
b (4 + 4) ÷ (20 – 4) [M1]
= 0.5 or $\frac{1}{2}$ [A1]

Question 8 – 2 marks
Number of tuna packets ÷ 30 = 0.3 [M1]
9 packets [A1]

Question 9 – 4 marks
a P(Late) = 1 – (0.18 + 0.31) [M1]
= 0.51 > 0.49
Yes [A1]
b 225 × 0.31 [M1]
= 69.75
→70 [A1]

Question 10 – 9 marks
a $\frac{3}{25}$ or 0.12 [B1]
b $\frac{2}{25}+\frac{9}{50}+\frac{3}{50}$ [M1]
$\frac{16}{50}=\frac{8}{25}$ or 0.32 [A1]
c $\frac{2}{25}+\frac{1}{25}+\frac{3}{50}+\frac{1}{10}$ [M1]
$\frac{14}{50}=\frac{7}{25}$ or 0.28 [A1]
d $\frac{3}{50}+\frac{4}{25}+\frac{1}{25}+0+\frac{1}{25}+\frac{7}{50}$ [M1]
$\frac{22}{50}=\frac{11}{25}$ or 0.44 [A2]
e P(Blue 4) = 0 [B1]

Question 11 – 7 marks
Answers must be fractions in their simplest form.
a 40 ÷ (40 +10 + 40 +10) = 40 ÷ 100
$\frac{2}{5}$ [B1]
b (10 + 10) ÷ 100 [M1]
$\frac{1}{5}$ [A1]
c (40 + 10) ÷ 100 [M1]
$\frac{1}{2}$ [A1]
d (10 + 40 + 10) ÷ 100 [M1]
$\frac{3}{5}$ [A1]

Question 12 – 12 marks
a i 102 is red and a multiple of 3. [M1]
No [A1]
ii 5 is blue and prime. [M1]
No [A1]
iii No white numbers are multiples of 7 [M1]
Yes [A1]
b i 81 is red and a multiple of 3. [M1]
No [A1]
ii 29 is blue and prime. [M1]
No [A1]
iii 84 is white and a multiple of 7. [M1]
No [A1]

Question 13 – 2 marks
Sunny and snowing are not mutually exclusive. [M1]
No [A1]

Question 14 – 5 marks
a Interior angle of pentagon = 180° – 360° ÷ 5
= 108° [B1]
Triangle angle = 360° – 90° – 90° – 108° [M1]
= 72° [A1]
P(blue) = 72 ÷ 360
= 0.2 or $\frac{1}{5}$ [B1]
b You have assumed that all angles are equally likely to be chosen. [B1]

Measures and accuracy

Learning outcomes

G14 Use standard units of measure and related concepts (length, area, volume/capacity, mass, time, money, etc.).

N13 Use standard units of mass, length, time, money and other measures (including standard compound measures) using decimal quantities where appropriate.

N14 Estimate answers; check calculations using approximation and estimation, including answers obtained using technology.

N15 Round numbers and measures to an appropriate degree of accuracy (e.g. to a specified number of decimal places or significant figures) use inequality notation to specify simple error intervals due to truncation or rounding.

N16 Apply and interpret limits of accuracy [including upper and lower bounds].

R1 Change freely between related standard units (e.g. time, length, area, volume/capacity, mass) and compound units (e.g. speed, rates of pay, prices) in numerical [and algebraic] contexts.

R11 Use compound units such as speed, [rates of pay, unit pricing,] density [and pressure].

Prior knowledge

Check-in skill

- Multiply and divide decimals by 10, 100, 1000.
- Accurately read divisions on a scale.
- Solve problems involving multiplication.

Online resources

MyMaths 1002, 1004, 1005, 1006, 1043, 1067, 1121, 1246, 1932, 1933

InvisiPen videos

Skills: 09Sa – f Applications: 09Aa – d

Kerboodle assessment

Online Skills Test 9 Chapter Test 9

Development and links

Construction, engineering, surveying, science, sport, design and technology all rely heavily on measurement. Inaccurate measurements could lead to a compromise in the strength of a structure or to incorrect ranking of competitors. Length and area are used throughout daily life, for example to calculate the number of rolls of wall paper required to decorate a room, the length of fencing required for a garden or the size of a carpet to cover a floor.

Chapter investigation

Using base ten for units of time was advocated because using decimals made calculations easier. The system was used briefly in France during 1793-4. The decimal system of time used ten decimal hours in a day, one hundred decimal minutes in an hour and one hundred decimals seconds in a minute: giving one decimal second equals 0.864 seconds. The French republican calendar also introduced twelve months each of three *decades* – ten day weeks (plus five or six complimentary days at the years end).

Suppose a machine produces 273 widgets an hour. Ask students to calculate how many it produces per day, per week and per month. Supposing decimal time these calculations are easy but not so if there are 24 hours in a day, 7 days in a week and between 28 and 31 days in a month.

Show how the later calculations can be made easier by using rounding to approximate the numbers by ones which are easier to calculate with: $273 \times 7 \approx 200 \times 10 \approx 2000$ (exact 1911). Develop the idea of using approximations to estimate answers [**9.1**].

Calculators are the obvious tool to use when faced by 'complex' calculations: take the opportunity to develop students' confidence using calculators [**9.2**]; emphasise how estimates provide a check of working An interesting problem, in non-metric time, is to convert one million seconds into days, hours, minutes and seconds.

Expand the discussion of metric units to those for length, mass and capacity/volume together with compound units such as speed and density [**9.3**].

9.1 Estimation and approximation

Objectives

① **N15** Round numbers to an appropriate degree of accuracy

② **N14** Estimate answers; check calculations using approximation and estimation

Useful resources

Place value table, mini whiteboards, estimation game (e.g. Maths in Schools, Resource Bank (MA) or DCSF Course Handbook for Part 1 Planning and Teaching HB 3.3; DCSF Y9 Booster Kit resource sheet M4.1) with counters and cards, A4 paper in various colours, calculators

Starter – Skills

Display a calculation and answer as the centre of a spider diagram on the board:

$32.4 \times 0.35 = 11.34$

Give one equivalent statement, $3.24 \times 3.5 = 11.34$, as a leg. Ask students to record others using whiteboards. Add some to the display. Now extend to related statements by adding a leg from an offered equivalent statement, say $3.24 \times 7 = 22.68$

Ask students for other related calculations and add some of these to the display.

Teaching notes – Skills

① and ② Refer to the starter and discuss how **rounding** can be used to approximate difficult calculations and check answers. Recap the rules of rounding, using an example. Write a number on the board, e.g. 8458, and discuss how to round it to the nearest 10, 100 and 1000. Highlight the relevant place value 'decider' (to round up or round down), eliciting that this is the *next* place value digit after the rounding digit. Extend this to decimals. Refer to examples to extend to **estimating calculations** using rounding. Discuss using an **appropriate degree of accuracy**, reminding students that they should choose approximate values that are easier to evaluate mentally. Organise pairs of students to play the estimation game. Show an **estimation of a calculation**, using one significant figure only. Make sure the estimation really represents 'thinking out loud'. Repeat with another calculation, this time asking students to offer reasons for your choice of, for example, 20 rather than 16. For consolidation, students should **match calculations to answers** by estimating. Encourage students to work in pairs, and to demonstrate the estimation stages by recording on coloured A4 paper that can be displayed, compared and discussed later in the lesson.

Plenary – Skills

Discuss some of the questions and focus on appropriate accuracy to obtain an estimate.

Exercise commentary – Skills

Questions 1 and **2** Drill in rounding numbers to a specified accuracy. Some students will be less confident in using significant figures, particularly in amounts such as in question **1g** and **1h**. a common error is to just give an answer with a single digit – students should appreciate that they will need to include zeros before the decimal point, to preserve place value.

Question 3 Students are required to estimate answers to multiplication and division calculations, with a specified accuracy. Ensure that they appreciate the distinction between decimal places and significant figures. Also ensure that they are not calculating it accurately, and then rounding at the end – that's not the point of this exercise.

Questions 4 to **7** Practice in estimating answers to decimal calculations, involving a mixture of arithmetical operations including powers and roots. No accuracy is specified – 1 sf is a good rule of thumb, but in some (mostly division) problems it may yield easier numbers to use a different estimate. In question **7**, students should be careful with order of operations.

Questions 8 to **10** A mixture of calculations involving square roots. These can be rather laborious, because even though they are estimates, they involve long multiplication. Students should be aware of the square numbers, so $\sqrt{26}$ would be a little bit more than 5; if $\sqrt{9}$ is 3 and $\sqrt{16}$ is 4, then $\sqrt{13}$ would be about halfway. In question **10d**, the square roots are close to square numbers.

Question 11 It will help to know how to multiply and divide by powers of 10, which is a useful technique in estimation. So dividing by 0.05 will be like dividing by 5 and then multiplying by 100. Alternatively use fractions, if students recognise 0.05 as 1/20.

Question 12 Estimation in a mundane context – some students will find it as easy to just work this out.

Question 13 Here is an example of where it doesn't make sense to round each number to 1 sf (the denominator should round to the nearest 10).

Simplification – Skills

Students should be given further opportunities to practise rounding, initially to given powers of 10, then to decimal places and significant figures, starting with one dp and one sf.

Extension – Skills

Students could be given further examples of calculations where rounding is appropriate. Providing examples where the answer is not given and students are required to work out their own estimates could also be used.

Recap – Applications

1 Round these numbers to the specified number of significant figures:

	1 sf	2 sf	3 sf
406 738			
646			
52.09			
0.612			
0.008971			

Answer:

	1 sf	2 sf	3 sf
406 738	400 000	410 000	407 000
646	700	650	646
52.09	50	52	52.1
0.612	0.6	0.61	0.612
0.008971	0.009	0.0090	0.00897

2 These statements are all incorrect.

Rewrite them correctly.

a 452 to the nearest 10 is 45

(452 to the nearest 10 is 450)

b 2495 to the nearest 100 is 2400

(2495 to the nearest 100 is 2500)

c 2.03 to 1 sf is 2

(2.03 to 1 sf is 2.0)

d 0.0234 to 2 sf is 0.02

(0.0234 to 2 sf is 0.023)

3 **Estimate** the value, to the nearest whole number of this calculation. Use your calculator to check your accuracy. Write your calculator results to 3 sf.

$$\frac{9.8^2 - 2.7\times 3.7^2}{9.62+3.33}$$

(4456)

Plenary – Applications

Use a statement where a wrong but close answer is offered to a simple problem. For example, $3.1 \times 0.42 = 13.02$

Ask students to discuss in pairs how they know it must be wrong and why. Share some of the comments and use them to reinforce the ideas of multiplying or dividing by numbers greater or less than 1 and the results. Highlight the importance of looking out for these 'clues' when estimating and checking answers.

Exercise commentary – Applications

Question 1 This is a standard estimation in order to convert between metric and imperial. Students may be uncomfortable in saying whether something is a good estimate or not – they may think that if it's not accurate, then it's not the right answer. Use it as a discussion point — it may be better to say 1 inch = 2.5 cm.

Question 2 In problems like this, students should appreciate that they will need to round up to ensure that there's enough for the job, even if there's lots left over.

Questions 3 and **4** Further practice in mental estimation, but including whether an estimate is likely to be under or over the real answer. This is a little bit trickier with division. In question **4**, students should try to suggest the simple mistake that Mark has made.

Question 5 here is another real-life problem involving metric-imperial conversion. It is really important to read the question carefully, and questions like this have occurred in past exams – in this case, it's how many *complete* jars that are important.

Question 6 Similar to question **4**, students are required to comment on given estimates, and suggest ways in which to improve them. Part **iii** is given as a fraction – discuss why it could be useful to leave it like this.

Questions 7 to **9** Real-life problems involving estimation in a variety of contexts. Beware of language issues, such as in question **9** where the word 'diesel' appears in **b**.

Question 10 This is a good example of what is referred to as 'Fermi estimation', similar to 'how many footsteps will you take today'. This provides a great opportunity for lots of good maths, including providing a model for the size of a jellybean.

Simplification – Applications

Students should be given more practice rounding to one significant figure before attempting to estimate the answers to calculations. Keep the calculations themselves simple.

Extension – Applications

Ask students to calculate the actual value of some of the examples. They could then try and work out the percentage error in their estimates.

9.2 Calculator methods

Objectives

ⓘ**N14** Estimate answers; check calculations using approximation and estimation, including answers obtained using technology.

Useful resources

Scientific calculators

Starter – Skills

Invite students to match each calculation with its correct answer:

$4 + 3 \times 5$	Answers:	12, 19, 35
$(4 + 2)^2 \times 2$		72, 16, 12
$3(4 + 1) + 4^2$		31, 29, 51

Ensure students recall the order of operations BIDMAS; Brackets, Indices, Division, Multiplication, Addition, Subtraction

Teaching notes – Skills

Provide students with scientific calculators and invite them to type in $4 + 3 \times 5$. Highlight that the scientific calculator follows the order of operations automatically. Highlight that calculators can enable more complex calculations to be done quickly. Ask students how many people have ever phoned a wrong telephone number. Highlight that mistakes can be made inputting values and link this to calculator use. Emphasise that estimation is always a good checking tool.

Work through the examples in the student book, inviting students to evaluate each calculation using their calculators. Encourage students to check their work using an approximated calculation.

Ensure students:

- Can find the bracket buttons and recall use of the x^2 button
- Check the display of the calculator to check the input
- Recognise the hidden brackets of a division and understand that these must be inputted into the calculator.

Discuss how to round the answers to 1 decimal place. Ensure students recall the second decimal place as the decider digit, indicating whether to round up or down. Discuss rounding the answer to an appropriate degree of accuracy, asking students to consider the degree of accuracy of the values in the question. Finally, discuss the rounding of a value where a 'double rounding' is required, for example 1.98 (1 dp). Link to 'carrying' a ten in addition and highlight that the answer must have 1 decimal place, for example 2.0.

Plenary – Skills

Refer to the calculations in one or more of the questions. Work through the answers, pointing out any areas where students went wrong. Discuss values used to estimate each calculation. Encourage students to consider making the approximate calculation as easy as possible to evaluate.

Exercise commentary – Skills

Questions 1 to **3** These questions provide drill practice in using a calculator to work out decimal calculations. Encourage students to estimate the answer first – there may be some resistance to this. In questions **2** and **3**, ensure that students use the correct order of operations.

Question 4 provides practice at calculating with time using a calculator, for which it is worth looking at the last example in the student book. Many students will not find this easy, and you might want to go through it as a class.

Question 5 Students are required to round their answer to 2 significant figures – ensure that they don't round the numbers in the question beforehand.

Questions 6 and **7** These are harder calculations involving division, but also including brackets and powers. Students could do this all in one go using brackets, or they could use the memory functions on their calculator (often quite different for different makes of calculator). Some students will want to work out top and bottom separately, writing down the answer to each.

Question 8 This is an interesting launchpad for an investigation into the Golden Ratio.

Simplification – Skills

Students may need lots of practice at using their calculators for simple calculations. Avoid hidden brackets and complex decimals.

Extension – Skills

Students could be invited to work out what other buttons on their calculator do. An example could be the factorial key ($x!$) that works out the product of all of the counting numbers from 1 up to x.

Recap – Applications

1 Use your calculator to work out the values, to 4 significant figures where necessary, of

a $(19.9 + 86.2) \times (1.34 - 0.766)$ (60.90)

b $\frac{3454+213.67}{(1.33+0.965)^2}$ (8.388)

2 Use your calculator to convert:

a 4 325 seconds into hours, minutes and seconds (1 hour, 12 min and 5 sec)

b 4 325 minutes into days, hours and minutes (3 days, 0 hours and 5 min)

c 4 325 days into years, weeks and days (11 years, 45 weeks and 6 days)

d 4 325 weeks into years and weeks. (Ignore leap years) (83 years and 9 weeks)

Plenary – Applications

This short exercise uses approximation to check answers found on a calculator. Students need to decide if these deductions are true or false. If false, they need to work out the correct values.

Fact	Deduction
1 km = 0.621 miles	52.5 km ≈ 33 miles
1 ounce = 28.3 grams	320 grams ≈ 110 ounces
£46 = 63 Euros	£599 ≈ 8200 Euros
1 sq foot = 0.093 m^2	108 m^2 ≈ 1200 sq feet

Exercise commentary – Applications

Question 1 Practice at using estimation to check an answer. It also hints at the fact that mistakes are often made when brackets are put in the wrong place, or calculations done in the wrong order.

Question 2 There is lots of information here, and it would be a mistake to just pick up a calculator and just punch the numbers in. Encourage students to write down the calculations that need to be made (RTQ and decide what to do), then perform a quick estimate, and then they can use their calculator.

Question 3 Again lots of information is given here so do encourage students to write down the calculations that need to be done. It may be a good idea to go through this together.

Question 4 None of the calculations give an answer that is exactly zero (but A is close to zero); similarly with the whole numbers.

Question 5 This is a fairly standard comparison of mobile phone offers, which should be a context of relevance to students. It is important that they get a feel for when a calculator method is more appropriate than a written or mental method – here it is clearly much more appropriate to use a calculator. Ensure that in part **b**, students use a clear coherent argument.

Question 6 This uses a formula that some students will find daunting. A common error will be to extend the square root over the whole numerator. In part **b**, it will be a good idea to jot down the actual calculation that is needed, ensuring correct order of operations, before reaching for the calculator.

Simplification – Applications

Students may need some help in extracting the calculation from the more complex problems and should be given more questions with minimal context. For example:

Estimate, then use your calculator to decide which of these calculations are correct:

$(5.7 \times 2.2) - (11.9 \div 3.5) = 9.14$ (yes)

$4.4 \div 1.6 + 2.8 = 10$ (no)

Extension – Applications

Use the formula for the distance, in metres, travelled in time t seconds, $s = \frac{1}{2}gt^2$, with $g = 9.81\text{ms}^{-2}$.

Ask students to find approximate values of s when

i $t = 0.52$ s

ii $t = 7.95$ s

and then work out exact values on their calculators.

Check they are working out gt^2 and not $(gt)^2$.

9.3 Measures and accuracy

Objectives

① **G14** Use standard units of measure and related concepts

② **N15** Round numbers and measures to an appropriate degree of accuracy

③ **N16** Apply and interpret limits of accuracy

Useful resources

Number line, place value table, mini whiteboards, rulers, everyday objects/containers

Starter – Skills

Invite students to write different metric units of measurement for mass, length and capacity and their abbreviations on the board in a table (headed mass/length/capacity). Note any suggested imperial measurements, but focus mainly on metric and highlight the link between metric measurements and the whole decimal system. Show a line with five equal intervals marked. Write different start and end numbers, e.g. 0–5, 10–60. Ask students to establish the size of each interval. Discuss strategies.

Teaching notes – Skills

① Following on from the starter, ask students to work in pairs to put the collected **units of measurement** from each heading in order of size from smallest to largest. Explore students' knowledge of metric prefixes and their meanings, including the possible confusion between milli- $\left(\frac{1}{1000}\right)$ and kilo- (1000). Highlight that you can use these prefixes to help remember the relationships between different units of measurement. Ask students to give examples of objects with estimated lengths of 1 cm, 1 mm, 1 m, etc. Discuss what units you would use to measure:

- The width of a paperclip (mm)
- The leaning tower of Pisa (m)
- The length of a mountain range (km)
- The length of a pencil (cm)

Extend to discussing units of mass and capacity, including their relative size. Discuss what units you would use to measure:

- The mass of a computer (kg)
- A feather (mg)
- A bus (tonnes)
- The capacity of a cup of tea (cl)
- A water droplet (ml)
- A barrel of oil (l)

②Ask students how accurately they can measure a line of approx. 6 cm. Can they measure it to the nearest mm? What difference would it make if the line was approx. 6 m? If they were measuring the length of a garden path, would they need to know the exact length to a mm? a cm? a m? How about the distance from home to school? In a practical situation, we have to decide about the degree of accuracy we require for a particular purpose and be realistic about how accurate our measurements can be. When we are told some measurements in an applications question, their accuracy will tell us how accurate the answer can be. If the length of a rectangular lawn is given as 4.8 m and the width as 2.6 m, then the area cannot be worked out to more than one decimal place with any accuracy.

③ Discuss where we see scales in real life. Highlight that most scales have major values sub-divided into smaller divisions (intervals). Consider the readings of various scales by addition or counting on in multiples of the smaller divisions. Highlight that any measurement might not be exact but given to the **nearest value**. Highlight the link to rounding to emphasise that **inaccuracy** may be up to a half of the division in either direction. Use a ruler to highlight that actual measurements of both 4.6 cm and 5.3 cm might both be rounded to 5 cm.

Plenary – Skills

Ask groups of students to recall and record conversion rules between the standard sets of metric units for length, mass and capacity, using multiplication and division by 10, 100 and 1000.

Then pose one or more problems involving writing values correctly and rounding values accurately.

Exercise commentary – Skills

Question 1 Students are expected to identify an appropriate metric unit to measure a particular quantity.

Question 2 Students should memorise the equivalences in the yellow panel, and be able to confidently convert between metric units of length, mass and capacity.

Questions 3 to **5** These questions focus on average speed, which is revisited in the section on compound units. In question **3**, students will need to think carefully about the compound units they decide to use.

Questions 6 to **9** These questions focus on density, which is again revisited later (chapter 22) when dealing with compound units. Students need to take care in giving the units in their answers, as this will vary. There is an inverse calculation to be done in **8b**.

Questions 10 and **11** Students often don't like error intervals and limits of accuracy. In question **10a**, assume the accuracy is given to 1 dp etc (this is implied accuracy). Question **11** is effectively asking the same thing as question **10**, just using different terminology.

Simplification – Skills

Give plenty of practice at conversions. Students may also need more questions on speed, using the S, D, T triangle to help them to remember the correct formula. Keep the wording very straightforward.

Extension – Skills

Students could be asked to work out the maximum and minimum areas of a rectangle in which both side lengths are given to the nearest centimetre.

Recap – Applications

1 Which units would you use to measure the
 - **a** length of grain of rice (mm)
 - **b** mass of a car (kg)
 - **c** capacity of a wine glass (ml)
 - **d** capacity of a bath (l)
 - **e** mass of a golf ball (g)
 - **f** distance from Paris to Rome (km)

2 The International Space Station travels for a day at an average speed of 7.66 km/s.
How many km has it flown? (661 824 km)

3 An iron ball has a radius of 20 cm and a density of 7.874g/cm^3. The formula for the volume of a sphere is $V = \frac{4}{3}\pi r^3$. What is the mass of the ball to the nearest kg? (264 kg)

Plenary – Applications

Read out the following conversions slowly, telling students to write True or False for each one.

1. 10 km ≈ 16 miles
2. There are 1000 millilitres in 1 litre
3. A car travels 95 miles in 5 hours. Its average speed is 19 mph.
4. A van travels 60 miles at an average speed of 36 mph. This takes 1½ hours.
5. A speed of 36 km/h is the same as a speed of 10 m/s

(F, T, T, F, T)

Exercise commentary – Applications

Question 1 Calculation involving time – students might prefer to work out the travelling time in minutes, then add to the start time.

Questions 2 and **3** Calculations involving speed, and unit conversion. In question **2**, students should be aware that m stands for metres, not miles.

Question 4 This is a problem involving metric-imperial conversion. Ensure that students read the question properly (particularly the crucial phrase 'at least').

Question 5 This is an error interval problem involving subtraction. It will be a good idea to go through this as a class, as a common mistake will be to neglect to find the error intervals for each of the two numbers.

Questions 6 to **8** These are mixed problems involving calculation, estimation, interpreting a calculator display in the context of the problem, and giving reasoning. It is important that students know when to round down or to round up when giving their final answer (in question **7**, they should clearly round down).

Question 9 Students need to convert miles per litre into miles per gallon (which is still usually quoted as a measure of fuel efficiency for a car). Ensure that students can give a clear concise argument for part **b**.

Simplification – Applications

Students should be given plenty of questions with relatively easy numbers and a limited context to gain confidence.

Extension – Applications

Working in pairs, students could write their own questions. Each of them devises a new question, works out the answer and then gives it to their partner to solve.

9 Measures and accuracy

Key outcomes	Quick check
N13 Use standard units of mass, length, time, money and other measures (including standard compound measures) using decimal quantities where appropriate.	**1** cm^2 m *cl* mm^3 g Choose from the cloud a unit of **a** length (m) **b** volume (mm^3) **c** capacity (*cl*) **d** mass (g) **e** area. (cm^2) **2** Simon stars cycling at 09:50 and continues for 85 minutes, at what time does he stop? (11:15) **3** Convert these measurements to kg. **a** 165 g (0.165 kg) **b** 1.5 t (17.5 kg) **c** 17500 g (1500 kg) **d** 1 000 000 mg (1 kg)
N14 Estimate answers; check calculations using approximation and estimation, including answers obtained using technology.	**4** Estimate the answers to these calculations. **a** 28 ÷ 10.3 (3) **b** $\frac{35}{\sqrt{3.8}}$ (20)
N15 Round numbers and measures to an appropriate degree of accuracy (e.g. to a specified number of decimal places or significant figures) use inequality notation to specify simple error intervals due to truncation or rounding. N16 Apply and interpret limits of accuracy.	**5** Round each of these numbers to **i** 3 sf **ii** 2 sf **iii** 1 sf. **a** 28 791 (28 800, 29 000, 30 000) **b** 723.89 (724, 720, 700) **c** 0.007 821 (0.007 82, 0.0078, 0.008) **d** 0.9057 (0.906, 0.91, 0.9) **6** A line of length x is measured to the nearest mm and found to be 5 cm. Write an inequality to show the range of possible lengths of the line. ($4.95 \le x < 5.05$)
G14 Use standard units of measure and related concepts (length, area, volume/capacity, mass, time, money, etc.).	**7** Potatoes cost 90p per kg. **a** How much will 600 g of potatoes cost? (54p) **b** What mass of potatoes will cost £2.25? (2.5 kg) **8** Alisha takes 30 minutes to walk home at a speed of 4 km/h, how far does she walk? (2 km)

Misconceptions and challenges	Solutions
Students often forget if there are 10, 100 or 1000 smaller units in the larger unit.	Centimetres cause the metric system to seem more confusing than it really is. Demonstrate how the rule for most metric conversions is multiply or divide by 1000. Discuss why we use cm if it causes such problems.
Students may not see that the number of decimal places used varies for different units of measure. Students might always want to use 2 dp.	Students are familiar with using 2 dp for money. Make sure you ask for answers to different numbers of decimal places for an exercise – even up to 10 dp. Students will then be able to write 15.3 mm as 0.0153 m and even 0.000 015 300 0 km.

Misconceptions and challenges	Solutions
Volume and capacity are difficult concepts to grasp intuitively. For example, quantities of liquids are very difficult to estimate.	Tackle this misconception practically. Use different shape containers to contain the same amount of water. Make predictions about what will fit and then observe the results.
Students face a fundamental problem if they do not have an understanding of the physical measurements they are working with. They will be unable to check if an answer is realistic, or get a sense of how to understand a problem.	All students benefit from practical experimentation, including holding kg weights, measuring in litres and ml, and investigating how units of $1 cm^3$ fit into different size cuboids. Use a range of standard and non-standard measures to increase understanding. A classic experiment is to estimate how many chocolate bars would fill the classroom.
Students are often very reluctant to make estimations or approximations, as they seem to be wrong.	Give situations in which it is hardly fathomable that someone would calculate exactly. Perhaps a footballer earns £234 129.63 a month. Are they really going to be worried about that 63 pence?
Using inequality notation in relation to rounding, students often don't spot occasions where a '≤' ought to be used.	Introduce this symbol in the context of expressing the rule for rounding (round down if <5, round up if ≥ 5) as a way of saving effort. Discuss how mathematical symbols save time and confusion (rather than the opposite!)

Review question commentary

Students need to know the correct shorthand notation for units of length, area, volume, time, speed and capacity. Use calculators where necessary.

Question 1 (9.1) – Remind students that the first significant figure is never zero.

Questions 2 and **3 (9.1, 9.2) –** Students should round to 1 significant figure.

Question 4 (9.3) – Volume and capacity could be seen as interchangeable.

Question 5 (9.3) – Use fact that 1 m = 100 cm = 1000 mm.

Question 6 (9.3) – Students must state units with their answers.

Question 7 (9.3) – Students should first write 300 minutes as 5 hours. Answer should not say 72.5. Units should be included.

Question 8 (9.3)– Students should use the fact that 0.5 km is 500 m, so calculation needed is 500 ÷ 20. Units should be included.

Question 9 (9.3) – Students need to learn the formula for density.

Question 10 (9.3) – Check that the strict inequality is in the correct place.

Question 11 (9.3) – Students can find the difference of the two masses to find that the measurement was to the nearest kg.

Review answers

1 a i 8 750 **ii** 8 800 **iii** 9 000
  b i 15.0 **ii** 15 **iii** 20
  c i 0.0682 **ii** 0.068 **iii** 0.07
  d i 0.509 **ii** 0.51 **iii** 0.5

2 a 200 **b** 103 **c** 5.5 **d** 4

3 a 8, 8.114 056 225 **b** 80, 81.312
  c 1, 1.052 060 738 **d** 300, 255.903 591 7

4 a cm **b** cm^3 **c** litres **d** kg **e** m^2

5 a 3.5 m **b** 0.145 m **c** 200 m **d** 9.32 m

6 1 hour 52 minutes / 112 minutes

7 a £72.50 **b** 9.5 hours/ 9 hours 30 minutes

8 a 5 seconds **b** 25 seconds

9 a 5 g/cm^3 **b i** 27 cm^3 **ii** 3 cm

10 $89.5 \leq x < 90.5$

11 The nearest kg.

Assessment 9

Question 1 – 6 marks

a 3.23 (3 sf) [B1]
b 29 (2 sf) [B1]
c 0.2 (1 sf) [B1]
d 310 (nearest 10) [B1]
e 5700 (nearest 100) [B1]
f 256 000 (nearest 1000) [B1]

Question 2 – 5 marks

a B [37.7] [B1]
b B [113.12] [B1]
c C [69.52] [B1]
d A [$5.\dot{0}7692\dot{3}$] [B1]
e C [$8.\dot{6}8131\dot{8}$] [B1]

Question 3 – 2 marks

$6 \times 60 \times 25 = 9000$ [B1]
Mia used 25 as an estimate for the number of hours in a day. [B1]

Question 4 – 3 marks

a 6 and 7 [B1]
b $6^2 = 36$ and $7^2 = 49$ [B1]
c 7 [46 is closer to 49] [B1]

Question 5 – 5 marks

a $2 \times 2^2 = 8$ [B1]
A better estimate $= (36 - 8) \div 15 = 28 \div 15$ [B1]
$= 2$ [B1]
b 0.886129… – 0.0775
= 0.808629471… [B2]
One mark for sight of 0.886129…

Question 6 – 2 marks

$3560 \div 88 \approx 3600 \div 90$ [M1]
40 [A1]

Question 7 – 11 marks

a $6.8 \times 9.6 + \frac{1}{2} \times 6.8 \times 8.5$
Or equivalent correct formula. [M2]
$= 65.28 + 28.9$
$= 94.18\ \text{m}^2$
1 mark value; 1 mark units [A2]
b 12.5 cm = 0/.125 m [B1]
94.18×0.125 [M1]
$= 11.7725\ \text{m}^3$ [A1]
c i density kg/m^3 = densiy $\text{g/cm}^3 \times 100^3 / 1000$ [M1]
0.3×1000
$= 300\ \text{kg/m}^3$ [A1]
ii 11.7725×300 kg $\div$ 1000 tonnes [M1]
= 3.53 tonnes [F1]

Question 8 – 10 marks

a $4.6 + (5.3 \times 2.6) = 18.38$ [B1]
b $14.9 - (6.8 \div 2.5) = 12.18$ [B1]
c $(3.4 \times 1.6) + 5.9 - 2.8) = 8.54$ [B2]
d $2.6 + (7.56 \div 1.8) - 0.72 = 6.08$ [B2]
e $(12.3 - 5.2 \times 1.6 + 3.4) \times 2 = 14.76$ [B2]
f $(5.9 + 2.2) \div 3.6 - 2.4 \times 0.3 = 1.53$ [B2]

Question 9 – 20 marks

Allow one mark for numerical value and one mark for the unit.

a ≈ 100 – 1000 litres [B2]
b ≈ 20 kilograms [B2]
c ≈ 2 grams [B2]
d ≈ 150 metres [B2]
e ≈ 50 – 300 tonnes [B2]
f ≈ 30 millilitres [B2]
g ≈ 15 millimetres OR 1 centimetre [B2]
h ≈ 40 kilometres [B2]
i ≈ 15 centimetres [B2]
j ≈ 300 millilitres [B2]

Question 10 – 6 marks

a £25.30 [B1]
b 25 m 30 cm [B1]
c 25 kg 300 g [B1]
d 25 cl 3 ml [B1]
e 25 hrs 18 min [B2]

Question 11 – 10 marks

a $165 \div 2.5$ [M1]
= 66 km/h [A1]
b $9.5 \div (3.8 / 60)$ [M1]
= 150 km/h [A1]
c 175×2.75 [M1]
= 481.25 km [A1]
d $465 \times 7\frac{1}{3}$ [M1]
= 3410 miles [A1]
e $14 \div 47$ [M1]
= 0.29787… hr = 17 min 52 s [A1]

Question 12 – 8 marks

a Density $= 158 \div 195$ [M1]
$= 0.81\ \text{g/cm}^3 < 1$ [B1]
Yes [F1]
b $44 \div 19.3$ [M1]
$= 2.28\ \text{cm}^3$ (3 sf) [A1]
c Volume $= 25 \times 15 \times 6 = 2250\ \text{m}^3$ [B1]
$2.4\ \text{g/cm}^3 = 2.4\ \text{tonnes/m}^3$ [B1]
Mass $= 2250 \times 2.4$
= 5400 tonnes [B1]

Question 13 – 7 marks

a	LB 221455	UB 221465	[B1]
b	LB 85 cm	UB 95 cm	[B1]
c	LB 452.5 g	UB 457.5 g	[B1]
d	LB 3 min 28.75 s	UB 3 min 28.85 s	[B1]
e	LB 238 bags	UB 242 bags	[B1]
f	LB 27.5 tonnes	UB 28.5 tonnes	[B1]
g	LB 585.5 mm	UB 586.5 mm	[B1]

Question 14 – 5 marks

a UB $45.5 \times 24.5 \times 0.35 = 390.1625\ \text{cm}^3$ [B1]
LB $44.5 \times 23.5 \times 0.25 = 261.4375\ \text{cm}^3$ [B1]
b 'Max = Max / Min', 'Min = Min / Max' [M1]
UB $76.5 \div 261.4375 = 0.293\ \text{g/cm}^3$ (3 sf) [A1]
LB $75.5 \div 390.1625 = 0.194\ \text{g/cm}^3$ (3 sf) [A1]

Equations and inequalities

Learning outcomes

A3 Understand and use the concepts and vocabulary of [expressions,] equations, [formulae,] inequalities, [terms,] factors [and identities].

A11 Deduce roots algebraically.

A17 Solve linear equations in one unknown algebraically (including those with the unknown on both sides of the equation); find approximate solutions using a graph.

A18 Solve quadratic equations algebraically by factorising; find approximate solutions using a graph.

A19 Solve two simultaneous equations in two variables (linear/linear) algebraically; find approximate solutions using a graph.

A21 Translate simple situations or procedures into algebraic expressions or formulae; derive an equation (or two simultaneous equations), solve the equation(s) and interpret the solution.

A22 Solve linear inequalities in one variable; represent the solution set on a number line.

Prior knowledge

Check-in skill

- Understand multiplication and division facts.
- Simplify algebraic expressions.
- Substitute numerical values into formulae and expressions.

Online resources

MyMaths 1154, 1161, 1162, 1169, 1175, 1176, 1181, 1182, 1319, 1395, 1925, 1928, 1930

InvisiPen videos

Skills: 10Sa – o Applications: 10Aa – g

Kerboodle assessment

Online Skills Test 10 Chapter Test 10

Development and links

Engineers use equations to model and calculate what will happen to a design under certain conditions. Buildings and bridges have to be able to withstand the worst conditions that might prevail, preferably with a safety margin. Structural engineers use equations to calculate whether or not the structure design can withstand maximum loads and stresses, whether the foundations are strong enough and how the materials used will behave under different conditions.

Chapter investigation

Students should start by generating some L-shapes and recording the corresponding L-numbers. By writing the numbers in L_n as n, $n-1$, $n-2$, $n-12$ and $n-22$ you can derive a general formula which can be extended to other grids.

Grid size	Total (n = L-number)
10 × 10	$5n - 37$
$m \times m$	$5n - 3m - 7$

Ask the problem, which L-number equals 293? This leads to the two-step equation $L_n = 293$ or $5n - 37 = 293$ (L_{66}) with the unknown on one side **[10.1]**. This can be solved analytically or using graphs, though the later will require either a very large graph or knowing that n can only be an integer.

An extension to equations involving the unknown on both sides follows from a problem of the type, the L-number of a number plus 120 equals the L-number of twice the number, what is the number? **[10.2]**.
$L_n + 120 = L_{2n}$ or $(5n - 37) + 120 = 5 \times 2n - 37$ (24)

Both of the problems above can be viewed as simultaneous equations: solve $y = 5x - 37$ and $y = 293$, and $y = 5x + 83$ and $y = 10x - 37$ **[10.4]** Show students how this type of equation can be solved by elimination, by substitution or using a graph.

To introduce quadratic equations ask the problem, which L-number squared is 6889? $L_n^2 = 6889$ or $(5n - 37)^2 = 6889$ (L_{24}) **[10.3]**. This equation can be solved by square-rooting both sides and knowing to discard the solution $n = -46/5$. Use simpler equations, with coefficient of n^2 equal to 1, to demonstrate how to solve a quadratic using factorisation or a graph.

To introduce inequalities ask the problem, which is the first L-number greater than 100? $L_n \geq 100$ or $5n - 37 \geq 100 \Rightarrow n \geq 27.4$ (28) **[10.5]**. Emphasise that the approach taken for inequalities is very much the same as for equations – do the same to both sides. The main difference to emphasise is how to treat division by a negative number.

10.1 Solving linear equations 1

Objectives

① **A17** Solve linear equations in one unknown algebraically

② **A21** Derive and solve an equation from a real-life or contextual situation and interpret the solution

Useful resources

Mini whiteboards, spider diagram display

Starter – Skills

Use a spider diagram display with an equation at the centre: $4x + 5 = 13$.

On one leg write $8x + 10 = 26$. Ask what you have done to get this. What would the next expression be if this continued?

On the second leg, write $4x + 6 = 14$. What has happened here? What would the next be? and the next?

On the third leg, write $4x + 4 = 12$ and repeat the procedure, asking for the next.

Continue to get to $4x = 8$. Prompt halving, and again, to give the equivalent statement as an answer.

Teaching notes – Skills

Write the equation $x + 5 = 7$.

Discuss what has been done to the unknown in the equation and how this will be undone. Recall inverse operations.

Highlight that an equation is like a set of scales; both sides must balance. Demonstrate how any operation performed on one side must also be performed on the other side to maintain balance. Emphasise that they should check the answer by substituting back into the equation.

Write the equation $3x = 21$.

Recall that $3x$ means $3 \times x$, the 'hidden' multiplication. Discuss what has been done to the unknown in the equation and how this can be undone. Recall inverse operations. Again, emphasise balancing the scales.

Write a two-step equation: $6x + 3 = 15$.

Demonstrate how to solve this algebraically, first getting the xs on one side and the numbers on the other, and then dividing to find the value of x. Show again how any operation performed on one side must also be performed to the other side to maintain balance.

$$6x = 15 - 3$$
$$x = 12 \div 6$$
$$x = 2$$

Work through examples to gain confidence; extend to equations with division.

Plenary – Skills

Show this solution to a problem and invite students to discuss whether it is correct. (It is not.)

$$x + 9 = 21$$
$$x = 21 + 9$$
$$x = 30$$

Highlight: Substitution to check an answer; using working out to check through an answer; using inverse operations to undo operations.

Exercise commentary – Skills

Question 1 These are mixed equations that involve only one operation. Show students how to check their answers by using substitution.

Questions 2 and **3** For these two questions provide examples that give students model solutions for solving these types of equations. In question **3** explain that the brackets will need to be expanded first, if need be recap on how to do this. It may be helpful for students to think of SAMDIB (reverse of BIDMAS) when considering what operation to deal with first.

Question 4 This question demonstrates that an alternative way of solving an equation is to plot the graph and find where the y-coordinate is the required value and read off the corresponding x-value.

Questions 5 and **6** Further practice on solving equations that involve two operations. Emphasise the importance of doing the same operation to both sides and remind students to take extra care with negative terms.

Questions 7 and **8** In each case in these questions students will need to start by expanding the brackets. Remind students to multiply both terms inside the bracket by the term on the outside.

Question 9 A set of equations to solve with two or more operations including division. Promote the importance of applying SAMDIB. Discuss as a whole class why $p - 3 = 48$ would not be a correct first step in part **c.**

Questions 10 and **11** Demonstrate how to draw on horizontal lines from the y-values to the graph and then vertical lines from the graph down to the x-axis.

Question *12 You may need to demonstrate how to plot this type of graph. Explain that $-10 \le x \le 10$ means that the x-coordinates need to go from -10 to 10. Part ***iv** may be best tackled as a whole class, first ask 'how do you think that the original graph has been transformed?'

Question 13 Demonstrate how to solve equations where the unknown is on both sides by making the first step to subtract the smallest x-term from both sides.

Question 14 As a whole class discuss how to find an expression for the perimeter and the steps needed to simplify this expression. Ask students what the final stage should be once x has been found.

Simplification – Skills

Students could work with single-step problems to gain confidence with the method. A writing frame may help them to structure their solutions.

Extension – Skills

Students could be challenged to solve equations where the unknown appears on both sides, such as $4x - 7 = 3x + 3$.

Recap – Applications

1 Solve these equations making sure the two sides always balance. Check each of your solutions.

a $7y = 77$ (11) **b** $8x = -16$ (–2)

c $\frac{w}{5} = 3$ (15) **d** $\frac{v}{12} = -2$ (–24)

e $u + 7 = 16$ (9) **f** $8 = s + 8$ (0)

g $14 = 1 + r$ (13) **h** $17 = 8 - p$ (–9)

i $5o + 7 = 17$ (2) **j** $6n - 8 = 13$ (3.5)

k $2 + 7m = 44$ (61) **l** $15 - 4k = 6$ (2.25)

m $j - 3.6 = 18.1$ (21.7) **n** $11.1 = 6.6 - i$ (–4.5)

o $23.9 = 79.7 + 5h$ (–11.16)

p $\frac{f}{11} + 9 = -12$ (–231)

q $55 + \frac{e}{9} = 22$ (–297) **r** $\frac{3}{d} = 5$ (0.6)

s $\frac{15}{b} = -2$ (–7.5) **t** $\frac{-14}{a} = -28$ (0.5)

2 Solve these equations:

a $7(3u + 2) = 56$ (2) **b** $51 = 3(8 - 6s)$ (–1.5)

c $-18 = 4(5 - 2r)$ (4.75)

d $6(2q + 5) = -3$ (–3.75)

e $\frac{5p + 7}{3} = 9$ (4) **f** $\frac{6 + 3n}{12} = 22$ (86)

g $\frac{-7 - 10m}{12} = 3.2$ (–4.54) **h** $\frac{18 - 5l}{19} 27$ (–99)

Plenary – Applications

Invite students to write the equation for a word problem: I have a number, I multiply it by 3, then add 4 and the answer is 19.

Discuss the order that operations were performed in and highlight that these must be undone in reverse order.

Work through the balance method highlighting the logical progression of the working out.

Exercise commentary – Applications

Question 1 Discuss how 5 lots of n pencils means $5 \times n$ and should be written as $5n$. Remind students to solve the equation using inverse operations.
Question 2 Ensure students realise that they need to write the equation using algebra letting x (or another letter) represent the unknown number.
Question 3 Students will probably attempt to solve each equation and compare the answers. Remind students to use SAMDIB to find which operation to deal with first.
Question 4 Initially students may attempt to create equations using the base bricks. Discuss why these would form identities rather than equations and therefore cannot be solved for a unique value of n or m.
Question 5 In parts **b** and **c** students will need to simplify their equations before solving them. Emphasise the importance of checking your answer using substitution. Part **c** provides an opportunity to reinforce the definition of a regular shape.
Question 6 It may be useful to check that students are comfortable solving two-step equations when the answer is a fraction before tackling this question. Some guidance on how to build up the equation may also be necessary, if the solution is to be $x = 4$, students could start with $3x = 12$, then subtract 1 from each side.
Questions 7 and **8** Encourage students to consider each part of the question and represent this using algebra. For example, in question **7** if Josh has twice as many sandwiches as Sarah and she has y sandwiches then he must have $2y$ sandwiches. Students should then put all their expressions together to form the equation.
Question 9 Stress the importance of reading the question carefully. A common error is to find the value of x and give this as the final answer when it is the side lengths that have been asked for.
Question 10 Check that students remember that the sum of the angles in a quadrilateral is 360. As an extension students could construct questions involving forming and solving equations using angles in polygons.

Simplification – Applications

Students should be given further examples which are routine practice in order to ensure an efficient (and correct) method is being used.
Some students may find handling negative values a challenge. Encourage the use of the number line as a support with negatives.

Extension – Applications

Students could devise their own 'I have a number' problems involving brackets and division, and ask a partner to solve them.

10.2 Solving linear equations 2

Objectives

① **A17** Solve linear equations in one unknown algebraically (including those with brackets and the unknown on both sides of the equation)

② **A21** Derive and solve an equation from a real-life or contextual situation and interpret the solution.

Useful resources

Mini whiteboards

Starter – Skills

Invite students to discuss what has gone wrong in the following equations and correctly solve them.

$$\begin{aligned} 2x + 7 &= 23 \\ 2x &= 30 \\ x &= 15 \end{aligned}$$

$$\begin{aligned} 3x + 2 &= 14 \\ 3x &= 14 \\ x &= 7 \end{aligned}$$

$$\begin{aligned} 2x - 4 &= 6 \\ x &= 7 \end{aligned}$$

Teaching notes – Skills

Refer to the starter and ensure students recall:

- using inverse operations to undo
- performing inverse operation on both sides of the equation
- using substitution to check solutions
- the importance of showing working out.

Recap how to solve an equation, such as

$$2x + 3 = 11$$

Write the equation $3(x - 2) = x + 4$

This equation contains brackets, and the unknown appears on both sides.

Recap how to expand a bracket.

Invite students to give the steps needed to solve the equation.

$$\begin{aligned} 3(x - 2) &= x + 4 \\ 3x - 6 &= x + 4 && \text{(expand bracket)} \\ 3x &= x + 10 && \text{(add 6 to both sides)} \\ 2x &= 10 && \text{(subtract } x \text{ from both sides)} \\ x &= 5 && \text{(divide by 2)} \end{aligned}$$

Putting $x = 5$ back into the original equation confirms the answer.

Plenary – Skills

Ask students to solve this equation with division:

$$\frac{x}{5} + 4 = 6$$

What should the first step be? Ask students to explain their solutions, clearly showing each step.

Emphasise the importance of checking the solution by substitution.

Exercise commentary – Skills

Questions 1 and **2** Tell students that when they rearrange an equation that has the unknown on both sides of the equation they should first rearrange the equation so that the unknown is just on one side.

Questions 3 to **5** Ensure students can confidently solve equations with unknowns on both sides by demonstrating the method with a few worked examples. Discuss why the first stage should be to subtract the 'smallest unknown term from both sides', would it matter if it wasn't the smallest? Also ask what the first stage should be if the smallest unknown term is a negative term (as in question **5**).

Question 6 This question demonstrates that you can solve an equation where the unknown is on both sides of the equation by considering two relevant straight-line graphs and finding the coordinates of where the two graphs cross.

Question 7 Ask students to think about what would happen if they were to plot both parts of the equation as straight-line graphs. Students may be unsure so you may need to demonstrate that both lines are parallel and will therefore never cross.

Questions 8 to **10** In these questions equations need to be formed first using the given information. You may need to remind students of relevant facts such as the sum of the angles inside a quadrilateral, the definition of a perimeter of a shape and how to find the area of a rectangle and triangle. Model the process of forming the equation, simplifying the equation, solving the equation and then actually answering the question (this is not always just the value of the unknown letter).

Question *11 Remind students to take care of negatives when expanding the brackets.

Question 12 Students will need to form the equation first. Tell students to allocate the unknown number a letter such as x, ask students, 'how will you represent what is happening to x using algebra?'

Question 13 You may need to recap on how to plot a straight-line graph in order for students to be able to access this extension question.

Simplification – Skills

Easier examples may need to be provided for consolidation work. Students should concentrate on solving these equations using an efficient method and layout.

Extension – Skills

Students could be given examples which involve brackets on both sides of the equals sign and division to extend this work.

Recap – Applications

1 Solve these equations:

a $3z + 2 = 5z$ (1)

b $4y - 9 = 6y + 11$ (-10)

c $5x - 6 = 7x - 10$ (2)

d $2v - 4 = 8 - 4v$ (2)

e $\frac{2}{5}(3t+2)=6$ $\left(-4\frac{1}{3}\right)$

f $\frac{1}{2}(2s-5)=2(s+1)$ $\left(-4\frac{1}{2}\right)$

g $\frac{1}{4}(5r+2)=\frac{5}{6}(2r+7)$ $\left(-12\frac{4}{5}\right)$

2 a A rectangle with sides 4 cm and 12 cm has the same perimeter as a rectangle with sides 8 cm and $4w$ cm. Use this information to find and solve the equation in w. (2)

b Arturo is 3 times as tall as his son. The sum of their heights is 184 cm.

How tall is Arturo? (1.38 m)

c A jug, holding y ml of milk, has a volume of 1 litre when full. It takes another $(3y + 10)$ ml to make the jug three quarters full.

What is the value of y? (185)

d There are m mint sweets in a bag. I gave 5 mints to each of four friends and still had one third of the mints left. Calculate the value of m. (30)

Plenary – Applications

Take a question that involves deriving an equation from a word problem. Ask as many individual students as possible to give their strategies for deriving suitable expressions and deciding what equation correctly describes the situation given.

Ask student to work through to the solution. Does this give a sensible answer? How can you check?

Exercise commentary – Applications

Questions 1 and **2** In these questions equations will need to be formed and then solved, encourage students to use a letter like n to represent the unknown number.

Questions 3 and **4** It is easy for students to confuse area and perimeter when questions appear on both alongside each other. Draw their attention to the fact that question **3** is about perimeter (a reminder that the shape shown is a square and that therefore all sides are the same length may also be welcome here) and question **4** is about area. When solving the equation in question **4** some students may take a first step that is to expand the brackets whilst others may begin by dividing both sides by 4, discuss why both these approaches are acceptable.

Question 5 This question provides good practice at solving equations with the unknown on both sides and where some answers are not whole numbers or positive. Remind students that they can leave answers that are not whole numbers as improper fractions or convert them to mixed numbers. As an extension you could tell the students that one equation cannot be solved, can they find the equation and explain why it cannot be solved?

Questions 6 and **7** Here equations need to be formed to represent equal perimeters (question **6**) and then equal areas (question **7**). Emphasise the importance of checking answers by substituting in the x-value found.

Question 8 Some students may need a little more guidance in this question. You may need to mention that they will need to form expressions for the total number of buttons on four blouses and three shirts and then form an equation as these are equal. A recap that three shirts with $m + 2$ buttons means $3 \times (m + 2)$ and can be written as $3(m + 2)$ may also be welcome.

Question 9 Further practice at forming equations where the unknown is on both sides. You could get students to form similar questions for each other to solve.

Questions 10 and **11** It would be easy to misread these questions and mistake the expression given for the side length rather than the perimeter.

Simplification – Applications

Writing equations from word problems can be difficult for students and they may benefit from working in pairs to discuss and derive each situation. Encourage students to consider the relationship being described before generalising it.

Extension – Applications

Students could be asked to devise their own word problems for others to solve.

10.3 Quadratic equations

Objectives

① **A18** Solve quadratic equations (including those that require rearrangement) algebraically by factorising

Useful resources

Graph-plotting tool, 2 mm graph paper, pre-drawn axes and tables, calculators

Starter – Skills

Ask what two numbers can you multiply to get the answer zero? Or phrase the question as, if $a \times b = 0$ what could a and b equal?

Establish that if two numbers are multiplied together and the answer is zero, then one or both of the numbers must be zero.

Teaching notes – Skills

Remind students how to expand and simplify.

$$(x + 8)(x - 2) = x^2 + 8x - 2x - 16$$
$$= x^2 + 6x - 16$$

Remind students that factorising involves putting terms back into brackets.

If a quadratic expression is equal to zero, it is sometimes possible to solve it by factorising the expression. For example,

$$x^2 + 4x + 3 = 0$$
$$\Rightarrow \quad (x + 1)(x + 3) = 0$$

$(x + 1)$ and $(x + 3)$ are both numbers, and so one of them must equal zero because their product is zero.

either $x + 1 = 0$, and $x = -1$,

or $x + 3 = 0$, and $x = -3$.

We can also find an approximate solution using a graph. Ask students to draw axes –4 to 4 for x and –4 to 10 for y.

Draw the graph of $y = x^2 - 1$ (compile a table first).

x	–3	–2	–1	0	1	2	3
y	8	3	0	–1	0	3	8

Now solve these equations.

$x^2 - 1 = 0$

Where on the graph is $y = 0$? (At $x = -1$ and $x = 1$: these are the solutions to the equation.)

$x^2 - 1 = x + 5$

What has y changed into? (y has changed into $x + 5$ or $y = x + 5$)

Draw this line and see where it intersects (crosses) the curve $y = x^2 - 1$. (At $x = -2$ and $x = 3$)

Plenary – Skills

Challenge students to attempt these three equations.

$x^2 = -25$ $\quad x^2 + 10 = 5$ $\quad x^2 + x + 10 = 0$

Suggest various approaches:

- different values of x in your head
- factorising
- trial and improvement with a calculator.

There are in fact *no* answers. Not all quadratic equations have solutions.

Exercise commentary – Skills

Questions 1 and **2** Emphasise that the first question has two solutions, a positive and negative solution. Show students how to factorise the expression in the second question and how the two solutions are derived.

Question 3 Demonstrate how the first part of this question is a special case and can be factorised using the difference of two squares.

Question 4 Stress the difference between factorising a quadratic expression and solving a quadratic equation. Explain that in order for the equation to be true either one or both the brackets will need to be equal to zero and that this is how the solutions are found. Ensure students realise that such equations have two solutions. Tell students to set out their working in the same way as shown in the first part of the second example on page 210. Also ask 'what do you notice about the solutions compared to the numbers found in the brackets?'

Questions 5 and **6** Further practice at solving quadratic equations but this time where some of the terms are negative. Remind students to take extra care with negatives and encourage them to check their factorised forms by expanding the brackets. A common mistake is to incorrectly factorise and give two numbers in brackets that multiply to give the coefficient of x and add to make the constant.

Question 7 The final two parts of this question will stretch the most able students. Students need to take out a numerical factor before they apply the normal method to factorise a quadratic with an x^2 coefficient of 1.

Question 8 In this question students will need to rearrange each equation so that it equals zero. Direct students to set out their method in the same way as shown in part **c** of the second example on page 210.

Question 9 Demonstrate how approximate solutions to quadratics can be found using graphs.

Question 10 This would be a good question to raise as a discussion point with the whole class. Can anyone justify why $x^2 - 4x = -5$ does not have a solution by looking carefully at the graph given?

Question *11 Ask students who are attempting this extension question to describe how they think the graph $y = x^2$ would be transformed to create the graph $y = x^2 + 20$. Hopefully this will enable them to figure out the answer without drawing the graph.

Question 12 Explain to students that they will need to form an equation to represent the given information, expand brackets and rearrange it so they can factorise to find the solutions. Some students may think that there is more than one solution. Ask them to think about the context of the question and what solutions are possible.

Simplification – Skills

Concentrate on the standard quadratics with straightforward factorisations and ensure students can communicate the method effectively while applying it.

Extension – Skills

Give the students (simple) examples where the coefficient of x^2 is not 1 and ask them to factorise these 'by inspection', if possible, and then solve.

Recap – Applications

1 a Factorise

- **i** $a^2 + 12a + 13$ $((a + 12)(a + 1))$
- **ii** $b^2 + 4b - 21$ $((b + 7)(b - 3))$
- **iii** $d^2 - 2d - 80$ $((d - 10)(d + 8))$
- **iv** $12 - 4f - f^2$ $((2 - f)(6 + f))$

b Put = 0 at the end of each of the expressionsyou factorised in part **a** and then solve the equations.

(**i** [-1, -12] **ii** [-7, 3] **iii** [-8, 10] **iv** [-6, 2])

2 Solve these equations:

- **a** $a^2 + 15a + 54 = 0$ ([-9, -6])
- **b** $c^2 + 9c - 22 = 0$ ([-11, 2])
- **c** $d^2 - 8d - 84 = 0$ ([-6, 14])
- **d** $f^2 - 9f = -18$ ([3, 6])
- **e** $g^2 + g = 110$ ([-11, 10])

Plenary – Applications

How could you solve the equation $x^2 = x^3 + 1$?

(Draw the graphs of $y = x^2$ and $y = x^3 + 1$)

Where they cross is the solution. ($x \approx -0.8$)

Exercise commentary – Applications

Question 1 This question covers an important misconception, 'If $(x + 4)(x - 2) = 0$ and either $x + 4 = 0$ or $x - 2 = 0$ which gives $x = -4$ or $x = 2$ then surely we can apply the same method when $(x + 4)(x - 2) = 7$ ...' Discuss why this method cannot be transferred to an equation that does not equal zero.

Question 2 A common error is to expand $2x(x - 1)$ as $2x - 2x$, show students this and ask them to tell you what error has been made. Stress that in order for this equation to be solved it will need to first be rearranged so that it is equal to zero.

Questions 3 and **4** In these questions quadratic equations will need to be formed and solved using the given information. Ensure students are confident about forming the initial equations, you could ask more able students 'does it matter if (in question **4**) the second number is expressed as $x - 4$ or $x + 4$?' Make sure students understand that two pairs of numbers will need to be found in both these questions, the second number in the pair found by substituting the first into the second expression. As a final stage each pair should be multiplied to check that they give the correct product.

Questions 5 and **6** Emphasise the fact that side lengths and angles cannot be negative numbers.

Question 7 A recap on the formulae for the area of a trapezium may be necessary here. Simplifying the expression for the area of a trapezium before writing this as an equation equal to 36 is a good strategy to employ, ask students to explain why they should dismiss negative solutions.

Question 8 Check students can find the area of a triangle. Ensure they are expanding brackets and rearranging correctly to give the equation in the format required in the question. Stress that for this type of question it is essential to show all stages of your working as the answer is given as part of the question.

Question 9 An easy mistake to make would be to write $4(3x - 2) = x(8x - 8)$. Discuss what error has been made and what the equation should be. Ensure students substitute the value of x found into the expression for the side length of the square and not just state the value of x as the answer.

Question 10 As a whole class discuss how you could form an equation to represent the given information, rearrange it to equate to zero and then begin to consider possible solutions. You may wish to allow students the use of a calculator to help find the answers.

Simplification – Applications

For questions where students draw graphs to find a solution, they could be given pre-drawn axes and tables to speed up this work.

Extension – Applications

Students could be given further examples where both functions are non-linear. They could be asked to rearrange one of these types of example and draw a single graph (subsequently equating it to 0).

10.4 Simultaneous equations

Objectives

① **A19** Solve two simultaneous linear equations in two variables algebraically; find approximate solutions using a graph.

② **A21** Derive and solve simultaneous equations from a real-life or contextual situation and interpret the solution

Useful resources

Mini whiteboards, graph-plotting tool, pre-drawn axes

Starter – Skills

Read out this problem.

The sum of two numbers is 12. The difference of the same two numbers is 4. What are the two numbers? (8 and 4)

How could we use algebra to find the solution?

$x + y = 12$ and $x - y = 4$

These are simultaneous equations. Adding the equations, $2x = 16$ so $x = 8$, and $y = 4$.

Repeat the problem with different values for the sum and difference, for example 28 and 16 (22 and 6)

Teaching notes – Skills

Discuss simultaneous equations where the coefficients of the variables are different.

$$2x + 3y = 12$$
$$5x + 4y = 23$$

Demonstrate the 'elimination' method. Make the number of xs the same by multiplying the first equation by 5 and the second by 2.

$$10x + 15y = 60$$
$$10x + 8y = 46$$

Subtract to eliminate one of variables (the xs) and solve.

$$7y = 14$$
$$y = 2$$

Put y into one of the original equations to find x.

$2x + 3y = 12 \Rightarrow 2x + 6 = 12 \Rightarrow x = 3$

Show that you can solve simultaneous equations using a graph. Draw axes from –10 to 10 on both axes. What values can you have for x and y if $y = 2x - 3$? Obtain three possible answers from the students and plot these points, then draw the line, extending as far as possible.

What other values for x and y can you find from the line? Discuss how the line gives you all the possible values, within the limits of the line.

Try the same for the line $x + y = 9$. From the graph can you tell what values of x and y will work in both equations at the same time (simultaneously)? Lines cross at $x = 4$ and $y = 5$. What you have done is solve the simultaneous equations.

Plenary – Skills

Ask students to draw axes from –10 to 10 on both axes. Plot the possible answers for $x + y = 12$, then join the points to make a line, and label it. Do the same for the possible solutions of $x - y = 4$.

Can you see how these graphs could help you to find how the solution to simultaneous equations? Where they cross is the answer.

When might this not be a good method? When the numbers are very big or when they cross at a point which is hard to read accurately from the graph.

Exercise commentary – Skills

Questions 1 and **2** Make sure students realise that when they solve simultaneous equations they will find two solutions, one for x and one for y. In this first question both equations contain identical positive y and x terms respectively, so students will need to subtract one equation from the other in each case.

Question 3 This question shows students that a single equation with two unknowns can have many possible solutions. When two linear equations are given, only one possible value for each unknown will fit both equations.

Question 4 Further practice at solving simultaneous equations which both contain an identical positive term.

Question 5 Here equivalent equations will need to be found so that either one of the unknowns have the same coefficient in both equations. Demonstrate how to multiply all of the terms in the equation to achieve this. Alternatively students could use the method of substitution. Parts **e** and **f** lend themselves to using a substitution method.

Question 6 Emphasise the importance of paying attention to negative terms. Remind students that the sign before the term belongs to the term in front of it. Why is $-4q = 2$ not the correct first stage for part **c**?

Question 7 Show students that in the first two parts of this question the identical terms have different signs and for this reason the first step for solving these pairs of simultaneous equations will be to add the equations. Part **b** of the second example on page 214 shows clearly how to set out the method for these types of questions, draw attention to the final stage, checking your answers.

Question 8 Use the final example on page 214 to demonstrate that the solutions to simultaneous equations can also be found by plotting graphs and writing the coordinates of where the graphs intersect. Ask 'why is difficult to give exact solutions in some cases?'

Question 9 Recap on how to generate coordinates so that the straight line can be drawn. Suggest that a suitable degree of accuracy will be to one decimal place when finding solutions for these questions. Invite students to suggest ways that accuracy of the solutions could be improved, for example, use graph paper or bigger axes etc.

Question 10 Students could use a substitution method to create a quadratic equation and factorise this to find the x-coordinates. A common error is to then forget to find the y-coordinates. Remind students that they need to substitute their x-values into one of the equations to find the y-values. Alternatively, demonstrate how a table of values can be used to generate coordinates and plot a quadratic graph, explain that the points should be joined with a smooth curve.

Question 11 You wish to model the process of forming a simultaneous equation in order that students can access this style of question.

Simplification – Skills

Students should be directed to attempt questions where it is the second term which is eliminated and only one equation needs to be multiplied.

Extension – Skills

Students could be given further examples which have non-integer solutions or where more initial manipulation is required.

Recap – Applications

1 Solve these equations simultaneously either by elimination, substitution or by using a graph. Make sure you use each of the three methods at least twice during your working.

a $a + b = 6$; $2a + b = 13$ $(a = 7, b = -1)$

b $2c - 3d = 5$; $c - 2d = 4$ $(c = -2, d = -3)$

c $2e + 7f = 67$; $3e - 2f = 13$ $(e = 9, f = 7)$

d $7i + 4j = 42$; $-2i + 9j = -12$ $(i = 6, j = 0)$

e $6k + 12l = 11$; $3k - 4l = -2$ $\left(k = \frac{1}{3}, l = \frac{3}{4}\right)$

f $10m - 6n = -7$; $20m + 12n = 6$ $\left(m = \frac{-1}{5}, n = \frac{5}{6}\right)$

Plenary – Applications

Discuss students' solutions to a question in which they derive their own simultaneous equations from a context or situation. Students often find it hard to form equations from word problems, so addressing misconceptions as a whole class will help.

Exercise commentary – Applications

Question 1 Students need to realise that the solutions have to fit both equations in order to be viable solutions.

Question 2 Emphasise that sometimes you have to multiply all the terms in one or both of the equations in order to make one of the unknowns have the same coefficient in both equations.

Question 3 Tell students that for some combinations they will need to rearrange the equations so that they are in the familiar format of $ax + by = c$. Challenge students to find the combination that gives the largest x value, the smallest y value etc...

Questions 4 and **5** In these questions students will need to form as well as solve simultaneous equations. Question **4a** is similar to the example on page 216, students could be given an extension task of creating similar types of problems for each other to solve. In part **b** students may initially miss or not recognise the isosceles triangle. In question **5** tell students to let one number be x and the other be y.

Question 6 It may be useful to point out that the number on the right hand side represents the sum of the numbers in that row.

Question 7 This could be a good question to go through as a whole class. It may not be obvious to some students how two different equations can be formed here, one for the total cost and one for the total number of people. Calculators should be allowed for this question.

Question 8 These questions are quite challenging, both in terms of forming the equations and in terms of plotting the points, they are probably best partially covered as a whole class. In each case let one variable be x and the other be y so that the equations formed are recognisable to students as straight-line graphs. Once the graphs are plotted emphasise that the solution is the coordinates of where the lines cross.

Question 9 In part **a** some students will realise from the equation that the graphs are parallel and will therefore never cross and have no solution. Others will need to plot them and then to see this. For these students try and relate the fact that they are parallel to the coefficient of x in each equation. In part **b** hint that they might need to consider graphs that are not straight lines.

Simplification – Applications

Students could be given further examples which require little initial manipulation.

Students could be given pre-drawn axes to help them with graphical questions, and should be directed to solve questions which are in the form $y = \ldots$

Extension – Applications

Students could be given further examples where they have to form the equations themselves from a contextual situation. Alternatively, they could be invited to solve a set of linear equations in three unknowns.

10.5 Inequalities

Objectives

① **A22** Solve linear inequalities in one variable; represent the solution set on a number line.

Useful resources

Number line, mini whiteboards

Starter – Skills

Ask students to respond to questions using whiteboards. Write on the board $n > 5$. Ask students to write any possible value for n. Share and discuss the responses.

Write $p < 4$ and request possible values for p. Share some of these responses, particularly if negative values are offered. Explore what students think might be the largest possible value of p.

Write a third statement, $m \geq 7$, and repeat. Share any fraction or decimal responses, and explore what the smallest value here might be.

Draw each solution on a number line, showing and discussing the open and closed circle convention.

Teaching notes – Skills

Write the statement $5 \leq y < 11$ and ask for possible values of y. What is the smallest value possible? What might be the largest value?

Introduce the word 'integer' and remind students of its meaning. If y is an integer what is the largest/smallest value of y? Ask students to represent this solution on a number line using mini whiteboards, and check the correct use of open and closed circles.

Now ask students to write an equivalent statement, to $5 \leq y < 11$, say by doubling or adding.

Select some of those offered to share with the whole group and ask if students can spot what has happened to reach this statement.

Address the possible correct statement: $11 > y \geq 5$, by exploring it on a number line, thus making the point that conventionally inequalities are written in ascending order.

Give students the statement $6x - 2 \leq 16$ and ask them to illustrate this solution on a number line. Prompt and model suggestions from students to 'simplify' and produce a solution. Ask for sketches from all students.

Write an example such as $-3 \leq 3m < 12$ on the board for students to 'simplify' and draw the number line solution.

Plenary – Skills

Ask students to respond on mini whiteboards. Give them a diagram showing a number line with values indicated and ask them to write the corresponding inequality. Share and discuss the answers. Repeat for two or three more examples.

Exercise commentary – Skills

Question 1 Students need to be clear about the meaning of the inequality signs, ask them to say in words what each inequality sign means. Recap that an integer is a whole number.

Question 2 Students need to remember that a filled circle is used if the number is included and that a hollow circle is used if it is not. Ask students to describe the inequality in words and then convert this into symbols.

Question 3 In parts **b** and **c** students need to rearrange the inequality so it is in terms of n. They should use the balance method but apply it to all three sides of the inequality in the same way as when solving equations.

Question 4 Discuss the first two parts of the second example on page 218. Again, students should apply the balance method but remind them that they must make sure that they give the solution using the inequality sign.

Question 5 Make sure students apply the same inverse operation to all three parts of the inequality. Go through an example as a whole class, such as part **c** of the second example on page 218.

Question 6 Remind students that when they expand brackets they must multiply the term on the outside of the brackets by both the terms on the inside.

Question 7 This question involves more complex inequalities that use a range of operations. Reinforce that the methods for solving inequalities are the same as those used for solving equations. Recap that when you solve an inequality you should use SAMDIB to identify which operations to tackle first.

Questions 8 and **9** These questions involve coefficients of x that are negative. A common mistake is to divide by the negative coefficient and not swap the inequality sign. If students struggle to understand why this is the case you could show students what happens to the statement $4 > 2$ when it is multiplied by -1, giving the obviously incorrect answer $-4 > -2$. Some students may prefer to rearrange the inequality instead of dividing by a negative number and swapping the signs.

Question 10 This question will help students to understand the meaning of the inequality signs and give them practice identifying which numbers are included in the inequality.

Question 11 Ask students to describe the inequality in words first and then convert this into a solution represented on a number line. Ensure they remember that a filled circle is used when the number is included and a hollow circle is used when it is not.

Question 12 Students will first need to solve the inequality and then show the solution on a number line. Reinforce the need to show all stages of working out.

Questions 13 and **14** Discuss whether 12 or 13 should be the answer to the first part of question **13** and why this is the case. Question **14** involves similar questions but with negative coefficients of x. Remind students that they either need to swap the sign when they divide by a negative number or rearrange the inequality to eliminate the negative coefficient.

Simplification – Skills

Students should concentrate on showing and interpreting two-sided inequalities with number lines.

Extension – Skills

Challenge students to solve simple(ish) two-sided inequalities using a balance method. An example could be $-1 < 2x - 3 < 7$.

Recap – Applications

1 **a** Represent these statements on a number line:

  i $x > 1$ **ii** $x < -1$ **iii** $-5 \leq x \leq 2.5$

 b Find **all** the **whole number** solutions to:

  i $-1 < 3p < 17$ ([0, 1, 2, 3, 4, 5])

  ii $-5 \leq 3q \leq 6$ ([−1, 0, 1, 2])

  iii $11 \geq 5r \geq -5$ ([2, 1, 0, −1])

 c Solve these inequalities:

  i $3s < -12$ ($s < -4$)

  ii $5t \geq -35$ ($t \geq -7$)

  iii $3u - 14 \geq 4$ ($u \geq 5$)

  iv $6v + 14 < 2v - 6$ ($v < -5$)

2 Solve these inequalities.

 a $4(a + 8) < 12$ ($a < -5$)

 b $3(b - 2) \geq 9$ ($b \geq 5$)

 c $12 < 4(e + 3)$ ($e > 0$)

 d $-25 \geq 5(f + 2)$ ($f \leq -7$)

 e $30 \geq 4(7 - g)$ $\left(g \geq -\frac{1}{2}\right)$

Plenary – Applications

Write the statement: $8 \leq p < 14$. Ask students to respond on whiteboards to the questions:

What would the statement involving $2p$ look like? What would the statement involving $5p$ look like? What would the statement involving $5p + 2$ look like? Share and discuss after each question.

Write the statement $10 \leq 3a + 4 < 22$. Ask students to 'simplify' this statement to one involving a only. 'What would the first action be?' 'The next?' and so on.

Exercise commentary – Applications

Question 1 Ensure students appreciate that for the inequality to be true it will need to fit all the values of x.

Questions 2 and **3** In these questions students need to form and solve inequalities related to perimeters and areas of shapes. In question **3** students will need to take care that they form correct expressions for the area and perimeter as it is easy to confuse the two or make mistakes when simplifying. Remind them to check part **b** by substituting the value in and checking that it 'fits'.

Question 4 This inequality should be split and solved as two parts, then put back together as a final stage.
Questions *5 and ***7** These questions would make suitable extension questions or you could cover them together as a class and invite students to discuss and explain their ideas. It might be helpful to demonstrate the solution to question **7** using a graphical method.

Question 6 As a whole class ensure all students are clear about the definition of obtuse and reflex angles. Demonstrate how two-sided inequalities can be set up to represent the information given.

Question 8 Encourage students to consider the possible values that y could be and then for each possible value of y list all possible values of x, emphasise that x and y must be positive whole numbers.

Question 9 Encourage students to solve each inequality separately, then consider the values of x that are true for both inequalities and put this together using the inequality symbols.

Question 10 This question ensures that students are clear about the meanings of the inequality symbols.

Questions 11 and **12** In question **11** ask 'how can we write an expression for angle x in terms of y?' Given the question gives $x < 30°$ students should then be able to form the required inequality. For part **c**, ask students to think about what would happen to the total angles inside the triangle if this was not true. A similar approach will be needed to answer question **12**.

Simplification – Applications

Students may find it easier to approach some problems using a trial-and-error approach, testing out possible numbers on a number line.

Extension – Applications

Give students inequalities involving 'negative-x' terms. For example,

$$6 - x > 3 \quad \text{or} \quad 4 - 2x \geq -6 \quad \text{or} \quad -2 < 3 - x \leq 4$$

Encourage an approach based on adding and subtracting terms in order to isolate x, rather than involve the complication of multiplying by a negative. Students should check their answers by back substitution.

10 Equations and inequalities

Key outcomes	Quick check
A3 Understand and use the concepts and vocabulary of equations and inequalities, terms and factors.	**1** Solve these equations. **a** $g + 17 = 19$ (2) **b** $6h = 30$ (5) **c** $3i - 7 = 23$ (10) **d** $8j + 15 = 7$ (−1) **e** $\frac{k}{3} = 12$ (36)
A17 Solve linear equations in one unknown algebraically <u>(including those with the unknown on both sides of the equation)</u>; find approximate solutions using a graph.	**2** Solve these equations with unknowns on both sides. **a** $4y + 8 = 3y + 20$ (12) **b** $10y - 22 = 4y - 10$ (2) **c** $10 - 2y = 15 - y$ (−5)
A11 Deduce roots algebraically. A18 <u>Solve quadratic equations algebraically by factorising.</u>	**3** Solve these quadratic equations by factorising. **a** $x^2 + 8x - 9 = 0$ (−9, 1) **b** $x^2 + 6x + 8 = 0$ (−4, −2) **c** $x^2 - 7x + 10 = 0$ (2, 5) **d** $x^2 - 4 = 0$ (−2, 2) **e** $2x^2 - 6x = 0$ (0, 3) **f** $x^2 + 3x = 4$ (−4, 1)
A19 <u>Solve two simultaneous equations in two variables (linear/linear) algebraically; find approximate solutions using a graph</u>	**4** Solve these pairs of simultaneous equations **a** $4x + y = 19, 4x - 2y = -2$ ($x = 3, y = 7$) **b** $3a - 2b = 7, 5a + 2b = 1$ ($x = 1, y = -2$) **c** $x + 7y = 1, 3x + 10y = -8$ ($x = -6, y = 1$) d $2v + 5w = 21, 3v - 2w = 3$ ($x = 3, y = 3$) **5** Use the graph to estimate the solutions to the simultaneous equations $y = 4x$ and $y = 4 - x$. ($x = 0.8, y = 3.2$)
A21 <u>Translate simple situations or procedures into algebraic expressions or formulae; derive an equation (or two simultaneous equations), solve the equation(s) and interpret the solution.</u>	**6** The price of a sandwich and two apples is £3.20. The price of two sandwiches and one apple is £4.30. Write a pair of simultaneous equations and solve them to find the price of a sandwich and an apple. ($s + 2a = 3.2, 2s + a = 4.3, a =$ £0.70, $s =$ £1.80)
A22 <u>Solve linear inequalities in one variable; represent the solution set on a number line</u>	**7** Solve these inequalities and show each solution on a number line. **a** $8x - 4 \geq 36$ ($x \geq 5$) 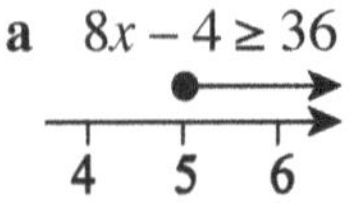 **b** $9x + 8 \leq 35$ ($x \leq 3$) 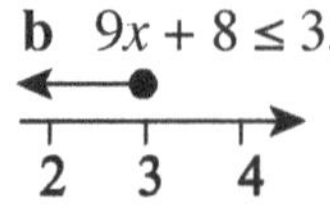 **c** $5x - 2 > 13 + 2x$ ($x > 5$) 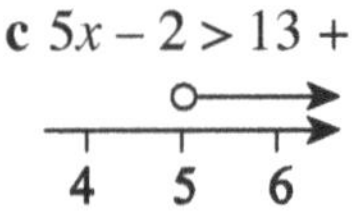 **d** $1 \leq x + 1 < 3$ ($0 \leq x < 2$) 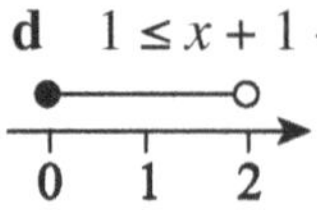

Misconceptions and challenges	Solutions
In equations where the solution is immediately clear by inspection, students are more likely to make an error in rearrangement. For example, when solving $7x + 21 = 56$ students add 21 to both sides.	Make sure that students check their answers by substituting back into the equation. Start with simpler equations such as $3x + 2 = 8$ that are easy to check.
Equations involving fraction notation, such as $\frac{x}{4} = 5$, can be difficult for students to interpret.	Make sure that students have a good understanding of the link between fractions, division, and BIDMAS. Look at the different ways of writing $\frac{x}{4}$. ($\frac{1}{4}$ times x, $\frac{1}{4}$ of x, x divided by 4, ...)

Misconceptions and challenges	Solutions
When solving linear equations with brackets, students misapply the BIDMAS rule, 'brackets first'. For example, when solving $5(x - 10) = 5$, students add 10 to both sides of the equation first.	Use a variety of visual images to support students' understanding. For example, put the expression in brackets in a box.
Students often make errors when rearranging formulae or solving equations. Encourage them to check their solutions in the original equation.	Spend some time looking at all the different kinds of errors that students can make. Give students a task that requires them to spot and explain different errors in a worked example.
Equations with unknowns on both sides can make students, who think they have grasped how to solve equations, lose confidence.	Encourage students to have a system, or a mental checklist, for how to solve the problem. For example, 1 Choose which side to cancel the unknowns on. 2 Cancel the unknowns.
In examples such as $\frac{x}{3} = 15$, students often give the solution $x = 5$, as 3 is a factor of 15.	Get students to make a list of things that make them 'trip up' in exams. This will help them to notice mistakes similar to this.
When deriving an equation from a context, students may avoid the question entirely, as it is not immediately obvious how to start.	Give students frequent practice of setting up and solving equations from contexts.
When solving inequalities involving negative numbers, such as $x > -5$, students show confusion about how to interpret the inequality sign.	Make sure that students have a number line to refer to for inequalities involving directed numbers.
Students write answers to inequalities with an equals sign.	This is indicates a common misconception of the '=' sign. Spend plenty of time working on the notion of '=' as equivalence and balance.

Review question commentary

Questions 1 and **2** (**10.1, 10.2**) – Encourage students to check their answers using substitution. Students should use the 'balance' method for question **2**.

Question 3 (**10.2**) – If necessary give a hint for an expression for Vicky's Mum's age $(x + 24)$.

Question 4 (**10.3**) – Students should give their factorisations in their solutions. In part **d** they need to spot difference of two squares.

Question 5 (**10.3**) – The quadratic equation needs to be rearranged first.

Question 6 (**10.4**) –When multiplying by a constant, a common error is to neglect to multiply the RHS.

Question 7 (**10.4**) – Students can work in kg or g as long as they are consistent.

Question 8 (**10.4**) – Students should find pairs of values that equal 4 for the $x + y = 4$ and think about gradient and y-intercept for $y = 2x + 1$.

Question 9 (**10.5**) – Check that the circles are not filled in for strict inequalities.

Question 10 (**10.5**) – Remind students to solve these in the same way as equations but take care with the direction and type of inequality sign.

Review answers

1 **a** 48 **b** 5 **c** 7 **d** 16.5
e 100 **f** –2

2 **a** 6 **b** 2 **c** –7

3 **a** $2x + 24 = 42$ **b** 9, 33

4 **a** –3, –5 **b** 1, 5 **c** –3, 2
d –8, 8 **e** 0, 12

5 $(x - 10)(x + 2) = 0, x = -2, 10$

6 **a** $x = 3, y = 5$ **b** $a = 1, b = -2$
c $x = 9, y = 3$ **d** $v = 2, w = -3$

7 **a** $2c + w = 3.75, 3c + 2w = 6$
b $c = 1.5$ kg, $w = 0.75$ kg

8 Graph of $y = 2x + 1$ and $x + y = 4, x = 1, y = 3$

9 **a**
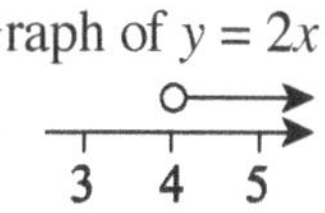

b
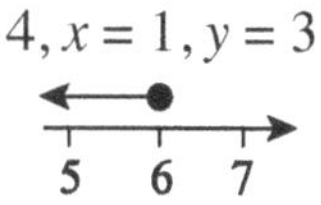

c
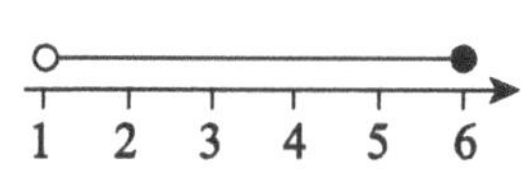

10 **a** $x > 5$ **b** $x \leq 3$ **c** $x \geq 1$ **d** $x > -1$
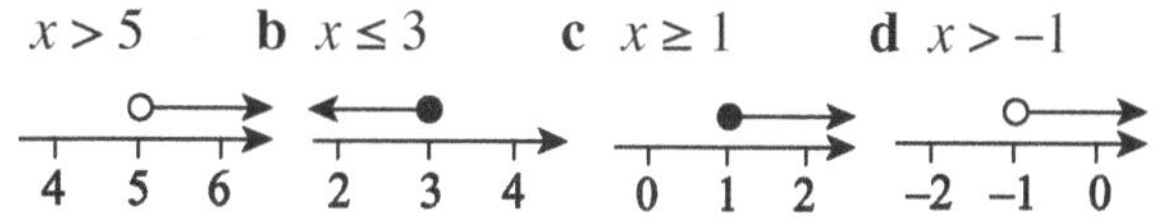

Assessment 10

Question 1 – 3 marks
$2(5 + 2s) = 49$ [B1]
$2s = 49 \div 2 - 5$ [M1]
$s = 4.9$ cm [A1]

Question 2 – 2 marks
$x + 4x = 55$ [B1]
11 years [B1]

Question 3 – 2 marks
$p + p + 22 = 27.5$ [B1]
2.75 kg [B1]

Question 4 – 4 marks
$x = 3y$ and $x = y + 6$ [B1]
$3y = y + 6$ [M1]
Albert 3, Oliver 9 [A2]

Question 5 – 4 marks
$y = z + 36,\ z = x - 22$ and $x + y + z = 454$ [B1]
$x + (x - 22 + 36) + x - 22 = 454$ [B1]
$x = (454 + 8) \div 3$ [M1]
154 g [A1]

Question 6 – 6 marks
a $x + \frac{1}{2}(x + 150) + (x + 150) = 2000$ [B1]
b $\frac{5}{2}x + 225 = 2000$
$5x + 450 = 4000$
$x = (4000 - 450) \div 5$ [M2]
$= 710$ [A1]
c Brendan €710, Arsene €430, José €860
Lose 1 mark for each error. [B2]

Question 7 – 8 marks
$a \times (a + 9) - a \times 5 = 45$ [B2]
$a^2 + 4a - 45 = (a + 9)(a - 5) = 0$
OR equivalent method of solution [M3]
$a = -9$ or 5 [A2]
$a > 0$ because it is a length [B1]

Question 8 – 7 marks
a $5k - 2(30 - k) = 115$ [B2]
$k = (115 + 60) \div 7$ [M1]
$k = 25$ [A1]
b $5k - 2(30 - k) > 0$ [B1]
$k > 60 \div 7 = 8.571\ldots$ [M1]
9 km [A1]

Question 9 – 3 marks
a $(w + 8)(w - 9)$ [B2]
b $w = -8$ or 9 [B1]

Question 10 – 6 marks
$a^2 - b^2 = (a - b)(a + b)$ [M2]
$(89 - 11)(89 + 11) = 78 \times 100 = 7800$ [A2]
$(6.89 - 3.11)(6.89 + 3.11) = 3.78 \times 10 = 37.8$ [A2]

Question 11 – 6 marks
$s^2 + (s - 2)^2 = 202$ [B1]
$s^2 + s^2 - 4s + 4 = 202$
$s^2 - 2s - 99 = (s - 11)(s + 9) = 0$ [M2]
$s = 11$ or -9 [A2]
$s > 0, s = 11$ cm [B1]

Question 12 – 4 marks
$n \times (n + 2) = 63$ [B1]
$n^2 + 2n - 63 = (n + 9)(n - 7) = 0$ [M1]
OR
$\sqrt{63} = 7.937\ldots \approx 8$ plus inspection [M2]
7 and 9 or 7 and –9 [A1]

Question 13 – 4 marks
$\frac{1}{2}n(n+1) = 5050$ [B1]
$n^2 + n - 10\,100 = (n + 101)(n - 100) = 0$ [M2]
$n = 100$ $[n > 0]$ [A1]

Question 14 – 5 marks
$h = 20t - 5t^2 = 15$ [B1]
$t^2 - 4t + 3 = (t - 1)(t - 3) = 0$ [M2]
1 s, going up and 3 s, coming down. [A2]

Question 15 – 4 marks
$n(n - 3) = 2 \times 54$ [B1]
$n^2 - 3n - 108 = (n - 12)(n + 9) = 0$ [M2]
12 sides $[n > 0]$ [A1]

Question 16 – 4 marks
$b + r = 46$ and $b - r = 10$ [B1]
$2b = 56$ and $2r = 36$ OR equivalent [M1]
Batman 28, Robin 18 [A2]

Question 17 – 4 marks
a $2a + 2c = 22$ and $2a + 5c = 35.5$ [B1]
$3c = 13.5,\ c = 4.5,\ a = 11 - 4.5$
OR equivalent [M1]
£6.50 [A1]
b £4.50 [B1]

Question 18 – 4 marks
$5b + g = 150$ and $8b + g = 210$ [B1]
$3b = 60,\ b = 20,\ g = 150 - 5 \times 20$
OR equivalent [M2]
50 g [A1]

Question 19 – 4 marks
$g - l = 2.5$ and $g + l = 40.5$ [B1]
$2g = 43$ and $2l = 38$ OR equivalent [M1]
Graham £21.50, Liz £19 [A2]

Question 20 – 5 marks
a $5d + 3c = 549$ and $3d + c = 279$ [B1]
$4d = 3 \times 279 - 549 = 288$ OR equivalent [M2]
72p [A1]
b 63p $[279 - 3 \times 72]$ [A1]

Question 21 – 5 marks
$3D + 2C = 4583$ and $D + 3C = 2692$ [B1]
$7C = 3 \times 2692 - 4583 = 3493$ OR equivalent [M2]
DVD £11.95, CD £4.99 [A2]

Question 22 – 5 marks
a $2s + 6c = 3500$ and $10s + 2c = 3500$ [B1]
$28s = 3 \times 3500 - 3500 = 7000$ OR equivalent [M2]
£250 [A1]
b £500 [A1]

Question 23 – 5 marks
a $5m + 6w = 38$ and $6m + 12w = 60$ [B1]
$4m = 2 \times 38 - 60 = 14$ OR equivalent [M2]
Maggot 4p, Worm 3p [A2]

Question 24 – 3 marks
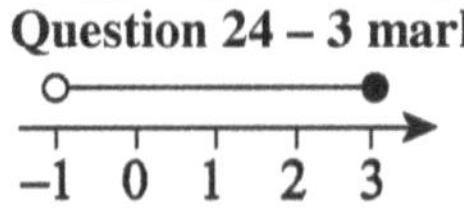

Correct end symbols [B2]
Correct line position [B1]

Question 25 – 3 marks
$14 \geq 4c \geq -3 \Rightarrow 3.5 \geq c \geq -0.75$ [M1]
3, 2, 1 or 0
Lose one mark for each missing integer. [A2]

Question 26 – 2 marks
$0 < z < 84$ $[= 180 - (35 + 61)]$ [B2]

Question 27 – 3 marks
a $\frac{1}{a} < 1$ [B1]
b Not true for, 0 ⍰ b ⍰ 1. No [M1, A1]

Circles and constructions

Learning outcomes

A5 Understand and use standard mathematical formulae; [rearrange formulae to change the subject].

G1 Use the standard conventions for labelling and referring to the sides and angles of triangles; draw diagrams from written description.

G2 Use the standard ruler and compass constructions (perpendicular bisector of a line segment, constructing a perpendicular to a given line from/at a given point, bisecting a given angle); use these to construct given figures and solve loci problems; know that the perpendicular distance from a point to a line is the shortest distance to the line.

G9 Identify and apply circle definitions and properties, including: centre, radius, chord, diameter, circumference, tangent, arc, sector and segment.

G15 Measure line segments and angles in geometric figures, including interpreting maps and scale drawings and use of bearings.

G17 Know the formulae: circumference of a circle = $2\pi r = \pi d$, area of a circle = πr^2; calculate: perimeters of 2D shapes, including circles; areas of circles and composite shapes.

G18 Calculate arc lengths, angles and areas of sectors of circles.

R2 Use scale factors, scale diagrams and maps.

Prior knowledge

Check-in skill

- Accurately measure line segments and angles.
- Calculate the area of rectangles.

Online resources

MyMaths 1083, 1088, 1089, 1090, 1118, 1147

InvisiPen videos
Skills: 11Sa – h Applications: 11Aa – e

Kerboodle assessment
Online Skills Test 11 Chapter Test 11

Development and links

Creating accurate mathematical constructions has important applications in architecture, graphic design, engineering and art. Police and Mountain rescue teams use loci to determine a search area based on the missing person's last known location and presumed travelling speed.

The circumference of the wheel is an exact length such as one metre. The distance is measured by rolling the wheel along the ground and counting the revolutions.

Chapter investigation

Careful investigation leads to the sequence 2, 4, 7, 11, 16, 32, … $\frac{1}{2}(n^2 + n + 2)$. Restricting the lines to chords joining points on the circumference (Moser's problem) gives the infamous misleading sequence 1, 2, 4, 8, 16, 31, …, $\frac{1}{24}(n^4 - 6n^3 + 23n - 18n + 24)$.

Return to the initial division problem and work through the associated language [**11.1**]. Extend this to looking at the lengths and areas of various shapes: focus on arcs and sectors. Start by looking at calculating the area and circumference. The two formulae can be related to each other by dividing the circle into lots of small triangles: these are all of height $\approx r$ and the total base length $\approx 2\pi r$.

The areas and arc lengths of semi-circles and quadrants are intuitively easy by dividing whole circle results into halves and quarters. Extend this idea to arcs and sectors with an arbitrary angle at the centre [**11.2**].

Consider a circle with a diameter drawn: ask students if they can quarter the circle without using a protractor. Use this to introduce the perpendicular bisector construction [**11.3**]. Asking for division into eighths would make use of angle bisection whilst division into sixths requires the construction of a 60° angle. Further constructions can be covered.

An interesting locus problem is to find a point equidistant from three points on the circumference of a circle. This requires finding the perpendicular bisectors of two chords which cross at the centre of the circle [**11.4**]. This is equivalent to finding the circumcircle of a triangle. A variant is finding a point that is equidistant from the three sides of a triangle which gives the incentre of a triangle. (The sides are tangents to the circle however at foundation knowledge of tangents is not required.) Expand the discussion to cover further locus problems.

11.1 Circles 1

Objectives

① **G9** Identify and apply circle definitions and properties, including centre, radius, diameter, circumference.

② **G17** Know the formulae for the circumference and area of a circle; calculate areas and perimeters of composite shapes involving circles

Useful resources

Mini whiteboards, pair of board compasses, OHT/whiteboard file of parts of a circle, calculators, string

Starter – Skills

Invite a student to describe a square, as if to someone (an alien?) who had no concept of different shapes. Encourage other students to draw the shape as it is being described. Highlight the importance of defining properties.

Repeat with different triangles and quadrilaterals.

Challenge a student to describe a circle. Demonstrate by playing 'devil's advocate' how descriptions such as 'round' are inadequate.

Teaching notes – Skills

Leading on from the starter, draw a circle using a pair of compasses. Explain that each point of a circle is exactly the same distance (equidistant) from the centre.

Define radius as the distance between the centre and the circle. Identify and label various parts of the shape:

centre radius chord diameter circumference
tangent arc sector segment

Take time to differentiate between straight and curved lines, and lines and areas.

Display the formulae for area and circumference of a circle:

$C = \pi d$ or $C = 2\pi r$

$A = 2\pi r^2$

Discuss the approximate values for π. Demonstrate that π is 'about 3' by cutting a piece of string to exactly the length of the diameter of circular object, such as a bin. Compare this with the length of string that wraps around it.

Highlight that the digits of π continue infinitely but that it is approximated to 3.142. Encourage students to find the π button on their calculators.

Work through some examples of finding circumference and area of circles. Remind students of the correct units for each.

Plenary – Skills

The circumference of the London Eye is 425 m. What is the length of each spoke?

Exercise commentary – Skills

Question 1 Students should use a calculator for this question. As an extension you could ask students to estimate the answers first for the questions with non-integer answers.

Question 2 This question should help students to visualise that the circumference is π times the diameter.

Questions 3 and **4** Students may confuse the two formulas $C = \pi d$ and $C = 2\pi r$. Point out that, in parts **a** and **c** they can double the radius first and use $C = \pi d$ or save the doubling and use $C = 2\pi r$. Potential errors include incorrect units. Answers can be given as decimals or in terms of π.

Questions 5 and **6** Both of these questions involve either rearranging the formulae and the substituting in the correct values or using the known values and then rearranging to find the required dimension. The second example on page 230 is a good example of the latter.

Question 7 For circles **c** and **d**, it would be good practice for students to use the basic equations $C = \pi d$, $C = 2\pi r$ and $A = \pi r^2$ and then find r or d by rearrangement, rather than by substituting into pre-rearranged formulae.

Question 8 Remind students that the perimeter includes the straight side as well as the semi-circular arc.

Question 9 This question is similar to the first example on page 230. Remind students that the area of a composite shape is the sum of its parts but that the perimeter is not.

Questions 10 and ***11** These questions are similar to question **9** but involve subtraction. In question ***11** remind students to use the perpendicular, not the slant, height of the trapezium.

Question 12 This question provides a useful opportunity to demonstrate during a whole-class discussion that, when working in terms of π, the answers are independent of π.

Simplification – Skills

Students could be given further examples where the dimensions are exactly what they need, so diameter for circumference and radius for area. Avoid having them work backwards.

Extension – Skills

Challenge students to work out the areas and circumferences of semi-circles and quarter circles.

Recap – Applications

1 a Calculate the circumference and areas of a circle with diameter 78 cm.

(Circumference = 245 cm, Area = 780 cm^2)

b A crop circle has a circumference of 25.1 m. Calculate its radius. (4.00 m)

c Another crop circle has an area of 302 ft^2. Calculate its radius. (9.80 ft)

2 A football club logo consists of a semi-circle on top of an equilateral triangle.

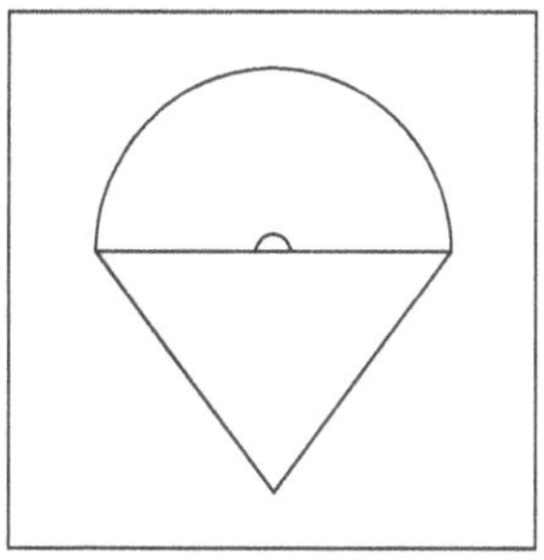

a On the players shirt, the diameter of the semi-circle is 3.5 cm. Calculate the circumference of the logo. (12.5 cm)

b On a hoarding outside the club ground, the radius of the semi-circle is 8 ft. Calculate the circumference of the logo. (41.1 ft)

3 a Find the area and perimeter of a **quarter circle** with diameter $d = 23.4$ m.

(Area = 108 m^2, perimeter = 41.8 m)

b A 30 m garden hose is wound on a wheel. The diameter of the wheel is 40 cm. Percy the Park Keeper completely unwinds the reel. How many times, to the nearest whole number, does the reel rotate? (Ignore the thickness of the hose)

(12 times)

Plenary – Applications

Sketch a circle with radius 5 cm and ask for its area. Now sketch a square around it, with sides as tangents. Discuss the area of the square.

Exercise commentary – Applications

In this exercise a complete answer will generally require some written explanation of the method. Students should be reminded to explain their method in writing as they work towards their answer. The worked examples on page 232 provide good models of writing. Encourage students to work in terms of π where appropriate.

Question 1 In this question it would be appropriate for students to leave their workings in terms of π until the very end.

Questions 2 to **4** A common error is that, when students are finding areas, they use d rather than r.

Question 3 In part **b**, remind students to use the perpendicular height (not the slant height) when finding the area of a trapezium. Refer to the first worked example on page 232.

Question 4 Part **a** is similar to the second worked example on page 232. Part **b** is more difficult as students have to see how the three semi-circles combine to be able to calculate the area.

Question 5 This question could prove tricky for some students as they need to spot that the diagonals of the hexagon form equilateral triangles in order to find the perimeter of the hexagon.

Question 6 Show students that the quickest way to find the area of two identical semi-circles is to find the area of one circle.

Question 7 A whole-class discussion may be necessary for students to realise that, in rotating once, the cycle has moved forward a distance equal to the circumference. A demonstration using a wheel or thin cylinder will help. Possible errors may occur in converting between km and cm.

Question *8 There are two methods to answer this question. One is to find $\frac{3}{4}$ of the square's area and compare this with the circle's area. The other is to write the circle's area as a fraction of the square's. The first method is likely to be the easier to understand.

Question *9 Compare this question to question **6**, and the method used to find the area of two semi-circles. Ask students for a quick way of finding the total length of the two semi-circular arcs.

Question *10 Students may not realise that the given diagram is not the whole sheet of metal, they may simply count the circles on the diagram. Students should draw their own sketch before starting their calculations.

Simplification – Applications

Students should be given more examples where they simply apply the formula. Check that they are setting out their work carefully and that they are consistently getting the answers right.

Extension – Applications

Students could consider how many revolutions a standard car tyre completes in a mile (or kilometre). How many would this be in a year, if the average mileage is 10 000 miles?

11.2 Circles 2

Objectives

① **G9** Identify and apply circle definitions and properties, including centre, radius, chord, diameter, circumference, arc, sector and segment

② **G18** Calculate arc lengths, angles and areas of sectors of circles

Useful resources

OHT/whiteboard file of the parts of a circle, calculators

Starter – Skills

I want to make a circle with a circumference of 120 cm. I will make it from a set of identical arcs.

One possibility is that I could use 4 arcs of 30 cm each. What other arc lengths could I use?

($1 \times 120,\ 2 \times 60,\ 3 \times 40,\ 4 \times 30,\ 5 \times 24,\ 6 \times 20$
$8 \times 15,\ 10 \times 12,\ 12 \times 10,\ 15 \times 8,\ 20 \times 6,\ 24 \times 5$
$30 \times 4,\ 40 \times 30,\ 60 \times 2,\ 120 \times 1$)

If you use 4 arcs of 30 cm each, then each arc makes an angle of 90° with the centre. How many degrees will the other possible solutions make?
(360°, 180°, 120°, 90°, 72°, 60°, 45°, 36°, 30°, 24°, 18°, 15°, 12°, 9°, 6°, 3°.)

You could do the same starter with sectors instead.

Teaching notes – Skills

Recap the formulae for area and circumference of a circle. Emphasise that there are two commonly used formulae for circumference.

Explain that the word circumference only applies to the whole of a circle. The area of a semi-circle is half the area of the circle, but the perimeter of a semi-circle is not half the circumference. Work through an example where you find the area an perimeter of a semi-circle, emphasising that the perimeter is half the circle plus the diameter.

Remind students of the terms arc and sector, referring to the mental starter. You could draw a circle and ask students to label its parts. Introduce the angle, θ, as the angle at the centre of a circle, and justify the formulae for arc length and sector area.

Work through several examples on finding arcs, sector areas and perimeters using a fractional multiplier. Give another example using a sector angle of 50° and radius of 10 cm, and ask for the sector area (43.5 cm^2 3 sf).

Plenary – Skills

For a sector of angle 45° and radius 4 m, find the arc length, sector area and perimeter either:

- in terms of π or
- as an estimate without a calculator.

Use π as 3 in all estimates unless told otherwise.
(arc = π m or 3 m, sector area = 2π m^2 or 6 m^2, perimeter = $\pi + 8$ m or 11 m.)

Exercise commentary – Skills

Some questions ask for answers in terms of π.

Question 1 Remind students how to cancel fractions and if necessary refer them to the example on page 96.

Questions 2 to **6** These questions are very similar to the first two examples on page 234. In question **5**, note that the diameter is given, not the radius. Students should give their answers to 3 significant figures, except in question **6**, where their answers should be left in terms of π.

Questions 7 and **8** These two questions involve students substituting the known values into the formulae and then rearranging to find the required dimension. Refer students to the third worked example on page 234 if they get stuck.

Question *9 This question is similar to question **2c** as students first have to find the area of a quarter circle. Students then need to calculate the area of the square and find the difference.

Question 10 This question involves rearranging the formula for the length of an arc to find the angle of the sector. Students then need to use this information to calculate the area of the sector.

Question 11 This question is very similar to question **6** as students need to find both the perimeter and area of the sector. In this question it would be more appropriate for students to give their answers to 3 significant figures.

Simplification – Skills

Students could be given further examples to consolidate the basic application of the methods. Half and quarter circles could also be given to avoid the need for ratios.

Extension – Skills

Set this question. It is designed to check on students' ability to sketch a diagram from a description in words. It also demonstrates that leaving an answer in terms of π is sometimes quicker as well as more accurate. Discuss why it is more accurate.

a *OPQ* is a sector of a circle of radius 5 cm. *O* is the centre of the circle. Angle *POQ* = 108°. Sketch the sector and work out the length of the arc *PQ* in terms of π. (3π cm)

b *CAB* is a sector of a different circle which has its centre at *C*. Angle *ACB* = 60°. The arc *AB* is equal in length to the arc *PQ*. Sketch this sector and find the radius, *AC*. (9 cm)

Recap – Applications

1 a Find the length of arc, perimeter and area of this sector:

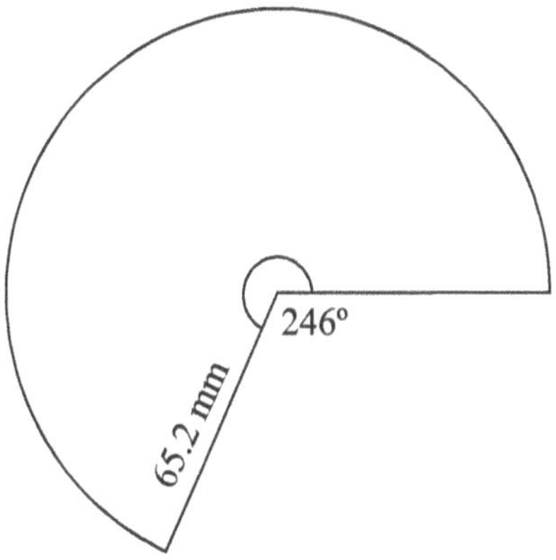

(Length of arc = 280 m, perimeter = 410 m, area of sector = 130 m^2)

b Find the angle at the centre of the circle for an arc with radius, $r = 4.6$ cm and arc length = 4.4 cm. (54.8°)

2 A right-angled triangle has a base of 13.86 cm and a height of 8 cm.

A circle with radius 2.928 cm, is cut from the triangle.

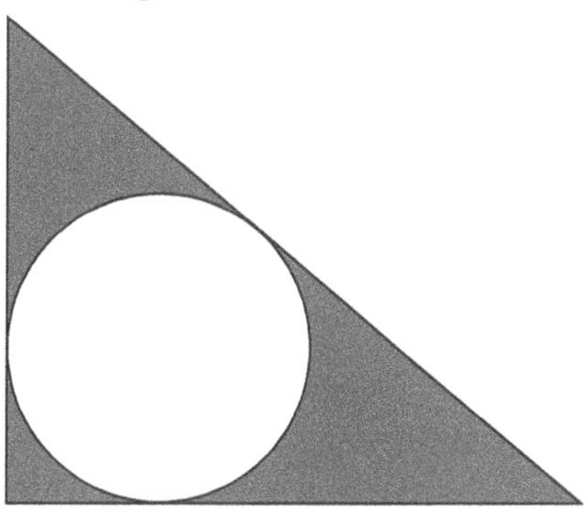

What is the area left? (28.5 cm^2)

Plenary – Applications

Set this question. The answer may surprise students.

Jayne buys three 8-inch pizzas for £9.99.

Kyle buys one 14-inch pizza for the same price.

Which person gets the most pizza for their money?

(Kyle (49π) gets more than Jayne (48π))

Exercise commentary – Applications

Question 1 Students need to spot that the hem is the length of the exterior arc and does not include the straight edges or the interior arc.

Question 2 Part **a** is fairly straightforward as students have to find the difference between the areas of the two sectors. In part **b**, remind students that the shaded area has two straight edges and two arcs.

Question 3 This question will need clear written explanation of students' methods. It might help students to draw a sketch of the diagram in the question and label each arc in order to keep track of their calculations.

Question 4 This question may require a whole-class discussion. Ask students what extra lines are needed on a copy of the diagram. Some students may think that they need to draw radii into the centre of the diagram when in actual fact the four arc lengths come from four separate circles.

Question 5 This question will also require a whole-class discussion. For part **a**, ask the question 'When the small cog rotates once, does the large cog also rotate once?' This will lead students to realise that the circumference of the small cog maps onto only an arc of the large cog. Part **a** can extend into part **b** by asking students 'When the small cog rotates once, what fraction of the circumference of the large cog does it engage with?'

Question 6 This question is a composite shape involving an equilateral triangle and a sector. Remind students that when calculating the area of the triangle they need to use the perpendicular height.

Question 7 Outlining one quarter circle in colour will help students to see the method for part **a**. For part **b**, it would help students to see the two quarter-circles cut out of paper and placed in position so that they overlap. Discuss how adding their areas relate to the area of the square.

Simplification – Applications

Students may need help in finding the relevant information from a diagram. Write up part-answers as they are found, to show how to build up the complete answer. A very common error in questions is forgetting to add on the straight sides so draw attention to this.

Extension – Applications

Students could be given further applied examples. They could also be asked to work backwards from a given area/arc length to find the angle/radius of the given sector.

11.3 Constructions

Objectives

① **G2** Use the standard ruler and compass constructions (perpendicular bisector of a line segment, constructing a perpendicular to a given line from/at a given point, bisecting a given angle)

Useful resources

Pairs of compasses for students and a board compass, rulers for students and a board ruler, tracing paper, geometry tool, pre-drawn diagrams

Starter – Skills

A snail crosses a railway track as fast as possible. It can move at a speed of 2 feet every 3 min. The track is 4 feet 8 inches wide. (There are 12 inches in a foot.)

How long will it take to cross the track?
(7 min)

What assumption must you make about the way the snail crosses the track?
(The rails are parallel and to cross at the shortest distance you must cross the rails at 90°.)

Teaching notes – Skills

What does 'bisect' mean? (Cut into two equal pieces.)

What is the difference between 'parallel' and 'perpendicular'? (Lines going in the same direction or lines crossing at 90°.)

Demonstrate bisecting an angle. Allow students time to draw their own, then to check that the two angles are indeed equal using tracing paper.

Ask students to choose a point on the bisector and then measure the shortest distance between the point and each of the two lines which form the original angle. These should be equal.

Demonstrate the construction of the perpendicular bisector of a line. Allow students time to draw their own, then to check that the two angles are indeed equal using tracing paper and to measure the two line segments. Ask students to choose a point on the bisector and then measure the distance between this point and the ends of the original line.

Demonstrate constructing a perpendicular from a point to a line. Allow students time to draw their own, then check that the two angles are equal using tracing paper.

Demonstrate constructing a perpendicular from a point on a line. Allow students time to draw their own, then check that the two angles are equal using tracing paper.

Plenary – Skills

How can you construct angles of 120°, 300°, 150° and 210° from an equilateral triangle using only a ruler and compasses?

Exercise commentary – Skills

Students should only use a pencil, pair of compasses and a ruler for constructions in this exercise. Protractors should only be used to check answers.

Questions 1 and **2** This question provides practice of a perpendicular bisector in different orientations. Students can refer to the first construction on page 238 for the method. If they get stuck drawing a perpendicular bisector in a different orientation remind them that they can turn their paper around!

Question 3 Students should extend the ends of their line beyond M and N before doing this construction.

Question 4 Remind students that the shortest distance from a point to a line is a perpendicular bisector. Students will not be penalised if their constructed line goes beyond the line QR but encourage them to only construct what is asked for.

Question 5 This question provides a useful demonstration that the construction of an angle bisector is the same for both acute and obtuse angles. As an extension you could ask students to do the same for a reflex angle.

Question 6 It might be useful for students to highlight this question in their books once it is complete as it will help them if they ever need to construct a 45° in future questions.

Question 7 In part **b ii** ask students for the sum of angles which make a straight line.

Question *8 Students have already constructed angles of 90°, 45°, 60° and 30°. Before they tackle this question ask students how they would theoretically combine these angles to make the required angles in the question. As an extension you could ask students to come up with some other combinations of these four angles and then attempt to draw them.

Question 9 Remind students that they are not allowed the use of a protractor for this question.

Question *10 This question provides useful practice of perpendicular bisectors. Remind students to extend their lines beyond those given.

Simplification – Skills

Students should be carefully monitored to ensure that they are constructing their bisectors correctly and should have further practice at both types before trying to apply the skills. Pre-drawn lines and angles will help.

Extension – Skills

Students could be encouraged to do the constructions to be discussed in the plenary.

Recap – Applications

1 **a** Draw a horizontal line, XY, 12 cm long.

b Using straight edge and compasses only, construct the perpendicular bisector of XY. Label it PQ and the point of intersection, O.

c Using straight edge and compasses only, construct the angle bisector of angle POY.

d Mark a point 5 cm from O on this bisector.

e Using straight edge and compasses only, construct the perpendicular line from this point to the line OY. Label this point Z.

f Measure and record the length OZ. (3.5 cm)

2 **a** Draw a horizontal straight line 6 cm long. Using straight edge and compasses only, construct an equilateral triangle of side 6 cm.

b Draw a horizontal straight line 15 cm long and mark two points A and B on it, where $AB = 2$ cm.

c Using straight edge and compasses only, construct the perpendicular to AB at the point A.

d Mark a point, C, on this line, 5 cm from A, and complete the triangle ABC.

e Measure and record the length CB. (13 cm)

f Using a protractor measure and record the angles ACB and ABC. (67°, 23°)

Plenary – Applications

Suppose you have a plate in the shape of an equilateral triangle. How can you find the point underneath it that it will balance on (centre of mass)?

(The intersection of the perpendicular bisectors of each side. Only two are necessary, but a third side is a good way to check the accuracy of the construction. Note this is *only* true for an equilateral triangle.)

Exercise commentary – Applications

Students should not use a protractor in this exercise.

Question 1 Refer to the worked example on page 240. Students could use tracing paper to copy the given diagram.

Question 2 Students may need reminding of how to construct a scale diagram, they could use the examples on pages 140 and 142 to help.

Questions 3 to **5** These questions explore the reasons why the constructions work. In question **4** students have to explain why a construction works using congruent triangles. Students may need to recap congruence using the examples on pages 56 and 58.

Question 6 Draw students' attention to the fact the coordinates of the intersection of the perpendicular bisector with the line is the midpoint.

Questions 7* and ***8** Emphasise that large triangles are requested for both of these questions, but not so large that the circumcircle does not fit the paper.

Simplification – Applications

Students can be provided with pre-drawn diagrams to help.

Extension – Applications

Students can investigate the various different centres of a triangle such as the incentre and the circumcentre. They could look at how these can be accurately constructed.

Loci

Objectives

① **G2** Use constructions to solve loci problems

② **G2** Know that the perpendicular distance from a point to a line is the shortest distance to the line

Useful resources

Mini whiteboards, geometry software, construction equipment for students, loci situations written on A5/A6 cards, pre-drawn diagrams

Starter – Skills

Ask students to imagine a pet dog on a lead that is fixed to a post in a field. Ask them to sketch the area that the dog can reach. Discuss the responses, and pick out any errors for further questioning.

Change the scenario by asking students now to imagine a person standing still, and a second person walking so that the first person is always 2 metres away.

Discuss the two scenarios, exploring the vocabulary and how certain changes affect the situations, for example, 'at least...', 'no more than...', 'equidistant from ...'.

Teaching notes – Skills

Explain that in the starter students were finding loci. A locus is the path formed by a point that moves according to a rule. Ask for explanations about how an accurate version of the locus could be produced.

Use an example to highlight the producing an accurate drawing in three stages:

visualise → sketch → construct

Discuss the main types of loci:

- constant distance from a point (circle)
- equidistant from two points (perpendicular bisector)
- constant distance from a line (parallel line)
- equidistant from two intersecting lines (angle bisector)

Distribute the loci cards to individuals or pairs. Ask students to work to produce diagrams. Encourage the students to continue with the visualise → sketch → construct stages, whether constructing by hand or computer.

Plenary – Skills

Discuss the types of construction used to find loci: circles, perpendicular bisectors, angle bisectors.

Ensure that students are comfortable with these constructions.

Exercise commentary – Skills

Questions **3**, **4**, **5**, **7** and **11** involve loci that are lines. Questions **6**, **8**, **9** and **10** involve loci that are regions. Questions **1**, **2** and **12** ask for sketches, these need not be accurate. However, the loci in these questions – except **12a** – could easily be drawn accurately.

Question 1 This question introduces students to the idea that a dotted line is used when the points on the boundary are not included and a solid line is used when they are.

Question 2 In part **a**, introduce the word 'equidistant' from *PQ* and *RS*.Note that the locus extends an infinite distance to the right and left. In parts **b** and **c**, question students carefully if their loci do not include circular arcs.

Questions 3 and **4** These two questions cover the locus of points that form a perpendicular bisector and an angle bisector.Students could refer to the second example on page 242 if they are stuck.

Question 5 This question is very similar to question **2** part **b**.

Question 6 This question should be constructed on one diagram (not two separate diagrams) so that the locus is the region within two overlapping circles.

Question 7 This question is very similar to question **2** part **c**.

Question 8 This question involves drawing two circles from the same point and shading the required region. Remind students that a dotted line is used when the points on the boundary are not included and a solid line is used when they are.

Question 9 This question combines the locus of points a given distance from a point with the locus of points a given distance from a line.

Question 10 In part **a**, the right angle should be constructed without using a protractor. In part **b**, students will readily interpret 'more than 7 cm from *C*' but some will struggle to realise that 'nearer to *A* than to *B*' involves a perpendicular bisector of *AB*.

Question 11 Ask students how the construction of a 60° angle on page 238 can be used in this question. Points equidistant from *AB* and *BC* lie on the bisector of angle *ABC*; so finding point *X* requires the construction of the three bisectors of angles *A*, *B* and *C*, although just two of them are sufficient to find *X*. Mention to students that *X* is called the in-centre of the triangle and they can use it to draw the in-circle. As an extension, students could draw the angle bisectors of any triangle to see if they produce an in-centre. A further extension would be to investigate the intersection of the perpendicular bisectors of the three sides of any triangle – and so find the circumcentre and the circumcircle.

Question * 12These two loci are initially best demonstrated physically to the whole class with a large circle and square cut from card. Students can then replicate the motion using constructions on paper.

Simplification – Skills

Students should practise basic loci constructions, using further examples if necessary. Ensure that students can construct the bisectors, etc. accurately before proceeding to formal loci.

Extension – Skills

Challenge the students to draw the locus of points equidistant from a line segment. (It looks like a running track with curved ends on it.)

Recap – Applications

1 Describe these loci.

a The locus of all points which are 10 cm from a fixed line *AB*.

b The locus of all points which are 4 cm from the circumference of a circle of radius 3 cm.

c The locus of all points which are closer to the centre of a square than they are to any of the other vertices.

(**a**

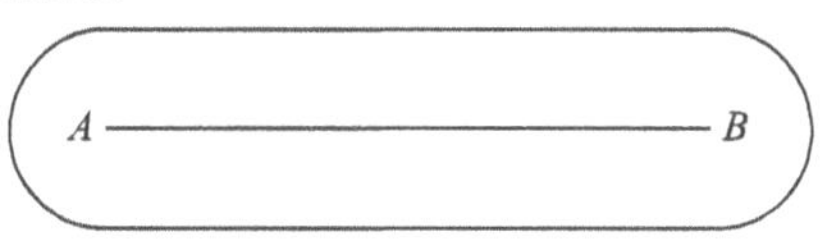

b

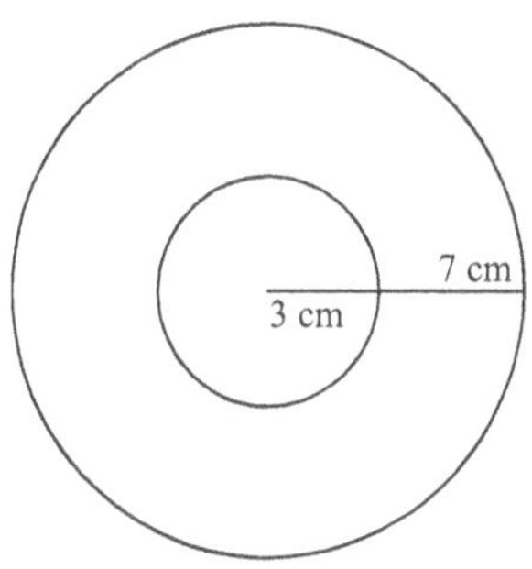

c)

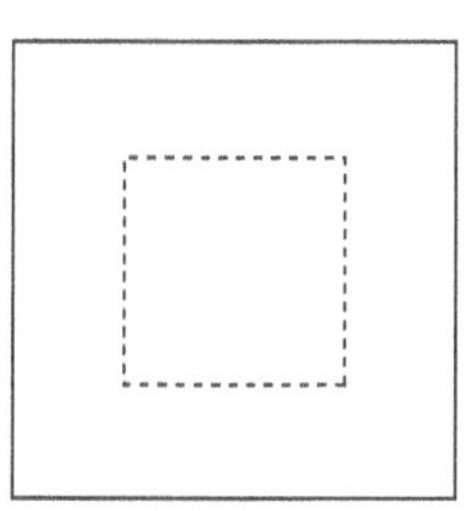

Plenary – Applications

Challenge students to draw the locus of the points an equal distance round the outside of these shapes. Split the class into groups and ask one member of each group to put their solution on the board. Remind students that sharp corners get rounded off, just like making something in DT, where you sand off sharp corners. Complete the first example as a demonstration.

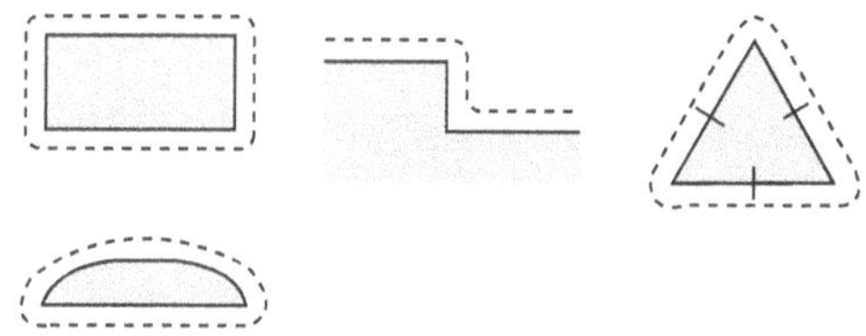

Exercise commentary – Applications

Squared paper can be used to help students draw shapes such as rectangles. Tracing paper is needed for question **6**. Revision of bearings will be essential for questions **2** and **4**, students could look back at the examples on pages 140 and 142 if they need additional help. There are many scale diagrams, the scale is sometimes given and sometimes not.

Question 1 This question is very similar to the example on page 244.

Question 2 Emphasise that the words 'the bearing of *B* from *A*' imply that the student is at *A* and looking away from *A* towards *B*, so that centre of the protractor is placed on *A* when measuring the bearing. An initial sketch will help students to position the scale drawing on the paper. A 360° protractor could be used as some students will need help with a 180° protractor.

Question 3 As part **a** asks students to 'draw' not 'construct' students do not need to use a pair of compasses to answer this part of the question. For part **b** a pair of compasses is essential.

Question 4 An initial sketch will help students to decide the scale and positioning of the diagram on paper.

Question 5 Students may find it difficult to answer part **b**, ask them 'which point in the garden is furthest from the power point at *P*?'

Question 6 For this question students should use tracing paper to copy the map.

Question *7 Challenge students to justify which sector will have the largest area before doing the calculations. To answer part **b ii** students may need to revise how to find the area of a sector using the example on page 232.

Simplification – Applications

Students could be given pre-drawn diagrams to help them.

Extension – Applications

Students can be given further examples that involve the application of loci to practical problems.

11 Circles and constructions

Key outcomes	Quick check
G1 Use the standard conventions for labelling and referring to the sides and angles of triangles; draw diagrams from written description. G2 Use the standard ruler and compass constructions (perpendicular bisector of a line segment, constructing a perpendicular to a given line from /at a given point, bisecting a given angle); use these to construct given figures and solve loci problems; know that the perpendicular distance from a point to a line is the shortest distance to the line.	**1 a** Use a protractor to draw an angle of 50°. (50° ±2°) **b** Use a ruler and a pair of compasses to bisect the angle. (25° ±2°, construction lines visible) **2 a** Draw a line exactly 8.6 cm long. **b** Use a ruler and a pair of compasses to accurately construct the perpendicular bisector of this line. **c** Mark a point P above your line. Construct a perpendicular from the point P to the line. (Check students' lines are 8.6 cm and perpendicular is 90°) **3** Use a ruler and compasses or a protractor to construct these triangles. **a** 8cm, 7 cm, 4 cm (30°, 61°, 89°) **b** 3 cm, 45°, 5 cm (36°, 3.6 cm, 99°) **c** 6 cm, 90°, 8 cm (37°, 10 cm, 53°) **d** 55°, 3.5 cm, 65° (3.3 cm, 60°, 3.7 cm)
R2 Use scale diagrams and maps. G15 Measure line segments and angles in geometric figures, including interpreting maps and scale drawings and use of bearings.	**4** A goat is tethered in the corner of a 30 m by 15 m field by a 20 m rope. Draw a scale diagram of the field and shade the locus of points that the goat can reach. Use a scale of 1 cm : 5 m. 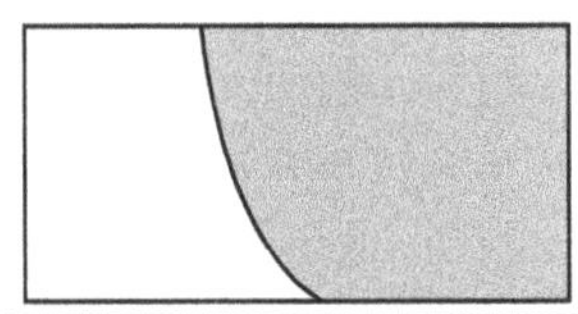
G9 Identify and apply circle definitions and properties, including: centre, radius, chord, diameter, circumference, tangent, arc, sector and segment.	**5** What term is used to describe **a** a line segment that joins two points on the circumference of a circle and passes through the centre (Diameter) **b** a curve that is part of the circumference of a circle? (Arc)
A5 Understand and use standard mathematical formulae. G17 Know the formulae: circumference of a circle = $2\pi r = \pi d$, area of a circle = πr^2; calculate: perimeters of 2D shapes, including circles; areas of circles and composite shapes. G18 Calculate arc lengths, angles and areas of sectors of circles.	**6** Calculate **i** the area **ii** the circumference of a circle with **a** $d = 12$ cm (113 cm^2, 37.7 cm) **b** $r = 9$ cm. (255 cm^2, 56.5 cm) **7** Calculate **a** the perimeter (51.4 m) **b** the area of this semi-circle. (157 m^2) 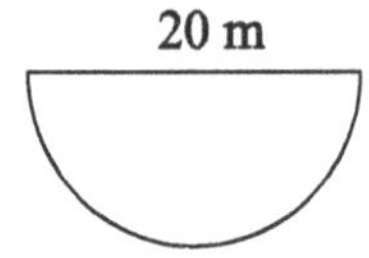 **8** Calculate **a** the are length (6.28 cm) **b** the area of this sector. (25.1 cm^2) 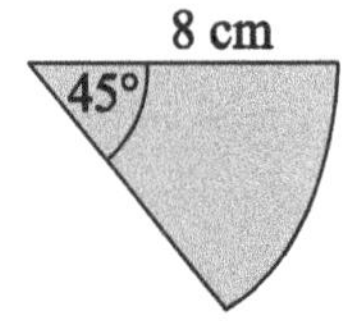

Misconceptions and challenges	Solutions
Students find it difficult to remember which formula to apply for the area and circumference of a circle.	This is a good opportunity to notice the dimensionality of area compared to length. You can link this to the formulae for area of different polygons.
Students multiply π by the radius and square the result when finding the area.	Remind students that they need to follow BIDMAS.
Students confuse the words segment and sector.	Ask students to design a mnemonic or other memory trick to remember which is which.

Misconceptions and challenges	Solutions
Students find it difficult to use a pair of compasses.	Look at different techniques, such as tilting the compasses, turning the paper around or drawing half of the circle at a time. Practice drawing circles often.
Students confuse the methods for constructing a perpendicular bisector with bisecting an angle.	Demonstrate on a large scale, using a whiteboard pen attached to a long piece of string to show that compasses produce two measured lengths that are exactly the same length. Use this to explain the first step in bisecting an angle.
Students do not notice whether the measurement given is the radius or the diameter.	This is a very common error. Make sure that students are aware of it, and model it as a mental check every time you solve a problem on the board.
Students forget to add the diameter when finding the perimeter of a semi-circle.	Students tend to put most of the effort into using the circumference formula, but they need to remember the final step. Make this the first step, as it is the easiest.
When solving problems about composite shapes involving circles, students find it difficult to adapt the circle formulae.	A visual understanding of fractions of a circle is important for this problem. Give students regular challenges of sketching a third of a circle, an eighth, and so on…
When calculating the arc-length or the area of a sector, students become confused about what multiplier to use.	Ask students to estimate the multiplier first, by making an approximation of how many times the sector would fit into the whole circle. They can use this to check their answer.

Review question commentary

Students will require rulers, pencils and pairs of compasses.

Question 1 (**11.1**) – If students are struggling with remembering the parts of the circle get them to create flashcards with a definition on one side and a labelled diagram on the other.

Questions 2 and **3** (**11.1**) – Students should use the π button on their calculator or $\pi = 3.142$
Answers should be given correct to 3 sf and units included.

Question 4 (**11.1, 11.2**) – For the perimeter students need to add on the length of the diameter (12 m) to the arc length (18.85 m).

Question 5 (**11.2**) – This question is aimed at the most able students.

Questions 6 to **9** (**11.3**) – Students must leave their construction lines visible.
Allow ±2 mm and ±2°.

Question 10 (**11.4**) – It is important that students are confident using a pair of compasses for simple constructions. Demonstrate good technique to students and set extra practice for homework where necessary.

Review answers

1 **a** Radius **b** Chord

2 **a** 50.3 cm^2 **b** 154 cm^2

3 **a** 25.1 cm **b** 44.0 cm

4 **a** 56.5 m^2 **b** 30.8 m

5 **a** 4.19 cm **b** 8.38 cm^2

6 Check students' diagrams (nearest mm, degree).
a 34°, 44°, 102°
b 6.4 cm, 48°, 62°.
c 6.7 cm, 27°, 63°.
d 120°, 3.4 cm, 4.6 cm.

7 **a, b** Check line of 7 cm with line crossing through midpoint (3.5 cm) at angle of 90°.

8 Check perpendicular (90°).

9 **a, b** Check both angles = 35°.

10 Check circle of radius 6 cm.

Assessment 11

Question 1 – 5 marks

a Check student's drawing: $r = 5$ cm ± 1 mm [B1]
b Check student's drawing: $r = 4.5$cm ± 1 mm [B1]
c Check student's drawings: chords 7cm ± 1 mm [B2]
d 11 cm > diameter of either circle; No [B1]

Question 2 – 6 marks

a i A $x = 61.58 \div (2\pi) = 9.80$ cm (3 sf) [B1]
ii C $2.10 \div (2\pi) = 50$ or $2\pi \times 0.32 = 2.01$ [B1]
iii B $314.16 \div (2\pi) = 50$ or $2\pi \times 50 = 314.16$[B1]
b i B $\pi \times 5.08^2 = 81.1$ or $\sqrt{81.1 \div \pi} = 5.08$ [B1]
ii A $\pi \times 7.5^2 = 176.7$ or $\sqrt{176.7 \div \pi} = 7.5$ [B1]
iii C $y = \sqrt{0.407 \div \pi} = 0.360$ m (3 sf) [B1]

Question 3 – 9 marks

a $10^2 - 5^2 \times \pi$ [M2]
$= 21.5$, **C** [A1]
b $3^2 \times \pi - \frac{1}{2} \times 6 \times 3$ [M2]
$= 28.27\ldots - 9$
$= 19.3$ cm^2 (3 sf)
Answer **A**, 29.3, is incorrect. [A2]
c $4.5^2 \times \pi - 2^2 \times \pi$ [M1]
$= 63.61\ldots - 12.56\ldots$
$= 51.1$ **B** [A1]

Question 4 – 4 marks

25 cm = 0.25 m [B1]
$50 \div (\pi \times 0.25)$ [M2]
= 63.7 times [A1]

Question 5 – 7 marks

a $4 + 4 + \pi \times 2$ [M2]
$= 14.3$ cm (3 sf) [A1]
b Radius = 1 cm [M1]
$\frac{1}{2} \times 4 \times 3.46 + 1^2 \times \pi$ [M2]
$= 10.1$ cm^2 (3 sf) [A1]

Question 6 – 3 marks

Angle = (arc length ÷ circumference) × 360° [M1]
= (10 ÷ (2 × π × 10)) × 360° [M1]
= 360° ÷ (2 × π)
= 57.3° (3 sf) [A1]

Question 7 – 8 marks

a

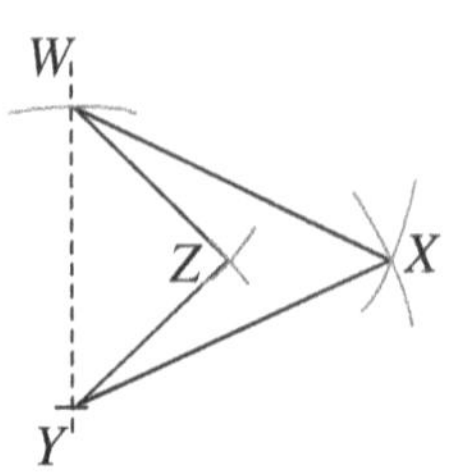

Base line *YW*
= 4 cm ± 1 mm [B1]
Arcs *WZ* = *YZ*
= 3 cm ± 1 mm [B1]
Arcs *WX* = *YX*
= 5 cm ± 1 mm [B1]

Construction lines visible. [B1]
b ∠ *WXY* = 47° ± 2° [B1]
∠ *WZY* = 276° ±2° [B1]
c Acute [B1]
d 2.3 cm ± 2 mm [B1]

Question 8 – 8 marks

a

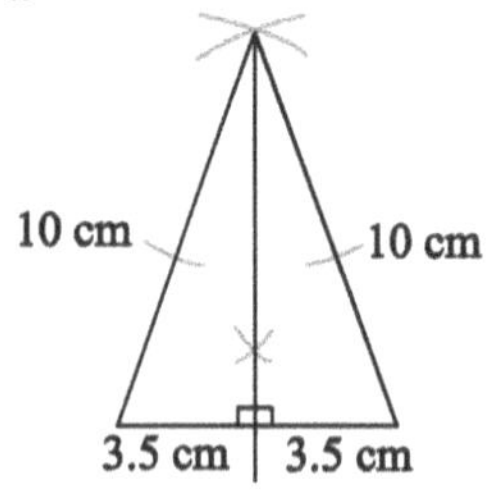

Base line
= 7 cm ± 1 mm [B1]
Equal sides
= 10 cm ± 1 mm [B1]
Construction lines visible. [B1]

b Two sets of equal length arcs [B2]
Line through smallest angle [B1]
c 90° ± 2° [B1]
d 9.4 cm ± 2 mm [B1]

Question 9 – 12 marks

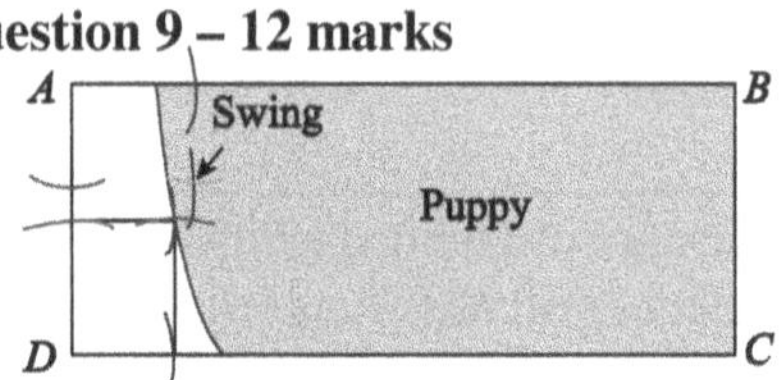

a A 20 cm ± 1 mm × 8 cm ± 1 mm rectangle [B2]
b Two arcs 4 cm ± 1 mm [B1]
Two arcs 3 cm ± 1 mm [B1]
Correctly positioned rectangle [B1]
c Two pairs of arcs of length 3.7 cm ± 1 mm and 3.0 cm ± 1 mm and their intersection marked. [B2]
OR
Line parallel to *AB* at 3.0 cm ± 1 mm away and parallel tp *AD* 3.7 cm ± 1 mm and their intersection marked. [B2]
d Arc of a circle, centre *B* [B1]
passing through corner [B1]
e 17.4 m ± 20 cm [B1]
f The swing is inside the locus of the puppy's lead. [M1]
Yes [A1]

Question 10 – 18 marks

a

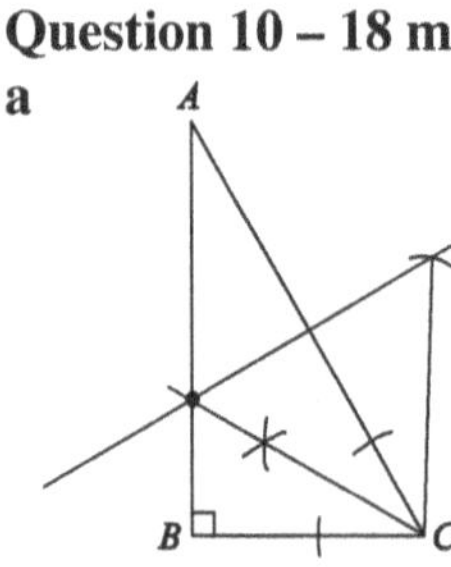

Vertical line, *AB*,
10 cm ± 1 mm [B1]
Horizontal line *BC* [B1]
∠ *BAC* = 90° – 60° [M1]
= 30° [A1]
60° angle constructed at *A* plus its angular bisector – *AC* [B4]

b Construction for the perpendicular bisector of *AC*. [B3]
Arc, centre *C* radius 7 cm ± 1 mm;
Sighting marked at intersection 'above *C*' [B1]
Construction of angle bisector at *C*;
AB and two bisectors should be coincident [B3]
c 7.3 miles ± 0.4 miles [B1]
d 7.3 ÷ 2.5 [M1]
= 2.9 miles/sec [F1]

Ratio and proportion

Learning outcomes

N11	Identify and work with fractions in ratio problems.
R2	Use scale factors, scale diagrams [and maps].
R3	Express one quantity as a fraction of another, where the fraction is less than 1 or greater than 1.
R4	Use ratio notation, including reduction to simplest form.
R5	Divide a given quantity into two parts in a given part : part or part : whole ratio; express the division of a quantity into two parts as a ratio; apply ratio to real contexts and problems (such as those involving conversion, comparison, scaling, mixing, concentrations).
R6	Express a multiplicative relationship between two quantities as a ratio or a fraction.
R7	Understand and use proportion as equality of ratio.
R8	Relate ratios to fractions [and to linear functions].
R9	Define percentage as 'number of parts per hundred'; interpret percentages and percentage changes as a fraction or a decimal, and interpret these multiplicatively; express one quantity as a percentage of another; compare two quantities using percentages; work with percentages greater than 100%; solve problems involving percentage change, including percentage increase/decrease and original value problems, and simple interest including in financial mathematics.
R12	Compare lengths, areas and volumes using ratio notation.

Prior knowledge

Check-in skill

- Convert between fractions and decimals.
- Understand simple proportion problems.

Online resources

MyMaths 1015, 1029, 1036, 1037, 1038, 1039, 1060, 1103, 1237, 1302, 1934

InvisiPen videos

Skills: 12Sa – i Applications: 12Aa – c

Kerboodle assessment

Online Skills Test 12 Chapter Test 12

Development and links

Applications of ratios include making scale models and reading maps. Automotive engineers use ratios when designing a transmission. The gear ratios determine the number of revolutions the engine must make to turn the car wheels though one complete revolution.

Proportionality has wide applications in everyday life. The techniques used in this chapter can be applied when calculating price rises, bank interest and VAT, calculating the nutrition value of food, making scale models, reading maps and converting currencies.

Metallurgists use proportion when creating metal alloys. Brass is an alloy of copper and zinc and its properties are determined by the proportions of the component metals. Different brasses can be created for different purposes by varying the proportions.

Chapter investigation

Start by discussing ratios, including how to handle units and simplify them [**12.2**]. Actual data on heights and head circumferences can then be collected from the students in the class. One way to compare the ratios is to write them all in the form 1 : n and look at the values for n. Another option is to plot a scatter graph [**16.3**] and see if the points lie about the line $y = 3x$.

In an adult a person's head height is approximately a seventh of their total height. Does this proportion apply to the students in your class [**12.1**]?

Many ratios and proportions have been suggested for the human body and these could be tested. The relative sizes of body parts in animals could be investigated. How big would your head be if you had the same head size to body size ratio as a koala bear or a snake?

People and faces are often shown in drawings – which are effectively scale drawings [**12.2**]. Ask students to create accurate scale drawings of each other based on measurement. Sometimes features are exaggerated for effect; for example in manga comics or in ancient depictions of the Egyptian royal family. Can students classify styles of depiction from measurements alone?

The relative proportions of the human body change significantly during childhood. For example, a baby's head is around a quarter of its height whereas for an adult it is about a seventh. These changes in dimensions can be described by percentage changes [**12.3**]. Challenge students to calculate new lengths given various percentage changes and to investigate the effects on given ratios and proportions.

12.1 Proportion

Objectives

① Express one quantity as a fraction of another

② Interpret percentages and percentage changes as a fraction or a decimal

③ Express one quantity as a percentage of another

Useful resources

Mini whiteboards, domino cards, pie chart display, spider diagrams for display and group work, recipe example(s) for display

Starter – Skills

Ask students some quick-fire questions based on fractions, decimals and percentages.

- What percentage is equivalent to $\frac{1}{2}$? 0.6? $\frac{9}{10}$?
- Which fraction is equivalent to 75%? 0.3? 20%
- Which decimal is equivalent to $\frac{1}{10}$? 40%? $\frac{7}{10}$?

Now show five domino cards and ask students how they could fit them into a loop. Give small groups of students copies of the cards to work with.

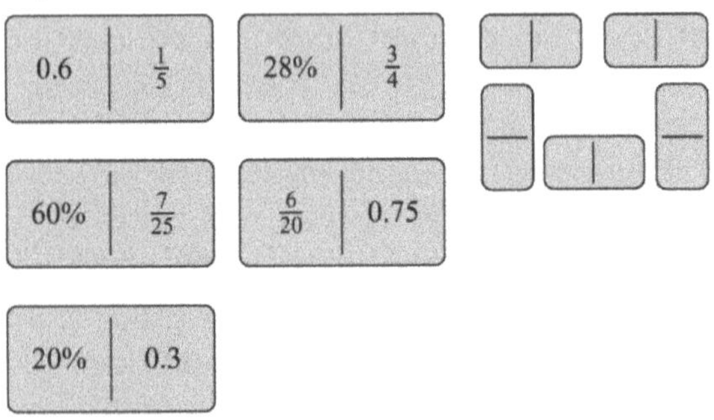

Teaching notes – Skills

① and ③ To revise and practise **finding a fraction or percentage of a quantity**, display a spider diagram with a number at the centre (say 90), and various fractions as the 'legs'. Discuss how to calculate the values for each fraction.

Ask students to work in pairs to complete their own versions of the diagram using £600 as the centre. Share results and explanations. Students should continue with different centre values and/or a value given in one of the legs. Differentiate by giving appropriate starting values to pairs of students. Repeat the activity using percentages instead of fractions, and/or a combination of both.

② Refer to the starter and recall that percentages, fractions and decimals are different ways of writing the same thing. Recall how to **convert from percentages to fractions or decimals**. Highlight that to convert:

- A percentage to a decimal, you divide by 100
- A percentage to a fraction, you write it as a fraction with denominator 100 and then simplify.

Write these notes clearly on the board for students to refer to throughout the exercise.

Emphasise that **proportion** compares a part with the whole and link this to previous work on fractions (and decimals and percentages). Ask students questions based upon the class group, for example:
What proportion of the class is female/male, or has blue eyes/brown hair? and so on.

Emphasise the need to first consider the *total* (the denominator of the fraction). Where possible, encourage students to simplify fractions and give decimal and percentage equivalents.

Plenary – Skills

Display a pie chart using angles 90°, 45°, 45°, 60° and 120° labelled and contextualised.

Ask students to respond to questions using whiteboards. Ask questions which focus on the language of proportion: fractions, decimals and percentages. What proportion *prefer*...? What percentage has...? What did a quarter of the survey...? Half of the survey preferred either ... or.... Explore alternative, equivalent values for the fractions, decimals and percentages.

Exercise commentary – Skills

Question 1 All of these will simplify as fractions.

Question 2 Ensure that numerator and denominator are the right way around. Students should cancel their fractions where possible. In parts **i** and **j** students should notice that units need to be the same.

Questions 3 to **5** These questions allow students to recap conversion between fractions, decimals and percentages.

Question 6 Students may wish to use a calculator for the percentage calculations.

Question 7 It may be worth a quick literacy session on identifying vowels. Make sure students count any double letters twice. This task can be linked to probability.

Questions 9 to **11** These are all problems in context, involving one quantity as a proportion of another. Ask what is easier to understand – fractions or percentages?

Question 12 Discuss how to deal with these large numbers. Students should appreciate that the first step is to find the total.

Simplification – Skills

Students should be given further simple examples in which they have to write proportions as fractions, and they may benefit from further practice at simplifying fractions. Students should work with finding 'one' part of quantities to get used to dividing by the denominator.

Extension – Skills

Students could be given multi-stage problems to solve, e.g 'what is three quarters of one third of…'.

Recap – Applications

1 What proportion of:

a 50 is 10 **b** £12 is £1.50 **c** 8 cm is 5 mm

(**a** $\frac{1}{5}$, 0.2 **b** $\frac{1}{8}$, 0.125 **c** $\frac{1}{16}$, 0.0625)

2 **a** Write these proportions as decimals and percentages.

i $\frac{3}{4}$ (0.75, 75%) **ii** $\frac{2}{3}$ $\left(0.6, 66\frac{2}{3}\%\right)$

b Write these proportions as decimals and fractions.

i 85% (0.85, $\frac{17}{20}$) **ii** 70% (0.7, $\frac{7}{10}$)

c Write these proportions as percentages and fractions.

i 0.375(37.5%, $\frac{3}{8}$) **ii** 0.3 $\left(33\frac{1}{3}\%, \frac{1}{3}\right)$

Plenary – Applications

Ask students, on whiteboards, how they would adapt a recipe for 4 people into one for 10 people. Examine the suggestions of double and half and add. What would need to happen to change 4 to 10? Develop, with the use of line segments, the move from 4 to 1 and to 10 into $\times\frac{10}{4}$ or $\times\frac{5}{2}$.

Explore such changes for other values.

Exercise commentary – Applications

Question 1 Students should convert all numbers to the same form. They should discuss which is the most appropriate/easiest.

Question 2 Comparison of proportions in a context that will be familiar to most students. Part **b** could raise some interesting group or class discussions.

Question 4 Some may need help with the more complex language here. A diagram such as a number line may be helpful.

Question 5 This question could be used as the start of a real-life investigation or homework task. Students will recognise this context as familiar in supermarkets and food labelling.

Question 6 Look out for students who do not realise that part **a** helps the solution to part **b**.

Questions 7 and **8** It may help students to draw these shapes on squared paper and cut them up to check their answers.

Question 9 The question needs to be read carefully. It requires 15% of 80%.

Simplification – Applications

Students should be encouraged to make effective use of a calculator and to estimate the size of the resulting answer.

Extension – Applications

Students could think about different scenarios involving proportion, not just direct. Consider the classic problems of people digging holes, for example, where if it takes three people two days to dig five holes, how long will it take six people? Or how long will it take them to dig eight holes? etc.

Ratio

Objectives

① Use and simplify ratios

② Divide a quantity into a given ratio

③ Understand and use proportion as equality of ratio

Useful resources

Mini whiteboards, sets of coloured paper, Cuisenaire rods

Starter – Skills

Describe this scenario: Two people, A and B buy a £1 lottery ticket. One contributed 75p to the ticket and the other, 25p. Ask students in what proportion or ratio were the payments? What if the amounts were 70p and 30p? 60p and 40p?

Take the last combination: If the ticket then won £250 000, what would be a fair way of dividing the winnings between the two? Discuss responses (including that 50–50 might be fairest) and explore the reasoning behind the use of the ratio 3 : 2.

Teaching notes – Skills

① Refer to the starter. Highlight that the **ratio**, 3 : 2, is used to divide the winnings in **direct proportion** to the original ticket payments. Formalise the idea of ratio as a means of **comparing two or more quantities**. Discuss the proportions of girls and boys in the class. Highlight that girls : boys = 12 : 16, for example, is *not* the same as 16 : 12. The ratio must be expressed in the same order as the parts (in words) that it represents. Discuss how to **simplify a ratio** by dividing by **common factors**, linking to work on fractions. Demonstrate scaling up (or down) to find **equivalent ratios** and increase (or decrease) each quantity in proportion; for example, using the 12 : 16 above (or the real girls : boys ratio if the numbers work).

② Discuss how to **divide a quantity in a given ratio**. For example: If £15 is shared between Tim and Rose in the ratio 1 : 4, how much do they each receive? Discuss the total parts of the ratio as 5 and highlight that you are therefore dividing the total amount of money, £15, into 5 parts. Discuss different possible strategies such as incrementally or directly scaling up each side of the ratio by the same factor. Demonstrate the shorter method used in the student book:

- find the total number of parts
- find the size of each part
- multiply by the ratio to find each share.

So: Total number of parts = 5

1 part is $15 \div 5 = 3$

So Tim gets $1 \times 3 = £3$,
and Rose gets $4 \times 3 = £12$.

③ Give sets of paper Cuisenaire rods to pairs of students and ask them to arrange the strips in order. Select the red and the yellow rods, then find another pair with a similar length ratio. Ask for the two sets of lengths as ratios. (2 : 5 = 4 : 10)

Ask students to look for three pairs with a similar length proportion. (such as 2 : 3 = 4 : 6 = 6 : 9)
Ask what the ratios remind students of to prompt the connections with fractions and simplest forms.

Give students several pairs of rod-pair ratios with a missing amount to find or work out; for example, 1 : 3 = 3 : ?, 5 : ? = 1 : 2, 4 : 2 = ? : 3, and so on. Discuss strategies and responses and use these to show how you can use **proportion as the equality of ratios** to find an unknown amount when problem solving. For example: Juice and water are mixed in the ratio 3 : 5. If 150 ml of juice is used, how much water was added?

Plenary – Skills

Use an art scenario about paint mixing: For a particular lilac colour, 3 parts of red are mixed with 4 parts of blue. Ask, for example: For 9 litres of red paint, how much blue do I need? For 21 litres of lilac, how much of each colour? and so on. Ask students to explain their reasoning.

Exercise commentary – Skills

Questions 1 and **3** Encourage students to make the link with using common factors to cancel fractions.

Questions 4 and **5** Practice in dividing a quantity in a given ratio, with just two parts (apart from **4e**, which has three parts). Students can use a calculator for question **5**.

Question 6 Remind students to check the units are the same before simplifying.

Question 7 Practice in dividing a quantity into three parts. For part **c** draw students' attention to the hint in the margin, 1 km = 1000 m.

Question 8 Ratios in unitary form 1: *n*. All of these work out as integers.

Questions 9 to **13** These types of question are often easier if students work out the scale as 1 cm = □ metres before attempting each part. This avoids the problem of losing or gaining zeros.

Simplification – Skills

Students may benefit from continued use of block diagrams and other visual strategies to support their understanding of ratio. They should practise simplifying ratios and concentrate on questions that require only one operation.

Extension – Skills

Students could be given further examples of triple ratios and asked to divide amounts into three parts. They could also extend this to examples where there are quadruple ratios.

Recap – Applications

1 Simplify each of these ratios.

a 6 : 2 **b** 27 : 6 **c** 84 : 156

(**a** 3 : 1 **b** 9 : 2 **c** 7 : 13)

2 **a** Write these ratios in the form n : 1.

i 5 : 4 **ii** 5 mm : 4 cm **iii** 75p : £3.75

(**i** 1.25 : 1 **ii** 0.125 : 1 **iii** 0.2 : 1)

b Write the following ratios in the form 1 : n.

i 8 : 5 **ii** 5 cm : 1.5 m **iii** 30 ml : 2.4 l

(**i** 1 : 0.625 **ii** 1 : 30 **iii** 1 : 80)

3 Divide 8 weeks in the ratio 4 : 3.

(32 days : 24 days)

Plenary – Applications

Discuss which pairs of quantities are in direct proportion, including cases with 'grey areas' or conditions (such as that unit cost must be the same). For example:

- number of cakes : number of eggs used
- number of pencils bought : cost of pencils
- number of builders building a house : hours spent building the house.
- number of painters painting a bridge: amount of paint used

Exercise commentary – Applications

Questions 1 and **2** These problems involve converting proportions expressed as a ratio into percentages, then using this to calculate a missing quantity. Go through question **1** as a class, then let them try question **2**.

Question 3 This problem develops proportional reasoning. The arrow diagrams as used in the examples will help with this type of problem.

Question 4 This question can be done using fractions alone. Students may wish to refer back to the examples on page 100 that show how to multiply fractions and add fractions with different denominators.

Question 5 Students will need a ruler to measure the height of the tower.

Question 9 Remind students to check their answer by adding up all the parts.

Question 10 In part **a** the algebraic language may need explanation, as it will put off some students.

Question 11 and **12** Check that students know the properties of regular polygons and trapezia. Students could look at pages 52 and 60 to recap these topics.

Simplification – Applications

Students should concentrate on examples that simplify to integer values, avoiding decimals. They could also concentrate first on double ratios, before moving on to triple ratios.

Extension – Applications

Students could devise their own similar ratio problems. They should test the problems themselves to ensure that they work, and then challenge a partner to solve them.

12.3 Percentage change

Objectives

① Compare two quantities using percentages

② Solve problems involving percentage change including percentage increase/decrease and original value problems and simple interest including in financial mathematics

Useful resources

Mini whiteboards, calculators, sets of number cards for group work, leaflet of bank interest rates

Starter – Skills

Draw a spider diagram with 800 in the middle. Discuss how to calculate various percentages of this amount, e.g. 50%. Encourage students to justify their answers. (50% is the same as $\frac{1}{2}$, so divide by 2.) Encourage students to derive harder percentages using the simple percentages, e.g. 17.5%.

Teaching notes – Skills

① Refer to the starter. Discuss how to find percentages of an amount. Recap that, for example, 12% means 12 parts out of 100 or $\frac{12}{100}$, and that to find 12% of an amount you divide it by 100 and then multiply by 12. Highlight that the easiest method, however, is often to express the percentage as a decimal and then multiply by this. Conversely, we can express fractions (or proportions) as percentages. This is useful for **comparing different fractional quantities using percentages**. E.g. In a test, A got 65%, B got 16 out of 25 and C got 27 out of 40. Who got the best mark? Write as fractions, then either convert to fractions with denominator 100, or to decimals and multiply by 100 to make percentages. $\frac{16}{25}=\frac{16\times4}{25\times4}=\frac{64}{100}=64\%$

$\frac{27}{40} = 27 \div 40 = 0.675$, and $0.675 \times 100\% = 67.5\%$

so C was first, A second and B third.

② Explore different methods of calculating **percentage increase/decrease**. Ask students to think in pairs of different methods they could use to decrease £50 by 20%. Share strategies and the reasoning behind them. Encourage more direct methods using 100% – 20% = 80%. For example:

- 1% of 50 is 0.5, so 80% is 40 ⇒ £40
- Same using 10 % or 20% rather than 1%
- $80\% = \frac{80}{100} = 0.8$, and $50 \times 0.8 = 40$ ⇒ £40

Ensure students understand why decreasing by 20% is the same as multiplying by 0.8. Use a similar method to increase 90 cm by 30%. Discuss how to find the **percentage profit or loss**, rather than the new amount. E.g. A shopkeeper bought some goods for £200 and sold them for £220. How much profit did she make?

Discuss **simple interest**. Ensure students understand that banks *provide* interest on money deposited and *charge* interest on money borrowed. Discuss the interest on £750 after one year, and after 5 years, at an interest rate of 8%. Highlight:

Simple interest = interest for one year × number of years

Reverse percentage problems involve finding the original amount after a percentage change. E.g. The price of a computer is increased by 25% to £625. What did it cost originally? Elicit and discuss the common error of calculating the percentage change directly on the given amount.

Plenary – Skills

Give groups a set of number cards, one per student. Each student must work out their number as a percentage of each other number, and express this as a percentage increase/decrease in each case. Discuss strategies, results, and links between the percentage increase/decrease found from paired numbers.

Exercise commentary – Skills

Question 1 A straightforward recap of percentages to decimals, but students will need to think carefully about parts **d**, **e** and **f**, to ensure they give the correct place value.

Questions 2 to **4** Remind students to estimate, to make sure their answers are reasonable (some will have no sense of what's reasonable, in which case discuss as a class).

Questions 5 and **6** As an extension, students could be challenged to do the calculations on a calculator as efficiently as possible, without writing down any interim figures.

Questions 7 and **8** Simple interest calculations including decimal percentage rates. Students should be encouraged to show their working clearly, and this will attract marks in an exam.

Questions 9 and **10** Bridging to a multiplier method – it is expected that Foundation students should know this more efficient technique.

Questions 11 and **12** These could be done using mental methods.

Question 13 Encourage a multiplier method.

Question 14 In parts **c**, **d** and **f**, ensure that the correct fractions/multipliers are used. Again encourage estimation, for example 0.9% is less than 1%

Simplification – Skills

Students should be given more practice at finding percentages of quantities before working with increase/decrease. Emphasise the 'two-stage' method to calculating percentage increase/decrease. On interest problems they should work with small numbers of years and with simple percentages.

Extension – Skills

Students could work on this problem:

> **SOFAS 4 YOU**
> Nothing to pay for 6 months then pay just £29.95 per month over 3 years.
> (Cash price £650)

Work out the extra cost of this sofa as a percentage of the cash price. (approx. 68%)

Recap – Applications

1 In a test Jamie scored 48 out of 75.
He needed 65% to obtain a grade A.
Did Jamie get his grade A? Explain. (No – he got 64%)

2 Calculate the simple interest paid on £4800 at an interest rate of 2.5% pa for 5 years. (£600)

3 Calculate these percentage changes. Give your answers to an appropriate level of accuracy.
a Increase £4540 by 17.6% (£53.39)
b Decrease 681g by 34% (449.46 g)

Plenary – Applications

Set pairs or small groups this problem: Two workers receive the same wage. One receives a rise of 10% at the end of the year, but the other only receives a rise of 5%. When the second worker discovers this he asks why. The boss agrees it was unfair. To put it right she will give the second worker a 10% rise next year instead, while the other worker will only have 5%. Will each worker now have the same wage? Is this resolution fair? Discuss and explain.

Exercise commentary – Applications

Questions 1 and **2** Basic practice in writing one number as a percentage of another, just to get students confident in the skill that they will then need to apply to problems. An accuracy of 1 dp should be fine for question **2**.

Questions 3 and **4** Students should read the question carefully and check their answer is sensible. A common misconception is to give the answer to **3a** as 80%, for example. Students should begin to appreciate that there is often a subtraction involved in first finding the absolute increase or decrease.

Question 5 Note that average percentage loss is not the same as annual depreciation.

Question 6 Bring students' attention to the first 'working backwards' problem, which can be discussed as a whole class as it highlights a common misconception.

Questions 7 to **13** These are all problems in context (apart from question **8**), involving applying 'reverse percentages' to find an original amount. As well as developing students' proportional reasoning skills, these problems will help with calculator skills.

Question 14 This task could be discussed as a whole class, and provides an opportunity to use powers.

Simplification – Applications

Students should concentrate on straightforward examples of percentage change, before moving on to reverse percentage problems.

Extension – Applications

Students could investigate paying off a loan and answer related questions. For example: Suppose they borrow £500 at 10% (simple) interest per year and pay off (up to) £100 at the end of each year. How long will it take them to pay off? How much will they have to pay in total? And so on.

12 Ratio and proportion

Key outcomes	Quick check
R2 Use scale factors, scale diagrams and maps.	**1** This rectangle is enlarged by scale factor 12. 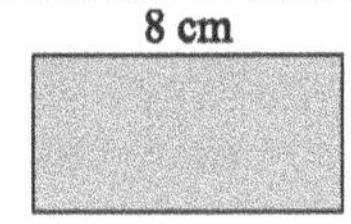 **a** What is the length of the enlarged rectangle? (96 cm) The width of the enlarged rectangle is 60 cm. **b** What is the width of the original rectangle? (5 cm) **2** A map is drawn using the scale 1 : 50000. **a** How far in real life is a length of 8 cm on the map? Give your answer in kilometres. **b** A road is 900 m long, how long will it be on the map? (1.8 cm)
N11 Identify and work with fractions in ratio problems. R3 Express one quantity as a fraction of another, where the fraction is less than 1. R4 Use ratio notation, including reduction to simplest form. R5 Divide a given quantity into two parts in a given part : part or part : whole ratio; express the division of a quantity into two parts as a ratio; apply ratio to real contexts and problems (such as those involving conversion, comparison, scaling, mixing, concentrations). R6 Express a multiplicative relationship between two quantities as a ratio or a fraction. R8 Relate ratios to fractions. R12 Compare lengths, areas and volumes using ratio notation.	**3** **a** What fraction of the stars are white?  Write your answer in its simplest form. $\left(\frac{3}{4}\right)$ **b** What percentage of the stars are grey? (25%) **4** Write these ratios in their simplest form. **a** 25 : 15 (5 : 3) **b** 24 : 32 (3 : 4) **c** 1 m : 5 cm (20 : 1) **5** Share **a** £42 in the ratio 1 : 2 (£14 : £28) **b** 88 kg in the ratio 6 : 5 (48 kg : 40 kg) **6** Lily's pay is twice as much as Dan's pay. Write the ratio of Lily's pay to Dan's pay. (2 : 1) **7** The ratio of sugar to flour in a recipe is 2 : 3 **a** How much sugar is needed for 450 g of flour? (300 g) **b** What fraction of the mixture is flour? $\left(\frac{3}{5}\right)$ **8** Aaron plays football 4 days a week and cricket the other days. **a** What fraction of the week does he play cricket? $\left(\frac{3}{7}\right)$ **b** Write the ratio of the amount of days he plays football to the amount of days he plays cricket. (4 : 3)
R9 Interpret percentages and percentage changes as a fraction or a decimal, and interpret these multiplicatively; express one quantity as a percentage of another; compare two quantities using percentages; work with percentages greater than 100%; solve problems involving percentage change, including percentage increase/decrease and original value problems, and simple interest including in financial mathematics.	**9** **a** Increase 35 by 58% (55.3) **b** Decrease 280 by 16% (235.2) **10** A bank pays 2% per annum interest on a savings account. £7000 is paid in at the beginning of the year and no further deposits or withdrawals are made. How much is in the account after 1 year? (£7140) **11** Adam gets a loan from the bank of £1500. In the first year he pays £75 interest. How much interest has he paid as a percentage of the amount borrowed? (5%) **12** **a** Shane is 20% older than his sister Lexie. If Shane is 36 years old, how old is Lexie? (30 years old) **b** A pair of trousers is reduced by 35% and now costs £18.20. What was the original price? (£28)

Misconceptions and challenges	Solutions
Students sometimes give 'silly' answers, for example giving an answer larger than the original quantity when asked to divide it in a ratio.	Discuss answers to practice problems in class. Ask students to decide whether the answer seems 'sensible' in the context of the problem.
Many students struggle with ratio questions if the context is unfamiliar.	Use as many contexts as possible, particularly where the units in a ratio might be different, and discuss the answers to the problems.
In 'best buy' problems, students often miss an efficient or elegant solution, where they do not need to work out all the information to solve the problem.	Model how 'best buy' problems often have a common sense element, and you do not need to calculate everything if you can find a reason why one must be more or less than the other.
Students do not know how to apply a percentage multiplier for a percentage increase or decrease. For example, multiplying by 0.88 for a 12% decrease.	Give students a percentage decrease example with a range of worked solutions and ask them to explain how each method works.
Some students confuse 3 : 4 and $\frac{3}{4}$	Spend time converting from fractions to ratios, and noticing the differences in calculating with them.
Many students will only partially simplify ratios, particularly where the two parts are not multiples of 2, for example, 30 : 42 partly simplified is 15 : 21	Give students plenty of practice with simplifying ratios that do not have 2 as a factor.
Some students are confident with ratios in the form $a : b$ but struggle with $a : b : c$ and relationships between quantities.	Expose students to problems involving long chains of ratios. For example, 1 : 1 : 3 : 5 : 10, model their solutions visually.
Students often struggle where ratio questions contain fractional reasoning. For example, $\frac{1}{3}$ of £180 shared in the ratio 2 : 3	Alert students to this kind of 'trick question', and model the mental check for every stage of working: 'is this a fraction or a ratio?'

Review question commentary

Students may use calculators, particularly in the percentage questions.

Question 1 (**12.1**) – In part **b**, students could write the answer as a fraction then convert to a percentage.

Question 2 (**12.1**) – Students could convert both values to decimals or convert the fraction to a percentage.

Question 3 (**12.2**) – In part **c** students should write the ratio without units.

Question 4 (**12.2**) – Encourage students to check their answer by making sure it adds up to the original amount.

Question 5 (**12.2**) – Make sure students write the ratio the correct way round.

Question 8 (**12.2**) – Students should give their 'real life' answer in kilometres.

Question 9 (**12.3**) – The most able students should be encouraged to use the multiplier method. (**a**1.1 **b** 0.71)

Question 10 (**12.3**) – Students must give the total amount in the account, not the interest. This is an opportunity for a discussion about interest rates.

Question 11 – (**12.3**) For part **b** students could calculate the interest first. (£180)

Question 12 – (**12.3**) The most able students should be encouraged to use the multiplier method. (**a** 1.05 **b** 0.75)

Review answers

1 **a** $\frac{2}{5}$ **b** 60%

2 Physics (72% > 60%)

3 **a** 6 : 7 **b** 3 : 5 **c** 1 : 400

4 **a** £7, £28 **b** £40, £50

5 **a** 1 : 3 **b** $\frac{1}{4}$

6 **a** Butter 240 g, Flour 600 g **b** 750 g **c** $\frac{5}{7}$

7 **a** 63 cm **b** 3 cm

8 **a** 10 km **b** 0.75 cm

9 **a** 57 **b** 106.5

10 £4060

11 **a** 2.5% **b** 30%

12 **a** £1.20 **b** £44

Assessment 12

Question 1 – 6 marks

a $\frac{1}{3}$ [B1] **b** $\frac{1}{6}$ [B1]

c $\frac{1}{8}$ [B1] **d** $\frac{1}{2}$ [B1]

e $\frac{3}{8}$ [B1] **f** $\frac{3}{4}$ [B1]

Question 2 – 3 marks

a 52% and 0.52 [B2]

b $\frac{13}{25} \times 225\,000$ OR $0.52 \times 225\,000$ [M1]

= 117 000 Rand [A1]

Question 3 – 3 marks

$1 - \frac{6}{25} = \frac{19}{25}$ [M1]

$\frac{19}{25} \times 17\,250$ [M1]

= £13 110 [A1]

Question 4 – 2 marks

a 12 : 5 [B1]

b 2.4 : 1 [F1]

Question 5 – 4 marks

1 'part' = 99 ÷ (5 + 4) [M1]

= 11 [A1]

Geography students = 5 × 11 = 55 [M1, A1]

Question 6 – 8 marks

a 1 'part' = 63 ÷ (3 + 4) = 9 [M1, A1]

No. plain biscuits = 3 × 9 = 27 [A1]

No. chocolate biscuits = 4 × 9 or 63 – 27 = 36 [F1]

b 1 'part' = 15 ÷ 5 = 3 [M1, A1]

5 + 6 = 11 'parts' [M1]

Total = 11 × 3 = 33 [A1]

Question 7 – 6 marks

a 8 : 2 : 3 [B1]

b 1 'part' = 160 ÷ 8 = 20 [M1, A1]

Ingredient = No. parts × 30 [M1]

Butter = 2 × 20 = 40 g; Cheese = 3 × 20 = 60 g [A2]

Question 8 – 4 marks

a 6 : 5 [B1]

b New ratio = 24 + 1 : 20 – 5 = 25 : 15 [M1, A1]

$= 1\frac{2}{3} : 1$ [B1]

Question 9 – 8 marks

a 1 'part' = 88 ÷ (4 + 7) = 8 [B1]

Gender = No. parts × 8 [M1]

Girls = 4 × 8 = 32; Boys = 7 × 8 = 56 [A2]

b Girls → 32 + 12 = 44 [B1]

Boys → 56 + 0.375 × 56 or 1.375 × 56 [M1]

= 77 [A1]

Ratio → 44 : 77 = 4 : 7 (Does not change.) [B1]

Question 10 – 5 marks

a 20 000 cm = 200 metres [B1]

b 5.85 × 20 000 [M1]

= 117 000 cm = 1.17 km [A1]

c 20.75 × 20 000 = 415 000 cm = 4.15 km [M1, A1]

Question 11 – 7 marks

a 8.1in × 5 [M1]

= 40.5 miles [A1]

b 128 ÷ 5 [M1]

= 25.6 inches [A1]

c 120.4 × 5 = 602 [B1]

838 – 602 [M1]

= 236 miles [F1]

Question 12 – 4 marks

a 5 × 0.04 × 2.50 [M1]

= £0.50 [A1]

b 4 × 0.035 × 5200 = £728 [M1, A1]

Question 13 – 6 marks

a Gavin [B1]

b Gemma [B1]

c 0.3 is 30% not 3% [B1]

90 + 0.03 × 90 or 1.03 × 90 = 92.7 kg [B1]

d 1 – 0.454 = 0.546 or 'subtract from original' [B1]

0.546 × 550 = 300.3 ml [B1]

Question 14 – 2 marks

(20 ÷ 45) × 100% [M1]

= 44.44% [A1]

Question 15 – 3 marks

25 – 17.5 = 7.5 OR 100 – (17.5 ÷ 25) × 100 [M1]

(7.5 ÷ 25) × 100% 100 – 70 [M1]

= 30% = 30% [A1]

Question 16 – 2 marks

2 500 000 + 0.85 × 2 500 000 or 1.085 × 2500 000 [M1]

= £2 712 500 [A1]

Question 17 – 3 marks

((164 300 – 86 100) ÷ 86 100) × 100% [M1]

= (78 200 ÷ 86 100) × 100% [A1]

= 90.8% [A1]

Question 18 – 4 marks

Areas: $6 \times 4 = 24\text{ cm}^2$ and $7 \times 5 = 35\text{ cm}^2$ [B1]

((35 – 24) ÷ 24) × 100 or (35 ÷ 24) × 100 – 100 [M1]

= 45.8%. [A1]

Yes; they are correct. [F1]

Question 19 – 4 marks

a (1 – 0.08) × 225 = 0.921 × 225 = 207 [M1, A1]

b 0.9442 × 207 = 195 (nearest crocodile) [M1, A1]

Question 20 – 2 marks

(1 – 0.12) × 2500 = 0.88 × 2500 = £2200 [M1, A1]

Question 21 – 2 marks

(2566.8 ÷ 103.5) × 100 [M1]

= £2480 [A1]

Question 22 – 2 marks

(251.34 ÷ 106.5) × 100 [M1]

= £236 [A1]

Factors, powers and roots

Learning outcomes

N4 Use the concepts and vocabulary of prime numbers, factors (divisors), multiples, common factors, common multiples, highest common factor, lowest common multiple, prime factorisation, including using product notation and the unique factorisation theorem.

N5 Apply systematic listing strategies.

N6 Use positive integer powers and associated real roots (square, cube [and higher]), recognise powers of 2, 3, 4, 5.

Prior knowledge

Check-in skill

- Multiply repeated numbers and divide by 100.
- Recognise prime numbers.
- Factorise whole numbers.

Online resources

MyMaths 1032, 1034, 1044, 1053, 1924

InvisiPen videos

Skills: 13Sa – f Applications: 13Aa – h

Kerboodle assessment

Online Skills Test 13 Chapter Test 13

Development and links

Squares and cubes are important in work on area and volume and have applications in technology, art and engineering. Square and cube roots are used to find distances from known areas or volumes, for example the diagonal length of a square pane of glass. Powers can be used to write very large numbers and are widely used in the scientific community and in finance to calculate some forms of interest. The encryption of credit card information relies on the difficulty of finding the prime factors of large numbers.

There are an infinite number of prime numbers and prizes are offered to anyone who discovers a new largest prime. A prime number with 13 million digits was discovered in August 2008. Powers have applications in finance to calculate compound interest.

Chapter investigation

The challenge is to find the prime factorisation of a given number. Start by discussing factors and their relationship to multiples [**13.1**]. Students should be shown the divisibility tests and what makes prime numbers special. Point out that students need to only test primes up to the square root of the number.

As a development look at finding the highest common factor and lowest common multiple of two, or more, numbers [**13.1**]. Initially this can be done using listing strategies

Next look at writing a number as a product of its factors. Challenge students to see how far they can go in breaking down a number. Draw out the points that they stop when they reach primes and that they always get a unique answer for each number [**13.2**].

Ask students to factorise $1024 = 2^{10}$. Checking the answer requires counting the factors of 2 and naturally motivates the introduction of index notation [**13.3**].

Ensure students see the factor tree and division by primes methods of factorisation. These can then be used to systematically investigate the two numbers given.

$702 = 2 \times 3^3 \times 13$ $\quad$ $703 = 19 \times 37$

Following the earlier development look at how to use Venn diagrams to calculate HCFs and LCMs of a pair of numbers.

Returning to index notation, explain that the powers 2 and 3 have special significance for squares and cubes [**13.3**]. Ask students to explain what this means for their prime factorisations: any factors are raised to an even power or multiple of three. Develop the discussion to look at square and cube roots, paying particular attention to the treatment of negative numbers.

13.1 Factors and multiples

Objectives

① **N4** Use the concepts and vocabulary of prime numbers, factors (divisors), multiples

② **N4** Use the concepts and vocabulary of common factors, common multiples, highest common factor, lowest common multiple and apply systematic listing strategies

Useful resources

Multiplication square, 100 square grids, digit cards

Starter – Skills

Write the numbers 14, 16, 8, 21, 100 and 54. Ask students to find the odd one out. Establish that all but one are multiples of 2; divisible by 2. Recall that any number with an even last digit is divisible by 2.
Write the numbers 12, 21, 54, 62, 111 and 153. Ask students to spot the odd one out. Establish that all but one are divisible by 3. Recall that any number where the sum of the digits is divisible by 3 is itself divisible by 3.

Teaching notes – Skills

① Refer to the starter and ensure students are comfortable with the key words **factor** and **multiple**. Link 'multiple' to 'multiply'. Recall that a factor of a number divides into it exactly leaving no remainders. Provide a clear example of both terms and invite students to give similar examples. Refer to the **tests of divisibility** from the starter and invite students to share any similar tests for numbers up to 10. Highlight that these can be used to find factors of larger numbers.

Recall the definition of a **prime number** as a number with exactly two distinct factors: 1 and itself. Highlight that 1 is therefore *not* prime. Ask students to identify the first six prime numbers or, if possible, the first 10.

Write the numbers 55, 63, 59 and 62 on the board and discuss which are prime numbers. Use the divisibility tests discussed earlier. Find opportunities to discuss aspects that may have been met before, such as factor trees, or factor properties of prime and square numbers.

② Ask students for multiples of 20, and for multiples of 15. Discuss and circle the multiples that appear in both lists. Emphasise that these are **common multiples**. Discuss which number is the **lowest common multiple (LCM)** (60)

Discuss and list the factors of 126, and then repeat for 120. Circle the factors common to 126 and 120 and emphasise that these are **common factors**.

Discuss which number is the **highest common factor (HCF)**. (6)

Encourage students to work *systematically* and justify their answers. Demonstrate using each factor identified to find another one, by considering factor pairs; for example, $2 \times \square = 120$

Plenary – Skills

Give out digit cards 0–9. Ask the class to display in turn the even numbers, the odd numbers, the square numbers and the prime numbers, the multiples of 3 and the factors of 8. Challenge students to count up to a given number doing this. Pairs or groups could be assigned a type of number to focus on.

Exercise commentary – Skills

Questions 1 and **2** Make sure students do not muddle factors and multiples. In question **1**, encourage students to be systematic in listing factor pairs.

Question 3 Student explanations should be concise, for example: 'Yes, because last digit is 5'

Question 4 As in question**1**, students should be systematic in finding the factor pairs. If they start from the extremes (1×24 etc.) and work towards the middle (6×4) then they should capture them all and avoid duplication.

Question 6 Students could list all factors of each number before looking for common ones; some students may identify them immediately.

Questions 8 and **9** HCF and LCM can confuse many students, so it may be worth going through the first one or two together as a class.

Question 10 This is commonly known as the Sieve of Eratosthenes. Students could research this Greek mathematician.

Simplification – Skills

Students should concentrate on listing the factors and multiples of (small) numbers before being introduced to the ideas of LCM and HCF. Recall of small prime numbers should be encouraged.

Extension – Skills

Students could be asked to find the HCF or LCM or three or more numbers by listing the factors and/or multiples of them.

Recap – Applications

1 a Write down all the factor pairs of these numbers.

i 35 $(1 \times 35; 5 \times 7)$

ii 60

$(1 \times 60; 2 \times 30; 3 \times 20; 4 \times 15; 5 \times 12; 6 \times 10)$

b Write down the first 3 factors of these numbers.

i 55 (1, 5, 11) **ii** 120 (1, 2, 3)

c Write down the first 3 multiples of the first 5 prime numbers.

(2, 4, 6; 3, 6, 9; 5, 10, 15; 7, 14, 21; 11, 22, 33)

2 a Find the highest common factors of

i 15 and 75 (15) **ii** 26 and 117 (13)

b Find the lowest common multiples of

i 6 and 18 (18) **ii** 32 and 112 (224)

Plenary – Applications

Show that the product of two numbers is equal to the product of their LCM and HCF. Challenge students to calculate the LCM of 12 and 9 given that the HCF is 3. Discuss how to rearrange the initial rule to give product ÷ HCF = LCM

Challenge students to calculate the HCF of 12 and 8 given that the LCM is 24.

Exercise commentary – Applications

Support students as they work through this exercise. The mathematics of factors and multiples is placed in real-life context questions which some may find confusing; however it will reap rewards with confidence for exam questions. The difficulty is often in knowing that LCM or HCF is required in the first place.

Questions 1 and **2** Fairly straightforward problems involving multiples. Students could tackle question **2** by taking each multiple of 6 in turn until they reach one that works – they won't have to go very far. As a discussion point, you could ask what the next age is that would satisfy this criterion. Some might realise that Joe's age needs to end in 4.

Questions 3 and **4** These are similar to the first example. A systematic approach could be used.

Question 5 Students should be given the opportunity to try this, perhaps in pairs; then bring it together, as an exercise in counter-example.

Questions 6 to **9** These are variants on classic LCM and HCF-type questions. A diagram might help, particularly in question **7**. Students might need help interpreting the meaning of question **8** (flower arrangements: 12 arrangements of 3 roses and 5 daisies).

Question 10 As an extension, students could play this game in pairs.

Question 11 This could be done in pairs, and strategies could be discussed as a whole class.

Question 12 A homework challenge might be to find the next perfect number after 496 (8128). This can be easily looked up on the internet, but students should be able to demonstrate that it is in fact perfect.

Simplification – Applications

Students may need practice at listing factors or multiples. Set these questions:

1 Two cyclists start together on a racetrack.

Cyclist A completes a lap every 6 minutes.

Cyclist B completes a lap every 8 minutes.

How long will it be before they pass the start line together? (List **multiples**:

A	6	12	18	<u>24</u>
B	8	16	<u>24</u>	32

They are together after 24 minutes.)

2 n is a positive odd number and $3n + 2$ is a multiple of 7. Find the smallest possible value of n.

(List **multiples** of 7:

7 14 21 28 <u>35</u> 42

Make a table of values of $3n + 2$ for $n = 1, 3, 5, 7, 9, 11, 13$ etc. $n = 11$)

Extension – Applications

You could extend this topic by introducing prime factors and linking with HCF and LCM.

Prime factor decomposition

Objectives

① **N4** Use the concepts and vocabulary of prime numbers, factors (divisors), prime factorisation, including using product notation and the unique factorisation theorem

Useful resources

Mini whiteboards, calculators, numbers displayed around the room (one of which is prime), sheets of A5 coloured paper

Starter – Skills

Using only the numbers 2, 3, 5, 7, 11 and 13, and the operation ×, make all the integers from 2 to 16. You can use one or more numbers in each answer; (for example, just use 7 to make 7), and you can use each number more than once per answer.

Ask students what type of numbers has been used. Ask: Can *any* integer be written as the product of prime numbers? (Yes.) Explain your answer.

Teaching notes – Skills

② Ask students to list the factors of 24, and to highlight which of them are **prime numbers**. Recall that a prime number is a number with exactly two distinct factors: 1 and itself (so 1 is *not* prime).

Demonstrate **prime factorisation** by breaking down 24 into a product of its **prime factors**, using a **factor tree**.

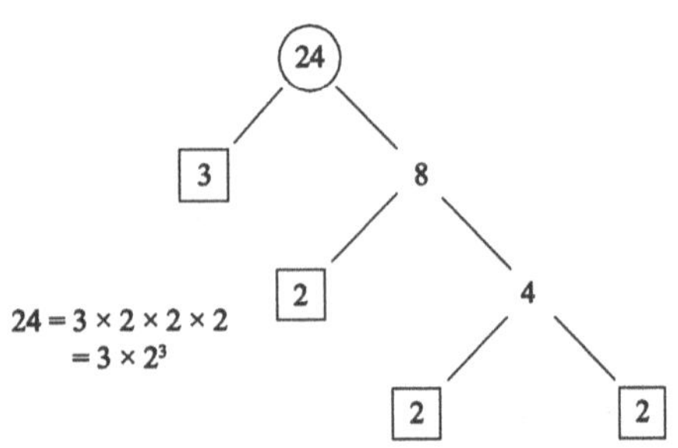

Emphasise that each branch *ends* at a prime factor, and write the factorisation using **product notation**. Use powers to simplify the calculation.

Ask students for input to demonstrate factor trees for 120 and for 13. Highlight that every number has a factor tree, *except* prime numbers, and can be expressed as the **product of its prime factors**. Students should know this process as **prime factor decomposition**.

Ask students to find the factor trees of numbers displayed around the room, recording the tree and the final product on coloured paper. These can be stuck close to the number in the room when completed.

After sufficient time for this, choose one of the numbers and look together at the different factor trees produced. While the final results should all be the same, the *branches* may well be different. Ask students if it matters which way the trees have been formed? Why not? Conversely, discuss whether any two numbers will have the *same* prime factorisation.

Emphasise that factor trees may be started using any obvious factors, whether or not they are prime, as long as the resulting smaller factors are then reduced and all the prime factors are collected at the end.

Plenary – Skills

Ask students to work in pairs on the question: Is the number 2011 a prime? (Yes)

Allow some activity time before asking for some sharing of strategies to help 'stuck' students. Allow calculator use. After some more time on the task, share more strategies and results. Explore how students check divisibility for certain numbers, such as 2, 3, 5. At what point was a calculator used? How far did they go in trying for factors? Is it a prime? Why?

Exercise commentary – Skills

Questions 1 to **4** These questions recap the earlier work on factors and multiples, reinforcing the meaning of each of these terms.

Question 5 Prime factors are introduced in this question. In part **f**, the two factors are 13 and 17.

Question 6 Enables students to become familiar with factor trees as a tool for identifying prime factors, with a simple number.

Questions 7 to **10** These questions all cover prime factor decomposition. Students should realise that using a factor tree or repeated division both reach the same result. Also it doesn't matter which pair of factors you start with. Encourage use of index notation.

Questions 11 to **14** Students may need help with drawing Venn diagrams. Once drawn correctly, it becomes very intuitive to identify the LCM and HCF.

Simplification – Skills

Students should concentrate on listing factors in pairs for further examples. Encourage them to consider factor pairs and work systematically, 1 × □, 2 × □, etc. Recall of small prime numbers should be encouraged. Students should practise factor trees extensively to gain confidence with the process.

Extension – Skills

Students could progress to using prime factorisation to find the HCF and LCM of two, three or more numbers, or of larger numbers than those in the examples.

Recap – Applications

1 Each of these numbers has just two prime factors, which are not repeated. Write each number as the product of its prime factors.

a 38 (2×19) **b** 65 (5×13)
c 85 (5×17) **d** 87 (3×29)
e 187 (11×17)

2 Express these numbers as products of their prime factors.

a 25 (5×5) **b** 30 $(2 \times 3 \times 5)$
c 36 $(2 \times 2 \times 3 \times 3)$
d 80 $(2 \times 2 \times 2 \times 2 \times 5)$
e 126 $(2 \times 3 \times 3 \times 7)$

3 Write the prime factor decomposition for each of the following numbers. Express them in powers of prime factors where appropriate.

a 2695 $(5 \times 72 \times 11)$
b 1815 $(3 \times 5 \times 112)$
c 22477 $(7 \times 132 \times 17)$
d 2601 (32×172)
e 12705 $(3 \times 5 \times 7 \times 112)$
f 23275 $(52 \times 72 \times 19)$

Plenary – Applications

Ask students to write 10, 100 and 1000 as products of the powers of their prime factors.

$$(10 = 2 \times 5,\ 100 = 2^2 \times 5^2,\ 1000 = 2^3 \times 5^3)$$

Ask: Can you spot a pattern? If so, how can you easily write one million and one billion as a product of their prime factors?

$$(1 \text{ million} = 2^6 \times 5^6,\ 1 \text{ billion} = 2^9 \times 5^9)$$

Exercise commentary – Applications

Question 1 Some students find it harder to spot an error than to make one! However, many will relish the challenge, and may find that it helps with the learning.

Question 2 Students could write down the factors of the required number and compare to the four numbers given in prime factor form.

Question 3 A good question to do in pairs. This could lead to an interesting investigation.

Questions 4 to **7** These are all problems in which the solution involves an understanding of multiples and factors. The trick is in realising this, and then working out if it's factors or multiples that are required. **Questions 4, 5** and **7** are about dividing a whole into smaller parts, so factors would probably be involved; question **6** is about repeated patterns at different rates, so multiples would be involved.

Question 8 Like question **3**, this could lead to an interesting investigation.

Questions 9 and **10** These are further problems involving factors and multiples. Some students may prefer to work out how many factors 108 has without using the prime factor decomposition.

Simplification – Applications

Correcting mistakes helps avoid making them. Students could be given questions in which they need to highlight and correct mistakes.

Extension – Applications

Ask students to solve 'reverse problems'. For example, given the HCF and LCM of two numbers, what are they? Will the answer ever be unique?

13.3 Powers and roots

Objectives

① **N6** Use positive integer powers and associated real roots (square, cube and higher) and recognise powers of 2, 3, 4, 5

Useful resources

Mini whiteboards, calculators, $2 \times 2 \times 2$ cube

Starter – Skills

Display these numbers:

1, 5, 4, 3, 8, 2, 12, 13, 16, 23, 25, 27

Ask students to find two numbers from the board which are square numbers; two prime numbers; two cube numbers; a number which is a multiple of ...; two numbers which are both factors of ...

Select some of the responses, and probe the reasoning: 'What is a square number?' and so on. Before showing some of the answers, ask students to check each other's responses in pairs, discussing and correcting as necessary.

Complete and record definitions for the key vocabulary from those offered by students.

Teaching notes – Skills

①Ask students to identify what the numbers 1, 4, 9 and 16 have in common by considering factors. Highlight that they have two equal factors that you multiply. Recall that when a number is multiplied by itself, the result is a **square number**.

Discuss why it is called a square number and link to the properties of a square (length and width are equal). Demonstrate how 1, 4, 9 and 16 counters can be arranged as squares.

Remind students of $\square^2$ notation and the key term **squared**. Build confidence with the notation by calculating square numbers. Provide calculators and demonstrate use of the squared button.

Show students a $2 \times 2 \times 2$ cube and ask for the name of the shape. Discuss properties of a cube: the length, width and height are equal. Ask students to calculate how many smaller cubes make the larger cube. Emphasise that 8 is a **cube number** as it is the result of multiplying a number by itself and then multiplying by that number again.

Introduce $\square^3$ notation and the key term **cubed**. Demonstrate use of the cube button on a calculator.

Write the calculation:

$\square^2 = \square \times \square = 144$

Ensure students understand 144 as the square number and discuss what number has been multiplied by itself to create 144. Formalise: 12 is the **square root** of 144.

Recall $\sqrt{}$ notation and provide calculators. Demonstrate use of the square root button and ask students to find the square root of:

625; 1 000 000; 676; 177 241; 25; 81; 63.

Use the last example to highlight that only square numbers have whole-number square roots.

Write the calculation:

$\square^3 = \square \times \square \times \square = 27$

Ensure students understand 27 as the cube number and discuss what number has been multiplied by itself and then again to make 27. Formalise: 3 is the **cube root** of 27.

Introduce $\sqrt[3]{}$ notation and ask students to find the symbol on their calculators. Demonstrate use of the cube root button and ask students to find the cube root of: 729, 1728, 3000.

Use the last example to highlight that only cube numbers have whole-number cube roots.

Formalise the superscript number as the **index** or **power**. Elicit that the index tells you how many times to multiply the number by itself.

Discuss the calculation required to evaluate 5^4. Ask students to use their calculators. Discuss how to evaluate 5^9. Emphasise the laborious calculator work and introduce students to the [x^y] (or equivalent) button. Demonstrate its use and ask students to evaluate: 9^4, 11^6, 10^5.

Plenary – Skills

Ask students to work in pairs and consider the statements $3^4 = 12$ and $3^0 = 30$. Are they true or false, and why?

Allow sufficient discussion time then share the results, selecting some student pairs to explain the reasoning to the group.

Exercise commentary – Skills

Question 1 Students should know the first 12 square numbers, and be able to work out cube numbers.

Question 2 How many solutions can the class find?

Questions 3 to **5** Students should take the opportunity to practise using the exponent functions on their own calculator. Ensure the order of operations in question **4**. In question **5** parts **k** and **l,** ensure correct units in the answer.

Question 6 Practice at finding square roots mentally.

Question 7 Encourage students to estimate these square roots before using their calculators.

Question 8 Students may need to rehearse cubing negative numbers.

Question 9 Students may need help in finding the cube root function on their calculator. In part **f**, ensure they use the sign key rather than the minus operation.

Question 12 Check that students are using the correct key here. A common misconception is to recognise 12^3 as being 36.

Question 16 Students could work in pairs or groups to discuss the fastest or easiest method to do each calculation.

Simplification – Skills

Students should concentrate on learning the values of the squares and square roots up to 10 and the values of 2 and 3 cubed, since they must recall them. Writing out a table of values for these will be a useful exercise since the repetition of writing the calculations will aid memory.

Extension – Skills

Students could be introduced to triangle numbers and other numbers based on geometrical arrangements similar to square and cube numbers (examples include pentagonal numbers and square pyramidal numbers).

Recap – Applications

1 **a** Find the first two square numbers, after 1, that are also cube numbers. (64 and 256)

b Find the smallest number, after 1, that is the sum of two different cube numbers. (8 + 27 = 35)

c Find the smallest number, after 1, that is the difference between a cube number and a square number. (8 – 4 = 4)

d Find the sum of the third cube number after 1 and the 6th square number after 1. (64 + 49 = 113)

2 Calculate the following values

a 3.6^3 (46.656) **b** -4^3 (-64)

c $(-4)^3$ (-64) **d** -4.2^4 (-311.1696)

e $(-4.2)^4$ (311.1696)

f $(-6.1)^5$(-8445.96301)

g $(18)^2 \div 2$ (164) **h** $(25)^3 \div 2$ (7812.5)

Plenary – Applications

Ask students to answer questions using whiteboards.

What is ... to the power of 4?
What is the value of anything to the power of 0?
etc.,

Include questions on squares and square roots, cubes and cube roots, and higher powers and roots.

Exercise commentary – Applications

Question 1 A systematic approach would be beneficial here. This could lead to an interesting investigation.

Question 2 A mapping diagram linking integers on to their squares might help students here and in question **5**, perhaps compiled together as a class and displayed on the board.

Questions 3 and **4** Semi-contextual problems involving square and cube numbers.

Question 5 This is a fairly common type of question to appear on exam papers. Ensure students understand the meaning of the term 'consecutive'. You could turn it into a pacey higher-or-lower game.

Questions 7 and **8** Intended to be non-calculator problems. Question **8** is interesting – some students may imagine that there should be more than one number that has a cube between 3000 and 4000 (others may not give it a second thought!). Could lead to an interesting discussion or investigation into how 'rare' cube numbers become the larger they are.

Questions 11 and **12** These problems contain algebraic symbolism which may confuse some students, who will be deterred from even starting. It is probably a good idea to start these together: 'What numbers would need to be inside the square root (1, 4, 9, 16, ...)'?

Question 13 An opportunity for class discussion. Students should be encouraged to present a clear, logical argument using counter-examples.

Question 14 An interesting application of prime factor decomposition to find square roots.

Simplification – Applications

Give students some 'mixed-up answers' to help them to master squares and roots of relatively small numbers. Model using known roots to estimate answers, for example:

$\sqrt{13}$ lies between $\sqrt{9}$ and $\sqrt{16}$, so between 3 and 4
$\sqrt{40}$ lies between $\sqrt{36}$ and $\sqrt{49}$ so between 6 and 7

$\sqrt{50}$ lies between $\sqrt{49}$ and $\sqrt{64}$ so between 7 and 8 *and quite close to 7 because 50 is close to 49*
$\sqrt{118}$ lies between $\sqrt{100}$ and $\sqrt{121}$ so between 10 and 11 *and quite close to 11*

Extension – Applications

Students could work with squares of numbers up to about 30, on the task of finding as many triples as possible where any two squares add to the third (Pythagorean triples).

13 Factors, powers and roots

Key outcomes	Quick check
N4 Use the concepts and vocabulary of prime numbers, factors (divisors), multiples, common factors, common multiples, highest common factor, lowest common multiple, prime factorisation, including using product notation and the unique factorisation theorem.	**1** List all the factors of these numbers. **a** 28 (1, 2, 4, 7, 14, 28) **b** 37 (1, 37) **c** 25 (1, 5, 25) **2** List the first 5 multiples of these numbers. **a** 4 (4, 8, 12, 16, 20) **b** 7 (7, 14, 21, 28, 35) **3** Are these numbers prime? Give your reasons. **a** 22 (no, 2 × 11) **b** 39 (yes) **c** 41 (yes) **d** 49 (no, square) **4** Find the HCF of each of these pairs of numbers. **a** 15 and 45 (15) **b** 14 and 35 (7) **c** 18 and 20 (2) **5** Find the LCM of each of these pairs of numbers. **a** 5 and 2 (10) **b** 8 and 12 (24) **c** 11 and 12 (121) **6** Find the prime factor decomposition of these numbers. **a** 44 (2 × 2 × 11) **b** 70 (2 × 5 × 7) **c** 48 (24 × 3) **d** 250 (2 × 53) **7 a** Copy and complete the Venn diagram to show the prime factors of 20 and 25. 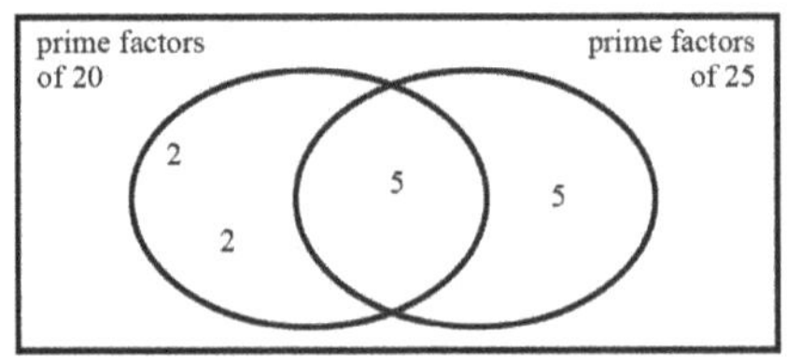 **b** Use the diagram to work out the **i** HCF (5) **ii** LCM 20 and 25. (100)
N6 Use positive integer powers and associated real roots (square, cube and higher), recognise powers of 2, 3, 4, 5.	**8** Calculate the value of these roots. **a** $\sqrt{25}$ (5) **b** $\sqrt{100}$ (10) **c** $\sqrt[3]{64}$ (4) **d** $\sqrt[3]{125}$ (5) **9** Calculate the value of these expressions. **a** 9^2 (81) **b** 6^2 (36) **c** 3^3 (27) **d** 2^4 (16) **10** What is the value of x in the equation? $10^x = 1000$ ($x = 3$)

Misconceptions and challenges	Solutions
Students calculate a^2 as $2a$, for example 5^2 given as 10.	Students need to know why square numbers are called square, with demonstrations using arrays and objects.
A common error is to interpret 2^3 as 2 × 3.	Looking at the effects of exponentiation (such as repeated scales of powers of 10) can help students grasp the difference between raising to powers and multiplication.
Pupils confuse 'factor' and 'multiple', and misinterpret problems as a result. The problem is that factors and multiples are related, but often taught in isolation.	Look at how 24 is a multiple of 12 because 12 is a factor 24. Look at how a number often has just a few factors (10 has 4 factors) but an infinite number of multiples (10, 20, 30, 40…). Ask questions such as 'Is zero a multiple of 12?' to prompt detailed discussion.

Misconceptions and challenges	Solutions
Students forget that '1' and the number itself are a factor of a number.	A systematic way of searching for pairs of factors, beginning with 1 can prevent this.
Students confuse finding the prime factors of a number with finding common factors.	Look at the subtle difference between the two tasks. A prime factor tree is a good way to find prime factors, but many pupils will become confused if they try to use this to find common factors. Encourage a simpler, systematic listing strategy for finding common factors.
Students cannot remember which method to apply when looking for HCF or LCM.	It may help to use a horizontal listing strategy for LCM, and a vertical listing strategy for HCF, so that the methods are visually distinct.

Review question commentary

Students should not use calculators in this exercise.

Questions 1 (13.1) – Students sometimes confuse the terms 'factor' and 'multiple'. Encourage them to list factors systematically, either in pairs or in ascending order.

Question 2 (13.1) – The first multiple of each will be the number itself.

Question 3 (13.1) – If a number is not prime, students should state the factors.

Question 4 (13.2) – Other methods are possible but the circled numbers should be the same.

Question 5 (13.2) – Students should write prime factors in ascending order with multiplication signs between them. Students could also use index form giving **a** 2×3^2, **b** $2^2 \times 7$

Question 6 (13.2) – To find the HCF students should multiply together the factors in the intersection. To find the LCM they should multiply all the numbers in the Venn diagram.

Question 7 (13.2) – Students could first list all the factors of each number. In part **c**, 7 and 9 are coprime as the highest common factor is 1.

Question 8 (13.2) – Students could start by listing the first few multiples of each number.

Question 9 (13.2) – Students should write the HCF as 2 not 2^1.

Questions 10 to **13 (13.3)** – Students could check their answers on a calculator.

Review answers

1 **a** 1, 2, 3, 4, 6, 12 **b** 1, 19
c 1, 2, 3, 4, 6, 8, 12, 16, 24, 48

2 **a** 5, 10, 15, 20, 25 **b** 13, 26, 39, 52, 65
c 18, 36, 54, 72, 90

3 **a** No, 5 is also a factor.
b Yes, exactly two factors.
c No, 3 and 19 are factors.

4 **a** 2, 3 **b** 1, 2, 3, 9, 18 **c** 18, 54, 72

5 Check students' factor trees, $72 = 2 \times 2 \times 2 \times 3 \times 3$

6 **a** $2 \times 3 \times 3$ **b** $2 \times 2 \times 7$

7 **a**

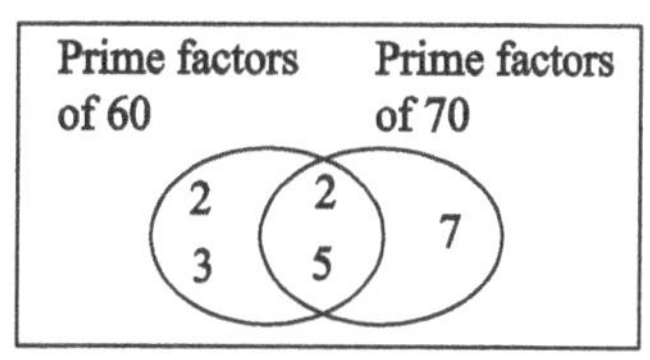

b **i** 10 **ii** 420

8 **a** 4 **b** 27 **c** 1 **d** 1

9 **a** 12 **b** 24 **c** 99 **d** 143

10 **a** **i** 2×3^3 **ii** $2^3 \times 5^2$
b $\text{LCM} = 2^2 \times 3^3 \times 5^2 = 900$, HCF = 2

11 **a** 4 **b** 9 **c** 2 **d** 10

12 **a** 9 **b** 49 **c** 125 **d** 32

13 **a** 3 **b** 3

Assessment 13

Question 1 – 2 marks

$\underline{1 \times 42}, 2 \times 21, 3 \times 14, \underline{6 \times 7}$ [B1]

No [F1]

Question 2 – 11 marks

a 3 is not a factor OR

$3454 \div 6 = 575$ r 4 [B2]

b **i** 100, 102, 104, 106, 108 [B1]

ii 102, 105, 108 [B1]

iii 100, 104, 108 [B1]

iv 100, 105 [B1]

v 102, 108 [B1]

vi 105 [B1]

vii 104 [B1]

viii 108 [B1]

ix 100 [B1]

Question 3 – 5 marks

a The last two digits are not divisible by 4

OR $110 \div 2 = 55$ and 55 is not divisible by 2 [B2]

b Factors of 110: 1, 2, 5, 10, 11, 22 55, 110 [M1, A1]

5, 10, 11 [F1]

Question 4 – 2 marks

Factors $54 = 2 \times 3^3$: 1, 2, 3, 6, 9, 18, 27, 54

Factors of $99 = 3^2 \times 11$: 1, 3, 9, 11, 33, 99 [B1]

HCF = 9, No [F1]

Question 5 – 3 marks

Multiples of $36 = 2^2 \times 3^2$: 36, 72, 108, 144, 180, … [B1]

Multiples of $60 = 2^2 \times 3 \times 5$: 60, 120, 180, … [B1]

LCM = $2^2 \times 3^2 \times 5 = 180$ [F1]

Question 6 – 2 marks

$6 = 2 \times 3$ $15 = 3 \times 5$ $21 = 3 \times 7$ $30 = 2 \times 3 \times 5$ [B1]

1st OR 3rd [F1]

Question 7 – 5 marks

$60 = 2^2 \times 3 \times 5$ $45 = 3^2 \times 5$ $25 = 5^2$ [B1]

LCM = $2^2 \times 3^2 \times 5$ [M1]

$= 180$ [A1]

6 am + 180 min = 9 am [M1]

9 pm [A1]

Question 8 – 3 marks

Factors of 28: 1, 2, 4, 7, 14, 28 [B1]

$1 + 2 + 4 + 7 + 14$ [M1]

$= 28$ [A1]

Question 9 – 9 marks

a $(16, 28) \to (16, 12) \to (4, 12) \to (4, 8) \to (4, 4)$ [B2]

HCF = 4 [F1]

b $(30, 66) \to (30, 36) \to (30, 6) \to (24, 6) \ldots (6, 6)$ [B2]

HCF = 6 [F1]

c $(252, 588) \to (252, 336) \to (252, 84) \to$

$(168, 84) \to (84, 84)$ [B2]

HCF = 4 [F1]

Question 10 – 3 marks

$19\,800 = 198 \times 10^2 = 2 \times 99 \times (2 \times 5)^2$

$= 2^3 \times 5^2 \times 9 \times 11 = 2^3 \times 3^2 \times 5^2 \times 11$

OR equivalent method of prime factorisation [B2]

Isa; must see supporting workings. [F1]

Question 11 – 6 marks

a $1024 > 625$; Yes [B1, F1]

b $1024 > 100$; Yes [B1, F1]

c $16 = 16$; No [B1, F1]

Question 12 – 8 marks

a $33 = 3 \times 11$ [B1]

It has four factors (1, 3, 11, 33) [B1]

b No, all the numbers are odd. [B1]

c All the numbers are even. [B1]

2 is the only even prime number

No [B1]

d 43 and 47 [B2]

e No; all the numbers are multiples of 4. [B1]

Question 13 – 8 marks

a $25 = 2 + 23$ [B2]

b $16 = 3 + 13 = 5 + 11$ [B2]

c $36 = 5 + 31 = 7 + 29 = 13 + 23 = 17 + 19$ [B4]

Question 14 – 4 marks

a Glen [B1]

3^5 [B1]

b Giorgia [B1]

14^6 [B1]

Question 15 – 4 marks

a Sam: negative numbers have no square roots;

0 has one square root [B1]

George, only positive numbers have two square roots [B1]

Neither

b All numbers (positive, zero and negative) have only one cube root [B2]

No

Question 16 – 4 marks

$M + C \approx 70$, $M \approx 2C$ and C is prime [B1]

$3C \approx 70$

$C \approx 23$ [M2]

23 is prime [A1]

Question 17 – 6 marks

a Correct interpretation of formula [M1]

$41 - 0 + 0^2 = 41$ (a prime) [A1]

$41 - 3 + 3^2 = 47$ (a prime) [A1]

$41 - 6 + 6^2 = 71$ (a prime) [A1]

b $41, 41 - 41 + 41^2$ OR $42, 41 - 42 + 42^2$ [B1]

$= 41^2$ $= 1763 = 41 \times 43$ [B1]

Graphs 1

Learning outcomes

A8 Work with coordinates in all four quadrants.

A9 Plot graphs of equations that correspond to straight-line graphs in the coordinate plane; use the form $y = mx + c$ to identify parallel lines; find the equation of the line through two given points, or through one point with a given gradient.

A10 Identify and interpret gradients and intercepts of linear functions graphically and algebraically.

A14 Plot and interpret graphs [(including reciprocal graphs)] and graphs of non-standard functions in real contexts, to find approximate solutions to problems such as simple kinematic problems involving distance, speed and acceleration.

A17 [Solve linear equations in one unknown algebraically (including those with the unknown on both sides of the equation);] find approximate solutions using a graph.

R14 Interpret the gradient of a straight line graph as a rate of change.

Prior knowledge

Check-in skill

- Substitute numerical values into expressions.
- Draw a coordinate grid.
- Plot coordinates in all four quadrants.

Online resources

MyMaths 1093, 1153, 1312, 1314, 1322, 1323, 1394, 1395, 1396

InvisiPen videos
Skills: 14Sa – k Applications: 14Aa – f

Kerboodle assessment
Online Skills Test 14 Chapter Test 14

Development and links

Graphs provide a visual means of representing a function and are important in fields where equations are used to model behaviour in the real world. They can be used to calibrate scientific instruments, convert currencies, convert from metric to imperial units and to display the results of a scientific experiment or geographical investigation. Finding the midpoint of a line has links to finding the centre of mass of an object which has applications in science and engineering.

Chapter investigation

Start by asking students how they would decide if a third point lies on the same line as two others. A likely answer is to draw all three points. Investigate this for the points given and for sets of points that span all four quadrants [**14.1**].

Suppose the point being tested was (1000, 2999) or (5.135, 13.405), could you draw a big enough or accurate enough diagram to be able to decide? Agree that having a formula for the points on a line would be a good idea.

Investigate how to read off the y-intercept and calculate the gradient from a line drawn through two points [**15.2**]. Pair up the students. Ask them first to each choose a pair of points and find the equation of the line through their points. Then ask them to swap equations and draw the lines – do the lines go through the original points? [**15.1**]

Move on to calculating the equation of a line using just the points without relying on a graph [**15.2**]. This can be developed to finding the equation of a line given a point on it and its gradient.

To answer the question, test if the point satisfies the equation of the line, $y = 3x - 2$. It does *not* so it does *not* lie on the line ($3x - 2 = 61 \neq 18$).

A scenario in which the investigation can be made a little more realistic is distance–time graphs [**15.3**]. If a train, travelling at a constant speed, passes two distance markers at given times will it pass through a third at a specific time? Ensure that students recognise that the '(average) speed = distance travelled ÷ time taken' is the formula for calculating the gradient of a straight line.

14.1 Drawing straight-line graphs

Objectives

① **A8** Work with coordinates in all four quadrants.

② **A9** Plot graphs of equations that correspond to straight-line graphs in the coordinate plane.

Useful resources

Mini whiteboards, display of marked axes, OHT/whiteboard files of coordinate grids (first quadrant and all four quadrants.), pre-drawn axes/blank tables of values

Starter – Skills

Show the four quadrants on an OHT with letters placed at various points. Write a word using coordinate code and challenge students to decipher the word. Ensure students understand that when a point is to the left of the y-axis then the x-coordinate is negative and when a point is below the x-axis the y-coordinate is negative.

Teaching notes – Skills

Write the equation $y = 2x$ and an incomplete table of values ranging from $x = -2$ to 3

Invite students to generate the y-values by substituting each x-value in separately.

Recall rules of multiplication.

positive × positive = positive

negative × negative = positive

positive × negative = negative

Highlight that each x has a corresponding y and demonstrate how to write as coordinates.

Show an OHT of the four quadrants and invite students to plot the coordinates.

Discuss the pattern shown. Discuss the y-value in non-integer x-values, for example, when $x = 1.5$

Highlight that all values that satisfy the equation would fit along the line and elicit that the points can be joined.

Write the equation $y = 2x + 1$ and invite students to complete a table of values and plot the graph.

Highlight that points that satisfy an equation will always create a straight line and demonstrate how the graph can be used to read corresponding pairs of values.

Ensure students understand the importance of finding the value given on the correct axis.

Plenary – Skills

On an OHT showing the first quadrant draw the line $x + y = 8$.

Invite students to give coordinates that fit the line, and to articulate the relationship between the coordinates.

Prompt and direct students with questions like, Will (4, 4) be on the line? Why or why not? What about (–1, 9)? Link worded reasoning with equation of line. Repeat for other lines and equations.

Exercise commentary – Skills

Question 1 It would be worth reminding students of the rule 'along the corridor and up or down the stairs' to be used when writing and plotting coordinates. Also highlight the fact that you plot the x-coordinate first and then the y-coordinate, (x, y).

Question 2 Encourages students to tell you the coordinates of the points given in the question, what do they notice? Which coordinate is the same? This should lead them to being able to name the line.

Question 3 Remind pupils that $2x$ means $2 \times x$. It may be suitable to work through part **a** of the first example given on page 290 so that students can see how the y-coordinates are generated.

Question 4 Some students may prefer to include an additional row to their tables used in question **3** with each coordinate listed, (1, 4), (2, 5) etc… Tell students to join their points with a straight line and extend the line so that it fits the grid.

Question 5 In each case encourage students to use a table of values. You may need to demonstrate how to find y when the equation is given in this type of format with the y-intercept first and the gradient second.

Question 6 Invite more able students to explore the connection between the coefficient of x and the steepness of the graph (gradient), also what do they notice about the constant value and the resulting graph?

Question *7 You may need to recap on the rules of multiplying with negative numbers in order to enable students to access this extension question.

Question 8 Suggest students choose 3 or 4 points that all lie on the same straight line and write down the coordinates, what do they notice? They should spot that all the x-coordinates or y-coordinates are identical and hence this is how the name of the straight line is formed. Direct students still struggling to look at the final part of the example on page 290.

Question 9 Tell students to write down 3 or 4 points where the x or y-coordinate is the required value, plot these points and then join to form a straight line.

Emphasise how $y = a$ lines are horizontal and how $x = a$ lines are vertical.

Question 10 Ask students to plot the points and then it should be easy enough for them to discover which point does not lie on the line.

Simplification – Skills

Students may benefit from pre-drawn axes and blank tables of values. Give them further examples of equations that involve just one operation to ensure they are competent at completing a table of values and then plotting the points.

Extension – Skills

Students could be given further examples of equations that have two operations. They could also investigate plotting simple quadratic graphs.

Recap – Applications

1 **a** Draw a grid with the x and y-axes from 0 to 6.

b On the grid draw the straight line for the graph of

i $y = 5$ **ii** $y = 2$

iii $y = x$ **iv** $y = x + 2$

c Write down the coordinates of the points where the line $y = 2$ meets the two other lines.

((0, 2); (2, 2))

d Write down the coordinates of the point where the line $y = 5$ meets the other two lines.

((3, 5); (5, 5))

e What is the shape made by the lines joining these 4 points? (parallelogram)

2 **a** Does the point (1, 3) lie on the line $y = 2x + 1$? (Yes)

b Does the point (–4, –5) lie on the line $y = 3x - 7$? (No. $3 \times -4 - 7 = -19$)

c The point (1, 3) lies on the line $y = 5x + c$. Work out the value of c. ($c = -2$)

d The point (m, –1) lies on the line $y = 4x - 9$. Work out the value of m. ($m = 4$)

Plenary – Applications

Display a set of axes to the whole group.

Ask the students to draw graphs in the air.

Where would this line be?

$x = 5$, $x = 12$, $x = -3$,
$y = 6$, $y = -2$, $y = x$,
$x + y = 4$, $x + y = 9$, etc.

Exercise commentary – Applications

Question 1 A quick reminder that a parallelogram has two pairs of parallel sides may be needed here. Part * **c** would be suitable for a whole class discussion. You may wish to demonstrate how other solutions could be generated on a coordinate grid as they are not easy to spot!

Question 2 Prior to this question show students how to find the coordinates of where the line cuts the two axes, plot the points and then join them to form the required straight-line graph. Explain that the additional coordinates they need to give are any points that lie on the straight-line graph but encourage students to use whole numbers.

Questions 3 and **4** Explain to the class that coordinates for graphs given in implicit forms can either be formed by finding the value of x when $y = 0$ (and vice-versa) or by first rearranging to make y the subject and then creating a table of values. Encourage students to try out both methods. Are there some situations where one method is easier than the other? Remind students to take care with negatives.

Question 5 Tell students to plot both lines in each part on the same grid and state the coordinates of where the line crosses. If the two lines don't appear to cross remind students to extend their lines so that they do cross.

Question 6 Remind students that an integer is a whole number. Explain that they should plot all the lines given on the same axes and find the coordinates of the point that fits all the descriptions given.

Question 7 Tell student to eliminate options by matching the graphs they recognise first.

Question *8 This would be a suitable question to go through as a whole class. Discuss how you would find the y-coordinate at the point where the lines cross and then how you can use this value to find the gradient and then the y-intercept of the red line.

Question 9 Demonstrate with a similar equation such as the second example shown on page 292 how you could set up equations that represent the two options. Show how you can substitute in the required value to answer part **a** and model drawing the graph and using the graph to answer the other parts of a question like this.

Simplification – Applications

Students should be encouraged to practise with equations of the form $y = mx + c$ rather than the implicit functions. Pre-drawn axes and tables may help students speed up their work.

Extension – Applications

Ask students to investigate a possible way of plotting implicitly defined functions without rearranging. Suggest that the standard tabular approach can be suitably modified.

14.2 Equation of a straight line

Objectives

① **A9** Use the form $y = mx + c$ to identify parallel lines; find the equation of the line through two given points, or through one point with a given gradient.

② **A10** Identify and interpret gradients and intercepts of linear functions graphically and algebraically.

③ **R14** Interpret the gradient of a straight-line graph as a rate of change.

Useful resources

Mini whiteboards, graph plotting software

Starter – Skills

Take two graphs: $y = x + 3$ and $y = 2x + 3$. Ask What is the same about the graphs and their equations? Use the keyword intercept. Ask What is different about the graphs and their equations? Use the keyword gradient. Ask students to show an equation which is parallel to $y = 2x + 3$, and ask how this is identified.

Teaching notes – Skills

Draw axes from –10 to 10 in both directions. Draw the lines $y = 2x - 1$ and $y = -3x + 2$ taking x values at 0, 2, 4. Show how to find the gradient by picking any two clear (integer) points on the line. Make a right-angled triangle and measure the height and the base. The gradient is the change in y divided by the change in x. Point out that lines that slope down have a negative gradient and lines that slope up have a positive gradient. Explain that the y-intercept is the number where the line cuts the y-axis. What is the y-intercept of each line? How are the values of the gradient and the y-intercept related to the equations of the lines?
(y = gradient × x + y-intercept)

Explain that the normal symbol for the gradient is m. The value of the y-intercept normally uses the symbol c. So the formula becomes

$y = m \times x + c$ or $y = mx + c$.

Notice that m can be positive or negative as can c. When c is negative you write – instead of +.

What can you say about the lines $y = 5x$ and $y = 5x - 4$? (They are parallel – both have gradient 5.)

Plenary – Skills

What is the gradient of $y = 5$? (Zero)

What is the gradient of $x = -2$? (Infinity or undefined)

This can be established by looking at steeper and steeper lines or flatter and flatter lines.

Exercise commentary – Skills

Questions 1 to **2** Ensure you have covered as a whole class the content given in the introductory section of page 294 before students embark on these questions. It is important that they fully understand what is meant by the gradient and can relate this to an actual graph and appreciate that the y-intercept is where the graph cuts the y-axis. The first two parts of the example show how these can be found.

Questions 3 to **5** In these questions students need to demonstrate that they can confidently find the gradient and y-intercept and then use these values to write the equation of a graph. Recap that the gradient is the coefficient of x and that the y-intercept is the constant value when the straight line is given in the form

$y = mx + c$.

Question 6 Students will need to show that they can find the y-intercept and gradient when given the equation. Emphasise that the equation first needs to be in the form $y = mx + c$ and as such the final two parts of this question require some rearranging. Once rearranged in the correct form will part **f** be $y = x - 10$ or $y = -x + 10$?

Question 7 Students may be unsure what to do when either the gradient or y-intercept is equal to zero. Reinforce that $0x = 0$ and that if the constant or gradient is 0 you would not need to write it. A common mistake is to mix up the gradient and y-intercept, to write the first answer as $y = x + 3$ for instance. Show students this and ask them to describe the mistake and state what the correct answer should be.

Questions 8 and **9** These questions help students to recognise the effect that the gradient and y-intercept have on the graph drawn. What do they notice in particular about parts **a** and **d** and can they explain why this is the case?

Question 10 In this question ask students to first plot the coordinates of where the y-intercept is and then think about the gradient. They could consider the gradient by drawing on a triangle to find another pair of coordinates that will lie on the line, this can be done in a similar way to that shown in the introductory section on page 294. Once they have found two pairs of coordinates on the straight line these can be joined and extended to form the required straight-line graph.

Question 11 Emphasise that parallel graphs have the same gradient and will never cross.

Question 12 It is important that students fully understand what is meant by the gradient and how it relates to an actual graph and that they appreciate that the y-intercept is where the graph cuts the y-axis.

Question 13 You may wish to allow students to first draw suitable graphs in order to answer part ***c**. As an extension you could ask them to comment on anything they notice about the gradients of the perpendicular lines.

Simplification – Skills

Concentrate first on examples where the gradient is positive. Avoid implicit functions and ones where the x-term is second on the right-hand side

Extension – Skills

Students could use the formula for gradient in the form: $\frac{y_2 - y_1}{x_2 - x_1}$ to calculate the gradient of a line through two points without drawing the line.

Recap – Applications

1 Find the equations of these lines. Write all your answers with whole number coefficients.
   - **a** gradient –1, intercept 7 ($y = -x + 7$)
   - **b** gradient –4 intercept –13 ($y = -4x - 13$)
   - **c** gradient $\frac{2}{3}$, intercept $\frac{1}{3}$ ($3y = 2x + 1$)

2 Write the equations of three lines which are parallel to the line $y = 6 - 3x$.
   ($y = d - 3x$, where d is any constant other than 6.)

Plenary – Applications

Helen cycles uphill for 2 km. She rises in height by 400 m and the ride takes her 8 min. Fran cycles uphill for 3 km. She rises in height by 300 m and the ride takes her 16 min. Who is faster? Explain.
(Helen. One solution is to look at what each rider can achieve in the same amount of time, say 8 min.)

Exercise commentary – Applications

Question 1 Remind students that the equation of a straight line can be written in the form $y = mx + c$. Recap that m is the gradient and c is the y-intercept. For parts **e** and **g** students will need to rearrange the given equation in order to find the gradient. The first part of the first example on page 296 provides an outline of the steps needed to do this.

Question 2 Show students that they can find the gradient by calculating the change in the y-coordinates divided by the change in the x-coordinates. Remind students that if the line slopes downwards from left to right then the gradient will be negative. They will then be able to give the equation using the y-intercept shown in the question and the calculated gradient value.

Question 3 Demonstrate that if the first set of coordinates is labelled (x_1, y_1) and the second set of coordinates is labelled, (x_2, y_2) then an alternative way of describing how to find the gradient is $\frac{y_2 - y_1}{x_2 - x_1}$. This method can be used in this question though students will have to take care with negatives in the final two parts.

Show students that to calculate the y-intercept they will need to substitute in their gradient and the respective x and y-coordinates from one of the coordinate points that lie on the line into the equation $y = mx + c$, then rearrange to find c, the y-intercept. Students will need to see a few worked examples before they attempt this sort of question, the second example on page 296 would be suitable.

Question 4 Completing this question should consolidate students understanding of what the y-intercept and gradient are and what impact they both have on a graph.

Question 5 Here students need to match graphs to equations but without having any numerical values on the axes. Encourage students to use a logical process of elimination, starting by matching the ones they can easily work out and reducing the options available. Ensure they recognise that part **d** has a negative gradient.

Questions 6 to **8** Work through at least one of these problem-solving style questions as a whole class. Discuss how these problems could be approached in different ways. For example one possible way of approaching question **7** would be to find the missing p-coordinate by considering how the x and y-coordinates have changed so far and then continuing this pattern. Alternatively, they could find the equation of the straight line that goes between the first two points and then use this equation to substitute the known value of p from the third coordinate in to find the q-coordinate.

Question 9 Encourage students to consider what 0 on the x-axis means and ask what is happening to the height each year, how does this relate to the gradient? As an extension task you could ask if they think this graph is a suitable representation of real life and to justify why.

Simplification – Applications

Students could be given graph drawing software and asked to plot different equations. Visualising the lines in this way should help to strengthen the interpretation of the form '$y = mx + c$'. It can also be used as a way of confirming the equivalence of various forms of the same rearranged equation.

Extension – Applications

Students could be asked to consider simple examples of perpendicular lines and to write down what they notice about the gradients in these cases.

14.3 Distance–time graphs

Objectives

① **A14** Plot and interpret graphs to find approximate solutions to problems such as simple kinematic problems involving distance, speed and acceleration.

Useful resources

Mini whiteboards, calculators, display of a journey mapped out on a distance–time graph

Starter – Skills

Describe your journey to school and sketch a graph on basic axes to illustrate this.

Invite students to sketch a graph that represents their journey to school. Ask them to describe their graphs. Discuss the label for each axis.

Teaching notes – Skills

Display a journey graph axes labelled Time and Distance with units. Check that students understand each of the scales by asking questions.

Discuss that different steepness in slope indicates faster and slower speeds. Highlight that a steeper line shows more distance is travelled over a shorter time.

Ask specific questions about the journey which involve time and distance. Divide the journey into sections (A, B, C, etc.). Ask students: Which is the fastest/slowest part of the journey? When is the vehicle not moving? and so on.

Extend to include speed over certain sections of the journey using the formula:

speed = distance ÷ time

Demonstrate how to calculate the speed for part of a journey by reading from the graph:

- distance travelled in that part of the journey
- time taken for that part of the journey.

Ensure students understand how to substitute the values correctly into the formula, and recognise that the units of speed must reflect the units of distance and time. Demonstrate use of a calculator, and discuss how to convert fractions of an hour into equivalent decimals ($\frac{3}{4}$ as 0.75).

Plenary – Skills

Refer to a question on the topic and encourage students to calculate the speed being travelled using their intuitive knowledge.

Emphasise that speed is usually a measurement given as distance travelled per hour.

Direct with questions such as: 'if George travelled 12 miles in $\frac{3}{4}$ of an hour, how far did he travel in $\frac{1}{4}$ of an hour?' and 'so how far in an hour?'

Exercise commentary – Skills

Question 1 Demonstrate with an example such as the first one shown on page 294 how to read and interpret a distance–time graph. Show students how you can draw vertical and horizontal lines on the graph to get the required information. Often mistakes are made as scales are not considered correctly; stress the importance of establishing what one square represents on both the x-axis and the y-axis.

Question 2 A student who has not read the question correctly may give the answer to part **a** as 2.45, discuss the error that has been made here. As a whole class discuss what each part of the graph means, the first slope, the horizontal section and the second (steeper) slope. Try and encourage comments referring to the speed of the sloped sections, ask the question 'in which part is Tamara travelling faster?' As an extension you could pose the question, 'why would it be impossible to have a vertical line on this sort of distance–time graph?'

Question 3 Ensure students can apply the formula speed equals distance divided by time to calculate the speed and that they recognise that the steeper the gradient the faster the speed. A common misconception is to not take care with the units, for example a student may incorrectly try and calculate the speed in part **e** as $\frac{40}{30}$. Show students this and discuss the error that has been made. Additionally, some may also initially struggle with calculating $\frac{40}{0.5}$ and incorrectly give the answer as 20. Discuss this and demonstrate why dividing by 0.5 is the same as multiplying by 2.

Question 4 Students need to be clear that the average speed is equal to the total distance travelled divided time taken. You may wish to tell them to exclude stops. The second example on page 294 shows how the average speed can be calculated.

Question 5 It may be worthwhile working through one part here as a whole class. Make sure students can calculate the speed for each part of the journey. Demonstrate how the axes will now have speed on the y-axis and time on the x-axis. Ask why this graph is not a true reflection of what happens in real life. Encourage answers that refer to the fact that speeds cannot change instantly and in reality you would have acceleration and deceleration, you could ask more able pupils how this would be shown on a speed–time graph.

Question 6 As an extension you could ask a student who uses more than one mode of transport to describe his journey. For example, Ben walks 1 km which takes him 10 minutes. He then catches a bus which takes 20 minutes to travel 10 km. Students could be asked to draw a distance–time graph to represent this situation.

Simplification – Skills

Students could be given graphs that have very simple two (or three) stages to the journey described and asked to write out what the journey is.

Extension – Skills

Challenge students to draw a distance–time graph from information given in a 'story'.

Recap – Applications

1 The distance–time graph shows a flight on the shuttle service of 'Jetoff' Airways between Manchester, Amsterdam and Vienna.

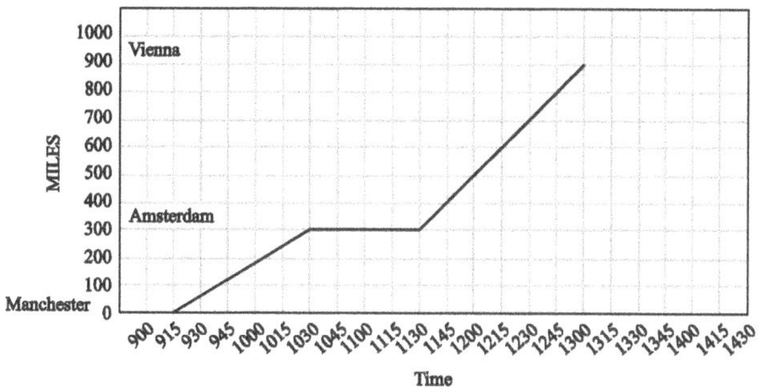

a How far is Amsterdam from Manchester by air? (300 miles)

b How far is Amsterdam from Vienna by air? (600 miles)

c How long was the stopover in Amsterdam? (1h)

d Calculate the average speed of the aircraft between Manchester and Amsterdam. (240 mph)

Plenary – Applications

Invite students to estimate the distance from school to home/a well-known landmark and so on. Encourage them to discuss how long it would take to walk/drive there.

Discuss how to use this information to calculate the speed that they would be travelling if they walked or if they drove.

Exercise commentary – Applications

Question 1 Consider asking students to write this question down and underline the key information. Discuss how to set out the axes, 'how far will the x and y need to go in each direction?' Use the information highlighted to find key coordinate points that need to be plotted, 'what will happen to the graph when he is resting? How long will the return journey take?' This could be found be rearranging the formula, speed = distance/time. Some students may take the approach, 6 km = 1 hour, 12 km = 2 hours, 15 km = 2.5 hours.

Question 2 Suggest to students that they find key coordinates for the distance–time graph using the information given in words. Remind students to convert units when necessary, here a mixture of metres and kilometres and minutes and seconds are used (if need be remind them of the conversions). Students may find the final part of the journey difficult to plot. You may need to show that 0.833... is equivalent to $\frac{5}{6}$ and demonstrate how this can be converted into metres per minute, alternatively you could allow students the use of a calculator for this question.

Question 3 Tell students that using a grid that goes across to 12.30 pm on the x-axis and up to 150 km on the y-axis is sufficient. Check students realise that when the two lines meet they represent when the trains are the same distance from the starting station.

Question 4 Make sure students are clear that the steeper the gradient of the graph the faster the speed. Recap that to calculate the speed they will need to find the distance travelled and divide this by the time taken, remind students to state the units in their answer. For the final part discuss how the easiest way to answer this question would be to just continue Asif's graph.

Question 5 This would be a question that could be effectively covered as a whole class where students are invited to discuss their reasons why each graph is impossible. Hopefully they will be able to recognise situations where time would go backwards, distances would be negative and distances are travelled in no time at all.

Question 6 Emphasise the importance of establishing how speed has varied in the journey. Some students may be unsure about part **c**, ensure they realise that the first part of the journey is outward and the last part is inward but that the speed has not varied.

Question 7 It is important that students appreciate that acceleration can be calculated from a speed–time graph and that this is change in speed divided by time taken. It would be worthwhile directing students to look through the final example on page 296 before attempting this question.

Simplification – Applications

Students may benefit from a list of basic equivalent fractions and decimals for questions involving fractions of an hour. Alternatively they could be restricted to examples where they are working in round hours.

Extension – Applications

Students could be given a journey described in terms of speed and either distance or time and asked to complete the distance–time graph for this journey.

14 Graphs 1

Key outcomes	Quick check
A8 Work with coordinates in all four quadrants.	**1 a** Write down the coordinates of A, B and C. $(A\ (2, -4), B\ (3, 5), C\ (-1, 0))$ **b** What is the gradient of the line shown? (2) **c** What is the equation of the line? $(y = 2x - 1)$ 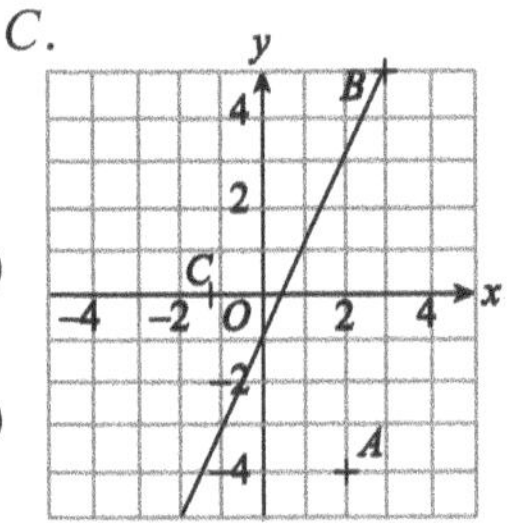
A9 Plot graphs of equations that correspond to straight-line graphs in the coordinate plane; use the form $y = mx + c$ to identify parallel lines; find the equation of the line through two given points, or through one point with a given gradient.	**2** Copy and complete a table of values for x between −1 and 3 for each equation. **a** $y = x + 5$ (4, 5, 6, 7, 8) **b** $y = 3x - 1$ (−4, −1, 2, 5, 8) **3 Draw** appropriate axes and plot the lines for each of the equations in question **2**. **4 Complete** a table of values and plot the graphs of these equations for values of x between −1 and 3 **a** $y = 2x + 2$ (0, 2, 4, 6, 8) **b** $y = -4x + 4$ (8, 4, 0, −4, −8) 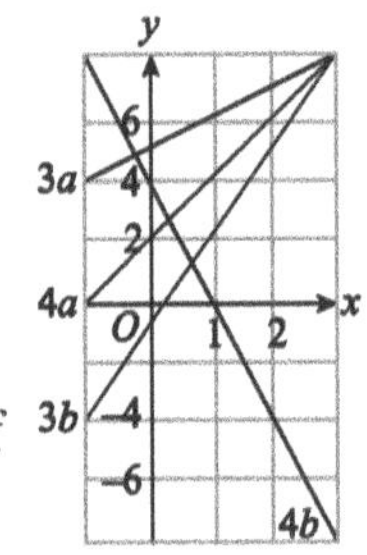
A10 Identify and interpret gradients and intercepts of linear functions graphically and algebraically.	**5** State the gradient and y-intercept of these lines. **a** $y = -3x$ $(m = -3, c = 0)$ **b** $y = x + 5$ $(m = 1, c = 5)$ **6** Write down the equation of any line that is parallel to the line with equation $y = 0.5x + 1$ $(y = 0.5x + c)$ **7** What is the equation of a line that has gradient 3 and crosses through the y-axis at the point (0, 6)? $(y = 3x + 6)$
A14 Plot and interpret graphs and graphs of non-standard functions in real contexts, to find approximate solutions to problems such as simple kinematic problems involving distance, speed and acceleration. A17 Find approximate solutions using a graph. R14 Interpret the gradient of a straight line graph as a rate of change.	**8** The distance–time graph shows Anna's bicycle ride from home to town and back again. 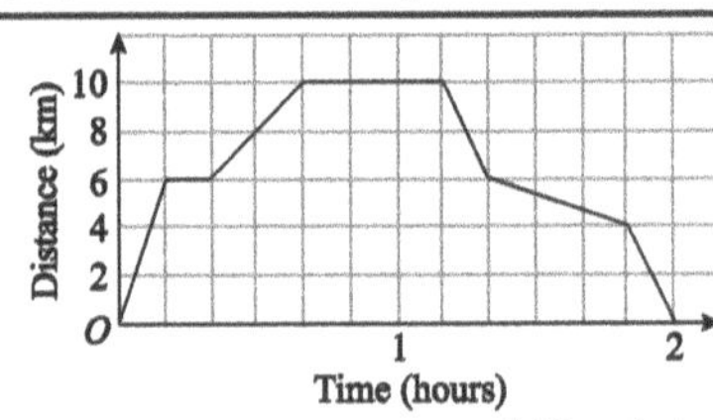 **a** What is the total distance Anna travelled? (20 km) **b** How long did she stop for? (40 min) **c** What was her fastest speed? (36 km/h) **d** What is her average speed over the whole journey? Give your answer in km/h. (10 km/h)

Misconceptions and challenges	Solutions
When working in four quadrants, students fail to plot x and y-coordinates in the correct order.	Students may well have learned memory tricks such as 'you go along the hallway before you go up the stairs', or 'x is a cross [across]'. Adapt the memory tricks, for example, 'you go along the hallway and up or down in the lift'.
Students may interpret a graph as being 'steeper'if it appears higher than another at $x = 0$.	Encourage students to visualise how the graph would continue beyond the scale of the axes.
Students plot the given points of a linear graph, but fail to join them with a line, or extend the line.	Model to students how intermediate points are also part of the graph, and so a line is the most efficient way of plotting all the points.
Students often think that a graph must pass through the origin, and so skew their line.	Introduce graphs that do not pass through the origin first, then introduce lines of the form $y = mx + 0$ as a special case.

Misconceptions and challenges	Solutions
Students need time to explore the effect of changing the gradient and y-intercept, to understand the equation $y = mx + c$.	Using graphing software, ask students to keep the gradient constant, and choose different values for the y-intercept.Then have students keep the y-intercept constant, and choose different values for the gradient.
Students do not fully understand how gradients can be interpreted as a rate of change, and struggle to model problems as a result.	Introduce a problem without mentioning that it can be modelled as a linear graph.After some guided exploration students will produce a model that clearly resembles the linear situation.Then explore why the link exists.
Students often confuse fractional and negative gradients.	Use graphing software or animations to allow students to manipulate graphs while displaying the changing gradients
Students may not understand that solutions are given by intersections between graphs generally, and often by intersections with the x-axis.	Spend time discussing the meaning of the word 'solution'and how it applies to the graph as well as the equation. Begin with very simple functions to demonstrate the link.

Review question commentary

Question 1 (14.1) Remind students that the horizontal coordinate comes first.

Question 2 (14.1) Negative numbers tend to cause issues. Students could attempt the positive x-values first then check that they get a continuation of the same pattern in the negative numbers.

Question 3 (14.1) – As an extension get students to mark on the y-intercept and draw triangles to illustrate the gradient.

Question 4 (14.1) – Remind students that '$y =$ ' lines are horizontal and that ' $x =$ ' lines are vertical.

Question 5 (14.2) – Students will need to consider the change in y-coordinates divided by the change in x-coordinates.

Question 6 (14.2) – Students can find drawing axes difficult. Use peer assessment to ensure scale on axes is even, axes have labels etc.

Question 7 (14.2) – Any constant (including zero) allowed for c.

Question 8 (14.2) – Remind students that that the y-intercept is where the line crosses the y-axis and at this point $x = 0$.

Question 9 (14.2) – It may help students to draw a diagram.

Question 10 (14.3) – In part **c**, the bus travels 2 km in 12 min so the average speed is $\frac{1}{6}$ km/min. Students need to × 60 to convert to km/h.

Review answers

1 A (2, 5), B (–3, 5), C (0, –4), D (3, 0), E (–2, 3)

2 **a** –6, –3, 0, 3, 6 **b** 3, 5, 7, 9, 11

3 **a**

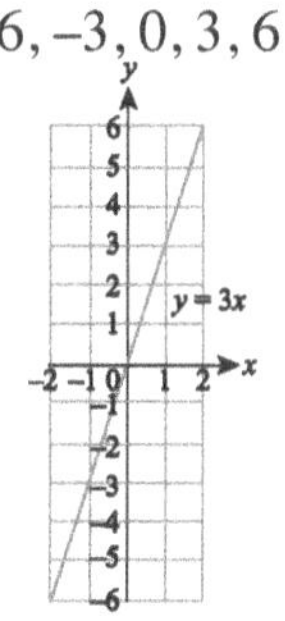

b

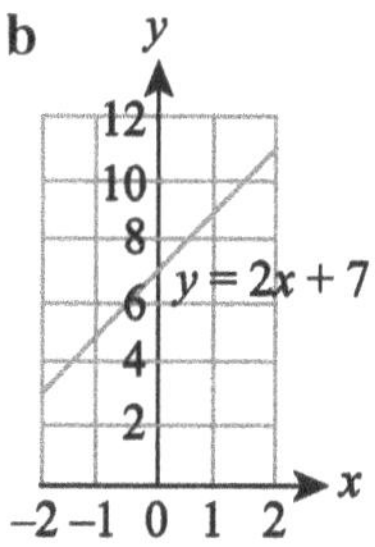

4

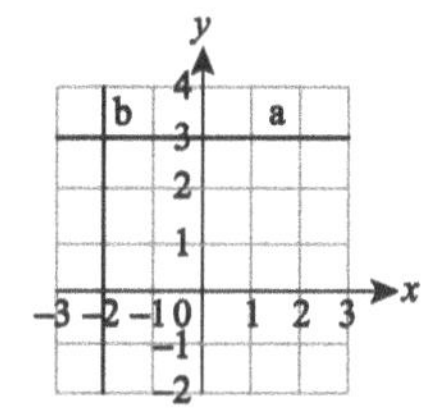

5 **a** 3 **b** $y = 3x + 1$

6 **a** $y = -4, -1, 2, 5, 8, 11$ **b** $y = 25, 20, 15, 10, 5, 0$

$m = 3, c = -1$ $m = -5, c = 20$

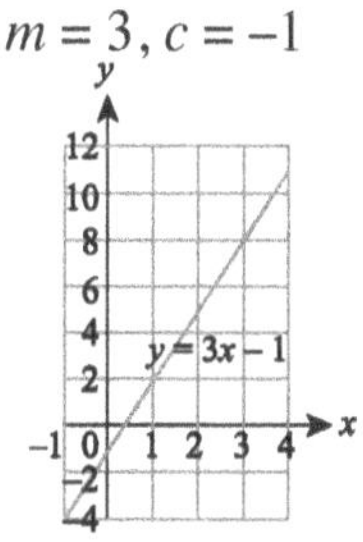

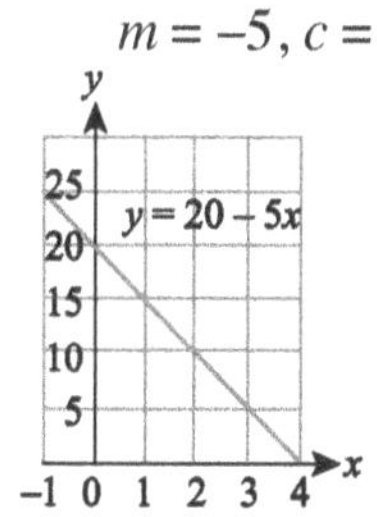

7 $y = 3x + c$, where c is any number.

8 $y = 7x - 4$

9 $y = 4x + 2$

10 **a** 4 km **b** Speed **c** 20 km/h

110 marks

Assessment 14

Question 1 – 5 marks

a

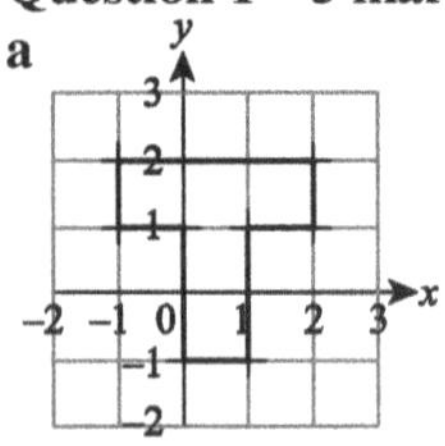

Correctly drawn and labelled axes [B1]

Minus 1 mark for each incorrectly plotted point [B3]

b T [B1]

Question 2 – 20 marks

a Lose 1 mark for each error in a row.

A -1, 1, 3, 5, 7, 9 [B2]

B 8, 7, 6, 5, 4, 3 [B2]

C $\frac{1}{2}, 1, \frac{3}{2}, 2, \frac{5}{2}, 3$ [B2]

D 10, 8, 6, 4, 2, 0 [B2]

b

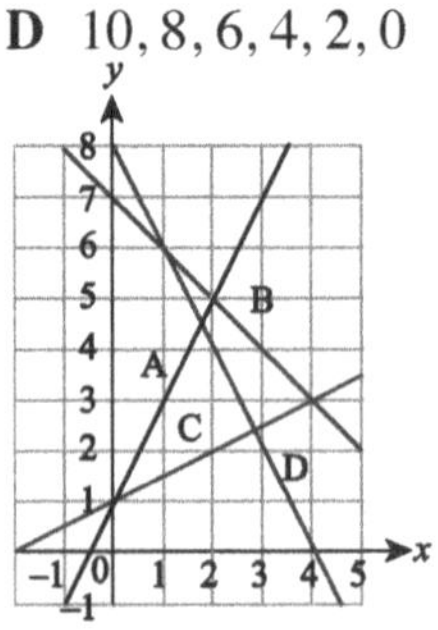

Correctly drawn and labelled axes. [B1]

Minus 1 mark for each incorrectly drawn point [B3]

Correctly drawn and labelled lines [B4]

c **i** (2, 5) [F1]

ii (0, 1) [F1]

iii (4, 3) [F1]

iv (1, 6) [F1]

Question 3 – 7 marks

a - c

d

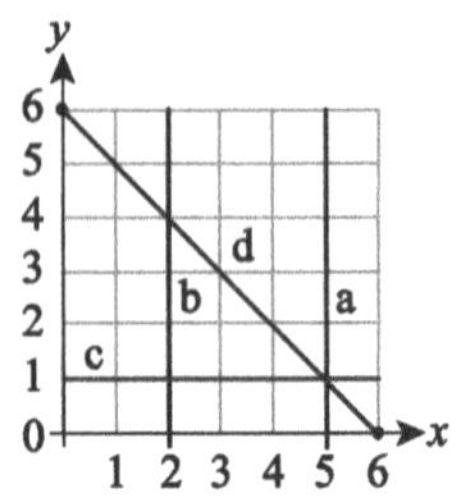

Correctly draw line [B3]

Two correctly plotted points [B1]

$y = 6 - x$ [F1]

e $\frac{1}{2} \times 3 \times 3 = 4.5$ [M1, A1]

Question 4 –3 marks

$2 \times -2 + 3 = -1$; $2 \times 0 + 3 = 3 \neq 2$; $2 \times 3 + 3 = 9$ [B2]

She is incorrect [F1]

Question 5 – 2 marks

a No [$3 \times 5 - 4 \times -4 = 31 \neq 30$] [B1]

b $y = x - 1$ [$1 - 7 = -6 \neq 6$; $7 - 1 = 6$] [B1]

Question 6 – 14 marks

a $m = 2, c = 27$ [B2]

b $m = 4, c = 9$ [B2]

c $m = 6, c = -11$ [B2]

d $m = -4, c = 12$ [B2]

e $y = \frac{4}{7}x - 2$ [M1]

$m = \frac{4}{7}, c = -2$ [F2]

f $y = -\frac{15}{14}x + \frac{35}{14}$ [M1]

$m = -\frac{15}{14}, c = \frac{35}{14} = 2\frac{1}{2}$ [F2]

Question 7 – 4 marks

a $y = x + 1$ [B1]

b $y = -x + 1$ [B1]

c $y = 2x + 6$ [B1]

d $y = -4x + 13$ [B1]

Question 8 – 6 marks

a **i** D to E

ii E to F

iii C to D

iv B to C

v A to B

Lose 1 mark for each pair of incorrect answers. [B4]

b The gradient is steepest along DE. [M1]

DE [A1]

Question 9 – 10 marks

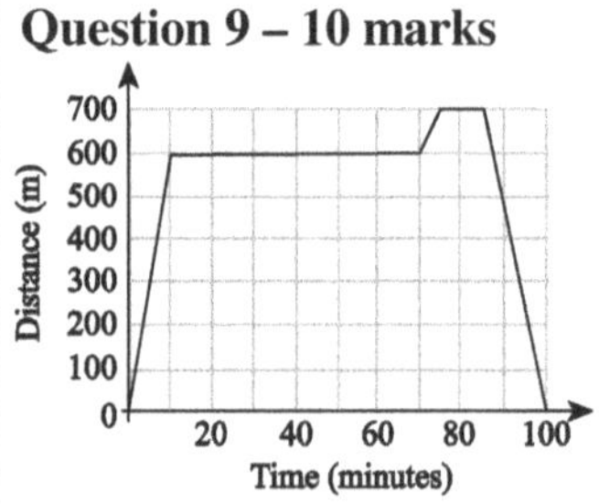

Correctly drawn and labelled axes. [B2]

Each section a straight line of correct slope and duration.

Allow follow through errors in start positions.

Lose 1 mark for each error. [B8]

Question 10 – 8 marks

a $(9 - 5) \div (5 - 1) = 1$ [M1, A1]

b $(-9 - 7) \div (8 - 2) = -8$ [M1, A1]

c $(6 - 5) \div (-4 - -3) = -1$ [M1, A1]

d $(-8 - 0) \div (5 - -11) = -\frac{1}{2}$ [M1, A1]

Question 11 – 6 marks

a $y = -5x - 16$ [B1]

b $y = 3x + c$ [B1]

$y = 3x - \frac{1}{2}$ [B1]

c $y = \frac{1}{3}x + c$ [B1]

$y = \frac{1}{3}x - 2$ [B1]

d $y = \frac{1}{4}x - \frac{3}{4}$ [B1]

Question 12 – 6 marks

a $y = 7x + 5$ [B2]

b $y = -3x - 7.25$ [B2]

c $y = -\frac{1}{3}x + 2\frac{2}{3}$ [B2]

Question 13 – 7 marks

a Gradient = change in y ÷ change in x [M1]

A 2 B $\frac{3}{2}$ C $-\frac{5}{3}$ D $-\frac{2}{3}$

Lose 1 mark for each error. [A3]

b **i** C

ii B

iii A

iv D

Lose 1 mark for each pair of incorrect answers. [B3]

Working in 3D

Learning outcomes	
A5	Understand and use standard mathematical formulae; rearrange formulae to change the subject.
G1	Use conventional terms and notations: vertices, edges, planes, draw diagrams from written description.
G12	Identify properties of the faces, surfaces, edges and vertices of: cubes, cuboids, prisms, cylinders, pyramids, cones and spheres.
G13	Construct and interpret plans and elevations of 3D shapes.
G14	Use standard units of measure and related concepts (length, area, volume/capacity).
G16	Know and apply formulae to calculate: area of triangles, parallelograms, trapezia; volume of cuboids and other right prisms (including cylinders).
G17	Know the formulae: circumference of a circle = $2\pi r = \pi d$, area of a circle = πr^2; calculate: perimeters of 2D shapes, including circles; areas of circles and composite shapes. Surface are and volume of spheres, pyramids, cones and composite solids.
R12	Compare volumes using ratio notation; make links to scale factors.

Prior knowledge

Check-in skill

- Calculate the area of rectangles and triangles.
- Understand the circle definitions of diameter, circumference and radius.

Online resources

MyMaths 1078, 1098, 1106, 1107, 1122, 1136, 1137, 1139, 1246

InvisiPen videos

Skills: 15Sa – I   Applications: 15Aa – g

Kerboodle assessment

Online Skills Test 15   Chapter Test 15

Development and links

Prisms have applications in optical equipment and in nature many crystals and molecules occur in regular 3D shapes. 3D shapes are widely used in the packaging industry to create novel designs, the volume of the container determining the amount of product that it can hold. Unlike liquids and solids, gases do not have a fixed volume and will take the shape and volume of any container.

Chapter investigation

Start by discussing the various shapes that are used for drinks containers, focus on simple shapes: cylindrical cans, cuboid cartons, tetrahedral cartons (Tetra Pak); pyramidal and spherical bottles. Introduce the correct language for describing the shapes and how they can be drawn on isometric paper and in projection [**15.1**]. Move on to consider how much material is needed to make a given shape and introduce nets.

Look at the formulae for the volumes of the basic shapes [**15.2**]. Ask students to find possible dimensions for cuboids with a volume of 1 litre (= 1000 cm^3). Start with integer values before encouraging the use of decimals. Extending this to cylinders will require students to solve the volume equation for h given r or r given h.

Next look at calculating the areas of the various shapes; start with cuboids before extending this to cylinders, etc. [**15.3**]. A formula for S in terms of r could be used in a spreadsheet.

For reference, the optimum cuboidal shape is a cube of side $\sqrt[3]{V}$ = 10 cm with S = 600 cm^2.

The optimum cylindrical shape has

$$r = \frac{h}{2} = \sqrt[3]{\frac{V}{2\pi}} = 5.4\text{ cm and } S = 3\sqrt[3]{2\pi V^2} = 554\text{ cm}^2$$

Mathematically the ideal shape is a sphere with

$$r = \sqrt[3]{\frac{3V}{4\pi}} = 6.2\text{ cm and } S = \sqrt[3]{36\pi V^2} = 484\text{ cm}^2$$

Students should compare their idealised solutions with the dimensions of actual containers. Ask what other considerations might need to be taken into account. For example, the need for tabs/overlaps for manufacturing, the ease of handling or how easily the containers can be packaged or stacked.

Finally ask students to make a net for a practical design.

15.1 3D shapes

Objectives

① **G12** Identify properties of the faces, surfaces, edges and vertices of cubes, cuboids, prisms, cylinders, pyramids, cones and spheres

②**G13** Construct and interpret plans and elevations of 3D shapes

Useful resources

Set of 12–15 mathematical solids, bag, multilink cubes, squared paper

Starter – Skills

Put a cuboid or cube in a bag. Invite a student to feel and describe the shape without naming it. The rest of the class must guess the name of the shape.

Highlight that the word side, as used when describing 2D shapes, in this case could be considered a face or edge and stress the need to differentiate between these. Highlight the key language to be used: face, edge and vertex.

Repeat with other 3D shapes, encouraging students to use the key terms.

Teaching notes – Skills

Show students a cuboid, a triangular prism, a cylinder and a cone and discuss which is the odd one out. Highlight key definitions:

- Prisms have a constant cross-section. Liken this to a loaf of bread – every 'slice' is the same shape and size. They are defined by the shape of their cross-section – cuboids, cubes and cylinders are specially named prisms.
- Pyramids taper to a point and are defined by their base shape – cones and tetrahedrons are specially named pyramids.

Ask students to visualise various 3D solids. Challenge them to give the number of vertices, edges and faces. Where possible, show each shape to check answers. Invite students to name 3D solids given various clues: I have 5 vertices, 5 faces, one face is square and the rest are isosceles triangles.

Using a cuboid as an example, discuss how to represent 3D objects on 2D paper. Introduce front and side elevation diagrams. Discuss how to represent other shapes.

Display the plan and elevations for an object made from 5 or 6 multilink cubes. Challenge students to work together to make the shape.

Plenary – Skills

Select some of the models used in the lesson and ask students to sketch possible nets for each. Compare different but viable nets for each solid selected.

Exercise commentary – Skills

Square grid paper and isometric paper (lined and dotted) will be needed for various questions. Card, scissors and adhesive are needed for question **10**. Interlocking cubes are useful for building certain shapes if students struggle to visualise them. Students should use the correct language: 2D shapes have sides; 3D shapes have edges and faces; a vertex (plural: vertices) is a corner of both a 2D and a 3D shape.

Question 1 Students can use the diagrams on page 308.

Question 2 Multiple answers are possible; as an extension ask students to think of a second answer for each part, then challenge them to refine the description so it fits only one of their answers.

Questions 3 to **5** Students can cut out these nets from square grid or isometric paper if needed. Commercial kits of interlocking 2D shapes can also be used to build 3D shapes.

Question 4 This can be extended by asking students to find all the possible nets – make sure they watch out for repetitions due to rotation.

Question 5 The net will need tabs to attach the faces; ask students 'On which edges of the net should tabs be placed?' (Alternate edges).

Question 6 Compare these with the shapes on page 308.

Questions 7 to **9** Physical objects which students can handle would be useful, such as interlocking cubes for questions **8** and **9**.

Question 10 Students could work in pairs to make shapes allocated by the teacher. Make sure they recall the rule for placing tabs on edges.

Simplification – Skills

Students should concentrate on writing down the correct names for the solids and counting things like vertices and edges. Avoid formally discussing Euler's relationship as this may confuse.

Extension – Skills

Students could be invited to complete a more formal investigation into Euler's formula that relates the number of faces, vertices and edges of 3D solids: $f + v - e = 2$.

Recap – Applications

1 What solid do you think each of the following descriptions show?

a I have six faces and they are all rectangles (cuboid)

b I have 3 faces and two of them are circles (cylinder)

c I have 7 faces and 7 vertices (hexagonal pyramid)

d I have 4 faces and they are all triangles (tetrahedron)

2 Draw the nets for each of these shapes:

a a cube with sides 5 cm

b a prism with triangular base 4 cm and height 6 cm

c a pentagonal pyramid with base length 5 cm and five isosceles triangles, 5 cm by 6 cm by 6 cm.

(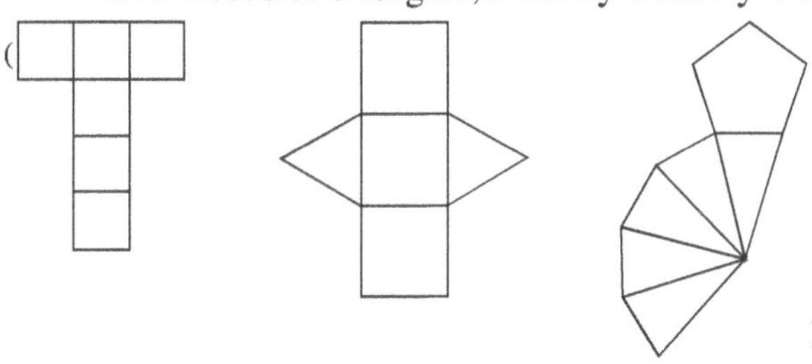)

3 Make an isometric drawing of each shape.

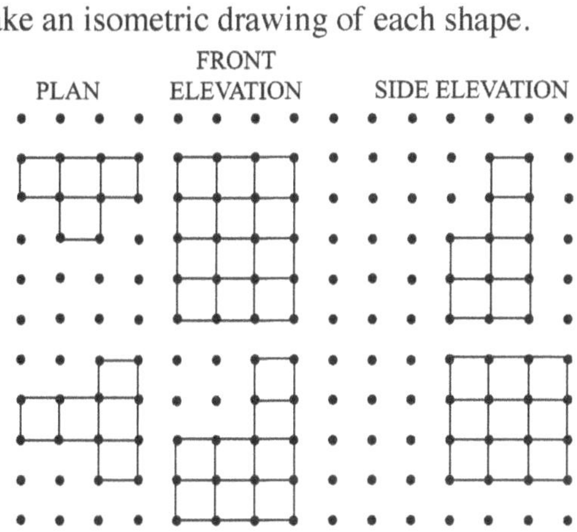

(**Answer**: 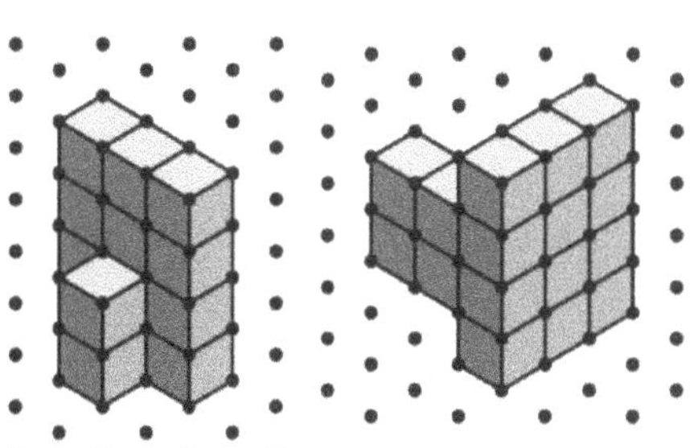)

Plenary – Applications

Students work in pairs. Give each student 5 multilink cubes. Sit students back to back. One student has to link the cubes together and then describe to his/her partner how the cubes are arranged so that he/she can replicate the arrangement. How successful were the students? What methods of communication worked best?

Exercise commentary – Applications

Students will need square grid paper, square centimetre paper or plain paper.

Question 1 You may wish to have this shape prepared so that students can see why it fails to be a net. Trimming two triangles will show them how to make it into a net.

Question 2 A common error here is to confuse the radius with the diameter.

Questions 3 Refer to the worked example (part **a**) on page 310.

Question 4 There are several possible nets. So, in part **c**, the minimum rectangle is for the particular net in part **b**.

Question 5 Interlocking cubes can be useful here.

Question 6 If students struggle to find a reason in part **b** they could cut out their nets and build the matchbox. If they have been precise they should find that the sleeve is very tight and may not fit.

Question 7 The length of the sloping edges can be found using a ruler or by Pythagoras' theorem.

Question 8 Students must consider the most appropriate net of all the possibilities by considering how they fit onto the rectangular card.

Simplification – Applications

When drawing plans and elevations, students may need squared paper and multilink cubes to build their models before attempting to draw the different aspects. Avoid questions with sloping faces.

Extension – Applications

Challenge students to build a more complicated model and get a partner to correctly draw the plan and elevations of it. Six or more cubes can make things interesting.

15.2 Volume of a prism

Objectives

①**G16** Know and apply formulae to calculate the volume of cuboids and other right prisms (including cylinders)

②**G14** Use standard units of measure for volume, capacity and mass

Useful resources

Sheets of A4 paper, rulers, mini whiteboards, set of prisms

Starter – Skills

Ask students, in pairs, to look at the sheets of A4 paper. Do students all agree that they have the same area? By joining either the widths or the lengths together two different cylinders can be formed. Ask students to try this and agree which of the two cylinders has the larger volume. Share the results, and ask how this might be tested.

From student responses, establish a reminder of how to find the volume of any prism. What shape is the cross-section? Estimating π as about 3, ask students to establish rough values for the volumes; hence which is larger. There is potential to examine methods of estimation here, if appropriate for the students' needs.

Teaching notes – Skills

Briefly discuss the meaning of volume measure.

Discuss the volume of a prism, and focus on three key points.

- Volume of a cuboid = length × width × height
- Volume of a prism = area of cross-section × length
- Volume of a cylinder = area of circle × height

Remind students that volume is measured in cubic units. Work through some examples with lengths in different units. For each prism, which shape is the constant cross-section?

Plenary – Skills

Challenge students to find as many different cuboids with volume 36 cm^3 as they can. Give thinking time before selecting various dimensions from the students. Are these all the possible ways? How do you know? What if half centimetres are allowed?

Exercise commentary – Skills

Use of calculators is at the discretion of the teacher.

Question 1 Students should pay attention to the units used.

Question 2 Students may confuse radius and diameter. They could work without a calculator to find answers in terms of π and then as decimals in the final step.

Question 3 Ask students to recall the formula for the area of a triangle.

Question 4 As an extension students could find the new volume if the radius and height are increased by 20%. (218 litres)

Question 5 Refer to the third worked example on page 312. Students could summarise this by writing each variable l, w, h, V in terms of the other three variables.

Questions 6 to **8** Students need to recall the area formulas (see page 144) and meet the density formula (see page 312). Refer to the second worked example on page 312.

Question 9 In part **b**, students must find the radius first and then the diameter.

Question 10 The method is similar to question **6**. Note that the length is in metres (not cm). A common error is to take the slant height rather than the vertical height when finding the area of the trapezium.

Simplification – Skills

Students should consolidate work on volumes of a cuboid before moving on to cylinders and triangular prisms. Complex shapes are best avoided or worked through as a group.

Extension – Skills

Students could be given further examples of compound solids and asked to find the volume.

Recap – Applications

1 Work out the volumes of these prisms:

- **a** A cylinder with base diameter 2 m and height 6 m. (18.8 m^3 (3 sf))
- **b** A right-angled triangular based prism with sides of length 8 cm, 15 cm and 17 cm and height 15 cm. (900 cm^3)

2 Hawking uses 1 cm cubes to make a 'tube'. These consist of a block, 14 cm by 15 cm by 16 cm with a hole 2 cm square through the middle.

- **a** How many cubes are in the 'hole'? (64)
- **b** Calculate the volume of the 'tube'. (3296)

Plenary – Applications

What possible formula do you think could be used to find the volume of an oblique cuboid? Encourage students to be imaginative and consider which measurements they will need to make.
(volume = area of base × perpendicular height.)

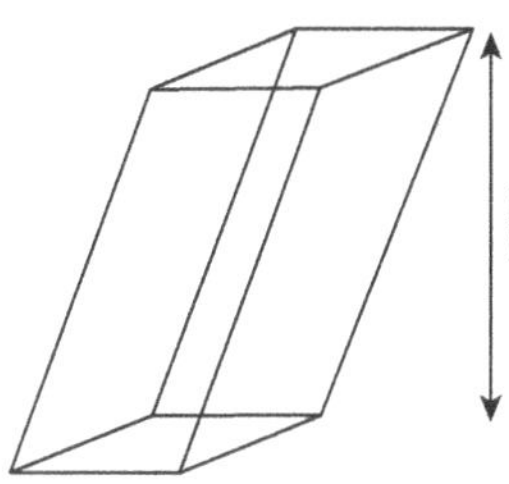

Exercise commentary – Applications

Several questions ask students to state their assumptions. These assumptions are best discussed as a whole class.

Questions 1 Part **a** involves a mix of units. Part **b** requires rearrangement of the formula.

Question 2 Remind students to use common sense in their answers – the answer here must be rounded *up* to the nearest whole number.

Question 3 Refer to the first worked example on page 314.

Question 4 Encourage students to think carefully about their assumptions. Would you fill a coffee cup to the top or would you leave space?

Question 5 Students might find the rate calculation tricky. Encourage them to try out a few values first: 2 litres takes 1 minute, 4 litres takes 2 minutes, … so the time (minutes) is always half the volume (litres).

Question 6 Consider the method of question **4** and ask if it is sensible to divide the two volumes to find the solution here.

Question 7 A common mistake here is to use the diameter instead of the radius.

Question 8 The $\frac{1}{4}$ kg is the weight of the *empty* box.
Ask students what their strategy will be before they start to calculate. They need the density formula (see page 314) and can refer to the first worked example (part **b**) on page 314.

Question 9 As an extension ask students how they would change the width so that the requirements are met. ($r \geq 3.08$)

Question 10 Students could draw a plan view to help with part **a**. In part **b**, students may need to be reminded how to convert a fraction to a percentage.

Simplification – Applications

Students should be given the opportunity to work on further examples of simple prisms and cylinders.

Extension – Applications

Challenge students to find the volume of a hexagonal prism. (The easiest way is as a compound of several equilateral triangular prisms.)

15.3 Volume and surface area

Objectives

① **G17** Know and apply formulae to calculate the surface area and volume of spheres, pyramids, cones and composite solids

Useful resources

OHT/whiteboard file of 3D shapes, a set of 3D shapes, measuring scales/water, calculators

Starter – Skills

Show a square-based pyramid and a cuboid of the same base area and height. Also show a cone and a cylinder of the same base area and height. Ask:

- How many square-based pyramids make the cuboid?
- How many cones make the cylinder?

Write estimates on the board and then weigh the shapes to demonstrate the solution. Alternatively, if the shapes are hollow containers, then show the amount of water displaced by the solids

Teaching notes – Skills

Recap the formula:

volume of a prism = area of cross-section × height

Use the mental starter to demonstrate that the volume of a pyramid is always $\frac{1}{3}$ of the prism it comes from.

Therefore,

volume of a pyramid = $\frac{1}{3}$ × base area × vertical height.

Relate to the formulae for volume of a cylinder and cone: $\pi r^2 h$ and $\frac{1}{3} r^2 h$.

Introduce the volume of a sphere of radius r:

volume of a sphere = $\frac{4}{3}\pi r^3$

Discuss what students understand by the term *surface area*. Emphasise that surface area is the total area of all of the faces (or the curved surface of a sphere). Display a cuboid. Discuss how students would calculate the surface area of a cuboid given a 2D drawing. Encourage them to consider the three views of the cuboid to establish the three faces to be calculated. Emphasise that the surface area of a cuboid is double the sum of the areas of the three views (plan, front and side).

Discuss the surface area of a pyramid, cylinder, cone and sphere.

Remind students that area is measured in square units: cm^2, m^2, etc.

Plenary – Skills

Show students a diagram of a triangular prism and discuss shape of faces, hidden faces and how to calculate its surface area.

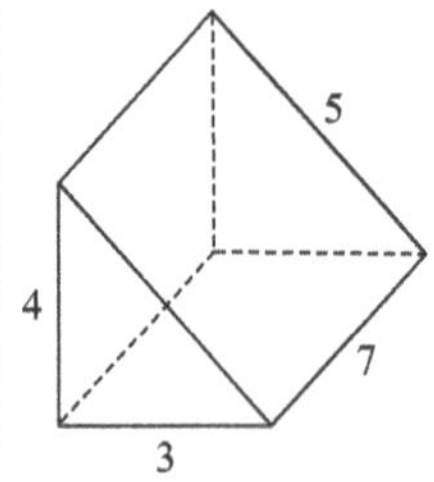

Exercise commentary – Skills

All questions involve choosing the appropriate formulae. Where appropriate, students should work in terms of π and give answers in terms of π before changing to decimals.

Question 1 The separation of parts **ii** and **iii** should help students to develop a strategy for finding the surface area of a cylinder, avoiding the common error of missing out the two discs.

Question 2 Students should pay careful attention to which units they are working in and which dimension they have been given, d or r. An example of the error created by using d in place of r may be useful here to show that the surface area will be multiplied by 4 and the volume will be multiplied by 8.

Question 3 Encourage students to use mental methods here if they can.

Questions 4 and **5** Students may confuse the vertical height (found in the volume formula) and the slant height (needed for finding surface area).

Question 6 Students must avoid confusing r and d on the diagrams and in the formulae. Encourage students to discuss the comparative benefits of giving answers in terms of π and as decimals (the former is exact but the latter is easier to visualise and to use in estimations).

Simplification – Skills

Students may benefit from access to a real cuboid to add relevance to the dimensions. Encourage drawing (and labelling) of the component rectangles.

Extension – Skills

Students could be asked to work out the surface area of further triangular prisms similar to the example given in the plenary.

Recap – Applications

1 a A waste paper basket is an **open** cuboid with a square base of side 10 in and a height of 15 in.

i Calculate its volume. ($1500\ in^3$)

ii Calculate the total surface area of the waste paper basket in in^2. ($800\ in^2$)

b A wooden door stop is in the shape of a prism with a right-angled triangular cross-section. The triangle has sides of 0.9, 4 and 4.1 in. The length of the prism is 4.5 in. Calculate:

i its total surface area ($76.5\ in^2$)

ii its volume. ($8.1\ in^3$)

2 An ice crystal has the shape of a parallelogram of cross-sectional area $14\ cm^2$. The length of the crystal is 16 cm.

a Calculate its volume. ($224\ cm^3$)

b The temperature rises and the crystal melts into a cylinder of base radius 2 cm. How high up the side of the cylinder does the water reach? (17.8 cm (3 sf))

3 An unsharpened wooden pencil is 20 cm long, with a hexagonal base of area $6.9\ mm^2$. Inside it is a graphite cylinder of radius 2 mm. Calculate:

a the overall volume of the pencil ($138\ cm^3$)

b the volume of the graphite ($2.51\ cm^3$ (3 sf))

c the volume of the wood. ($135.5\ cm^3$ (4 sf))

Plenary – Applications

Compare the formula for the surface area of a sphere with the formula for the area of a circle. What does this tell you about the surface of a sphere?
(It is identical to 4 circles with the same radius as the sphere.)

If you circumscribe a sphere inside a cube so that it just fits, what fraction of the cube does it take up?

Approximate π as 3 to show that it is about half. Then challenge students to decide if the fraction is actually larger or smaller than half. (a little larger $\frac{\pi}{6}$).

Discuss the real-life issue with packaging. You may wish to show, for example, a squash ball inside a cubical box.

Exercise commentary – Applications

Question 1 Encourage students to use sketches to help them break down these problems into component parts.

Question 2 Ask students if the answer would change if the top vertex was not central. How can they use the formula to show that it would not?

Question 3 Remind students to consider the order of operations here.

Question 4 Students may need to be told that the word similar is used here in a mathematical sense.

Question 5 The rearrangement in this question involves dividing by $\frac{4}{3}$. Some students may need to take this in two stages, first multiplying by 3 and then dividing by 4. Some students may need to use a function machine.

Questions 6 and **7** These exciting results would be good choices for paired presentation work.

Question 8 Encourage students to develop their own strategies.

Question 9 Students can repeat their method from question **8** part **b**.

Question 10 Students may not notice that the radius of the cone is the same as the radius of the hemisphere (given).

Question 11 Ask students what is needed which is not provided (the radius). Ask them for a strategy before they begin to calculate.

Question 12 Students may not remember that $1\ cm^3$ and 1 ml represent the same volume.

Question 13 Measurements taken from an accurate drawing of a net are quicker than doing any calculation. A reminder is likely to be needed when calculating the percentage. This question would benefit from a whole-class discussion.

Question 14 Students could agree a strategy in a whole-class discussion. They can draw on their work of finding a percentage from the previous question **13**.

Simplification – Applications

Students should practise the formal application of formulae in this section rather than trying too many problem solving type questions.

Extension – Applications

Ask students to work out the surface area and/or volume of a compound shape such as a triangular prism combined with a cuboid. Ask them to determine the minimum amount of information necessary to work these out.

15 Working in 3D

Key outcomes	Quick check
G1 Use conventional terms and notations: vertices, edges; draw diagrams from written description. G12 Identify properties of the faces, surfaces, edges and vertices of: cubes, cuboids, prisms, cylinders, pyramids, cones and spheres.	**1** **i** What are the names of these 3D shapes? **ii** How many faces, edges and vertices does each have? **a** 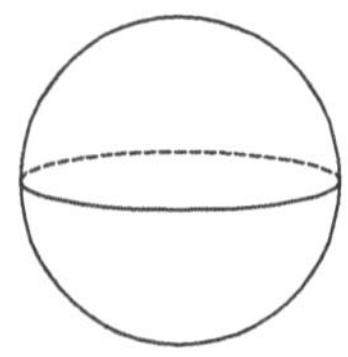 **b** 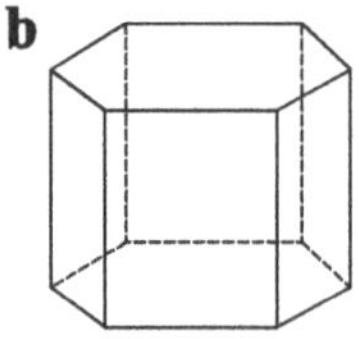 **c** 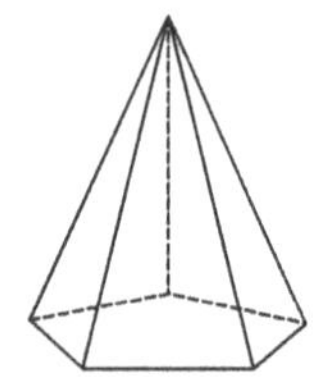 **(Sphere, 1, 0, 0)** **(Hexagon-based prism, 8, 18, 12)** **(Pentagon-based pyramid, 6, 10, 6)**
G13 <u>Construct</u> and interpret <u>plans and elevations of 3D shapes.</u>	**2** Draw the front elevation and plan view of question **1c**. 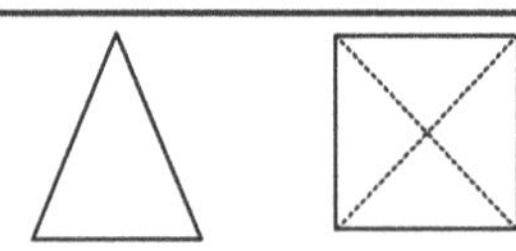 **3** Here are three elevations of a 3D solid made from cubes. 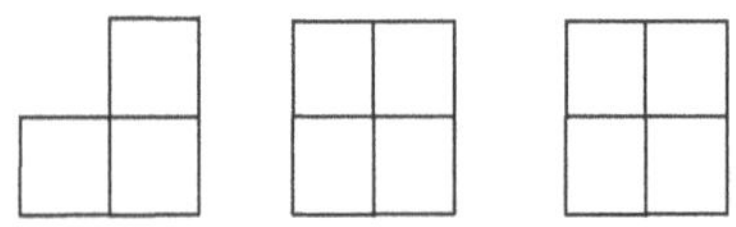 **Front** **Plan** **Side** 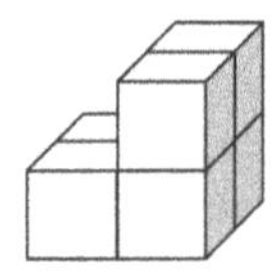 Draw the 3D solid these views come from.
A5 Understand and use standard mathematical formulae. R12 Compare volumes using scale factors. G14 Use standard units of measure and related concepts (volume/capacity). G16 Know and apply formulae to calculate: volume of cuboids and other right prisms (including cylinders). G17 <u>Surface area and volume of spheres, pyramids, cones and composite solids.</u>	**4** A cube has a side length of 9 m. Calculate the **a** volume ($729\ m^3$) **b** surface area of the cube. ($486\ m^2$) **5** Calculate the **a** volume ($48\ cm^3$) **b** total surface area ($108\ cm^2$) of the prism. 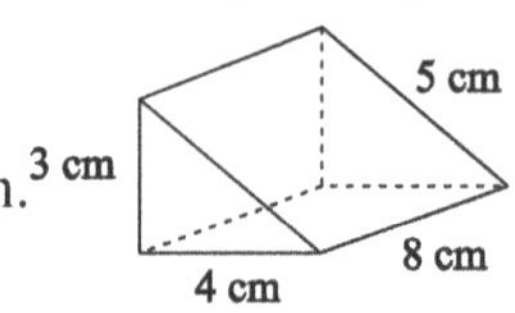 **6** Thevolume of a cone is given by the formula $V = \frac{1}{3}\pi r^2 h$. What is the volume of this cone? Give your answer to 3 sf. ($75.4\ cm^3$) 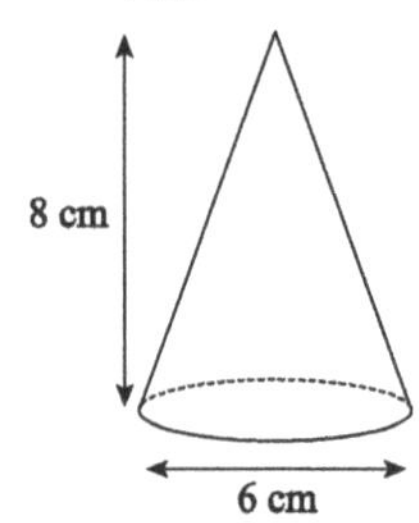

Misconceptions and challenges	Solutions
Students often forget to give the correct units for surface area and volume.	This is a good opportunity to give a context to squares and cubes as powers. Students can begin to link their learning in number and algebra to shape.
Students do not distinguish correctly between prisms and pyramids.	Ask questions such as 'What's the same and what's different about a pyramid and a prism with an odd number of vertices?' to help reinforce the differences.
Students find it difficult to visualise a 3D shape from 2D representations such as plans and elevations.	Spend some quiet reflective time at the end of a lesson on visualisation exercises. 'Imagine a cube, now imagine it stretches out into a cuboid. How many edges have changed length?' and so on.
When calculating the surface area of a triangular prism, students do not use the correct measurements for the rectangular faces.	This is especially common for a face hidden from view. Ask students to draw the net of the 3D shape and remind them that the edges that meet must have the same length.

Misconceptions and challenges	Solutions
Students do not notice if the radius or the diameter is given in the question, and do not adapt their approach accordingly.	This is a common problem. Students need to remember to make this their first check if they are calculating with circles.
Students often do not see how the circumference of the circular face of a cylinder relates to the surface area of the curved face.	To give students an understanding of how it relates, they can be given a challenge to make a net for a cylinder that fits exactly around a given circle. Allow students to try different strategies before guiding them towards the circumference.
For some students, learning the formulae may take precedence over learning how to apply them.	Combine application of formulae with memorisation and frequent revision. Students should not try to learn them all at once. Teach students revision techniques, such as the use of cards, spider diagrams and pictures to aid memorisation.
When working with composite shapes, students may include or exclude important calculations. For example, they might forget to add the rectangular face to the surface area of a cylinder cut in half or add the areas of two faces that are touching.	Have physical shapes for students to examine. Send students out to find composite shapes around the school site (where classroom buildings adjoin, for example), and have them calculate approximations of the surface area and volume. Look in particular at situations where there are hidden faces.

Review question commentary

Question 1(15.1) – Check that students understand the difference between edges and vertices.

Question 2 (15.1) – Spelling does not need to be completely accurate as long as it is intelligible. However, it is worth spending time practising the correct spellings.

Question 3 (15.1) – The front view may confuse some students, it should be a normal rectangle not curved in any way.

Question 4 (15.1) – Students could use isometric paper for this question.

Question 5 (15.2) – Units should be given with answers. For part **c** students will need to use the relationship mass = density × volume.

Question 6 (15.2, 15.3) – You may need to remind students that the curved area will be a rectangle with the circumference as its width. It is useful to demonstrate this.

Questions 7 and **8 (15.3)** – Students are not expected to memorise these formulae.

Review answers

1 **a** 6 faces, 12 edges, 8 vertices
b 5 faces, 8 edges, 5 vertices

2 **a** **i** Cone
ii 1 curved and 1 flat face, 1 curved edge, 1 vertex
b **i** Triangular prism
ii 5 faces, 9 edges, 6 vertices

3 **a** 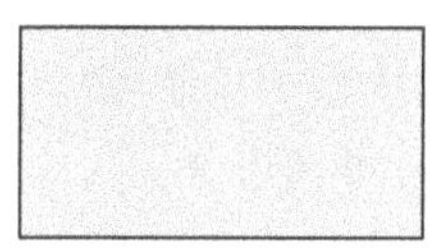 **b** 

4 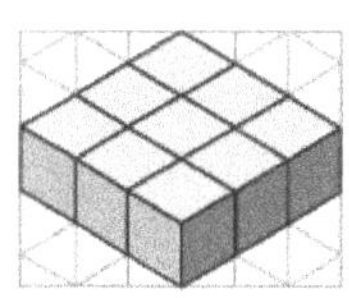

5 **a** 12 m^3 **b** 34 m^2 **c** 30 kg

6 **a** 7 600 cm^3 **b** 1 380 cm^2 **c** 2 140 cm^2

7 37.7 cm^2

8 2 140 cm^3

Assessment 15

Question 1 – 3 marks
a Correct
b Tetrahedron or triangular-based pyramid
c Sphere
d Correct
e Hexagonal-based prism
Minus 1 mark for each error. [B3]

Question 2 – 4 marks
a Triangle-based pyramid [B1]
b

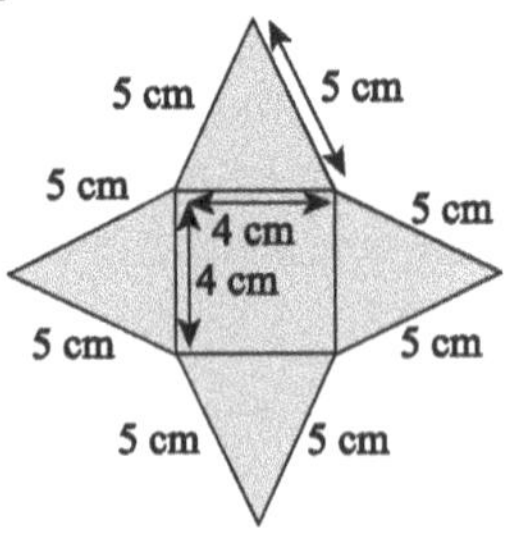

Correct shape [B1]
Square side length 4 cm ± 1 mm [B1]
Isosceles triangles equal sides 5 cm ± 1 mm [B1]

Question 3 – 2 marks
Must see a valid reason to obtain marks: 'width of base'.
a A [B1]
b B [B1]

Question 4 – 6 marks
0.372 2.75 5 8 9 6.25 [B6]

Question 5 – 8 marks
a 512 [B1]
b $512 \div 2^3$ or $(8 \div 2)^3 = 64$ [M1, A1]
c $512 \div 4^3$ or $(8 \div 4)^3 = 8$ [M1, A1]
d $512 \div 3^3 = 18$ r 26 [M1]
i 18 [A1]
ii 26 [A1]

Question 6 – 6 marks
$1 \times 1 \times 60, 1 \times 2 \times 30, 1 \times 3 \times 20, 1 \times 4 \times 15,$
$1 \times 5 \times 12, 1 \times 6 \times 10, 2 \times 2 \times 15, 2 \times 3 \times 10,$
$2 \times 5 \times 6, 3 \times 4 \times 5$
Minus 1 mark for each error or missing answer [B6]

Question 7 – 3 marks
Each answer must include an explanation
a Correct $1\text{ m} \times 1\text{ m} \times 1\text{m} = 1\text{ m}^3$ [B1]
b Incorrect $(100\text{ cm})^3 = 1\,000\,000\text{ cm}^3$ [B1]
c Incorrect $(1000\text{ mm})^3 = 1\,000\,000\,000\text{ mm}^3$ [B1]

Question 8 – 10 marks
a '$V = abc$' [M1]
$(24 \times 30 \times 36) \div (6 \times 5 \times 2)$
or $(24 \div 6) \times (30 \div 5) \times (36 \div 2)$ [A1]
$= 432$ [A1]
b Ratio of volumes = 432 : 1 [B1]
SA = '$2(ab + bc + ca)$' [M1]
Large SA = $2(24 \times 30 + 30 \times 36 + 36 \times 24)$
$= 5328$ [A1]
Small SA = $2(6 \times 5 + 5 \times 2 + 2 \times 6) = 104$ [A1]
Ratio = 5328 : 104 [M1]
= 51.2307… : 1 [F1]
No $[51.2 \neq 432]$ [F1]

Question 9 – 6 marks
a $\pi \times 14^2 \times 36$ [M1]
$= 22\,200\text{ cm}^3$ (3 sf)
b $[1 \times]\ \pi \times 14^2 + 2\pi \times 14 \times 36$ [M2]
$= 615.75\ldots + 3166.72\ldots$
$= 3780\text{ cm}^2$ (3 sf) [A1]
$= 0.378\text{ m}^3$ [B1]
OR convert at the start 14 cm = 0.14 m, etc.

Question 10 – 6 marks
a Recognising 3.9 is the hypotenuse [B1]
$2 \times \frac{1}{2} \times 1.5 \times 3.6 + (1.5 + 3.6 + 3.9) \times 5$ [M2]
$= 50.4\text{ in}^2$ [A1]
b $\frac{1}{2} \times 1.5 \times 3.6 \times 5 = 13.5\text{ in}^3$ [M1, A1]

Question 11 – 6 marks
$V = \frac{1}{3}\pi r^2 h$ [M1]
'Outer volume' = $\frac{1}{3} \times \pi \times 4^2 \times 12$ [M1]
$= 201.061\ldots\text{ cm}^3$ [A1]
Height of inner cone = $12 \times (3.9 \div 4) = 11.7$ [B1]
'Inner volume' = $\frac{1}{3} \times \pi \times 3.9^2 \times 11.7$
$= 186.356\ldots\text{ cm}^3$ [F1]
Difference = 14.7 cm^3 [F1]

Question 12 – 7 marks
a $\frac{1}{3} \times 55 \times 40 \times 65$ [M2]
$= 47666.7\text{ cm}^3$(1 dp) [A1]
b Radius = 5 cm [B1]
V sphere = $\frac{4}{3} \times \pi \times 5^3$ [M1]
$= 130.899\ldots$ [A1]
Number = $47\,666.7\ldots \div 130.899\ldots = 364$ [F1]

Question 13 – 5 marks
a $0.5^2 \times \pi \times 8 - 0.25^2 \times \pi \times 8$ [M2]
$= 4.71\text{ cm}^3$(3 sf) [A1]
b $4.71\ldots \times 2.6$ [M1]
= 12.3 g (3 sf) [F1]

Question 14 – 6 marks
a $13.5 \times 0.3 \times 0.3 = 1.215\text{ cm}^3$
$6 \times 0.45 \times 0.45 = 1.215\text{ cm}^3$ [B1]
Yes [B1]
b SA = '$2(ab + bc + ca)$' [M1]
$2(13.5 \times 0.3 + 0.3 \times 0.3 + 0.3 \times 13.5)$
$= 16.38\text{ cm}^2$ [A1]
$2(6 \times 0.45 + 0.45 \times 0.45 + 0.45 \times 6)$
$= 11.205\text{ cm}^2$ [A1]
Fat chips $[11.205\text{ cm}^2 < 16.38\text{ cm}^2]$ [F1]

Question 15 – 12 marks
a radius = 3 cm height = 4 cm [B1]
$\frac{1}{2} \times \frac{4}{3} \times \pi \times 3^3 + \frac{1}{3} \times \pi \times 3^2 \times 4$ [M3]
$= 94.2\text{ cm}^3$(3 sf) [A2]
b $\frac{1}{2} \times 4 \times \pi \times 3^2 + \pi \times 3 \times 5$ [M4]
$= 104\text{ cm}^2$ (3 sf) [A2]

Handling data 2

Learning outcomes	
A17	[Solve linear equations in one unknown algebraically (including those with the unknown on both sides of the equation);] find approximate solutions using a graph.
S2	Interpret and construct tables, charts and diagrams, including [frequency tables, bar charts, pie charts and pictograms for categorical data, vertical line charts for ungrouped discrete numerical data,] tables and line graphs for time series data and know their appropriate use.
S4	Interpret, analyse and compare the distributions of data sets from univariate empirical distributions through: - appropriate graphical representation involving discrete, continuous and grouped data - appropriate measures of central tendency (median, mean, [mode] and modal class) and spread (range, [including consideration of outliers]).
S5	Apply statistics to describe a population.
S6	Use and interpret scatter graphs of bivariate data; recognise correlation and know that it does not indicate causation; draw estimated lines of best fit; make predictions; interpolate and extrapolate apparent trends whilst knowing the dangers of so doing.

Prior knowledge

Check-in skill

- Interpret two-way tables.
- Interpret frequency tables.

Online resources

MyMaths 1193, 1196, 1198, 1201, 1202, 1213, 1250

InvisiPen videos

Skills: 16Sa – I   Applications: 16Aa – d

Kerboodle assessment

Online Skills Test 16   Chapter Test 16

Development and links

Analysing and interpreting data plays a crucial role in many different organisations including the government, the pharmaceutical industry, manufacturing industries, research facilities and the NHS. Official statistics in the UK are collected and published by the Office for National Statistics (ONS), the executive office of the UK Statistics Authority. The ONS collects information from a wide range of sources including the UK Census, public surveys and organisations such as the NHS.

Chapter investigation

Start by asking students to say what they think it means to say an animal, say a dog, lives 11 years. Explain that the question isn't trivial and that it will need to be investigated.

Start by collecting data on the lifetimes of dogs, either from student experience or from the internet, and discuss how this can be shown in a continuous data frequency diagram [**16.1**].

Move on to investigate how to calculate the various types of average and spread for the lifetime data [**16.2**]. Ensure that (some of) the data is grouped so that students have to work with finite class widths.

Settle on a definition of lifetime, either an average or a maximum, and collect data on size and lifetime for various animals. This data is naturally displayed in a scatter graph [**16.3**]. Discuss how to establish a correlation and the role of outliers.

Other correlations that could be investigated are animal mass and size (height), which will be positive, or animal heart rate and lifetime. It is often claimed that each animal has a fixed number of heartbeats, in which case lifetime and heart rate will be inversely proportional.

Finally consider how the size of an animal, for example the mass of a human, changes over its lifetime. This leads naturally to looking at time series and discussing spotting trends within the data [**16.4**].

16.1 Frequency diagrams

Objectives

① **S3** Construct and interpret diagrams for grouped discrete data and continuous data

Useful resources

Mini whiteboards, examples of different data sets

Starter – Skills

Recall the definitions of 'discrete' and 'continuous'. (**discrete**: you can count it; **continuous**: you can measure it) Give students a number of examples of different data. Ask them to decide whether each one is discrete or continuous. For example: height, number of siblings, time in minutes to get to school, percentage scores in an exam. Ask students to think of further examples of each type of data.

Teaching notes – Skills

① Recall previous work on collecting and tallying data, then representation on a bar chart.

For example: The Country Choir has members from six villages, as shown on the bar chart.

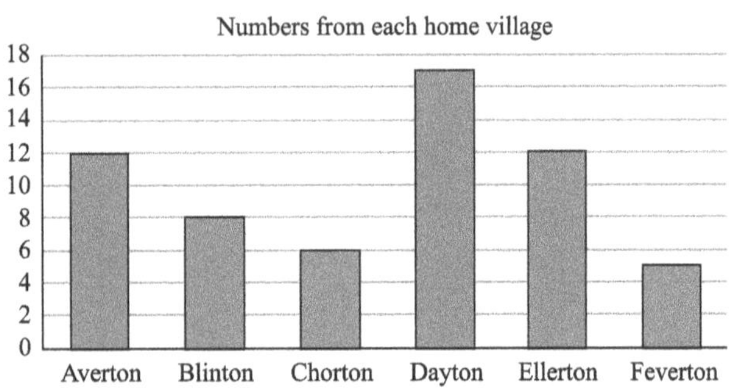

Discuss the type of data (discrete) and how it might be collected. Note the spaces between the bars.

The ages of the choir members are shown on the next frequency diagram.

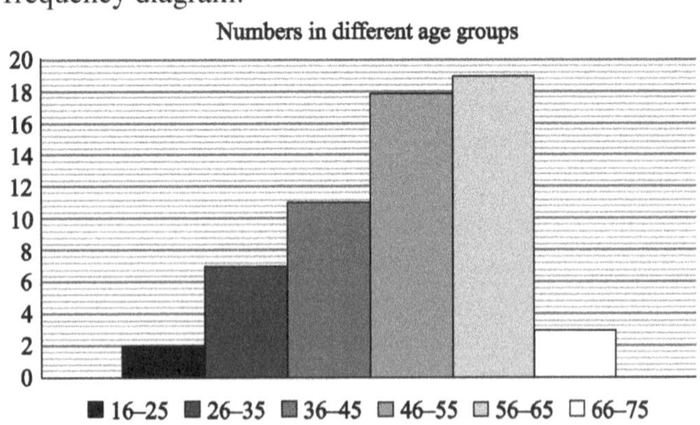

Discuss the type of data (continuous) and the way the histogram shows this. Discuss why the data has been grouped. How is this shown on the histogram?

Use the histogram to complete this frequency table:

Age	16–25	26–35	36–45	46–55	56–65	66–75
Frequency	2					

Explain that a histogram usually has a continuous scale on the horizontal axis, so remove the 16–25 etc. and put in 15, 25, 30, 35, ... 75.

Discuss the problem of the boundary values.

Introduce class intervals, e.g. $15 < a \leq 25$, $25 < a \leq 35$. Highlight that class intervals are equal in size and must not overlap.

Plenary – Skills

Sketch these types of diagram on the board: bar chart (grouped and ungrouped) and histogram.

Ask students to sort the diagrams into two groups: used for *discrete* or *continuous* data.

Ask questions: How do you recognise discrete/continuous data? What part of the graph are you looking at to help you decide? What are you looking for? Select the diagram likely to be the most controversial: a grouped bar chart. Who put this in the discrete group? Give praise. Why is this discrete? What part of the diagram gives you this information?

Exercise commentary – Skills

Question 1 This question is useful as a tallying exercise. Ask the students to consider how this table could be used. By introducing the idea of class mid-point, it may provide a good introduction to calculating the mean from a grouped frequency distribution.

Questions 2 and **3** Two very useful questions which give the students a chance to develop skills in drawing histograms. This is notoriously tricky because of the class boundaries and later, the introduction of frequency density. Be very careful about the inequalities – in question **2**, the upper value of each interval is **not** in the interval. In the worked example and in question **3**, the **lower** value of each interval in not in that interval. Generally speaking, the presentation of question **2** is to be preferred. The ideas in question **2d** and **e** are also important. Presenting raw data and calculating summary statistics is all about simplifying in order to make more manageable and more informative. However, if too much simplifying is done, detail is lost and the results become less useful again.

Question 4 This could be the right time to explain that the frequencies in this question can be compared directly because the class intervals are equal. This could usefully be used as an assessment.

Question 5 This question could be used to emphasise the difference between bar charts (question **5**) and histograms (question **4**). As discussed in the student book, very often this corresponds to the difference between discrete and continuous data. The students should be aware that much more care is needed for continuous data.

Simplification – Skills

Students may need time to look at and discuss the grouping notation and how to place 'borderline' values. Students could be given the axes and scales they need for the questions. Emphasise the need for a continuous scale on the x-axis for histograms.

Extension – Skills

In pairs, students could find some continuous data on the internet and decide on suitable intervals for grouping in a frequency table. Try choosing two different intervals, then proceed to draw the related histograms. Are they similar in shape?

Recap – Applications

1 The average monthly hours of sunshine in a holiday resort are shown. Draw a bar chart to illustrate this data.

Month	Jan	Feb	Mar	Apr	May	Jun	Jul	Aug	Sep	Oct	Nov	Dec
Hours	5	2	5	6	6	8	10	12	10	8	4	4

(
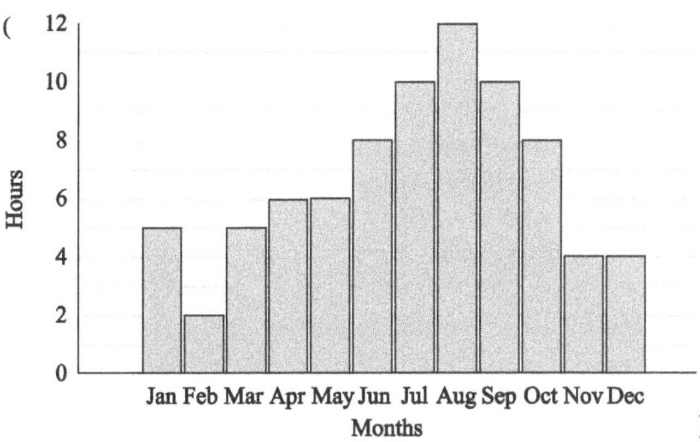

)

Plenary – Applications

Ask each student to write four key points they would make to help other students read diagrams or charts carefully. Share key points and explanations of why they are important.

Exercise commentary – Applications

Question 1 This is a fairly standard question on interpreting histograms and as such, may be useful for quiet, individual work or for an assessment. It may be worth introducing the concept of modal interval as opposed to modal value. Also, it is possible to use this question and the next to introduce ideas related to symmetry, or lack of it, in distributions. Both of these distributions are positive skew.

Question 2 Part **a** is tricky! If the inequalities are as in the table in question **4**, the largest value is 200 or more and the smallest is 39 or less; hence, a range of 161 is possible. If the inequalities are the other way, these values are 201 and 40, therefore also allowing 161. Part **c** allows a discussion on ideas of experimental probability given earlier in this course.

Question 3 A question which lends itself to group work. Let the students work out for themselves how the value of x should be found. This would be a very useful exercise because there are many contexts (probability distributions, bivariate tables, ...) where unknown values are found from known totals.

Question 4 Values to be found by subtraction – a nice twist to test the clear thinking of the students!

Simplification – Applications

Students will need plenty of practice at interpretation of histograms before they are ready to switch between frequency tables and histograms to work out missing information.

Extension – Applications

Students could be asked to look for charts and diagrams in newspapers or on the internet and describe what they show.

16.2 Averages and spread 2

Objectives

① **S4** Interpret and analyse distributions of data sets through the median, mean, mode and modal class

Useful resources

Mini whiteboards, calculators, grouped distance data, paired histogram and frequency polygon, grouped frequency data

Starter – Skills

Display some grouped data of, for example long jump distances. Ask questions such as: Give an example of any distance that is in this group. What might the smallest distance in this group have been? What might the biggest distance in this group have been? Could the statement, 'no one jumped more than 252 cm' be correct? What is the modal group (modal class)? Can you state the actual mode length? Explore responses and reasoning.

Teaching notes – Skills

① Discuss how you can find the **range**, **mode**, **median** and **mean** when you have all the data, either as raw data or in a frequency table. But if the data is represented in a **grouped frequency table** you can only find *estimates* for these values.

Remind students of the work done on frequency tables and **grouped data**. Recall techniques for finding the range and averages of **ungrouped data**.

Show this grouped frequency table:

Number of homeworks per week	Number of students (frequency)
0–6	2
7–9	3
10–20	10

Discuss and work through these questions.

i What is the **modal class** interval? (10–20)

ii Which **class interval contains the median** result? (15 results, the middle one is the 8th result which is in the 10–20 group.)

iii Estimate the mean number of homeworks.

Begin by asking students what they might *estimate* it to be. Explore their strategies and ask: Why can the result only ever be an estimate?

Emphasise that the 'estimated' part is our use of the **midpoint** of each class interval: Assume that 2 people have 3 homeworks, 3 people have 8, and 10 people have 15. Total: $2 \times 3 + 3 \times 8 + 10 \times 15 = 180$

Divide by the total **frequency** (or *number of results* – in this case, students) $180 \div 15 = 12$ homeworks per person.

iv What is the **range**? $(20 - 0 = 20$ [not $10 - 2$!])

Show a **histogram** to the class. Point out key features such as the scaling used because of the nature of the data and the labelling. Now show a **frequency polygon** of the same data. Again point out the key features. If possible, superimpose the polygon onto the histogram, illustrating how one is constructed from the other.

Plenary – Skills

Ask students to complete these instructions.

1 To find the modal class, look for the class interval with the ....

2 To find the class containing the median, find the total of the ...., halve this and count through the class intervals to find where the .... lies

3 To estimate the mean, use the ...... of each class interval. Multiply it by the ....., add up the results and ...... by the total of the ......

(**1** highest frequency **2** frequencies, middle item of data **3** midpoint, frequency, divide, frequencies)

Exercise commentary – Skills

Question 1 The table's class intervals raise interesting questions. Note that the intervals have gaps between them – the upper limit of the first interval is 64 kg, the lower limit of the second 65 kg. However, we have agreed that continuous variables like mass shouldn't have gaps between intervals. This problem is resolved by recognising that data relating to continuous variables becomes discrete data when it is rounded – in this case to the nearest whole number. These ideas should probably be raised only with the brightest students, or those who raise these issues. Remember, the median of 25 observations is the $\left(\frac{25+1}{2}\right) = 13$th value.

Question 2 To illustrate the problematic nature of all this work on continuous variables, note that, if all the speeds are given to the nearest integer, all 6 cars in the second interval could be travelling at 20.4 mph and therefore breaking the speed limit. However, common sense has to prevail here and the answer should therefore be 3. In cases where the mid-point is not obvious, tell the students that its value is the mean of the upper and lower limits.

Question 3 This question provides good practice for calculating these measures, particularly the mean, from grouped frequency distributions. The use of the word 'estimate' is important – as discussed before, when data is put in a more convenient form (in this case, in a table) information is lost. The problem can be extended by asking students to compare and contrast the groups of people to whom these tables relate.

Question 4 A good, straightforward assessment question – if, after all the practice, students can't do this question, they probably haven't been listening or doing their homework!

Simplification – Skills

Students should be given plenty of support. They could also be given partially completed tables (for example, with the midpoints already filled in) when calculating an estimate for the mean.

Extension – Skills

Students could be given a question that extends the use of an estimated mean to work backwards to find missing data.

Recap – Applications

1 A speed camera was placed in a 40 mph zone and the speeds of 200 vehicles were noted.

Speed (mph)	N°. of vehicles
$0 < V \le 20$	5
$20 < V \le 30$	42
$30 < V \le 40$	75
$40 < V \le 45$	34
$45 < V \le 50$	26
$50 < V \le 70$	18

a How many motorists broke the speed limit? (78)

b The police prosecute any motorists who are driving at more than 10% above the 40 mph limit. How many motorists are prosecuted? (44)

c Write down

i the modal class of the data ($30 < V \le 40$)

ii the class interval containing the median. ($30 < V \le 40$)

d Calculate an estimate for the mean driving speed. (37.425 mph)

Plenary – Applications

Give out grouped frequency data to small groups of students. Ask: How could you find a more accurate estimate of the median? Ask questions such as: Will the median be closer to the lower end or the upper end? How much closer? And so on.

Exercise commentary – Applications

Question 1 In this question, it would certainly be worthwhile producing two separate tables, one for each month, and adding columns for mid-point and '$x \times f$' for each one. Compare only measures of average but perhaps make the student aware that further comparisons are possible and will be made in later questions.

Question 2 As discussed before, it begs the question, which is the best measure of average for this data? Well, journey time to work is the sort of variable which may well be normally distributed and, if this is the case, then the mean is probably the most useful. These ideas may be of interest to the higher attaining students.

Question 3 An interesting question and one which could easily lead to (qualitative) ideas about hypothesis testing. The question which students will be able to cope with is, 'How far from the Granny Smith mean and range do the table values have to be before we can say that the apples are almost certainly not Granny Smiths?'

Question 4 Lots of interesting ideas here. First of all students should be aware that a sample of size 1000 is large, a sample of size 10 may not say much about the daily output. Secondly, maybe set some limits on what is an acceptable sample mean before working on the sample values; perhaps 25 ± 5% of 25. Anyway, is it ok for the sample mean to be significantly over 25 g? It's never too early to get these ideas over to students.

Question 5 This raises many of the points given in the commentaries for the last two questions. Perhaps stick to just mean and range in order to make the comparisons.

Simplification – Applications

Remind students that statistical comparisons usually depend on consistency, for which we use the range, and an average value. They could be told which average to use for their comparison.

Extension – Applications

Once students have mastered finding averages and ranges, they can try open-ended questions which test their ability to think what averages and ranges do and do not tell us. For example:

10 girls and 10 boys took the same test, which was marked out of 20. The mean of the girls' scores was 14 and their range was 11. The mean of the boys' scores was 12 and their range was 5.

Write down two sets of marks which would give these results and collect up the suggestions. Did the girls or the boys produce the better performance?

16.3 Scatter graphs and correlation

Objectives

① Construct scatter graphs and recognise correlation and know that it does not indicate causation

② Draw estimated lines of best fit and make predictions

Useful resources

Mini whiteboards, pre-drawn axes, various display scatter graphs

Starter – Skills

Display three sketch graphs showing axes and plotted points for the three situations of correlation (positive, negative, none), labelled A, B and C. Recall that graphs like this can be used to show how one data set relates to another. Ask students to select which of the graphs indicate(s) some sort of relationship between the two data sets (positive/negative correlation), such that an increase/decrease in one set of values allows you to make predictions about what will happen to the other set of values. In pairs, ask students to think of real situations which might have a positive or negative correlation. Share ideas and draw out the key features underlying the concept of correlation.

Repeat this for no correlation: ask for pairs of unrelated values. Again, share ideas and discuss the underlying concepts.

Teaching notes – Skills

① Students work in pairs to provide some explanation and conclusions from scatter graphs. Emphasise that they will need to study the diagrams carefully to see what they are about. They will need to see if any relationships or **correlations** are likely, and why. Ensure that students understand the terms: **positive correlation**, **negative correlation** and **no correlation**. Prompt pairs with questions such as: What is the graph about? What are the two axes measuring? How large is the survey illustrated? Are any connections between the data likely? If so, in which direction (positive/negative)? Could the diagram be used for any predictions? How reliable do you think the data is? Would you agree with it?

Allow time for each pair to examine at least two diagrams. Ask pairs to share findings with each other first and compare notes. Then share and discuss more widely students' responses and the reasoning behind them.

Move on to discussing the concept of **causation** *vs.* correlation. Show students some scatter graphs where variables show correlation without being causally related, for example: ice-cream sales and incidences of jelly fish stings. Challenge students to explain how the data is correlated but with no *causal* connection. (Hot weather is the common or connecting variable.) Offer other examples and ask them to think of examples of their own.

② Display one set of correlated data plotted as a scatter graph. Discuss the drawing of a **line of best fit** with the whole group. Stress the need to look at the line as a best fit overall, by eye – with roughly but not necessarily *exactly* the same number of points on each side of it. Ask students to suggest how they would position the line and add these to the display. Discuss how a line of best fit might help with some predictions. Emphasise the difference between **interpolation** and **extrapolation**.

Plenary – Skills

Ask students for examples of positive correlation. E.g. 'If the temperature goes up the sales of ice-cream also go up'. How about the sales of sun protection creams? garden chairs? heating boilers? coats? Try other scenarios.

Exercise commentary – Skills

Question 1 It's always interesting to try to think of other variables which have a certain type of correlation – and the most difficult one is negative correlation. Queuing times and the number of cashiers for a given number of people in a store is one option.

Question 2 A good question for group work. After the students have done this question and fully understood the implications of a cross in a certain position on the graph, perhaps they could discuss what the correlation would actually look like in real life. They could even make up more imaginative scenarios – for example, exam mark and hours of revision *for a student who doesn't know how to revise very well!*

Question 4 A practical question to reinforce the ideas talked about so far. This might be a good time to raise the question of causality in correlation. As it says in the text, correlation doesn't necessarily mean causation. However, there could be a causal connection and in this case we can assume that there is. For example, if the watering was automatic, high temperatures *cause* dry soil which *causes* increased water flow. The great examples of non-causation are stork population and human population over a 20 year period and number of radio licences sold (back in the day) with admission to psychiatric hospitals. Storks don't bring babies and radios don't make you mad!

Question 5 Point out that discrete variables don't necessarily take integer values. This could be a good question for an assessment or for quiet, individual work since it covers most of the theory and is fairly straightforward.

Simplification – Skills

Students could be given pre-drawn axes for scatter diagram questions.

Extension – Skills

Students could make predictions based on lines of best fit.

Recap – Applications

1 This table shows the results of a group of students who had done a test in Science and Music.

Sc	20	21	26	33	38	42	44	57	59	62
Mu	88	76	22	77	65	66	59	58	49	51
Sc	66	70	76	81	83	87	90	91	91	94
Mu	47	49	42	42	40	36	34	34	89	28

a Plot a scatter diagram of this data.

b Draw the line of best fit.

c Comment on the type of correlation. (Strong negative)

d Comment on the two outliers.

e Use your line to estimate the:

i Science mark corresponding to a Music mark 60 (50)

ii Music mark corresponding to a Science mark 60. (53)

Plenary – Applications

Each student draws on their whiteboard a scatter graph showing the exam marks of 10 students in a pair of subjects of their choice. The scatter graph can show positive, negative or no correlation and, if there is correlation, it should include an outlier. Pick three students to show their graph and to talk about what conclusions might be drawn from it.

Exercise commentary – Applications

Question 1 In describing a relationship between two variables, it is good practice to comment on the correlation (positive, negative, zero, strong, weak) and also answer in terms of the specific variables (a good mark in paper 1 tends to go with...). Parts **c** and **d** relate to interpolation and extrapolation, respectively.

Question 2 This question is suitable for this level of work. However, it's probably worth remembering that in most cases, these lines of best fit are either used for predicting y-values from given x-values **or** x from y-values, not both. For details, consider the OUP A level statistics texts.

Question 3 This is the first question where the student has to draw the line of best fit. Two points to note: ensure that there are roughly the same number of points above and below the proposed line (which by itself is absolutely no guarantee that the line is any good) and that the line follows the general trend of the dots. For extension work, it is possible to add a third criterion; that is, that the line of best fit should pass through the point with coordinates (the mean of the xs, the mean of the ys). Part **f** is, of course, the difference between interpolation and extrapolation.

Question 4 Again, a good, straightforward question covering much of the theory and therefore appropriate for both assessment and quiet, individual work.

Simplification – Applications

Some students may find it hard to plot points accurately for a scatter diagram. They'll need plenty of practice. Start with simple scales and work on achieving a satisfactory line of best fit. Many students will feel there is one perfect line of best fit which they must achieve to gain marks. Show examples where different lines would be valid.

Extension – Applications

Students could be asked to interpret and describe the correlations in terms of real-life situations.

16.4 Time series

Objectives

① Interpret and construct tables and line graphs for time series data and know their appropriate use

Useful resources

Mini whiteboards, 2 mm graph paper, computers, rainfall graphs for starter activity, time series data in table form

Starter – Skills

Display two time-line graphs on rainfall and say that they are showing 'weather' at two different places (in the world/England). Ask students to use whiteboards to answer questions about the graphs: What do the letters on the horizontal axis refer to? When was the highest/lowest rainfall? What was the highest/lowest? Which of the two places is the drier/warmer? Where might they be? Explore some of the answers offered. Introduce the keyword, 'trend', into the discussion about the graphs.

Teaching notes – Skills

① Recap the use of statistical diagrams – to display a picture of data to highlight patterns and trends. Recall:

- **Pictograms** use quantities of pictorial symbols to show sizes of categories, allowing us to compare categories with each other.
- **Bar charts** and **histograms** use bars to show sizes of categories, allowing us to compare categories with each other.
- **Pie charts** use parts of a circle to show sizes of categories, allowing us to see each category as a fraction of a whole.

Recap **discrete and continuous data**. Highlight that the latter is often a measurement: height, weight or temperature.

Discuss the **line graphs** from the student book. Emphasise that a line graph shows how something changes over time and discuss the axes labels. Highlight that time is always recorded on the horizontal axes, and that the axes do *not* have to start from zero. Recall the **zigzag symbol** used to 'squash' axes from zero to the first required reading.

Look at the first example in the student book. Discuss how to read the graph and the trends it shows, focusing on increasing and decreasing temperatures. Emphasise that steeper lines indicate a sharper increase or decrease in temperature. Highlight that the intermediate points are not actual readings, but could be used to estimate temperatures.

Tell students that they are going to use data already saved on the computers, and that their task is to explore the graphs possible with the chart wizard, selecting the most appropriate ones for the data. Remind them that their decision must reflect the need for charts to be clear and give helpful and convincing information about the data. Allow students to compare a variety of charts and graphs. Offer support if required to ensure correct labelling of axes and scales. Groups of students working with similar sets of data should then compare results, and decide as a group which diagram(s) offer the best illustration of the data, and why.

Plenary – Skills

Display a set of time series data in table form. Ask students in pairs to decide how they would display this data as a graph. Explore the stages of construction of the graphs offered. Ask students why certain features are so important. Ask them to give three main points they would say were crucial when drawing graphs.

Exercise commentary – Skills

Question 1 As an extension, students should look for patterns in the data and describe what is happening over the course of the holiday.

Question 2 The three points to consider when choosing a scale: the smallest value (therefore where to start the scale, at zero or not), the largest value and therefore where to end the scale, and from these, the intervals. In this case, start at zero and go up in 10s.

Question 3 It's interesting to consider the relationship between these two variables. In pure mathematics, it is usual to talk about independent and dependent variables. Here, more helpful terms are explanatory and response variables. Of these two variables, it is weight which is 'explained' by age, so age is the explanatory variable and weight the response variable. As such, age should go on the x-axis. This is called 'regression on a fixed variable' since only weight is a random variable.

Questions 4 and **5** If the students start the vertical axis at a value other than zero, it is probably worth mentioning the errors in interpretation that can follow; for example, changes appearing more dramatic than they actually are.

Simplification – Skills

Students could be given pre-drawn axes to allow them to focus on the content of the graphs.

Extension – Skills

Students could be asked to plot two time-series graphs on the same axes and make comparisons. For example, the average monthly temperature in Britain could be compared to that in South Africa.

Recap – Applications

1 The temperature from 0600 to 1800 at hourly intervals in Vic's garden are shown:

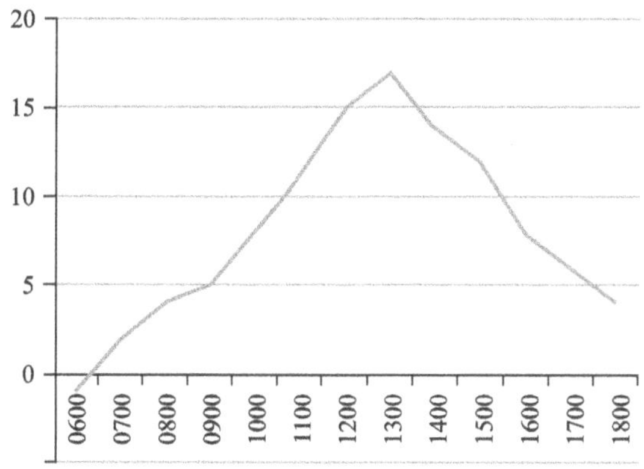

a What was the temperature at 1000? (8 °C)

b What was the temperature at 1300? (17 °C)

c What was the temperature at 1430? (13 °C)

d Why is your answer to **c** only an approximation?

(Because the graph just shows a trend and there are no actual figures recorded at this time.)

e What are the minimum and maximum temperatures recorded? (-1 °C and 17 °C)

f For how long was the temperature on or above 8 °C? (8 hours)

Plenary – Applications

Emphasise that a line graph may sometimes be misleading, as the lines between the data points do not always have meaning. Ask students for examples where this might be the case, in particular where the variable plotted on the vertical axis is discrete (usually frequency).

Exercise commentary – Applications

Questions 1 to **4** Four questions which are extremely useful in developing graph drawing skills. Encourage the use of pencils and rulers and remember that the most difficult part for many students is likely to be plotting the axes and making decisions on scale.

Question 2 Treat each time period as a single point not a set of three separate months. For example, think of Jan–March as Quarter 1. As it says in the text, the three types of pattern likely to occur are short term trends, long term trends and seasonal variation.

Question 3 Discuss the second peak in this data in December – can the students give possible reasons for this?

Question 4 This provides a good opportunity for interpreting data – is the library becoming more popular amongst teenagers or is the data insufficient to show this? Would the students answers change if they discounted 2005?

Question 5 The ranges are about the same so it's a question of comparing measures of average. Ask the students which measure can be estimated from the graphs. It's not really possible to get much of an idea about the mean directly. The mode is easily obtained, and on this measure the answer is Sell-a-lot. Medians divide areas into two equal parts and on this measure the answer is also Sell-a-lot. A good question for talking about the different types of average.

Simplification – Applications

Pre-drawn axes would be very helpful for applications and the variety of time labels on the horizontal axis needs some discussion.

Extension – Applications

Students could find data on the internet relating to e.g. traffic crossing a bridge each day for a month, daily footfall at airports, number of swimmers at the local pool etc. Plotting this over different time intervals could reveal unexpected trends.

16 Handling data 2

Key outcomes	
A17	Find approximate solutions using a graph.
S2	Interpret and construct tables, charts and diagrams, including frequency tables, bar charts, tables and line graphs for time series data and know their appropriate use.
S4	Interpret, analyse and compare the distributions of data sets from univariate empirical distributions through: - appropriate graphical representation involving discrete, continuous and grouped data - appropriate measures of central tendency (median, mean, mode and modal class) and spread (range, including consideration of outliers).
S5	Apply statistics to describe a population.
S6	Use and interpret scatter graphs of bivariate data; recognise correlation and know that it does not indicate causation; draw estimated lines of best fit; make predictions; interpolate and extrapolate apparent trends whilst knowing the dangers of so doing.

Quick check

1 The frequency table shows the number of miles Amber drives before having to put petrol in her car.

Miles	Frequency
$200 \le m < 220$	5
$220 \le m < 230$	8
$230 \le m < 240$	9
$240 \le m < 250$	2
$250 \le m < 260$	1

a In which group would the value 240 miles be placed? ($240 \le m < 250$)

b What is the modal class? ($230 \le m < 240$)

c In which class does the median lie? ($220 \le m < 230$)

d Estimate the mean number of miles before filling up. (228.4 miles)

Darcy travels a mean of 250 miles before having to fill up with petrol. Her range is 70 miles.

e Compare their fuel consumption. (Mean: Amber < Darcy, Range: Amber 60 < Darcy)

2 The table shows Ian's earnings.

Year	Earnings (£)
2009	29 000
2010	21 000
2011	22 000
2012	28 000
2013	30 000
2014	35 000

a Draw a line graph for this time series data.

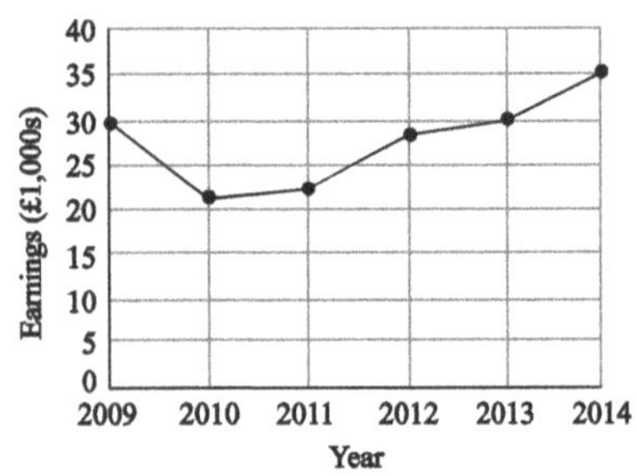

b Describe what happened between 2009 and 2014. (Earnings decrease sharply then steadily increased.)

Student	A	B	C	D	E	F	G	H	I	J
Test A	14	13	9	6	5	12	10	7	8	6

3 The table shows results of two different tests.

a Represent this data on a scatter diagram.

b What type of correlation does the diagram show? (Negative)

c Draw a line of best fit on the graph.

d Estimate the result in Test B of a student who scored 11 on Test A. (5)

e Explain why it may not be sensible to use this graph to estimate the scores of students who got below 4 in either test. (Unreliable estimate because there is no data in this range.)

Misconceptions and challenges	Solutions
Grouped continuous data can appear to be discrete to some students, and this makes deciding which class to put data in confusing.	Using data collection from the class can help students to understand the difference as it puts data collection into context.
When grouping data, students are often confused about when to use ≤ or <.	Play games such as 'I am thinking of a number between 37 and 73' to prompt students to ask if those boundaries are included or excluded. Model these different options using inequality symbols.
Estimating the mean of grouped data, students do not multiply the frequency by the mid-point before dividing, but rather find the mean of the frequencies.	You can demonstrate this by showing very simple data sets, and pointing out inappropriate results.
When drawing the line of best fit, students join the lowest and highest values plotted on each axis.	Ensure that students know that the line of best fit does not have to pass through these values or the origin.
When drawing estimated lines of best fit, students can err on the side of too much caution, and can allow outliers greater weight than necessary.	Encourage students to apply visual common sense to the line of best fit, circling outliers before drawing the line can help students to exclude these from consideration.
Students find it difficult to understand when causation is not implied by correlation, or how to describe a correlation.	Students should be able to interpret scatter graphs using the language of correlation, and need to qualify correlations with 'weak' and 'strong' rather than 'bad' or 'good'.
When finding the median class, students look for the centre of the range.	Visual images could help here. Get students to draw the classes as bars and stack them, in order, one on top of the other. Then ask them to find the middle. Once students are comfortable with this idea ask them to find the total frequency and then count through until they reach the middle.
Students' explanations are often vague or repetitive, missing out on marks but taking a long time to complete.	Make sure that students know to compare at least one measure of central tendency (mean, median, mode) and a measure of spread (range).

Review question commentary

Question 1 (16.1) – Students should be careful to read the inequality signs correctly. The value 10 should go in $10 \le l < 12$ not $8 \le l < 10$.

Question 2 (16.2) – For the mean, midpoints must be used (9, 11, 13, 15). Incorrectly dividing by number of groups instead of total frequency will give 46 (which students should be directed to notice is not a sensible answer).

Question 3 (16.3) – Students should appreciate that correlation does not necessarily imply causation.

Question 4 (16.3) – Ensure axes are labelled and scales are even.

Question 5 (16.4) – Ensure axes are labelled and scales are even. Students should join points using straight lines.

Review answers

1 4, 5, 6, 1

2 **a** $12 \le l < 14$ **b** $10 \le l < 12$ **c** 11.5 cm

3 **a** Negative

b No, the correlation may be a coincidence or y may have the effect on x.

4 **a, c**

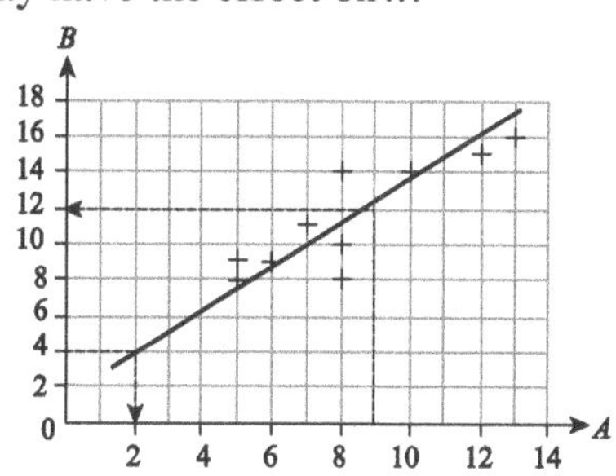

b Positive

d 12–13

e **i** 2–3

ii Unreliable estimate because there is no data in this range.

5

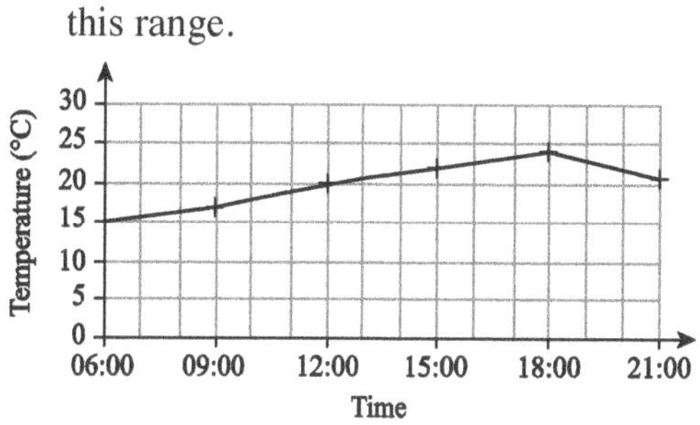

Assessment 16

Question 1 – 5 marks

a

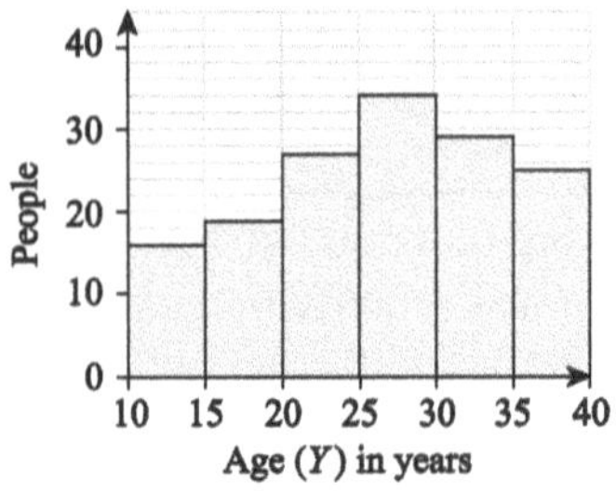

Correctly drawn and labelled axes. [B1]
No gaps. [B1]
Correct height bars.
Lose 1 mark for each error. [B2]

b 35 [16 + 19] [B1]

Question 2 – 2 marks

Accept sensible answers.
Split 60 – 80 at the speed limit: 60 – 70 and 70 – 80
Since 0 – 10 is empty, change 0 – 20 to 10 – 20 [B2]

Question 3 – 6 marks

a 20 – 30 [B1]
b It is the highest bar. [B1]
c 24 guest = 12 'cells' [B1]
38 'cells' in total [M1]
$38 \times 2 = 76$ [A1]
d 20 – 30 [B1]

Question 4 – 10 marks

a

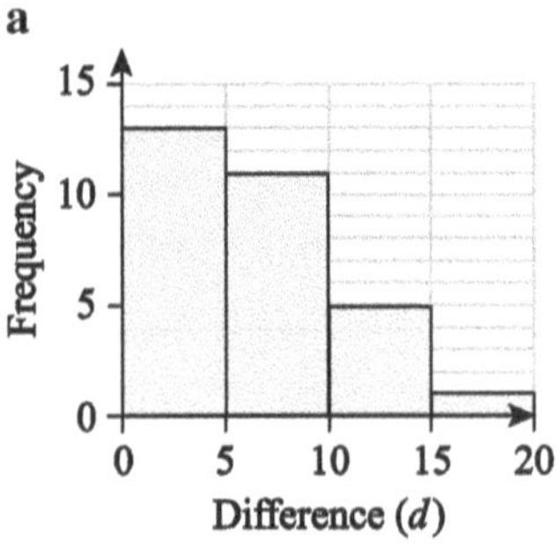

Correctly drawn and labelled axes. [B1]
No gaps. [B1]
Correct height bars.
Lose 1 mark for each error. [B2]

b Total frequency = 30 [B1]
Est total diff = $13 \times 2.5 + 11 \times 7.5 + 5 \times 12.5 + 1 \times 17.5$ [M1]
= 195 [A1]
Est mean = $195 \div 30$ [M1]
= 6.5 [F1]
c *d* is always recorded as positive.
d = 5 for both 395 and 405 tea bags [B1]

Question 5 – 11 marks

a

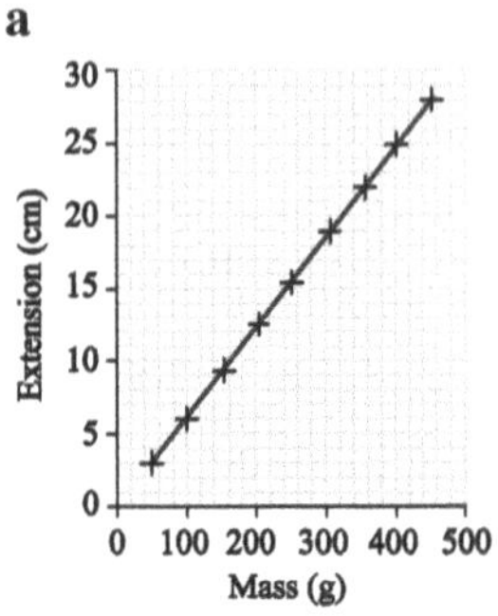

Correctly drawn and labelled axes. [B1]
Correctly plotted points.
Lose 1 mark for each error. [B3]

b Straight line drawn through points [B2]
Strong positive [B1]
c **i** 20 ± 0.5 cm [B1]
ii 230 ± 10 g [B1]
d This is outside the data values collected [B1]
No [B1]

Question 6 – 10 marks

a

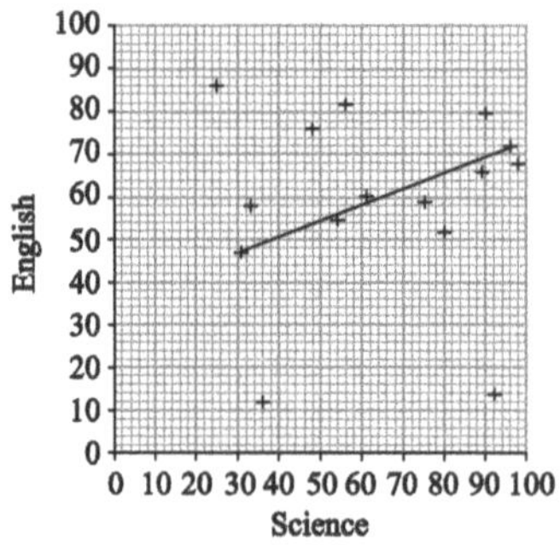

Correctly drawn and labelled axes. [B1]
Correctly plotted points.
Lose 1 mark for each error. [B3]

b Straight line drawn through points [B2]
Weak positive [B1]
c (93 Sc, 15 E) and (25 Sc, 86 E) [B1]
d **i** 41 ± 1 [B1]
ii 56 ± 1 [B1]

Question 7 – 6 marks

a 22 ± 1 [B1]
b 18 ± 1 [B1]
c 23 ± 1 [B1]
d The graph just shows a trend and there are no actual figures. [B1]
e 41 ± 1 [B1]
f Any valid reason.
It coincides with morning, lunchtime and afternoon/evening surgeries. [B1]

Question 8 – 10 marks

a

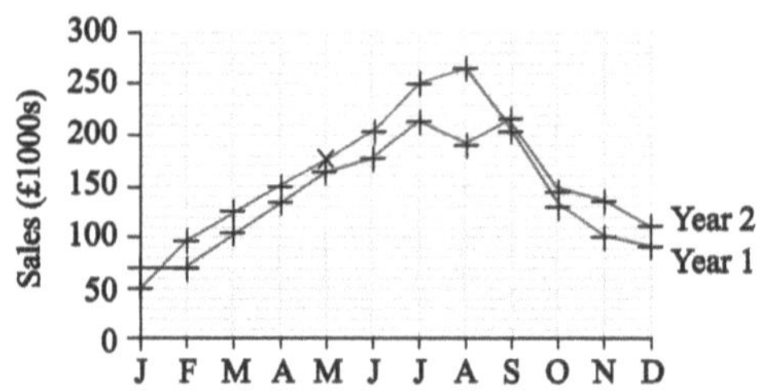

Correctly drawn and labelled axes [B1]
Correctly plotted points; lose 1 mark for each error [B3]
Two sets of points joined by lines [B1]
Labels on the two lines [B1]
b Two valid comparisons each supported by evidence from the graphs [B4]
Summer sales in Year 1 were higher than in Year 2.
Winter sales in Year 1 were lower than in Year 2.

Calculations 2

Learning outcomes

N2 Apply the four operations (+, -, ×, ÷), including formal written methods, to integers, decimals [and simple fractions (proper and improper), and mixed numbers – all both positive and negative]; understand and use place value (e.g. when working with very large or very small numbers, and when calculating with decimals).

N6 Use positive integer powers and associated real roots (square, cube and higher), recognise powers of 2, 3, 4, 5.

N7 Calculate with roots, and with integer indices.

N8 Calculate exactly with fractions and multiples of π.

N9 Calculate with and interpret standard form $A \times 10^n$, where $1 \le A < 10$ and n is an integer.

Prior knowledge

Check-in skill

- Calculate the product of simple powers.
- Convert between metric units of length.

Online resources

MyMaths 1017, 1033, 1040, 1047, 1049, 1050, 1051, 1924

InvisiPen videos

Skills: 17Sa – c Applications: 17Aa – c

Kerboodle assessment

Online Skills Test 17 Chapter Test 17

Development and links

Standard index form is extremely important in science where scientists use it to describe small quantities such as the diameter of an atom and large quantities such as distances across the Universe.

Rounding and estimation are used in business and industry to ascertain whether there are sufficient resources to complete a project.

Chapter investigation

Scientific measurements often use very small or very large units. For example, named SI units of distances range from a yoctometre, 1×10^{-24} m, to a Yottametre, 1×10^{24} m. Written as decimals these numbers are unwieldy so students should quickly see the merit of writing them using standard form [**17.3**].

Consider problems involving the multiplication and division of numbers, such as the perimeter and area of a rectangle, and how to do these when numbers are given in standard form. This will require knowledge of how to manipulate indices [**17.1**]. Problems such as finding the side length of a cube given its surface area or volume will lead on to handling square and cube roots.

Problems should be tackled both using written and calculator methods.

Historically the UK used inches as a unit of length and it was commonplace to use quarters, eighths, sixteenths, etc. as sub units. A length of 10 cm is very nearly $3\frac{15}{16}$ inches. What is the perimeter and area of a 10 cm square in inches and inches^2? Treating this, and similar, problems exactly requires knowing how to work with fractions [**17.2**]. Extending the shapes to circles and cylinders will involve learning how to treat π in exact calculations.

17.1 Calculating with roots and indices

Objectives

① **N7** Calculate with roots and integer indices

Useful resources

Place value tables, mini whiteboards, calculators

Starter – Skills

Ask students to work out the value of:

$2^3, 5^2, 4^3, 3^1, 3^4, 2^8, 5^0, 6^3$

(8, 25, 64, 3, 81, 256, 1, 216)

Making sense of the powers 0 and 1 can be picked up further on in the lesson.

Teaching notes – Skills

① Recap that the **square root** of a number (say, 9) is the number you multiply by itself to get the starting number; and that the **cube root** of a number (say, 8) is the number you multiply by itself and by itself again to get the starting number. Refer to the starter and formalise the superscript number as the **index** or **power**, discussing the relevance of this number to the calculation. Elicit that the index tells you how many times to multiply the number by itself. Ask students to work in pairs to decide whether these statements are true, and to come up with reasons to justify their answers:

$4^3 \times 4^2 = 4^5$
$2^8 \div 2^3 = 2^5$
$(2^3)^2 = 2^6$

Work through the rules for simplifying calculations with indices, showing all stages of working.

i **Multiplying** with indices (or the **addition rule**):

$5^3 \times 5^4 = (5 \times 5 \times 5) \times (5 \times 5 \times 5 \times 5) = 5^7 (= 5^{3+4})$

Highlight: ADD the indices.

ii **Dividing** with indices (or the **subtraction rule**):

$$6^5 \div 6^2 = \frac{6 \times 6 \times 6 \times \cancel{6} \times \cancel{6}}{\cancel{6} \times \cancel{6}} = 6 \times 6 \times 6$$

$$= 6^3 \qquad (= 6^{5-2})$$

Highlight: SUBTRACT the indices.

iii Raising a **power to a power**:

$(3^4)^3 = 3^4 \times 3^4 \times 3^4 = 3^{12} \qquad (= 3^{4 \times 3})$

Highlight: MULTIPLY the indices.

Discuss the **power 0**. Any number (except 0) to the power of 0 is 1. For example, using the subtraction rule for dividing indices, $4^3 \div 4^3 = 4^{3-3} = 4^0$. But any number divided by itself gives the answer 1, so $4^0 = 1$. Discuss the **power 1**. Any number to the power of 1 is itself. Show this similarly using one of the index laws.

Plenary – Skills

If you want to divide an amount by 100 you can do so in two identical smaller steps by dividing by 10 twice. What number can you divide by twice so that overall you divide by:

9, 4, 25, 1, 144? (3, 2, 5, 1, 12)

How are these answers connected? (square roots)

Exercise commentary – Skills

Question 1 These will all yield integers, and students should memorise these square roots.

Questions 2 and **3** Practice at square roots and cube roots, with decimal answers that will need to be rounded to 2 dp. A recap on rounding may be helpful here.

Questions 4 to **6** Practice at evaluating powers – question **4** should be attempted without a calculator. Go through **4a** together, to quickly dispel the notion that 5^2 is 10. Check that students can find the correct keys for their own calculator.

Question 7 Part **e** is a kind of 'trick' question, but hopefully parts **c** and **d** should help to instil the fact that anything to the power of zero is 1.

Questions 9 to **13** Support students as they practise using the rules of powers; particularly in questions **12** and **13** where the calculations are multi-step. For division calculations, students could use 'cancelling', but this needs caution as it comes with lots of misconceptions.

Question 14 A challenging task, perhaps best tackled in pairs. Remind students about the correct order of operations.

Simplification – Skills

Students should concentrate first on using the rules of indices with questions that have only two terms.

Extension – Skills

Students could be asked to interpret the meaning of a negative index. Can they write this down clearly to enable someone else to understand it as well?

Recap – Applications

1 a Calculate these square roots using a calculator where appropriate. Give your answers to 3 sf as necessary.

i $\sqrt{256}$ (16) ii $\sqrt{76}$ (8.76)

b Calculate these cube roots using a calculator where appropriate. Give your answers to 3 sf as necessary.

i $\sqrt[3]{1000}$ (10) ii $\sqrt[3]{206021}$ (59.1)

2 a Evaluate the following without using a calculator:

i 5^4 (625) ii $\sqrt[3]{-8}$ (-2)

iii $(-5)^3$ (-125) iv $(1^4)^2$ (1)

3 Write the answers to these multiplications in index form:

a $8^3 \div 8$ (8^2)

b $15^3 \times 15^6 \div 15^9$ (1)

c $(12^2)^7$ (12^{14})

d $(3.2)^4 \times 3.2$ (3.2^5)

e $(21.6)^{12} \div (21.6)^4$ (21.6^8)

4 Find the value of:

a $17^8 \times 17^3 \div 17^9$ (289)

b $\dfrac{6^2 \times 3^4}{6^3 \times 3}$ (4.5)

c $\dfrac{6^2 + 3^4}{6^3 + 3^2}$ (0.52)

Plenary – Applications

Challenge students to make as many numbers as they can using four 4s, brackets and any operators; with a particular emphasis on using roots and indices where possible. It may help to compile a list on the board so that students' efforts can be focused on filling in any gaps.

Exercise commentary – Applications

Question 1 requires students to mark some incorrect work and identify the error (taking the power outside the bracket). Discuss as a whole group why this is incorrect (indices before addition).

Question 2 The structure of this question reflects some exam questions, where students are required to use given facts to work out unknown facts.

Question 3 You may need to remind some students that the laws of indices need all the base numbers to be the same.

Question 4 some students will not know where to start with this – suggest they try it to see if it's true. It actually leads to a nice investigation – some students will appreciate that the factors are always 1, the number, the number squared, and the number cubed.

Question 7 Students could work in pairs on this, and try to proceed systematically with pairs of numbers.

Question 8 This task could be extended to look at other logarithmic scales (decibels) or to research recent earthquakes.

Question 9 Part **a vi** involves the term 'reciprocal', which will need revisiting.

Question 10 This highlights the inverse nature of powers and roots, and can be discussed as a learning point. As a challenge, students can try to check on their calculators.

Question 11 some students will realise that because the base numbers are the same, they can be ignored and the index laws can be applied.

Simplification – Applications

Work on eradicating common errors.

Encourage students to write e.g.

$2^5 \times 2^2$ as [2 × 2 × 2 × 2 × 2] × [2 × 2] and count up the 2s to get 2^7.

Set questions, for example:

1 $7^2 \times 7^x = 7^6$ Lee says $x = 3$

Explain why Lee is wrong.

2 $3^8 \div 3^4 = 3^y$ Mo says $y = 2$

Explain why Mo is wrong.

3 $[11^3]^2 = 11^k$ Olly says $k = 9$

Explain why Olly is wrong.

Extension – Applications

Students could be given a problem such as $2^3 \times 4^2$ to solve. They could be prompted to notice that 4 can be written as a power of 2.

17.2 Exact calculations

Objectives

① **N8** Calculate exactly with fractions and multiples of π

Useful resources

Mini whiteboards, calculators

Starter – Skills

Revise the four rules applied to fractions and BIDMAS for the order of operations.

Teaching notes – Skills

① Different **fractions** have different types of decimal equivalent. So, for example:

$\frac{73}{100}$ can be written as 0.73

$\frac{2}{3}$ can be written as 0.666…

$\frac{13}{42}$ can be written as 0.309 523…

But the decimal equivalents are not always helpful to use when calculating accurate answers.

Explore the different types of decimals: **terminating** (0.73), **recurring** (0.666…), and **continuing without recurrence** ($\frac{13}{42}$ = 0.309 523…, π = 3.141 592…, $\sqrt{3}$ = 1.732 050…)

Terminating decimals come only from fractions with a denominator whose only prime factors are 2 and/or 5, so it is usually more accurate to **leave fractions in your answer**.

Similarly, **leaving π in your answer** gives a more accurate answer, and is often easier than writing out the answer with lots of decimal places.

Multiples of π behave like algebraic terms in calculations.

For example: $4\pi + 5 + 3\pi = 7\pi + 5$

Decimal approximation can be useful in practical contexts, but it is often more accurate to simplify an expression first, and *then* find an approximation if need be. For example:

$4\pi + 5 + 3\pi = 7\pi + 5$

$\approx 7 \times 3.1 + 5$

$= 26.7$

Plenary – Skills

Look at examples that show that an answer may be solely a multiple of π. For example:

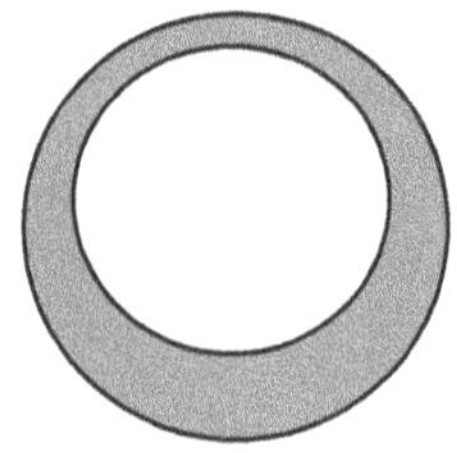

The radius of the inner circle is 5 cm and the radius of the outer circle is 6 cm. Calculate the area of the blue ring. (11π cm^2)

Exercise commentary – Skills

Questions 1 and **2** Basic skill questions involving arithmetic with fractions. In question **1**, the first step for students will be in remembering that they need to find the LCM of the denominators. Some students will struggle with mixed numbers; in question **2**, it's best to convert to improper fractions. Encourage correct use of 'cancelling' where possible.

Question 3 Recap of converting from fractions to decimals. Some parts will include recurring decimals, for example 5/3.

Question 4 Use this as an opportunity to consolidate the order of operations.

Questions 5 and **6** These all involve π, and many involve expansion of brackets. The third example will help here.

Question 7 This context shows that you often multiply by a fraction when working with scale.

Question 8 Students need to calculate area and perimeter using fractions. This is similar to the sorts of exam questions that involve running tracks, and many students fall prey to the common errors – here, the perimeter of the entire shape does not include the short sides of the rectangle.

Question 9 This provides reinforcement of arithmetic applied to fractions.

Simplification – Skills

Students should practise more questions on fractions.

Extension – Skills

Set two fraction sums, one addition and one multiplication, half of the group working in fractions and the other half working in decimals, all without calculators. Check that the answers match and decide on the quicker method.

Recap – Applications

1 Expand and then write these expressions in their simplest and exact form.

a $12 + 3\pi - (7 + 4\pi)$ $(5 - \pi)$

b $3\pi(13 - 4^2)$ (-9π)

c $(10 - \sqrt{16})\pi \div 2$ (3π)

d $\sqrt{48} + \pi(3^3 - 5^2)$ $(4\sqrt{3} + 2\pi)$

e $\sqrt{3}(3\pi - \sqrt{3})$ $(3\sqrt{3}\pi - 3)$

f $\pi(\sqrt{81} + 5\pi) + (3\pi)^2$ $(9\pi + 14\pi^2)$

g $(5\pi)^3 - 2\pi(\pi^2 - \sqrt{11}\pi - 6)$

$(123\pi^3 - 2\sqrt{11}\pi^2 + 12\pi)$

Plenary – Applications

Ask: What is the circumference of a circle whose diameter is 5 m? Give the exact answer, without using a calculator. $(5\pi$ m)

Exercise commentary – Applications

Many students will think that calculations are only exact if they are done on a calculator, so it's a good idea to discuss this before proceeding with the exercise.

Question 1 This problem is set around the scenario of a bicycle wheel, so involves calculating circumference. Ensure that students use π.

Question 2 Some students will reach for their calculators; discourage this as they should be simplifying the expressions, after which their relative magnitude should be clearer.

Question 3 This is an interesting diversion into old paper sizes, which could be investigated alongside the modern standard A series.

Question 4 this gives students practice in piecing together expressions. Part **b** is more of a challenge, and relates to the formula for the area of a circle (remembering that this is a quarter of a circle).

Question 5 Make sure all students understand the question. A real can and label may help. Note the use of imperial measure in this question, and check the units of the answers. Students will need to know the surface area and volume of a cylinder.

Question 6 This is another problem relating to the surface area of a cylinder, in this case a cake. In part **d**, assume that the icing covers the same dimensions as in part **b**.

Simplification – Applications

Students could practise finding area and perimeter of circles in terms of π.

They could also practise finding volume and curved surface area of cylinders in terms of π.

Extension – Applications

Students could find volumes of composite figures such as a cone on a hemisphere, or a hemisphere on a cylinder, in terms of π.

17.3 Standard form

Objectives

① **N9** Calculate with and interpret standard form $A \times 10^n$, where $1 \leq A < 10$ and n is an integer

Useful resources

Place value table, OHT/whiteboard file of powers of 10, calculators

Starter – Skills

Write 10, 100 and 1000 on the board. Give students a number and invite them to multiply it by 10, 100 and 1000. Repeat with a decimal number. Discuss the effect of multiplying by each. Use place value columns to demonstrate the digits moving one, two or three places to the left. Give more practice with decimal numbers. Repeat for division.

Teaching notes – Skills

① Refer to the mental starter. Ensure students recognise that 'adding/removing a zero' does not work for decimal numbers. Highlight that the decimal system is based upon **powers of 10**. Recap that the index or power tells you how many times to multiply the number by itself.

Discuss the calculation 3.2×10^1 and highlight this as equal to 3.2×10. Discuss the effect of multiplying by 10. Repeat for 3.2×10^2, link to $\times$ 100 and discuss the effect of multiplying by 100.

Highlight that the index indicates how many places the digits move. Discuss the movement of the digits for 3.2×10^5. Establish that each digit will move 5 times as indicated by the power. Extend to division by powers of 10. Ask students for the largest number that they have encountered in a context; encourage cross-curricular links with science. Repeat the discussion using the smallest number; again, science is an obvious context to draw on.

Describe the use of **standard form** as a convenient way of writing large and small numbers, in the form of two numbers multiplied together:

$A \times 10^n$,

where $1 \leq A < 10$ and n is an integer

Give examples. Emphasise that to find the power/index of 10 you should always count the number of places the digits have to move relative to the decimal point, not the number of zeros.

Use examples, discussing whether the operation, in real-world terms, is multiplication or division, and how the digits are 'moving' in each case. Include examples of: writing numbers in 'ordinary' form, writing numbers in standard form, multiplying and dividing with numbers in standard form using the rules of indices and adding and subtracting with numbers in standard form.

Plenary – Skills

Target 36

Challenge students to give calculations using powers of 10 where the answer is 36.

Exercise commentary – Skills

Questions 1 to **4** These questions provide practice in converting between powers of 10 and ordinary numbers, including both positive and negative indices. Students should appreciate that large numbers → positive powers of 10, and small numbers → negative powers of 10

Questions 5 and **6** Practice in calculating with powers of 10 using the index laws. In **6d** and **6f**, students should appreciate that $10 = 10^1$, and in **6e**, $1 = 10^0$.

Questions 7 to **9** These provide practice in converting between standard form and ordinary numbers. Question **9** reinforces the constraint that the number on the left should be between 1 and 10.

Questions 10 to **12** Calculations involving standard form, using all four main arithmetical operations. In questions **10** and **11**, students should refrain from using a calculator; encourage them to multiply or divide the numbers first, then the powers. In question **12**, they can use a calculator, but ensure that they both identify and use the standard form key correctly. Discuss any common calculator errors. Students could also discuss how to do these questions without a calculator.

Simplification – Skills

Students should concentrate on working with positive integer powers of 10, and on multiplying and dividing by powers of 10 not given using index notation before gaining confidence in understanding and using the notation of standard form.

Extension – Skills

Students could practise tackling calculations involving addition and subtraction by manipulating the numbers to give the same powers of 10 in each part and using BIDMAS, rather than working out each number in 'ordinary' form first.

Recap – Applications

1 a Write as powers of 10:

i 1 000 000 000 (10^9)

ii 0.000 000 1 (10^{-7})

b Write as 'ordinary' numbers:

i 10^7 (10000000)

ii 10^0 (1)

iii 10^{-4} (0.001)

c Write as powers of 10:

i $10^6 \times 10^5$ (10^{11})

ii $10^{12} \div 10^{15}$ (10^{-3})

iii $10^{-8} \times 10^{-12}$ (10^{-20})

iv $10^{-3} \div 10^{-2}$ (10^{-1})

2 a Write in standard form

i 3 (3×10^0)

ii 256 (2.56×10^2)

iii 0.44 (4.4×10^{-1})

iv 186.2×10^{-1} (1.862×10^1)

b Write as 'ordinary' numbers:

i 9.9×10^7 (99000000)

ii 11.11×10^{-2} (0.1111)

3 Calculate, giving your answers instandard form:

a $(1.2 \times 10^3) \times (5.4 \times 10^0)$

($9\,648 \times 10^3$)

b $(5 \times 10^6) \div (20 \times 10^4)$

(2.5×10^1)

c $(5 \times 10^{-4}) \div (4 \times 10^3)$

(1.25×10^{-7})

d $1.8 \times 10^2 + 5.2 \times 103$

(5.38×10^3)

e $9.81 \times 10^{-2} + 7.22 \times 10^{-1}$

(8.201×10^{-1})

f $6.6 \times 10^{-4} - 8.9 \times 10^{-3}$

(-8.24×10^{-3})

Plenary – Applications

There are approximately 64 000 000 people living in the UK. Can this number be written by multiplying two numbers together? Challenge students to do this, using 10, 100, 1000, ... for one of the numbers. How many combinations are there? Share responses. Include examples like 0.64 × 100 000 000. How can each answer be simplified using powers of 10? Write down solutions and ask: Which of these possibilities is written in standard form?

Repeat this exercise for the mass of one grain of salt which is approximately 0.000 001 7 kg.

Exercise commentary – Applications

This exercise provides real-life problems involving large and small numbers, and requiring calculation using standard form. Students should be encouraged to use their scientific calculator correctly.

Question 1 Students will first need to write each value as a decimal number, so a recap on metric units would be good here.

Question 2 This would be a good question to revise the correct/incorrect use of brackets.

Question 3 Students could research other units that are the same/different between US and UK.

Questions 4 to **6** Students often need help deciding which operations are required in standard form questions. Ask them to think of similar examples using ordinary numbers.

Question 7 Students should have met this in science. Students could research the distance to the nearest star, and then consider how long ago the light from that star was actually generated.

Question 8 Some students may wonder how to apply significant figures to standard form; they just need to focus on the number on the left.

Question 9 It will be worth discussing what is an appropriate degree of accuracy for the answer to this problem.

Questions 10 and **11** These problems involve addition and subtraction, whereas previous problems have involved multiplication and division. Many students will find this harder, particularly if the powers of 10 are different.

Simplification – Applications

Students may need help to interpret many of the questions to decide what calculation they have to make. Help them to produce a list such as:

Difference → subtract one number from another; Total → add the numbers together; How many times smaller was A than B → divide B by A; How many times larger was P than Q → divide P by Q.

Extension – Applications

Students could investigate the prefixes used to describe certain powers of 10 such as giga-, mega-, milli- and micro-.

Calculations 2

Key outcomes	Quick check
N7 Calculate with roots, and with integer indices.	**3** Calculate the value of these expressions. **a** $9 + 8 \times 2$ (25) **b** 2×5^2 (50) **c** $24 \div (8 - 2)$ (4) **d** $\dfrac{13+18\div 9}{\sqrt{16}+1}$ (3) **4** Simplify these expressions, giving your answers in index form. **a** $2^3 \times 2^2$ (2^5) **b** $3^4 \div 3$ (3^3) **c** 12^1 (12) **d** $4^3 \times 4^{-2}$ (4) **e** 5^0 (1) **f** $8^7 \div 8^5$ (8^2) **g** $\sqrt{121}$ (11) **h** $\sqrt[3]{64}$ (4)
N8 Calculate exactly with fractions and multiples of π.	**2** Calculate the answers and write in the simplest form. **a** $\frac{2}{7}\times 3$ $\left(\frac{6}{7}\right)$ **b** $\frac{5}{8}\times\frac{2}{3}$ $\left(\frac{5}{12}\right)$ **c** $\frac{4}{9}+\frac{2}{9}$ $\left(\frac{2}{3}\right)$ **d** $\frac{7}{10}-\frac{1}{3}$ $\left(\frac{11}{30}\right)$ **e** $\frac{5}{3}+\frac{1}{4}$ $\left(\frac{17}{12}=1\frac{5}{12}\right)$ **f** $5\frac{1}{2}-2\frac{1}{3}$ $\left(3\frac{1}{6}\right)$ **g** $\frac{10}{7}\times\frac{2}{5}$ $\left(\frac{4}{7}\right)$ **h** $2\frac{1}{3}\times\frac{3}{4}$ $\left(\frac{7}{4}=1\frac{3}{4}\right)$ **i** $\frac{8}{5}\div 4$ $\left(\frac{2}{5}\right)$ **j** $\frac{1}{8}\div\frac{3}{4}$ $\left(\frac{2}{12}=\frac{1}{6}\right)$ **5** Calculate the exact area and perimeter of these shapes. All measurements are in metres. **a** 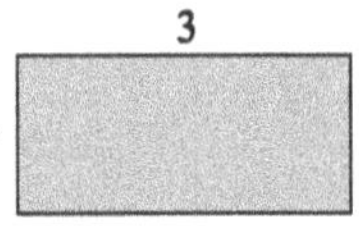 $(4\text{ m}^2, 8\frac{2}{3}\text{ m})$ **b** 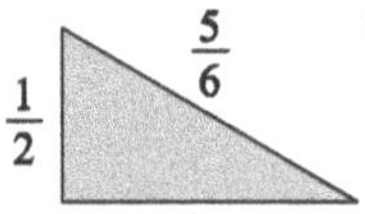 $(\frac{1}{3}\text{ m}^2, 2\text{ m})$ **c** 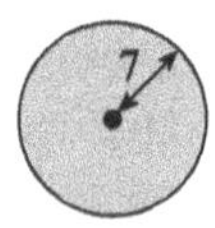 $(49\pi\text{ m}^2, 14\pi\text{ m})$ **d** 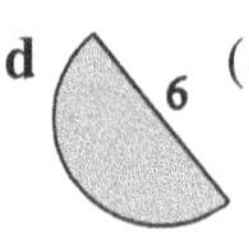 $(4\frac{1}{2}\pi\text{ m}^2, 6 + 6\pi\text{ m})$
N9 Calculate with and interpret standard form $A \times 10^n$, where $1 \le A < 10$ and n is an integer.	**8** Write these ordinary numbers in standard form. **a** 143 000 000 (1.43×10^8) **b** 629 000 000 000 m $(6.29 \times 10^{11}\text{ m})$ **c** 0.000 149 g $(1.49 \times 10^{-4}\text{ g})$ **d** 1 mm in km $(1 \times 10^{-6}\text{ km})$ **9** Write these as ordinary numbers. **a** 2.9×10^4 (29 000) **b** 5.62×10^9 (5 620 000 000) **c** 3.8×10^{-2} (0.038) **d** 9.04×10^{-8} (0.000 000 090 4) **10** Calculate these and leave your answer in standard form **a** $(4 \times 10^5) \times (2 \times 10^4)$ (8×10^9) **b** $(2.6 \times 10^8) \times (4 \times 10^{-4})$ (1.04×10^5) **c** $(9 \times 10^8) \div (3 \times 10^5)$ (3×10^3) **d** $(2.8 \times 10^{-5}) \div (2 \times 10^{-1})$ (1.4×10^{-4}) **e** $(3.2 \times 10^5) + (2 \times 10^4)$ (3.4×10^5) **f** $(2.8 \times 10^9) - (5 \times 10^7)$ (2.75×10^9)

Misconceptions and challenges	Solutions
When learning standard form $A \times 10^n$, students frequently give A as less than 1 or greater than (or equal to) 10.	To promote greater understanding, students should not see standard form in terms of counting 0s, but as how many places left or right the digits have moved.

Misconceptions and challenges	Solutions
Students confuse standard form with ordinary indices for example $2000 = 2^3$ or $2000 = 2.0 \times 2^3$	Encourage students to think of the powers of 10 and their ordinary number equivalents as being the same mathematical object with different names. For example, 10^{-1} as another name for 0.1 and 10^3 as another name for 1000. It is then easier to see standard form as a multiplication.
Students make errors when adding terms with powers by misapplying the index laws. For example, errors such as $x^a + x^b = x^{a+b}$ or $3x^a + 4x^b = 7x^{a+b}$.	Write indices in expanded form, for example a^4 as $a \times a \times a \times a$, to help students see how the index laws can be correctly applied.
In calculator questions, students make mistakes entering roots containing multiple terms, for example entering $\sqrt{1.4^2 + 2.33^2}$ as $\sqrt{1.4^2} + 2.33^2$	This often occurs when students have not had enough practice with their calculators. Give students plenty of practice entering complex calculations involving fractions, powers and roots.
Common errors include squaring $2r$ to get $2r^2$, squaring $\sqrt{3}$ and leaving the answer as $\sqrt{9}$	Students could check answers by substituting values into both the simplified and non-simplified version of the expression but should be aware that this is not a guarantee, merely a good way of spotting an error.
Students often do not feel comfortable giving their answers exactly as a fraction or in terms of π.	Remind students that it is more accurate than a decimal answer, since a decimal can only ever be an approximation to a number such as π, or $\sqrt{3}$. It may help to research digits of π and discover that such a search can never be complete.

Review question commentary

Students should not use calculators in this exercise.

Question 1 (**17.1**) – Index laws should be used to simplify these expressions. Remind students of BIDMAS for part **f**.

Question 2 (**17.1**) – Index laws should be used to simplify before evaluating. This is particularly important in part **f** where students should not be calculating the value of 3^{12}!

Question 3 (**17.2**) – It will usually be easier to convert mixed numbers to improper fractions first. Likely correct but not simplified answers are shown in brackets, encourage students to always cancel down.

Question 4 (**17.2**) – Calculations required are

a $2 \times \frac{3}{5}$ **b** $\frac{1}{2} \times \frac{1}{2} \times \frac{5}{2}$

Question 5 (**17.2**) – Remind students to collect like terms.

Question 6 (**17.2**) – In part **a ii** remind students to work to use the radius. For part **b ii** the diameter of the semi-circle should be included in the perimeter.

Questions 7 and **8** (**17.3**) – Students should leave answers with the same degree of accuracy (3 sf except **8a** and **8c**).

Question 9 (**17.3**) – Students should use laws of indices to simplify the powers of 10. Part **d** is 0.6×10^{-1}, students need to rewrite this in standard form.

Review answers

1 **a** 5^{10} **b** 3^4 **c** 7^{12} **d** 2^0
e 3^3 **f** 4^4

2 **a** 128 **b** 16 **c** 5 **d** 64
e 1 **f** 27 **g** 6 **h** 2

3 **a** $\frac{3}{5}\left(\frac{6}{10}\right)$ **b** $\frac{3}{14}\left(\frac{6}{28}\right)$ **c** $\frac{3}{5}$ **d** $\frac{13}{24}$
e $\frac{31}{24}\left(\frac{62}{48}\right)$ **f** $\frac{41}{20}\left(2\frac{1}{20}\right)$ **g** $\frac{22}{9}\left(2\frac{4}{9}\right)$ **h** $\frac{11}{14}\left(\frac{22}{28}\right)$
i $\frac{2}{7}\left(\frac{6}{21}\right)$ **j** $\frac{1}{6}\left(\frac{3}{18}\right)$

4 **a** $1\frac{1}{5}\,\text{m}^2$ **b** $\frac{5}{8}\,\text{m}^2$

5 **a** $3\pi + 2$ **b** 5π **c** $\frac{5\pi}{12}$ **d** $\frac{9\pi}{2}$

6 **a** **i** 64π **ii** $\frac{25}{2}\pi$
b **i** 16π **ii** $5\pi + 10$

7 **a** 1.37×10^9 **b** 5.46×10^7
c 6.97×10^{-2} **d** 6.25×10^{-5}

8 **a** 350 000 **b** 821 000 000
c 0.0027 **d** 0.000 000 207

9 **a** 6×10^{10} **b** 7×10^4
c 4×10^5 **d** 6×10^{-2}
e 2.424×10^5 **f** 3.42×10^3

Assessment 17

Question 1 – 3 marks

a Soraya [B1]
b Peter [B1]
c Soraya [B1]

Question 2 – 6 marks

a 9.261 [B1]
b 2687 (3 sf) [B1]
c 974 (3 sf) [B1]
d 29 [B1]
e 8.77 (3 sf) [B1]
f 8.68 (3 sf) [B1]

Question 3 – 5 marks

a No 15^{12} [B1]
b Yes 3^{20} [B1]
c Eliza [B1]
$(3^4)^0 = 3^0 = 1$ OR $x^0 = 1$ [B1]
d $7^{7+2-6} = 7^3$ [B1]

Question 4 – 2 marks

$(2.3\text{ cm})^3 = 12.167\text{ cm}^3$ [M1, A1]

Question 5 – 4 marks

a $6 \times 6 \times 6$ $[=6^3]$ [M1]
$= 216$ [A1]
b $x^3 = 125 = 5^3$ [M1]
$x = 5$ [A1]

Question 6 – 6 marks

a $4^2 \times 4^3 = 4^{2+3} = 4^5$ [M1]
$a = 5$ [A1]
b $(2^3)^b = (2^2)^6 \Rightarrow 2^{3b} = 2^{12} \Rightarrow 3b = 12$ [M1]
$b = 4$
c $3^8 = (3^2)^c \Rightarrow 3^8 = 3^{2c} \Rightarrow 2b = 8$ [M1]
$c = 4$ [A1]

Question 7 – 4 marks

Students' answers, for example, [B4]
$\frac{1}{4} + \frac{2}{8} = \frac{1}{2}$ or $\frac{1}{3} + \frac{2}{12} = \frac{1}{2}$, etc.
Lose 1 mark for each incorrect equation or equation with a repeated digit.

Question 8 – 3 marks

a $\frac{48}{240} = \frac{1}{5}$ [M1, A1]
b = 192 [240 – 48] [B1]

Question 9 – 3 marks

a $\frac{8}{11} \times 55$ OR $55 \div 11 = 5$ [M1]
$= 40$ $5 \times 8 = 40$ [A1]
b 15 [55 – 40] [F1]

Question 10 – 7 marks

a $\frac{3}{5} + \frac{1}{3} = \frac{9+5}{15} = \frac{14}{15}$ [M1, A1]
b $\frac{1}{15}$ $[1 - \frac{14}{15}]$ [F1]
c 1 fifteenth of vegetables = 4 [M1]
vegetables $= 4 \times 15 = 60$ [A1]
potatoes $= \frac{3}{5} \times 60 = 36$ [M1, A1]

Question 11 – 6 marks

a Romeo $\frac{7}{25} \times 15\,500$ OR $15\,500 \div 25 = 620$ [M1]
$= 4340$ $620 \times 7 = 4340$ [A1]
Juliet: $\frac{7}{20} \times 13\,400$ OR $13\,400 \div 20 = 670$
$= 4690$ $670 \times 7 = 4690$ [A1]
4690 – 4340 = 350
Juliet saves £350 more per year [F1]
b £4340 + £4690 [M1]
= £9030 [F1]

Question 12 – 3 marks

$9\frac{5}{8} \div 13\frac{3}{4} = \frac{77}{8} \div \frac{55}{4}$ [M1]
$= \frac{77}{8} \times \frac{4}{55}$ [A1]
$= \frac{7}{10}$ [A1]

Question 13 – 15 marks

a English Channel 29 000 mi^2
Baltic Sea 1 46 000 mi^2
BeringSea 876 000 mi^2
CaribbeanSea 1 060 000 mi^2
Malay Sea 3 140 000 mi^2
Indian Ocean 28 400 000 mi^2
Lose 1 mark for each incorrect conversion [B3]
Correct ascending order. [B1]
b 1×10^9 [B1]
1 [1 000 000 000 999 999 999] [B1]
c **i** 4 [B1]
ii 2 [B1]
iii 6 [B1]
iv $2.75 \times 10 \times 10^n = 2.75 \times 10^{-2}$ [M1]
-3 [A1]
d **i** 0.0008 joules [B1]
ii 10 763 km
[B1]
e 4×10^{-6} km [B1]
f 4 mm [B1]

Question 14 – 4 marks

a $2.96 \times 10^6 \div 3.4 \times 10^2$ [M1]
$= 8.71 \times 10^3$ or 8710 [A1]
b $2.179 \times 10^3 \times 10^3 \div (60 \times 60)$ m/s [M1]
= 605 m/s [A1]
= 605.277… ÷ 3.04 [M1
= 199 [F1]

Question 15 – 3 marks

a $5.776 \times 10^3 \div 4.336 \times 10^9$ [M1]
1.332×10^{-6} [A1]
b 1 ÷ 751 000 [B1]

Question 16 – 4 marks

a 180 km + 42 km + 3.8 km [B2]
= 226 km (3 sf) [F1]
b 2.26×10^2km [B1]

Graphs 2

Learning outcomes

A11 Identify and interpret roots, intercepts, turning points of quadratic functions graphically; deduce roots algebraically.

A12 Recognise, sketch and interpret graphs of linear functions, quadratic functions, simple cubic functions, the reciprocal function $y = 1/x$ with $x \neq 0$.

A14 Plot and interpret graphs (including reciprocal graphs) and graphs of non-standard functions in real contexts, to find approximate solutions to problems such as simple kinematic problems involving distance, speed and acceleration.

A18 [Solve quadratic equations algebraically by factorising;] find approximate solutions using a graph.

Prior knowledge

Check-in skill

- Substitute numerical values into expressions.
- Complete a table of values for a given linear function.

Online resources

MyMaths 1168, 1169, 1071, 1172, 1180, 1184, 1316, 1322

InvisiPen videos

Skills: 18Sa – d Applications: 18Aa – c

Kerboodle assessment

Online Skills Test 18 Chapter Test 18 8

Development and links

Real-life graphs can be used to identify trends in data and to predict future behaviour. Distance–time graphs have wide applications in mechanics and are used in motor sports to analyse the performance of the driver and the car from data collected during a lap. Another form of a distance–time graph is a tachograph which records the speed of a lorry or coach during a journey and is used to calculate the driver's speed, distance travelled and hours worked.

Chapter investigation

The key to this problem is to take the total number of man hours required as fixed at $20 \times 18 = 360$. So that one person would take 360 days, two people 180 days, etc. This naturally leads to the reciprocal graph $y = 360/x$ [**18.2**].

As a variant of this problem suppose that the job is unpopular in such a way that the number of people who will commit to working decreases according to the length of the job. If the job lasts y days then $42 - y$ people will commit to it. For this to be viable requires $y \times (42 - y) = 360$.

Solving this problem is equivalent to finding when the curve $y = 42x - x^2$ (swapping x and y) takes the value 360. Ask students to plot the function $y = 42x - x^2$ and to investigate its properties [**18.1**]. It has roots at 0 and 42 and has a turning point at (21, 441). Adding the line $y = 360$ gives intersections at $x = 12$ and 30: the job could be done in 12 days with 30 people or 30 days with 12 people.

What happens if you changed the number 42 to 36? Encourage students to focus on the position of the turning point, which becomes (18, 324). Since this is below 360 there can be no intersection and no solution.

Invite students to investigate the graphs you get for other quadratic [**18.1**] and cubic functions [**18.2**].

As part of the building work consider a water container that is variously filled and emptied. Show a graph of the depth as a function of time and invite students to interpret it [**18.3**]. For example, how long did it take to fill, when and how much water was taken to mix cement, etc.

Ask how, if water is poured in at a constant rate (volume per unit time), the shape of the vessel affects the depth of the water as a function of time? Alternatively can students match a depth–time graph to variously shaped vessels [**18.3**]?

18.1 Properties of quadratic functions

Objectives

① **A12** Recognise, sketch and interpret graphs of quadratic functions

Useful resources

Mini whiteboards, prepared sets of coordinates for display, prepared axes for quadratic function drawing, display of $y = x^2$ plotted on a graph

Starter – Skills

What is the value of x^2 when $x = -5$? (25)

What is the value of $2x^2$ when $x = 5$? $(2 \times 5^2 = 50)$

What is the value of $-x^2$ if $x = -6$? (–36, squaring –6 gives 36, so –36 is negative.)

Invent other questions of this type.

Teaching notes – Skills

Show this set of coordinates on the board, in order.

(–2, 4) (–1, 1) (2, 4) (3, 9) (4, 16) (7, 49)

Ask the students to work out missing coordinates: (5, ?), (6, ?). What is the relationship between these coordinates? Write as an equation.

Distribute prepared axes and ask the students to plot the points carefully for the function $y = x^2$. Go through the stages carefully with the whole class, including completing a table and identifying the coordinates to plot. Discuss the overall shape then ask students to draw the curve. Emphasise the curve should be smooth – demonstrate using a display of the graph. Say that it may help if students turn the axes upside down or sideways to use the natural sweep of the arm and hand for the curve. Students should now try to draw the curve. Leaving the set of coordinates up on the board for $y = x^2$, ask the students to find coordinates for the graph $y = x^2 + 2$ and draw this on the same set of axes.

Plenary – Skills

Revisit the graphs of $y = x^2 + 2$ and $y = x^2 + 3$ asking students what they notice. Ask them to draw the graph $y = x^2 + 5$ in the air, then $y = x^2 - 2$. What might $y = -x^2$ look like? Recap with some simple linear graphs to finish.

Exercise commentary – Skills

Question 1 A common misconception is to think that when you square a negative number the answer is also negative. Reinforce the point that $(-3)^2 = -3 \times -3 = 9$, two negatives multiplied together give a positive answer.

Question 2 Emphasise that they should plot the points accurately and then join them with a smooth curve. What do they notice about part **e** and can they explain why this has happened?

Question 3 Challenge students to find a link between the y-intercept and the equation in each case. What kind of equation goes with a y-intercept 0?

Question 4 Hopefully students should spot that the inclusion of $-x^2$ in the equation causes the shape of the graph to be an 'n-shaped' curve.

Question 5 Ensure students realise that they will need to construct and use their own table of values in order to find the points that lie on the curve. In part **a** make sure they realise that the graph will have a minimum y-coordinate that is lower than –3, that the graph will have a u-shaped curve between (–1, –3) and (0, –3) and not just a horizontal line. Stress that estimates should be as accurate as possible and that using graph paper could improve the accuracy.

Questions 6 and **7** You may wish to allow students to use calculators for these questions If this is the case they should put the x^2 term in brackets, this is particularly important for negative values of x.

Question 8 You may wish to go through part **f** as a whole group. Remind students they can check their factorisation be expanding the resulting brackets.

Question 9 As an extension task you could ask students to complete a table of values, then draw the graph for part **c**. When substituting into $2x^2$ ensure students realise they need to square before multiplying by 2.

Simplification – Skills

Students should concentrate on practising the plotting of quadratic functions using a table. Ensure that negative x values are correctly dealt with.

Extension – Skills

Challenge students to draw the graph of $y = x^3$ for values of x from –3 to 3

Recap – Applications

1 a Copy and complete the tables of values for each of these functions:

A $y = 6 - x^2$

x	-3	-2	-1	0	1	2	3
y					5		

B $y = x^2 + 4x + 4$

x	-4	-3	-2	-1	0	1	2
y							16

(**A** -3, 2, 5, 6, 5, 2, -3; **B** 4, 1, 0, 1, 4, 9, 16)

b For each function draw the graph of the function for the values in your table.

c For each function write:

i the value of the y-intercept

ii the coordinates of the turning point

iii the value of the x-intercepts

iv the equation of the line of symmetry.

(**A i** (0, 6) **ii** (0, 6) **iii** $x = \pm\sqrt{6}$ **iv** $x = 0$)

(**B i** (0, 4) **ii** (-2, 0) **iii** $x = -2, x = -2$)

Plenary – Applications

Can you find values of x and y that fit the equation $x^2 + y^2 = 25$?

Hint that the answers are integers and lie between –5 and 5 inclusive. Encourage students to start with a table.

Can you draw it?

(A circle, centre at (0, 0) with a radius of 5 units.)

Exercise commentary – Applications

Question 1 Encourage students to complete part **a** by substituting rather than factorising. This reinforces the understanding that a root is a value such that $f(x) = 0$.

Question 2 Ask students if they can find a way to write down the turning point without drawing the graph (use the symmetry of the curve to find the x-coordinate and substitute into $f(x)$ to find the y-coordinate).

Question 3 Remind students that a y-intercept is always a value $(0, a)$ so a curve with y-intercept 0 passes through (0, 0). They can tell 0 is a root if they can identify that it has y-intercept 0.

Question 4 You may wish to cover part **c** as a whole class, see if the students can tell you what effect having $2x^2$ at the start of the equation will have on the shape of the graph.

Question 5 Some students may need to look back to chapter 13 to remember how to interpret a Venn diagram. Peer assessment could be used to good effect here.

Questions 6 and **7** If using graphing software to answer these questions ensure all students are familiar with it and understand how to use it, remind them to make sure that the ranges of x and y-values are suitable and sufficient to see the shape of the graph. Encourage everyone to think about the shape of the graph before plotting the graph and double check that they get the shape that they expect. Students could also read through the second example on page 374 if they are still finding these types of questions difficult.

Question 8 Reinforce the fact that the solutions are the roots of the equation and are found when the graph cuts the x-axis. Show the students examples of quadratic graphs with two solutions, one solution and no solutions.

Question 9 In this question students begin to explore what effect simple transformations have on a quadratic curve. Encourage students to write down a statement summarising their findings for each question. As an extension you could ask them to investigate what effect changing a has on the graph $y = ax^2$.

Question 10 This is a good opportunity to clarify the meaning of the word 'root'. It is often taken to mean the solution to $f(x) = 0$ but in truth simply means solution. Students who take the more narrow description as a definition may get confused with questions of the form $f(x) = g(x)$.

Simplification – Applications

Give students pre-drawn axes and tables. Emphasise that it is the *interpretation* which is most important. If needed, provide the graphs already drawn.

Extension – Applications

This question extends the use of a quadratic graph to the solution of an inequality:

- Draw the graph of $y = 8 + 2x - x^2$ for values of x from –3 to +5
- Use your graph to find the range of values of x for which $5 + 2x - x^2 > 3$

  ($-1.45 < x < 3.45$)

18.2 Sketching functions

Objectives

① **A12** Recognise, sketch and interpret graphs of simple cubic functions and the reciprocal function.

Useful resources

Mini whiteboards, graph-plotting tool, 2 mm graph paper, pre-drawn axes and tables

Starter – Skills

What happens to the sign if you square a negative?
(The number becomes positive.)
What happens if you cube a negative?
(It stays negative.)

Give examples to back up these statements.

What value will $(-1)^5$ have? (–1)
What value will $(-1)^4$ have? (1)
What can you say about the powers of a negative number? (If the power is even then the answer is positive, if the power is odd the answer is negative.)

Teaching notes – Skills

Ask for examples of equations that give straight lines; then parabolas (quadratics). Sketch some graphs. Ask what makes the graph a curve. Elicit that the x^2 term produces a symmetrical curve.

Some equations produce more complex shapes, for example $y = x^3$. Ask students to complete this table.

x	–3	–2	–1	0	1	2	3
y	–27	–8	–1	0	1	8	27

Draw axis from 30 to –30 for y; use each square for two units; x-axis from –3 to 3, use two squares for each unit.

Use a whole page to draw the graph. Why do you get such a different sort of graph? (Because of the x^3 term.) Repeat for $y = -x^3$. How is the shape different?

Ask students to draw the graph of $y = \frac{1}{x}$ by making a table of values. Take x values from –4 to 4. Can you find the y value if $x = 0$? (No – error message on calculator.)

The graph is known as a reciprocal or a hyperbolic graph (a rectangular hyperbola). It has curves that stretch towards infinity. The curve approaches the axes in this case, but never touches either of them.

The lines that the curves approach are known as 'asymptotes'.

Plenary – Skills

Use the graph of $y = \frac{1}{x}$ from the main lesson to sketch the graphs of $y = \frac{2}{x}$ and $y = -\frac{1}{x}$.

Exercise commentary – Skills

Question 1 A likely problem here is errors when substituting negative values in part **b**. Remind students to count the negative signs – an even number of negatives will multiply to give a positive.

Question 2 Watch out for students joining up the two parts of the reciprocal graph. If this occurs, encourage them to describe what happens to y when x is 0.1, 0.01, 0.001, …

Questions 3 and **4** 'Sketch the graph' is often interpreted as 'plot the graph' by students. Remind them that when you 'sketch' a graph you do not plot all the points but instead find key features of the graph using the equation (such as intercepts, gradients for straight-line graphs, turning points for quadratic graphs, etc.) and use these to show the shape and where the graph cuts the axes.

Question 5 In each case discuss how to determine whether the curve will be a 'u-shaped' or 'n-shaped' curve. Remind students to label on their sketches key points that they have been given.

Question 6 Recap on how to find the roots when the equation has been factorised. Explain that once they expand the brackets they can see if the function has a positive or negative value of x^2 and hence are able to determine the correct orientation to draw the curve. Also remind students that they can substitute in $x = 0$ to find where the graph cuts the y-axis.

Question 7 Prior to this challenging question make sure students are familiar with the shape of a cubic graph and in particular draw their attention to the fact that they may have 1, 2 or 3 roots.

Question 8 Show students a reciprocal graph, you could use the one in the final example on page 372. Emphasise the fact that the graph is rotationally symmetrical, has two parts that don't meet and that the curves do not touch the axes. Encourage students to think about what the y-coordinate would be when the x-coordinate is 1, 2, 3, … in each case.

Question 9 Students could check the accuracy of their answers using graphing software.

Questions 10 and **11** Encourage students to create a general statement for each transformation, to test their statement and make sure it applies in all situations.

Simplification – Skills

Pre-drawn tables and axes can be used to help students set out their work neatly and provide them with a structure.

Extension – Skills

Students could be given an example of a quartic equation which gives a 'w'-shaped graph and asked to plot it, for example $y = x^4 - 4x^2 + 1$.

Recap – Applications

1 a Copy and complete the tables of values for each of these functions.

A $y = 3 - x^3$

x	-3	-2	-1	0	1	2	3
y	30						

B $y = \frac{2}{x}$

x	-5	-4	-3	-2	-1	1	2	3	4	5
y										

(**A** 30, 11, 4, 0, 2, -5, -24;

B -0.4, -0.5, $-\frac{2}{3}$ -1, -2, 2, 1, $\frac{2}{3}$, 0.5, 0.4)

b Draw the graph of the function of each function.

c For each function, write:

i the value of the y-intercept

ii the value of the x-intercepts

(**A i** (0, 3) **ii** $x = 1.4$ (2sf)

B i No y-intercept **ii** no roots)

Plenary – Applications

Present the function $y = x^4 - 5x^2 + 4$

This is called a quartic. Take integer x values from –3 to 3 inclusive and sketch it.

You could also find points where the quartic crosses the x-axis by solving first for x^2 and then for x.

Exercise commentary – Applications

Question 1 Students need to be clear about the shape of each type of graph and be able to match this to the correct equation. A linear graph is a straight-line graph and can be written in the form $y = mx + c$. A quadratic graph is a 'u-shaped' and the function contains an x^2 term. A cubic graph is an 's-shaped' curve and the function contains an x^3 term. A reciprocal graph has two separate parts and contains a $\frac{n}{x}$ term.

Question 2 Working through the first example given on page 374 would be wise before asking students to complete these questions. Show them that in these questions the x-axis is called the s-axis and the y-axis is called the P-axis. Discuss how in part **iii** the maximum value of P is needed and this will be found at the maximum value for the graph, recap on how to find this if need be using the symmetrical properties of the graph.

Question 3 In order to answer part **b** encourage students to think about what happens to the profit when s is below 15 or above 60.

Question 4 Students will need to draw a sketch to complete this question.

Question 5 This may be a good question to complete as a whole class. Explain that this type of question is often much easier to visualise and hence answer when a graph has been sketched. Take it step by step asking questions such as, 'What shape graph will be produced?' 'Where will the graph cut the axes ?' 'How does knowing this help us with part **a**?' 'How can we establish the maximum height as needed in part **b**?' Model sketching the graph as you ask these questions.

Question 6 Encourage students to narrow down possibilities by first looking at the shape of the graph and matching possible options. Then ask them to consider the roots, how many roots are there? Are they just positive? Or is one positive and one negative? Remind students they can double check their factorising by expanding the brackets.

Questions 7 and **8** Ensure students are familiar with the shape of a cubic graph and demonstrate how all the roots can be found from the factorised form. Make sure they label key coordinates on their sketches, such as where the graph cuts the axes.

Simplification – Applications

Students could be given pre-drawn axes and tables and work out their points step-by-step.

Extension – Applications

Students could be invited to plot two curves on the same set of axes and asked to find, approximately, the points of intersection.

18.3 Real-life graphs

Objectives

① **A14** Plot and interpret graphs (including reciprocal graphs) and graphs of non-standard functions in real contexts

Useful resources

Different shaped clear containers and a jug of water, mini whiteboards, pre-drawn axes

Starter – Skills

A robot is given these instructions for running a bath.

1 Turn on the taps.

2 When the bath is $\frac{3}{4}$ full the task is complete.

What will happen if the robot follows these instructions? What is wrong with these instructions? (Did not mention putting in the plug, does not tell you to turn off the taps, and does not take any notice of the temperature of the bath.)

Teaching notes – Skills

Draw a number of different-shaped containers. In each case ask students to imagine filling the container with a constant flow of water; as the water pours in the depth will increase, but in some containers the speed at which the depth is increasing changes. Think of filling a water bottle at the sink. The depth increases steadily, then suddenly the water rushes to the top. Demonstrate with some different shaped transparent containers and water from a jug. With the whole class, sketch the shape of each graph on the board. Emphasise that time is always plotted on the horizontal axis. Ask what is happening at each part of the graph. Ensure students appreciate the difference between a sudden change in depth of water which is shown by a steep gradient and a gradual change shown by a shallow gradient.

Plenary – Skills

Ask students to use whiteboards and list three or four key advice points they would give to other students about reading a graph. Share some of the suggestions, building up a general list of recommendations from the students.

Exercise commentary – Skills

Question 1 Challenge students to put an equation to this line graph. What do the y-intercept and gradient represent in this case?

Question 2 Emphasise that on this graph the y-axis is the speed not the distance. Is the train travelling at a constant speed or stationary at 2.5 minutes? Who can justify why?

Question 3 Ensure students notice that this graph is a distance–time graph. Recap that speed can be found by dividing the distance by the time and that the speed is faster when the gradient of the line is steeper.

Question 4 If students find it difficult to answer part **b** ask them 'who has travelled further after one minute?' Encourage students to write as much as they need to in this question, they can rationalise their answers after they have thought the situation through.

Question 5 Encourage students to use a process of elimination in order to establish the type of graph shown and hence answer part **c**.

Question 6 You may need to recap on how to use a distance–time graph to draw a speed–time graph. Remind students how to calculate the speed for each section of the journey and mention that the speed will be 0 when the graph is horizontal on the distance–time graph. Discuss part **b** as a group and make sure students realise that in real life speed would not have these constant intervals.

Simplification – Skills

Students often find it very difficult to construct axes. Highlight the equal space between intervals (including 0 and 1). Alternatively, provide students with pre-drawn axes.

Extension – Skills

Students could be given bottles with complicated shapes or asked to draw their own bottle and challenge a partner to sketch the resulting graph.

Recap – Applications

1 The velocity–time graph of a plane, flying between two airports, is shown:

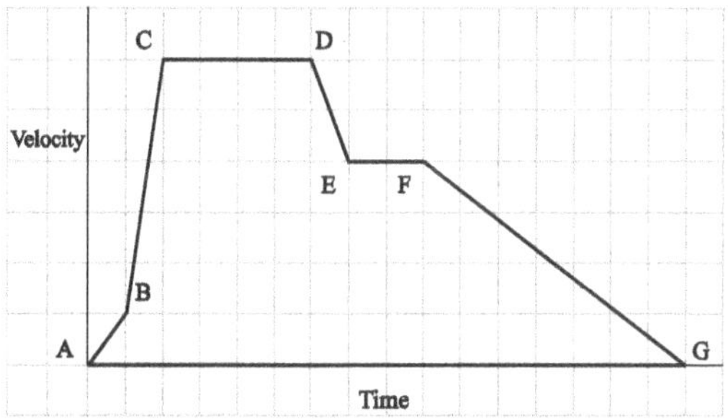

Comment on the movement of the plane during each of the lettered sections.

(AB: Taxiing to runway, small acceleration;
BC: Takeoff and climb to cruising height - larger acceleration;
CD: Constant velocity at cruising height;
DE: Deceleration to lower velocity;
EF: Constant velocity at cruising height;
FG: Deceleration to lower velocity and landing at airport)

Plenary – Applications

£1 = \$1.80 and \$1 = €0.80. Ask students to draw a conversion graph for pounds to Euros.

£	0	5	10
\$	0	9	18
€	0	7.20	14.20

Exercise commentary – Applications

Question 1 This would be a good question to discuss as a whole class. It would be wise to explain that the graphs represent water being poured in at a constant rate. Who can match up a graph with a container and justify their answer? Promote discussions about how the shape of the container would affect the depth, would the depth get deeper more quickly? If so is this change gradual or sudden? These visualisation questions can be challenging, a good support activity is to complete a practical experiment using a variety of different vessels. Students should predict how rapidly the water level will rise at different stages if water is poured in at a constant rate and then test their assumptions by filling the vessels.

Question 2 Make sure students realise that the total number of sandwiches needs to be shared amongst the number of people, if there are 20 people they get an average of 15 sandwiches each (300 ÷ 20), if there are 40 people they get an average of 7.5 sandwiches each (300 ÷ 40) etc.

Question 3 Allow students to use graph paper for this question. Ensure they use a scale that accommodates all the points. Once the graph has been plotted parts **b** and **c** would make effective whole-class discussions. Which types of functions are ruled out by the information given in part **c**? Are there any other values that students would like to be given in order to confirm their choices for part **b**?

Question 5 Students will initially adopt a trial and error type of approach but try and steer them towards using a trial and improvement approach where they think about the impact that changing each number within the equation has on the shape of the graph.

Simplification – Applications

Students can be given pre-drawn axes (with scales) for some of the questions. Further examples which show proportional relationships can be used.

Extension – Applications

Ask students to find the real charging structures of various utility companies and work out which you should be with based on your approximate usage.

18 Graphs 2

Key outcomes	Quick check
A11 Identify and interpret roots, intercepts, turning points of quadratic functions graphically. A18 Find approximate solutions using a graph.	**1** Use the graph of $y = x^2 - 2x - 3$ to write down **a** the y-intercept of the graph **b** the x-intercepts of the graph **c** the roots of the equation $x^2 - 2x - 3 = 0$ **d** the coordinates of the turning point of the curve.
A12 Recognise, sketch and interpret graphs of simple cubic functions, the reciprocal function $y = \frac{1}{x}$ with $x \neq 0$.	**2 a** Complete a table of values for $y = x^3$ for values of x between –3 and 3. (–27, –8, –1, 0, 1, 8, 27) **b** Sketch the graphs of $y = x^3$ and $y = \frac{1}{x} (x \neq 0)$ for values of x between –3 and 3. 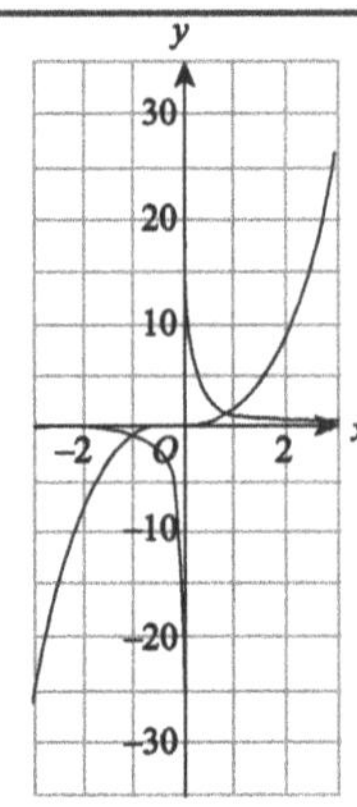
A14 Plot and interpret graphs (including reciprocal graphs) and graphs of non-standard functions in real contexts, to find approximate solutions to problems such as simple kinematic problems involving distance, speed and acceleration.	**3 a** How far was travelled in the first 3 hours? (9 km) **b** What was the average speed over the 4 hours? (4 km/h) 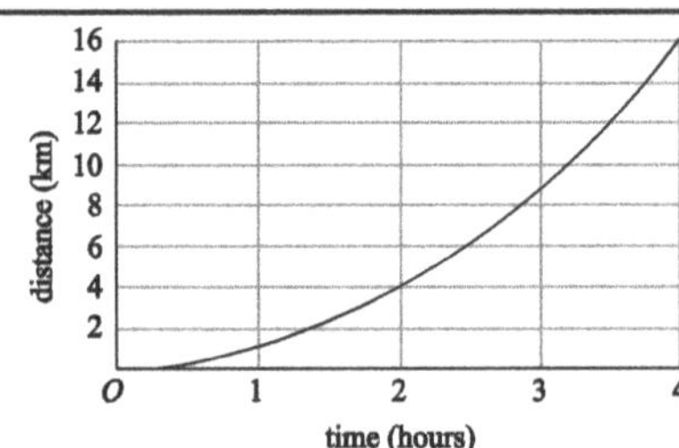 **5 a** Plot a speed–time graph for the information in the table. **b** What is happening to the speed during the first 5 s? (Increasing) **c** What is happening between 5 s and 7 s?(Constant speed 6 m/s) **d** What is the rate of change of speed during the final 2 s? (3 m/s^2) 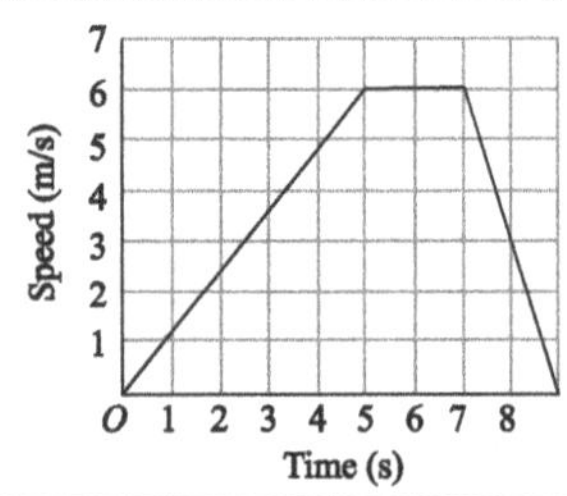

Time (s)	0	5	7	9
Speed (m/s)	0	6	6	0

Misconceptions and challenges	Solutions
Students interpret the word 'sketch' artistically, and do not see that sketches of quadratic graphs must include specific mathematical information.	Model how to begin a sketch by marking the x and y-intercepts and then looking at the gradient before sketching.
Students join the points of a quadratic function with straight lines.	Students need practice sketching curves, especially turning points. Some students will find it easier to begin from the turning point, and drawing the curve in two arcs from the centre.
Students do not understand how cubics behave for negative values of x.	Students' understanding of how negative numbers behave for different powers can hamper their understanding of cubics. Get students to look at what happens to the powers of –1.
Students struggle to understand how reciprocal graphs behave for very small values of x.	Look at unit fractions, and how they diminish as the denominator increases. This can be extended to looking at larger numerators as well, through questions such as, 'if $\frac{2000}{x} < 1$, what could x be?'

Misconceptions and challenges	Solutions
Students do not recognise the shapes of common functions.	It may well be that students have not linked the shape with *the reasons for* that shape. Students should be in the habit of trying out specific cases (what happens to a function at $x = 0$, for large x, for negative x...).
When looking at functions from real-life contexts (including distance, speed and time), students find it difficult to interpret the graph in relation to its context. Students frequently confuse changes of distance with changes in speed, for example.	Ideally, introduce these graphs through a practical activity. This offers an excellent opportunity to make cross-curricular links with science (especially physics).

Review question commentary

Students need to understand that, as the value of y is zero on the x-axis then setting $y = 0$ in any equation will give the roots for x. Similarly, setting $x = 0$ will give the y-intercepts.

Students should draw their own axes. Scales should be even and axes labelled.

Question 1 (18.1) – Students should be able to identify the x-coordinate of the turning point from the symmetry of the curve.

Question 2 (18.2) – If students have an approximate idea of what this curve will look like then it will help them not to make errors with the negative x-values.

Question 3 (18.2) – If students are stuck ask them what has happened to 'y' and how they would draw this on the graph. Remind students that '$y =$' lines are horizontal.

Question 4 (18.2) – This can just be a sketch showing the approximate shape.

Question 5 (18.2) – As an extension ask students to think of further equations that could match each sketch.

Question 6 (18.3) – Remind students if necessary that speed = distance ÷ time.

Question 7 (18.3) – Some students may confuse this with a distance–time graph. A zero gradient here indicates constant speed not standing still.

Review answers

1 a (0, –5) **b** (–1, 0), (5, 0)

c –1 and 5 **d** (2, –9)

2 a $y = 16, 9, 4, 1, 0, 1, 4, 9, 16$

b

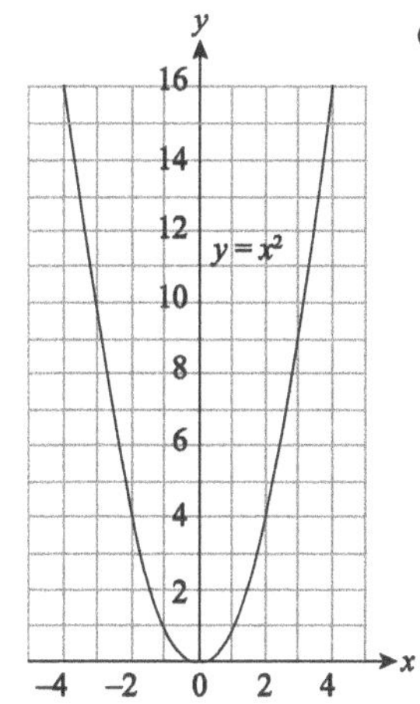

c (0, 0)

3 a

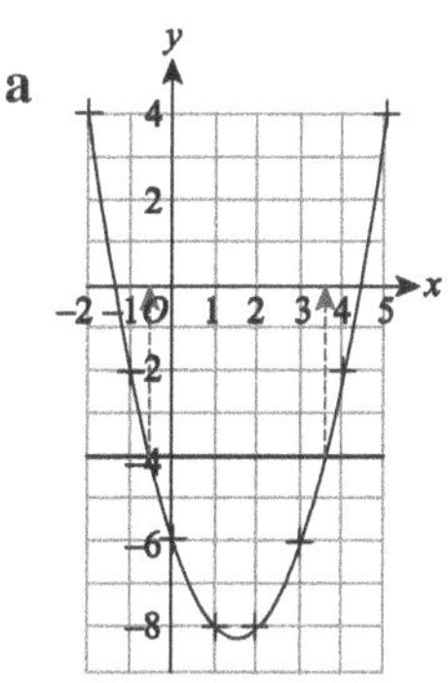

4

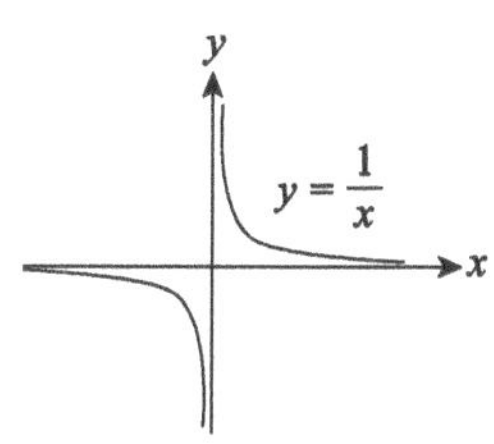

b i –1.4, 4.4 (1 dp) **ii** –0.6, 3.6 (1 dp)

5 a Reciprocal, $y = \frac{2}{x}$ **b** Linear, $y = 2x + 3$

c Quadratic, $y = x^2 + 3x$ **d** Cubic, $y = x^3 - 4x$

6 a 0.25 km/min or 15 km/h **b** 20 km/h

7 a

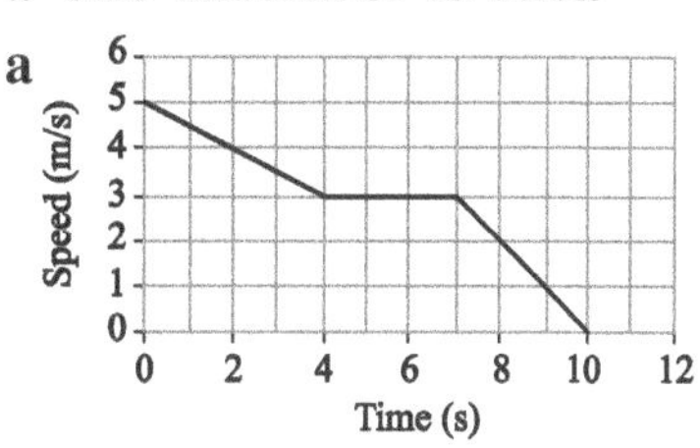

b Speed is decreasing. **c** Constant speed, 3 m/s

d 1 m/s^2

Assessment 18

Question 1 – 12 marks

a

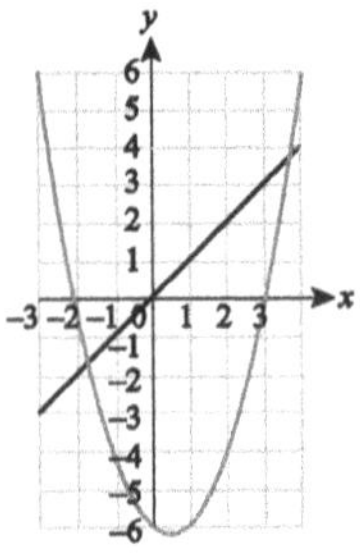

Correctly drawn and labelled axes. [B1]
Minus 1 mark for each incorrectly calculated and drawn point [B4]
Smoothly drawn and labelled lines. [B1]

Allow ± 0.2 in coordinates read off the graphs.

b (−1.6, −1.6) and (3.6, 3.6), [F1]

c (0.5, −6.25) [F1]

d $x = -2, 3$ [F2]

e $(x - 3)(x + 2) = 0$ [M1]
$x = -2, 3$ They are the same [A1]

Question 2 – 8 marks

a $d = 8.7, 9.3, 10, 10.7, 11.3, 12, 12.7, 13.3, 14, 14.7$
Minus 1 mark for each error. [B2]

b

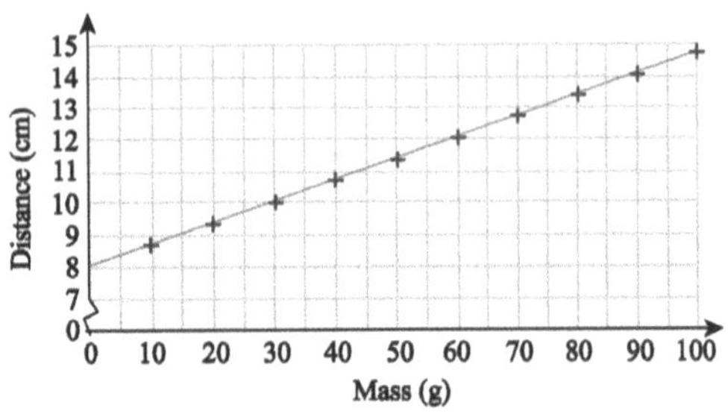

Correctly drawn and labelled axes [B1]
Correctly plotted points with a straight line through them. [B1]

c **i** 13 cm [F1]
ii 15 g [F1]

d $\frac{1}{15}$ [B1]

e 8 cm [B1]

Question 3 – 9 marks

a $d = 0, 6, 17, 33, 53, 79, 110, 146, 187, 233, 283$
Minus 1 mark for each error. [B3]

b

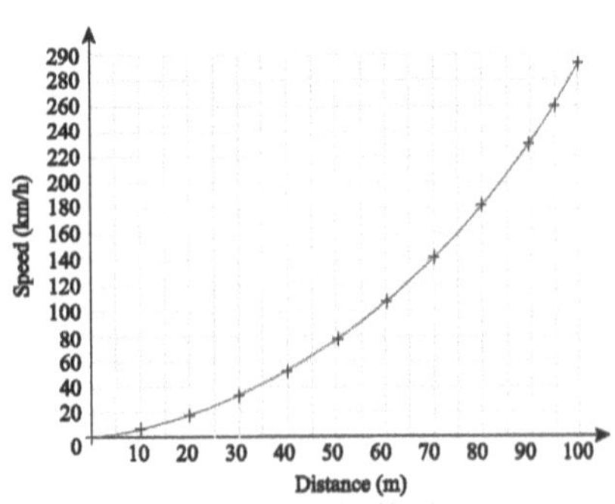

Correctly drawn and labelled axes [B1]
Correctly plotted points [F1]
Smooth curve through points. [B1]

c **i** 24 m [F1]
ii 58 m [F1]
iii 174 m [F1]

Question 4 – 14 marks

a $y = -2, 0.25, 3.25, 4, 4.25, 4, 3.25, 2, 0.25, -2$
Minus 1 mark for each error. [B3]

b

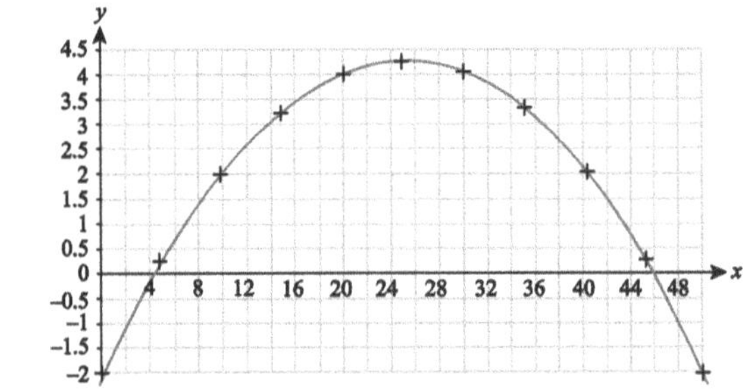

Correctly drawn and labelled axes [B1]
Correctly plotted points [F1]
Smooth curve through points. [B1]

c Allow ±£100 and ± 50 in coordinates read off the graphs.

i	£1690	[F1]	**ii**	£2688	[F1]
iii	1793, 3207	[F1]	**iv**	£4250	[F1]
v	2500	[F1]	**vi**	438	[F1]
vii	4562	[F1]	**viii**	1177 to 3823	[F1]

Question 5 – 4 marks

a E **b** C **c** B **d** A **e** D
Lose 1 mark for each *pair* of incorrect answers. [B4]

Question 6 – 17 marks

a Correct 'table' of values; lose 1 mark for each error.
0, 21, 24, 15, 0, −15, −24, −21, 0 [B3]

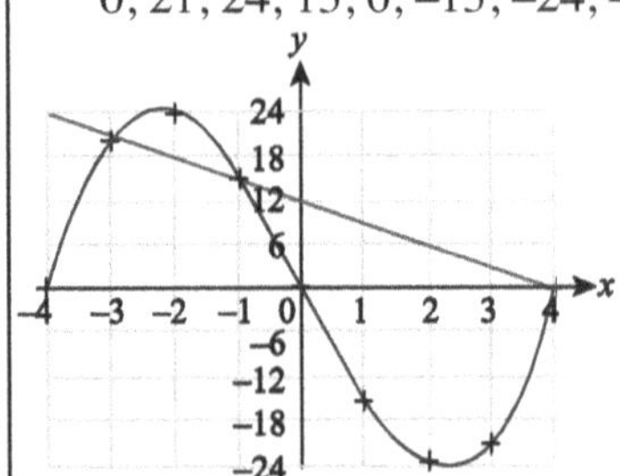

Correctly drawn and labelled axes. [B1]
Correctly drawn points. [B1]
Smoothly drawn and labelled line. [B1]

b Correctly drawn straight line [B2]

c $x = 4$ [B1]

d $x = -4, 0, 4$ [B3]

e (−3, 21), (−1, 15), (4, 0) [F3]

f $x^3 - 13x - 12 = 0$ [B2]

Question 7 – 11 marks

a $y = 36 \div x$ [B1]

b A 'table' of values with sufficient points to draw a smooth curve; lose 1 mark for each error.

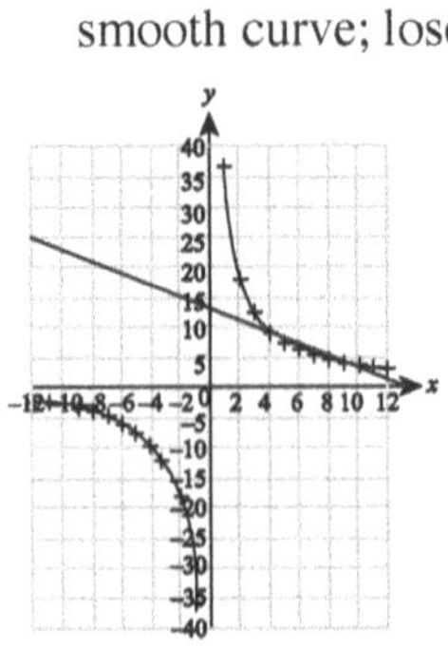

(±12, ±3), (±9, ±4), (±6, ±6), (±4, ±9), (±3, ±12), (±2, ±18), (±11, ±36);
no value for $x = 0$ [B3]
Correctly drawn and labelled axes. [B1]
Correctly drawn points. [B1]
Smoothly drawn and labelled line. [B1]

c Accurately drawn line $x + y = 36$ [B2]
Points of intersection (4, 9) and (9, 4) [B1]
Solutions are mirrors 4 × 9 and 9 × 4 [B1]

Pythagoras and trigonometry

Learning outcomes

G6 Apply Pythagoras' theorem to obtain simple proofs.

G19 Apply the concepts of congruence and similarity, including the relationships between lengths.

G20 Know the formulae for: Pythagoras' theorem, $a^2 + b^2 = c^2$, and the trigonometric ratios, $\sin\theta$ = opposite/hypotenuse, $\cos\theta$ = adjacent/hypotenuse and $\tan\theta$ = opposite/adjacent; apply them to find angles and lengths in right-angled triangles in two dimensional figures.

G21 Know the exact values of $\sin\theta$ and $\cos\theta$ for $\theta = 0°, 30°, 45°, 60°$ and $90°$; know the exact value of $\tan\theta$ for $\theta = 0°, 30°, 45°$ and $60°$.

G25 Apply addition and subtraction of vectors, multiplication of vectors by a scalar, and diagrammatic and column representations of vectors.

R12 Compare lengths, make links to similarity (including trigonometric ratios).

Prior knowledge

Check-in skill

- Substitute numerical values into expressions involving squares.
- Calculate squares and square roots.

Online resources

MyMaths 1053, 1112, 1131, 1133, 1134, 1135, 1145

InvisiPen videos

Skills: 19Sa – c Applications: 19Aa – d

Kerboodle assessment

Online Skills Test 19 Chapter Test 19

Development and links

Pythagoras' theorem has important applications in mathematics, science, engineering and geography and is used in surveying, navigation, construction, astronomy and optics. In construction, Pythagoras theorem is used to make sure that the corners of foundations are completely square. Ancient Egyptian land surveyors used a method based on dividing a rope into twelve equal parts using knots or paint to create a 3 : 4 : 5 right angled triangle. In the packaging industry, surface area influences the cost of the packaging but volume determines the amount of product that the package can hold.

Chapter investigation

Suggest students start by using a scale drawing: a height of 4.5 cm and hypotenuse of 20 cm gives a base of 19.5 cm; equivalent to 195 m. Answers are likely to differ according to the accuracy of students' drawings.

Introduce Pythagoras' theorem [**19.1**] which gives the exact answer 194.8717...= 195 (3 sf). Develop the investigation by asking for the length of the cables required for different horizontal ranges.

Pythagorean triples can be presented as special cases with whole number sides; three directly relevant cases are [45, 60, 75], [45, 108, 117] and [45, 200, 205]. By using scale drawings to measure the angle of elevation, which case would make the safest ski-lift?

A further variant is to suppose the ski-lift stops after travelling, say, 80 m, what is its vertical distance from the ground? This introduces similar triangles that all share the same angle of elevation and have the same, tangent, ratio of height to base. Explain how these ratios are tabulated as a function of angle so that you don't need to use scale drawings to find sides or angles. [**19.2**, **19.3**]

Show how to use the tangent function to find the height or base given the base or height and the angle of elevation and how to find the angle from the tangent ratio. Extend this to include the sine and cosine functions when you know the hypotenuse. Returning to the original scenario students should check that a 200 m cable length gives the angle 12.68...°, which is too steep, and that the minimum safe cable length is 216.4 m. How high could the lift safely go if the cable was fixed at 200 m? (41.6 m)

Suppose the engineering company builds two types of ski-lift and specifies the base and height (in m) using vectors where lift 1 = $\begin{pmatrix}200\\45\end{pmatrix}$ and lift 2 = $\begin{pmatrix}120\\20\end{pmatrix}$. [**19.4**]

What combination of lifts should be used to construct a multi-stage lift with a base of 760 m? What would be the total base and total length of cable required? The required combination is

$2\begin{pmatrix}200\\45\end{pmatrix} + 3\begin{pmatrix}120\\20\end{pmatrix} = \begin{pmatrix}760\\150\end{pmatrix}$ where the order does not matter. The height is 150 m and, using Pythagoras, the total length of cable is 774.7 m. [**19.4**]

19.1 Pythagoras' theorem

Objectives

① Know the formulae for: Pythagoras' theorem, $a^2 + b^2 = c^2$ and apply it to find lengths in right-angled triangles in two-dimensional figures.

Useful resources

Calculators in degree mode, geometry tool, mini whiteboards

Starter – Skills

Ask students to estimate square roots, for example of 10, 12, 18 and 20. Accuracy should be initially between two integer values, then to an approximate first decimal point. These can be checked with a calculator.

Teaching notes – Skills

① Remind students of the properties of equilateral, isosceles, scalene and right-angled triangles.

Draw two **right-angled** triangles with sides 6, 8, 10 and 5, 12, 13. Square each length and write it near the original length.

What is the relationship between the squared lengths of the sides?
($6^2 + 8^2 = 10^2$ and $5^2 + 12^2 = 13^2$)

Remind students of **Pythagoras' theorem**.

Students may be familiar with any of $c^2 = a^2 + b^2$ or $a^2 = b^2 + c^2$ or $h^2 = a^2 + b^2$, depending on the diagrams used in other textbooks.

Emphasise the fact that it is the squares of the two shorter sides that add to make the square of the longest side (**hypotenuse**).

Plenary – Skills

Take a straightforward question on the topic, extending it with further questions if necessary. Ask as many individual students as possible to give strategies or procedures for each stage of the question, building up the solution from the whole group. Ask others to help in corrections if necessary, or to disagree and offer alternatives, finally showing a complete and thorough solution.

Exercise commentary – Skills

Question 1 Students could memorise these squares and the corresponding square roots. Students could make a set of 30 cards with the first fifteen positive integers and the first fifteen square numbers and use them to play snap to develop rapid recognition.

Questions 3 and **4** Encourage students to complete as many of these as possible without a calculator. In question **4** students should use estimation to check their place value.

Question 5 This reinforces Pythagoras' theorem visually.

Question 6 A common error is to fail to take the square root when finding the hypotenuse. This question is a good way to introduce Pythagorean triples – can students find any other right-angled triangles with three integer sides?

Question 7 One common error here is to add the squares of the two given sides, heedless of which side the hypotenuse is. Students who make this error should be referred back to question **5** where the relationship between squared sides is more visually apparent.

Question 8 A possible error is not to halve the 60 mm when using the isosceles triangle.

Question 9 Students must take care with units in this question.

Question 10 A good reminder of the practical uses of Pythagoras' theorem.

Simplification – Skills

Students may need guidance on the correct way to set out their working. Further simple practice will almost certainly be required to cement the process in their minds.

Students may need more practice at finding the hypotenuse in order to secure their knowledge of before moving on to use it in finding a shorter side.

Extension – Skills

Ask students to research a proof of Pythagoras' theorem. Simple dissection proofs are accessible to higher ability Foundation-tier candidates.

Recap – Applications

Find the length of each missing side.

1

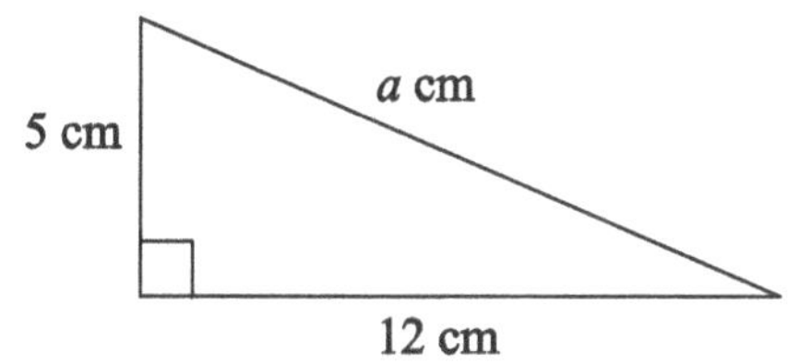

($a = 13$)

2

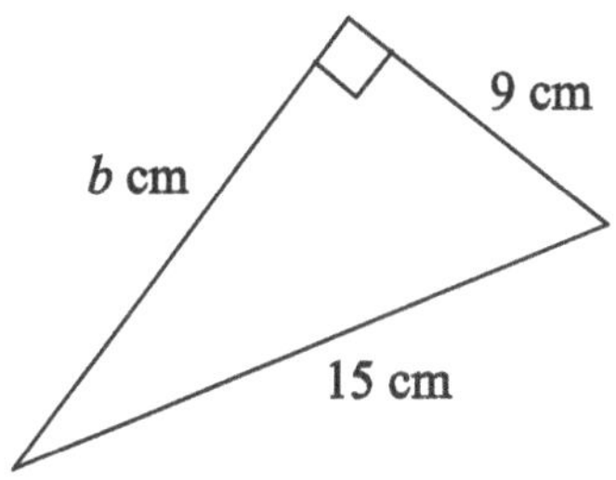

($b = 12$)

3

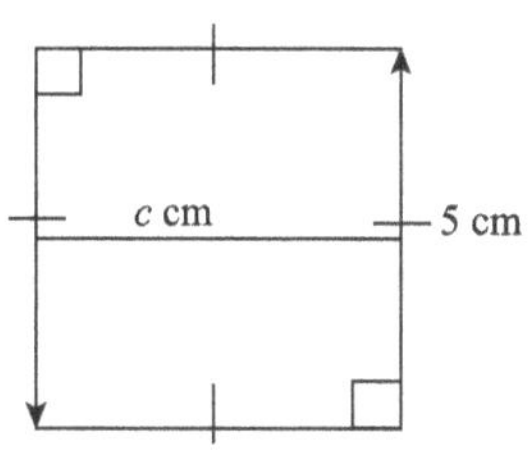

($c = \sqrt{50}$)

Plenary – Applications

Show the students the points A (1, 2), B (13, 2), C (13, 7) marked on a grid. Which journey is shorter: A to C or A to B to C? What is the length? How would we find it? By how much is it shorter? What strategies from given group advice are you using?

Exercise commentary – Applications

Question 1 A sketch reveals two right-angled triangles. Students may not notice the change of units. Refer to the first worked example on page 390.

Question 2 Encourage students to estimate the answer first.

Question 3 Students need to sketch a diagram for each part and write the lengths on it. They should pay careful attention to the difference between the two parts.

Questions 4 and **5** Students could model the situation using a desk against a wall and a ruler; if the hypotenuse is fixed but the other two sides can vary, what is the relationship between the varying sides? Can students represent this on a graph? (Shorter sides with lengths x and y obey the rule $x^2 + y^2 = c$, the graph will be the first quadrant of a circle with radius c, the square of the length of the ruler).

Question 6 Refer to the third worked example on page 390. A sketch on square grid paper which shows the right-angled triangle in each case will help avoid errors.

Question 7 This can be extended to a kinematics question: if a woman walks at 1.4 m/s how much time will the shortcut save her? (21.0 seconds)

Question 8 In part **a**, students need to draw an extra line to create right-angled triangles. A likely error is not to halve the 20 cm. In part **b**, students use Pythagoras' theorem to calculate the base length.

Questions 9 and **10** These involve the converse of Pythagoras' theorem. In question **9** part **a**, ask students to decide which side is the hypotenuse (10 cm). Then discuss the relative sizes of $6^2 + 8^2$ and 10^2. Sketch diagrams will help the students' explanations.

Question 11 In part **a** some students may assume that ABC and ACD are congruent isosceles triangles. If this assumption emerges get students to work in groups to *prove* that they cannot be isosceles or congruent.

Question 12 This multistep problem is a good candidate for poster work. Students could look out for interesting questions throughout the topic and construct a series of posters showing annotated worked examples to be used for revision later on.

Question 13 As there are many Pythagorean triples with $c < 100$, the students can be set a time limit for part **a**. Alternatively, the task can be set as a class project over several days. This question deserves a whole-class effort.

Simplification – Applications

Students will need constant reminding whether to add or subtract and a copy of both versions of the formula can be displayed on the boards for easy reference.

Extension – Applications

Ask students how they might go about finding the length of the long diagonal across the classroom. Suggest modelling the classroom and extracting triangles as a possible strategy.

Students could investigate the life and work of Pythagoras or look into the generation of Pythagorean triples in more depth, perhaps even looking at possible formulae used to generate them.

19.2 Trigonometry 1

Objectives

① Know the formulae for the trigonometric ratios:

$$\tan\theta = \frac{\text{opposite}}{\text{adjacent}}$$

② Apply the trigonometric ratios to find angles and sides in right-angled triangles.

Useful resources

Calculators in degree mode, geometry tool, mini whiteboards

Starter – Skills

Display two similar right-angled triangles, sides marked a, b, c and p, q, r. Explain that the triangles are similar – one an enlargement of the other. Record that these triangles are in the ratio 1 : 3.

Students write their answers on whiteboards: If $a = 3$ cm and $b = 4$ cm, what is the ratio of a to b? p to q?

If angle ... is ..., what size is this angle? and so on.

Teaching notes – Skills

① Recap how in similar triangles there is a constant ratio between sides. This lesson looks at the ratio between the sides in a right-angled triangle. The first step in any problem is to label the sides of the triangle as hypotenuse, opposite (to the marked angle) and adjacent (to the marked angle).

Ask students to construct right-angled triangles of differing sizes, all with a common angle of 30°, and measure the opposite and adjacent lengths. They then calculate the ratio with a calculator. Pool results to 1 significant figure (0.6). Define the tangent ratio.

② Encourage students to see tan as a function that links the size of the angle to the ratio of the sides.

$$\text{Angle} \rightarrow \tan \rightarrow \text{ratio of } \frac{\text{opposite}}{\text{adjacent}}$$

$$\text{Ratio of } \frac{\text{opposite}}{\text{adjacent}} \rightarrow \tan^{-1} \rightarrow \text{angle}$$

Check that all students have their calculators in degree mode and that they can find the $\tan^{-1}$ function.

The algebraic manipulation required when finding the length of the adjacent side using a tangent ratio may cause problems.

Plenary – Skills

Set up equations using trigonometry on the board, for example $\tan\theta = 0.5$ and $\tan\theta = 0.2$.

Ask students to label a triangle with opposite side, adjacent side and angle that correspond to each equation. Ask students to find the hypotenuse (using Pythagoras' theorem) and third angle.

Exercise commentary – Skills

Exercises **19.2S** and **19.2A** are given to calculating lengths of sides rather than angles.

Question 1 Ask students to imagine themselves standing at the vertex labelled θ and then to give names to the three sides. Ask them to name the hypotenuse.

Question 2 Refer to the first worked example on page 392, especially for parts **d**, **e**, and **f** of this question.

Question 3 Encourage students to run through the question and decide which rule to use in each part before attempting the question.

Question 4 This involves finding unknowns in the denominator. It may be worth revising simple equations such as $3 = \frac{6}{x}$ and $4.2 = \frac{5.04}{x}$ with students who struggle.

Question 5 Students can use a variety of different approaches here, encourage them to discuss the different approaches possible and make sure the inclusion of Pythagoras' theorem is mentioned here.

Question 6 A combination of trigonometry and Pythagoras makes this a challenging question that may need a whole-class approach.

Question 7 Remind students to draw sketches here and to pay attention to the units in use.

Question 8 This is deceptively challenging. A whole-class discussion may be needed to plan a strategy, e.g. finding angle *CBD* from the angle sum of a triangle leads to an easier method for calculating length *CD*.

Question 9 This deserves a whole-class approach with the teacher asking questions leading to the required results. Having completed this question, a few extra supplementary examples would help students to consolidate their results.

Question 10 In practice, a safety constraint would give a range of values for the base angle. If the base angle has to be between 70° and 80°, what are the corresponding values for d and h? (d between 0.87 m and 1.71 m, h between 4.70 m and 4.92 m) Does a small value for the base angle lead to a maximum or minimum value of d? (Maximum)

Simplification – Skills

Students should be encouraged to draw labelled sketches of the triangles and check that their answers are sensible.

Extension – Skills

Students could be provided with a practical example, using bearings perhaps, where unknown distances or angles have to be found from the information given.

Recap – Applications

1 Calculate to 2 decimal places

a tan 27° (0.51) **b** tan 51° (1.23)

2 Calculate to the nearest degree

a $\tan^{-1}(0.7)$ (35°) **b** $\tan^{-1}(1.6)$ (58°)

3 Find the angles marked by letters to 1 decimal place.

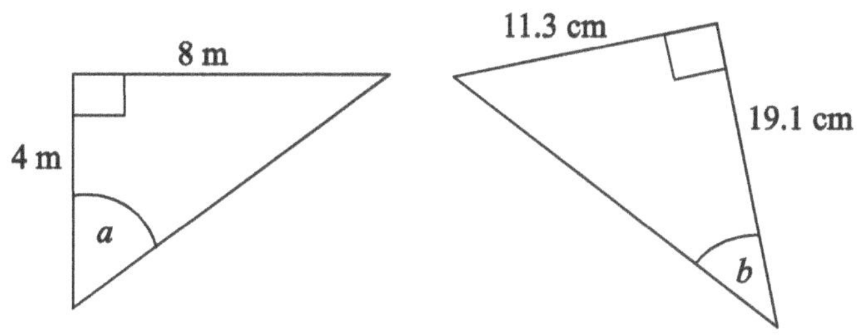

(63.4°) (30.6°)

Plenary – Applications

Discuss appropriate accuracy in questions involving trigonometrical ratios. Emphasise that in an exam, accuracy is often specified. However, 3 significant figures are quite standard for most purposes.

Exercise commentary – Applications

Questions 1 and **2** Refer to the first worked example on page 394. For question **2** part **b**, the major reason is likely to be that the base of the tower is higher than the beach.

Question 3 This presents a good opportunity for students to research sundials.

Question 4 This involves the sine ratio, and finding the opposite side. Students should not just respond 'yes' or 'no' (no, in this case), but give a clear reason.

Questions 5, 6 and **9** The word '*exact*' implies that surds should be used when using 30° and 45°. For question **5**, refer to the second worked example on page 394. Questions **6** and **9** need extra lines to create right-angled triangles. In question **9**, students need to recall the size of the angles of an equilateral triangle.

Question 7 As an extension students could imagine the plane altering its angle to the horizontal to 28° after the first kilometre and travelling at this angle for a further 2 kilometres. What is its height now? (1.47 km)

Question 8 Just calculating the opposite side is insufficient; students will need to take into account Beth's height.

Question 10 A multi-step question, students will need to find the height of the building, and subtract this to find the height of the flag. Discuss a sensible degree of accuracy, and encourage students to check if their answer is sensible. Ensure that they give units in their answer (metres).

Question 11 In problems like this, encourage students to estimate yes or no by looking at it – in real-life situations they won't always have a calculator at hand. Students should appreciate that this is an isosceles triangle, and therefore they can split it into two right-angled triangles (this deductive leap should start to become intuitive with familiarity). This is a multi-step problem involving sine; encourage students to show all their workings out coherently on separate lines, and discourage rounding too early (if they do, you can use this as a learning opportunity, and involve the whole class in discussion about when to round).

Simplification – Applications

Students should be encouraged to draw labelled sketches of the triangles and check that their answers are sensible.

Extension – Applications

Students could be asked to measure the height of a school building using a clinometer, trundle wheel, sketch diagram and the tangent ratio.

Trigonometry 2

Objectives

① Know the formulae for the trigonometric ratios:

$$\sin \theta = \frac{\text{opposite}}{\text{hypotenuse}}$$

$$\cos \theta = \frac{\text{adjacent}}{\text{hypotenuse}}$$

$$\tan \theta = \frac{\text{opposite}}{\text{adjacent}}$$

② Apply the trigonometric ratios to find angles and sides in right-angled triangles.

Useful resources

Calculators in degree mode, geometry tool, mini whiteboards

Starter – Skills

Write these equations on the board and ask students to solve them.

$0.5 = \frac{x}{16}$ $(x = 8)$ $12x = 108$ $(x = 11)$

$\frac{m}{2} = 0.72$ $(m = 1.44)$ $\frac{r}{9.7} = 0.1$ $(r = 0.97)$

Extend to harder examples of the type

$\frac{3}{v} = 0.6$ $(v = 5)$

Teaching notes – Skills

① In this lesson, all three trigonometrical ratios are used to find angles. Check that all students have their calculators in degree mode and that they can find the inverse trigonometry functions.

As before, students should label the sides of the triangle, identify the ratio which is needed and write down the equation to find the angle.

② Encourage students to use the bracket function on their calculators so that to find x from the equation $\cos x = \frac{6}{10.5}$ the key operations are $\cos^{-1}(6 \div 10.5) =$.

Recap the steps in solving trigonometry questions.

- Label the sides, hyp, opp, adj.
- Identify the two sides that are involved in the question.
- Select the formula that uses the two sides identified.
- Write the equation using the numbers and letters given.
- Solve the equation.

Remind students that they always require an inverse function when finding an angle.

Plenary – Skills

Ask students to use a calculator to find values of cos θ and sin θ up to 360°, using 20° intervals. Plot the values on a graph of sin θ against cos θ.

Ask students what they notice.

Exercise commentary – Skills

Question 1 Students practise using the inverse trigonometric functions on their calculators.

Question 2 In parts **b** and **d** students should be aware there are two possible answers.

Question 3 Students have to name the sides of the triangle before choosing the correct trig function. Refer to the first worked example on page 396.

Questions 4 and **5** Trigonometry and Pythagoras are both used as required, as is the angle sum of a triangle. There are three unknowns in each diagram and students will need different strategies in each part. It may help to discuss the possible strategies as a class first. Refer to the second worked example on page 396.

Questions 6 to **9** These questions are similar to question **4** in that students call on trigonometry, Pythagoras' theorem and the angle sum of a triangle as required. Remind them that, where possible, it is better to use the data given rather than data which the student has calculated, as it reduces the chance of error.

Question 10 Students need to draw a right-angled triangle (not a triangle as on the sign!) and label it with the given data. Note that 'the hill goes down by 20 m' means that it drops vertically by 20 m.

Simplification – Skills

Students should be encouraged to draw labelled sketches of the triangles and check that their answers are sensible.

Extension – Skills

Students could be provided with a practical example, using bearings perhaps, where unknown distances or angles have to be found from the information given.

Recap – Applications

Find the angles marked by letters.

1

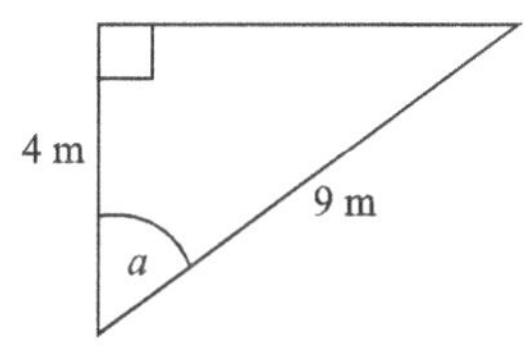

(63.6°)

2

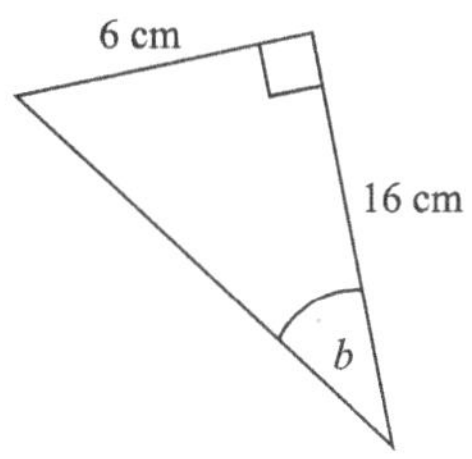

(20.6°)

3

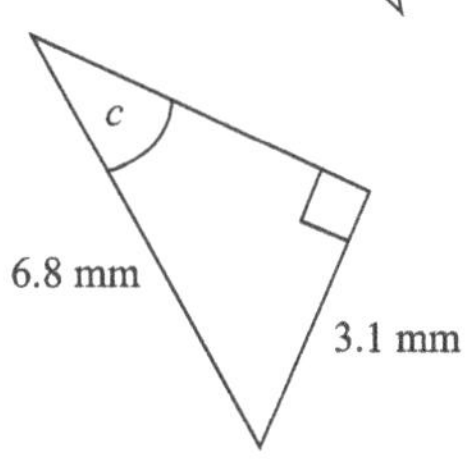

(27.1°)

Plenary – Applications

Discuss appropriate accuracy in questions involving trigonometrical ratios. Emphasise that in an exam, accuracy is often specified. However, 3 significant figures are quite standard for most purposes.

Exercise commentary – Applications

The beginning of the exercise asks students to check for reasonable answers. Discuss this with them.

Questions 1 to **3** could be solved by scale drawings (see **7.1S** and **7.1A**, pages 140–143). Ask which method is the more accurate. Refer to the worked example on page 398. Remind students that bearings are measured clockwise from the north and that 'the bearing of *A* from *B*' means that you imagine yourself at *B* looking towards *A*.

Questions 5 and **6** Students need to make a sketch for each question, For question **5**, they add an extra line and find *h* in two parts.

Question 7 To calculate tan θ, students need to draw right-angled triangles on the graphs. As a check, they could use a protractor to find θ and then use a calculator to find its tangent.

Question 8 In part **a**, students use trigonometry but in part **b** they use angle facts they have learned earlier.

Question 9 Students draw their own diagrams, add extra lines and create right-angled triangles.

Question 10 Students draw a right-angled triangle and enter 40° as one angle. Ask them what the third angle of the triangle is. Label the sides *a*, *b*, *c* (in any order) and so write the two values required.

Question 11 In both parts, as a first step, use Pythagoras' theorem to find the length of the third side.

Simplification – Applications

Students will benefit from the questions being grouped according to the ratios used. Also, encourage clear labelling of the sides and the use of either ratio triangles or SOHCAHTOA.

Extension – Applications

Students could be given further problems that require either multi-stage calculations or the application of trigonometrical ratios to practical problems.

19.4 Vectors

Objectives

① Describe translations as 2D vectors.

② Apply addition and subtraction of vectors, multiplication of vectors by a scalar, and diagrammatic and column representations of vectors.

Useful resources

5 mm square grid paper, tracing paper, mini whiteboards

Starter – Skills

A football is made from 20 congruent hexagons and 12 congruent pentagons. How many vertices and edges are there? (60 vertices and 90 edges)

You could give the hint that each pentagon is surrounded on each side by hexagons.

Teaching notes – Skills

① Recap any student knowledge of vectors, for example in translation of 2D shapes (chapter 7).

In particular focus on column vectors, such as $\begin{pmatrix}3\\4\end{pmatrix}$ meaning 3 up and 4 along.

② Highlight the use of bold font in naming a vector, such as **a**, but students and teachers tend to write them with a line underneath. Also show the notation $\overrightarrow{AB}$ and emphasise that the arrow shows the direction of the vector.

Show graphically how vectors can be added and subtracted from each other, and introduce the term 'resultant vector'. Highlight the notation used for resultant vectors.

Demonstrate how you can add vectors in any order. Draw an analogy with giving the directions: 'Walk three paces forwards then two paces to the left.' The result should be the same as if the instructions were in reverse order.

Show graphically how this would look with two vectors and their resultant. Introduce the term 'commutative'.

Illustrate multiplying a vector by a scalar, by showing it as repeated addition of the vector. Progress to the key point: vectors represented by parallel lines are multiples of each other. Emphasise that this works both ways – if two vectors are multiples of each other, then they are parallel.

Plenary – Skills

Discuss how you can add and subtract vectors in the form $\begin{pmatrix}x\\y\end{pmatrix}$.

For example, $\begin{pmatrix}5\\2\end{pmatrix}+\begin{pmatrix}3\\1\end{pmatrix}=\begin{pmatrix}8\\3\end{pmatrix}$

$\begin{pmatrix}-3\\2\end{pmatrix}-\begin{pmatrix}4\\-1\end{pmatrix}=\begin{pmatrix}-7\\3\end{pmatrix}$

Exercise commentary – Skills

Students will need square grid paper in several questions. The whole class will need reminding that, for a column vector, the x-component is positive for a move right and negative for a move left, whereas the y-component is positive for a move up and negative for a move down.

Questions 1 to **3** Refer to the first worked example on page 400. In question **2**, the axes and their labels can be ignored. Question **3** part **a** may be difficult for some students to visualise, in which case they could do part **b** first.

Question 4 Refer to the top of page 400 and especially the diagram on the right. Remind students that, for parts **d** to **i**, arrows should be drawn nose-to-tail. Some students are likely to struggle with subtracting a vector in parts **g, h, i**, this question may benefit from peer assessment.

Question 5 Refer to the second worked example on page 400. For part **a**, students work with the x and y components separately, taking particular care with negative signs. Part **b** is similar to question **4**.

Question 6 This is best attempted on squared paper as for question **3** part **b**.

Question 7 In part **b** students should remember to change *both* signs to reverse the direction.

Question 8 Students must be careful when subtracting negatives. This is a particular pitfall in part **a vi** where students will have halved the values of **c** so may think their job is done.

Question 9 Drawn on isometric paper this is similar to question **4**. Remind students that subtracting a vector is the same as adding its negative. Students should position diagrams so they fit the isometric grid.

Simplification – Skills

Suggest that students use a piece of tracing paper to test the equality of vectors by overlaying one on top of the other. To do this properly the orientation of the paper must not be changed – it may help to start by drawing a 'North arrow' on the tracing paper.

It may help students to think of each vector as a translation of a point, with –**v** being the reverse of translation **v**.

Extension – Skills

Pairs of equal vectors can often be identified by inspection. Challenge students to prove that pairs of vectors are equal based on the geometric properties of the various shapes: both their lengths and directions.

Recap – Applications

1 Draw each vector on squared paper.

a $\begin{pmatrix}2\\3\end{pmatrix}$ **b** $\begin{pmatrix}3\\2\end{pmatrix}$ **c** $\begin{pmatrix}-1\\4\end{pmatrix}$ **d** $\begin{pmatrix}-1\\-4\end{pmatrix}$

2 $\mathbf{p}=\begin{pmatrix}4\\1\end{pmatrix}$, $\mathbf{q}=\begin{pmatrix}-2\\5\end{pmatrix}$

Calculate

a $3\mathbf{p}$ **b** $\mathbf{p}+\mathbf{q}$ **c** $2\mathbf{p}+5\mathbf{q}$

Answers:

1

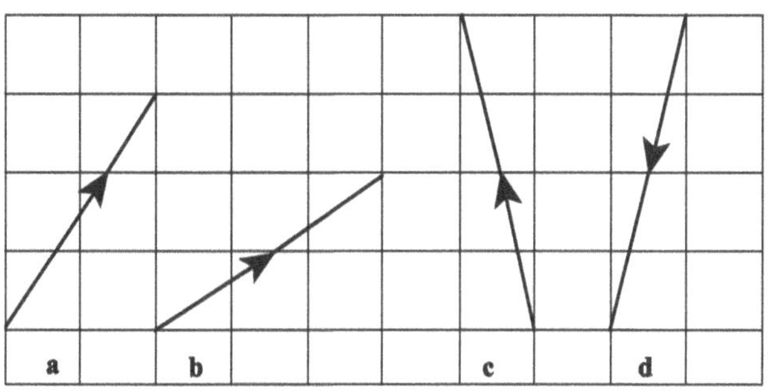

2 a $\begin{pmatrix}12\\3\end{pmatrix}$ **b** $\begin{pmatrix}2\\6\end{pmatrix}$ **c** $\begin{pmatrix}-2\\27\end{pmatrix}$

Plenary – Applications

One of the following pairs of vectors are not parallel. Which pair is it?

i 3**a** and 12**a**

ii 4**b** – 3**a** and 2**b** – 1.5**a**

iii **a** + $\frac{2}{3}$ **b** and 3**a** + 2**b**

iv 4**p** – **q** and –6**p** + 2**q**

v 6**a** – 4**b** and –15**a** + 10**b**

(**iv** is not in a pair)

Exercise commentary – Applications

Square grid paper is needed in the exercise. Isometric paper is needed for question **2**.

Questions 1 and **2** For these, refer to the first worked example on page 402. Mention to students that the vectors **a, b, p, q** are called *unit vectors* because they have a length of 1 unit. Emphasise that a unit vector doesn't have to be horizontal or vertical.

Questions 3 and **4**: Ask the question 'What do I multiply (or divide) this component by to get that component?' to find the scale factor which transforms the first vector into the second vector. Refer to the second worked example on page 402.

Question 5 A copy of the island and its grid would be useful for part **c**. Part **c ii** gives a check as the vector sum is the zero vector. Ask students why this is so.

Question 6 Some students may not need a diagram but others will find a diagram on square grid paper necessary.

Question 7 Students may attempt to construct complicated methods here. Remind them that the horizontal and vertical components can be treated separately resulting in linear equations.

Question 8 This links with previous work on Pythagoras' theorem and trigonometry making it an excellent assessment question.

Question 9 Higher achieving students will be able to complete this using Pythagoras' theorem and trigonometry but others may need to use a scale drawing. The easiest method is to use square grid paper, but ruler and protractor (or compasses) provide a more demanding method.

Question 10 A whole-class approach is useful here.

Question 11 This will produce an equation similar to those in question **7**. Students deal with x and y-components separately.

Question 12 Some students will be able to complete this without using the grid but should still be instructed to use the grid to check their answers.

Simplification – Applications

It may help to start students on questions that use orthogonal basis vectors so that the coefficients of **x** and **y** can be thought of as the more familiar (x, y) coordinates. One the basic idea is grasped students could then look at questions with oblique basis vectors.

Extension – Applications

Students could be asked to think about how they might specify an arbitrary point on a straight line. First specify one point on the line and then move some multiple of a vector parallel to the line.

Are the starting vector and parallel vector unique? If not, then how are they related?

19 Pythagoras and trigonometry

Key outcomes	Quick check
R12 Compare lengths, using similarity (including trigonometric ratios). G19 Apply the concepts of congruence and similarity, including the relationships between lengths.	**2** The two triangles shown below are similar. Calculate the lengths x and y. ($x = 5$ cm, $y = 48$ cm) 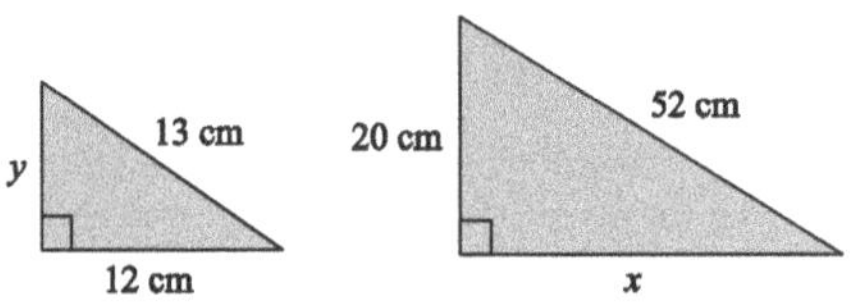
G6 Apply Pythagoras' theorem to obtain simple proofs. G20 Know the formulae for: Pythagoras' theorem, $a^2 + b^2 = c^2$, and the trigonometric ratios, $\sin\theta$ = opposite/hypotenuse, $\cos\theta$ = adjacent/hypotenuse and $\tan\theta$ = opposite/adjacent; apply them to find angles and lengths in right-angled triangles in two dimensional figures. G21 Know the exact values of $\sin\theta$ and $\cos\theta$ for $\theta = 0°, 30°, 45°, 60°$ and $90°$; know the exact value of $\tan\theta$ for $\theta = 0°, 30°, 45°$ and $60°$.	**1** Calculate the lengths a and b in these right-angled triangles. Give your answers to 1 dp. ($a = 10.8$ cm, $b = 11.0$ cm) 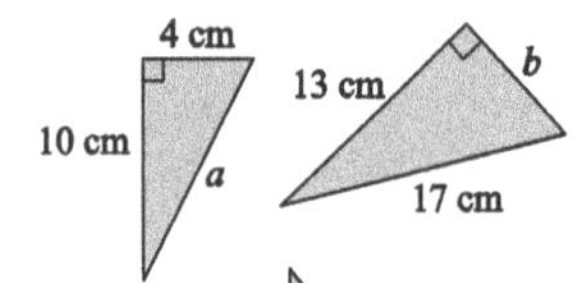 **3 a** Write as a fraction the value of **i** $\sin x$ $\left(\frac{4}{5}\right)$ **ii** $\cos x$ $\left(\frac{3}{5}\right)$ **iii** $\tan x$ $\left(\frac{3}{4}\right)$ **b** Work out the size of the angle x. (53.1°) 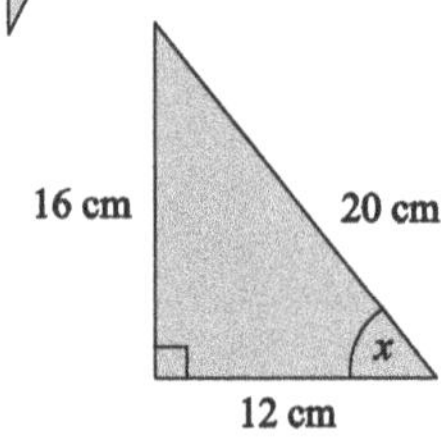 **4** Calculate the lengths a, b and c to 3 sf. 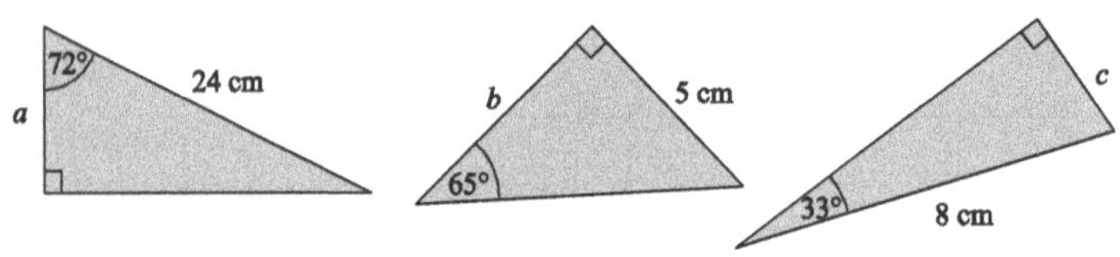 ($a = 7.41$ cm, $b = 2.33$ cm, $c = 4.36$ cm) **5** Without using a calculator, select the correct value of each ratio from the cloud. 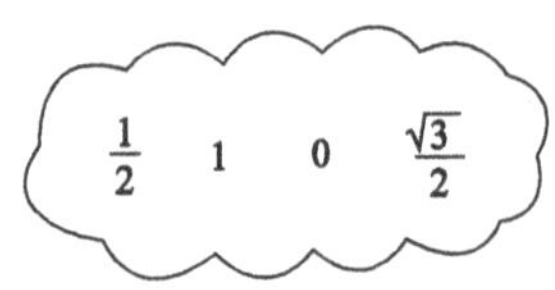 **a** $\cos 60°$ $\left(\frac{1}{2}\right)$ **b** $\sin 90°$ (1) **6** A ladder of length 5 m rests against a wall, the base of the ladder is 2 m from the base of the wall. **a** How far up the wall does the ladder reach? (4.6 m) **b** What angle does the ladder make with the ground? (66.4°)
G25 Apply addition and subtraction of vectors, multiplication of vectors by a scalar, and diagrammatic and column representations of vectors.	**7** Work out these vector sums **a** $\begin{pmatrix}3\\5\end{pmatrix} - \begin{pmatrix}2\\8\end{pmatrix}$ $\left[\begin{pmatrix}1\\-3\end{pmatrix}\right]$ **b** $\begin{pmatrix}7\\-3\end{pmatrix} + \begin{pmatrix}-5\\2\end{pmatrix}$ $\left[\begin{pmatrix}2\\-1\end{pmatrix}\right]$ **c** $\frac{1}{2}\begin{pmatrix}-2\\6\end{pmatrix}$ $\left[\begin{pmatrix}-1\\3\end{pmatrix}\right]$ **d** $4\begin{pmatrix}2\\6\end{pmatrix} - 3\begin{pmatrix}-1\\8\end{pmatrix}$ $\left[\begin{pmatrix}11\\0\end{pmatrix}\right]$ **8** Write down the column vectors to describe vectors **u** and **v**. (**u** = $\begin{pmatrix}-1\\4\end{pmatrix}$, **v** = $\begin{pmatrix}3\\-2\end{pmatrix}$) 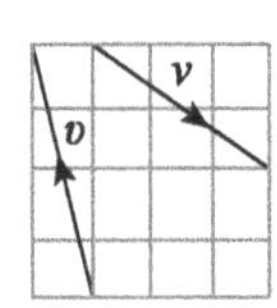

Misconceptions and challenges	Solutions
Students forget to find the square root as the final stage when finding missing lengths using Pythagoras' theorem.	Help students to lay out their work in a systematic way. This will help students who lack confidence to solve problems more easily.
If the missing length is not the hypotenuse, students still add the squares of the other sides.	This is a common error. Help students by modelling the question 'Do I know the hypotenuse?' before the start of each example. Encourage students to draw a sketch of the problem and label the hypotenuse at each stage.
When applying trigonometry, students make errors when finding missing lengths, as they use reasoning for finding missing angles, and vice-versa.	Encourage students to write out all the information, including what they know and what they do not know, before starting the problem. If they have a clear way of writing out the formulae with known values substituted in, then they will find it easier to see what to do.
Students assume that the values of cos 0°, sin 0°, and tan 0° are all zero.	Look at the values of sin, cos and tan for 1 degree, and half a degree, and gradually get closer and closer to zero to show students what happens as these functions tend to zero.
Memorising the exact values for sin, cos and tan (30°, 45°, 60°, ...) can be very tricky, especially given that cos 60° = sin 30°, for example.	Keep these displayed in the classroom, with the triangle diagrams used to derive them (include labels for the opposite, adjacent and hypotenuse with their values).
Students often make errors when finding an unknown in a denominator, for instance the hypotenuse when using SOH and CAH, and the adjacent when using TOA.	Give students practice with equations in the form $2 = \frac{4}{x}$, and $\frac{2}{3} = \frac{6}{x}$, to help them with these questions.
Vector addition can be confusing when there is a mixture of positive and negative numbers.	Encourage students to sketch the vectors as they can then check their answer with their diagram.

Review question commentary

Students will need calculators and should check that they are in 'degrees' mode.

Question 1 (**19.1**) – Encourage students to check that the hypotenuse is the longest side.

Question 2 (**19.2**) – For part **b**, students can use either the similarity of the triangles or Pythagoras' theorem.

Question 3 (**19.2**) – Students need to learn the sine, cosine and tangent ratios. They can use any of their answers from part **a** to answer **b**. Discuss why this is the case.

Question 4 (**19.2**) – The necessary calculations are **a** 18 ÷ tan 67, **b** 4 ÷ sin 57, **c** 12 × cos 75.
If students are stuck, give them a hint as to which ratio to use. If students find rearranging difficult, get them to represent the equation in a triangle.

Question 5 (**19.2**) – Students could use calculators to check their answers.

Questions 6 and **7** (**19.3**) – Students should be writing column vectors not coordinates.

Review answers

1 $a = 21.6$ cm, $b = 10.7$ cm

2 **a** $x = 9$ cm, $y = 5$ cm **b** Yes, scale factor 3

3 **a i** $\frac{5}{13}$ **ii** $\frac{12}{13}$ **iii** $\frac{5}{12}$ **b** 22.6°

4 $a = 7.64$ cm, $b = 4.77$ cm, $c = 3.11$ cm

5 **a** $\frac{\sqrt{3}}{2}$ **b** 1 **c** 1 **d** $\frac{\sqrt{3}}{2}$

6 **a** $\mathbf{u} = \begin{pmatrix} 2 \\ 4 \end{pmatrix}$, $\mathbf{v} = \begin{pmatrix} -3 \\ -2 \end{pmatrix}$

b

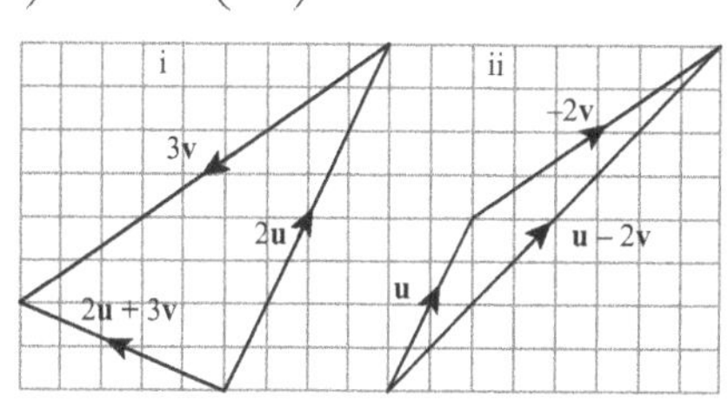

7 **a** $\begin{pmatrix} 5 \\ 9 \end{pmatrix}$ **b** $\begin{pmatrix} 6 \\ -6 \end{pmatrix}$ **c** $\begin{pmatrix} 15 \\ -5 \end{pmatrix}$ **d** $\begin{pmatrix} 1 \\ 0 \end{pmatrix}$

115 marks

Assessment 19

Question 1 – 7 marks

a $a = \sqrt{10^2 + 9^2} = \sqrt{181}$ [M1]

$= 13.45$ (2 dp) [A1]

She did not take the square root. [B1]

b $b = \sqrt{14.2^2 - 6.1^2} = \sqrt{164.43}$ [M1]

$= 12.82$ (2 dp) [A1]

$14.2^2 + 6.1^2 = (15.4547\ldots)^2$ [B1]

He added the two squares. [B1]

Question 2 – 4 marks

a $2^2 + 3^2 = 4 + 9 = 13$ [M1]

$\neq 13^2$ [A1]

b $20^2 + 99^2 = 400 + 9801 = 10\,201$ [M1]

$100^2 = 10\,000$ but $101^2 = 10\,201$

100 should be 101 [A1]

Question 3 – 3 marks

$d^2 = (6 - -3)^2 + (-1 - -5)^2$ [M1]

$= 9^2 + 4^2$ [A1]

$d = \sqrt{97} = 9.85$ (3 sf) [A1]

Question 4 – 9 marks

a 1 and 28 2 and 14….4 and 7 [B3]

b 1 and 28 $d = \sqrt{1^2 + 28^2}$ [M1]

$= \sqrt{785} = 28.02$ (4sf) [A1]

2 and 14 $d = \sqrt{2^2 + 14^2}$ [M1]

$= \sqrt{200} = 14.14$ (4 sf) [A1]

4 and 7 $d = \sqrt{4^2 + 7^2}$ [M1]

$= \sqrt{65} = 8.062$ (4 sf) [A1]

Question 5 – 15 marks

a $9^2 + 12^2 = 81 + 144 = 225$ [M1]

$15^2 = 225$ [A1]

Yes [F1]

b $9^2 + 14^2 = 81 + 196 = 227$ [M1]

$17^2 = 289$ [A1]

No [F1]

c $1.6^2 + 3.0^2 = 2.56 + 9 = 11.56$ [M1]

$3.4^2 = 11.56$ [A1]

Yes [F1]

d $11^2 + 19^2 = 121 + 361 = 482$ [M1]

$22^2 = 484$ [A1]

No [F1]

e $3.6^2 + 7.7^2 = 12.96 + 59.29 = 72.25$ [M1]

$8.5^2 = 72.25$ [A1]

Yes [F1]

Question 6 – 10 marks

a Evidence of a logical argument. [M1]

∠HBS = 62° (Alternate) [A1]

∠SBL = 180°– 152° = 28° [A1]

$x = 62° + 28° = 90°$ [A1]

OR

∠HBN = 180° – 62° = 118° [M1,A1]

$x = 360° - 152° - 118° = 90°$ [A1]

b $(LH)^2 = 2.5^2 + 3.6^2 = 19.21$ [M1,A1]

$LH = \sqrt{19.21} = 4.38$ mi (3 sf) [A1]

c 10.5 mi (3 sf) [2.5 + 3.6 + 4.38] [F1]

d ∠NHL = ∠HLS = 62° + 55° = 117° [M1]

Bearing = 180° + ∠HLS = 297° [A1]

Question 7 – 6 marks

a **i** $\sin\theta = 4 \div 6$, $\theta = \sin^{-1}(0.6667) = 41.8°$ [B1]

ii $\cos\theta = 15 \div 19$, $\theta = \cos^{-1}(0.7895) = 37.9°$ [B1]

iii $\tan\theta = 29.6 \div 34.5$, $\theta = \tan^{-1}(0.8580) = 40.6°$ [B1]

b **i** $a = 6 \times \cos(41.8°) = 4.47$ cm (3 sf)

OR $a = 4 \div \tan(41.8°) = 4.47$ cm (3 sf) [F1]

ii $b = 19 \times \sin(37.9°) = 11.7$ (3 sf)

OR $b = 15 \times \tan(37.9°) = 11.7$ cm (3 sf) [F1]

iii $c = 34.5 \div \cos(40.6°) = 45.5$ cm (3 sf)

OR $c = 29.6 \div \sin(40.6°) = 45.5$ cm (3 sf) [F1]

Question 8 – 5 marks

a $\sin 12.5° = 1.75 \div L$ [M1]

$L = 1.75 \div \sin(12.5°)$ [M1]

$= 8.09$ m (3 sf) [A1]

b $h^2 = 8.09^2 - 1.75^2$ OR $h = 8.09 \times \cos(12.5°)$ [M1]

$h = 7.89$ m (3 sf) $= 7.89$ (3 sf) [A1]

Question 9 – 34 marks

a Check students' drawings. [B8]

b Check students' drawings.

i $\begin{pmatrix} 2 \\ 13 \end{pmatrix}$ [B2] **ii** $\begin{pmatrix} -6 \\ 1 \end{pmatrix}$ [B2]

iii $\begin{pmatrix} 6 \\ -1 \end{pmatrix}$ [B2] **iv** $\begin{pmatrix} 8 \\ 12 \end{pmatrix}$ [B2]

v $\begin{pmatrix} 4 \\ -14 \end{pmatrix}$ [B2] **vi** $\begin{pmatrix} 14 \\ -9 \end{pmatrix}$ [B2]

c **i** $\sqrt{2^2 + 13^2} = \sqrt{173}$ [M1, A1]

ii $\sqrt{(-6)^2 + 1^2} = \sqrt{37}$ [M1, A1]

iii $\sqrt{6^2 + (-1)^2} = \sqrt{37}$ [M1, A1]

iv $\sqrt{8^2 + 12^2} = \sqrt{208}$ $[= 4\sqrt{13}]$ [M1, A1]

v $\sqrt{4^2 + 14^2} = \sqrt{212}$ $[= 2\sqrt{53}]$ [M1, A1]

vi $\sqrt{14^2 + (-9)^2} = \sqrt{277}$ [M1, A1]

d The vectors are parallel, [B1]

The vectors are the same length [B1]

Question 10 – 10 marks

a Correct [B1] **b** $-2\mathbf{x} + 7\mathbf{y}$ [B2]

c $-6\mathbf{y}$ [B2] **d** Correct [B1]

e $2\mathbf{x} + 3\mathbf{y}$ [B2] **f** Correct [B2]

Question 11 – 12 marks

a $\begin{pmatrix} 35 \\ -10 \end{pmatrix}$ [B1] **b** $\begin{pmatrix} 16 \\ -10 \end{pmatrix}$ [B1]

c $\begin{pmatrix} -1 \\ 3 \end{pmatrix}$ [B1] **d** $\begin{pmatrix} 3 \\ -3 \end{pmatrix}$ [B2]

e $\begin{pmatrix} 3 \\ 4 \end{pmatrix}$ [B2] **f** $\begin{pmatrix} -40 \\ 18 \end{pmatrix}$ [B2]

g $\begin{pmatrix} 28 \\ -8 \end{pmatrix} + \begin{pmatrix} 12 \\ 3 \end{pmatrix} + \begin{pmatrix} 16 \\ -10 \end{pmatrix} = \begin{pmatrix} 56 \\ -15 \end{pmatrix}$ [M1, A2]

The probability of combined events

Learning outcomes

N5 Apply systematic listing strategies.
P1 Record, describe and analyse the frequency of outcomes of probability experiments using [tables and] frequency trees.
P6 Enumerate sets and combinations of sets systematically, using tables, grids, Venn diagrams and tree diagrams.
P7 Construct theoretical possibility spaces for single and combined experiments with equally likely outcomes and use these to calculate theoretical probabilities.
P8 Calculate the probability of independent and dependent combined events, including using tree diagrams and other representations, and know the underlying assumptions.

Prior knowledge

Check-in skill

- Cancel fractions to their simplest form.
- Add and subtract fractions and decimals.
- Recognise types of number.

Online resources

MyMaths 1199, 1208, 1262, 1263, 1334, 1921, 1922, 1935

InvisiPen videos
Skills: 20Sa – g Applications: 20Aa – d

Kerboodle assessment
Online Skills Test 20 Chapter Test 20

Development and links

Probability has applications wherever it is necessary to predict how likely it is that a random or unpredictable event will happen, for example to produce a weather forecast, to predict the effects of climate change or to predict the chance of winning a prize in any game of chance. It is important in the workplace as all employers are required by law to carry out risk assessments to minimise the chances of an accident. Companies use probability to make risk/reward assessments for calculating insurance premiums or to determine the likelihood of a product breaking down during a warranty period.

Chapter investigation

Encourage the students to predict the answer to this question in advance. Students should then tackle the problem by experiment and record the number of times they get each possible pairing. These results should be used to compute experimental probabilities using both individual and 'pooled' data.

A possibility space diagram [**20.2**] should help students work out the theoretical probabilities, the largest of which are $P(7) = \frac{6}{36} = \frac{1}{6}$ for addition and $P(6) = P(12) = \frac{4}{36} = \frac{1}{9}$ for multiplication. Comparing the experimental and theoretical probabilities can be used to recap FDP conversions and how to write probabilities.

Move on to consider two-stage games, for example, if you roll an even number on the first go then you win if you score 3 or more on the second go but if you roll an odd number first then you must roll 4 or more to win on the second go. Analysing such games is naturally done using tree diagrams [**20.3**]. Experimental results can be shown on a frequency tree which can be related to the required theoretical calculations: multiplying probabilities along branches and add the probabilities of mutually exclusive events.

Finally return to the original games and use them to look at how the language of sets can be used to describe probabilities [**20.1**]. For example, let A = {The answer is even} and B = {The answer is a multiple of 3}. Then in the first game (add scores) $P(A) = \frac{18}{36} = \frac{1}{2}$, $P(B) = \frac{12}{36} = \frac{1}{3}$ and $P(A \cap B) = \frac{6}{36} = \frac{1}{6}$ whilst in the second game (multiply scores) $P(A) = \frac{27}{36} = \frac{3}{4}$, $P(B) = \frac{20}{36} = \frac{5}{9}$ and $P(A \cap B) = \frac{15}{36} = \frac{5}{12}$

20.1 Sets

Objectives

① **P6** Enumerate sets and combinations of sets systematically, using tables, grids, Venn diagrams

Useful resources

Mini whiteboards, pre-made Venn diagram templates

Starter – Skills

Ask students to choose three two-digit numbers (e.g. 12, 15 and 17). 'Randomly' generate one- and two-digit numbers and ask students to tick off each time they get a factor of one of their three numbers (each generated number can be used for more than one of theirs). The winner is the person who collects all their factors first.

Teaching notes – Skills

Students need to be able to comprehend the general language of sets and the structure of the Venn diagram and explain, in words, what each region represents. Encourage them to do this first rather than diving straight into the questions. They can produce a glossary of terms since much of the language will be unfamiliar.

Work on Venn diagrams follows and there are two main things to think about: Firstly, how can probabilities be worked out from the Venn diagram, and secondly, the shading of specific regions. Students may have trouble visualising the regions indicated by the notation so further practice on this could be provided, or word descriptions instead of notation.

A two-way table provides a good way to link work on sample spaces, etc. with this work on Venn diagrams. For example, consider a two-way table showing two types of chocolate split into 'like' and 'dislike':

	Like B	Dislike B
Like A	18	6
Dislike A	12	15

How can this information be translated into a Venn diagram? Students should be able to see that the four numbers in the table match the four regions in the Venn diagram and they can use this to complete the diagram. Follow-up questions can then be used such as 'What is the probability that…?'

Plenary – Skills

Identify the region. By taking a standard '2-circle' Venn diagram, ask students to write down, either using notation or in words, the regions indicated by, for example, the 'moon-shaped' section of B plus the 'moon-shaped' section of A (A or B but not both). This can be tailored for ability and regions combined as appropriate.

Exercise commentary – Skills

Question 1 Since this question asks for a list of elements, it is not strictly necessary to use set notation, but the students should get used to using it, curly brackets and all! $P = \{1, 4, 9, ...\}$

Question 2 Ask the students whether a commutative rule operates here; that is, is $P \cap T = T \cap P$, ...

Question 3 Students may need an example to get started: **a** factors of 10... Has anyone got an alternative valid answer to the one in the back of the book?

Questions 4 and **5** These two questions are very similar to questions **1** and **2**; you may wish to discuss questions **1** and **2** with the whole class and then get the students to solve questions **4** and **5** themselves. It is a good idea to revise a little number theory – square numbers, prime numbers etc.

Question 6 While talking about subsets, mention the distinction between subsets which necessarily have fewer elements that their parent set (sometimes called real subsets) and subsets which can equal the parent set. Get the students to think of examples of each.

Question 7 Since these are infinite sets, the lists of common elements may either be represented by a clear pattern or a rule.

Students who find this challenging may use a defined universal set for the problem; for example, the set of all integers less than 50. Encourage the use of the sign for the intersection of two sets.

Questions 8 and **9** Question **8** naturally leads to questions about probability and question **9** actually does this. Use question **8** to discuss these ideas and then let the students solve question **9** on their own. Emphasise that finding probabilities in this context is only possible because all elements are equally likely to be chosen.

Simplification – Skills

The notation associated with the Venn diagrams could be explained in words rather than symbols to help the students visualise the regions of the Venn diagram they are to consider.

Extension – Skills

Give students a sketch of a Venn diagram that has three overlapping circles. Say, students who like pasta, students who like pizza, and students who like pickles. Point out the link between a description of one particular student and where they would be placed on the Venn diagram, e.g. 'Steve likes pickles and pasta but he is not keen on pizza'. Steve's preference would be placed where the pasta and pickles circles overlap, outside of the central region where all three circles overlap. Ask: Where does a student go who likes all of these foods? And what about a student who likes none of these foods?

Recap – Applications

1 **a** List the elements of these sets:

i N: The first 10 odd numbers ($\{1, 3, 5, 7, 9, 11, 13, 15, 17, 19\}$)

ii M: The first 5 multiples of 7 ($\{7, 14, 21, 28, 35\}$)

b Hence list the elements in these sets:

i $N \cap M$ ($\{7\}$)

ii $N \cup M$

($\{1, 3, 5, 7, 9, 11, 13, 14, 15, 17, 19, 21, 28, 35\}$)

2 The Venn diagram shows information about the decisions that all Year 9 students made in selecting their GCSE Options for History (H) and/or Geography (G).

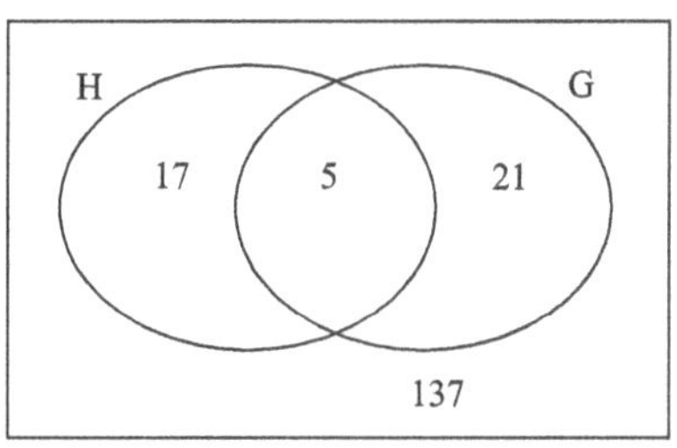

How many students

a studied both History and Geography? (5)

b studied History but not Geography? (17)

c studied Geography but not History? (21)

Plenary – Applications

Ask students to come up with their own problem similar question **7**. Can they give *just enough* information so that a partner can solve the Venn diagram?

Exercise commentary – Applications

Question 1 Challenge students to write down the sets A = {**prime** factors of 42} and B = {**prime** factors of 63}. Can they describe in words $A \cap B$ (prime factors of the HCF of 42 and 63) and $A \cup B$ (prime factors of the LCM of 42 and 63)?

Question 2 It may be useful, before even considering the questions being asked of these two diagrams, to discuss the sets with the students. Make up your own questions. 'What characterises the three pupils in the middle of the diagram? (They're dark haired girls.) Get the students to make up problems – it's a great way of really understanding theory.

Question 3 Ask the students to attempt to draw the Venn diagram, including scalene triangles. Be careful: is E a subset of I?

Question 4 Changing the value of x changes the situation in interesting ways. It will almost certainly be necessary to remind students what mutually exclusive events are and this time they can be explained in set notation as well.

Question 5 This is a good question for paired work. Students may need a hint to set up two simultaneous equations – ask them to write down all the information they have, remind them that to find two unknowns (the number of participants for each activity) they need two separate equations.

Question 6 The classic Venn diagram problem. With a possible change of sports, it may be interesting to construct a similar diagram for the class being taught.

Question 7 Encourage students to discuss the *order* in which they use these facts. If they use a Venn diagram they can put in the value 32 straight away, despite it not being the first item in the list.

Question 8 Encourage students to use probability notation in this question. Emphasise that its intuitive nature means that rather than being more arbitrary mathematical notation they are expected to use it is, in fact, useful shorthand.

Simplification – Applications

Use ready prepared Venn diagrams to illustrate. See http://www.cram.com/flashcards/venn-diagrams-notation-3411256 for examples.

Extension – Applications

Students could be encouraged to explore the idea of conditional probability.

20.2 Possibility spaces

Objectives

① **P7** Construct theoretical possibility spaces for single and combined experiments with equally likely outcomes and

② **P7** Use possibility spaces to calculate theoretical probabilities

Useful resources

Mini whiteboards, two display spinners for starter

Starter – Skills

Show two large spinners with 4 to 6 numbered sides each. Ask students for examples of different outcomes you could get from spinning both spinners and adding the results. How you could record these outcomes if you wanted to be sure not to leave out or repeat any outcome? Record different suggestions. Encourage a two-way table approach for maximum clarity and efficiency. Ask students to draw up and complete such a two-way table for the two spinners. Discuss and compare results.

Teaching notes – Skills

① Recap **equally likely outcomes**. Refer to the starter. Emphasise that the sort of two-way table or possibility space used in the starter is only suitable for recording events with equally likely outcomes. Ask students what other equally likely **combined events** they could record in this way. (dice, coins, etc; combinations of same)

Emphasise the need to be careful and systematic when recording outcomes in a possibility space. Highlight that there are often patterns to be found in the tables, and that identifying these can be helpful when using the data to calculate probabilities.

Ask students to draw up two possibility spaces for the outcomes of throwing two dice, one for the sum and one for the product. Use these to find and discuss patterns in the tables.

② Ask students what a possibility space would look like for throwing a dice and tossing a coin (both fair). Ask a variety of questions to practise **calculating theoretical probabilities** of different combined outcomes. Revise P( ) notation.

Referring to the possibility spaces looked at so far, ask students to find the rule for the relationship between the total number of combined outcomes and the number of outcomes for each event. (Total number of outcomes = number of outcomes of event A × number of outcomes of event B)

Ask if this formula will work for all combined events. If not, why not? This could be extended to dependent events, by asking students to come up with scenarios for such cases. If they need a prompt, give them a hint such as coloured balls in a bag: how could they make two events out of this, and why might the formula not work?

Plenary – Skills

Display a completed two-way table of either the products or sums of throwing two dice. Ask students questions referring to the table: What is the most likely result? Give a result with probability 1. What is the probability of getting a multiple of …? Etc.

Allow/encourage answers in different forms (fraction, decimal, percentage). Why is the fraction form the most obvious?

Exercise commentary – Skills

Questions 1 to **3** Remember that for any given random experiment there is any number of sample spaces, each corresponding to a different random variable. In the picturesque language of gambling, if you bet on a product of 36, it is entirely immaterial what the sum of the two numbers is or what each one is individually. These questions could be extended to include constructing a table showing the possible values of the random variable ($X \times Y$ or $X + Y$) and their probabilities.

Question 4 The important thing here is to list the different outcomes systematically; for example, 0 heads, 1 head, … And remember, when you come to 2 heads, it may be easier to think of 1 tail, which is the same thing.

Questions 5 to **7** These questions deal with the same experiment but with different random variables or events. Question **7** uses a straightforward but important idea – that, in these equiprobable outcomes problems, the more ways an event can happen, the more likely it is to happen. These questions provide good practice at forming two-way tables.

Question 8 An estimate for the number of times 10 occurs in 100 throws is, of course, the product of the probability and the number of throws. This seems intuitively correct and this explanation will suffice for the students. It's worth having the real explanation at the back of your mind, though: The number of 10s in 100 throws is a binomial random variable, $n = 100$, p = probability of a 10 in any one throw, and the mean of a binomial random variable is np.

Question 9 The important difference in this question is that one of the dice has numbers repeated, and these correspond to repeated rows.

Simplification – Skills

Students should practise listing the outcomes for simpler examples. They could also be given prepared tables to complete.

Extension – Skills

Students could think of a different situation which involves two successive events, draw up a possibility space showing all the outcomes, and then write five questions to be answered from the table.

Recap – Applications

1 This sample space shows the results when two pentagonal spinners are thrown and the scores on each one added:

	1	2	3	4	5
1	2	3	4	5	6
2	3	4	5	6	7
3	4	5	6	7	8
4	5	6	7	8	9
5	6	7	8	9	10

Write down, the probabilities of a score of

a exactly 10 (0.04)
b exactly 7 (0.16)
c exactly 3 (0.08)
d at least 8 (0.24)
e less than 6 (0.4)
f a square number (0.2)
g a prime number (0.44)
h an even number. (0.52)

Plenary – Applications

Ask students to draw a 2 × 3 grid on their whiteboards and to work in pairs to prepare these 'cards' for a game of bingo. They can put any six different numbers of their choice on the cards. For each 'call', the scores from throwing two dice are called, for students to add up and cross off their cards if present. Play one game. Ask if any students would now like to change the numbers on their cards. Why? Refer to the possibility spaces encountered and questions from the lessons, and discuss how to go about choosing the most advantageous numbers. Repeat the game with revised rules as discussed, or using the product or difference of two dice, or some other combination of events. Each time design, play and discuss.

Exercise commentary – Applications

Question 1 From the wording of this question, the draws are without replacement, make sure students are aware of this.

Question 2 Repeated, identical and independent trials like these are called Bernoulli trials. This may be a good opportunity to get the students to do some research in mathematics history such as finding out about the life and work of Jacob Bernoulli.

Question 3 The student should spend time understanding the experimental set up. This can sometimes be done most effectively by actually doing the experiment. In this case, it is as if the yellow areas on the spinner are labelled 0.

Question 4 Further to the hint in the text for this question, get the students to find a strategy for obtaining the number of cards with two digits. Clearly, it is 100 – (the number of cards with 1 or 3 digits).

Question 5 Students should have developed the skills required for two-way tables by now. The slightly tricky part of this question relates to the phrase 'at least twice the score on the other spinner' – 'at least' **includes** twice the score itself.

Question 6 This is an interesting question which requires careful, logical thinking. The student has to realise that, in **a**, the game necessarily ends after the first pair of throws and, since a draw is allowed, the answer isn't 0.5. If a draw isn't available as the result of the game, one of them must win. Now, is there any reason to believe that one of the players has an advantage over the other? This should give the answer without any counting.

Question 7 A good assessment question as it covers several concepts from this chapter.

Simplification – Applications

Students could be given more scenarios where a possibility space is appropriate for working out the probabilities.

Extension – Applications

Students could be asked to draw up their own two-way tables based on features of people in the class. They could consider whether to record the actual outcomes (and if so, how to do this most clearly and efficiently) or the probability of each one.

20.3 Tree diagrams

Objectives

① **P8** Calculate the probability of independent and dependent combined events, including using tree diagrams

Useful resources

Mini whiteboards, dice, coins, bags of counters/marbles

Starter – Skills

Ask students to find products of fractions and to simplify their answers. For example:

$\frac{1}{2}\times\frac{5}{12}$ $\frac{1}{3}\times\frac{6}{7}$ $\frac{2}{5}\times\frac{3}{4}$ $\left(\frac{5}{24}, \frac{2}{7}, \frac{3}{10}\right)$

Extend this to finding some decimal products. E.g.: $0.6 \times 0.4, 0.3 \times 0.8, 0.25 \times 0.6$ (0.24, 0.24, 0.15)

Teaching notes – Skills

① Recall that two-way tables (possibility spaces) can be used for two combined events with equally likely outcomes. When there are more than two events combined (such as tossing three coins), and/or when the events do *not* have equally likely outcomes, a **tree diagram** is better for recording outcomes and giving the data to calculate different probabilities. Using a simple example, ask students what outcomes are possible when tossing two coins. Explore different possible recording methods and emphasise the need to record HT *and* TH, and suggest that it helps to think of two *different* coins to ensure listing all possibilities. Ask students to record the outcomes in a list and a two-way table. Then recall how to do the same with a tree diagram.

Extend this to looking at the possible outcomes of tossing three coins and recording these on a tree diagram. Highlight the convention of writing the individual outcome at the *end* of a branch, the probability *along* the branch, and a label or heading for the event above each *stage* of branching.

Explore how to use tree diagrams when calculating probabilities. Start with simple examples from the two-coin diagram, and build up to more difficult ones with two coins, before moving on to examples from the three-coin diagram. Use plenty of examples to illustrate and emphasise the difference between probabilities involving 'and' (**multiplying** *along* the path of two or more branches) *vs*. 'or' (**adding** *across* different outcome paths), where a given outcome could happen in more than one way.

Sometimes the outcome of one event has no effect on the outcome of another event. These events are called **independent events**. Sometimes the outcome of one event does affect the outcome of another event. These events are called conditional or **dependent events**. For example:

If I throw a dice and get a 6, and then flip a coin and get tails, are these events independent or dependent? (Independent. Getting a 6 doesn't make getting tails more or less likely.)

Suppose it rains one day and I decide to come to school by car, are these two events independent?
(No. I am more likely to use a car if it rains than if it is dry, so one event is dependent on the other.)

Plenary – Skills

Display a tree diagram from a past GCSE exam question to the whole group. Ask the students to work in pairs, and say they will have one minute each to tell their partner as many probabilities of events from the diagram as possible. Give all the students two minutes to study the diagram carefully and make some rough notes for themselves before allowing the first person to report to their partner. Ask if any mistakes were noticed, and then allow the second person one minute. Share some of the comments or questions with the whole group.

Exercise commentary – Skills

Question 1 As this is a frequency tree, remind students to convert the proportions to numbers first.

Question 2 Students could use this to investigate the concept of weighted means. As an extension, in small groups students could give Lydia a target to reduce her lateness to less than 12% of the time over all. In order to achieve this, how many days should she drive each month? (More than 16 days out of 20.) They can use trial and error for this and should check their values satisfy $0.1D + 0.2T < 0.12$ and $D + T = 1$. By only changing the proportion of days she drives and gets the train is it possible to reduce her overall lateness to 8%? (No as both modes of transport make her late more than 8% of the time.)

Question 3 A lot of information is presented in this question, students may benefit from discussing this scenario in pairs to make sure they understand what each number represents.

Question 4 This is an important question. In part **b**, the probability should be found by using a two-way table or equivalent method, not by finding the separate probabilities first. If the probabilities in **b** and **c** are equal, the events are independent – this can be thought of as a **definition** of independent events.

Question 5 The first stage of this tree diagram relates to brakes (faulty or not faulty) and the second to lights. As usual, multiply probabilities along the branches and then add the final probabilities of the relevant three branches.

Question 6 An interesting question which could be used to connect mathematics to the wider world. For example, one of the arguments against mass screening for certain diseases, notably cancer, is the relatively high rate of false positive results which can cause significant and unnecessary worry for patients. This type of discussion can bring mathematics alive for students.

Simplification – Skills

Students may need some revision on multiplying fractions. Pre-drawn tree diagrams could be used.

Extension – Skills

Students could be asked to complete further examples of three-stage tree diagrams where the probabilities are not equally likely.

Recap – Applications

1 Anna eats two pieces of toast each day at breakfast, with either marmalade, honey or lemon curd on them. The probability that she chooses marmalade is 0.6; the probability she chooses lemon curd is 0.24.

a Explain why the probability that Anna chooses honey for a piece of toast is 0.16.

(The probabilities must add up to 1)

b Draw a tree diagram to show Anna's possible choices. Use your tree diagram to calculate the probabilities that Anna chooses

i honey on the first piece and lemon curd on the second (0.0384)

ii marmalade on both pieces (0.36)

iii lemon curd on the second piece only (0.24)

iv honey on at least one piece. (0.3648)

Plenary – Applications

Give students the scenario of coloured marbles in a bag. Two marbles are taken out, without replacement. Are these independent or dependent events? Ask students to work in pairs to construct a tree diagram for the two events. Make sure they care to adjust the total number of marbles and the number of each colour to take account of the first marble. Finally, discuss and work through how to calculate the probabilities for the four individual outcomes (YY, YB, BY, BB) and combinations.

Exercise commentary – Applications

Question 1 It is very often necessary in these probability questions to re-express the event in question. In this problem, the student has to ask, 'What has to happen in order that the team has at least three points after 2 games?' The independence assumption is very important; make sure that the students don't get confused with mutually-exclusive events. Finally, even if the assumption of independence is thought to be a bit dubious, it is not a reason for rejecting the approach completely – the student has simply to be a little cautious in drawing conclusions.

Question 2 In part **b** students should be aware that they only need to use the first two stages of the tree diagram. Ensure that students use their common sense here – it is not uncommon for a student to add the probabilities of 'fail, pass' and 'pass, pass' in part **b ii,** ignoring the fact that a pupil who passes will not take the test a second time.

Question 3 Students may need to discuss this situation in order to draw the probability tree. They should not include a pair of branches for 'catches the bus' or 'does not catch the bus' as this is given.

Question 4 This is a good choice for class discussion. If students struggle with part **a** ask them to describe an element that is in Z but not Y, or an element in Z but not X, or in X and Y but not Z.

Question 5 This emphasises important concepts and notation. It's worth linking this with question **1** and using it to revise the notion of independence, one of the most important words in this subject. Encourage students to write down the formula
$P(X \cap Y) = P(X) \times P(Y)$ for **independent X and Y**.

Question 6 To support differentiation, it may be helpful to give this problem to one group of students who should solve it collectively on a large piece of card. This would then free some teacher time to focus on more routine problems with students who are struggling with these important ideas.

Simplification – Applications

Giving the students a page of blank diagrams will certainly speed up the process of drawing the tree diagrams. If necessary, make the numbers smaller.

Extension – Applications

A bag contains 3 red and 2 blue balls. I take out two balls. Find the probability they are the same colour.

This is a very tough question without a tree diagram. Note that this time the probabilities of the colour of the second ball depend on what is picked as the first ball; this is dependent or conditional probability.

20 The probability of combined events

<table>
<tr><th>Key outcomes</th><th>Quick check</th></tr>
<tr><td>P1 Record, describe and analyse the frequency of outcomes of probability experiments using frequency trees.</td><td>
1 The probability Andre wins a game of chess is 0.7.
He plays two games.
a Copy and complete the tree diagram to show all the possible outcomes.
b Andre plays two games of chess with 200 different people. Fill in the frequencies on your tree diagram.
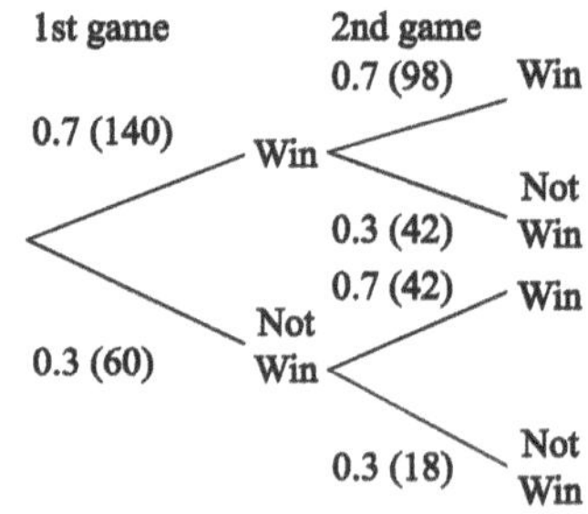

c Calculate the probability that Andre
i wins both games (0.49)
ii loses both games. (0.09)</td></tr>
<tr><td>P6 Enumerate sets and combinations of sets systematically, using tables, grids, Venn diagrams <u>and tree diagrams.</u></td><td>
2 Copy and complete the Venn diagram by adding in all the integers up to and including 8.
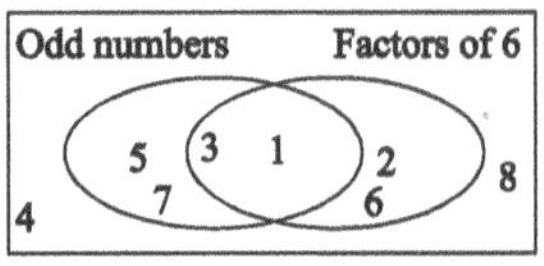
</td></tr>
<tr><td>N5 Apply systematic listing strategies.

P7 Construct theoretical possibility spaces for single and combined experiments with equally likely outcomes and use these to calculate theoretical probabilities.</td><td>
3 A spinner has four colours, blue, red, green and yellow.
The spinner is spun and at the same time a coin is tossed.
a Draw a table to show all the possible outcomes.
<table>
<tr><th></th><th>B</th><th>R</th><th>G</th><th>Y</th></tr>
<tr><td>H</td><td>HB</td><td>HR</td><td>HG</td><td>HY</td></tr>
<tr><td>T</td><td>TB</td><td>TR</td><td>TG</td><td>TY</td></tr>
</table>
b The spinner and the coin are both fair.
What is the probability of getting
i heads on the coin $\left(\frac{1}{2}\right)$
ii blue on the spinner and tails on the coin $\left(\frac{1}{8}\right)$
iii heads on the coin and red or green on the spinner? $\left(\frac{1}{4}\right)$</td></tr>
<tr><td>P8 <u>Calculate the probability of independent and dependent combined events, including using tree diagrams and other representations, and know the underlying assumptions.</u></td><td>
4 The probability that Layla falls off her bike is 0.3
The probability that Luke falls off his scooter is 0.1
The probabilities are independent. Calculate the probability that
a Layla and Luke both fall off (0.03)
b only one of them falls off. (0.34)
5 A bag contains 5 blue and 2 green counters. A counter is removed at random and not put back in. A second counter is then removed. Calculate the probability that
a both counters are blue $\left(\frac{10}{21}\right)$
b both counters are green $\left(\frac{1}{21}\right)$
c the counters are different colours. $\left(\frac{10}{21}\right)$</td></tr>
</table>

Misconceptions and challenges	Solutions
Students think that the content of an outcome of an experiment affects its probability. For example, they may think the probability of rolling a 1 and a 6 on two dice is $\left(\frac{7}{36}\right)$.	Introduce the topic using non-numerical outcomes. For example, the chances of picking a tabby and a tortoiseshell cat from a selection of cats.
Students make assumptions when reading probabilities from sample space diagrams. They may spot a pattern and assume it continues for all possibilities.	A good example to disprove this is the sum of two dice. The pattern appears to show the probabilities increasing $\frac{2}{36}, \frac{3}{36}, \frac{4}{36}$ etc. Draw students' attention to the fact that the pattern starts decreasing halfway through the possibilities.

Misconceptions and challenges	Solutions
Students may find it difficult to trace probability paths through a tree diagram where the probabilities are dependent, and so different for each branch of an event.	Make sure that students understand independent events are a special case, and give them plenty of chance to practise with dependent events where the probabilities vary between branches.
Students underestimate the amount of information contained in a Venn diagram and when calculating the probability of events they may forget to include a part of the diagram in their calculations.	Give students plenty of time using Venn diagrams to organise and classify results in a number of areas of maths (factors, primes, upper and lower bounds, properties of shapes, etc). This will make them more aware of the different parts of the Venn diagram.
Students often want to add probabilities to calculate the probability of multiple events. For example, they will try to calculate the probability of tossing three heads in a row as $\frac{1}{2}$, $\frac{1}{2}$, $\frac{1}{2}$.	Help students see that additive reasoning does not apply in this case by drawing out a probability tree. It is worth giving this error a name, decided in class, so that students look out for it.
When using a tree diagram for events where there is 'no replacement' students often forget to reduce the denominator for subsequent events.	Students are used to the fact that the denominator represents the total number of outcomes, and so it is very likely they will think that this is set from the beginning. Use practical contexts to demonstrate that the number of outcomes can decrease. For example picking cubes from a bag without replacement.

Review question commentary

Use fractions for probabilities except in question **4**. Simplify all fractions fully.

Question 1 (**20.1**) – Remind students that integers are whole numbers.

Question 2 (**20.1, 20.2**) – Students do not necessarily need to fill in the middle of the table, headings are sufficient.

Question 3 (**20.2, 20.3**) – Students need to use the fact that mutually exclusive and exhaustive events sum to 1 to give the probabilities of the lights not being red.

Question 4 (**20.4**) – Consider that it could be either only Robbie ($0.6 \times 0.9 = 0.54$) or only Rachel ($0.1 \times 0.4 = 0.04$) jumping over 4 m.

Question 5 (**20.4**) – This could be done as a practical activity. Students need to understand to multiply the probabilities together. **a** $\frac{3}{5} \times \frac{2}{4}$,

b $\frac{2}{5} \times \frac{1}{4}$, **c** $\frac{3}{5} \times \frac{2}{4} + \frac{2}{5} \times \frac{3}{4}$ or $1 - \frac{3}{10} - \frac{1}{10}$

Review answers

1 a

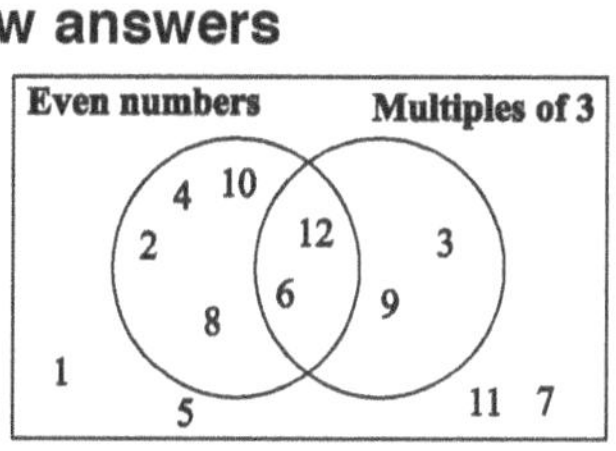

b 2 **c** $\frac{2}{12} = \frac{1}{6}$

2

		Plate		
		Red	Blue	Green
Cup	Red	R, R	R, B	R, G
	Blue	B, R	B, B	B, G
	Green	G, R	G, B	G, G

2 b i $\frac{1}{9}$ **ii** $\frac{1}{3}$ **iii** $\frac{1}{3}$

3 a, b

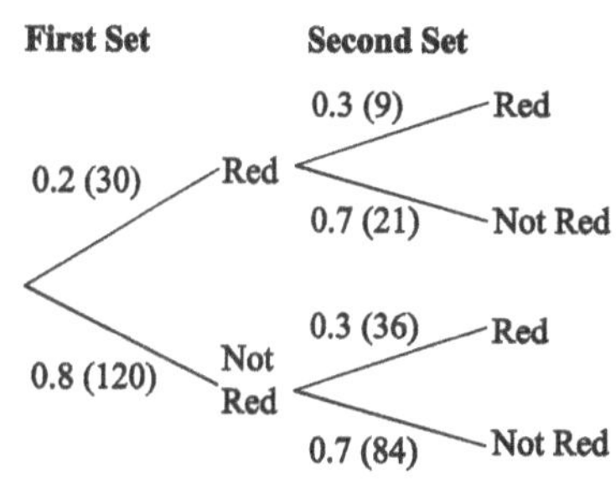

c i 0.06 **ii** 0.56

4 a 0.06 **b** 0.58

5 a $\frac{3}{10}$ **b** $\frac{1}{10}$ **c** $\frac{3}{5}$

Assessment 20

Question 1 – 12 marks

a **i** N = {2, 3, 5, 7, 11, 13, 17, 19, 23, 29} [B1]
ii M = {3, 6, 9, 12, 15, 18, 21, 24, 27, 30} [B1]
iii P = {a, d, e, i, l, p, r} [B1]
iv F = {F, a, h, r, e, n, i, t, 4, 5, 1} [B1]

b **i** {3} [F1]
ii 2, 3, 5, 7, 11, 13, 17, 19, 23, 29, 6, 9, 12, 15, 18, 21, 24, 27, 30} [F1]
iii {5} [F1]
iv {a, r, e, i} [F1]
v {p, a, r, e, l, i, d, F, h, n, t, 4, 5, 1} [F1]
vi {5} [F1]
vii {} [F1]
viii{2, 3, 5, 7, 11, 13, 17, 19, 23, 29, 6, 9, 12, 15, 18, 21, 24, 27, 30, p, a, r, e, l, i, d, F, h, n, t, 4, 1} [F1]

Question 2 – 7 marks

a

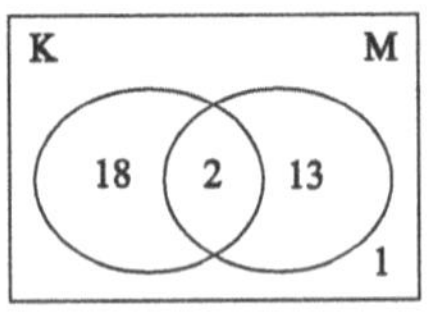

Two overlapping sets correctly labelled [B1]
Correct numbers in each region. [B3]

b 1 [B1]

c 18 + 13 = 31 [M1, A1]

Question 3 – 8 marks

a

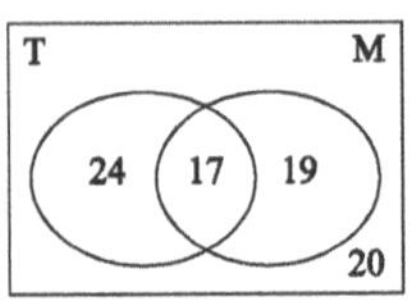

Two overlapping sets correctly labelled [B1]
Correct numbers in each region. [B3]

b **i** $\frac{41}{80}$ or 0.5125 or 51.25% [B1]
ii $\frac{44}{80} = \frac{11}{20}$ or 0.55 or 55% [B1]
iii $\frac{60}{80} = \frac{3}{4}$ or 0.75 or 75% [B1]
iv $\frac{17}{80}$ or 0.2125 or 21.25% [B1]

Question 4 – 8 marks

a Heads 8, 7, 9, 6, 7
Tails 16, 12, 18, 9, 10
Lose 1 mark for each error. [B4]

b $\frac{2}{10} = \frac{1}{5}$ or 0.2 or 20% [B1]

c $\frac{6}{10} = \frac{3}{5}$ or 0.6 or 60% [B1]

d $\frac{4}{10} = \frac{2}{5}$ or 0.4 or 40% [B1]

e $\frac{5}{10} = \frac{1}{2}$ or 0.5 or 50% [B1]

Question 5 – 8 marks

a

+	1	2	3	4	5	6	7	8
1	2	3	4	5	6	7	8	9
2	3	4	5	6	7	8	9	10
3	4	5	6	7	8	9	10	11
4	5	6	7	8	9	10	11	12
5	6	7	8	9	10	11	12	13
6	7	8	9	10	11	12	13	14
7	8	9	10	11	12	13	14	15
8	9	10	11	12	13	14	15	16

Correct diagram [B1]
Minus 1 mark for each incorrect entry [B2]

b **i** $\frac{2}{64} = \frac{1}{32}$ [B1]
ii $\frac{7}{64}$ [B1]
iii $\frac{5}{64}$ [B1]

c 9 [B1]

d All outcomes were assumed to be equally likely. [B1]

Question 6 – 7 marks

a

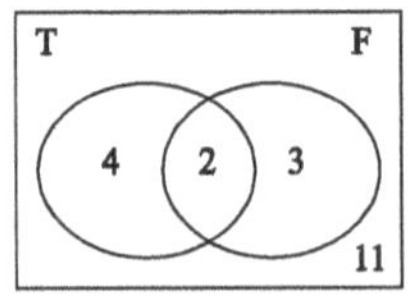

Two overlapping sets correctly labelled [B1]
Correct numbers in each region. [B3]

[n(F) = 0.2 × 20 = 4, n(T ∩ F) = 4, n(T ∪ F) = 9]

b n is less than or equal to 20; has 5 factors, 2 of which are factors of 18 [M2]
n = 16 [A1]

Question 7 – 4 marks

Tea	17	Tea-Chocolate	12
		Tea-Plain	17 – 12 = 5
Coffee	32 – 17= 15	Coffee-Chocolate	22 – 12 = 10
		Coffee-Plain	15 – 10 = 5

Minus 1 mark for each error. [B4]

Question 8 – 8 marks

a B 0.1 + 0.15 = 0.25, $\frac{1}{4}$ BB 0.25 × 0.25 = 0.0625, $\frac{1}{16}$
BA 0.25 × 0.75 = 0.1875, $\frac{3}{16}$
A 1 – 0.25 = 0.75, $\frac{3}{4}$ AB 0.75 × 0.25 = 0.1875, $\frac{3}{16}$
AA 0.75 × 0.75 = 0.5625, $\frac{9}{16}$
Lose 1 mark for each error. [B3]

b 0.25 × 0.25 = 0.0625 or $\frac{1}{16}$ [M1, A1]

c 0.25 + 0.75 × 0.25 [M2]
= 0.4375 or $\frac{7}{16}$ [A1]

Question 9 – 17 marks

a 0.1 [1 – (0.65 + 0.25)] [B1]

b [5]

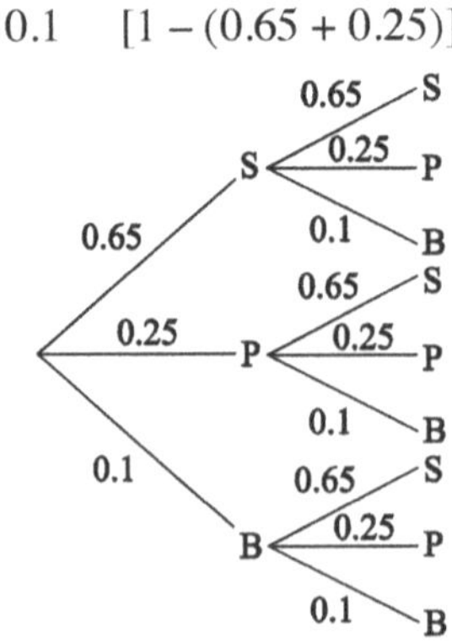

Correctly drawn and labelled tree. [B1]
Correct numbers at end of each branch. [B4]

c **i** 0.1 × 0.25 = 0.025 [M1, A1]
ii 0.65 × 0.65 = 0.4225 [M1, A1]
iii 0.65 × 0.25 + 0.1 × 0.25 [M2]
= 0.1875 [A1]
iv 0.65 × 0.1 + 0.25 × 0.1 + 0.1 [M3]
= 0.19

Sequences

Learning outcomes

A23 Generate terms of a sequence from either a term-to-term or a position-to-term rule.

A24 Recognise and use sequences of triangular, square and cube numbers, simple arithmetic progressions, Fibonacci type sequences, quadratic sequences, and simple geometric progressions (r^n where n is an integer, and r is a rational number > 0).

A25 Deduce expressions to calculate the nth term of linear sequences.

Prior knowledge

Check-in skill

- Calculate the difference between pairs of numbers.
- Understand and calculate multiples.
- Substitute numerical values into expressions.

Online resources

MyMaths 1053, 1054, 1165, 1173, 1920

InvisiPen videos

Skills: 21Sa – h Applications: 21Aa – e

Kerboodle assessment

Online Skills Test 21 Chapter Test 21

Development and links

Knowledge of sequences was vital to decoding the German Enigma code at Bletchley Park during World War II. Sequences are commonly used in encoding and encryption, and have applications in finance, security and telecommunications. They occur in the natural world in the arrangement of leaves and petals and are important in art and architecture to achieve pleasing proportions. In medicine, DNA sequencing has been responsible for huge leaps forward in research as scientists understand more about the human genome and the causes of disease.

Chapter investigation

Start by reviewing the language of sequences and how they are described by term-to-term and position-to-term rules [**21.1**].

Abi's sequence is $T(1) = 1$ and $T(n + 1) = T(n) + 3$ or $T(n) = 3n - 2$.

Bo's sequence is $T(1) = 1$ and

$T(n + 1) = T(n) + (3n - 2)$ or $T(n) = \frac{1}{2}(3n^2 - 7n + 6)$.

Cara's sequence is $T(1) = 1, T(2) = 2$ and

$T(n + 2) = T(n + 1) + T(n)$.

Ask students to create a few sequences of their own using the three sets of rules and then plot the terms against positions for each sequence.

Abi's sequence is clearly linear, the gradient given by the constant difference [**21.2**].

Bo's sequence is quadratic [**21.3**]; the method of construction suggesting a way to identify the type. The constant second difference is 3.

Using the natural numbers and odd numbers in Bo's method gives the triangular and square numbers respectively.

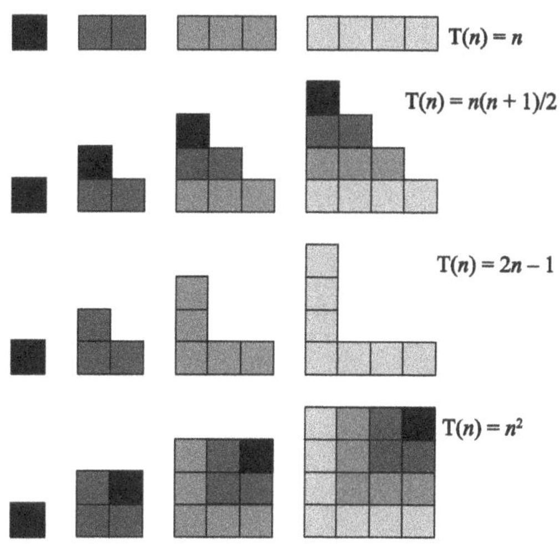

Cara's sequence is Fibonacci-type. On a graph it will quickly settle to show exponential growth.

This is equivalent to the ratio of terms in the sequence tending to have a constant value, here

$\varphi = (1+\sqrt{5})/2 = 1.6180339\ldots$

This means that the sequence approaches a geometric sequence with $T(n) \sim C\varphi^n$.

21.1 Sequence rules

Objectives

① A23 Generate terms of a sequence from either a term-to-term or a position-to-term rule

Useful resources

Mini whiteboards, number lines

Starter – Skills

Give students a start number (say 17). Work around the class asking students to count up in 2s. Repeat with different start numbers. Extend to decreasing steps, then progressing to negative numbers.

Teaching notes – Skills

Write the sequence 13, 15, 17 and 19 on the board. Remind students of key terminology of sequence, term. Discuss what the next term will be. Elicit that the difference between terms is 2, so the rule is 'add 2'. Repeat for different sequences, such as 25, 20, 15, 10, …

Highlight that sequence rules indicate how to move from one term to the next. Formalise as *term-to-term* rules. Highlight that each sequence has a start number and a rule.

Ensure students recognise the difference between the position of the term, and its value by asking questions such as: What is the value of the 5th term in this sequence? What position is x in?

Display the sequence 3, 6, 9, 12, …

Ask for the term-to-term rule. Discuss the value of the 10th and 100th terms.

Emphasise that this would be easier if you had a rule linking the position and the term.

Discuss such a rule and elicit: 3 × position = term. Highlight this as the *position-to-term* rule.

Explain that the letter n is often used to represent the position: 3 × position = $3 \times n = 3n$. Explain this is known as the nth term. Ask what value the 100th and 200th terms would have.

Plenary – Skills

Invite students to give the terms of a linear sequence where the difference is 3. Collect sequences and highlight that some sequences are ascending and some are descending. Invite students to give the first five terms of an ascending linear sequence where the difference is 4. Highlight that you need a further piece of information to generate a specific sequence; the *first term*.

Exercise commentary – Skills

Question 1 Emphasise that the rule given is applied to the last term in order to find the new term. Ask 'will the second term for part **h** be -13 or -7?'

Questions 2 to **4** In each part students will need to apply a given rule to the term before to generate the next term. Ask 'will the second term for question **4** part **f** be 1 or 4?' As an extension, students could present each set of sequences on a graph with term number along the x-axis and investigate the different patterns they create. Is there a connection between the pattern seen in **3** part **a** and **4** part **a**?

Question 5 As an extension students could be asked to pose similar or more challenging problems of this style for each other.

Question 6 This would make a suitable question to discuss as a whole class; for different reasons any one of the three sequences given could be classed as the odd one out.

Question 7 As an extension pose 'find the error' questions for these sequences. For example, in part **a** 'Jay says that the term 49 is in this sequence – show that he can't be right'. Some students will solve the equation $3n + 3 = 49$ and others will recognise that this sequence only contains multiples of 3.

Question 8 Remind students to follow the principles of BIDMAS when substituting, this is particularly important in parts **f** and **h**.

Question 9 As an extension or a homework task students could be asked to research the Fibonacci sequence, where does this sequence arise in nature?

Simplification – Skills

Students should concentrate on generating the terms of simple linear sequences. Allow them to work with linear sequences which contain negative values and which go down as well as up.

Extension – Skills

Students could be asked to generate sequences from position-to-term rules involving powers such as n^3, $2n^2$ and $n^2 + 1$.

Recap – Applications

1 For each of these sequences:

i find the next two terms

ii fill in any missing spaces

iii write down the term-to-term rule.

a -15, -12, ... , ..., -3

(i 0, 3 ii -9, -6 iii +3)

b 9, 6.5, 4, ... , ... , -3.5

(i -6, -8.5 ii 1.5, -1 iii -2.5)

c 256, 64, ... , 4, 1

(i $\frac{1}{4}$, $\frac{1}{16}$ ii 16 iii ÷4)

d 400, 640, 1024

(i 1638.4, 2621 iii ×1.6)

e 2, -6, 18, ... , ... , -486

(i 1458, -4374 ii -54, 162 iii × -3)

f ... , 500, -100, 20, ... ,0.8

(i -0.16, 0.032 ii -2500, -4 iii × -5)

2 Generate the first five terms of the sequences with these position-to-term rules.

a $T(n) = 7n$ (7, 14, 21, 28, 35)

b $T(n) = 23 - 5n$ (18, 13, 8, 3, -2)

c $T(n) = n^2 + 1$ (2, 5, 10, 17, 26)

d $T(n) = \dfrac{60}{n}$ (60, 30, 20, 15, 12)

e $T(n) = (-2)^n$ (-2, 4, -8, 16, -32)

Plenary – Applications

Show students a two-step position-to-term pattern:

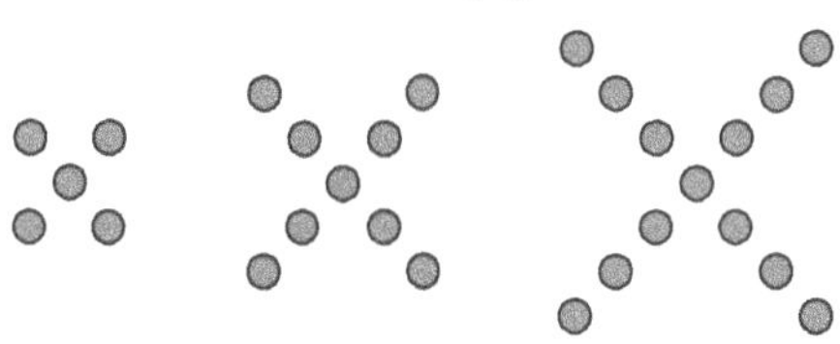

Discuss the term-to-term rule, what the difference is. Re-emphasise the limitations of the term-to-term rule. To derive the position-to-term rule suggest students write out the four times table (4 is the term-to term difference) and compare it to the actual number of dots in the patterns. In each case they need to add 1, so the position-to-term rule is '4 × pattern number + 1'. This should be checked on, say, the fourth pattern.

Exercise commentary – Applications

Question 1 Ask students to describe in words how each new diagram differs from the previous one, they should then be able to draw the next diagram. For the final part ask students to make it clear in their diagram exactly how many matches they have used.

Question 2 Tell students to use a process of elimination here, match up the ones that seem easiest first of all.

Question 3 You may wish to allow students to use a calculator for this question. If they don't find the term 1021 when they apply the term-to-term rule then they know they have made a mistake. More advanced students should be encouraged to use the inverse rule.

Question 4 Students may initially take a time consuming approach when attempting this question. To speed up this question show students that they can find the difference between 1000 and the first term given and then see if this is divisible by the number that is being added or subtracted each time.

Question 5 Here students become familiar with the fact that the coefficient of x in the term-to-term rule determines what is added or subtracted each time.

Question 6 Encourage students to come up with a general statement that proves what Belle thinks, along the lines of 'if you multiply any number by four then it will be an even number and if you subtract two from any even number it will still remain even.'

Question 7 Encourage students to try out this process for at least 3 positive values as well as negative and fractional values. Once they see that the statement seems to work, model using n why this will work for any given value generating the sequence $n, 4n, 5n, 9n, 14n, 23n, 37n, 60n$.

Question 8 This would be a suitable question to go through as a whole class. Build up to the answer by asking how would we find the 30th term? How about the 29th term? And the 28th term? Can we extend this approach to finding the 1st term? Promote responses that involve taking away multiples of 5, try and encourage students to explain why to find the 1st term we take away 30 × 5 from 159.

Question 9 A useful extension task where the answer is likely to surprise some students.

Simplification – Applications

Students can be given further practice at writing out the terms of a sequence, given a simple rule. Students should be encouraged to continue patterns and identify term-to-term rules for further examples. Avoid position-to-term rules from patterns.

Extension – Applications

Students could create their own patterns and challenge a partner to continue the pattern and find the number of dots/sticks, etc. in the 10th pattern, for example.

21.2 Finding the *n*th term

Objectives

① A25 Deduce expressions to calculate the *n*th term of linear sequences

Useful resources

Mini whiteboards

Starter – Skills

Write these expressions on the board.

$3n - 1$	$12 - 2n$
$2n + 4$	$3n^2 + 1$

For each expression, ask students to substitute the values $n = 1, 2, 3$ and 4. Students should write the values of the expression as a list of numbers.

Teaching notes – Skills

Refer to the sequence $3n - 1$ from the starter:

2, 5, 8, 11, …

Explain that a sequence that goes up or down by the same number is called a linear sequence. What is the term-to-term rule? (+3)

How do we find the 257th term? We need a position-to-term rule. This sequence has a rule of 'position × 3 + 2'

The 7th term is $7 \times 3 - 1 = 20$

The 257th term is $257 \times 3 - 1 = 770$

The rule is normally called the '*n*th term' or 'T_n'.

Instead of writing 'position × 3 + 2' you use the letter *n* to stand for the position so '$3n + 2$'.

How do you find the rule for the *n*th term?

Look at the sequence 2, 5, 8, 11, 14, …
Because the sequence goes up by 3 each time, the rule will begin with $3n$.
The positions *n* are 1, 2, 3, 4, 5, …
Using $3 \times n$ for each term, leaves you 1 above the sequence: 3, 6, 9, 12, 15, …
So the *n*th term, T_n, is $3n - 1$.

Look at the sequence 14, 8, 2, −4, −10, …
Because the sequence goes down by 6 each time, the rule will begin with $-6n$.
The positions *n* are 1, 2, 3, 4, 5, …
However using $-6 \times n$ for each term leaves you 20 below the sequence: −6, −12, −18, −24, −30, …
So the *n*th term, T_n, is $6n + 20$.

Plenary – Skills

Show the whole group a sequence written in vertical table form. Ask students to use whiteboards. What is the next number in the sequence (the fifth term)? Is this a linear sequence? How is a linear sequence recognised? Which multiplication table is involved? What tells us this? Find the sequence rule. Write the rule for the *n*th term.

Exercise commentary – Skills

Questions 1 and **2** Ensure that students understand that *n* represents the term number, if you want to find the 1st term then you make $n = 1$ and substitute this into the given *n*th term rule, the 2nd term will be found when $n = 2$ and so on.

Question 3 Make sure students realise that the notation $T(n)$ is just another way of representing *n*th term. To find the value of the required term you just need to substitute *n* into the given expression.

Question 4 Any student who is finding this question difficult should look through part **b** of the first example on page 438.

Question 5 Reinforce the fact that a linear sequence goes up *or* down by the same amount each time. Students may benefit from representing some sequences on a set of axes to see why they are called 'linear'.

Question 6 This question gently guides students in the direction of being able to find the general term for a linear sequence.

Question 7 As an extension challenge students to create sub-sequences using every third term of one of the sequences and write down the new *n*th term. How does this relate to the original rule?

Question 8 Discuss the circumstance where the sequence goes *down* by the same amount each time, what will the coefficient of *n* be in this situation? As an extension you could ask students to explain why the *n*th term rule is a much more useful rule than the term-to-term rule.

Question 9 Some students may predict that the 10th term is 42, $4 \times 10 = 40$ and $2 + 40 = 42$. This question challenges this misconception and ensures students follow the correct process when calculating the *n*th term.

Question 10 Encourage students to generate the first few terms of the sequence that has the *n*th term $5n - 3$. They should then be able to see that the units digit is always 2 and then 7: 2, 7, 12, 17… This should enable them to answer the question quickly. As an extension you could pose similar questions to this based on different *n*th term rules and challenge students to find another method of answering the question.

Simplification – Skills

Provide students with a pre-drawn table to help with setting out their answers. This can be withdrawn once they appreciate what needs to be done.

Extension – Skills

Students could be given linear sequences that involve decimals or fractions.

Alternatively they could be challenged to write the nth term for 'obvious' non-linear sequences such as,

$2, 5, 10, 17, 26, \ldots\ n^2 + 1$

$2, 8, 18, 32, 50, \ldots\ 2n^2$

$1, 8, 27, 64, 125, \ldots\ n^3$

Recap – Applications

1 The nth term of a sequence is $T(n) = 21 - \frac{5}{n}$
Find
a T(1) **b** T(50) **c** T(100)
(**a** 16 **b** 20.9 **c** 20.95)

2 Find the nth term of these sequences:
a 20, 16, 12, 8, ... $(24 - 4n)$
b $1, 3\frac{1}{2}, 6, 8\frac{1}{2}, \ldots$ $\left(2\frac{1}{2}n - 1\frac{1}{2}\right)$
c $10\frac{1}{4}, 10\frac{1}{2}, 10\frac{3}{4}, 11, \ldots$ $\left(10 + \frac{n}{4}\right)$
d $14, 12, 11\frac{1}{3}, 11, \ldots$ $\left(10 + \frac{4}{n}\right)$

3 Here is the start of a sequence of patterns:

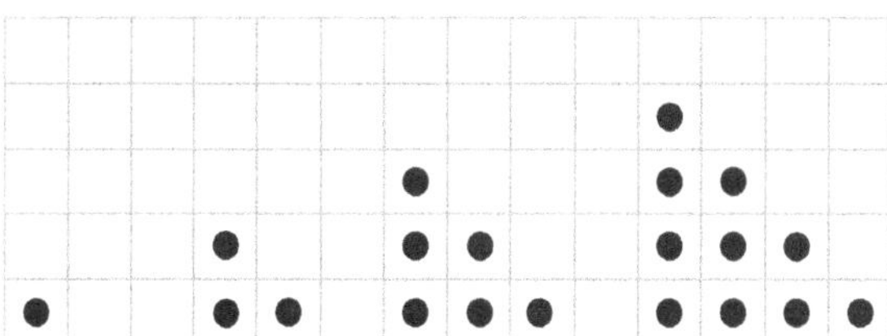

a Draw the next pattern.
b Show that the number of terms in each pattern is given by the formula $T(n) = \frac{n(n+1)}{2}$

Plenary – Applications

Say you are going to give the students a challenging sequence to look at.

Write 1, 4, 9, 16, 25, 36, ... on the board.

Ask the students to work in pairs to look for any patterns that they can spot in this sequence. The most likely response is that of 'adding odd numbers'. Do the students recognise these numbers? What might the nth term look like? Discuss the findings. Sometimes the 'obvious' is overlooked.

Exercise commentary – Applications

Question 1 Some students will answer this question by continuing the sequence and establishing if 36 is in the sequence or not. Others may form an equation with the nth term equal to 36 and then solve to see if n is a whole number. Discuss in what type of situation the latter approach becomes more suitable.

Question 2 This question addresses a common misconception. Ensure students realise that the common difference is represented by the coefficient of x in the nth term expression.

Question 3 These sequences and expressions could be written on cards and used to play snap.

Question 4 For part **d** students will need to set up and solve an inequality, they must remember to look for the integer solution nearest the boundary.

Question 5 Encourage use of the nth term here. If students want to draw the pattern use peer assessment as errors are likely in such a large figure.

Question 6 Emphasise the fact that there are lots of correct ways in which the diagrams could be drawn.

Question 7 Make sure students realise that the posts are vertical and that the planks are horizontal. Encourage students to create a table showing the pattern number, the number of posts and the number of planks.

Question 8 Students need to describe in words how the sequence starts and how it increases each time.

Question 9 Once students have found the first few terms they should be able to establish that all terms are multiples of 5. Try and ask them to prove this in more general terms. When you multiply any number by 10 what sort of number do you always get? What happens if you subtract 5?

Question 10 The second part of the last example on page 440 demonstrates the method here.

Question 11 Encourage students to look for the equation of the line. Emphasise that nth term formulae are special because n can only take integer values.

Simplification – Applications

Students should concentrate on finding the nth term of linear sequences which *ascend* before attempting descending sequences.

Extension – Applications

Give students examples of non-linear sequences and ask them to investigate a possible method (with guidance) for generating the nth term formula.

Special sequences

Objectives

① A24 Recognise and use sequences of triangular, square and cube numbers, simple arithmetic progressions, Fibonacci type sequences, quadratic sequences, and simple geometric progressions

Useful resources

Mini whiteboards, OHT/whiteboard file of pattern sequences, matchsticks

Starter – Skills

How many squares can you see in these four grids?

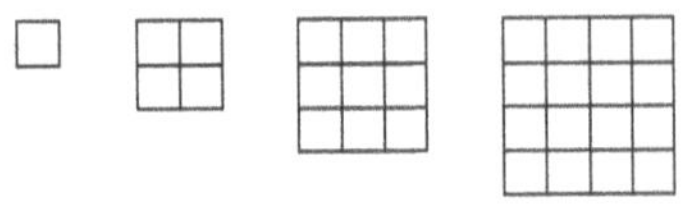

Write down how you counted up to your answer.
(1; 1 + 4 = 5; 1+ 4 + 9 = 14; 1 + 4 + 9 + 16 = 30)

How many squares could you see on a chessboard (an 8 by 8 grid)?

(30 + 25 + 36 + 49 + 64 = 204)

Teaching notes – Skills

Sometimes you don't have a sequence of numbers, but a sequence of diagrams.

Display a pattern of dots in triangle shapes (the triangle numbers). Show how you can use a table to find the sequence of triangle numbers:

1, 3, 6, 10, 15, …

Extend to the square numbers, and then to a cube sequence, which offers a 3D example.

Consider hexagons are joined together to form a chain.

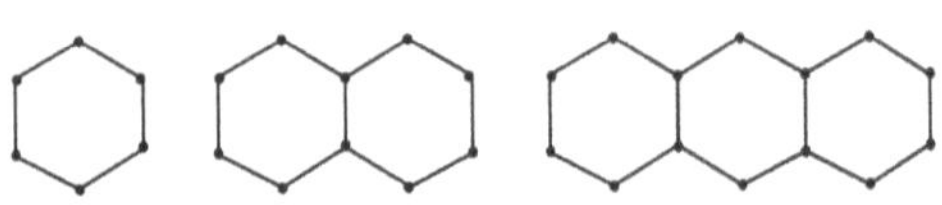

When 3 hexagons are joined you need 16 lines. How many lines for n hexagons?

To form the sequence of numbers you need to imagine 1 hexagon, then 2, 3 and so on. The sequence is 6, 11, 16, 21, …

Number of lines = $5n + 1$.

This can also be done by recognising that each extra hexagon drawn needs five lines, so the formula must start with $5n$, but you need to add 1.

Plenary – Skills

What is the sequence obtained by dividing the square number sequence by the cube number sequence, one term at a time?

$\left(\frac{1}{1}, \frac{4}{8}, \frac{9}{27}, \frac{16}{64}, \frac{25}{125}, = \frac{1}{1}, \frac{1}{2}, \frac{1}{3}, \frac{1}{4}, \frac{1}{5}, \ldots\right)$

Can you see why it works out this way?
(Each term is made by squaring on top and cubing underneath, this means multiplying twice on top and multiplying three times underneath. Cancelling leaves a single term in the denominator.)

Exercise commentary – Skills

Question 1 Ensure you have defined triangular, square and cube numbers before asking students to complete this question.

Question 2 Emphasise that triangular numbers form a right-angled isosceles triangular shape when drawn out.

Question 3 Arithmetic sequences are easiest to spot, tell students to find these sequences first. Stress that when they think they know how the sequence is formed they should ensure this works for all terms and not just the first term. Question **4** supports this as all types of sequences can start with the same first two numbers.

Question 4 As an extension you could give students a more challenging pair of starting numbers and ask them to repeat the question for example, -3, 12 or 5, 2.5

Question 5 Initially students may find part **d** difficult, ask '*if* the second difference is a constant number what must it be? What must be happening with the first difference?'

Question 6 This question clarifies the essential meaning of an important term.

Questions 7 to **9** In these questions students will need to demonstrate that they can apply the rule given to generate the terms in the sequence. They should then be able to compare the sequence found to the type of number sequence specified in the question.

Question 10 An explanation of how to multiply surds will also probably be welcome in order to be able to answer the last part, ensure students know to leave the terms in surd form.

Question 11 Ask students to describe the property of a Fibonacci sequence, on realising that the next term is found by adding the previous two terms together they should be able to find possible values for a and b. Ask 'does it matter which one is the bigger number?'

Question 12 As an extension challenge students to write a formula for this using T(n) notation. Can they use this to write the 50th term in terms of T(40), T(41) and T(42)?

Question 13 You may wish to allow students the use of a calculator for this question. As an extension to part **c** you could ask them to investigate if what they have found out applies to all geometric sequences or just to some, how can they tell whether this property will apply or not?

Questions 14 and **15** As an extension you could ask students to set up similar style problems for each other to solve.

Simplification – Skills

Concentrate on patterns which have a simple linear rule and which can be easily visualised.

Extension – Skills

Students could be asked to investigate other sequences similar to the Fibonacci sequence.

Recap – Applications

1 The first four terms of another sequence are:
100, 85, 70, 55

  a Write down the next two terms of this sequence. (40, 25)

  b Find the nth term of the sequence. ($T(n) = 115 - 15n$)

  c Write down the 50th and 100th term of this sequence. ($T(50) = -635$, $T(100) = -4885$)

2 a Complete this sequence with the missing numbers:
1, 8, ..., 64, 125, ..., 343, ...
(27, 216, 512)

  b What is the name of this Familiar sequence? (Cube numbers)

3 Find the first 3 terms, the 10th and the 100th for the sequence where $T(n) = n^2 + 25$
(26, 29, 34, 125, 10 025)

Plenary – Applications

Draw a 4 × 4 square. There are 30 squares inside it. Can you find all of them?

How many squares are there in a 3 × 3 square? (14)

Draw a 10 × 10 square. How long might it take to count all the squares inside?

Fortunately there is a formula for finding the number of squares inside. For an $n \times n$ square grid the number of squares inside it is

$$\frac{1}{6}n(n+1)(2n+1)$$

Using the formula what is the answers for a 10 × 10 square?
($10 \times 11 \times 21 \div 6 = 2310 \div 6 = 385$ squares)

Exercise commentary – Applications

Questions 1 and **2** Ask 'If you know a term-to-term rule how can you create different sequences?' Students should realise that choosing a different starting number will result in a different sequence.

Question 3 As an extension challenge students to find another number that is both a square and cube number.

Question 4 Encourage using diagrams to explain why this is the case – showing diagrammatically that the sum of two consecutive triangular numbers is equal to a square number (putting the diagrams of the triangular numbers together – drawing one diagram rotated by a half turn).

Question 5 Once again suggest to students that their response should relate to the diagram, each time how many more dots are being added?

Question 6 It is likely that students will produce a wide variety of different sequences for this question, you could look at some answers as a whole class and discuss whether they are correct or not.

Questions 7 to **10** These questions would make appropriate homework tasks or activities for students to work on in small groups – you could give a different task to each group. Once completed, each group could present their findings and explanations to the whole class.

Question 11 Make available a calendar so that the number of months and days can be agreed. A spreadsheet and graphing software would help students appreciate the linear and exponential growth rates for the options. Students could be asked to investigate the work of Thomas Malthus who claimed the growth in population is geometric whilst that in resources (food production) is arithmetic.

Question 12 This question could be copied and the options cut out and matched physically.

Simplification – Applications

Work on just one of the special sequences at a time, before mixing them up. Students could write out the first 10 square numbers and the first 10 cube numbers (using a calculator after the 5th one). For triangular numbers, students will need to draw the patterns so squared paper would help them to do this neatly. Invite them to make up their own Fibonacci sequences and draw out the conclusion that once you have decided on two starter numbers, the Fibonacci sequence can be generated.

Extension – Applications

Students could explore the number of diagonals in an n-sided polygon, by continuing this table:

Sides	4	5	6	7	8	...	...
Diagonals	2						

21 Sequences

Key outcomes	Quick check
A23 Generate terms of a sequence from either a term-to-term or a position-to-term rule.	**1 a** What are the next three terms and the term-to-term rule for these sequences? **i** 8, 11, 14, 17, … (20, 23, 26, add 3) **ii** 25, 19, 13, 7, … (1, –5, –11, subtract 6) **iii** 0.2, 0.4, 0.6, 0.8, … (1, 1.2, 1.4, add 0.2) **2** Calculate the 7th term for these sequences. **a** $T(n) = 5n - 3$ (32) **b** $T(n) = 10n + 4$ (74) **c** $T(n) = -2n + 8$ (–6) **3** Matchsticks are arranged into triangles as shown.  Draw the fourth pattern in the sequence. ()
A24 Recognise and use sequences of triangular, square and cube numbers, simple arithmetic progressions, Fibonacci type sequences, quadratic sequences, and simple geometric progressions (r^n where n is an integer, and r is a rational number > 0).	**4** The nth term of a sequence is given by $2n^2$. Calculate the **a** 3rd term (18) **b** 7th term (98) **c** 10th term. (200) **5** This sequence is formed by adding the two previous terms to get the next term. 3, 4, 7, 11, … Write down the next three terms of the sequence. (18, 29, 47) **6** Write down the next two terms of these sequences **a** 1, 4, 9, 16, … (25, 36) **b** 1, 3, 9, 27, … (81, 243)
A25 Deduce expressions to calculate the nth term of linear sequences.	**7** Write a rule for the nth term of these sequences. **a** 8, 16, 24, 32, … ($8n$) **b** 2, 8, 14, 20, … ($6n - 4$) **c** 9, 11, 13, 15, … ($2n + 7$) **d** 10, 0, –10, –20, … ($-10n + 20$)

Misconceptions and challenges	Solutions
Students find it difficult to move from the concept of term-to-term rule to the reasoning involved in position-to-term rules.	Begin with sequences given by simple expressions such as $3n$ for the nth term. Then look at $3n + 1$, $3n + 2$, and so on.
Students find it difficult to remember the procedure for producing the formula for the nth term of a sequence, especially when the sequence decreases.	Students need list the sequence systematically and compare it with the sequence given by looking at the term-to-term difference alone, as an intermediary stage. Students who structure their working clearly will find this much easier to tackle.
Students are unlikely to recognise key sequences automatically, particularly where they have not often had success with learning about properties of number.	You can revise sequences of numbers in other topics by having every number in an exercise being a cube, or triangle number. For example, 'Using only triangle numbers, how many pairs of equivalent fractions can you make?'
It is very common to think that the 100th term of an arithmetic sequence will be 10 times as large as the 10th term, or other similar reasoning.	Allow students to make this prediction then demonstrate that it doesn't work in most cases. Look at $n + 1$. Here, the tenth term is 11, so students think the 100th term is 110 instead of 101. Challenge students to classify the expressions that produce the results they are after (nth term = $an + 0$), and those that won't.

Misconceptions and challenges	Solutions
When asked to 'Explain why x is not in the sequence…' students' reasoning is often vague or incomplete.	Model how explanations can include calculations, and must contain precise mathematical information. Look at how answers such as '… because it ends in a …' are often incorrect.
Some students struggle to recognise square numbers individually or in sequence.	Students will need regular practice with square numbers, and must rehearse them frequently. You can play square number bingo, or guess the square number, and so on.
Students find it difficult to apply their knowledge of sequences to practical contexts despite having confidence with a sequence of numbers.	Encourage students to sketch the images of a pictorial sequence, and ask themselves 'what's the same, and what's different?' about subsequent terms. They can then look at the numbers associated with the sequence, and see how they relate to the structure of the sequence itself.
Looking for a linear expression of the form $an+b$, students can make mistakes finding b in cases where a is negative.	If students calculate that $a = -2$, encourage them to generate the result for $n = 0$, and use that to calculate b. Alternatively, if students are more confident working with $n = 1$, then they need to be careful with their negative coefficients.
When asked if a number is in a sequence, students find it difficult to know how to re-arrange the algebraic expression so try to calculate every term until they reach or go past the given number.	Clearly, calculating every term is an inefficient method. Students can spend time organising and classifying numbers based on a sequence, and then looking for patterns (perhaps in the units digits for a start), before looking at how to apply numeric or algebraic reasoning to the problem.
Questions that are 'reversed', such as 'What position does the term 356 hold in the sequence given by $7n - 1$?' can cause confusion for many students.	Make a link between nth term expressions and work on solving equations. Students will need to understand the difference between expressions and equations.

Review question commentary

Calculators should not be necessary for this exercise.

Question 1 (21.1) – Students need to know the difference between term-to-term rules and position-to-term rules (also known as the nth term).

Question 2 (21.1) – Need to substitute $n = 9$ into each rule.

Question 3 (21.1) – Correct order of operations needs to be applied here otherwise will get 49, 196, 10 404.

Question 4 (21.2) – Students should check their answers by substituting $n = 1$ for first term, $n = 2$ for second term etc.

Question 5 (21.2) – Discuss what a formula will look like, i.e. it will have an 'equals' sign not just be an expression.

Questions 6 and **7 (21.3)** – An extension task would be to consider what the nth term would be. Question **6** is $3n$ (tricky!), **7a** is x^3, **7b** is $\frac{1}{2}n(n+1)$ – tricky but can discuss how these are triangle numbers and where they come from.

Question 8 (21.3) – Encourage students to give reasons for their answers.

Review answers

1 **a i** 21, 25, 29 **ii** 4, –6, –16 **iii** 2.7, 3.3, 3.9
b i +4 **ii** –10 **iii** +0.6

2 **a** 29 **b** 61
c 3 **d** $8\frac{1}{2}$

3 **a** 27 **b** 146 **c** 10 002

4 **a** $3n$ **b** $5n - 1$ **c** $6n + 2$ **d** $22 - 2n$

5 **a**

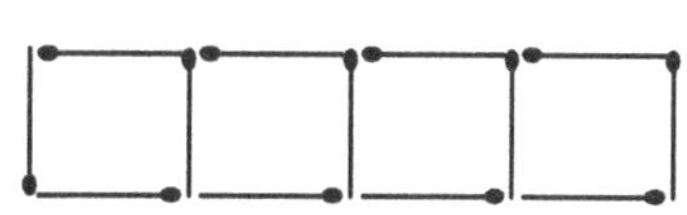

b Number of matchsticks = 4, 7, 10, 13, 16, 19
c $m = 3s + 1$

6 **a** 24, 48, 96 **b** Geometric

7 **a i** 125, 216 **ii** 15, 21
b i Cubic **ii** Triangular

8 **a** Geometric **b** Fibonacci-type
c Arithmetic **d** Quadratic

105 marks

Assessment 21

Question 1 – 65 marks

a **i** −20, −30 [B1] **ii** 30 [B1]
iii ↓ [B1] **iv** −10 [B1]
v −10 [B1]

b **i** 188, 210 [B1] **ii** 154 [B1]
iii ↑ [B1] **iv** 22 [B1]
v +22 [B1]

c **i** 3, 6 [B1] **ii** −9, −3 [B1]
iii ↑ [B1] **iv** 3 [B1]
v +3 [B1]

d **i** −10, −21 [B1] **ii** 12 [B1]
iii ↓ [B1] **iv** −11 [B1]
v −11 [B1]

e **i** 49, 54 [B1] **ii** 34, 39 [B1]
iii ↑ [B1] **iv** +5 [B1]
v +5 [B1]

f **i** 3.1, 3.5 [B1] **ii** 1.9 [B1]
iii ↑ [B1] **iv** +0.4 [B1]
v +0.4 [B1]

g **i** 84, 96 [B1] **ii** 24, 60 [B1]
iii ↑ [B1] **iv** 12 [B1]
v +12 [B1]

h **i** 1.07, 1.06 [B1] **ii** 1.09 [B1]
iii ↓ [B1] **iv** −0.01 [B1]
v −0.01 [B1]

i **i** −1.15, −1.20 [B1] **ii** −1, −1.1 [B1]
iii ↓ [B1] **iv** −0.05 [B1]
v −0.05 [B1]

j **i** 1 000 008, 1 000 0111 [B1]
ii 999 999, 1 000 002 [B1]
iii ↑ [B1] **iv** 3 [B1]
v + 3 [B1]

k **i** −0.75, −1.5 [B1] **ii** 0.75 [B1]
iii ↓ [B1] **iv** −0.75 [B1]
v −0.75 [B1]

l **i** −38, −45 [B1] **ii** −24 [B1]
iii ↓ [B1] **iv** −7 [B1]
v −7 [B1]

m **i** 6.625, 6.75 [B1] **ii** 6.125 [B1]
iii ↑ [B1] **iv** 0.125 [B1]
v + 0.125 [B1]

Question 2 – 7 marks

a – v, b – iv, c – vii, d – vi, e – ii, f – iii, g – viii, h – ii
Lose 1 mark for each incorrect *pair* of answers. [B7]

Question 3 – 3 marks

a +10 [B1]
b Comparison of $10n$ to 1, 11, 21, … [M1]
$10n - 9$ [A1]

Question 4 – 4 marks

a Jack

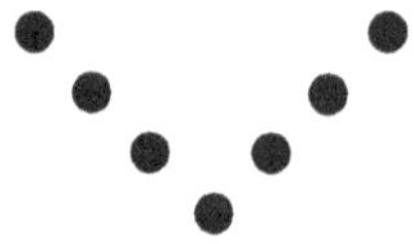

[B1]

b Common difference = 2
Comparison of $2n$ with 1, 3, 5, 7, .. [M1]
$2n - 1$ [A1]
c 19 [2 × 10 − 1] [B1]

Question 5 – 3 marks

a 16, 49, 144, 196
Lose 1 mark for each error [B2]
b Square numbers; $1 = 1^2, 4 = 2^2, 9 = 3^2, \ldots$ [B1]

Question 6 – 4 marks

a 9 red, 10 blue [B1]
b 49 red, 50 blue [B1]
c 99 red, 100 blue [B1]
d $n - 1$ red, n blue [B1]

Question 7 – 6 marks

a **i** 10, 12, 14, 16, … Common diff = 2 [M1]
$2n + 8$ [A1]
ii 4, 6, 8, 10, … Common diff = 2 [M1]
$2n + 2$ [A1]
b 54 cm^2 [P(n) = A(n) − 6] [B1]
c 42 cm [B1]

Question 8 – 6 marks

a $3n - 1$ [B1]
b Each term is 6 less than the previous term [M1]
3, −3;. [A1]
c Comparison of $-6n$ to 27, 21, 15, 9, … [M1]
$33 - 6n$ [A1]
d −279 [−267 − 6 − 6] [B1]

Question 9 – 5 marks

a Correct $2 \times 10 + 7 = 27$. [B1]
b Incorrect 1, 7, 13. [B1]
c Incorrect $13 - 3 \times 100 = -287$ [B1]
d Incorrect $102 - 10 = 100 - 10 = 90$ [B1]
e Correct $15 - 3 \times 100^2 = 15 - 30\,000$
$= -29\,985$ [B1]

Question 10 – 2 marks

Ratios = 1 : 2, 1 : 4, 1 : 6 [M1]
No [A1]

Units and proportionality

Learning outcomes	
R1	Change freely between related standard units (e.g. time, length, area, volume/capacity, mass) and compound units (e.g. speed, rates of pay, prices) in numerical and algebraic contexts.
R6	Express a multiplicative relationship between two quantities as [a ratio or] a fraction.
R7	Understand and use proportion as equality of ratios.
R8	Relate ratios [to fractions and] to linear functions.
R10	Solve problems involving direct and inverse proportion, including graphical and algebraic representations.
R11	Use compound units such as speed, rates of pay, unit pricing, density and pressure.
R12	Compare lengths, areas and volumes using ratio notation; and scale factors and similarity (including trigonometric ratios).
R13	Understand that X is inversely proportional to Y is equivalent to X is proportional to $1/Y$; construct and interpret equations that describe direct and inverse proportion.
R14	Interpret the gradient of a straight line graph as a rate of change; recognise and interpret graphs that illustrate direct and inverse proportion.
R16	Set up, solve and interpret the answers in growth and decay problems, including compound interest.

Prior knowledge

Check-in skill

- Understand direct proportion.

Online resources

MyMaths 1036, 1048, 1059, 1061, 1070, 1121, 1238, 1246

InvisiPen videos

Skills: 22Sa – e Applications: 22Aa – f

Kerboodle assessment

Online Skills Test 22 Chapter Test 22

Development and links

Problems involving proportionality in daily life include bank interest and VAT, scaling recipes, making scale models, reading maps and converting currencies. In ballistics, gravity causes a shell shot towards a target to fall towards the ground at a rate which is proportional to the square of the time since leaving the barrel of the gun.

Chapter investigation

Wages, salaries and pay is likely to be a topic of practical interest to students: where possible examples should be based on situations they may encounter.

Start by considering wages paid at an hourly rate or a 'per unit' – a piece rate. Investigate how long you need to work/many items need to be produced in order to earn a certain amount [**22.1**]. Look at changing an hourly rate into a daily, weekly or annual rate and how a piece rate compares to an hourly rate.

The amount earned per unit time is an example of direct proportion [**22.2**]. Introduce graphical representations and make links to other cases of direct proportion such as currency exchange rates, unit conversions or 'best buy' problems. For example, if company A pays £X for n hours work and company B pays \$$Y$ for m hours work then who should you work for? Look at related questions, e.g., if it takes n people to do X then how many people does it take to do Y?

The time taken to earn a given amount is an example of inverse proportion [**22.3**]. Again introduce graphical representations and related problems.

Finally return to the original question and focus on Jeannie whose pay increases are compounded [**22.4**]. Aim to develop the multiplicative formula for repeated increases. The actual question can be answered by creating a table: at the end of year 6 Ian earns £32 000 and Jeannie earns £31 737.49 and at the end of year 7 Ian earns £34 000 and Jeannie earns £34 276.49 This data can usefully be shown on a graph. Percentage decreases can be investigated in the context of depreciation.

22.1 Compound units

Objectives

① Change freely between related standard units (e.g. time, length, area, volume/capacity, mass) and compound units (e.g. speed, rates of pay, prices, density, pressure) in numerical and algebraic contexts

② Use compound units such as speed, rates of pay, unit pricing, density and pressure

Useful resources

Mini whiteboards, calculators, OHTs/whiteboard files of formulae triangles for density/speed/rate of flow, table of distances and times suitable for mental calculation of speed

Starter – Skills

Ask some questions based around travelling at 60 km per hour.

For example, how long would it take to travel 240 km?

What distance would be covered in $5\frac{1}{2}$ hours?

Ask which is faster: 60 miles per hour or 60 km/hr.

Teaching notes – Skills

① and ② Ask students for examples of **units of measurement** for **speed** (m/s, km/h, miles per hour or mph). '/' or 'per' means 'divided by', so

speed = distance ÷ time

Remind students of the **S–D–T triangle** and how to use it.

Similarly, **density** is measured in g/cm^3 or kg/m^3, so

density = mass ÷ volume

Recap density as a measure of how tightly the atoms are packed inside an object. Remind students of the D–M–V triangle.

Population density is population/km^2, so

population density = population ÷ area.

Remind students of the D–P–A triangle.

In all these formulae the units of measurement give a clue to the relationship between the quantities. Recap how knowing one relationship helps in drawing the triangle.

Plenary – Skills

Display a table of various different times and distances, with different units and figures suitable for mental calculation. Ask students to calculate associated speeds from the table, using whiteboards. Emphasise inclusion of appropriate units, and explore the reasoning behind the answers offered.

Exercise commentary – Skills

Questions 1 to **3** These focus on working out speed, distance and time given the other two quantities, without context. Ensure students use the correct units.

Questions 4 to **6** Density is the focus with these contextual questions. Beware of units, particularly in question **6** which uses kg and g.

Question 7 Students need to complete a table for pressure, force and area. A common error is to divide the wrong way around, or to multiply when they should divide. The triangles are useful if students can remember where the letters go; otherwise the clue is in the units.

Questions 8 to **9** These mini-problems involve money in simple contexts, including rates of pay.

Questions 10 to **11** This pair of questions focus on rates of flow in litres per second.

Questions 12 to **13** Energy usage and fuel efficiency provide standard contexts for compound units. In question **13**, students need to convert between miles and kilometres.

Question 14 Another standard context is exchange rates – students should appreciate that UK currency is commonly referred to as pounds sterling.

Simplification – Skills

Students may need more practice at examples where the numbers are easy to work with. This will encourage them to focus on the process and gain an understanding as to what they are doing (and why). They should be encouraged to use a formula triangle in each case, to ensure that they multiply or divide correctly. You could display these triangles on the board for ease of reference.

Extension – Skills

Students could be asked to think about other compound measures they might encounter (for example, GDP per capita), and to think about how to construct formulae for them.

Recap – Applications

1 a 1 paving slab, 0.5 m square costs £3.75. Find the price of laying a patio 8 m by 3.5 m.

b Lucy is paid £470 for a 40 hour week.

i What is her hourly rate of pay? [£11.75]

ii Overtime is paid at 'time and a half'. How much does Lucy earn if she works 46 hours in a week? [£575.75]

2 Light travels at 186 000 miles per second. Mars is, on average, 140 000 000 miles from earth.

Using these estimates, calculate how long, in minutes and seconds, it takes for light from Mars to reach the Earth. [12 minutes 33 secs]

3 A Eurostar train has reached a British train speed record of 208 mph (334.7 km per hour).
Calculate its speed in:

a miles/minute [3.47(3 sf)] b ft/sec [305 (3 sf)]

c m/minute [5 578 (3 sf)] d m/s [93.0 (3 sf)]

4 a A Bafta Award trophy has a mass of 3.7 kg and a volume of 3024 cm^3. What is its density?
[1.22 g/cm^3 (3 sf)]

b A jar of mercury has a density of 13.6 g/cm^3 and a mass of 3.4 kg. What is its volume? [250 ml]

c The air in a room 5 m × 6 m × 2.25 m has a density of 0.001 293 g/cm^3. What is the mass of the air in the room? [87 300 g (3 sf), or 87.3 kg]

Recap the different main types of compound quantities – density, speed, pressure. You might want to invite students to draw formula triangles, and ask for how they can remember which way around the letters go – students are often better at remembering if they make up their own aide memoires.

Discuss the different rates that students are aware of – rates of flow, currency exchange, also quantities such as interest rates. What is it about them that makes them a rate?

The examples in the student book give fairly standard contexts for compound units, such as the average speed of a train (discuss why this is 'average', and recap the definition of this term). In the third example, there is a kg to g conversion – students should be aware of these potential pitfalls. It may be worth quickly revising the standard metric conversions.

Plenary – Applications

Arrange these countries in ascending order of population density = the number of people/km^2.

	Russia	USA	Monaco	India	China
Population	145 M	281 M	32 k	1045 M	1284 M
Area (km^2)	17 M	9 M	1.5	3 M	10 M

(In people/km^2 the order is: Russia 8.5, USA 31, China 130, India 350 and Monaco 21 000.)

Exercise commentary – Applications

Questions 1 to **3** These are very similar to the worked examples, so provide a gentle start to the exercise. Remind students of the need to convert units in question **3**.

Questions 4 to **5** These questions provide simple practice at calculating speed/distance/time.

Questions 6 to **8** These are problems relating to density. Questions **7** and **8** require conversion between mm and cm (also m), and also kg and g. Question **8** particularly requires conversion between cubic units of length, which will need going through as a class.

Questions 9 to **10** These problems involve money – ensure appropriate units of currency are given in the answer.

Question 11 Students who struggle with this question could be prompted to work out the time of the winning yacht from what they know.

Question 12 Two similar problems involving pressure exerted on the ground. In part **b**, students will need to halve their answer.

Simplification – Applications

Stripping out the contexts, or providing simpler contexts, will help. Avoid problems involving the need to convert, particularly units of volume.

Extension – Applications

Provide more challenging problems involving density, or perhaps other contexts involving compound units encountered in physics, for instance in the study of electricity.

22.2 Direct proportion

Objectives

① **R10** Solve problems involving direct proportion, including graphical and algebraic representations

② **R13** Construct and interpret equations that describe direct proportion

③ **R14** Interpret the gradient of a straight line graph as a rate of change; recognise and interpret graphs that illustrate direct proportion

Useful resources

Mini whiteboards, calculators, wages/time scenario and table, square graph paper

Starter – Skills

Describe this scenario: A jeweller can make seven necklaces in two days. How many complete necklaces can she make in 8 working days? 2 weeks? 5 weeks? (Assuming a 5-day week.)

(28, 35, 87.5)

Discuss responses and strategies, recording different ways of approaching the problem, for later use.

Teaching notes – Skills

① ② and ③ Ask students what it means if two quantities are in **direct proportion** to each other. Elicit and explore key ideas:

- When one quantity goes up (or down), the other goes up (or down) at the same **rate**, or by the same **scale factor**.
- The ratio between each pair of corresponding values stays the same.
- Another way of saying 'directly proportional to' is 'varies (or changes) directly with'.

Emphasise that **proportionality is a multiplicative relationship**, so problems involving proportion are solved by **multiplying or dividing**. Draw at least one pair of similar shapes to illustrate, and ask questions about scale factors and the operation used to go from one length to its corresponding pair – such as 'double', 'halve' and so on.

Give students a scenario such as wages earned for a given time and say that the money earned and time worked are in proportion. Ask students to record on their whiteboards as many other wages and times as they can which would be equivalent.

Share responses and add these to a display of a table showing wages and time. Notate the table, showing the reasoning given by students as relationships to link these values. Explore real-world concepts such as hourly rate.

Demonstrate **proportionality notation** and how to interpret it. If x and y are in direct proportion, then

$y \propto x$

We read this as 'y is *proportional* to x' and it means that 'y is equal to $x \times$ a scale factor'. This scale factor is usually written as k, and its proper name is the **constant of proportionality**.

We can then write the same thing as an equation, which is much more useful for solving problems:

$y = kx$

Ask students what this would look like as a graph and sketch a representation of $y = kx$ on the board. Give students a few different values of k to sketch some graphs of $y = kx$ on whiteboards, to show how the graph changes with k. Ask for examples of possible coordinate pairs from their sketch graphs, verbalised in terms of proportion (for example, 'x is … and y is …, so y is … times as big as x').

Discuss these three methods for solving problems: the unitary method and the algebraic method always work, but the informal scaling method is often quicker and easier to use.

Guide students through a number of example questions, modelling a clear step-by-step approach and logical layout for their working.

Plenary – Skills

Brainstorm common conversions between metric and imperial units. Although students are not required to know imperial units for the exam, they are useful in everyday life. Turn this into a quick-fire exercise: 'how many miles in 10 km?'

Exercise commentary – Skills

Questions 1 to **2** Simple drill questions on cost per metre.

Questions 3 to **4** These require scaling – encourage students to use the unitary method i.e. find the value of one item (1 metre, 1 bucket).

Questions 5 to **8** questions involving cost per gram of various items in a shop. Question **7** includes an extra layer of complication, as students need to find answers relating to a single teabag.

Question 9 Here is another scaling question; students should realise that the numbers given are in the 7 × table.

Questions 10 to **11** These questions involve converting between different units (metric–metric, and metric–imperial). Students are required to draw a conversion graph – this could present some problems, and it may be worth talking through appropriate axes.

Question 12 This question involves interpreting a conversion graph between miles and kilometres. The final part relates gradient to rate, and asks students to find an algebraic formula. You should go through this together with the class.

Simplification – Skills

Students may need help in reading problems and making sense of what is being asked. They should be given further guidance in setting their work out, and encouragement to develop a clear step-by-step method that they can use.

Extension – Skills

Students may need help in reading problems and making sense of what is being asked. They should be given further guidance in setting their work out, and encouragement to develop a clear step-by-step method that they can use.

Recap – Applications

1 The air resistance (R) on a body falling varies directly as its speed (V) varies. When R is 1.8, V is 360. Find

a the formula connecting R and V

b the value of R when $V = 500$

c the value of V when $R = 5$.

(**a** $R = 0.005V$ **b** 2.5 **c** 1 000)

2 **a** A pack of 7 printer cartridges cost £17.50. How much would 10 printer cartridges cost?

b Nigella can cook 6 pancakes in 21 minutes. How long would it take her to cook 11 pancakes?

c A bricklayer can build a wall of length 15 m in $3\frac{1}{2}$ days. What length wall of the same height could he build in 14 days?

(**a** £25 **b** 38 min **c** 60 m)

3 An electric cooker uses 12.25 units of electricity over a period of 3.5 hours.

a What is the hourly rate of consumption of electricity by the cooker?

b If used continuously, how many units of electricity would the cooker use in a day?

(**a** 3.5 units/h **b** 84 units)

Recap the meaning of direct proportion, and how to use scaling or the unitary method to solve proportion problems. Students should begin to realise that these problems all involve multiplication or division, and the key is in finding the scale factor – this is the basis of multiplicative reasoning.

Discuss proportion graphs, and their main features – direct proportion graphs go through the origin, and the gradient gives the rate of change.

The first example in the student book can be worked through as a class – even though students may not be making consumer choices relating to olive oil just yet, this type of scenario is common in a supermarket, and has appeared in exams. These problems typically require use of a calculator, and appropriate rounding. There is also the need for correct interpretation – if it costs less per ml, then it's better value.

The second example is also highly useful in being a confidently numerate adult: being able to scale recipes up or down. In this case a unitary method has been used – find the number of grams for 1 person, then scale up.

Plenary – Applications

Find some recipes, either from a book or from the internet – these are often given for 4 or 6 people. Challenge students to scale to 2/3/8 people etc.

Exercise commentary – Applications

Questions 1 to **2** These problems relate to cost of packs containing multiple items. Best value type problems should be rehearsed thoroughly, not just for the exam but also for adult life.

Questions 3 to **4** These are standard recipe problems, although the numbers are not easy. Students should be confident with using a calculator, and giving an answer to an appropriate accuracy, and with the correct units.

Question 5 This problem includes ratio in a fairly complex (but realistic) scenario. You could go through this as a class, and recap ratio at the same time.

Question 6 Students should be able to decide whether two quantities are directly proportional, given the right information. In this case they're not – ensure students appreciate why.

Question 7 This problem includes a formula expressed in words – it's worth going through this together, because there's a general point in the term that's added (that should be multiplied).

Question 8 Here is an interesting problem that could be turned into an investigation on paper sizes.

Simplification – Applications

Avoid mixing ratio and proportion in the same problem; use simpler numbers for scaling.

Extension – Applications

Ask students to write a coherent report on standard paper sizes.

22.3 Inverse proportion

Objectives

① **R10** Solve problems involving direct and inverse proportion, including graphical and algebraic representations

② **R13** Interpret equations that describe direct and inverse proportion

③ **R14** Recognise and interpret graphs that illustrate direct and inverse proportion

Useful resources

Mini whiteboards, calculators

Starter – Skills

Ask the class for pairs of numbers that multiply together to give 360. Write them as coordinates, and ask what the graph would look like if it was plotted (invite sketches).

Teaching notes – Skills

① Recap definitions of direct proportion. Ask students what it might mean if two quantities are in **inverse proportion** to each other. Start from the idea that when one quantity goes up (or down), the other goes up (or down) at the same rate, or by the same scale factor: How could you adapt this description to fit inverse proportionality?

Use a simple visual example to illustrate, such as the lengths and widths of two rectangles with the same area: if the lengths double, then the widths must halve for the area to stay the same.

② Emphasise that if two quantities are inversely proportional, then the product of each pair of values is constant. This leads naturally to the equation $xy = k$, where k is the constant of proportionality. Revisiting changing the subject of the formula will elicit the equation $y = \frac{k}{x}$. Solving the equations such as $5 = \frac{20}{x}$ to find unknown x values may prove problematic; some students may prefer to interpret the equation as '20 divided by … is 5' as this removes the need to rearrange the equation.

③ Ask students what $y = \frac{k}{x}$ would look like as a graph and sketch a representation of $y = \frac{k}{x}$ on the board. Ask for examples of possible coordinate pairs from the sketch graph, verbalised in terms of proportion (for example, 'x is … and y is …, so y times x is …).

Plenary – Skills

Ask how you can tell whether two quantities are inversely proportional to each other – give some paired sets of numbers, some of which have a fixed product and some that don't.

Exercise commentary – Skills

Questions 1 to **2** These questions examine the effects of scaling up and down when quantities are directly or inversely proportional to each other.

Questions 3 to **5** These are fairly standard 'how-long-to-build-a-wall' type, questions. Students should start to think in terms of 'person-hours' or 'passenger-weeks'. There is a note of caution in the student book for question **5** – students should think whether two quantities are directly or inversely proportional.

Question 6 This links direct and inverse proportion to their algebraic representation. It will be highly useful to draw out the learning points here. Some of these formulae are designed to tease out misconceptions.

Question 7 This links inverse proportion to its graphical representation. You could ask how this could be adapted for the starter exercise.

Question 8 This provides an algebraic formula to represent the situation in question **3**.

Simplification – Skills

Promote the idea that if two variables are inversely proportional, then their product remains constant. Make links with factor pairs.

Extension – Skills

Ask students to write down possible dimensions of a rectangle with area 120 cm^2. They could then plot width against length and write a formula that connects the sides. Ask students to then create a formula connecting length and width for a rectangle with an area of 20 cm^2, and extend to triangles with a fixed area.

Recap – Applications

1 It takes 12 bricklayers 5 hours to build a wall.

a How long will it take for 6 bricklayers to build the same wall? (10 hours)

b How many bricklayers are needed to build the wall in 4 hours? (15 bricklayers)

2 x is inversely proportional to y with $y = \frac{8}{x}$.

a Complete this table of values.

x	0.5	1	2	4	8	16
y						

b Plot each pair of values and join your points with a smooth curve.

(Points plotted at (0.5, 16), (1, 8), (2, 4), (4, 2), (8, 1), (16, 0.5)).

Provide further recap with a simple scenario – London to Leeds, straight up the M1, roughly 200 miles. Ask how long it would take to travel from London to Leeds, driving at an average speed of 50 miles per hour. How long for 40 miles per hour? Try some other values (stick within the 70 speed limit!), not all of which should give integral answers.

Draw a table of values.

Ask students to trace the shape of the graph in the air, and invite someone to the front to sketch it on the board.

Ask what the relationship is between average speed and time (and encourage the response that they are inversely proportional).

Give the quantities letters: S and T. Challenge the class to identify a formula relating them ($ST = 200$). Ask how this could be rewritten to make S the subject.

Ensure that students understand how the table of values relates to the graph, and how they both relate to the formula. Also ensure that students understand the term 'reciprocal'.

Work through the example in the student book, which relates to work that students may have done in Science. Ask what the current reading at 15 ohms should actually be (probably 5.2 rather than 4.2). Ask what a suitable formula would be in this case.

Plenary – Applications

Discuss question **5** in the exercise, and ensure that students appreciate the relationship between length, width and perimeter for a given area. Extend to consideration of a triangle with a fixed area.

Exercise commentary – Applications

Question 1 Here is a simple question on the inverse relationship between speed and time.

Question 2 This is slightly different in that one of the quantities (power level) is qualitative rather than numerical (you could ask students to imagine that 'Warm' was 1 and 'Full' was 5).

Question 3 There is a considerable amount of language here, and the situation is slightly complex because there are two proportionalities. It may be a good idea to work through this together, particularly part **b**.

Question 4 This is a fairly straightforward puzzle to complete, although the challenge is knowing where to start. Once students have realised that the product is 24 (they may need a clue), then it should be easy.

Question 5 This problem explores the relationship between the length and width of a rectangle with a fixed area. The question could be extended for rectangles with different areas.

Simplification – Applications

Quantities can be given in simpler contexts, or with the context removed (or language stripped out), until students are confident in working with inverse proportion.

Extension – Applications

More problems can be derived from physics or other areas of science, involving reciprocal laws. Students could be asked to investigate quantities that only display direct or inverse proportion over a range of values. And are they ever really proportional in the real world, or is it just an approximation (what other factors are involved)?

22.4 Growth and decay

Objectives

① **R16** Solve and interpret the answers in growth and decay problems, including compound interest

Useful resources

Calculators, mini whiteboards

Starter – Skills

Ask students to work in pairs, with a whiteboard. Say that a bank gives customers interest on money left in an account. Is it better to leave this interest in the account or take it out? Allow a few minutes to discuss this before sharing some reactions. In order to model the situation, say the amount is £500 and the interest rate is 5% p.a. Ensure students understand the meaning of p.a. What interest would be earned after one year? If the interest is taken out, what is the interest for the next year? What would it be if the previous year's interest is not taken out?

Teaching notes – Skills

① Recap **simple interest** and establish the difference between simple interest and **compound interest**. Set up a table to illustrate the compound interest concept: Amount/Interest/New amount, and label rows with time. Demonstrate how to complete the table, asking students to fill in one row at a time, then checking as a class. Highlight that compound interest is just a repeated percentage increase, and extend this to encourage the use of a multiplier.

Discuss 'depreciation', using a car or similar as an example. Highlight interest and depreciation as being good examples of functional mathematics in the real world.

Students should be introduced to the term 'multiplier', which is usually given as a decimal. Show with examples how this can be easily found from a given percentage change. Give some percentages (such as 130%) and ask for the multiplier (1.3).

Students may be put off by the formulae given at the top of the page, but to solve most problems they don't actually need to learn these – just how to identify the multiplier from the context given, and then use it to find the required values.

Introduce the phrases 'exponential growth' and 'exponential decay', with examples.

Plenary – Skills

Students should use whiteboards. Describe an octopus that has a starting weight of 200 g and increases its weight by 5% each day. Ask for the weight after 1 day, after 2 days, and after 3 days. Share answers and reasoning. Ask what methods you could use to find an increase of 5%. Prompt if necessary to establish three methods (half 10% and add, × 0.05 and add, × 1.05). Which is the most efficient calculator method and why?

Exercise commentary – Skills

Students may use the opportunity to explore the functions on their scientific calculator; it is particularly helpful to discover the ability to perform iterative calculations quickly.

Question 1 This provides drill-based practice in finding the multiplier associated with given percentage change values.

Question 2 This is exponential (population) growth, and students should appreciate how numbers start off small but get very large very quickly.

Question 3 Here is an example of exponential (radioactive) decay. You might want to explain the concept of half-life, to ensure that everyone understands what it implies. Students should appreciate that the substance just keeps getting smaller and smaller but never quite disappears.

Question 4 This is a standard price decrease problem – students may need help with the wording of part **b**, which might appear ambiguous.

Questions 5 to **6** These problems include formulae – it will be helpful to use a scientific calculator efficiently with the repetitive calculations. Students may need help in understanding what is required from them in question **5**, where they have to show that a formula works for the situation.

Question 7 Compound interest appears in this question, and again the power to do iterative calculations will be helpful. Students will need to round to two decimal places for money calculations. Ensure that students are able to apply the formula given.

Simplification – Skills

Students should be confident with simple interest calculations over multiple years before moving on to problems involving compound interest.

Extension – Skills

Students could examine the use of powers of the multiplier with the number of years, when calculating compound interest.

Recap – Applications

1 **a** Find the compound interest on £350 invested for 4 years at 4% pa. (£409.45)

b Davinder bought a motor bike for £8500. Each year it depreciates in value by 12.5%. How much is the bike worth after 3 years?

(£5694.34)

2 A city is planning a new ring road. Before construction the average rate of traffic flow was measured as 1250 vehicles per hour. The planners predicted that the average rate of flow would rise by 6% per year.

Write down, in the form, $1250 \times r^n$, where r is a constant, and n is the number of years, the average rate of traffic flow after 1, 2 and 3 years. Explain why this predicts that the average rate of traffic flow after n years is 1250×1.06^n.

(1325, 1404.5, 1488.77)

Plenary – Applications

Look again at the second example (population of the village). At what point would there be no people left (when will the population round to zero)? Students could be asked to create a spreadsheet.

Exercise commentary – Applications

Questions 1 and **2** These are compound interest problems. In question **1**, students should try to do all the calculations efficiently on their calculator, only rounding at the end (not as they are going along). Question **2** highlights the difference between simple and compound interest.

Questions 3 and **4** Depreciation and population growth provide the contexts for these growth and decay problems. It is fairly standard in exams to get questions like part **b** in both questions ('after how long will the value reach/fall below/exceed ...?')

Questions 5 and **6** Both problems use formulae, with a crucial difference – in question **5**, the scenario is decay and in question **6** it is growth. Ask how the multiplier gives you a clue as to which type it is. As with question **4**, the questions invite the student to challenge the assumptions – they should appreciate that real life is only approximated to by these models, which provide a simplification.

Questions 7 and **9** These are problems in which students have to compare two accounts. In part **b** of question **7**, students should consider that they are given no information as to how the interest rate in account B progresses beyond year 3. Question **9** could lead to a nice investigation into how the frequency of adding interest can affect the amount returned.

Question 8 This puzzle should highlight the difference between multiplicative and additive growth, and how they are represented graphically.

Simplification – Applications

Keep problems to no more than 3 'years'; avoid 'reverse' questions of the type in questions **3b** and **4b**; avoid interpretation of modelling assumptions, particularly linked to formulae.

Extension – Applications

Extend to creating spreadsheets to simulate a growth or decay model over a large number of years. Explore the effects of changing the values in the formula.

22 Units and proportionality

Key outcomes	Quick check
R1 Change freely between related standard units (e.g. time, length, area, volume/capacity, mass) and compound units (e.g. speed, rates of pay, prices) in numerical and algebraic contexts.	**1** Convert **a** 2.4 km to cm (240 000 cm) **b** 500 min to hrs and min (8 hrs 20 min) **c** 520 cm^3 to litres (520 litres) **d** 10.8 km/h to m/s. (3 m/s) **2** Convert 385 000 cm^3 into m^3. (0.385 m^3) **3** A cube of side length 2.5 cm is enlarged by scale factor 4. **a** What is the volume and surface area of the **i** small cube (15.625 cm^3, 37.5 m^2) **ii** enlarged cube? (1000 cm^3, 600 m^2)
R6 Express a multiplicative relationship between two quantities as a fraction.	**4** Two variables, x and y, are directly proportional to each other. When $x = 5, y = 30$. **a** Write a formula to link x and y. ($y = 6x$) **b** What is the value of **i** y when $x = 10$ (60) **ii** x when $y = 42$? (7) **5** X is inversely proportional to Y. When $X = 2, Y = 1.5$. **a** Write a formula to link X and Y. ($Y = \frac{3}{X}$) **b** What is the value of **i** Y when $X = 5$ $\left(\frac{3}{5}\right)$ **ii** X when $Y = 3$? (1) **6** Sketch a graph to show the relationship between X and Y in **a** **i** question 3 **ii** question 4. 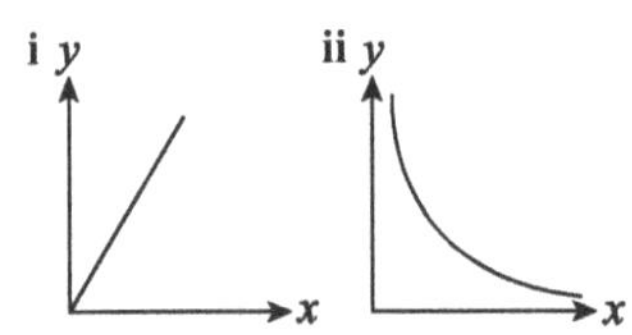 **b** x is the number of tickets sold and y is the cost of attending a concert. What does the gradient of the graph represent in question **5 a i**? (Price per person)
R7 Understand and use proportion as equality of ratios.	
R8 Relate ratios to linear functions.	
R10 Solve problems involving direct and inverse proportion, including graphical and algebraic representations.	
R13 Understand that X is inversely proportional to Y is equivalent to X is proportional to $1/Y$; construct and interpret equations that describe direct and inverse proportion.	
R14 Interpret the gradient of a straight line graph as a rate of change; recognise and interpret graphs that illustrate direct and inverse proportion.	
R11 Use compound units such as speed, rates of pay, unit pricing, density and pressure.	**7** A force of 15 N acts over an area of 3 m^2. What is the pressure? (5 N/m^2) **8** A packet of butter costs £1.20 for 250 g. What is the cost per 100 g? (£0.48 per 100 g)
R16 Set up, solve and interpret the answers in growth and decay problems, including compound interest.	**9** Ivan invests £1500 in a bank account that pays 3% interest per year. **a** How much is in the account after **i** one year (£1545) **ii** four years? (£1688.26) **b** Write a formula to find the value of the account (V) after t years. ($V = 1500 \times 1.03^t$)

Misconceptions and challenges	Solutions
Students only understand gradient as part of $y = mx + c$, or as the 'steepness of a graph', and do not understand how it applies to a rate of change.	Look at graphs in contexts such as distance–time, without numerical information on the axes. Ask questions such as 'When is the car travelling fastest?', to draw out how the steepness of the graph relates to the rate of change.
Students find it difficult to extract information from a context such as 'The ball falls a distance *d* metres in a time *t* seconds'.	First have students underline any phrases that refer to proportionality. This will give them the type of equation they need to generate, and then they can look for the algebraic notation.
Some compound units are so familiar, that students find it difficult to recognise them as compound.	In particular, speed and rates of pay are often very familiar to students. This can be an excellent way to begin discussion of compound units, and to dispel this misconception. Students could spend time working out their rate of pay per second, the speed of a cyclist in metres per decade, and so on.
Students frequently forget a multiplier for inverse proportionality. For example, if told a is inversely proportional to t, they write $a = \frac{1}{t}$.	Challenge students to spot the difference between $a = \frac{1}{kt}$ and $a = \frac{k}{t}$ for a value of k and different values of t. What do they notice if they rearrange the equation to make k the subject?

Review question commentary

Students can use calculators in this exercise. Units should always be included with answers.

Question 1 (22.1) – Students need to learn that $1000\ \text{cm}^3 = 1$ litre. In part **d**, they could first convert to km/s (5000).

Question 2 (22.1) – Students should state their units.

Question 3 (22.1) – It is easier to convert pence to pounds in this question.

Question 4 (22.1) – A diagram of $1\ \text{m}^2$ split into $10\ 000\ \text{cm}^2$ may remind students why they cannot simply multiply by 100.

Question 5 (22.1) – Students could check their answers by working out the side length of the enlarged cube (24 cm).

Questions 6 and **7 (22.2, 22.3)** – Any students struggling with the algebra may still be able to spot the patterns and answer part **b**.

Question 8 (22.2) – Make sure that students make the link between price per magazine and the gradient of the graph.

Question 9 (22.2, 22.3) – If students get stuck ask them to think about the gradient of each graph and how this relates to the formulae in **6** and **7**.

Question 10 (22.4) – Compound interest is used here so the interest remains in account to earn interest the next year.

Review answers

1 **a** 0.14 m **b** 16 min, 40 s
  c $3000\ \text{cm}^3$ **d** 18 km/h

2 $2.5\ \text{N/m}^2$

3 £0.24 or 24p per 100 g

4 $18\ 000\ \text{cm}^2$

5 **a** **i** $64\ \text{cm}^3$ **ii** $1728\ \text{cm}^3$
  b **i** $96\ \text{cm}^3$ **ii** $864\ \text{cm}^3$

6 **a** 32 **b** 11

7 **a** $\frac{2}{3}$ **b** 9

8 **a** $P = 3N$ **b** 3 **c** Price per magazine

9 **a** A **b** C

10 **a** **i** £2040 **ii** £2122.42
  b $V = 2000 \times 1.02^t$

Assessment 22

Question 1 – 7 marks

a $(88 - 68) \div 40 = 0.5$ hrs [M1]
$= 30$ min [A1]

b $20 \div (18{:}55 - 18{:}15) = 20 \div \frac{2}{3}$ mph [M1]
$= 30$ mph [A1]

c $68 \div 1\frac{1}{3} - 20 \div 1\frac{1}{3}$ [M1]
$= 48 \div 1\frac{1}{3}$ or $51 - 15$ [A1]
$= 36$ mph [F1]

Question 2 – 3 marks

$93\,000\,000 \div 186\,000$ [M1]
$= 500$ s [A1]
$= 8$ min 20 s [F1]

Question 3 – 6 marks

a $100 \div 2.54$ [M1]
$= 39.37$ in [A1]

b 1 costs $6.50 \div 8$ OR $12 = 8 + \frac{1}{2} \times 8$
12 cost 0.8125×12 $6.50 + ½ \times 6.50$ [M1]
$= £9.75$ $= £9.75$ [A1]

c 1 omelette $15 \div 8$ OR $28 = (3 + ½) \times 8$
28 omelettes 1.875×28 $3 \times 15 + ½ \times 15$ [M1]
$= 52$ min 30 s $= 52$ min 30 s [A1]

Question 4 – 4 marks

$100 \div 40\,000 = 0.0025$ hr [M1]
$= 0.15$ min [M1]
$= 9\text{ s} < 9.8\text{ s}$ [A1]

OR

$100 \div 9.8 = 10.204\ldots$ m/s [M1]
$= 0.010\,204\ldots \times 60 \times 60$ km/h [M1]
$= 36.73 < 40$ km/h [A1]
The wombat [F1]

Question 5 – 6 marks

a $3850 \div 529$ [M1]
$= 7.28$ g/cm^3 [A1]

b $250 \div 10.5$ [M1]
$= 23.81$ cm^3 [A1]

c $1.03 \times 1000 = 1030$ g or 1.03 kg [M1, A1]

Question 6 – 8 marks

a 1 day $3 \div 2 = 1.5$ OR $30 = 15 \times 2$
30 days 30×1.5 15×3 [M1]
$= 45$ tins $= 45$ tins [A1]

b $67 \times 1.5 = 100.5 > 100$ tins
OR $100 \div 1.5 = 66.7 < 67$ [M1]
No [A1]

c Second dog $2 \times 1.5 = 3$ tins per day [M1]
Total $1.5 + 3 = 4.5$ tins per day [A1]
$30 \div 4.5 = 6.67 < 14$ days
OR $14 \times 4.5 = 63 > 30$ tins [M1]
No [A1]

Question 7 – 6 marks

a $17.5 \times 60 = 1050$ s [B1]
$150 \times 1050 = 157\,500$ ml [M1]
$= 157.5$ litres [A1]

b $157\,500 = \pi \times (23 \div 2)^2 \times h$ [M1]
$h = 157\,500 \div (\pi \times 11.5^2)$ [M1]
$= 379$ cm [F1]

Question 8 – 8 marks

a $9600 \times 7.2 = 69\,120$ g [M1]
$= 69.12$ kg [A1]

b $0.7 = (9.8 \times 69.12) \div A$ [M1]
$A = 677.376 \div 0.7 = 967.68$ [A1]
$= 40 \times x$ [M1]
$x = 967.68 \div 40 = 24.192$
$x = 24$ cm [A1]

c $9600 = 40 \times 24 \times y$ (Allow previous x value) [M1]
$y = 10$ cm [A1]

Question 9 – 7 marks

a $\tan x = 0, 0.0175, 0.0349, 0.0524, 0.0699, 0.0875, 0.1051, 0.1228, 0.1405, 0.1584, 0.1763$
Minus 1 mark for each error. [B3]

b

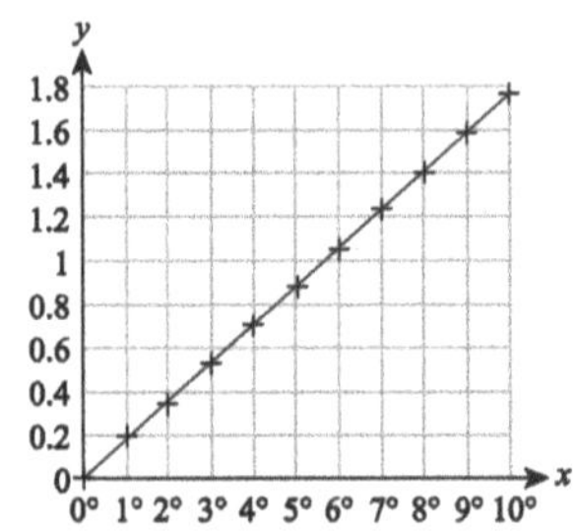

Correctly drawn and labelled axes. [B1]
Correctly drawn points. [B1]
Line drawn through points. [B1]

c The graph is a straight line in this range.
Yes [B1]

Question 10 – 6 marks

a

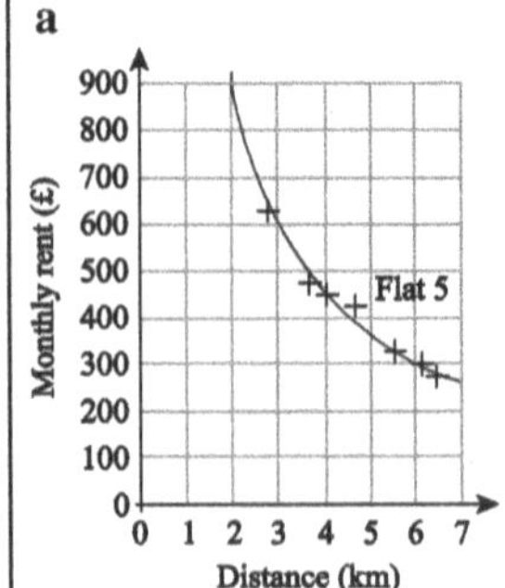

Correctly drawn and labelled axes. [B2]
Correctly drawn points.
Lose 1 mark for each error. [B2]

b Flat 5 does not lie on the curve though thepoints. [B1]

c 3.5 km [B1]

Question 11 – 7 marks

a Multiplier $= 1.032$ OR $2500 + 0.032 \times 2500$ [B1]
2500×1.032^5 $2580 + 0.032 \times 2580$ etc. [M1]
$= £2926.43$ $= £2926.43$ [A1]

b Year 6 2500×1.032^6 or 1.032×2926.43
$= 3020.08$ [B1]
$3020.08 - 500 = 2520.08$ [B1]
$2520.08 \times 1.032^4 = £2858.46$ [M1,A1]

Question 12 – 7 marksp

a £27 000, 5% [B2]

b $27\,000 \times 0.95^{10} = £16\,165.90$ [M1, A1]

c Multiplier $= 1 - 0.10 = 0.9$ [B1]
$16\,165.90 \times 0.90^5 = £9545.80$ [M1, A1]